Failure of a Dream?

Essays in the History of American Socialism

Failure of a Dream?

Essays in the History of American Socialism

☆

Edited by

John H. M. Laslett

and

Seymour Martin Lipset

REVISED EDITION

UNIVERSITY OF CALIFORNIA PRESS

Berkeley, Los Angeles, London

University of California Press
Berkeley and Los Angeles, California

University of California Press, Ltd.
London, England

Published by arrangement with Doubleday & Company, Inc.

Library of Congress Cataloging in Publication Data

Main entry under title:
Failure of a dream?

Bibliography: p.
Includes index.
1. Socialism—United States—History—Addresses, essays, lectures. I. Laslett, John H. M. II. Lipset, Seymour Martin.
HX83.F34 1984 335′.00973 77–80472
ISBN 0–520–03539–9
ISBN 0–520–04452–5 (pbk.)

Printed in the United States of America

1 2 3 4 5 6 7 8 9

CONTENTS

Preface to the Revised Edition *ix*

Preface to the First Edition *xi*

Chronology of Important Dates *xv*

PART ONE: INTERNAL PROBLEMS: THE SOCIALIST MOVEMENT AND AMERICAN SOCIALISM

1. *The Problem of Ideological Rigidity*—DANIEL BELL *3*
   Comment—JOHN H. M. LASLETT *30*
   Reply—DANIEL BELL *46*

2. *Radicalism and the Agrarian Tradition*—THEODORE SALOUTOS *52*
   Comment—MICHAEL ROGIN *65*
   Reply—THEODORE SALOUTOS *75*

3. *Catholic Anti-Socialism*—MARC KARSON *82*
   Comment—HENRY J. BROWNE *103*
   Reply—MARC KARSON *113*

4. *Socialism and American Trade Unionism*—JOHN H. M. LASLETT *118*
   Comment—PHILIP S. FONER *151*
   Reply—JOHN H. M. LASLETT *162*

5. *Socialism and Syndicalism*—MELVYN DUBOFSKY 170
Comment—ROBERT L. TYLER 204
Reply—MELVYN DUBOFSKY 213

6. *Socialism and Race*—SALLY MILLER 218
Comment—THEODORE KORNWEIBEL 232
Reply—SALLY MILLER 241

7. *Socialism and Ethnicity*—CHARLES LEINENWEBER 244
Comment—RUDOLPH J. VECOLI 269
Reply—CHARLES LEINENWEBER 285

8. *Socialism and Women*—SALLY MILLER 291
Comment—MARY JO BUHLE 318
Reply—SALLY MILLER 329

PART TWO: EXTERNAL PROBLEMS: AMERICAN SOCIETY AND AMERICAN SOCIALISM

9. *The Liberal Tradition*—LOUIS HARTZ 333
Comment—KENNETH MCNAUGHT 345
Reply—LOUIS HARTZ 357

10. *The Relevance of Marxism*—CLINTON ROSSITER 362
Comment 1—TOM BOTTOMORE 389
Comment 2—ANN J. LANE 398

11. *Socialism and Social Mobility*—STEPHAN THERNSTROM 408
Comment—SEYMOUR MARTIN LIPSET 427
Reply—STEPHAN THERNSTROM 446

12. *American Capitalism's Economic Rewards*—WERNER SOMBART 452
Comment 1—ADOLPH STURMTHAL 468
Comment 2—IRING FETSCHER 477

13. *The Role of Intellectuals*—ADOLPH STURMTHAL *484*
Comment—PAUL BUHLE *498*
Reply—ADOLPH STURMTHAL *508*

14. *Pluralism and Political Parties*—NORMAN THOMAS *516*
Comment 1—MICHAEL HARRINGTON *523*
Comment 2—LEON D. EPSTEIN *530*

Selected Bibliography *537*

Index *541*

Grateful acknowledgment is made for the use of the following:

Portions of *The End of Ideology: On the Exhaustion of Political Ideas in the Fifties* by Daniel Bell. Reprinted by permission of the author.
From *Marxism: The View from America.* Copyright © 1960 by Clinton Rossiter. Reprinted by permission of Harcourt Brace Jovanovich, Inc.
From *The Liberal Tradition in America,* copyright © 1955 by Louis Hartz. Reprinted by permission of Harcourt Brace Jovanovich, Inc.
"Comments on Selig Perlman's *A Theory of the Labor Movement,*" by Adolf Sturmthal. Reprinted from the *Industrial and Labor Relations Review,* Vol. 4, No. 4, July 1951. Copyright © 1951 by Cornell University. All rights reserved.
"The Catholic Church and the Political Development of American Trade Unionism (1900–1918)," by Marc Karson. Reprinted from the *Industrial and Labor Relations Review,* Vol. 4, No. 4, July 1951. Copyright © 1951 by Cornell University. All rights reserved.
Portions of *Socialism Re-examined.* Reprinted from *Socialism Re-examined* by Norman Thomas. By permission of W. W. Norton & Company, Inc. Copyright © 1963 by Norman Thomas.
"Working Class Social Mobility in Industrial America" by Stephan Thernstrom. Reprinted by permission of the publishers from Melvin Richter, ed., *Essays in Theory and History: An Approach to the Social Sciences.* Cambridge, Mass.: Harvard University Press, Copyright, 1970, by the President and Fellows of Harvard College.
Portions of *We Shall Be All: A History of the Industrial Workers of the World.* Reprinted by permission of Quadrangle Books from *We Shall Be All: A History of the Industrial Workers of the World* by Melvyn Dubofsky, copyright © 1969 by Melvyn Dubofsky.
"Women in the Party Bureaucracy: Subservient Functionaries," taken from *Flawed Liberation: Socialism and Feminism,* edited by Sally M. Miller and used with the permission of the publisher, Greenwood Press, a division of Congressional Information Service, Inc., Westport, Connecticut, copyright © 1981.
"The Socialist Party and the Negro, 1901–1920," by Sally Miller, *Journal of Negro History,* 56, 3 (July 1971), pp. 220–229, and used with the permission of the journal. "The American Socialist Party and 'New' Immigrants," by Charles Leinenweber, *Science and Society,* 32, 1 (Winter 1968), pp. 2–25, and used with the permission of the journal.

PREFACE TO THE REVISED EDITION

Publication of a revised edition of this work was made desirable by the decision of Doubleday and Anchor to let the first one go out of print in 1975, despite a generally favorable response. One of their reasons for doing so was the excessive length of the first edition, which came to 750 pages. Partly as a consequence of this, in this revised edition we have cut approximately one-third of the material presented in the earlier version, including the entire first and fourth parts. Part One of the earlier version consisted of two introductory chapters, the first analyzing explanations put forward by old socialists for the exceptional weakness of American socialism, and the second presenting a dialogue between the two editors on the subject. Although both contained valuable material, they are now somewhat out of date. The same thing was true of Part Four of the first edition, which consisted of two essays on the then current status and prospects of the New Left, a movement that has since largely collapsed. The new version, therefore, contains only two, renumbered sections. Part One deals with the internal difficulties that the American socialist movement encountered in its efforts to become a mass party, unlike the socialist movements in western Europe. Part Two examines the external or societal reasons for its lack of success.

In response to reviewers' comments on the first edition and in order to bring Part One up to date, three new chapters have been added to that section. The first one, a new Chapter 6, deals with the inhibiting effect on efforts to develop a mass socialist movement in America of racial divisions within the working class. Chapter 7, on ethnicity and class, attempts the same thing in relation to immigrant workers coming to the United States from abroad. Chapter 8, on socialism and women, deals with a similar issue from a somewhat different point of view. Beyond this, the various disclaimers that were put into the first edition concerning the limited nature of this work and on other matters still stand.

It is hoped that the briefer nature of this volume and the new material that has been added to it will make it attractive as a collection of readings in history, sociology, and political science for both the general reader and for use in college courses. The debate format—with scholars currently working in the field writing essays of comment on the previously published material and the previous authors writing a brief reply—has been retained to liven up the issues under discussion.

For readers who would like to pursue the subject further, a chronology or list of important dates has been added at the beginning of the book, and a selected bibliography at the back. Even though the bulk of the essays concern the American socialist movement, which reached its peak before the First World War, because of numerous references to the Communist Party in the text, both of these lists cover later radical movements as well. Readers interested in the views of the two editors on the relative weakness of American socialism are referred to our various works cited in the bibliography and to our essay in the first edition of this book, Laslett and Lipset, "Social Scientists View the Problem," pp. 25–82.

November 1983

John H. M. Laslett, U.C.L.A.
Seymour Martin Lipset, Stanford University

PREFACE TO THE FIRST EDITION

Contrary to most popular beliefs, the United States has an indigenous socialist tradition, if only a small one by European standards, which exerted a significant influence both in the labor movement and in American politics in the years before the First World War. In 1912, the Socialist Party of America had more than a thousand of its members in public office as mayors, state assemblymen, and other elected officials, and Eugene V. Debs received nearly a million votes in his campaign for the presidency that year. Yet by 1919, with the reforms of the Progressive movement, the Red Scare, and the split over Bolshevism, the American socialist movement received a setback from which it never recovered, not even during the Depression of the 1930s.

The purpose of this book is to examine the reasons for the relative weakness of American socialism with respect to the internal problems of the party and the movement in matters of tactics, ideology, and leadership. It also deals with the negative effects on socialism stemming from the nature of American society itself —for example, the relatively high degree of social fluidity, the pervasive character of American liberalism, or the nature of the political system. Part Two addresses itself largely to the first of these two sets of factors, and Part Three to the second. Part One consists of two chapters providing a general overview of the subject, with which the non-specialist reader is urged to begin. Chapter One represents, in summary form, portions of a series of interviews with old socialists giving their views of why the Socialist Party of America failed to attract more than a very small number of American voters to its banner. Chapter Two takes the form of a dialogue between the two editors, giving their respective views as students of the subject. Though they disagree over specific areas of interpretation, both authors consider the extent to which American society has differed from other societies in those elements which make for the growth of a strong socialist tradition crucial to an understanding of the problem.

The question "Why is there no socialism in the United States?" —the title of a famous essay published in 1906 by the German sociologist Werner Sombart, parts of which are reproduced in this volume in English for the first time—is not simply an academic one. In the 1840s Karl Marx and Friedrich Engels were only the first in what has since become a long line of foreign and domestic observers who still continue to discuss the absence of a strong socialist movement in what is by now by far the most advanced capitalist country in the world. This phenomenon has also been used by scholars as one of their major arguments in the continuing debate over America's alleged "exceptionalism"—how far, that is to say, American development has differed from that of other industrial societies in the West. Given the immense contemporary influence of the United States in other parts of the world, the question also has important consequences which go beyond understanding America's own history. It affects our judgment of what may happen elsewhere, as both Europe and Japan appear to take as many of the characteristics of mass industrial society which first appeared in the United States.

The issue has taken on added interest and importance with the rise of the New Left, both in the United States and abroad. When the idea for this book was first conceived, in 1969, it appeared for a time as though the American independent Left might break out of the mold of frustration, cooptation, repression, and failure which has so often dogged its footsteps in the past; and perhaps even establish a mass movement which would belie the terms in which Sombart's original question had been posed. Since then the New Left has failed to maintain its momentum. In our view, however, its collapse has increased, instead of diminished, the need for the kind of symposium presented here. Part Four of the work consists, therefore, of two essays by prominent representatives of the New Left which discuss both the differences between the Old Left and the New in American society, and the prospects for the New Left at the present time. Taken in conjunction with the largely historical materials presented in Parts Two and Three, they should enable the general reader, as well as the specialist, to form a clearer judgment about the past character and likely direction of American radicalism as a whole.

Previously published material which in our judgment incorporates a significant proportion of the important scholarly work which has hitherto been done on the subject constitutes only about half of the essays included in this book. The remainder consists of invited essays of Comment on these writings by distinguished scholars presently working in the field, followed by Replies from the original authors where they are still living, or by a second essay of Comment where they are not.

A deliberate effort has been made to solicit contributions both from scholars who have written on the subject, and from activists presently involved in the New Left movement, as well as to include representatives of different generational and ideological points of view. Inevitably, however, in dealing with so large a subject the collection is not wholly comprehensive. Some of the invited contributors were unable to participate in the symposium, and some previously published material could not be reproduced. Constraints of space have also meant that a number of important questions are not explored as fully as they might be. These include the issue of the frontier as a "safety valve" for working-class discontent, ethnic fragmentation as a problem in American working-class consciousness, and the role of blacks and other oppressed racial minorities as an "absentee proletariat" in the nineteenth-century American economy.

There are also a number of deliberate omissions. No attempt, for example, has been made to deal comprehensively with the issue of communism—even though many of the arguments made by the contributors to the symposium concerning the weakness of American socialism can equally be made with respect to American communism. Our central focus has been upon socialism and the Socialist Party; to deal with communism in detail would require another volume. We have largely found it necessary to ignore other radical tendencies as well.

Despite these limitations, these essays are offered in the belief that they represent the most comprehensive collection of scholarly work on the subject now available. For the general reader, we hope that they will satisfy at least part of his curiosity about the historical background which lies behind the present ferment on the American Left. For the student and the scholar we hope that they will stimulate further study and research into a question which has always been at the center of American historical and political debate.

One further point should be made. Although some scholars would undoubtedly argue to the contrary, as Betty Yorburg implies at the beginning of Chapter One, the reasons which they have chosen to emphasize in their explanations for the relative absence of socialism from America often reflect, either directly or indirectly, their own value judgments concerning both the nature and purposes of socialism as an ideology, and the merits or defects of American society itself. Many on the political Left, for example, regard the weakness of socialism in America as a regrettable but by no means inevitable occurrence which resulted from oppression, corruption, or inefficient leadership, or from the idiosyncrasies of the American electoral system or of American historical development generally. Others, usually associated of course with the political Right, regard it as a generally beneficent development which grew out of the generally successful character of the United States as an equalitarian society, or perhaps out of the virtually inevitable triumph of a liberal (as opposed to a Marxist or a conservative) form of political consensus.

A wide variety of other, more or less conscious, value judgments concerning this issue are embedded at various places in the scholarship which has been carried out on this topic, as the reader will soon discover for himself. The use of the word "failure" in the title of this volume, as elsewhere in its pages, should not be taken to imply either a pejorative or a deterministic judgment concerning the past performance or present fortunes of the American Left. Our opinions concerning the reasons for the weakness of the American socialist movement are made clear in various of our own contributions to this symposium, revealing along with them, of course, our own particular political points of view. The use of the word "failure" is a shorthand way of stating what seems to us the obvious fact that neither in America nor in Europe (or in any other part of the world, for that matter) have either the socialists, the Communists, or any other ideological grouping of revolutionary radicals yet succeeded in implementing even the most obvious of those common characteristics of a future society which are advocated by all socialists alike.

September 1973

John H. M. Laslett, U.C.L.A.

Seymour Martin Lipset, Harvard

CHRONOLOGY OF IMPORTANT DATES

1857	Communist Club of New York founded by Forty-Eighters Friedrich Sorge and Joseph Weydemeyer.
1872	Headquarters of Marx's First International (1864) transferred from London to New York; supported by a few hundred German and other immigrant workers, but few native-born Americans.
1877	Socialist Labor Party established in New York City as an alliance of Marxist (trade union) and Lassallean (political) socialists; reaches peak membership, still largely immigrant, of approximately 6,500 in 1890s.
1886	*May*: Haymarket riot in Chicago, followed by Red Scare; *November*: American Federation of Labor (AFL) founded under cigarmaker Samuel Gompers; a conservative craft union body, it follows a nonpartisan political policy of "reward-your-friends, punish-your-enemies."
1893–94	AFL rejects T. J. Morgan's Political Programme calling for an independent labor party and collective ownership of industry; also refuses to endorse Populists.
1895	Socialist Labor Party leader and editor of *The People* Daniel De Leon, angered by defeat of Morgan Programme, establishes Socialist Trades and Labor Alliance as rival to AFL.
1897	Eugene V. Debs founds Social Democracy of America.
1898	Social Democratic Party founded by Victor Berger, Morris Hillquit, and others; gains support of Debs.

1901 Socialist Party of America established, with headquarters in Chicago; a coalition of anti-De Leonite Marxists, Social Democrats, Christian socialists, and Bellamyite Nationalists, it repudiates dual unionism and seeks to "bore from within" the AFL.

1905 Industrial Workers of the World (IWW), known as "Wobblies," founded in Chicago as a revolutionary industrial union and rival to the AFL; initially incorporates De Leon's Socialist Trades and Labor Alliance, AFL seceders, and the Western Federation of Miners, led by Big Bill Haywood; at its peak, includes about 70,000 members, many of them migrant workers, compared to AFL's two million in 1917.

1906–10 Conflict within IWW, which endorses syndicalism in 1908, brings withdrawal of Western Federation of Miners, bitter conflict with AFL, and expulsion of De Leonites, who set up rival faction in Detroit; Wobblies undertake "free speech fights."

1912 *March*: IWW victory in Lawrence textile strike, aided by Haywood, Ettor and Giovanitti, and Emma Goldman; *May*: Socialist Party convention breaks with IWW, alleging anti-political stand and advocacy of violence; *November*: Debs receives 897,011 votes as Socialist Party presidential candidate, highest proportion of the popular vote ever received by a Socialist Party candidate.

1917–19 Because of opposition to April 1917 entry of U.S. into First World War and endorsement of October 1917 Russian revolution, most Socialist Party leaders are jailed; subsequent Red Scare emasculates party, dropping its peak membership of 125,740 in 1912 to 74,519 in 1918.

1919 *April*: Lenin's recently formed Third International urges all socialists to endorse "immediate revolution" under Moscow's leadership; *May*: rejecting this, Socialist Party expels Foreign-Language Federations and other revolutionary elements, loses one-third of remaining members; *July-September*: Communist Party of America and Communist Labor Party set up by breakaway Socialists.

1921 Workers Party of America, later Communist Party U.S.A., unites most revolutionary socialists, except Trotskyites, who form the Socialist Workers Party (1937); initially, Communist Party is composed of ex-Wobblies, intellectuals, Jews and other immigrants; Socialist Party, down to 12,000 members, never fully recovers.

1928–35 Communist Party, now in its revolutionary Third Period, replaces "boring from within" policy of Trade Union Educational League (1920) by dual unionist Trade Union Unity League (1928); limited success among coal, textile, and maritime workers; Communist and Socialist Parties try to organize unemployed from Great Depression.

1936 President Roosevelt's New Deal, bringing social security, relief, farm and labor legislation, attracts many farmers and workers, including southern blacks, into Democratic Party; in 1936 election, FDR receives nearly 28 million votes, compared to 187,342 for Socialist Norman Thomas, and 80,181 for Communist Earl Browder.

1936–37 Socialist Party, under Norman Thomas and H. L. Mitchell, organizes Southern Tenant Farmers Union, its only major trade union success of 1930s.

1936–39 Communist Party, following Popular Front policy, secures major influence in one-third of unions of Congress of Industrial Organizations (CIO), formed in 1936 by John L. Lewis, Philip Murray, and Sidney Hillman as an industrial union federation seceding from the AFL; Lee Pressman, Len DeCaux, and other Communists become part of official CIO leadership;

	Communist Party support for civil rights attracts votes of some blacks.
1939–41	Nazi-Soviet pact leads Communist Party to oppose U.S. rearmament.
1942–45	After German invasion of Russia (1941), Communist Party and much of Socialist Party support U.S. in Second World War, downplaying domestic grievances of workers.
1945–48	Emerging from war with a peak membership of 70,000, Communist Party rapidly loses support by defending Soviet interests in emerging Cold War.
1948	By endorsing third-party Progressive candidacy of Henry A. Wallace, Communist Party forfeits much union support.
1949	Communist-influenced unions expelled from AFL.
1950	Ten Communist-led unions expelled from CIO.
1950–56	Most remaining Socialists join the Democratic Party; McCarthyism destroys most remaining Communist influence in unions and among intelligentsia.

Part One

Internal Problems: The Socialist Movement and American Socialism

Chapter 1

THE PROBLEM OF IDEOLOGICAL RIGIDITY*

Daniel Bell

> The Rabbi of Zans used to tell this story about himself:
>
> "In my youth when I was fired with the love of God, I thought I would convert the whole world to God. But soon I discovered that it would be quite enough to convert the people who lived in my town, and I tried for a long time, but did not succeed. Then I realized that my program was too ambitious, and I concentrated on the persons in my own household. But I could not convert them either. Finally it dawned upon me: I must work upon myself, so that I may give true service to God. But I did not accomplish even this."
>
> Hasidic Tale

> He who seeks the salvation of souls, his own as well as others, should not seek it along the avenue of politics.
>
> Max Weber

Socialism was an unbounded dream. Fourier promised that under socialism people would be at least "ten feet tall." Karl Kautsky, the embodiment of didacticism, proclaimed that the average citizen of the socialist society would be a superman. The flamboyant Antonio Labriola told his Italian followers that their socialist-bred children would all be Galileos and Giordano Brunos. And the

* Chapter 12 from Daniel Bell, *The End of Ideology: On the Exhaustion of Political Ideas in the Fifties* (Glencoe: Free Press, 1960), originally entitled "The Failure of American Socialism: The Tension of Ethics and Politics."

high-flown, grandiloquent Trotsky described the socialist millennium as one in which "man would become immeasurably stronger, wiser, freer, his body more harmoniously proportioned, his movements more rhythmic, his voice more musical, and the forms of his existence permeated with dramatic dynamism."

America, too, was an unbounded dream. When the American colonies broke away from England, they inscribed upon the back of the great seal authorized by Congress *Novus Ordo Seclorum*—we are "the new order of the ages," the beginning of the American era. The American continent, with its vast lands and mighty riches, was destined to be a great social laboratory. Here the unfolding design of "God, Master Workman," would be manifest. Such a disguised deism, emphasizing the aspect of God as a craftsman rather than as a fixed revelation, was congenial to the growth of a pragmatic temper. It was a society which, if it did not welcome, would at least abide without scorn the efforts of small bands to explore the design of the millennium. And if in places the response was hostile, there was the Icarian wilderness, stretching from Texas to Iowa, in which Utopian colonies might find refuge, safe from prying eyes, to continue their chiliastic search. Small wonder then that such colonies arose in prodigal number.

Here, too, it seemed as if socialism would have its finest hour. Inspired, perhaps, by the expanse of the virgin wilderness, Marx and Engels felt a boundless optimism. In 1879 Marx wrote, "the United States have at present overtaken England in the rapidity of economical progress, though they lag still behind in the extent of acquired wealth; but at the same time, the masses are quicker and have greater political means in their hands to resent the form of a progress accomplished at this expense." Engels, who wrote a score of letters on the American scene in the late 1880's and early nineties, repeated this prediction time and again. In his introduction to the American edition of *The Conditions of the Working Class in England,* written at the height of enthusiasm over the events of 1886—notably the spectacular rise of the Knights of Labor and the Henry George campaign in New York—he exulted: "On the more favored soil of America, where no medieval ruins bar the way, where history begins with the elements of modern bourgeois society, as evolved in the seventeenth century, the working class passed through these two stages of its development [a national trade-union movement and an independent labor party] within ten months." And five years later, his optimism undiminished by the sorry turn of events, Engels wrote to Schleuter: ". . . continually renewed waves of advance followed by equally certain set-backs are inevitable. Only the advancing waves are becoming more powerful, the setbacks less paralyzing. . . . Once the Americans get started it will be with an energy and violence compared with which we in Europe shall be mere children."[1]

But there still hovers the melancholy question posed by Werner Sombart at the turn of the century in the title of a book, *Why Is There No Socialism in the United States?* To this Sombart supplied one set of answers. He pointed to the open frontiers, the many opportunities for social ascent through individual effort and the rising standard of living. Other writers have expanded these considerations. Selig Perlman, in his *Theory of the Labor Movement,* advanced three reasons for the lack of class consciousness in the United States: the absence of a "settled" wage-earner class; the "free gift" of the ballot (workers in other countries who were denied such rights—for example, the Chartists in England—developed political rather than economic motivation); and third, the impact of successive waves of immigration. It was immigration, said Perlman, which gave rise to the ethnic, linguistic, religious, and cultural heterogeneity of American labor and to the heightened ambitions of immigrants' sons to escape their inferior status. Count Keyserling, a traveler here in the twenties, observed that Americanism, with its creed of egalitarianism, was a surrogate for socialism; and the "conversions" of many German socialists who came here in the late nineteenth century attests to the acuity of this remark. Some writers have stressed the agrarian basis of American life, with the farmer seesawing to radicalism and conservatism in tune to the business cycle. Others have pointed to the basically sectional rather than functional organization of the two-party system, with its emphasis on patronage, its opportunism, and its vacuity of rhetoric as the mode of political discourse; hence compromise, rather than rigid principle, becomes the trading concern of the interest-oriented political bloc. In the end, all such explanations have fallen back on the natural resources and material vastness of America. In awe of the fact that the Yankee worker consumed almost three times as much bread and meat, and four times as much sugar, as his German counterpart, Sombart exclaimed: "On the reefs of roast beef and apple pie, socialistic Utopias of every sort are sent to their doom."[2]

Implicit in many of these analyses was the notion, however, that such conditions were but temporary. Capitalism as an evolving social system would of necessity "mature," crisis would follow crisis, and a large, self-conscious wage-earner class and a socialist movement on the European pattern would emerge. The great depression was such a crisis—an emotional jolt which shook the self-confidence of the entire society. It left scar tissue on the minds of American workers. It spurred the organization of a giant trade-union movement which, in ten years, grew from less than three million to over fifteen million workers, or almost 30 per cent of the wage and salaried force of the country. It brought in its train smoking-hot organizing drives and sit-downs in the Ohio industrial valley which gave the country a strong whiff of class warfare. It spawned strong anticapitalistic and antiplutocratic populist movements (e.g., Huey Long's share-the-wealth, Father Coughlin's social justice, Dr. Townsend's old-age pension scheme). Here, seemingly, was the fertile soil which socialist theorists had long awaited.

Yet no socialist movement emerged, nor did a coherent socialist ideology take seed either in the labor movement or in government. It would seem that the general reasons adduced earlier simply held—and that the New Deal, like the earlier ideology of Americanism, had become a somewhat different surrogate for socialism. But all such explanations are "external," so to speak, to the radical movement, and, even if true, are simply one side of the coin. The other is: How did the socialist see the world, and, because of that vision, why did the movement fail to adapt to the American scene? Why was it incapable of rational choice?

A general answer why the socialist movement did not face up to the real situation—and these judgments are always after the fact—involves *the interplay of social character* (i.e., the social composition of the movement and the kind of allegiance it demanded of its members), *the degree of "access" to other institutions,* and *the nature of its ideology.*[3] A full explanation of the failure—or success—of a social movement would have to describe how these three elements affect each other. Thus, a movement completely alienated from the society, for ethnic or emotional reasons, would find it harder to make compromises with an existing order; in such cases, the social character of the movement might be the decisive explanation for its failure to adapt to changing reality. A social movement with a high proportion of union members, one with a high proportion of professional persons, might have an easier "bridge" to other political groups; hence, "degree of access" might be the important factor. In other instances, the nature of the ideology might be the agent that creates the dilemma of action. For some movements, ideology is a pose, easily dropped; for others it is a bind.

This chapter concerns itself with the ideology of socialism. It is my argument that the failure of the socialist movement in the United States was rooted in its inability to resolve a basic dilemma of ethics and politics: the socialist movement, by the way in which it stated its goal, and by the way in which it rejected the capitalist order as a whole, could not relate itself to the specific problems of social action in the here-and-now, give-and-take political world. In sum: it was trapped by the unhappy problem of living *in* but not *of* the world; it could only act, and then inadequately, as the moral, but not political, man in immoral society. It could never resolve, but only straddle, the basic issue of either accepting capitalist society and seeking to transform it from within, as the labor movement did, or of becoming the sworn enemy of that society, like the Communists. A religious movement can split its allegiances and (like Lutheranism) live *in* but not *of* the world (after all, it is not concerned with this life but the after-life); a political movement cannot.

The Two Ethics

In the largest sense, society is an organized system for the distribution of rewards and privileges, the imposition of obligations and duties. Within that frame, ethics deals with the *ought* of distribution, implying a theory of justice. Politics is the concrete *mode* of distribution, involving a power struggle between organized groups to determine the allocation of privilege. In social action there is an ineluctable tension between ethics and politics. Lord Acton posed the problem in a note: "Are politics an attempt to realize ideals, or an endeavour to get advantages, within the limits of ethics?" More succinctly, "are ethics a purpose or a limit?"[4]

In some periods of history, generally in closed societies, ethics and politics have gone hand in hand. There, in theory, the moral law and the just price rule, and each stratum receives its privileges according to fixed status. But a distinguishing feature of modern society is the separation of ethics and politics—since no group can, through the civil arm, impose its moral conceptions on the whole society; and ideology—the façade of general interest and universal values which masks specific self-interest—replaces ethics. The redivision of the rewards and privileges of society can only be accomplished in the political arena. But in that fateful entry into politics, an ethic stated as purpose (or end), rather than as a limit (or simply the rules of the game), becomes a far-reaching goal which demands a radical commitment that necessarily transforms politics into an all-or-none battle.

Acton's dilemma was most clearly reformulated by Max Weber in his discussion of politics as a way of life. One can see the political game, he said, as an "ethic of responsibility" (or the acceptance of limits), or as an "ethic of conscience" (or the dedication to absolute ends). The former is the pragmatic view which seeks reconciliation as its goal. The latter creates "true believers" who burn with pure, unquenchable flame and can accept no compromise with faith.

Weber, arguing that only the ethic of responsibility is possible in politics if civil peace is to be maintained, writes: "The matter does not appear to me so desperate if one does not ask exclusively who is morally right and who is morally wrong, but if one rather asks: Given the existing conflict how can I solve it with the least internal and external danger for all concerned?"[5]

Such a view of politics, rather than the dedication to some absolute (whether it be Bolshevism as an active, disruptive force of society or religious pacifism as a passive withdrawal from society) is possible, however, only when there is a basic consensus among contending groups to respect each other's rights to continue in the society. The foundation of a pluralist society rests, therefore, on this separation of ethics and politics and on the limiting of ethics to the formal rules of the game. In practice, the socialists accepted this fact; in theory, because of its root rejection of the society, the socialist movement could never wholeheartedly accept this basic approach, and on crucial doctrinal issues it found itself stymied.

The question of which ethic one accepts becomes crucial, for the distinctive character of "modern" politics is the involvement of *all* strata of society in movements of social change, rather than, as in feudal or peasant or backward societies, the fatalistic acceptance of events as they are. The starting point was, as Karl Mannheim elegantly put it, the "orgiastic chiliasm" of the Anabaptists, their ecstatic effort to realize the Millennium at once. Martin Luther had torn down the monastery walls which separated the sacred from the profane life. Each man now stood alone, in the "equality of believers," forced to make his affirmation and to realize the Christian life himself, directly, rather than through the vicarious atonement of the saints. But if all men were equal, how could there be master and servant? If all men stood naked before God in the matter of salvation, should they not be equal in sharing the material goods of the worldly life? These were the disturbing questions asked by Thomas Munzer and the radical Anabaptists. Suddenly, other-worldly religious quietism became transformed into a revolutionary activism to realize the Millennium in the *here and now*. Thus the religious frenzy of the chiliasts which burst the bonds of the old religious order threatened to buckle the social order as well; for unlike previous revolutions, which aimed at single oppressors, chiliasm sought to overthrow the entire existing social order.†

The characteristic psychological fact about the chiliast is that for him "there is no inner articulation of time"; there is only "absolute presentness." "Orgiastic energies and ecstatic outbursts began to operate in a worldly setting and tensions previously transcending day to day life became explosive agents within it."[6] The chiliast is neither in the world nor of it. He stands outside of it and against it because salvation, the Millennium, is immediately at hand.

Where such a hope is possible, where such a social movement can transform society in a cataclysmic flash, the "leap" is made, and in the pillar of fire the fusion of ethics and politics is possible. But where societies are stable and social change can only come piecemeal, the pure chiliast, in despair, turns nihilist, rather than

† Munzer's millenarian dreams kindled the literary utopias, more than a century later, of Robert Burton's idyllic land, in his preface to the *Anatomy of Melancholy*, and the technological paradise of Bacon's New Atlantis, and found political expression in the egalitarian demands of the Levellers and Diggers during the Cromwell rebellion. A century and a half later, the same impulses flickered strongly, during the French Revolution, in Gracchus Babeuf's "conspiracy of the equals," and passed into the common currency of the revolutionary movements of the nineteenth century.

make the bitter-tasting compromises with the established hierarchical order. "When this spirit ebbs and deserts these movements," writes Mannheim, "there remains behind in the world a naked mass-frenzy and despiritualized fury." In a later and secularized form, this attitude found its expression in Russian anarchism. So Bakunin could write: "The desire for destruction is at the same time a creative desire."

Yet not only the anarchist, but every socialist, every convert to political messianism, is in the beginning something of a chiliast. In the newly found enthusiasms, in the identification with an oppressed group, there is the unsuppressed urgency and hope that the "final conflict" might soon be in sight. ("Socialism in our time" was the banner which Norman Thomas raised for the new recruits to the Socialist party in the 1930's.) But the "revolution" is not always nigh, and the question of how to discipline this chiliastic zeal and hold it in readiness has always been the basic problem of radical strategy.

The anarchist had the vision of *die Tat,* "the deed." Like Paul Munnumit, in Henry James's *Princess Casamassima,* he could live a drab, humdrum life because of his secret, omnipotent conviction that "a shot" could transform the world in a flash and that he could command the moment when the shot would come. Powerful as the image was, its believers could only live, like sleepwalkers, in a fantasy world. Yet only through fantasy could the anarchists keep the believer from becoming tired or dispirited. The most radical approach was that of Georges Sorel, with his concept of the revolutionary myth (*images de batailles*), a myth which, for the anarcho-syndicalists, functioned as a bastardized version of the doctrine of salvation. These unifying images, Sorel wrote, can neither be proved nor disproved; thus they are "capable of evoking an undivided whole" from the mass of diverse sentiments which exist in society. "The syndicalists solve this problem perfectly by concentrating the whole of socialism in the drama of the general strike; thus there is no longer any place for the reconciliation of contraries in the equivocations of the professors; everything is clearly mapped out so that only one interpretation of socialism is possible." In this "catastrophic conception" of socialism, as Sorel called it, *"it is the myth in its entirety which is alone important."*[7]

But how long can a myth sustain, when the reality constantly belies it?

The Veils of the Proletariat

What of the proletariat itself? What is its role in the socialist drama of history? How does the proletariat see through the veils of obscurity and come to self-awareness? Marx could say with Jesus, "I have come to end all mysteries, not to perpetuate them." His role, in his own self-image, was to lay bare the fetishes which enslave modern man and thus to confute Hegel's claim that freedom and rationality had already been achieved. But, like his old master, he could only deal with "immanent" forces of history, not the mechanics of social action.[8]

All political movements, Marx wrote, have been slaves to the symbols of the past. ("Thus Luther donned the mask of the Apostle Paul, the Revolution of 1789 to 1814 draped itself alternately as the Roman Republic and the Roman Empire," he wrote in *The Eighteenth Brumaire.*) But history is the process of progressive disenchantment; men are no longer bound to the river gods and anthropomorphic deities of the agricultural societies; nor need they be bound to the abstract impersonal deity of bourgeois Protestantism. Man was potential. But how to realize his potentiality? The intellectual was, in part, capable of self-emancipation because he possessed the imagination to transcend his origins. But the proletariat, as a class, could develop only to the extent that the social relations of society itself revealed to the slave the thongs that bind him. Man is not freer, said Marx in *Das Kapital,* because he can sell his labor power to whom he wishes. Exploitation is implicit in the very structure of capitalist society, which, in order to live, must constantly expand by extracting surplus value and accumulating new capital. In the process, the proletarian would be reduced to the barest minimum of human existence (the law of increasing misery) and thus be robbed of any mark of distinction. In the agony of alienation he would realize a sense of identity which would unite him with others and create a cohesive social movement of revolution. In action he would no longer be manipulated but would "make" himself.[9]

Thus the scene is set for the grand drama. Out of the immanent, convulsive contradictions of capitalism, conflict would spread. The proletariat, neither in nor of the world, would inherit the world.

But History (to use these personifications) confounded Marx's prophecy, at least in the West. The law of increasing misery was refuted by the tremendous advances of technology. The trade-union began bettering the workers' lot, and, in the political struggles that followed, the proletariat found that it could sustain itself not by becoming a revolutionary instrument against society but by accepting a place within society.

A Place in the Sun

In the America of the nineteenth century, almost every social movement had involved an effort by the worker to escape his lot as a worker. At times the solution was free land, cheap money, producer's co-operatives, or some other chimera from the gaudy bag of utopian dreams. The rise of the American Federation of Labor signaled the end of this search for the land of Prester John. "The working people," said Gompers, "are in too great need of immediate improvement[s] in their condition to allow them to forego them in their endeavour to devote their entire energies to an end however beautiful to contemplate. . . . The way out of the wage system is through higher wages."[10]

It was the obstinate manner in which the sectarians ignored the bread-and-butter aspect of the situation that soured him completely on the political socialists. In the 1880's, the cigarmakers union, headed by Gompers, sought legislation outlawing the manufacture of cigars in tenement homes. He marked for reprisal those legislators who voted against the measure and called for support of those who voted for the bill. But the political socialists were dead-set against voting for old-party candidates, even the pro-labor ones, charging that such a move might provide temporary gains for the cigarmakers but would "corrupt" the labor movement. Even when the first tenement-house bill was enacted, the socialists refused to support for re-election Gompers' man, Edward Grosse, who had been instrumental in pushing through the measure. It was a lesson that Gompers never forgot.

But there was another side to the seeking a place in the world to which Gompers was no less sensitive, though he was more masked in his statement of the case. Gompers, the son of Dutch-Jewish parents, came to the United States at the age of thirteen and, for most of his life, was acutely aware of his foreign birth. Most of the leaders of American labor have been immigrants or close to immigrant stock, and the desire to be accepted, as Marcus Lee Hansen has noted, was part of the intense status drive of most immigrants. In effect, the immigrant has not been a radical force in American life; on the contrary, the immigrant generation has tended to be conservative. When in the early 1900's the AFL took the much debated step of entering the National Civic Foundation, an organization headed by Republican political boss and president-maker Mark Hanna, Gompers explained the move in the following terms: "It helped to establish the practice," he wrote, "of accepting labor unions as an integral social element and logically of including their representatives in groups to discuss policies."[11] This was labor's single ambition: to win acceptance as a "legitimate" social group, equal with business and the church as an established institution of American life. For Gompers, the immigrant boy, it was a personal crusade as well. He sought to win recognition for labor in all civic aspects of American life: an entry and a hearing at the White House, an official voice in government, and acceptance in the community at large. To become respectable—this was Gompers' and labor's aim. And, by the mid-century, labor had indeed become the new parvenu force of American life.

Waiting for Socialism

Neither nineteenth-century American radicals nor the American socialists faced up to this problem of social compromise. The utopias that were spun so profusely in the nineteenth century assumed that in the course of evolution, "reason" would find its way and the perfect society would emerge. But so mechanical were the manikin visions of human delights in such utopias that a modern reading of Bellamy, for example, with its plan for conscript armies of labor ("a horrible cockney dream," William Morris called *Looking Backward*), only produces revulsion.

The "scientific socialist" movement that emerged at the turn of the century mocked these utopian unrealities. Only the organization of the proletariat could bring a better world. But this apparent relatedness to the world was itself a delusion. The socialist dilemma was still how to face the problem of "in the world and of it," and in practice the early socialist movement "rejected" the world; it simply waited for the new. Although the American Socialist party sought to function politically by making "immediate demands" and pressing for needed social reforms, it rarely took a stand on the actual political problems that emerged from the everyday functioning of society. "What but meaningless phrases are 'imperialism,' 'expansion,' 'free silver,' 'gold standard,' etc., to the wage worker?" asked Eugene V. Debs in 1900. "The large capitalists represented by Mr. McKinley and the small capitalists represented by Mr. Bryan are interested in these 'issues' but they do not concern the working class."

These "issues" were beside the point, said Debs, because the worker stood outside society. Thus Debs and the socialist movement as a whole would have no traffic with the capitalist parties. Even on local municipal issues the party would not compromise. The socialist movement could "afford" this purity because of its supreme confidence about the future. "The socialist program is not a theory imposed upon society for its acceptance or rejection. It is but the interpretation of what is, sooner or later, inevitable. Capitalism is already struggling to its destruction." So proclaimed the Socialist national platform of 1904, the first issued by the Socialist party.

And the Socialist party and its leader, Gene Debs, waited. To the extent that any one person can embody the fantastic contradictions inherent in the history of the socialist movement—its deep emotional visions, its quixotic, self-numbing political behavior, its sulky, pettish outbursts—it is Eugene Debs. Debs had what the theologians call charisma, the inner light of grace, or, as put by a laconic southerner, "kindlin' power." "He was a tall shamblefooted man, had a sort of gusty rhetoric that set on fire the railroad workers in their pine-boarded halls . . . made them want the world he wanted, a world brothers might own where everybody would split even," wrote Dos Passos.

Yet while Debs fully *realized* the messianic role of the prophet, he lacked the hard-headedness of the politician, the ability to take the moral absolutes and break them down to the particulars with the fewest necessary compromises. He lacked, too, the awareness that a socialist leader must play both of these roles and that in this tension there arise two risks—the corruption of the prophet and the ineffectuality of the politician. But Debs never even had the strength to *act* to the hilt the role of the prophet. A shallow dogmatism gave him the illusion of an inflexible morality. "If his mind failed to grasp a direct connection between a proposed reform and socialism," writes a sympathetic biographer, "he refused to waste time with reform. Then argument became futile; he could not be swayed."[12]

This dogmatism had its roots not in an iron revolutionary will, as with Lenin, but in an almost compulsive desire to be "left" of orthodox labor opinion. Nor did this thick streak of perpetual dissidence flow from the spirit of a dispossessed rebel, like Haywood. Its wellspring was a sentimental nineteenth-century romanticism. He had been named for Eugene Sue and Victor Hugo, and their concern for the underdog, as well as the naive optimism of a Rousseau, soared in him. Yet in his personal life, manner, and habits (except for a later private addiction to drink), Debs was respectable and almost bourgeois; his wife Kate was even more so. His literary tastes were prosaic: his favorite poet was Elbert Hubbard. But in his politics Debs wore romanticism like a cloak–and this was his strength as well as his weakness. It allowed him to be rhetorical and emotional, touching people at the ragged edge of their desire for a purpose outside themselves. But it also caused him to shun the practical and to shirk the obligations of day-to-day political decision. His fiercest shafts were reserved for the bureaucrat and party boss; his warmth and affection for those who led turbulent and dissident careers like his own. But, at bottom, it was the easiest path.

Withal, the lonely figure of Debs, his sagging, pleading gauntness, pierced all who beheld him. It was perhaps because, in a final sense, he was the true protestant. Debs stood at the end of the long road of the Reformation. He had an almost mystical–at times omniscient–faith in the dictates of his inner self. Like the Anabaptists of old, all issues were resolved by private conscience. From the priesthood of all believers he had become the solitary individual, carrying on his shoulders the burdens of humanity. That sense of loneliness–and grandeur–touched others who were equally afflicted with the terrible sense of isolation. By his standing alone, he emphasized the individual and his rights, and at best, such an attitude of "autonomy" provides a unique defense of the dignity of the person. But in its extreme antinomianism, in its romantic defiance of rational and traditional norms, it shirks the more difficult problem of living in the world, of seeking, as one must in politics, relative standards of social virtue and political justice instead of abstract absolutes. It is but one pole—a necessary one—in creating standards of action. But as the isolated protestant refuses to join the community of "sinners," so the isolated prophet evades the responsibility of political life. The prophet, Max Scheler once said, stands on the mountain as a signpost; he points the way but cannot go, for if he did, there would no longer be a sign. The politician, one might add, carries the sign into the valley with him.

Straddling for Socialism

Unlike the other-worldly movements toward salvation, which can always postpone the date of the resurrection, the Socialist party, living in the here and now, had to show results. It was a movement based on a belief in "history"; but it found itself outside of "time." World War I finally broke through the façade. For the first time, the party had to face a stand on a realistic issue of the day. And on that issue almost the entire intellectual leadership of the party deserted; and, as a result, the back of American socialism was broken.

The socialist movement of the 1930's, the socialism of Norman Thomas, could not afford the luxury of the earlier belief in the inevitable course of history. It was forced to take stands on the particular issues of the day. But it too rejected completely the premises of the society which shaped these issues. In effect, the Socialist party acknowledged the fact that it lived "in" the world, but refused the responsibility of becoming a part "of" it.

But such a straddle is impossible for a *political* movement. It was as if it consented to a duel, with no choice regarding weapons, place, amount of preparation, etc. Politically, the consequences were disastrous. Each issue could only be met by an ambiguous political formula which would satisfy neither the purist nor the activist, who lived with the daily problem of choice. When the Loyalists in Spain demanded arms, for example, the Socialist party could only respond with a feeble policy of "workers aid," not (capitalist) government aid; but to the Spaniard, arms, not theoretical niceties, were the need of the moment. When the young trade-unionists, whom the socialists seeded into the labor movement, faced the necessity of going along politically with Roosevelt and the New Deal in order to safeguard progressive legislative gains, the socialists proposed a "labor party," rather than work with the

Democrats, and so the Socialist party lost almost its entire trade-union base. The threat of fascism and World War II finally proved to be the clashing rocks through which the socialist argonauts could not row safely. How to defeat Hitler without supporting capitalist society? Some socialists raised the slogan of a "third force." The Socialist party, however, realized the futility of that effort; in characteristic form, it chose abnegation. The best way to stem fascism, it stated, "is to make democracy work at home." But could the issue be resolved other than militarily? The main concern of the anti-fascist movement had to be with the political center of fascist power, Hitler's Berlin, and any other concern was peripheral.

In still another way the religious, chiliastic origin of modern socialism revealed itself: in the multiplication of splits, in the constant formation of sectarian splinter groups, each hotly disputing the other regarding the true road to power. Socialism is an eschatological movement; it is sure of its destiny, because "history" leads it to its goal. But though sure of its final ends, there is never a standard for testing the immediate means. The result is a constant fractiousness in socialist life. Each position taken is always open to challenge by those who feel that it would only swerve the movement from its final goal and lead it up some blind alley. And because it is an ideological movement, embracing all the realm of the human polity, the Socialist party is always challenged to take a stand on every problem from Vietnam to Finland, from prohibition to pacifism. And, since for every two socialists there are always three political opinions, the consequence has been that in its inner life the Socialist party has never, even for a single year, been without some issue which threatened to split the party and which forced it to spend much of its time on the problem of reconciliation or rupture. In this fact lies one of the chief clues to the fecklessness of American socialism as a *political movement* in the last thirty years.‡ But if in politics it proved to be impotent, it remained a moral force, and in Norman Thomas it had a new signpost.

‡ Beyond the reaches of this essay is the problem of the psychological types who are attracted by a sectarian existence. Yet one might say that the illusion of settling the fate of history, the mimetic combat on the plains of destiny, and the vicarious sense of power in demolishing opponents all provide a sure sense of gratification which makes the continuance of sectarian life desirable. The many leadership complexes, the intense aggressiveness through gossip, the strong clique group formations, all attest to a particular set of psychological needs and satisfactions which are filled in these opaque, molecular worlds.

If Debs was, at bottom, the sentimentalist of American socialism, Norman Thomas has been its moral figure. A communist critic once sneered at Norman Thomas for entitling his study of poverty in the United States *Human Exploitation* rather than *Capitalist Exploitation*. The critic, unwittingly, had a point, for what aroused Thomas was not the analytical and sociological but the ethical and emotional. Intellectually, Thomas would know that "the system" is to blame; but such abstractions rarely held meaning for him. His interest had always been the personal *fact* of injustice, committed by individuals; and while socialism might analyze the impersonal "basic" causes, he was always happiest when he could *act* where the issue was immediate and personal. In speaking out against sharecropper terror in Birdsong, Arkansas; in defying martial law in Terre Haute, Indiana; in exposing the Klan in Tampa; in uncovering the municipal corruption of Jimmy Walker's New York; in combating the anti-free-speech ordinances of Jersey's Boss Hague–in all these instances, Thomas' voice rang out with the eloquent wrath of an Elijah Lovejoy or of a William Lloyd Garrison.

These impulses came naturally to Norman Mattoon Thomas. Religion, orthodox Presbyterianism, was the center of his boyhood home. His father was a minister, as was his Welsh-born grandfather. He was raised in a strict sabbatarian code, but the harshness of his ancestral Calvinism was modified by the kindness of his parents. "My father who believed theoretically in eternal damnation," wrote Thomas, "would never say of any one that he was damned."[13]

Thomas, born in Marion, Ohio, in 1884, was a sickly little boy who grew too fast, became an awkward, skinny kid, shy with his peers and talkative with his elders, and who found his main satisfaction in reading. Norman was the eldest of six children, and the family was always busy with household chores and other activities of small-town middle-class life. Of the parents, Emma Mattoon was the more outstanding personality, and "father was content to have it so." In thinking back on his boyhood in the small Ohio town, Thomas remarked: "What a set-up for the modern psychologically-minded biographer or novelist. A study in revolt born of reaction from Presbyterian orthodoxy and the Victorian brand of Puritanism in a midwest setting. The only trouble is that this isn't what happened."

With the financial help of an uncle, Thomas satisfied a boyhood dream and entered Princeton, graduating in 1905 as class valedictorian. Entering the ministry was a more or less destined fact. But in the age of genteel faith in progress, acceptance of the old orthodoxies seemed out of place. As with many social-minded ministers of the day, the modernist and liberal gospel of Walter Rauschenbusch had its appeal. But it was the filth and poverty of the cold-water flats of the Spring Street slums on New York's west side that turned Thomas actively to social reform. And it was World War I and the influence of the Fellowship of Reconciliation, a religious pacifist organization, that made him a socialist. "God, I felt, was certainly not the 'God and Father of Our Lord Jesus Christ' if his servants could only serve him and the cause of righteousness by the diabolic means of war." Thomas' stand took him from the ministry into politics and journalism. (Rather than endanger the financial support his church received, he resigned the pastorate.) A tall handsome man with strongly-etched patrician features, rich resonant voice, and fine American credentials, he quickly became an outstanding leader in a party depleted of public figures. In 1924 he was nominated for governor of New York; four years later—because the two veteran party leaders, Morris Hillquit and Victor Berger, were European-born and because Dan Hoan was busy being mayor of Milwaukee—Thomas was nominated for the presidency.

As a party leader, Thomas had two serious flaws. For one, he strikingly distrusted his own generation and surrounded himself with considerably younger men who stood in an admiring and uncritical relation to him. The other was a profound fear of being manipulated, so that every political attack was taken personally. Unlike Debs, Thomas was intent on being party leader. Often a situation would develop—particularly in the late thirties—when, if party policy tended in a direction other than his, Thomas would threaten to resign (otherwise how could he speak on an issue with pure conscience?). Yet many of Thomas' decisions were made not with an eye to the political results but to the moral consequences as he saw them. Moreover, by background and temperament, Thomas was concerned largely with issues rather than ideas. In a party whose main preoccupation has been the refinement of "theory" even at the cost of interminable factional divisions, Thomas' interest in specific issues often meant shifting alliances with different factions while maintaining aloofness from the jesuitical debates that gave rise to these groups. Thus in the late thirties Thomas was with the right wing on the labor-party issue and shifted to the pacifist and left wing on the war problem. Thomas was probably most unhappy during the early and middle thirties, when, as a professed non-Marxist, he was involved in the conflicts of fifty-seven varieties of claims to revolutionary orthodoxy.

As a man whose instincts were primarily ethical, Thomas was the genuine moral man in the immoral society. But as a political man he was caught inextricably in the dilemmas of expediency, the relevant alternatives, and the lesser evil. As a sophisticated modern man, Thomas was acutely aware of his ambiguous role and felt he made the political choice. "One is obliged," he wrote in 1947, "to weigh one's actions in terms of relative social consequences . . . and the tragedy is that no choice can be positively good. . . . Positively [the pacifists] had nothing to offer in the problem of stopping Nazism before its triumph could not only enslave but corrupt the world. Nothing, that is, except for a religious faith in the power of God, a faith stronger if it could include a belief in immortality. It was something but not enough to affirm that the method of war was self-defeating for good ends. It was not enough to say 'if all Americans would act like Gandhi' we should more surely defeat avowed fascism. Possibly, but since almost no Americans would thus act the question remained of the lesser evil." Thomas did learn the lesson of the lesser evil: instead of being an absolute pacifist, however, he became an indecisive one. When the Franco rebellion broke out, Thomas gave up his religious pacifism, but was led to an ambiguous distinction whereby he supported the right of individuals to volunteer and fight but not "American official intervention by war which would involve conscription." After Pearl Harbor, Thomas came out in "critical support" of the United States government, a position which consisted in the first years largely of ignoring foreign policy and of speaking out against injustices on the home front. Fearful of another split, the Socialist party adopted a formula sufficiently elastic and ambiguous to permit pacifists, anti-war socialists, and pro-war socialists to continue together inside the party.[14] But to little avail. No one was satisfied with the compromise, and since factions were robbed of the incentive to split, the members simply resigned. From that point on, the Socialist party simply wasted away.

The Alien Outsider

For the twentieth-century Communist, there are none of these agonizing problems of ethics and politics. He is the perpetual alien living in the hostile enemy land. Any gestures of support, any pressure for social reforms, are simply tactics, a set of Potemkin villages, the façades to be torn down after the necessary moment for deception has passed. His is the ethic of "ultimate ends"; only the goal counts, the means are inconsequential.[15] Bolshevism thus is neither in the world nor of it, but stands outside. It takes no responsibility for the consequences of any act within the society nor does it suffer the tension of acquiescence or rejection. But the Socialist, unlike the Communist, lacks that fanatical vision, and so faces the daily anguish of participating in and sharing responsibility for the day-to-day problems of the society.

It is this commitment to the "absolute" that gives Bolshevism its religious strength. It is this commitment which sustains one of the great political myths of the century, the myth of the iron-willed Bolshevik. Selfless, devoted, resourceful, a man with a cause, he is the modern Hero. He alone, a man of action, a soldier for the future, continues the tradition of courage which is the aristocratic heritage bestowed on Western culture and which has been devitalized by the narrow, monetary calculus of the bourgeoisie. (Can the businessman be the Hero?) Such is the peculiar myth which has taken deep hold among many intellectuals. It is a myth which is also responsible for the deep emotional hatred and almost pathologic resentment felt most keenly by the ex-communist intellectual, the "defrocked priest," toward the party. For the "Bolshevik," through the myth of absolute selflessness, claims to be the "extreme man," the man of no compromise, the man of purity. The intellectual, driven to be moral, fears the comparison and resents the claim. Thus he bears either a sense of guilt or a psychological wound.

In addition to the myth of the Bolshevik as iron-willed Hero, twentieth-century communism has made several other distinctive contributions to the theory and practice of modern politics. Like so many other social doctrines, these were never put down systematically in a fully self-conscious fashion; yet over the years they have emerged as a coherent philosophy. Of these contributions some five can be linked schematically. These are central for understanding the history of the Communist party in this country.

One of the major innovations of the Bolsheviks is their theory of power. Against the nineteenth-century liberal view which saw social decisions as a reconciliation of diverse interests through compromise and consensus—this was a theory which social democracy gradually began to accept after World War I, when it was called upon to take responsibility for governments—power was defined as a monopoly of the means of coercion. Power was thought of almost in terms of physics, its equation being almost literally "mass times force equals power." The individual, central to the liberal theory of a market society, was for the Bolshevik a helpless entity. Only the organized group counted, and only a mass base could exert social leverage in society.

But a mass requires leadership. The great unresolved dilemma of Marxian sociology was the question of how the proletariat achieves the consciousness of its role. To await the immanent development of history was to rely on the fallacy of misplaced abstraction. "Spontaneity" was not for Lenin a reality in mass politics; nor was the trade-union an effective instrument. His answer, the most significant addition to revolutionary theory, was the vanguard role of the party.

Against the "economism" which glorified the role of the trade-union, Lenin argued that the mere organization of society on a trade-union basis could only lead to wage consciousness, not revolutionary consciousness; against the spontaneity theories of Rosa Luxemburg he argued that the masses, by nature, were backward. Only the vanguard party, aware of the precarious balance of social forces, could assess the play and correctly tip the scales in the revolutionary direction. This was the classic formulation of revolutionary avant-gardism which Lenin outlined in his *What Is to Be Done?*

In it he wrote that without the "dozen" tried and talented leaders —and talented men are not born by the hundred—professionally trained, schooled by long experience, and working in perfect harmony, no class in modern society is capable of conducting a determined struggle. "I assert," said Lenin, "(1) that no movement can be durable without a stable organization of leaders to maintain continuity; (2) that the more widely the masses are spontaneously drawn into the struggle and form the basis of the movement, the more necessary it is to have such an organization and the more stable must it be (for it is much easier for demagogues to sidetrack the more backward sections of the masses); (3) that the organization must consist chiefly of persons engaged in revolution as a profession."[16]

If the party were to become a vanguard, it needed discipline in action, and thus there arose the principle of party hierarchy and "centralism." A line was laid down by the leadership which was binding on all. Lenin's promulgation of these doctrines in 1903 split Russian socialism and brought about the emergence of the Bolshevik and Menshevik factions. In the beginning Trotsky opposed Lenin's ideas, but later he capitulated. As he wrote in his autobiography: ". . . there is no doubt that at that time I did not fully realize what an intense and imperious centralism the revolutionary party would need to lead millions of people in a war against the old order. . . . Revolutionary centralism is a harsh, imperative and exacting principle. It often takes the guise of absolute ruthlessness in its relation to individual members, to whole groups of former associates. It is not without significance that the words 'irreconcilable' and 'relentless' are among Lenin's favorites."[17]

From the principle of power and the theory of party organization rose two other key tenets of Bolshevism. One was the polarization of classes. Because it looked only toward the "final conflict," Bolshevism split society into two classes, the proletariat and the bourgeoisie. But the proletariat could only be emancipated by the vanguard party; hence anyone resisting the party must belong to the enemy. For Lenin, the maxim of the absolute ethic meant that "those who are not for me are against me." Hence, too, a formulation of the theory of "social fascism," which in the early 1930's branded the Social Democrats rather than Hitler as the chief enemy and led the Communists to unite, in several instances, with the Nazis in order to overthrow the German Republic.

The second tenet, deriving from the backward nature of the masses, was the key psychological tactic of formulating all policy into forceful slogans. Slogans dramatize events, make issues simple, and wipe out the qualifications, nuances, and subtleties which accompany democratic political action. In his chapter on slogans[18] Lenin wrote one of the first manuals on modern mass psychology. During the Revolution, the Bolsheviks achieved a flexibility of tactic by using such slogans as "All Power to the Soviets," "Land, Peace, and Bread," etc. The basic political tactic of all Communist parties everywhere is to formulate policy primarily through the use of key slogans which are transmitted first to the party rank and file and then to the masses.

The consequence of the theory of the vanguard party and its relation to the masses is a system of "two truths," the *consilia evangelica,* or special ethics endowed for those whose lives are dedicated to the revolutionary ends, and another truth for the masses. Out of this belief grew Lenin's famous admonition: one can lie, steal, or cheat, for the cause itself has a higher truth.

Except for the period from 1935 to 1945, the decade of fascism and war, the Communist party did not achieve any sizable following in the United States. In the misnamed "Red Decade," the Communist party, though never a national political force, did achieve important influence in the CIO (controlling at one time unions with about 20 per cent of the membership of the Congress, but, more important, holding almost all the major staff positions in the national CIO and running the large state and city CIO councils in New York, Illinois, California, and other key states) and did attain a position of respectability in the liberal and cultural community of the country.

The greatest triumph of Communist propaganda—the fifth innovation—was the creation of the papier-mâché front organizations. These fronts, sought to "hook" famous names and exploit them for Communist causes by means of manifestoes, open letters, petitions, declarations, statements, pronouncements, protests, and other illusions of opinion ground-swells in the land. The viciousness of the front technique was that it encouraged a herd spirit whereby only "collective opinion" carried weight; and if a critic dared challenge a tenet of Soviet faith, he was drowned out by the mass chorus of several score voices. As Eugene Lyons put it: "Did rumor-mongers charge that a horrifying famine had been enforced by the Kremlin to 'punish' forty million Soviet citizens in an area as large as the United States? Half a hundred experts on nutrition and agronomy, all the way from Beverly Hills to Park Avenue penthouses, thereupon condemned the capitalists and Trotskyites responsible for the libel, and the famine was liquidated."

The corruption of the front technique was that many poor dupes, imagining that they were the leaders of the great causes, found themselves enslaved by the opium of publicity and became pliable tools of the Communist manipulators behind the scenes. In other instances upper-class matrons and aspiring actresses found in the Communist "causes" a cozy non-conformism to replace their passé conventions. The ultimate betrayal was of the masses of front members who gained a sense of participation which they sadly discovered to be spurious when the party lines changed and they found that they themselves were victims of party manipulations.

But such influence was only possible because the Communist party was, at the time, moving in parallel direction with the liberal community whose emotions had been aroused by Hitler and Franco. Because of its superior organization, the Communist party was able to assume the leadership of many "causes." And yet, curiously enough, its very success was almost a corrupting influence. In the late 1930's, in the days of the Popular Front, the Communists suddenly found themselves accepted in areas (labor movement, Hollywood, urban politics) where they had been ostracized or scorned. But the Popular Front was a tactic. It had been dictated by Moscow as part of its policy of seeking national alliances. The Communists had not given up their belief in revolution or power; the liberals were a force to be manipulated. In 1943, however, in the so-called Teheran phase of national unity, there was a new phase. Browder took the decisive step of dissolving the Communist party as a political party and reconstituting it as a political association. But more than tactics was involved. The previous success in the Popular Front had given the party a new perspective. Browder himself was pleased by the new recognition and respectability of the party. In place of the Socialist party, it was becoming the acknowledged "left," occupying a "legitimate" place in American life. How far this revisionism would have gone is a moot point, for in 1945, abruptly and savagely, Browder was dumped, and the party was ordered into a new, sectarian phase, in accordance with the new, anti-Western aggressive line of Moscow. The Wallace campaign of 1948 was a desperate effort to salvage the old liberal support for the new extreme line. But the effort only resulted in isolating the Communists from the labor and liberal movements and leading to their exclusion.

In sum, the main appeal of the Communist party was to the dispossessed intelligentsia of the depression generation and to the "engineers of the future" who were attracted by the elitist appeal described above. It stirred many Americans to action against injustices and left them with burnt fingers when, for reasons of expediency, the party line changed and the cause was dropped. It provided an unmatched political sophistication to a generation that went through its ranks, and it gave to an easy-going, tolerant, sprawling America a lesson in organizational manipulation and hard-bitten ideological devotion which this country, because of its tradition and temperament, found hard to understand. But most of all, through the seeds of distrust and anxiety it sowed, communism helped spawn a reaction, a hysteria and bitterness that democratic America may find hard to live down in the years ahead.

From the sixteenth-century chiliast, burning with impatient zeal for immediate salvation, to the twentieth-century American labor leader, sunning himself on the sands of Miami Beach, is a long, almost surrealist jump of history. Yet these are antipodal figures of a curving ribbon which binds all movements that have sought to change the hierarchical social order in society.

The chiliast and the anarchist live in crisis, at the edge of History, expecting the world to be changed in a flash. The Bolshevik identifies himself with History and confidently expects that the turn of the wheel will put him forward, replacing the old. For these, then, the questions of social compromise, of the tension of ethics and politics, have had no meaning. But for others, particularly the socialists, the dilemma has been insoluble.

Living in the world, one cannot refuse the responsibility of sharing in the decisions of the society. In the here and now, people do not live at the extreme (in the "entirety" which was Sorel's myth), but they live "in parts," parceling out their lives amidst work, home, neighborhood, fraternal club, etc. Nor does History, as Acton put it, "work with bottled essences." Compromise is the "soul if not the whole of politics . . . and progress is along diagonals." For the socialist movement, living in but not of the world, it was a wisdom which it could not accept. Doctrine remained; but the movement failed.

NOTES

1. Letter to Danielson, No. 169, and Letter to Schleuter, No. 222, in *Karl Marx and Friedrich Engels; Selected Correspondence, 1846–1895* (New York, 1934), pp. 360 and 497.

2. Quoted in Goetz A. Briefs, *The Proletariat* (New York, 1937), p. 193. Communist economists, embarrassed by this situation, have tried to deny this material gain. A statistician, Jurgen Kuczynski (now an official of the East German government), argued, in an effort to defend Marx's proposition of the growing impoverishment of the working class under capitalism, that the living conditions of the American workers in the nineteenth century had actually deteriorated. Confronted from his own evidence with the fact that real wages had increased from 1790 to 1900, Kuczynski fell back on the Leninist theory that capitalism divided the workers into a labor aristocracy that did benefit and that in effect was bribed by higher wages, and a larger group of exploited masses. But this was only a rhetorical rather than a statistical claim. See Jurgen Kuczynski, *A Short History of Labour Conditions under Industrial Capitalism* (Vol. II of *The United States of America, 1789 to the Present Day*) (London, 1943).

3. A general hypothesis, such as the one above, can, however, only suggest an answer. It states conditions; it sensitizes one to questions. But the empirical inquiry into the fate of social movement has to be pinned to the specific questions of time, place, and opportunity. A social movement, like an individual, defines its character in the choices it makes. Therefore, one has to locate the "crisis points," define the alternatives which confronted the movement, and understand the motives for the choices made. In my monograph "The Background and Development of Marxian Socialism in the United States," I have tried to locate such turning points in American Socialism. (See Egbert and Persons [eds.], *Socialism and American Life* [Princeton, 1952], pp. 215–404.)

4. Cited in Gertrude Himmelfarb, "The American Revolution in the Political Theory of Lord Acton," *Journal of Modern History*, December 1949, p. 312.

5. "Politics as a Vocation," in *From Max Weber: Essays in Sociology*, eds. H. H. Gerth and C. W. Mills (New York, 1946), pp. 119ff.; also p. 9.

6. Karl Mannheim, *Ideology and Utopia* (New York, 1936), pp. 190–93.

7. Georges Sorel, *Reflections on Violence* (3d ed.; Glencoe, Ill., 1950), p. 140.

8. In *The German Ideology* Marx poses the question of how self-interest becomes transformed into ideology. "How does it come about," he asks, "that personal interests continually grow, despite the persons, into class-interests, into common interests which win an independent

existence over against individual persons, in this independence take on the shape of general interests, enter as such into opposition with the real individuals, and in this opposition, according to which they are defined as general interests, can be conceived by the consciousness as ideal, even as religious, sacred interests?" But Marx, exasperatingly, never goes on to answer the question. (See *The German Ideology* [New York, 1939], p. 203.) Sidney Hook, in his article on "Materialism" in the *Encyclopedia of the Social Sciences* (New York, 1933), X, p. 219, sought to rephrase the problem of consciousness in these terms: "What are the specific mechanisms by which the economic conditions influence the habits and motives of classes, granted that individuals are actuated by motives that are not always a function of individual self-interest? Since classes are composed of individuals, how are class interests furthered by the non-economic motives of individuals?" But having phrased it more sharply, he too left it as a question. So far no Marxist theoretician has yet detailed the crucial psychological and institutional nexuses which show how the "personifications" or masks of class role are donned by the individual as self-identity.

9. The question of how the proletariat achieves self-consciousness, and of the role of the intellectual, a person from another class, as the leader of the proletariat, long bedeviled the radical movement. In Marx's writings there are three different conceptions of class. In the *Communist Manifesto* there is the eschatological view in which the *Götterdämmerung* of history polarizes society into two classes and awareness of class position arises from beholding the widening abyss. In the conclusion to *Das Kapital,* Marx begins a simplified analysis of "essential" class division (i.e., as ideal types, rather than as reality) on the basis of source of income; but the conversion of income groups into congruent categories still begs the question of what the mechanisms of self-awareness are. Marx's actual historical analyses, as in *The Eighteenth Brumaire,* show a subtle awareness of the complex shadings of social divisions, which in action give rise to many varied social categories and diverse political interest groups. It is only, then, in "final" instances, rather than day-to-day politics, that class division and identity become crucial for Marxist politics. (For a discussion of Marx's theory of class, see Raymond Aron, "Social Structure and the Ruling Class," *British Journal of Sociology,* March 1950.)

10. It was in this statement, in the course of a debate with the Socialists, that Gompers first used the phrase, which later was to become the common description of the AFL, of unionism pure and simple. See Samuel Gompers, *Seventy Years of Labor,* I, pp. 286–87.

11. Ibid., II, p. 105.

12. Ray Ginger, *The Bending Cross* (New Brunswick, N.J., 1949).

13. Thomas made some autobiographical references in his *As I See It* (New York, 1932). The above questions, as well as some description of Thomas' beliefs, are from an unpublished memoir which Thomas wrote for his family in 1944 and to which this author had access.

14. A situation which provoked from Dwight Macdonald the comment: "The failure to split on the war issue has always seemed to me an indication of a certain lack of political seriousness in all the S.P. factions" ("Why I Will Not Support Norman Thomas," *Politics,* October 1944, p. 279).

15. "The believer in an ethic of ultimate ends," wrote Max Weber, "feels 'responsible' only for seeing to it that the flame of pure intention is not quenched."

16. V. I. Lenin, *What Is to Be Done?* (New York, 1929), p. 116.

17. Leon Trotsky, *My Life* (New York, 1930), pp. 161–62.

18. V. I. Lenin, "On Slogans," in *Toward the Seizure of Power, Collected Works* (New York, 1932), XXI, Book I, pp. 43–50.

COMMENT

John H. M. Laslett

Bell's major argument in this essay, which is probably the most influential attempt to explain the failure of American socialism to appear in the last twenty years, is that socialism failed in the United States because of its excessively dogmatic and chiliastic ideology, and because of continuing internal disagreements over the nature and purposes of the movement, which prevented it from translating its essentially revolutionary ideology into meaningful political action.[1]

In making this argument Bell aligns himself with those, on both the left and right wings of the political spectrum, who find the explanation for the difficulties which the socialist movement has always experienced in America in the internal dynamics of the movement, not in the exceptionalist character of American society.[2] Structural factors in the society which may have inhibited the growth of a strong socialist movement, such as those described by Sombart or Perlman in Part Three of this book, are dismissed by Bell as "conditions," not "causes," or "even if true, . . . [as] simply one side of the coin." The root cause of the problem, he argues in a much quoted passage, was that the socialist movement (although not the trade union movement, which made the necessary adjustments to American life) "was trapped by the unhappy problem of living *in* but not *of* the world: it could only act, and then inadequately, as the moral, but not the political man in an immoral society."[3] In the preface to a later version of his essay, Bell expands his theory (like Perlman attempting to generalize the presumed exclusive "job consciousness" of the American worker to include British, German, and Russian workers as well) to explain not simply the failure of the Old Left in America but also the difficulties faced by European socialism, and by the New Left, on both continents.[4] It was the ideological rigidity imposed by

Marxist theory, he argues, which prevented the German Social Democratic Minister of Finance, Rudolf Hilferding, from solving the economic problems of the Weimar Republic, because of the lack of sound Marxist teaching on remedying the shortcomings of a capitalist economy in the short run.[5]

Although the original "in" "of" metaphor derives from Martin Luther, the essential framework for this argument comes, as Bell acknowledges, from Max Weber's discussion of politics as a way of life. This is an important matter, since in the essay of Weber which Bell cites, Weber appears at first to confine legitimate politics to those which are limited to an "ethic of responsibility" (i.e., to "is" or present-oriented politics), and to reject those which are devoted to an "ethic of absolute ends" (i.e., "ought" or future-oriented politics), which are unacceptable if civil peace is to be maintained. Bell accepts this distinction, arguing that "the foundation of a pluralist society rests . . . on this separation of ethics and politics and on the limiting of ethics to the formal rules of the game."[6]

Aside from the inherent oversimplifications of this pluralist model, which presents a static, essentially ahistorical view of American society, and which—like the more extreme form of its corollary, the conflict model espoused by radical critics of recent American historiography—runs the risk of avoiding difficult historical questions by the way in which they are posed, this view comes close to imposing a moral imperative upon socialists *not* to interfere with the basic structure of the society, because to do so would run counter to the "rules of the game." It also betrays a major misunderstanding of Max Weber's meaning. Writing in the First World War under the impending chaos of the abortive German revolution of 1918, Weber's purpose was by no means simply to uphold the "ethic of responsibility" (i.e., the politics of minor adjustment and piecemeal change, now espoused by the older generation of American liberals, like Bell himself) as in all cases superior to the "ethic of conscience" (i.e., the politics of passion and commitment, now fashionable among their offspring), but to treat both kinds of politics as complementary to the other, and each as necessary to a dialectical process of social change. Weber certainly chided political chiliasts who ignored social realities, or who failed to take responsibility for their actions. But he disapproved also of political opportunists who sought to enhance their own position in society without any vision of a future world in mind. "Certainly all historical experience," Weber wrote later in the same essay, "confirms the truth—that man would not have attained the possible unless time and again he had reached out for the impossible."[7]

But the major issue is whether Bell's thesis itself is adequate as an historical explanation for the failure of the socialist movement in America, or for its limited success in other countries as well. And on this matter it is possible to have grave doubts.

In the first place, the distinction between "is"- and "ought"-oriented politics is, in the context which Bell is describing, very largely misplaced. All future-oriented social movements, whether political or not, suffer from an inherent tension between "is" and "ought," from feminism, which is semi-political, to the Committee for a More Effective Congress, which is overtly so; and one index of the health of a modern society (perhaps even of modernization itself) is the presence of an institutional framework which provides some means of resolving this tension in a rational way, usually through the medium of political parties. Nowhere is this more true than in the United States, where attempts to resolve the inherent tension between the future-oriented promises of the Declaration of Independence and *de facto* inequalities in the society have for two hundred years provided the major source of ammunition for political debate. (What other country has striven so mightily to translate the moral imperatives of the eighteenth century into twentieth-century political practice? Certainly not Great Britain or France, with their supposedly more ideology-laden revolutionary traditions.[8])

Seen from this point of view, the crucial issue becomes whether or not the American socialist movement, or any other socialist party, has been significantly less able than other future-oriented political movements to state its aspirations in realistic terms, and, when given the opportunity, to pursue them realistically as a matter of political practice. Bell answers this question in the negative, arguing that up until the First World War the American Socialist Party's supposed concern for converting the proletariat and advocating "immediate demands" was not pressed with any real vigor. Instead, the party refused to face up to the realities of the then contemporary political world, and simply "waited for the new." The war itself was the first major issue on which the Socialist Party took a genuine stand, forcing it "in" to the real world, but not yet making it a part "of" it. Thereafter, it "straddled" issues such as the Spanish Civil War and the Second World War, declining feebly into ineffectiveness in the period after 1945.[9]

Many of the assertions contained in this analysis are simply not borne out by the facts. Like the socialist parties of Europe, the Socialist Party of America had a long list of "immediate demands" attached to its Marxist preamble (several of which, like conservation, public ownership of the railroads, employees' compensation, and a graduated income tax, were also included in the platforms of reform-oriented parties such as the Populists, the Progressives, and the Wilsonian Democrats in 1912[10]). Like their European counterparts also, when presented with the opportunity it was these reform measures which the American socialists sought to implement, leaving the revolutionary phraseology of the preamble to rest in the shadows. In his longer essay Bell points to the antipathy displayed by the socialists toward their colleagues who gave support to reform-oriented groups such as the Nonpartisan League in North Dakota. But he ignores the much more widespread and characteristic examples of moderate, reformist activity which the socialists themselves undertook when elected to office. In Milwaukee, for example (the most important city in which the socialists held office), or in Berkeley, California, in Butte, Montana, or in various Massachusetts towns at the turn of the century, the socialists built moderately successful municipal administrations around hostility toward corruption, public works, improved sanitation, and a whole range of "gas and water" reformist measures which were no different from those being enacted in Birmingham or in Bordeaux. Such evidence makes nonsense of Bell's claim that, "Even on local municipal issues the party would not compromise."[11]

Socialist attitudes toward the official trade union movement were indeed somewhat more ambivalent, since Debs and a minority of more radical elements briefly supported revolutionary movements such as the IWW as alternatives to the AFL. Nevertheless, as I have argued in detail elsewhere, despite the attention which has been paid to them by labor historians, in the period before 1914 the influence of the "impossibilists" or extreme left-wing socialists in the labor movement was in fact very small. The IWW did not, unfortunately, secure more than a very limited foothold in any of the industries and trades then being organized by the AFL, with the possible exception of metal mining and coal, even during the period of its greatest strength (1905–17). And its dual-union activities did not prevent very considerable efforts being made—if one is to judge by money collected for union-led strikes, Socialist Party speakers invited to union conventions, and Socialist candidates elected to union office—to secure the support of the existing, frequently conservatively oriented trade unions.[12]

It is true that the First World War was the first important issue on which the American socialists took a virtually unanimous stand (the membership ratified the April 1917 St. Louis Declaration against the war by 21,639 votes to 2,752).[13] But it is wholly misleading to give the impression that the Socialist Party moved from a position of total rejection of American society in the period before 1914 to one of "straddling" it thereafter, and that in the 1930s it "acknowledged the fact that it lived 'in' the world, but refused the responsibility of becoming a part 'of' it." As already indicated, in its pre-1914 municipal and trade union policies the party had already made strenuous efforts to attract reform-minded moderates in the bourgeois world. It also "straddled" political issues just as frequently before the First World War as it did after. It is perfectly true, for example, that on the question of the Spanish Civil War (the touchstone of all left-wing consciences in the 1930s), the socialists "straddled" the issue insofar as they favored voluntary aid to Spain instead of direct government intervention—a position, incidentally, which was similar to that of most European socialist movements. But this was no different from the kind of "straddling" which the party had undertaken before 1917 on such issues as immigration, race, or the agrarian question.[14] In any event, "straddling" in the sense of obscuring ideological differences for the sake of united front is a sign of realism, not of rigidity; and far from being a vice, it is a time-honored American political virtue.

It is hard to escape the conclusion, moreover, that for Bell becoming a "part 'of' the world" in the 1930s would have meant little more for the socialists than becoming a pressure group within the reform wing of the Democratic Party. This was a course of action which by the 1950s the Socialist Party found itself impelled to take because of its continuing weakness—probably rightly if it was to avoid the total futility which remaining independent had brought to the SLP. But throughout the 1930s, with the communists monopolizing the fascism issue, and moderate CIO reformists usurping whatever position the socialists had made for themselves in the labor movement, the party leadership was aware that if it was to have any chance of exploiting the opportunities opened up for it by the Depression, to endorse the New Deal in its entirety—as Norman Thomas showed in his famous pamphlet *A Socialist Looks at the New Deal*[15]—would have meant committing political suicide. The party had come close to doing that once before—when it endorsed Robert M. La Follette for the presidency in 1924—and thereafter it was continually faced with the dilemma of trying to maintain a separate program which would be meaningful to the American electorate, while at the same time trying not to appear irrelevant. It was a dilemma created by attempting to come to terms with the realities of American politics, not by failing to do so.

More fundamentally, it may be argued that most of the difficulties with Bell's argument stem from the fact that he attempts to deal with both the socialist and communist movements in the same analytic framework, seeking to impute to the first of these two movements characteristics which more properly belong to part of—and only to a part of—the second. Throughout his essay Bell makes great play with the view that socialism as a movement originated with the impulse toward a secular form of chiliasm (deriving in turn from the spiritual chiliasm of the Reformation), the inability to find fulfillment for which allegedly leads to nihilism and despair—a final remark which reveals more about the contemporary New Left than it does about the Old. In fact, however, this chiliastic form of millenarianism describes only one psychological dynamic out of many which draw people to socialism (ranging from such apparently contradictory movements as anti-clericalism and Christian humanitarianism, to poverty and an aristocratic distaste for the brutalities of the industrial world), few of which, in themselves, imply the cataclysmic world view which Bell describes.

It may be true—it probably is true—that the communism of the 1930s, like other extreme revolutionary movements, attracted particularly those who had a desire to realize the millennium in the here and now. But by no means all socialists can be characterized in this way. Bell's oversimplifications here, as elsewhere in his book, result from his confusing the demise of the Old Left of the 1930s, and particularly the death of the old CP (i.e., the *End of Ideology,* or the end of the dominant radical impulse for Bell's own particular generation), with the death of socialist idealism generally, which as the rise of the New Left has effectively demonstrated is still very much alive. This confusion goes back, in turn, to Bell's excessively rigid distinction between Weber's "ethic of responsibility" and "ethic of conscience," which makes it difficult for him to recognize any form of politics which goes beyond the first to embrace the second.

In the 1890s, Daniel De Leon's Socialist Labor Party (which in its strict internal discipline and revolutionary commitments strongly resembled the Communist Party of post-1919) did indeed behave in a rigid and doctrinaire manner, repudiating the established labor movement in favor of dual unionism and dismissing "immediate demands" for legislative reform as irrelevant and "infantile." Similarly, the post-1919 Communist Party, acting this time at the bidding of Moscow and the Third International, showed little understanding or regard for the realities of American political life.[16] But in between these two dates, the Socialist Party of America (which was much more important than either of these other two movements) was—Bell's own remarks in the preface to his later essay notwithstanding—in many respects a genuine American political party, a regional and ethnic coalition of Marxists, ex-Populists, Bellamyites, trade unionists, and reformers which responded as pragmatically as could be expected of any future-oriented party, and certainly as pragmatically as most of its European counterparts, to the everyday exigencies of political life.

Bell's discussion of socialist personalities (limited to Debs and Norman Thomas) also reflects the dangers of attempting to encompass an entire movement within a single stereotype. His reference to the messianic character of Debs's rhetoric rings true, but here again his "is"-"ought," present-future dichotomy leads him astray. Most political rhetoric—virtually all American political rhetoric—is in some sense visionary or future-oriented, whatever ideology it purports to represent, and its function is to emphasize vote-catching generalities, not to indicate how a political party would act when once in power. Both Debs's sentimentalism and Thomas' moralism reflected quite different, but effective and respected elements in the American political tradition, the one redolent of William Jennings Bryan, and the other of Woodrow Wilson: both of them great contemporaries whom the two socialist leaders respectively resembled and admired.

It is true that neither Debs nor Thomas was a particularly effective party leader, and both tried to disassociate themselves from the Socialist Party's internal debates. But there were other men in the party, such as the machine-oriented Victor Berger or the practical Morris Hillquit, who were quite different from both Debs and Thomas—and who were in fact considerably more important than either of them in formulating party policy, at least until 1933—both of whom had the requisite "hard-headedness of the politician."[17] It was probably a net advantage to the party to have as its presidential candidates two men who tried to avoid being identified with any particular faction (although both were generally regarded as "left-wing" and after 1933 Thomas did intervene in party disputes, sometimes with disastrous results) around whom the faithful could rally at election time. It is worth adding, moreover, that neither Thomas nor Debs was quite as otherworldly even in their political rhetoric as Bell suggests. For example, Bell cites two or three phrases from a 1900 Debs article to suggest that Debs considered imperialism and the gold standard to be "meaningless phrases," and of no importance to the proletariat. In fact, the remainder of that article is devoted to an extensive attack on McKinley's foreign policy, showing Debs to be fully aware of its importance as an issue.[18] Thomas, by Bell's own admission, was not even a Marxist, but an issue-oriented reformer who was at his best, like the English Fabians, in delineating specific grievances and correcting them—hardly a chiliastic ideologue of the Daniel De Leon or William Z. Foster variety.[19]

It may still be said that even if the Socialist Party of America did resemble other political parties in the looseness of its structure and the diversity of its appeal, it still carried too much intellectual baggage to be a genuine American political party, and that it broke down because it quarreled over issues on which its members could not afford to disagree. There may be something to this, although my own view is that this has far more to do with a lack of access to power—or to influence in "other institutions" in the society, as Bell himself acknowledges, without exploring the idea fully—than it does with the character of socialist beliefs. It was no coincidence, for example, that the major splits in the Socialist Party occurred in the period after 1919, when it had been reduced to political impotence, and not in the period before World War I, when it was growing rapidly and had over a thousand of its members in federal, state, and local office. It is a truism of party theory that sectarianism and factionalism are diseases of political impotence, which diminish with the prospect of office; and it might well be illuminating to inquire more deeply into the influence erected by the Socialist Party's proximity to power upon the character of its ideology. Its conduct when in office, in Milwaukee, Reading, or Lynn, Massachusetts, suggests an ongoing conflict between an almost pusillanimous degree of pragmatism when in power and a narrower form of ideological militancy when out of it—a conflict which in itself may account for many of the party's internal conflicts, but which did not derive from the nature of its ideology as such. European comparisons make an even stronger case for the view that the successful growth of a socialist movement depends far more, as both Perlman and Sombart suggest, upon the presence or absence of certain structural factors in the society than it does upon the character of socialist ideology. (By "structural factors," I mean the nature of the class system, the extent of democracy, the distribution of wealth, and—although this is not usually included in a Marxist definition of structure—the character of the dominant values, as the Italian Marxist Antonio Gramsci, for example, defines them in his recently translated *Prison Notebooks*). Indeed, such comparisons appear to render almost ludicrous any argument which relies upon the nature of that ideology alone. In Germany, for example, the Social Democratic Party grew most rapidly in the first decade of the twentieth century during the period of the great revisionist controversy, which threatened to undermine the whole edifice upon which European Marxism had been built, and made the American socialists' quarrels over tactical and ideological matters seem petty by comparison. In England, the Labour Party took office in 1924 as much because of a split in the Liberal Party and the effects of the Lloyd George coalition upon the general political situation as because of any significant growth in working-class socialist convictions. And in Russia, the Bolsheviks clearly took power because of the collapse of the Czarist regime and the weakness of the Kadets and other liberal elements in the Provisional Government, despite the fact that by 1917 Lenin's doctrinaire (but tactically brilliant) insistence upon a revolutionary putsch had alienated not only the moderate Social Revolutionaries (who were prepared to establish a reformist government along Western political lines) but also many of his former Menshevik and Bolshevik supporters as well.[20]

How socialist parties behave when actually in power at the national level is, of course, a wholly different matter, and one on which the American experience can throw little light above the municipal level—although Victor Berger and Meyer London (the only two Socialists ever elected to Congress, and the nearest the Socialist Party of America ever came to power at the federal level) certainly showed no sign of being paralyzed by being "in" but not "of" the world.[21] Europe is a very different and much more important story, but even here it may be suggested that the inhibitions felt by Hilferding in Germany, by the second Labour government in Britain, or by the Popular Front in France resulted as much from the inherent difficulties of coalition government, from the preoccupation with fascism, and from a lack of political courage as they did from the rigidities or inadequacies of socialist theory.

It is true, as Adolph Sturmthal has pointed out, that in the depression years of the early 1930s the socialist (or socialist-dominated) governments of Britain and Germany (and in 1936 to some extent the Popular Front government in France also) remained prisoners of traditional laissez-faire economics (balanced budgets, stable currency, and reduced government spending), in part because orthodox Marxism provided few guides on how to counteract the cyclical operation of a capitalist economy, believing it necessary to allow the depression to run its course instead.[22] But in Sweden already in the 1930s, and in England and other European countries after the Second World War, once the lessons of Keynes had been fully learned social democratic regimes were able to operate a mixed economy and take steps toward social equality with at least some degree of success, without being caught up in the "in the world, not of it" conflict which Bell appears to believe dooms moderate socialist regimes inevitably to failure.

It can seriously be questioned whether the compromises which Attlee, Blum, or more latterly Brandt found it necessary to make with welfare capitalism in order to remain in power emasculated their earlier radicalism to such a degree that they could no longer be called socialists. In the same way it can be argued that after 1936 a similar rightward drift in the Socialist Party of America made it so reformist as to abandon all serious attempts at socialism—a development which was all the more serious for the American movement, since once Norman Thomas and Michael Harrington had made the American party virtually indistinguishable from the Democrats, they estranged the radicals without winning any new support elsewhere. But it cannot seriously be argued that these socialist leaders were chiliasts who had neither understanding of nor concern for the realities of political life. If anything, of course, precisely the opposite was true; almost to a man, the European so-called socialist statesmen of the 1930s and the 1940s (if they can be dignified with such a contradictory set of terms) were pusillanimous accommodationists who neither knew how to nor basically had any interest in fundamentally altering the capitalist system over which they temporarily exercised control. Even if either of these two qualifications had been present, however, myriads of other factors besides their particular brand of Marxism would have contributed to determining how successful or not they would have been.

Thus, the most serious weakness of Bell's argument is that he gives no satisfactory means of weighing the relative importance of ideology versus structural factors in assessing the reasons for socialism's failure, but simply *assumes* the primacy of ideological rigidity as the "root" cause, with only a passing reference to other possible factors. For the serious historian (and surely also for the serious sociologist) such mono-causal explanations as this must by definition be suspect; and in the absence of overwhelming evidence that ideological rigidity, or the difficulty of translating ideology into practice, *was* the main reason for the failure of socialism in America—which the evidence presented in this brief essay has attempted to refute—other explanations must be brought into play.

None of what has been written above should be taken to imply that the Socialist Party of America did not have a powerful left wing, or that there were not those who pressed it to behave in a more revolutionary way. Sometimes a Right-Center coalition dominated the Socialist Party, and sometimes a Left-Center one (as in the period from 1917 to 1920 or again in the 1930s).[23] But the ideological stand which the party took appeared to bear little relationship—although of course it bore some—to the size of its vote, or to the degree of its acceptance in the society generally. Viewing the American socialist movement as a whole (and including for this purpose both its socialist and communist wings, as Bell does), it is apparent that it went through periods in which "ought" or future-oriented elements were dominant, as well as periods in which “is” or present-oriented factions were in control. Neither approach worked. This surely implies strongly that we must look, not only at the nature of the movement’s ideology, but also at the nature of the society in which it operated, if we are to arrive at a full explanation for its lack of success.

NOTES

1. Bell first put forward this thesis in a longer essay, "The Background and Development of Marxian Socialism in the United States," in D. D. Egbert and S. Persons, *Socialism and American Life,* 2 vols. (Princeton: Princeton University Press, 1952), pp. 213–405, the first portion of which constitutes the article under review. The entire essay was republished in book form fifteen years later as *Marxian Socialism in the United States* (Princeton: Princeton University Press, 1967), partly, as Bell rightly says in his preface, because "the theoretical and interpretative framework . . . has influenced many of the subsequent studies in the field" (p. vii). My own comments here are directed to the shorter essay, save where there are specific references to the longer one.

2. On this point (although on little else) Bell agrees with radical historians of American socialism, such as Ira Kipnis, James Weinstein, or Gabriel Kolko, who also espouse the internal dynamics explanation. This shows that arguments over American exceptionalism do not necessarily correspond to arguments between the political Left and Right, although they are often thought to do so.

3. Bell, *End of Ideology,* p. 268.

4. I intend no such blanket statement. By "failure" in this essay, as implied in the Preface to the book as a whole, I mean simply the inability of the Old Left in the United States (the SLP, the IWW, the SP of A, and the CP) to convert any significant number of Americans to the need for overthrowing or seriously modifying the capitalist system. Although I make some interim observations concerning the difficulties encountered by the European social democratic parties later on in this essay, I intend no judgment here as to the ways in which socialist beliefs may have influenced American intellectuals or writers, stimulated social reforms carried out by others, etc., nor as to the past or future prospects of the New Left.

5. Bell, *Marxian Socialism in the United States,* p. viii.

6. Bell, *End of Ideology,* pp. 269–70; Max Weber, "Politics as a Vocation," in H. H. Gerth and C. Wright Mills (eds.), *From Max Weber: Essays in Sociology* (New York, 1958), pp. 120–27.

7. Max Weber's meaning is important, for his distinction (which Bell wrongly erects into a dichotomy) between the "ethic of conscience" and the "ethic of responsibility" is a key element in the current academic debate over the "end of ideology"—and by extension in the debate over the failure of American socialism also, since Bell's interpretations of Weber lead him as if by logic to exclude the "politics and conscience" (including socialist politics) from the realm of the politically possible. See Weber, op. cit., p. 128; Stephen W. Rousseau and James Farganis, "American Politics and the End of Ideology," in *Brit-*

ish Journal of Sociology, XIV, 4 (1963); Chaim Waxman (ed.), *The End of Ideology Debate* (New York, Funk & Wagnalls, 1968).

8. Indeed, it may be argued that future-oriented political parties have a continued guarantee of relevance by virtue of their very future orientation (provided they espouse at least some of the ideals enshrined in their nation's political culture), just as conservative parties do, by virtue of embodying natural traditions. This is less true both of reactionary parties, and of middle-of-the-road parties whose ideology becomes anachronistic or obsolete, such as the British Liberal Party or the French Radical Party.

9. Bell, *End of Ideology,* pp. 274–77.

10. Kirk H. Porter, *National Party Platforms* (New York, Macmillan, 1924), pp. 323, 329, 336–37, 339, 343, 347, 361–68ff. In his longer essay Bell also argues that despite these "immediate demands" the Socialist Party of America rarely took stands on "current issues agitating the American body politic." On this matter, however, the presence or absence of specific demands in the party platform is not a reliable guide. The socialist press, which included over three hundred periodicals at its peak, frequently carried articles discussing issues of national importance, and leading party figures such as Debs, Victor Berger, and Meyer London wrote and spoke out often on agrarian issues, immigration, American foreign policy, the Negro problem, and other matters of contemporary concern. See Bell, *Marxian Socialism in the United States,* pp. 54, 74; Arthur M. Schlesinger, Jr. (ed.), *Writings and Speeches of E. V. Debs* (New York, Macmillan, 1948), pp. 63–73, 271–74, 293–310, 326–28, 337–40ff.; Victor Berger, *Broadsides* (Milwaukee, Social-Democratic Publishing Co., 1912), pp. 54–59, 60–68, 97–114, 121–26, 146–55, 256–63ff.; Melech Epstein, *Profiles of Eleven* (Detroit, Wayne State University Press, 1965), pp. 175–85.

11. Bell, *End of Ideology,* p. 274; Ira Kipnis, *The American Socialist Movement, 1897–1912* (New York, Columbia University Press, 1952), pp. 359–62; Edward Muzik, "Victor L. Berger: Making Marx Respectable," *Wisconsin Magazine of History,* LXVII (Summer 1964), pp. 301–8; Henry Bedford, *Socialism and the Workers in Massachusetts, 1886–1912* (Amherst, University of Massachusetts Press, 1966), pp. 69, 85, 102–4, 121, 131ff.

12. See Laslett, *Labor and the Left, A Study of Socialist and Radical Influences in the American Labor Movement, 1881–1924* (New York, Basic Books, 1970), pp. 289–90ff.

13. James Weinstein, *The Decline of American Socialism, 1912–1925* (New York, Monthly Review Press, 1967), p. 127.

14. Kipnis, op. cit., pp. 127–34, 217–19, 276–88.

15. Norman Thomas, *A Socialist Looks at the New Deal* (New York, pamphlet, Socialist Party of America, 1933), pp. 18–19ff.

16. *Daniel De Leon, The Man and His Work: A Symposium* (New York, Socialist Labor Party, 1919), pp. 26–30, 63ff. For the Communist Party, see I. Howe and L. Coser, *The American Communist*

Party, A Critical History (Boston, Beacon Press, 1957), pp. 73–76, 96–106, 236–72, 319–86ff.

17. For Berger, see Edward Muzik, "Victor Berger: A Biography" (Ph.D. Thesis, Northwestern University, 1960); for Morris Hillquit, see Robert W. Iverson, "Morris Hillquit: American Social Democrat" (Ph.D. Thesis, University of Iowa, 1951).

18. For this, see David Shannon's review of Bell in *Pennsylvania History,* XIX, 4 (October 1952), pp. 511–12.

19. This view of Thomas is sustained by Bernard Johnpoll's recent biography of him, which shows Thomas to have been most successful when he behaved like a liberal Democrat (over civil liberties, Jewish refugees, or the plight of southern sharecroppers) rather than as a third-party leader. Although undoubtedly a sincere social gospeler and democratic socialist in the early part of his career, by 1944 Dwight Macdonald could make a comment on him which still holds true: "My objection to Norman Thomas can be put briefly: he is a liberal, not a socialist. A socialist, as I use the term anyway, is one who has taken the first simple step *at least* of breaking with present-day bourgeois society. . . . His role has always been that of left opposition *within the present society,* the fighting crusader on small matters (like Hague-ism and other civil liberty issues) and the timid conformist in big matters (like the present war)." See Bernard K. Johnpoll, *Pacifist's Progress: Norman Thomas and the Decline of American Socialism* (Chicago, Quadrangle Books, 1970), pp. 146–52, 196–98, 200–4, 218–20; Harry Fleischman, *Norman Thomas, A Biography* (New York, Norton, 1964), p. 303.

20. On this point, see also the interesting remark made by an old socialist (unidentified) to Betty Yorburg in the collective biography of American socialists excerpted in Chapter One, as follows: "Danny Bell, in his analysis of the decline of the Socialist Party, talks about the [sic] 'program was in but not of the world'. Well, it's nonsense because everything that he said about the Socialist Party in the United States applied equally to the Socialist Party in France, in the Scandinavian countries, the labor parties or social democratic parties, the British Labour Party. The same kinds of compromises had to be made there. You had the same problems of factionalism within the parties. You had the right wings and the left wings." Yorburg, *Utopia and Reality: A Collective Portrait of American Socialists* (New York, Columbia University Press, 1969), p. 127.

21. During their congressional terms both Victor Berger and Meyer London pressed vigorously for nationalization of the railroads, a national insurance system, mitigation of unemployment, an end to child labor, and numerous other social reform measures which were also being sought by socialists in Europe. See Muzik, op. cit., pp. 143–68ff.; Harry Rogoff, *An East Side Epic: The Life and Work of Meyer London* (New York, The Vanguard Press, 1930), pp. 85–88, 229, 235ff.

22. Adolph Sturmthal, *The Tragedy of European Labor, 1918–1939* (New York, Columbia University Press, 1943), pp. 83–175.

23. See Weinstein, op. cit., pp. 119–33; David Shannon, *The Socialist Party of America, A History* (New York, Macmillan, 1955), pp. 204–48.

REPLY

Daniel Bell

The limitations of space imposed by the editors forbid a detailed reply. I will cleave, therefore, to the main problem: the Socialist Party "failed" in American life, failed to the extent that it did not have any significant influence *qua* party (I leave aside the influence of its ideas) in the politics of the society. Why?

Mr. Laslett has posed the issue as "ideology versus structural factors," but this is wrongly put, logically and methodologically. Structural conditions can never account for or explain social movements, for they can only specify *contexts* and *constraints;* what they omit is human agency. What my explanation sought to do—accepting the structural conditions—was to locate the failure of American socialism in the human agency, *the character of the party,* and to pose the question: why did not the Socialist Party perceive the structural constraints that are so evident to us now, and why did it fail to adapt to the conditions of American life—as, eventually, the European socialist parties adapted to the circumstances of their societies?

The root of the problem, for all socialist parties, goes back to the historic inevitabilism which was promulgated by Marx himself. As Marx wrote in the author's preface to *Capital:*

> In this work I have to examine the capitalist mode of production and the conditions of production and exchange corresponding to that mode. Up to the present time, their classic ground is England. That is the reason why England is used as the chief illustration in the development of my theoretical ideas. If, however, the German reader shrugs his shoulders at the condition of the English industrial and agricultural laborers, or in optimist fashion comforts himself with the thought that in Germany things are not nearly so bad, I must plainly tell him, *'De te fabula narratur.'*
>
> Intrinsically, it is not a question of the higher or lower degree of

development of the social antagonisms that result from the natural laws of capitalist production. It is a question of these laws themselves, of these tendencies *working with iron necessity* towards inevitable results. The country that is more developed industrially only shows, to the less developed, the image of its own future.[1]

But history has not been that deterministic and the fate of countries, politically and industrially, has diverged markedly despite a similar capitalist foundation. One has only to compare the diverse fates of England, the United States, Nazi Germany, and imperial Japan.

The second fact is that the labor issue, as a class issue, which Marx thought would become the single overriding issue around which all society would be polarized, has not developed in that direction at all. Again, in *Capital,* Marx wrote:

Along with the constantly diminishing number of the magnates of capital . . . grows the revolt of the working class, a class always increasing in numbers. . . . Centralization of the means of production and socialization of labor at last reach a point where they become incompatible with their capitalist integument. This integument is burst asunder.[2]

But the working class has not grown in numbers but, in fact, relative to the work force has shrunk considerably while the major expansion, since 1910, had been in the professional and technical employments.[3] Equally important, the labor issue, while still rancorous, occasionally, as an *economic* issue, has become institutionalized and encapsulated while the occupational role has lost much of its force in molding the character and desires of the worker.[4] In advanced Western societies, the labor issue is no longer the single overriding issue with the ability to polarize the society and divide it solely into two irremediable and hostile camps. Institutionally, the trade union has become integral to the social structure of industrial society, and, in the process, has also transformed it. Those socialist movements which have been deeply engaged with the labor movements of their countries became transformed as well. (One can see this, finally, in the 1959 Bad Godesberg declaration of the German Social Democratic Party, which, revising the historic declarations from Gotha to Erfurt, declared that it was no longer a class party.)

This has been the main structural transformation of Western industrial society in the last fifty years. Those parties which have been under the compelling myth of Marx's earlier vision, or been seduced by the idea of revolution for the sake of revolution, never could understand the changed reality.

If one looks specifically at the American socialist movement, before 1917, the party was basically a chiliastic party in that it felt, as all socialist movements, that it was on the express track of History. The mood of the party was one of confidence, the confidence of all true believers that they know the path to salvation. It is no accident that a recurrent theme in party conventions was the question whether newcomers would be given the "front seats" in the party pews, since after all the leadership of the party carried with it the tickets to the doors of the future. The fundamental theme was the "purity" of the party and the unthinkability of any compromise with the bourgeois parties. That schisms existed was inevitable; they occur in all sects and churches. That some persons wanted immediate reforms and others only immediate revolution is true. But, at bottom, all factions agreed on this question of socialist purity. Left-wing historians assume that because there was a right wing in the Socialist Party (the extent of its rightism was that *some,* in 1910, wanted a Labor Party!), this right wing was "conservative" and willing to compromise. But that is not true. The right wing was united largely against the use of violence (though there was always the orthodox belief that if the party received "51 per cent" of the vote but was denied peaceful power by the capitalist class it would then resort to arms), but in its own way—on the issue of socialist purity—it was as dogmatic and sectarian as any left-wing group in the party. One has only to consider the views of Victor Berger in this light. He was right-wing, but equally a sectarian. The ideological blinkers were on tight for both groups.

After 1919, the Socialist Party was divided and confused. It now favored a Labor Party, rather than a pure-and-simple Socialist Party, and in 1924 it supported, of course, the La Follette-Wheeler campaign; but the weakness of the trade union movement precluded any labor political party. In the early 1930s, there was a chance for a reorientation of the socialist movement, but the influx of young, inexperienced, unemployed college youths and dispossessed lawyers led to a wholly new confusion. The Depression made it seem as if a revolutionary situation could develop in the United States. Franklin D. Roosevelt was seen as only a stopgap. The sense of *Götterdämmerung* was vivid. Much of Europe was going fascist and the young militants in the Socialist Party assumed, along with the communists, that as a capitalist society America, too, would inevitably go fascist, since fascism was the "last stage" of monopoly capitalism, and that the world had reached the showdown that Marx had predicted. So the party attacked Roosevelt, and went "left."

Again, history was misread and badly so. But the misreading of history was responsible for the split in the Socialist Party in 1935 and the weakening of the movement. From 1936 on, the rapid growth of the CIO led to the development of a progressive wing in the Democratic Party. Ironically, the CIO unions drew some of their strength from the very left-wing elements in the Socialist Party who a few years back had been most vocally "left and revolutionary," men like the Reuthers, Leonard Woodcock, Andrew Biemiller, Paul Porter, Jack Altman, and others. But by that point the Socialist Party had become almost completely sectarian and eventually these men left the party and joined the Democrats.

There is little point in rehearsing, again, this singular fact: at every possible turning point, e.g., the possibility of making a realistic adaptation to the political conditions of American life and joining with the labor movement as a ginger group, the forces of sectarianism won out in the American socialist movement. It is this which the historians have to explain in detail. It is this fact which is the historical puzzle regarding the failure of the American socialist movement, *qua* political party, to become a force in American life.

A note on Weber and the problems of ethics and politics: In Weber's view one could, ethically, adopt a "politics of responsibility," or a "politics of ultimate ends," and under certain situations both are moral stands. Each, pushed to a limit, however, ended in corruption: that of the politics of responsibility in hopeless opportunism, that of ultimate ends in a fanaticism and self-righteousness which results in the totalitarian confusion of means and ends. But central for Weber was the proposition that "the decisive means for politics is violence," and the question, therefore, is under what conditions can violence be justified ethically.

In a democracy, where peaceful means of persuasion are open to all viewpoints, it seems to me that the argument for a "politics of responsibility" is nigh irrefutable. What is important is the "rules of the game," the conditions of freedom which permit the play of all points of view. Where the socialist movement, until about thirty or so years ago, found itself in a profound confusion was the acceptance, from a vulgarized Marxism, of a historicized and relativized view of democracy. Democracy, thus, was seen not as a condition which men have repeatedly struggled for through the ages, and as a condition of the free political life, but as a class instrument and as "bourgeois democracy." In a different sense, Marxists could not believe in the relative autonomies of the economic and political systems and that, historically, political democracy had different roots and traditions in its conceptions of liberty than capitalist economics. For this reason, until quite late, the socialist movements were not prepared to defend democracy as a political fact independent of its economic substructure. The communists, never accepting democracy, were prepared to jettison it, and in the notorious instances in Germany in the 1930s, united with the Nazis to tear down the Weimar Republic. The socialist movements before World War II always faced the ambiguity of not accepting the ethics of ultimate ends but not, wholly, coming to accept the ethics of responsibility either. It was one of the fruits of living so long "in the world, but not of it."

NOTES

1. Karl Marx, *Capital,* Vol. I (Chicago: Charles Kerr, 1906), p. 13. (Emphasis added.)

2. Ibid., pp. 836–37.

3. For an elaboration of this argument and the statistical evidence, see my book, *The Coming of Post-Industrial Society* (New York: Basic Books, 1973).

4. This is a major argument of Ralf Dahrendorf in *Class and Class Conflict in Industrial Society* (Stanford: Stanford University Press, 1959).

Chapter 2

RADICALISM AND THE AGRARIAN TRADITION*

Theodore Saloutos

Agrarian discontent reached a boiling point during the late 1880s and early 1890s because of the sweeping changes that had brought about a downgrading of agriculture as an occupation and the upgrading of the non-agricultural pursuits geared to profit-making. The farmers felt especially grieved because they believed they deserved a better fate than the one wished on them. They reasoned they comprised the bulk of the population, paid most of the taxes, produced most of the food that sustained life and the raw materials that kept the wheels of finance, industry, and commerce going; and furthermore they were convinced they would continue to be the mainstay of American society in the future as they had been in the past. For this reason the economic health of the farmers had to be restored; for farming, in their opinion, was the most fundamental of all occupations, so fundamental that the survival of the nation hinged upon agriculture being elevated to a status of prosperity and prestige commensurate with its contributions to civilization.

Out of the welter of schemes advanced during this period to promote and protect the interests of the farmers, three stand out most conspicuously. The first sought to provide them with more and better social, cultural, and educational opportunities than they had in the past and enable them to enjoy some of the advantages long enjoyed by city people. The second was designed to right the economic imbalance from which the farmers suffered by bringing them higher prices for their goods and lower costs in terms of better marketing facilities, cheaper interest rates, lower taxes, and group buying. And the third was to resort to direct political action that would result in electing farmers, or friends of farmers, to represent them and their interests in public office. Since the main purpose of this volume is to deal with the question of why the

* Previously unpublished essay written for this collection.

American socialist movement failed to develop a major political movement based on all segments of the American working class, it is to the third, a political alternative, that I will address myself here. Each of these approaches was attempted, we shall see, and each of them was found wanting.

At least two courses of action were open to the political agrarians. At first the plan was to agree on a needed reform and then endeavor to persuade each political party to legislate to that effect; and if that failed, to devise some other method aimed to succeed. Although the conviction had grown that reform would have to come through legislative channels, this did not mean that a separate political party would be organized at the very outset. This, of course, was the other alternative.[1] But at first the agrarian politicos refused to attach themselves to either the Republican or Democratic parties, hoping to make both parties serve them.[2]

The agrarians were helped in their efforts by the crop failures and the low prices of the years just prior to 1890, and the existence of branches of farmers' organizations originally established to discuss issues of concern to farmers. Now these groups were being converted into political caucuses that were to aid the political transformation.[3] Many politicians were frightened by the thought of politically aroused farmers. Perhaps the words of a state president of a Farmers' Alliance served as a warning of what the farmers had in mind: "Being Democrats and in the majority, we took possession of the Democratic party. . . ."[4] In the South the farmers worked with the Democratic Party in 1890; but in the western states they worked for the most part outside of both the Republican and Democratic parties, although their strength was drawn more largely from the Republicans. In the general elections of 1890 the farmers elected governors in Georgia, Tennessee, South Dakota, and South Carolina. They also carried state tickets in Kansas, Nebraska, and South Dakota, and sent a total of thirty-eight representatives to the House and several senators to the United States Senate.[5]

Meanwhile the agrarian triumphs of late 1890 opened the floodgates of political action in a manner unprecedented in scope and intensity. Now the question had become not one of trying to get both parties to serve the interests of the farmers, but of whether to try and gain control of the Democratic Party or form a new party of their own. Opinion was badly divided. The southern agrarians for the most part were terrified by the thought of a third party because of the race question, but a small minority was willing to experiment with it; while the Middle Westerners were more favorable, but not overwhelmingly so, to the new party idea. Considerable thought also was given to the role that organized labor would play in such a new alignment. But in the meantime, the more persistent advocates of a new party had grown impatient and arranged for a meeting of the malcontents in Cincinnati on May 19, 1891, who assembled with representatives of organized labor and fired the opening salvo of the campaign of 1892. The net result was the formation of the Populist Party.[6]

The Populist Party, which in fact was the first farmer-labor party of major consequence, was based on the premise that the farmers and laborers had a common foe in monopoly, which had a stranglehold on the Republican and Democratic parties as well as on the arteries of money and banking, manufacturing, transportation, trade, and other facets of American life. Only when the forces of agriculture and labor were aligned into an effective political party could the interests of the farmers and laborers be protected. Naturally the support of the followers of Henry George, Edward Bellamy, the free silver advocates, and other reformist elements was sought in the crusade to wrest control of the government from the special interests and place it in the hands of the people where it belonged. The Populist Party believed that this could be accomplished with a platform asking for the free and unlimited coinage of silver, an increase in the amount of money in circulation, the graduated income tax, the secret ballot, the shorter workday, equality for women, the direct election of United States senators, and other proposals.

The results of the election of 1892 were encouraging, if not spectacular. The most impressive gains were scored in Kansas, where Weaver, the Populist candidate for President, aided by the Democrats, carried the state; and the entire state slate and five of the seven congressional seats were carried by Populists. Half of the votes received by Weaver in 1892 came from the Far West because of the singular interest of the states in this region to silver and not because of any broad commitment to the principles of Populism. One doubts whether the Populist Party would have made much of a dent there if it had not been for silver. In the South the achievements of the Populist ticket at the state level were minimal, and the results in the states east of the Mississippi River were hardly encouraging.

The reasons for the failure of the Populists to make headway in the eastern half of the United States were twofold. The agricultural economies of these states differed from those of the states in the Great Plains, hence their needs were different. The farmers in the older sections of the East had suffered from the expansion of agriculture in the newer sections and were disinclined to support the demands of the farmers of Kansas, Nebraska, and the Dakotas. The eastern farmers diversified their production and did not rely on a single crop such as wheat. Likewise the eastern wage earners continued to support the candidates of the two major parties, despite the special appeal the Populists made to them.[7]

How effective was this effort to achieve a working coalition between the farmers and the wage earners? As a rule the wage earners have been viewed as being more receptive to the farmer-labor ideal than the farmers, but the argument has been made, particularly by Norman Pollack in his book *The Populist Response to Industrial America,* that the Populists failed to develop a viable, long-range national farmer-labor party as a new alternative within the existing two-party system, because labor refused to give them the kind of support which the farmers gave. According to this line of reasoning, historians have erred in assuming that the real barriers to a viable farmer-labor party were the farmers because the favorable response they gave to it in 1891 would refute this. Perhaps the major obstacle in the way of this new alignment, the argument continues, was the lack of full cooperation from organized labor, especially from the American Federation of Labor.[8]

The validity of this thesis is open to serious doubts. The evidence in support of it is flimsy and tends to ignore the effects of the American experience on organized labor and the failures which labor had suffered from in the past when it chose to travel the road of politics; it also presupposes a strength and influence on the part of the American Federation of Labor which it did not have, and exaggerates the willingness on the part of the farmers to coalesce with labor.[9]

The position of the American Federation of Labor, when agitation for the formation of a third party began shaping up late in 1890 and early in 1891, was that of a relatively young and insecure organization seeking to become a fixture on the American trade union scene. For all practical purposes it was still feeling its way. Although the Federation was founded in 1881 it did not begin to get off the ground until 1886. More than anything else the Federation craved a secure footing, for the record of labor in general from the Civil War down to 1886, as its founders knew, had been one of youthful uncertainty, instability, and frustrated ambitions.[10] For one to suggest in the light of this evidence that the farmer-labor coalition failed because the Federation withheld its support is to overlook the impracticality of adopting such a course. It could have been suicidal for the Federation in particular if it had followed this course, and to the cause of the trade union movement in general.

One of the very things that the founding fathers of the Federation wanted to avoid was precisely the kind of entangling political party that the advocates of the third party were proposing. When the Federation was reorganized in 1886, the reorganization proceeded along lines that took cognizance of the prevailing conditions in labor circles and the political climate of the times. The men who helped organize and shape the policies of the Federation in the early years were men of experience. Some had once been members of, or had strongly opposed, the National Labor Union, the Greenback Labor Party, and the largest of the labor organizations prior to the formation of the American Federation of Labor—the Knights of Labor—who were disorganized, bankrupt, and almost extinct after having tried the political formula.[11]

Each of these movements, and the experiences shared by their former members, contributed in one fashion or another to the molding of the philosophy underlying the Federation. They had tasted the bitter fruits of political defeat and wanted to avoid it in the future. From the experiences of the National Labor Union and the Greenback Labor Party, for instance, leaders of the Federation had learned it was futile to try and build a political party based on alliances of farmers and small-business men pitted against the bankers and large-business men. Such alliances flourished in slump periods at best and then dissolved. Labor could not be lifted, and banking and big business could not be defeated, en masse. The immediate targets of the wage earners were the competing employers in the same line of business, and the ones most capable of taking effective aim were the employees of these competing employers, and no others. Finally, the cautious Federation leaders also knew only too well that hitherto no major labor organization had succeeded in surviving a major depression; consequently their primary task was not one of organizing to win political battles by direct political action, but of building a permanent organization capable of withstanding the ups and downs of the business cycle.[12]

The attitudes of the trade unionists, organized and unorganized, hardly lent themselves to the forging of an effective farmer-labor alliance. The trade unionist was interested in higher wages, lower prices on what he bought, and better working conditions today, tomorrow, next week, or next month at the latest, and not in the building of a millennium that would free men from the oppressions of an industrial society. Populism was as much a bread-and-butter proposition to those trade unionists who adhered to its principles as it was to those farmers who believed in it. Why should the trade unionist campaign for the free and unlimited coinage of silver which went to the essence of Populism, when this meant paying more for his food, clothing, and shelter?[13]

Another flaw in the argument that the Federation was a major obstacle to the formation of a farmer-labor coalition is that it exaggerates the importance of the Cincinnati meeting of May 19, 1891. In the first place the role of the farmers and their representation in the Cincinnati conference was minimal. When news of the forthcoming meeting was released the *National Economist,* the official organ of the National Farmers' Alliance and Industrial Union, better known as the Southern Farmers' Alliance, responded that the Cincinnati meeting "had no official sanction whatever from the National Farmers' Alliance and Industrial Union." The *Economist* also complained that the organizers of the meeting made no provisions "to get representation from the rural districts, and when the meeting is opened it will be found to consist of the same old crowd who have been at all times pulling so fast that they have discouraged thousands from joining the move. . . ."[14]

Just how one can imply that sheer attendance at the Cincinnati meeting was *ipso facto* evidence of success in the formation of a farmer-labor alliance is unclear. The Cincinnati meeting was not an Alliance meeting and it never was intended to be that. The Alliance at its last national meeting in Ocala, Florida, had provided for a general conference of all organizations of producers willing to cooperate to secure political reforms to be held in February 1892, agreeing at the time that all delegates from all organizations would meet on an equitable basis of representation, agree upon a set of demands and a method of enforcing them. Whatever action was taken in the February meeting on direct political action was to be taken with the understanding that the Alliance as an organization was to remain non-partisan.[15]

Among the most active advocates of the formation of a new political party, as Pollack points out, were the delegates from Kansas. However, many of these were of dubious agrarian origin, and felt that they were entitled to representation simply because they had left the Northern Farmers' Alliance to join the Southern. It is true that the Kansas delegates were very anxious to get the whole Alliance to support the third-party movement, but the large majority of the southern farmers who comprised the bulk of the membership were unprepared to desert the major party of the South. This reluctance of the Southerners to sever their relations with the Democratic Party did not deter the political ambitions of the third-party advocates from Kansas. The three Vincent brothers, the ones credited with drawing up the call, made the movement appear to have a broader base than it actually had.[16]

Observers substantiated the claim that representation from the South in the Cincinnati meeting was small; according to the *Daily Register* of Mobile, Alabama, the number of delegates in attendance from the entire South was thirty-six. Texas with a delegation of twenty-six had the largest representation by far, while Virginia, South Carolina, North Carolina, and Alabama were without any representation. If anything, the representation was largely Middle Western. The *Clarion Ledger* of Jackson, Mississippi, placed the number of delegates at about fourteen hundred, of which seven hundred were from Kansas and Ohio alone. To the *Times-Democrat* of New Orleans the meeting was more of "a gathering of all the political odds and ends in the country."[17]

The program of the agrarians was appropriated by the third-party people, if not the membership, and the editor of the *Economist,* who was opposed by many inside the Alliance, joined in the chorus of praise this time: ". . . the course pursued by the meeting has been so wise and conservative," he wrote, "that instead of conflicting (with the meeting of February 1892) [it] is destined to prove an actual benefit and supply the link that will unite the farmers with all other occupations in the great approaching conflict." He added that "the reformers of the country have met in mass meeting and unanimously agreed that the platform of the farmers adopted at Ocala, including the sub-treasury plan, shall be the basis of the great and inevitable reform fight which is now on, and that they desire to unite with the farmers and laborers to fight under the banner as a people's party in 1892; . . ."[18]

The Cincinnati meeting was neither the first nor the last of the political meetings attempting to capitalize on the popularity of the farmers' platform and to divert it onto a farmer-labor course. Witness, for instance, the developments in Chicago in the fall of 1894 in which the name of the People's Party was used in the campaign and on the official ballot. "But in all essentials the movement was a labor movement, having its first inception in a labor union, supported throughout by the efforts of organized labor and drawing its principal support at the polls from the manual working classes." Apparently, the aim of the driving forces behind this effort was to give the labor movement "a national character and an enthusiasm it can in no other way attain."[19]

The evidence is all too clear that the Cincinnati meeting, which was heralded as the great opportunity in forming a farmer-labor coalition, was not a farmers' meeting extending the hand of cooperation to laborers to join them in a great crusade. It was dominated by non-farmers with driving political ambitions. The astute reformers, labor leaders, crusaders, and other third-party advocates who sponsored the meeting were prepared to use the farmers, their organization, platform, and any other vehicle at their disposal to achieve their objectives. Some farmers, to be sure, were present but they were unrepresentative of the rank and file, and were too small in number to be significant.[20]

Gompers, in short, in pleading with members of his organization to avoid entangling political alliances, knew of what he spoke. He had no desire of belittling the efforts of the farmers or of withholding sympathy due them in their crusade; he was just looking after what he believed were the best interests of the workingman. He knew the history of the labor movement of this country, its strength and weaknesses, its hopes and frustrations; and he was most anxious to protect what gains had been made in a hostile climate. Future as well as past experiences were to bear out the wisdom of his decision.[21]

Radical analysts of Populism also seek to draw analogies and detect similarities between Populism and Marxism.[22] Unfortunately this analysis is built on shaky foundations. Populism, according to most experts, was an indigenous product, born on American soil and conditioned by the American experience. The European influence on Populism, except that emanating from the small minority residing in urban-industrial centers attracted to it because it was about as well organized and publicized a protest movement as any of its kind at the time, was minimal and found among the more labor-oriented members of the party. If it was radicalism, it was radicalism of the American variety rooted in the traditions of the Grangers, the Farmers' Alliance, the various farmer-labor coalitions formed at the state level, the monetary and bank reformers, and those hell-bent on raising the level of the common folk who for the most part were farmers.[23] To the Marxists this was rank opportunism, compromise, reformism, a sellout, nothing more, nothing less.

If Populism was more than agrarianism, as is claimed, it was only slightly more so, especially beginning in 1891, when nonfarmers sought its protective covering and tried to capture the organization lock, stock, and barrel in the name of the farmers. Prior to that the farmers' movement was chiefly agrarian, farmer-oriented, and farmer-directed.

The attempt to view Populism through the eyes of the radical industrial workers of the East and Europe, instead of through the eyes of the disconsolate American farmers of the Middle West, Southwest, and South is tempting, but it is also misleading. This amounts to a certain torturing of the facts. To the more radical industrial elements both Marxism and Populism might have meant the alienation of man from his product, but to the agrarian Populist it was largely alienation from his land, his equipment, his animals, and his personal belongings which made it difficult for him to raise a good crop, market it at a profit, sustain his family, educate his children, and discharge his obligations. One cannot help but believe that the downgrading of the agrarian aspects and elevating of the radical industrial phases of Populism also has caused a number of observers to minimize the importance of the free silver issue, low farm prices, indebtedness, high interest and taxation rates. An understanding of the farmer sentiments on these issues is crucial to any understanding of the farmer-labor relationship that failed to materialize. The farmers might have felt sorry for the workers being exploited by the large corporations, but they also viewed themselves as being a cut or two above the wage earners.[24]

Much is also made in Pollack's book of the creation of tramps and vagabonds who were forced to wander in search of work.[25] That they were a product of the industrial system and a cause of great concern to society is beyond doubt, but others indicate that this has been overstated. Professor Jessy Macy of Iowa College, Grinnell, Iowa, attributed the great attention given to tramps to "the industrious writing of the newspapers," and added that "Iowa has not been greatly afflicted by tramps." J. W. Gleed of Topeka, Kansas, said pretty much the same thing. "Nothing would probably ever have come of the Coxey movement, but the newspapers took it up, and day after day and week after week we had columns of it in the papers all over the West." He also noticed that "the Coxies armies have come almost entirely from large cities and mining country."[26]

A more realistic and immediate concern of the agrarians was not so much the specter of tramps and vagabonds as it was the desertion of the farm, the exchange of the values of rural life for those of the "corrupt" cities, the breakup of the family, and the turning of one's back on the virtuous agrarian way of life. The protests of the more industrial-oriented members of the party that found their way into print in papers carrying the Populist label only after the party had been disappointed elsewhere have been over-emphasized and, as a consequence, left the impression of a party with a greater industrial complexion than the facts justify.

The farmers were genuinely worried about the corporations and monopolies. That there was a growing concentration of wealth is a matter of elementary knowledge. Agrarian suspicions and distrust of the bankers and banks, the railroads, large industrial corporations, the cities, the East, and urban-industrial opposition to the income tax which was designed to lift some of the tax burdens from the land of the farmers and place them on the earnings and profits of those who escaped paying their fair share of the load are traditional but valid arguments.[27]

In effect the third party, or farmer-labor party, failed in 1892 and again in 1896 not because of the unwillingness of labor to give it the support that farmers gave it, but because of certain deep and almost irreconcilable differences. In the first place it was very difficult to bring the farmers of the various sections, let alone of the nation, into an effective political organization because of regional variations and conflicting commodity interests. The race question was a barrier to the third party in the South and the crops produced in the states east of the Mississippi created interests and attitudes different from those of farmers living in the states west of the Mississippi. The farmers in the East suffered in part because of the expansion of agriculture into the West; why should they become a part of a movement designed to bring these farmers more money, cheaper credit, lower transportation rates, greater representation in government, and higher prices for their products?

Finally, the willingness of the farmers to enter into a direct political alliance with the city workers likewise has been overstated. The attitudes of the wage earners, organized and unorganized, hardly lent themselves to the forging of an effective farmer-labor alliance. The wage earners were pragmatists interested in higher wages, lower prices, and better working conditions as soon as possible, and not in building a millennium that would free men from the oppressions of an industrial society. Populism reflected a high degree of idealism, but it also was a bread-and-butter proposition to the rank-and-file farmers supporting it. The wage earner viewed it in the same light. Why should he campaign for the free and unlimited coinage of silver, which went to the essence of Populism, when this meant paying more for his needs?

NOTES

1. *Appleton's Annual Cyclopaedia, 1890,* p. 299.
2. Washington Gladden, "The Embattled Farmers," *Forum,* X (November 1890), p. 319.
3. Fred Emory Haynes, "The New Sectionalism," *Quarterly Journal of Economics,* X (April 1896), p. 271; *Appleton's Annual Cyclopaedia, 1890,* p. 301.
4. *Appleton's Annual Cyclopaedia, 1890,* p. 301.
5. Ibid.
6. William Peffer, *The Farmer's Side* (New York, 1891), pp. 159–60; Helen Blackburn, "The Populist Party in the South, 1890–1898" (M.A. Thesis, Howard University, 1941), pp. 8–9; *Nation,* 52 (May 28, 1891), p. 431.
7. John D. Hicks, *The Populist Revolt* (Minneapolis, 1931), pp. 254–69.
8. See Norman Pollack, *The Populist Response to Industrial America: Midwestern Populist Thought* (Cambridge, 1962), pp. 43–67ff.
9. *Report of the Industrial Commission on the Relations and Conditions of Capital and Labor,* VII (Washington, 1911), pp. 108–10, contains some informative statistical data on the strength of the major labor organizations and their weaknesses.
10. Ibid., VII, p. 108. Gompers pointed out that from 1868, when the National Labor Union held its last convention, until 1881 the country lacked a general labor organization built around a trade union basis.
11. John R. Commons, *History of Labor in the United States,* II (New York, 1918), pp. 482 and 495. See also *Report of the Industrial Commission . . . ,* VII, p. 110, on the mistake made by the Knights of Labor in entering politics. Norman J. Ware, *The Labor Movement in the United States 1860–1895* (New York, 1929), p. 351, points out that "the American Federation of Labor has been the least political of all."
12. Ware, op. cit., pp. 351–52.
13. Ibid., pp. 352–53.
14. *National Economist,* IV (February 21, 1891), p. 357.
15. Ibid., V (May 30, 1891), p. 161.
16. Pollack, op. cit., p. 63; Helen M. Blackburn, "The Populist Party in the South, 1890–1898" (M.A. Thesis, Howard University, 1941), pp. 8–9.
17. Ibid., pp. 15–16.
18. *National Economist,* V (May 30, 1891), p. 161.
19. Willis J. Abbot, "The Chicago Populist Campaign," *Arena,* XI (February 1895), p. 330.
20. Ware erroneously assumes that the Cincinnati meeting of May

19, 1891, was a farmer-dominated meeting (Ware, op. cit., p. 369). See Commons, op. cit., II, p. 494.

21. Samuel Gompers, "Organized Labor in the Campaign," *North American Review,* CLV (July 1892), pp. 93–95.

22. See Pollack, op. cit., pp. 68–84; Anna Rochester, *The Populist Movement in the United States* (New York, 1943).

23. The best analysis of grievances leading to the formation of the Populist Party is still found in John D. Hicks, *The Populist Revolt* (Minneapolis, 1931), pp. 54–95. Walter T. K. Nugent, *The Tolerant Populists* (Chicago, 1963), pp. 167–74, suggests that the foreign-born were receptive to the Populist program, but presents no evidence suggesting that their European experiences influenced it.

24. Theodore Saloutos, "The Agricultural Problem and Nineteenth-Century Industrialism," *Agricultural History,* XXII (July 1948), pp. 169–73; Theodore Saloutos, "The Populists and the Professors," Ibid., XL (October 1966), pp. 245–46.

25. Pollack, op. cit., pp. 25–42.

26. J. W. Gleed, "A Bundle of Western Letters," *Review of Reviews,* X (July 1, 1894), pp. 43 and 46.

27. Theodore Saloutos, *Farmer Movements in the South, 1865–1933* (Berkeley and Los Angeles, 1960), pp. 282–84.

COMMENT

Michael Rogin

Young American historians, seeking to ground the 1960s' radical revival in a usable past, turned to agrarian radicalism. Some offered Populism as an American equivalent for European Marxism.[1] Populism, however, was a movement of farm-owning proprietors, not property-less workers. It attempted to reassert local community control against the economic and political centralization of corporate capitalism.[2] Professor Saloutos, rightly seeing that Populism was not Marxism, has mistakenly read back the triumph of narrow, elitist, interest group politics into the Populist period.

Populism was a radical alternative to the political and economic forces dominating America, and its radicalism had deep and genuine agrarian roots. It did grow out of more moderate, rural efforts at business cooperation and major party pressure politics. But it was a striking departure from those activities. While much of the broad and respectable support mobilized by the Farmers' Alliances, particularly among town merchants, businessmen, and bankers, dropped away from third-party Populism, masses of southern and western farmers adhered to it. If, as Saloutos indicates, the 1891 Cincinnati meeting which pushed for a national third party was dominated by professional reformers rather than farmers, the degree of agrarian support for the third party is all the more significant. In 1892 Populism won more than one third of the vote in eight of the twelve northern states west of the Mississippi, and more than 20 per cent of the vote in every one but California. In 1894 Populist or fusion tickets won 25 per cent of the vote or more in eight of the eleven former Confederate states. Populism was strongly regional; it was weak in the Midwest, and non-existent in the Northeast. Nevertheless, it represented a sharp break with major party traditions and ruling elites in the South and West. In several southern states Populism even overcame the resistance of white farmers to political cooperation with blacks; it remains the only significant example of black and white farmer solidarity in southern history. A radical third party, advocating substantial government ownership and making a powerful attack on finance and industrial capitalist control of the country, evoked enormous grass roots loyalty and participation from southern and western farmers.[3]

It is misleading, moreover, to attribute Populist voting strength primarily to the issue of free silver. While half of the Populist 1892 *electoral* vote came from the western mining states, less than 8 per cent of its total popular vote did.[4] The silver issue did not dominate Populism until the last years of the movement, and even in the mining states, as we shall see, its significance was different than Saloutos suggests.

The Populist image was communal, not Marxist, but it was radical within the American context. Its lack of Marxism hardly alienated American workers. More significantly, many workers were attracted rather than repelled by Populist agrarian appeals. Saloutos believes that the conflict between rural and urban interests—symbolized by the inflationary silver issue—created an impassable gulf between farmers and workers. But the story is more complex. Populism was not a rural interest group simply, but an agrarian crusade. And the traditions of native American workers were agrarian and communal too. The American labor movement had historically aimed at independent producership, even land, for laborers. Like Populism, workers' organizations attacked monopolies in the name of community control. By the same token American workers often shared with Populism a fundamentalist, Protestant mentality, transmuted into movements for social reconstruction—the "holy work" as one southern worker called it.[5] In its religious and fraternal character the pre-industrial labor movement paralleled English developments, although in England the weight lay with workers, in America with farmers. This American working-class tradition culminated in the 1880s with the Knights of Labor.[6]

The Knights had disintegrated by the 1890s, but labor unrest remained widespread. Populism understood the strikes of the 1885–95 decade as worker efforts to reassert popular control over centralizing, capitalist society. In this savage, visible, and prolonged industrial class conflict Populists sided with the working class. They supported the railroad strikes which climaxed in the Pullman boycott of 1894. Local Populist newspapers served as Pullman strike organs, and some Populist clubs collected food for the strikers. Populists sided with workers against the militia in the 1892 Homestead Steel strike and massacre. They supported the coal and metal mining strikes of the 1890s. The Populist governor of Colorado intervened to protect striking miners from a local militia, the reverse of the usual procedure. Populists sympathized with the tramps and vagabonds roaming the country in the wake of the 1893 depression, either alone or in peaceful "armies," seeking redress of grievances. Coxey's Army was the most famous of these, but there were others as well; their presence was more widespread than Saloutos' sources, unsympathetic to Populism, indicate. It is particularly noteworthy that a movement of hard-working Protestant farmers sympathized with men who could not find jobs, and understood, as Kansas Populist governor L. D. Lewelling's Tramp Circular shows, the social causes of their itinerancy. Populists also supported a shorter working day for urban workers. Finally, they attacked the Pinkerton "hireling army" of private strikebreakers employed by capitalists to war on strikers and work in their place.[7]

Both Saloutos on the one hand and Pollack on the other have wrongly minimized the extent to which workers reciprocated Populist support. Yeoman farmers feared that the invasion of powerful, mechanized, external forces would destroy their independent farms and communities. Artisans in several trades faced a similar threat, as the rapid introduction of machinery undermined their autonomy, reduced their income, and devalued their skills. Whether shoe workers in Massachusetts or machinists in the South and West, many such artisans supported Populism. The railroad was perhaps the central Populist symbol of mechanized, external control, and workers in the railway towns of the South and West often voted Populist. Much of the membership of the International Association of Machinists worked in railway shops and supported Populism. The party also received votes in the coal-mining towns of the South and Midwest, and from metal miners in the Rocky Mountain states. The President of the United Mine Workers became a Populist after the disastrous coal strike of 1894. The UMW gave Populism active support, and several miners ran on Populist tickets. The silver issue in the Rocky Mountains, far from splitting farmers from workers, led to a farmer-miner alliance against the silver and copper mineowners. The 1895 convention of the Western Federation of Miners endorsed the Populist Omaha platform. In Montana, Idaho, and

Colorado workers played the most significant role in Populism, and their struggles with the mineowners gave the movement "much more of a revolutionary flavor" than in the non-mining states. In many of the mining and railroad towns of the South and West there were traditions of worker-agrarian radical cooperation going back to the Greenback-Labor Party of the late 1870s, and these bore fruit in Populism.[8]

It is difficult to estimate the actual size of the working-class Populist vote. Among railway workers and miners, particularly in selected areas, the proportions were substantial. Among southern and western artisans as a whole the percentages were much smaller. Even so, Populism received the support of a substantial fraction of organized workers. Moreover, European socialism and syndicalism also began with minority working-class support. What is significant in the Populist case is not the small beginning, but the failure to endure and grow. The Populist-worker alliance was the end of an old tradition, not the beginning of a new one. How is this to be explained?

First of all, leaders of the emerging craft unions represented a new direction in American labor. Instead of resisting the centralizing, bureaucratic tendencies of American society, these craft unionists identified with them. AFL unions organized skilled workers around high-dues, narrow, craft-conscious organizations. These craft unions would cooperate with the "trusts," seeking neither to abolish or regulate them, nor to organize their unskilled workers. The national trades unions would exercise centralized control over local constituent bodies, which had heretofore enjoyed virtually complete autonomy. It was, point by point, the opposite solution to that tried by the Knights of Labor, and implied in a worker-Populist alliance.[9]

These emerging craft leaders opposed not merely Populism but all radical political and industrial action. They claimed to oppose politics, but most had ties to dominant, urban political machines. In part the union leaders were self-serving, but they also believed, with good evidence, that radical political and economic action would continue to decimate labor organizations, as it had in the past. Thus not only was Samuel Gompers hostile to Populism; the president of the International Association of Machinists opposed the Pullman boycott, although most members of the IAM worked in railroad shops, and thousands flocked to the American Railway

Union during the strike. At least one IAM local provided strikebreakers, in a pattern that would become increasingly prevalent in the industrial conflicts of the new century. In Chicago—also a harbinger of things to come—craft union leaders tied to the Democratic machine sought to sabotage a Populist-labor alliance, and opposed the Populist ticket in the elections of 1894 and 1895.[10]

Many of these conservative craft leaders were Irish, which reenforced their hostility to Populism. They had ties both to the Democratic Party and to the Catholic Church; the Church would shortly begin anti-radical activity in the labor movement. Although the American Irish were not immune to radicalism, the provocation had to be strong, and the commitment was generally short-lived.[11] In addition, the rural Protestant Populist flavor, while congenial to Protestant workers in southern and western towns, had little appeal to urban Irish workers and union leaders in the Northeast.

Craft union leaders erected a barrier between workers and Populism, but their power was hardly overwhelming. AFL unions were tiny in the Populist period, organizing only a small percentage even of the skilled workers prior to 1898. Perhaps Gompers was right that support for Populism would have decimated the labor movement once again. Certainly the AFL unions, hostile to reform, were the first in America to last through a severe depression. But in Europe many abortive efforts preceded successful syndicalist and socialist organizations. The key factor in the survival of AFL unions may well have been not their hostility to reform, but the existence for the first time of a substantial, permanent wage-earning class. Perhaps conservative craft unions were not the only kind that could have survived in America. Perhaps union leaders could have moved into the forefront of a reform-oriented labor movement, which might have survived and grown after 1896, as the AFL unions did. Craft union leaders certainly resisted this possibility, but they alone cannot be blamed for its failure. Populism and its labor allies could not attract any urban, eastern working-class support, skilled or unskilled, union or non-union.

Populism appealed to native artisans, railway workers, and miners, with local community loyalties and visions of social reconstruction. But workers like these could not take the lead in an expanding American labor movement, as happened with French syndicalism.[12] The eastern industrial working class was too immigrant-dominated, too ethnically fragmented, and too demoralized—by the shock of transplantation, by the depression, and by the alliance of state and industry which crushed efforts at revolt. Even in Chicago, where there was significant support for Populism among craft unionists independent of the Democratic machine, workers failed to vote for the party. Of the ten largest American cities, only San Francisco produced a significant Populist working-class vote.[13]

The new European working class emigrating from the countryside to the cities of Europe at least had ties of nationality, local place, and sometimes even political tradition to urban radicalism. In America the ties had to be to agrarian radicalism, and, except for Scandinavian and British immigrants, these ties were absent. Yeoman farmer communal appeals made little sense to the experience of immigrant workers. Eventually, and not without important, temporary exceptions, the immigrant unskilled followed the pattern set by the AFL.

One must not overdo the specifically working-class character of northeastern opposition to Populism. There was simply no Populist electoral or organizational strength here at all, and farmers were no more likely than workers to vote for the party. Populism was born from particular southern and western conditions; the very regional concentration that gave it initial state and local successes doomed it as a national movement. Equally important to the failure of Populism, it lacked staying power in the areas of its greatest strength.

The Populist effort to reassert community control could not embody itself in lasting institutions. Marxism in Europe, as Adam Ulam has written, tapped the anti-industrial emotion accompanying capitalism to industrial logic; workers did not destroy the machines and factories they hated, but organized and voted to overthrow the capitalist system instead.[14] But in America the forces of local control did not transmute themselves through Populism into a permanent, centralized, powerful socialist movement. With its program of nationalization and social control, and with its support for industrial labor, Populism took steps in this direction. But the external forces of resistance and the anti-monopoly, localistic agrarian traditions were too strong. Industrial logic, split from anti-industrial emotion, became embodied in the AFL and parallel farm organizations like the American Farm Bureau Federation. In Europe Marxian socialism emerged as the working class and its leaders recognized the permanence of an industrial capitalist system, until ended by seizure of state power. But in America that recognition led to accepting and working within the industrial capitalist structures, not seeking their overthrow. The dialogue in America—as the 1960s showed—remained one between a dominant, centralizing conservatism and sporadic reassertions of utopian communitarianism.

Less industrialized European countries offered a radical alternative to social democracy. Spain, Italy, and France produced lasting anarcho-syndicalist movements, sustained by rural workers, or workers with powerful local ties.[15] But American agrarian communities could not generate lasting organizations of this sort either. American farmers, sustained in part by cooperative frontier traditions, had produced a long tradition of agrarian protest. As Marx insisted, however, it was more difficult for farmers than for workers to form themselves into cohesive, independent organizations. In addition, industrial giants dominated society far more in America than in France or Spain. The European communities, finally, were in irrevocable opposition to centralizing tendencies within their societies; American rural communities were badly ambivalent. Western farmers, and those in the southern hill country areas of Populist strength, owned their own land. Many aspired to own more. Large numbers speculated and increased their mortgaged indebtedness in good times, and believed in the possibility of individual advancement. American farmers aimed for property-owning independence, not communal control of work. They wanted, and believed they could get, the new consumption goods, railroads, and telephones offered by homogenizing industrial capitalism. For the upper and most conscious strata of farmers and workers, individual mobility within capitalism seemed more possible than it did in Europe; this attenuated permanent and deep social divisions.

There is another side to this story. Sharing the American dream, most Populists spoke for a tradition they believed had once been dominant in America. They saw themselves not as reviving an ancient opposition, but as reasserting a claim to rule as once they had. This perspective gave them temporary confidence, but was not one from which an enduring opposition could be built. The European socialists and anarchists, not imagining themselves as dispossessed rulers, built more slowly and permanently. The American agrarian radical perspective could not stand adversity.

Populism lacked staying power as an independent alternative to industrial capitalism. It needed—as Populist visions of apocalypse and urgency suggested—to win immediately or not at all.

This very sense of crisis sent Populism in a moderate, single-issue direction. Although the Populist vote rose dramatically from 1890 through 1894, this success did not satisfy. In their search for immediate victory, writes John Hicks, Populists moderated their radical economic program, and emphasized the silver issue. This implied a return to the pre-Populist alliance of local businessmen and farmers, and the end of organizationally independent radical Populism. Support for Bryan, with his focus on the single issue of silver, was the logical outcome of these developments. Bryan emphasized the religious, panaceaic side of agrarianism, rather than its economic program.[16] He drove eastern workers and Catholics into the GOP, and ended the Populist Party's independent existence.

Populism did make a contribution to the future Socialist Party. Some areas of Populist strength later voted Socialist, and some Populist trade unionists and other activists joined the party. At the same time western farmers continued to sustain local agrarian radical movements, often attracting local working-class support as well.[17] But Populism had failed, either to reassert farm community control over the forces transforming American society, or to remain as a permanent opposition to those forces.

This is not to say that Populist leaders could have preserved the party by running their own candidates in 1896. The decision for fusion reflected longings in the Populist base as well as in its leadership, and Bryan would surely have swept Populist constituencies whether the party supported him or not. America did not provide Populism with the resources either to sustain itself as a community-based opposition to industrial capitalism or to evolve into socialism. As John Laslett writes, "the intense strains created by the process of rapid industrial change, which in Europe served to accentuate profound divisions which already existed in preindustrial society, in America found no such permanent roots in which to grow."[18] In Louis Hartz's language, the American liberal tradition, rooted in the absence of feudal class loyalties, defeated from within all potentially cohesive cultural alternatives to bureaucratic capitalism. Populism offers American radicals, once again, only nostalgia for a community lost.

NOTES

1. Norman Pollack, *The Populist Response to Industrial America* (Cambridge, Mass.: Harvard, 1962), pp. 68–84; Staughton Lynd, *Intellectual Origins of American Radicalism* (N.Y.: Random House, 1968); Michael Paul Rogin, *The Intellectuals and McCarthy: The Radical Specter* (Cambridge, Mass.: MIT, 1967), pp. 168–91; Michael N. Shute, "Populism and the Pragmatic Mystique" (unpublished ms., Berkeley, 1965).

2. Robert Wiebe, *The Search for Order, 1877–1920* (N.Y.: Hill & Wang, 1967), pp. 11–110.

3. The interpretation here follows John R. Hicks, *The Populist Revolt* (Lincoln, Neb.: University of Nebraska Press, 1961), pp. 128–300. Voting data is on pp. 263, 337. For further evidence of Populism's appeal to farmers cf. Rogin, op. cit., pp. 109–15, 138–43, 175–80, and sources there cited.

4. U. S. Bureau of the Census, *Historical Statistics of the United States; Colonial Times to 1957* (Washington, D.C., 1960), p. 688.

5. H. G. Gutman, "Black Coal Miners and the Greenback-Labor Party in Redeemer Alabama: 1878–79," *Labor History,* X (Summer 1969), p. 510.

6. Wiebe, op. cit., pp. 67–68. Cf. Norman J. Ware, *The Labor Movement in the United States, 1860–1895* (N.Y.: Appleton, 1929).

7. Pollack, op. cit., pp. 25–61; Norman Pollack (ed.), *The Populist Mind* (Indianapolis: Bobbs-Merrill, 1967), pp. 403–66; George Brown Tindall (ed.), *A Populist Reader* (N.Y.: Harper & Row, 1966), pp. 165–68; Leon W. Fuller, "Colorado's Revolt Against Capitalism," *Mississippi Valley Historical Review,* XI (Dec. 1934), pp. 355–57; Hicks, op. cit., p. 444; Wiebe, op. cit., p. 91; "A Bundle of Western Letters," *Review of Reviews,* X (July 1, 1894), pp. 43, 46. The Cincinnati meeting of third-party reformers, stressed by Saloutos but barely mentioned by Pollack, has little bearing on the widespread evidence of Populist support for labor.

8. John H. M. Laslett, *Labor and the Left* (N.Y.: Basic Books, 1970), pp. 59–63, 144–45, 148–54, 193, 200–1, 244–45, 278, 299; Fuller, loc. cit.; Gutman, op. cit., pp. 507–20; Michael Paul Rogin and John L. Shover, *Political Change in California: Critical Elections and Social Movements, 1890–1966* (Westport, Conn.: Greenwood, 1971), pp. 17–18; Chester McArthur Destler, *American Radicalism 1865–1901* (N.Y.: Octagon Books, 1965), pp. 175, 202, 208.

9. Michael Rogin, "Nonpartisanship and the Group Interest," in Philip Green and Sanford Levinson (eds.), *Power and Community* (N.Y.: Random House, 1970), pp. 120–36; Michael Rogin, "Voluntarism: The Political Functions of an Anti-Political Doctrine," *Industrial and Labor Relations Review,* XV (July 1962), pp. 521–35; Lewis L. Lorwin, *The American Federation of Labor* (Washington, D.C.:

Brookings, 1933), pp. 301–5, 447–52 *passim;* Wiebe, op. cit., pp. 124–25; Laslett, op. cit., pp. 81–88, 110–14.

10. Laslett, op. cit., pp. 150–51; Destler, op. cit., pp. 171–72, 181–88, 201–9; Rogin, *Power and Community,* pp. 126–29.

11. Laslett, op. cit., pp. 29, 77, 180; Destler, op. cit., p. 190; Marc Karson, *American Labor Unions and Politics 1900–1918* (Carbondale, Ill.: Southern Illinois University, 1958), pp. 212–84; David J. Saposs, "The Catholic Church and the Labor Movement," *Modern Monthly,* VII (May 1933), pp. 225–30 (June 1933), pp. 294–98.

12. Louis L. Levine, *The Labor Movement in France* (N.Y.: Columbia, 1912), pp. 21–68; Val R. Lorwin, *The French Labor Movement* (Cambridge, Mass.: Harvard, 1954), p. 41.

13. Destler, op. cit., pp. 250–51; Rogin and Shover, op. cit., pp. 17–18. German Socialist workers also voted Populist in Milwaukee. (Rogin, *Intellectuals and McCarthy,* p. 66; Destler, op. cit., p. 202.)

14. Adam Ulam, *The Unfinished Revolution* (N.Y.: Random House, 1960), pp. 28–57.

15. Levine, op. cit., pp. 164–95; V. R. Lorwin, op. cit., pp. 36–43; Gerald Brenan, *The Spanish Labyrinth* (Cambridge, Eng.: University Press, 1943), pp. 134–202.

16. Rogin and Shover, op. cit., pp. 22–24.

17. Laslett, op. cit., pp. 298–99; Rogin, *Intellectuals and McCarthy,* pp. 64–80, 116–31, 187–91.

18. Laslett, op. cit., p. 304.

REPLY

Theodore Saloutos

There is much in what Rogin says that I agree with and much that I disagree with. On the whole I agree with his conclusions on Marxism and Populism; his observations that Populists supported the strikes of the workers against the common enemy, the large corporations; that Populism had its greatest strength in the South and West; that some Populists became Socialists; that the American Federation of Labor had little to offer in the way of a radical past; and that the Populists disliked being ruled from a distance.

Rogin claims that I present a narrow group interest interpretation of Populism. I, of course, disagree. This is largely a matter of research, definition, and interpretation. Rogin, I fear, writes about the agrarians from the vantage point of the present when the farmers constitute but a fraction of the total population and their limited numbers make them appear self-centered, instead of from the early 1890s when the farmers and their families represented a very large part of the total population, and when the distances between rural and urban were not drawn as hard and fast as they are at the present. Nowhere does he allude to the over-all acceptance by the farmers of the principles of agricultural fundamentalism which governed so much of their thinking and so many of their actions. They, and many non-farmers as well, were convinced that the fortunes of America weighed heavily on the fortunes of the farmers. As the farmers went so did the rest of the country. If the farmers prospered the nation prospered; if the farmers were depressed the nation was depressed. This was a compelling argument in an age when the bulk of the population and the wealth of the nation were tied up in agriculture.[1]

Rogin, in my opinion, has not presented substantial evidence in support of his claim that the industrial working-class complexion of Populism was as great as he suggests. Personally I feel that he has overworked this point. True, the working-class population of the industrial East consisted of many immigrants; but this immigrant background is more of an explanation of why they, the immigrants, failed to join or be accepted by the trade unions which were biased against them than of why they did not embrace Populism. The bulk of these former European peasants established themselves in the urban-industrial centers and not in rural America; hence the union and its affiliates, political and non-political, and not the agrarian-oriented Populist movement, are what they would have most likely joined—if they joined anything.

The cooperation between labor and the agrarian Populists was more rhetorical than real. The suspicions of the farmers ran strong. If the working-class influence was as formidable as has been suggested why was not a representative of the working classes put up by the Populists as a presidential or vice-presidential candidate to prove that the farmers and wage earners had reached a genuine and comprehensive agreement on political cooperation? My argument is that the labor leaders of the Knights of Labor variety, representatives of a decadent labor organization at the time the Populists reached their peak, sought the cooperation of the politically oriented farmers; and the Knights who were on the decline wanted this affiliation with the hope of pumping new life into their lingering organization; and that they, as a consequence, were more or less tied to the skirts of the agrarians. The overwhelming agrarian basis of Populism is attested to by the geography of the Populist vote, the South and the West, the two preponderantly agricultural sections of the country.

That the Populists sympathized with labor that was victimized by organized capital—that is, the corporations—as the farmers believed they also had been, is beyond doubt. The farmers and laborers had a common foe in "monopoly," and when the circumstances permitted they combined to resist the encroachments of the so-called "monopolists." The evidence that Rogin has mustered of farmers sympathizing and coming to the assistance of the striking workers is but an elaboration of this argument. What evidence of cooperation does he present when their interests collided?

The assertion has been made that the "emerging craft unions" represented a new direction in American labor. Certainly the idea of the craft union was not new. The first unions, according to labor historians, were ushered into existence by members of the crafts—the skilled workers, the shoemakers, the carpenters, the printers, and other artisan groups. Hence it would be closer to the truth to argue that the American Federation of Labor, seen in historical perspective, was in part a reaction against the ineffectiveness of the kind of industrial unionism preached by the Knights of Labor and a reassertion of old craft union principles.[2]

Rogin also speaks of working-class opposition to Populism and the wisdom of deemphasizing this argument. I think it more accurate to say that it was not so much working-class opposition to Populism as much as it was the lack of appeal that Populism had for the wage earners of the East and their tendency to associate the free silver arguments and other Populist demands with an increase in the prices and services of the things they bought. Contrary to what Rogin claims this was a real and genuine argument. These were years of hard times, a fact that does not come out very clearly in his statement, as well as a matter of self-interest. The wage earners, as American Federation of Labor leaders knew, were more concerned about their jobs, the size of their earnings, and the working conditions than in building an ideal world.

Rogin, I further believe, grievously errs in not making better use of agrarian sources and particularly the writings of southern scholars whose works have appeared since *The Populist Revolt* was first published in 1931; and in relying on resolutions, convention platforms, and other surface bits of information instead of going behind the scenes and digging up the hard facts of what actually happened. Years ago my own research in southern sources and the writings of southern scholars convinced me that the reformers were unwelcomed by the rank-and-file farmers, because they were suspicious of them and they wanted to incorporate their own pet schemes into an already long and unwieldy platform that would tend to confuse the voters and defeat their purpose.[3]

Rogin is right in stating that the religious impulse was manifest among the agrarians. My own research into the subject led me to conclude that this influence was felt especially at the local level, among organizations such as the Agricultural Wheel, which was absorbed by the Farmers' Alliance, rather than among the Populists. However, there is little proof that religious leaders or ministers of the gospel assumed a dominant role in organizing the Populist Party or in heading it. Ministers, often without churches, and broken-down preachers were attracted to Populism as lecturers and organizers of locals; and the Populists, as was brought out, won the support of preachers such as Washington Gladden and probably other preachers of the social gospel.

A state by state study of Populism in the southern states is likely to reveal something less encouraging than what Rogin suggests in the form of black and white cooperation; in fact, the picture is somewhat uglier than is implied. The resistance to Populism was great; apprehension and fear over what black and white cooperation would bring was formidable; and the force and violence considerable. Furthermore the reactions of the blacks themselves to a black and white alliance were mixed. This phase of the story has to be told along with the more favorable, if we want a better-balanced picture of what happened. The white backlash was substantial.

The resistance to black and white cooperation was greatest in the areas in which the Populists sought to operate. Once "the back of Populism was broken," "the black belt whites"—the most vigorous foes of the third party—solidified their position and recruited "enough upcountry support to adopt poll taxes, literacy tests, and other instruments to disfranchise the Negro. . . ." In fact, this began with the Mississippi Constitutional Convention of 1890, before Populism reached its peak, and continued until new constitutions were adopted by seven states from 1895 to 1910. ". . . 'understanding clauses' and the white primary provisions of constitutions and laws were of major importance in reducing the number of votes. . . ." Populism, by threatening white supremacy, backfired and strengthened the one-party system.[4]

Although I agree that Populism had some little influence on the growth of socialist thought and the American Socialist Party, especially in the Great Plains states rather than in the urban-industrial centers of the nation, the influence on the Progressive movement was greater. Socialists made some headway in Oklahoma, Kansas, and North Dakota before the rise of the Nonpartisan League in 1915, but their numbers were small compared with those of the Progressives in the Middle West, the East, and the South. By this one is not inferring that Populism alone accounted for the growth of Progressivism. Certainly the lily-white platforms of the Progressives in the South attracted larger numbers than their Populist forebears and the socialists. Rightfully or wrongfully, the bulk of the farmers believed that under socialism their lands would come under government control, and that the most hopeful among the tenants would be unable to achieve proprietorships. The ambitions of many, probably most, farmers who expected to climb the agricultural ladder to farm ownership would be quashed. Actually relatively small numbers achieved this, but the expectations were still there.

Populism in an ideological sense survived long after the formal party structure collapsed, and many, if not most, of its ideas were incorporated into Progressive platforms at the state and federal levels. By 1912 when Woodrow Wilson was elected President, much of what the Populists had proposed had gained a wide following. Of special concern to the farmers was the income tax, designed at least in part to lift some of the tax burden from the land which was the base for most of the taxes they paid, and later the Federal Reserve Act which was the most important piece of financial legislation to be passed since the Civil War. Still later, the Federal Farm Loan Act and the Federal Warehouse Act, both of which to a degree were of Populist vintage, were calculated to overcome the defects of the Federal Reserve Act and bring to the farmers more of the kind of assistance they sought.[5]

Populism by and large was grass roots in character, folkish in its ways of thinking and behavior, and certainly not an intellectual movement, as is sometimes imagined. The reactions of the agrarians stemmed from a feeling of insecurity brought on by the relegation of agriculture to a subordinate position in society, the upgrading of the money-maker and the downgrading of the farmer, the end of the era of cheap lands, the growing importance of the cities, the drift of farm children from the countryside to urban communities, the belief that youth was turning its back on the virtuous life of the farmer, the breakup of the farm family, and the gradual disappearance from the scene of the America the farmers idolized and wanted to preserve.

I find Rogin's argument that businessmen, merchants, and bankers who joined the Farmers' Alliance did not follow them into the Populist Party a bit difficult to accept. In most, if not all, instances the Farmers' Alliance aroused fear among the town merchants, the businessmen, and the bankers; and as a rule, the official business of the Alliance was conducted in secret as a means of preventing outsiders from knowing what they were doing. The Farmers' Alliance had an anti-business attitude directed against the large and more traditional business agencies, which its members suspected of defrauding or working against the interests of the farmers. Many of the local Alliances harbored a deep distrust of the business community, and as a consequence set up their own business arrangements as a means of obtaining better prices for what they sold and cheaper prices for what they bought. To say that town merchants, businessmen, and bankers who joined the Alliance were drawn away from third-party participation is misleading, because there were few, if any, to draw away.[6]

On the whole I believe that Rogin is stretching his argument too much in trying to build a broad popular base for Populism. The great majority of Populists were farmers and their allies. That the Populists attracted some reformers, some wage earners, some preachers, and some members of the professional classes is beyond question, but by no means as many as is inferred or suggested. Some Populists were attracted to the socialist movement after the Populist Party declined, but many more either were attracted to the Progressives or abandoned politics as a way of reform. In general the political and psychological ties between Populism and Progressivism were greater than between Progressivism and socialism.

NOTES

1. In 1890 almost 65 per cent of the total population of the United States lived in rural districts. *Abstract of the Fourteenth Census of the United States, 1920* (Washington, 1923), p. 77. The farm population of the United States in 1966, for instance, was only 5.9 per cent of the total. *Statistical Abstract of the United States, 1967* (Washington, 1967), p. 605.

2. George R. Taylor writes: ". . . unions of such skilled craftsmen as printers, carpenters, shoemakers, and tailors were common immediately following the War of 1812 in the larger cities such as Philadelphia, Pittsburgh, Baltimore, New York and Boston. . . ." George R. Taylor, *The Transportation Revolution, 1815–1860* (New York, 1951), pp. 251–52.

3. *Western Rural and American Stockman,* XXX (April 16, 1892), p. 243; St. Louis *Post-Dispatch,* February 19–23, 25, 1892; John D. Hicks, *The Populist Revolt* (Minneapolis, 1931), pp. 226–27; Theodore Saloutos, *Farmer Movements in the South, 1865–1933* (Berkeley, 1960), pp. 123–24; Mary Earhart, *Francis Willard* (Chicago, 1944), p. 234; James Reddick, "The Negro and the Populist Movement in Georgia" (M.A. Thesis, University of Atlanta, 1937), pp. 34–35; Helen M. Blackburn, "The Populist Party in the South, 1890–1898" (M.A. Thesis, Howard University, 1941), pp. 22–23.

4. V. O. Key, Jr., *Southern Politics* (New York, 1951), pp. 7–8, 117–18; Gunnar Myrdal, *An American Dilemma* (New York, 1944), p. 453; Albert D. Kirwan, *Revolt of the Rednecks* (Lexington, 1951), pp. 58–84; Cortez M. Ewing, *Presidential Elections* (Norman, 1940), p. 68; Joseph H. Taylor, "Populism and Disfranchisement in Alabama," *Journal of Negro History,* XXXIV (October 1949), pp. 410–27; A. A. Arnett, *The Populist Movement in Georgia* (New York, 1922); John B. Clark, *Populism in Alabama* (Auburn, 1927); Robert L. Hunt, *Farmer Movements in the Southwest, 1873–1925* (College Station, Texas, 1935); Roscoe Martin, *The People's Party in Texas* (Austin, 1933); W. Du Bose Sheldon, *The People's Party in Virginia* (Princeton, 1935); Robert F. Durden, *The Climax of Populism* (Lexington, 1965); William W. Rogers, *The One-Gallused Rebellion: Agrarianism in Alabama, 1865–1896* (Baton Rouge, 1970).

5. Theodore Saloutos, "The Professors and the Populists," *Agricultural History,* XL (October 1966), pp. 235–54.

6. Theodore Saloutos, *Farmer Movements in the South, 1865–1933,* pp. 88–101.

Chapter 3

CATHOLIC ANTI-SOCIALISM*

Marc Karson

A number of years ago Dr. David J. Saposs declared in an informal essay that the "significant and predominant role of the Catholic Church in shaping the thought and aspirations of labor is a neglected chapter in the history of the American labor movement. Its influence explains, in part at least, why the labor movement in the United States differs from others. . . ."[1] On the basis of the material which the author has accumulated, it appears that this generalization has considerable merit.

Papal Encyclicals

One of the first papal encyclicals which suggested that the Roman Catholic Church intended to modify its opposition to certain aspects of nineteenth-century social change was seen in Leo XIII's pronouncement regarding labor, *Rerum novarum* of May 1891. In essence the encyclical called for strong support of the doctrine of private property, unqualified rejection of and opposition to socialism, and acceptance of trade unions indoctrinated with Catholic social principles.[2] Devout Catholics were accordingly influenced by this important encyclical, which made it clear that impartiality for Catholics in the labor-capital conflict was an impossibility and that henceforth their intervention in modern social disturbances was mandatory.

Pope Pius X reiterated the Church's opposition to socialism in his first encyclical letter of 1903, *E supremi.* In 1912, he again warned, in the encyclical *Singulari quadam caritate,* that "unions, in order to be such that Catholics may join them, should abstain

* Marc Karson, "The Catholic Church and the Political Development of American Trade Unionism (1900–1918)," *Industrial and Labor Relations Review,* 4 (July 1951), pp. 527–42.

from all principles and acts which are not in accord with the teachings and regulations of the Church or the legitimate ecclesiastical authority." As a result of such papal pronouncements, Vincent McQuade declared that "opposition to socialism was acknowledged by devout Catholics to be the fundamental issue" within trade unions.[3] . . .

Catholic Strength in the AFL, 1900–1918

In interviews with persons who had firsthand contact with the trade union movement during the years 1900 to 1918, the present writer found opinion unanimous that Catholics were the largest religious group within the AFL. This was primarily because of the Irish Catholic membership, although other nationalities, particularly the Germans, also helped to account for this fact. As late as 1928, Professor Selig Perlman wrote that it was "the Catholics who are perhaps in the majority in the American Federation of Labor."[4] Seven years later Norman J. Ware stated that the AFL was composed of "predominantly Irish leadership of the national unions."[5] Of the eight vice-presidential offices on the AFL Executive Board from 1900 to 1918, Catholics numbered at least four during any one year. Additional research by the author concerning the number of Catholics who were presidents of the AFL international unions in the years 1900 to 1918 reveals an incomplete list of more than fifty Irish Catholics.[6]

The Position of the Cardinals

The highest American dignitaries of the Catholic Church in the first two decades of the twentieth century were three cardinals—William O'Connell, James Gibbons, and John Farley. Each of them, in their sermons and writings, vigorously espoused the doctrines set forth in *Rerum novarum.*

Cardinal Gibbons' biographer declared that the Cardinal felt that "the Church must be aroused to resist the threatened danger of socialism, [and] prepared to throw the whole force of the Church against the further progress of the [socialist] movement. . . ." Preaching in the Cathedral of Baltimore on February 4, 1916, Gibbons said that inequality of rank, station, and wealth was inevitable and "must result from a law of life established by an overruling Providence."[7] In his reminiscences, the cardinal reiterated Leo XIII's view that social organizations must be based on Catholic ethics. He wrote:

> All social schemes based on the assumption that man's good lies in the natural order alone, must fail. The brotherhood of man is a dream unless it be founded in the Fatherhood of God. The Catholic Church is the authorized representative and exponent of the supernatural order. True, it is not her official duty to devise special social schemes for special social disorder; but it is her duty to see to it that all schemes devised are founded on Christian principles and do not antagonize the law of nature and the law of God.[8]

Gibbons' views on trade unions followed the principles of *Rerum novarum.* The employers' Anti-Boycott Association reprinted in pamphlet form, with his permission, the text of one of his addresses. In it he declared that trade unions needed leaders who would not infringe "on the rights of their employers." He advised the unions to select conservative leaders and to be on guard against socialists who would make the organization "subservient to their own selfish ends, or convert it into a political engine."[9]

Cardinal O'Connell was equally definite and outspoken in making known his views on trade unions. In a pastoral letter read in all the churches of the Archdiocese of Boston on Sunday, December 1, 1912, he announced that Catholic principles must dominate trade unions and that employer-employee problems could only be adjusted through the media of Catholic ideals. He denounced socialism and socialists at some length and emphasized that, as Leo XIII had shown in *Rerum novarum,* "there cannot be a Catholic socialist." The Holy Name Societies and workmen were exhorted to study the social pronouncements of the Church and "those having care of souls" were told to instruct the workmen "in the true doctrine of the Church concerning their duties in the realm of labor."[10]

Cardinal Farley of New York also closely followed the authoritative intention of *Rerum novarum.* At the annual convention of the Confraternity of Christian Doctrine, in 1909, he referred to socialism as "the heresy of the hour—a rampant heresy" which was a serious obstacle to the success of Catholic teachers in keeping Catholic workers true to the faith. He concluded by suggesting methods for Catholics to "combat the common enemy."[11]

Teachings of Bishops and Priests

In order that the papal pronouncements be understood and acted upon by Catholic workers, it was necessary for the bishops and priests to give time and effort to interpreting these encyclicals for the workmen. The devotion of these officials to Church authority accounted for the extensive number of addresses and writings that were directed toward the American Catholic workers. This duty was well stated by Father Kerby of Catholic University, in 1907, when he wrote:

> The Church has entered the conflict as the avowed enemy of Socialism. Our colleges teach against it; we lecture and write, preach and publish against it. We have abundant official pronouncements against it, and an anxious capitalistic world looks to the Church, nervous with gratitude for the anticipated setback that Catholicism is to give to Socialism.[12]

Bishop James McFaul by 1908 had established a Labor Day Sunday in the Diocese of Trenton, and he directed "the priests of each parish on this day to speak to their people on the relations between Capital and Labor."[13] Likewise Bishop James Quigley of Buffalo in 1902 had issued a pastoral letter in his diocese in which he asked the priests to "warn their people against the theories advocated by the socialists through the means of labor unions." He also had requested that there be organized "circles in every parish in the diocese, to which both workingmen and employers shall belong."[14] In Kansas City, in 1912, Bishop Thomas Lillis reminded 110 priests who were meeting in a diocesan synod of the "inviolability of private property" and the Catholic conflict with socialism.[15] Archbishop Ireland told the trade unionists of St. Paul in a Labor Day sermon in 1903 that the "most sacred right of man is his right to private property" and, therefore, the Church was "opposed to the state socialism that is now and then preached as the panacea of labor grievances."[16]

At times Catholic clergymen spoke to AFL conventions or to the Catholic unionists attending AFL conventions. For example, Bishop John Carroll of Helena told the AFL delegates in 1913 that the Church had been a powerful body for over 2,000 years and would be more desirable as an ally than as an enemy of unionism. Therefore, he cautioned that "it would be very impolitic for labor to favor any theory of economics . . . that must incur the enmity of the Church." There were millions of Catholics who were trade unionists, and these men, Carroll declared, because they "love their religion as their very lives," would be obliged to depart from a trade union whose doctrines threatened their Church.[17]

Father Charles Bruehl, Professor of Sociology in St. Charles Seminary, Philadelphia, also made this point in 1914 when he addressed the Catholic delegates who had gathered for the AFL convention in his city. He warned them that if the principles of the AFL came into conflict with Catholic teachings, the Church would be unable to continue its endorsement of the organization. And this meant, Bruehl added, that "what the Church cannot approve, God will not bless and prosper." A conservative union, he said, was "in harmony with the Church" because she, too, "loves order and prefers to preserve rather than to destroy." He felt that those listening to him were not "dreamers of dreams" and "seers of visions" but instead were "conservative, pillars of order, and a bulwark against revolution" who wisely accepted the existing economic system and merely desired "a fair share of remuneration." Therefore, he said, he wished to "hail labor organizations as one of the conservative forces of the community." The AFL properly recognized that there was no basic conflict between labor and capital but that socialism was the enemy of both. The "Catholic element" in the unions, however, Bruehl asserted, would "overcome the contagion of socialism."[18]

The reception of Pope Pius X's encyclical *Singulari quadam caritate* brought forth two editorials from the German Roman Catholic Central Verein, an organization of German-American Catholics, vividly explaining the Catholic position on trade unions. . . . The second editorial specifically interpreted *Singulari quadam caritate* as a guide to the position that Catholic workers could take toward trade unions. It said that the Pope's words[19]

> would exclude from the ranks of unions to which Catholics might belong all organizations influenced by and fostering socialism. . . . In short, in socialistic organizations we must behold a danger to society, morality and faith, Catholics therefore cannot be members of organiza-

tions founded and directed by Socialists or for Socialistic purposes as e.g., The Industrial Workers of the World, The American Railway Union, The Western Federation of Miners, the Socialistic Trades and Labor Unions, the Knights of Labor, etc., if they are what they are said to be.

Similarly, to give briefly an example of another kind, the Farmers Educational and Co-operative Union of America is not in conformity with the above teaching. From the *America* of November 26, 1912, we learn that this union is interdenominational; advocates—these are the objectionable points—religious interdenominationalism and puts aside the true standards of morality by declaring its aim and purpose to be "to secure equity, establish justice and apply the Golden Rule." These objectionable features make it fall under the unions censured by the Pope.

As for the AFL, the Central Verein editor wrote that it "has not adopted these pernicious and morally unsound principles. It intends to be a purely economic organization." He warned, however, that should the minority who were advocating such dangerous views as revolutionary strikes, free public school textbooks, and women suffrage gain in influence in the AFL, the Catholics would have no alternative but to depart. If this radical element "ever as some fear, comes into power, then the movement will be near the danger line at which all Catholics will have to halt and at which they would have to leave the Federation." Catholics could only remain in interdenominational unions "provided the latter are not opposed to the moral laws as regards membership and action. But, we repeat, this makes the adoption of safeguard, yea, of special assistance peremptory."[20]

Doubtless the writings and addresses of bishops and priests, such as those mentioned above, were partly responsible for Aaron Abell's conclusion that "to the very end of the pre-war era, despite efforts to strike a positive and constructive note, warring upon socialism seemed to most people perhaps the main interest of the American Catholic."[21]

The Role of Father Peter E. Dietz

In the period under consideration one priest, more than any other member of the American Catholic clergy, deserved credit for devoting himself unceasingly to the practical organizational tasks that would carry the principles of *Rerum novarum* into daily practice by devout Catholics. He was the Reverend Peter E. Dietz, who has been largely ignored by labor historians, but who is finally beginning to gain from Catholic historians the recognition long overdue him.[22]

In 1940 Father Dietz answered a letter from Sister Joan de Lourdes Leonard concerning his activity in the American trade union movement.[23] In this letter he told that he had led a defeated minority of AFL delegates out of the Ohio Federation of Labor convention in Toledo in October 1909 because "the socialists carried the convention." For several years, Dietz declared, he fought the socialist-controlled Ohio Federation and finally helped to bring about its defeat. From 1909 to 1917 he attended the AFL national conventions as fraternal delegate of the American Federation of Catholic Societies and in 1921, at the request of the AFL executive board, gave the opening prayer at the AFL convention in Cincinnati, Ohio.

His letter to Sister Joan stated that it was "impossible to recall the innumerable occasions" over a period of fifteen years when he was able to champion "Leo XIII's famous Encyclical" within the AFL. Nor could he estimate, as a result of his espousal of Catholic social principles within trade unionism, the many "friendships made, the enemies disarmed, the reconciliations effected, the policies considered and reconsidered, conflicts avoided or tempered." Dietz even admitted that Samuel Gompers had once informed him that he held "the unique distinction of having secured a reversal of decisions by the Executive Board of the AFL." . . .

The Militia of Christ for Social Service

Probably Dietz's most significant accomplishment for translating *Rerum novarum* into effective daily action occurred at the time of the AFL 1910 convention. In an address before the assembled delegates at St. Louis, he assured them of the Church's support of conservative trade unions.[24] What wins for him a place in the labor history of America, however, is the organizing work he did outside the convention hall itself. At this St. Louis convention he met privately with outstanding Catholic trade union leaders and discussed with them the value of creating an organization that would defend and advance Catholic principles in the labor movement. Out of these discussions during the AFL convention there evolved a constitution and program for an organization envisaged by Father Dietz. A committee consisting of Dietz and visiting trade union executives was formed, and they called on the Archbishop of St. Louis, John J. Glennon, for his official blessing. Once this was received on November 22, 1910, the Militia of Christ for Social Service had become an actuality.[25] Father Dietz was named executive secretary, and other officers and the directorate included an imposing array of prominent Catholic trade union leaders in America at that time. The stationery of the Militia listed the following trade union leaders as the directorate: Denis A. Hayes, President, International Association of Glass Bottle Blowers (and AFL Vice-President); James O'Connell, President International Association of Machinists (and AFL Vice-President); John R. Alpine, President, International Association of Plumbers and Steam Fitters (and AFL Vice-President); John Moffat, President, International Association of Hatters of North America; John Mitchell, Chairman, Trades Agreement Department, National Civic Federation (and AFL Vice-President and former President, United Mine Workers); T. V. O'Connor, International President of the Longshoremen; John Golden, International President of the Textile Workers.

The general officers of the Militia of Christ were listed as follows: President, Peter J. McArdle (President, Amalgamated Association of Iron, Steel and Tin Workers); Vice-President, John S. Whalen (Ex-Secretary of the State of New York); Second Vice-President, Peter Collins (Secretary, International Brotherhood of Electrical Workers); Third Vice-President, John Mangan (Editor, *The Steamfitters Journal*); Recording Secretary, Thomas Duffy (President, National Brotherhood of Operative Potters, and Ohio State Deputy, Knights of Columbus); Executive Secretary, Reverend Peter E. Dietz.

As its "Motto," the Militia of Christ for Social Service adopted the precept, "Thy Will be Done." Its "Object," according to its Constitution, was "The defense of the Christian order of society and its progressive development." The Militia's "Platform" read: "The economic, ethical, sociological and political doctrines of Christian philosophy as developed in the course of history—the legacy of tradition, interpreted to modern times in the letters of Leo XIII and Pius X."

To implement this platform, a twofold method was to be followed: first, "The Promotion of Social Education," and second, "The Compelling of Social Action."

"Social Education" was to be furthered by:

(1) syndicate letters to the Catholic and Labor Press;
(2) social lectures and conferences;
(3) student apostolates in the colleges and universities;
(4) lyceum co-operation with diocesan apostolates, mission bands, K. of C. lectureships, societies, and parishes;
(5) social emphasis upon Confirmation sponsorship;
(6) a social reference bureau, social science libraries, social centers;
(7) the publication of leaflets, pamphlets, monograms, and a Journal of Social Service.

"Social Action" was to be spurred by:

(1) personal propagandist service and volunteer distribution of literature;
(2) the advocacy of Christian principles in trade unions;
(3) intelligent and active interest in the problems of labor legislation; municipal reform, civil service and general administration, industrial education, prevention of industrial accidents and diseases, workmen's compensation, workshop, factory and mine inspection, and uniform state legislation;
(4) the cultivation of fraternal relations with all Catholic societies and conservative social movements;
(5) yearly programmatic convention conjointly with the convention of the American Federation of Labor;
(6) a Catholic celebration of Labor Day;
(7) a policy of conciliation, trade agreements, arbitration of industrial difficulties.

Dr. David Saposs has been one of the very few labor historians to pay more than a passing word to the Militia. In his opinion[26] it was:

a secret organization of Catholic labor leaders designed to combat radicalism. It counted among its members the leading Catholic labor leaders, and had the approval of Gompers and the handful of other Catholic conservative labor leaders. The Militia of Christ was an auxiliary of the Church. It had large funds at its disposal. It was manned by an able staff. It immediately became a formidable factor in the fight against radicalism. It issued literature and retained a corps of propagandists and lecturers. In addition it routed outstanding labor leaders, and priests who had distinguished themselves in labor affairs, on tours where they spoke to working class audiences against radicalism and for the conservative brand of laborism.[27]

The recent opinion of Professor Abell on the purpose and influence of the Militia is quite similar to that of Dr. Saposs. He has written: "Members of the society, mostly Catholics in key positions in labor unions, helped conservative trade unionists, 'the pure and simplers' to thwart the continuous endeavors of the Socialists to capture the AFL. . . ."[28]

At the end of one year's work with the Militia, Father Dietz announced that "the earliest hopes of the Militia of Christ are not fulfilled, yet I am equally sure that the movement has justified itself." He acknowledged that the Militia had several hundred subscriptions, but he was not yet satisfied. He hoped to establish a school of social service which would turn out a trained corps of priests who could devote themselves entirely to Social Service as defined in the pronouncements of Church authority. Since he estimated it would take ten or fifteen thousand dollars "for the foundation of the School" he suggested to Mitchell that "if we could talk the matter over with some men of means, who are glad of your acquaintance and friendship, matters would soon be arranged."[29]

Faced with financial difficulties and a huge amount of work which was impossible for him to do without some assistance, Father Dietz gradually turned more and more to the Social Service Commission of the American Federation of Catholic Societies, which had been established to promote "the further amelioration of conditions among the working people for the propagation and preservation of the faith."[30]

This was not a defeat for Father Dietz, but, as he admitted, a victory. "You are aware that for years I have been trying to influence Catholic Federation into this field. The Militia of Christ was organized largely as a lever for that body. . . . I am satisfied to relinquish the title of Militia of Christ."[31] The first published Catholic paper on Father Dietz holds that "the continuance of Dietz's work of conducting lectures, attending conventions, and issuing a weekly syndicated letter to the Catholic Press, seems to indicate that the Commission became a kind of enlargement of the Militia."[32]

By 1917 Dietz reported that the Commission was sending out about 10,000 press letters and about an additional 4,000 other letters annually.[33] In the early 1920's, "the AFL gave him a gift of $2,500 in token of their friendship and esteem for a priest who had attended their annual conventions since 1909 and whom they had 'known, admired and heeded.'"[34] In the opinion of Father Henry Browne the work of Peter E. Dietz had helped to "make the word of Leo XIII's *Rerum novarum* come alive."[35]

American Federation of Catholic Societies

As noted, the Militia of Christ after a few years was absorbed by the Social Service Commission of the American Federation of Catholic Societies. The latter organization represented a movement, between 1901 and 1917, to unite existing Catholic organizations into a federation for the main purpose of defending the Church's interests and "to promote social reform along the lines of Leo's Encyclical."[36] The AFCS's constitution stated that the organization intended to spread Catholic principles in "social and public life, in the State, in business, in all financial and industrial relations."[37] By 1917 over forty Catholic societies representing three million Catholics were affiliated with the AFCS. Resolutions at the organization's annual convention regularly urged "Catholic trade unionists' faithful attendance to trade union duties, active participation in the affairs of their unions, and unceasing opposition to the abuse of their organizations by the destructive propaganda of Socialism."[38]

The German Roman Catholic Central Verein

Probably the most socially conscious of all the Catholic societies affiliated with the AFCS was the German Roman Catholic Central Verein, an association of Catholic men of German extraction, founded in 1855. The Verein in 1908 established a Central Bureau so that Catholic ethics could be more widely and effectively interpreted to the United States. The bureau sponsored study courses and discussion clubs for considering the Church's principles as applied to social reconstruction and for training Catholics for social leadership. It also issued *Central Blatt and Social Justice,* a widely circulated monthly published in German and English for the benefit of the clergy and devoted to the discussion of social problems. In addition, it issued weekly press bulletins in both German and English to one hundred Catholic newspapers.[39]

The fear of socialism and the call to social action given by Leo XIII's *Rerum novarum* led the Central Verein and the local vereins "to take an active interest in the labor movement."[40] Mr. Gonner, the president of the GRCCV, in an address to the delegates at the annual convention in 1909, explained that the Verein could have a strong influence on Catholic workmen and on trade unions through utilizing a Catholic social reform program, an effective organization, and zealous Catholic leaders. The Verein president explained that the Catholic social reform program "becomes clear when we say that for us the words 'To Restore All Things in Christ' mean the promotion and defense of Christian Order in society, especially against the dangers of Socialism and Anarchy in any form."[41] He asserted that the duty of Verein members was to contact Catholic unionists in the AFL, to arouse them against socialist penetration, and to teach them Catholic social principles. In addition, he proposed the establishment of Catholic workers' associations when he said:

> . . . The Central Society is urging its more influential members in the various cities of the U.S. to gather around themselves in groups and circles, Catholic laboring men, members of the American Federation of Labor to instruct them on their duties and the Christian principles in the Labor Question, to enable these to counteract the baneful activity displayed by Socialistic agitators among the laboring men of the United States and thus while leaving intact American organized labor yet safeguarding Catholic religious and civic rights. . . . As a permanent solution of the problem of safeguarding Catholic laboring men, the Central Society advocates the formation of Catholic laboringmen's organizations, of course, without detriment to the American Federation of Labor.[42]

As the close of this address suggests, the AFL was well regarded by the Central Verein. That fact was confirmed by a letter in 1911 from F. P. Kenkel, the Central Bureau's director, to Samuel Gompers. Mr. Kenkel wrote that the Verein was interested in the AFL and was seeking to mold the opinion of Catholic unionists "in a manner favorable to the real interests of labor." The AFL President was informed that the Verein's 1910 Newark convention had adopted a resolution urging "Catholic workingmen to join the Trade Unions wherever possible [and] to combat the propaganda of Socialism in the Unions." Mr. Kenkel added that the Verein was pleased with Gompers' ideological leadership of the AFL because it was in consonance with the social teachings expounded by the Catholic Church. Gompers was extended the Verein's "best wishes for the success of organized labor along the lines most conducive to its real welfare, and to the real good of the working classes, to the good of society, of which you are so important a factor in conformity with Christian principles."[43]

An article in the Verein's official journal by a Catholic spokesman made even plainer that the attitude of the Catholic Central Verein toward trade union political thought and practice was one and the same as that of the Gompers administration. The workers were told to prize what their union had gained for them through their economic methods and to avoid any political policies that would be a departure from the slogan, "reward your friends, punish your enemies."

> There is no graver danger lurking about than when trade unionists themselves fail to appreciate what their unions have done for them. It is then that the devils of disruption get in their underhanded, their hellish work. There is one other grave danger threatening us as trade unionists. Its onward march should meet with determined resistance. "No politics in trade unions" may be trite but it is a true guide to safe conduct. The attempt to commit our unions to a specific political party should not be tolerated in our midst, neither by resolution, by financial aid, by giving politicians special privileges to carry on a campaign in our unions or in our official journals. . . . Our business is not politics but economics. The friends of labor are the men for unionists to support and the policy of unionists is well expressed in the shibboleth that "we should reward our friends and punish our enemies."[44]

Another crusader for the Catholic social cause, Peter W. Collins, former secretary of the Electrical Brotherhood, was also provided with space in the Verein's journal. Collins reminded his readers that Catholic trade unionists represented "almost one half of the men of organized labor." Since they had the numerical strength to defeat socialism in the trade unions, he considered the moral guilt would be theirs if socialism triumphed. His positive proposal for a Catholic victory was put in these words:

> We advocate Catholic workingmen's societies to be founded in each parish, whose members shall be instructed as to their special duties to church and society according to precepts laid down by Leo XIII . . . only when so instructed and fortified will Catholic laboringmen be able to do their full share in preventing the insidious enemy from capturing the Trade Union Movement and turning it into a recruiting ground for Socialism, into an appendix of the Socialist Party of the United States.[45]

The Central Verein, however, did more than propagate theory in its desire to educate Catholics on the proper application of the Church's doctrines to trade unions. It actually entered the sphere of social action by forming "Catholic workingmen's societies in several cities."[46] Director F. P. Kenkel mentions that two of these societies were the St. Anne's Arbeiterverein, formed in Buffalo in 1909 by Father Meckel (S.J.), and the Arbeiterwohl, organized in St. Louis by a number of German American priests, led by the Reverend Albert Mayer.[47] The St. Louis association's birth was in part due to the priests' fear of the influence of socialists in the brewing industry. The Arbeiterwohl's paper, *Amerika,* edited by Kenkel, "was read by every German speaking priest in St. Louis and could be found in most of the taverns frequented by German speaking workingmen."[48]

The social diligence of the Central Verein in translating the Church's doctrines to the American people earned the praise of Father John A. Ryan. He commended the Verein for recommending, as he said, "that Catholic workingmen take an active part in the regular trade union instead of forming separate organizations. In this way the Catholic workers will be able to oppose most effectively Socialism, unwise radicalism, and every other tendency or method that is hostile to genuine reform."[49]

The Catholic Press

A survey of the Catholic journals and newspapers from 1900 to 1918 reveals that the Catholic press was in accord with the principles laid down in *Rerum novarum,* and quite consistently advanced them. Leo XIII himself reminded the hierarchy of the importance of the press when he said: "All your work will be destroyed, all your efforts will prove fruitless if you are not able to wield the defensive and offensive weapon of a loyal and sincere Catholic press."[50] The wisdom of these words was not lost on the American hierarchy and in the "plenary councils, the bishops of the country have time and again pronounced on its importance, furthered it by every means within their power, urged and commanded and pleaded with the Catholic laity for its support."[51] A pastoral letter of Bishop McFaul of Trenton early in the twentieth century urged:

> Every Catholic family should subscribe for a Catholic newspaper and a Catholic magazine. . . . Catholics should ask their newsdealers for such newspapers as *The Freemen's Journal* of New York, *The Pilot* of Boston, *The Pittsburgh Observer,* and other religious newspapers published in their respective localities. They should also seek the inestimable Catholic periodicals like *The Messenger* and *The Catholic World* of New York, *Donahue's Magazine* of Boston and a host of others. . . . No better example of the power and influence of the press can be given than the results achieved in Germany. It was due to public opinion created by the Catholic press that the Center Party remained undivided and steadfast, triumphed over Kulturkampf, sent Bismarck to Canossa, and organized the Catholics of Germany so that they presented an unbroken front to their enemies.
>
> We will never attain the position due to us in the civil and religious life of America, unless we employ this powerful lever in the creation of public opinion.[52]

Besides drawing attention to Catholic publications, Church leaders also pointed out improper reading material. Husslein cautioned the Catholic trade unionists that, if they were to remain "men of clear insight and strong Catholic principles," they would not "endorse the socialist publications which were recommended to them." To accept socialist publications, he declared, meant bringing "into the house of the laborer a weekly apostle of radicalism in almost every shape condemned by the Church."[53]

The period 1900–1918 saw the birth of about fifty Catholic weekly publications, of the Catholic Press Association, and of several publications specifically dedicated to combating socialism.[54]

The Catholic Press Association was established in August 1911 at Columbus, Ohio, by Catholic editors convening in that city.

In New York City two anti-socialist publications were founded shortly before World War I by devoted Catholic sources. One was a newspaper, *The Live Issue,* the other a journal, *The Common Cause. The Live Issue*'s "Declaration of Principles," featured above its editorial page, stated that the paper "utterly repudiates and fearlessly combats Socialism." In consideration of the spirit and purposes of *Rerum novarum,* the editor saw his duty was to teach the workers the values of the Catholic social movement. "*The Live Issue*'s mission," he announced, "was to make our workingmen conscious factors in the moulding process which society is now undergoing. And it is to achieve this result that true social enlightenment is an imperative necessity no less than to expose the dangers and fallacies of Socialism."[55]

The Common Cause likewise proclaimed itself a journal which "comes to the defence of right-reason in things economic as against the theories of Socialism."[56] Its issues regularly contained indictments against socialism, and it periodically republished antisocialist articles originating elsewhere. The appearance of *The Common Cause* not only elicited an enthusiastic reception from a number of Catholic publications, but its editors also received a letter from Samuel Gompers complimenting its purpose.[57]

Conclusions

The weakness of socialism in the American Federation of Labor at the close of World War I was, in part, a testimonial to the success of the Catholic Church's opposition to this doctrine. The Church could credit itself with having waged an effective campaign in checking socialism within the trade union movement. Many other factors which labor historians have carefully brought out have accounted for the weakness of socialism within American trade unions, but certainly the definite opposition of the Catholic Church should be added to the reasons usually advanced. Professor Selig Perlman was evidently aware of this when he wrote in 1928 that for the American labor movement "to make socialism or communism the official 'ism' of the movement, would mean, even if the other conditions permitted it, deliberately driving the Catholics, who are perhaps in the majority in the American Federation of Labor, out of the labor movement, since with them an irreconcilable opposition to socialism is a matter of religious principle."[58] As can be readily understood, a labor party in an industrialized country derives its main strength from the support of the trade union movement. Where a trade union movement has neither socialist leadership nor a socialist political consciousness among its rank and file, it will not possess the ideology that would find its political expression in a labor party. The important generalization which Perlman has suggested, and which the research for this present study has confirmed, is that the failure of socialism and a political labor party to evolve in America were in some measure due to the hostility of the Catholic Church. Catholicism created a "bridge between the Church in America and the labor movement" enabling it to "take hold of the labor movement."[59]

It is also of importance to note that Catholicism engaged in this task during a period when American trade unionism, still in its infancy, was developing its institutional traditions. Like all traditions, these would prevail during future generations and tend to become almost conditioned responses. Furthermore, this period also began as one in which the socialist movement seemed on the threshold of becoming a major American political force. The awareness of these two facts on the part of the Catholic Church was evident in the extent of its exertions against socialist penetration of the trade unions. The victory achieved by Catholicism at the close of this period was shown by the weakness of the socialists in the AFL and the dominance of an antisocialist administration. At the conclusion of World War I, the similarity between the *AFL's Reconstruction Program* and the *Bishops' Program of Social Reconstruction* was more than a coincidence.[60] It was to some degree the result of the intensive efforts made by the Catholic Church to permeate the AFL with social principles. Aided by the predominantly Catholic officers of the international unions and by the large Catholic rank and file in the AFL responsive to their Church's views on socialism, Catholicism could take partial credit for the political philosophy and policies of the federation, for socialism's weakness in the trade union movement, and the absence of a labor party in the United States.

NOTES

1. David J. Saposs, "The Catholic Church and the Labor Movement," *Modern Monthly,* 7 (May–June 1933), p. 225.

2. Pope Leo XIII, *Rerum novarum,* May 15, 1891 (New York: Paulist Press, 1939).

3. Vincent A. McQuade, *American Catholic Attitude on Child Labor Since 1891* (Ph.D. Dissertation, Catholic University of America, 1938).

4. Selig Perlman, *A Theory of the Labor Movement* (New York: Macmillan, 1928), p. 168.

5. Norman Ware, *Labor in Modern Industrial Society* (New York: Heath, 1935), p. 35.

6. This list was prepared after consultation with Frank Morrison, AFL Sec. 1896–1929, and Dr. David J. Saposs. It does not include any Socialists.

7. Allen S. Will, "Checking the Tide of Socialism," in *Life of Cardinal Gibbons, Archbishop of Baltimore* (New York: Dutton, 1922), II, ch. 37.

8. Cardinal James Gibbons, *A Retrospect of Fifty Years* (Baltimore: Murphy, 1916), pp. 258–59.

9. Cardinal James Gibbons, *Organized Labor,* reprinted by Anti-Boycott Association as part of a pamphlet, *The Morals and Law Involved in Labor Conflicts,* in the New York Public Library.

10. Cardinal William O'Connell, "Pastoral Letter on the Laborer's Rights," *The Church and Labor* (New York: Macmillan, 1920), pp. 177–86.

11. *America,* vol. II, no. 13, January 8, 1910.

12. William Kerby, "Aims in Socialism," *The Catholic World,* 85 (July 1907), p. 511. Father Kerby was a good friend of Samuel Gompers. Occasionally he took his Catholic University Social Economy students to AFL headquarters for a lecture by Gompers on trade unionism.

13. Rev. James Powers (ed.), *Addresses of Bishop McFaul* (Trenton: American, 1908), p. 375.

14. *Messenger,* 38 (September 1902), p. 246, quoting Buffalo *Catholic Evening News,* July 5, 1902.

15. Kansas City *Journal,* April 10, 1912.

16. Archbishop John Ireland, *Labor and Capital,* p. 343 (in the New York Public Library).

17. *AFL Proceedings,* 1913, pp. 207–10.

18. Rev. Charles Bruehl, "The Conditions of Labor," in *Addresses at Patriotic and Civic Occasions by Catholic Orators* (New York: Wagner, 1915), I, pp. 63–82.

19. *Central Blatt and Social Justice,* 5 (February 1913), pp. 243–45.

20. Ibid. For a discussion of Catholic trade union leaders in Belgium and Germany who "separated themselves from unions that had fallen under socialist domination" and established Catholic unions see Henry Sommerville, *Studies in the Catholic Social Movement* (London: Burns, etc., 1933), pp. 5–6.

21. Aaron Abell, "The Reception of Leo XIII's Labor Encyclical in America 1891–1919," *The Review of Politics,* 7 (October 1945), p. 493.

22. Professor Abell in an essay, "Monsignor Ryan: An Historical Interpretation," *The Review of Politics,* 8 (January 1946), says that Ryan "left to others, notably the Rev. Peter E. Dietz, the organizational task involved in the [Leo's] Encyclical's official reception." Cf. Harrita Fox, "Peter E. Dietz, Pioneer in the Catholic Social Movement" (Ph.D. Dissertation, University of Notre Dame, 1950). In a letter to the author (March 14, 1948) she writes: "The influence of Father Dietz in the AFL was great since he numbered Samuel Gompers, John P. Frey and Matthew Woll among his friends. The fact, too, that he contributed to the *American Federationist* would indicate an appreciation of his opinions."

23. Sister Joan de Lourdes, now teaching at St. Joseph's College for Women, Brooklyn, kindly made this letter available to the writer. (Dietz to Leonard, Milwaukee, July 19, 1940.)

24. *AFL Proceedings,* 1910, pp. 202–3. At the 1911 Atlanta, Ga., convention Dietz preached the sermon at the Immaculate Conception Church on "The Relation of the Catholic Church to the Labor Movement" (*AFL Proceedings,* 1911, p. 184). At the 1912 convention he again spoke before all the delegates (*AFL Proceedings,* 1912, p. 223). He warned that even if the workers were able to carry out the slogan "workers of the world unite . . . you have a world to win," it would not "profit a man even if he does win the world but suffer the loss of his soul."

25. A copy of the Militia's constitution and platform and endorsement of Archbishop Glennon was seen by the author among the John Mitchell papers at Catholic University of America. A photostat of this document is now in the author's possession. The Reverend Henry J. Browne, while working on his Ph.D., realized the significance of the Mitchell papers and kindly introduced the author to them.

26. *The Catholic Church and the Labor Movement.*

27. The Militia, apparently, was no secret to the Socialist press. A news story in the Schenectady *Daily Union,* January 9, 1911, relating that "the work of getting Schenectady Catholic union men into the Militia will begin at once by the men in charge here," brought forth a vituperative editorial by De Leon in his *Daily People,* January 14, 1911. The *International Socialist Review* declared: "Every American Unionist knows how bitterly the Catholic Church has fought Socialism in the labor unions through its servile tools, such as the Militia of Christ and similar secret alliances" (Richard Perrin, "The German Catholic Unions," *International Socialist Review,* January 1914, p.

398). *The Masses,* in an editorial on AFL and Catholic Church opposition to Socialism, wrote: "The AFL is getting more and more into the hands of the Militia of Christ" (*The Masses,* July 1912, p. 3).

28. "The Reception of Leo XIII's Labor Encyclical," *The Review of Politics,* 7 (October 1945).

29. Dietz to Mitchell, December 30, 1911. In regard to raising funds, Mitchell proposed instead a circular letter of appeal for "small subscriptions from a large number of men" (Mitchell to Dietz, January 3, 1912).

30. Quoted by Aaron Abell, "The Reception . . . ," op. cit., p. 490, from *Catholic News,* September 2, 1911.

31. Dietz to Mitchell, Milwaukee, August 3, 1912.

32. Henry J. Browne, "Peter E. Dietz, Pioneer Planner of Catholic Social Action," *The Catholic Historical Review,* XXXIII (January 1948), p. 454.

33. *Bulletin* of AFCS, 12, nos. 8–10 (August–September 1917), p. 11.

34. Browne, op. cit., p. 456.

35. Ibid., p. 449.

36. Abell, op. cit., p. 479.

37. Matre, op. cit., IX, pp. 247–59. The present-day descendant of this organization is now known as the National Catholic Welfare Conference.

38. *Bulletin* of AFCS, 12, nos. 8–10 (August–October 1917), p. 11.

39. *The Central Verein: History, Aims and Scope,* Leaflet no. 82, published by the GRCCV's Central Bureau. This leaflet was kindly loaned to the author by Sister Joan de Lourdes.

40. Sister Mary Brophy, *The Social Thought of the German Roman Catholic Verein* (Ph.D. Dissertation, Catholic University of America, 1941), pp. 72–83.

41. Ibid.

42. Ibid.

43. *Central Blatt and Social Justice,* 4 (December 1911), p. 204.

44. David Goldstein, "Trade Unions: Their Foundation, Achievements, Dangers and Prospects," *Central Blatt and Social Justice,* 3 (December 1910), p. 189.

45. Peter W. Collins, "Catholic Workingmen's Association," *Central Blatt and Social Justice,* 5 (May 1912), pp. 35–36. Goldstein and Collins were two especially colorful lecturers routed on tours by the Militia of Christ and the AFC's Social Service Commission. Goldstein had been a member of the Socialist Labor Party before accepting the Catholic faith. Cf. David Goldstein, *Socialism: The Nation of Fatherless Children* (Boston: Union News League, 1902). Professor Abell rates Collins as second only to Father Dietz in extending Catholic principles within the trade unions at this time (Abell, op. cit., p. 489).

46. Abell, op. cit., p. 487.

47. F. P. Kenkel to Sister Joan de Lourdes, June 24, 1940. This letter was kindly loaned to the author by Sister Joan.

48. F. P. Kenkel to Norman McKenna, April 29, 1940, quoted by Sister Joan de Lourdes Leonard in "Catholic Attitude Towards American Labor 1884–1919" (unpublished M.A. Thesis, Columbia University, 1940).

49. John A. Ryan, "The Central Verein," *Catholic Fortnightly Review,* 16 (first March issue, 1909), p. 132. The devotion of Father Ryan to major social reform is well known. His support of AFL, its economic demands and strikes, endeared him to many. Space, however, prevents a consideration of Ryan's contributions (cf. Richard J. Purcell, "John A. Ryan–Prophet of Social Justice," *Studies,* June 1946).

50. Quoted by John Burke, "Convention of Catholic Editors," *The Catholic World,* October 1911, p. 9.

51. Burke, op. cit., p. 81.

52. James A. McFaul, "Some Modern Problems," *Pastoral Letter* (Trenton: American Publishing Co., 1908).

53. Joseph Husslein (S.J.), *The Catholic's Work in the World* (New York: Benziger Bros., 1917), pp. 112–16.

54. Cf. Apollinaris W. Baumgartner, *Catholic Journalism in the United States* (New York: Columbia University Press, 1931).

55. *The Live Issue* (New York City), April 11, 1914, p. 2.

56. *Socialism: The Nation of Fatherless Children.*

57. Gompers to *The Common Cause,* Washington, D.C., December 14, 1911, in *Gompers Correspondence,* AFL headquarters, Washington, D.C.

58. Perlman, op. cit., p. 169.

59. Dietz to Cardinal O'Connell, March 15, 1913, quoted by Sister Harrita Fox, op. cit., p. 105.

60. *Bishops' Program of Social Reconstruction* (Washington, D.C.: National Catholic Welfare Conference, n.d.).

COMMENT

Henry J. Browne

Religion traditionally gets blamed and credited for many things. In the history of the United States Catholicism has come in for more than its fair share of blame for being superstitious, priest-ridden, and out of step with prevailing American ways—if not actually politically subversive. Shortly before some of its devotees would credit it for producing John—or at least mother Rose—Kennedy, Marc Karson, a budding young scholar under Professor Harold Laski at the London School of Economics, blamed it for stopping the advance of socialism in the American labor movement, and hence for lessening the impact of socialism in the United States.

Karson's approach has always appeared to this writer to be essentially naïve and simplistic in a way almost mirroring the devotional believer's overclaim that when the Pope coughed all Catholics at least sneezed. Even the gently apologetic second statement of his thesis, which emphasized the unconscious brainwashing impact of a tradition of anti-socialism on Catholic trade unionists, only added to its gratuitous character. The argument's ideological milieu is more precisely that of the 1950s when the Kremlin-Vatican parallel was being made into an American secular dogma by Paul Blanshard.[1]

That there was a deviously organized and Church-directed Catholic bloc in the labor movement continued as part of the lore of the Left well into contemporary labor history. Catholic trade union enthusiasts did not always help to allay that suspicion. Father Peter Dietz, with what seems a kind of embarrassed encouragement from Catholic John Mitchell of the miners' union, did in 1912 organize the Militia of Christ for Social Service to encourage support of the American Federation of Labor. Though such a pious label telegraphed an image of religious proselytizing, the

Militia's work was mostly a one-man paper show in the form of press releases, prospectuses, and polemics.[2] Dietz, fortunately for Church and labor, soon moved into the more harmless field of educating Catholic social workers.

Some of Dietz's Militia activity indicated further the paradox of American Catholic trade unionists: at the very time they were supposedly infiltrating to keep the labor movement at least safe from socialism, if not Church-dominated, they were seeking clarification from Rome about their right to belong to a union that was not Catholic or at least interconfessionally Christian in character. Actually it was not until 1931 in *Quadragesimo anno* that such an explicit endorsement of Catholic membership in a so-called neutral or non-religious union was forthcoming from suspect Vatican headquarters.

In the Progressive era the most organized and people-connected Catholic voice of social reform was the German Catholics' Central-Verein. A recent sober and insightful account of that organization's conservative venture into the social question in 1908 leaves no doubt of its anti-socialist stand, its primary reason in fact for adding its program of social reform to those concerned with religion and ethnic identity. The real question of its real impact remains more mysterious, however. An intellectual director with a medieval orientation, editing a dull magazine in German, to be read mostly by priests and farmers, arranging lectures and pamphlet publication, and drawing inspiration from a very German and philosophic pattern of total social reorganization called "solidarism" hardly presents a picture of powerful influence. Outside the organization's own public statements, and the socialists' reciprocal claims about the power of the opposition, it is hard to find more than a rhetorical reality in that particular version of the mythic Catholic slaying of the red dragon among workers.[3]

On the other side is the evidence that some ethnic influence seems to have been at work in cases of Catholic flirtation with American socialism. In the mid-eighties New York Irish with more the auld sod than their own city tenements on their mind, in great numbers, and against the authority of the Church and their regular political party, backed Henry George's unsuccessful bid for mayor. His Single Tax platform denying private ownership in land had the endorsement of Dr. Edward McGlynn, who led largely by charisma instead of logic. Though the standard account of Catholic social action in the first two decades of the twentieth century is given to detailing the intellectual opposition to socialism, one can dig out Poles in Milwaukee, Italians in Colorado, Germans and Irish in Cleveland, and an organization of Christian Socialists in Chicago whose balloting proves that municipal socialism appealed to some Catholic laborers despite direct Church opposition. Clearly the intellectual's argument that made socialism intrinsically anti-religious did not have the impact claimed for it.[4]

Within the ranks of labor the Catholic-socialist debate was, in the final analysis, a conflict of power rather than of theory. American Catholics did not in any real conscious and effective way bring their ethical values to bear within the movement until 1937 with the Association of Catholic Trade Unionists. At least that was its manifest function. History might question its latent one, considering the success of many of its former members in positions with government, organized labor, and even as management consultants. The case in point may illustrate how long-abiding was the myth of the Catholic monolith sending tremors on every social and political doctrine from the Pope to the humblest parishioner. The ACTU was based on a paragraph in Pius XI's labor encyclical which advocated the creation of organizations, paralleling the unions, to inculcate Catholic ethical and religious principles. The training of unionist leaders and the education of rank and file for more active participation were pursued through labor schools and a lively newspaper, *The Labor Leader*. One of the chief focuses of organizational strength was the New York metropolitan area where the group had begun. Academic discussions sometimes led to action groups for reform within individual unions. The "bad guys" were usually racketeers or communists. Such specific union "conferences" were never restricted to Catholics nor were they clerically controlled, but of course they risked being labeled a religious caucus.

So it was that the issue of organized Catholic factionalism and anti-radicalism in unions did not get its real testing until the late 1940s. The question fought out was communist control of the United Electrical, Radio and Machine Workers of America. The ACTU concern began in their labor school conducted at New Rochelle College. For our purpose it may suffice to recall Michael Harrington's study of the case. He may be considered impartial since he is readily described as a Christian Socialist who was turned on by the Catholic Worker movement. Never were American Catholics so ready for such action against radicalism. There was a network of organizations across the country with competent unionist laymen working from a body of literature based on the social encyclicals. There was even a tie-in with the organizational power of the Church through the chaplains. Nonetheless, Harrington's detailed and detached study found that not only was the ACTU leadership opposed to a sectarian approach and religious factionalism but also that as a national force in the struggle it was not "cohesive and identifiable." A potpourri of organizations and personalities, clerical and lay, including the classic stimulant of anti-Catholic bile, Jesuits (in this case conducting labor schools), involved themselves in the fight. The conclusion, however surprising, is that the struggle which resulted in a victory for the newly established IUE was not a religious one but based on their convincing workers of their better delivery of union benefits. Indeed, the one priest who from the pulpit declared it sinful to vote for the communist leadership, was repudiated by the electrical workers of his community.[5]

This well-documented case seems to be the only available study of a confrontation between organized radicalism and organized Catholicism within the labor movement in the United States. Much research, it is suggested, remains to be done on the influence of the Church's teaching, particularly the role of its leadership, often both an ethnic and intellectual as well as a religious one, on the success or failure of trade unions in a specific locality. From the Molly Maguire pastors of the Pennsylvania coal fields to the as yet unsung priest members of mediation and arbitration boards who emerged in the 1930s, some interesting clerical examples of the interplay of religion and labor are being discovered. In general they indicate that no simple picture is to be drawn either depicting a Catholic rejection of Left extremism as evil or identifying the workers' efforts with radical and anti-social philosophy.

My own earlier research also points to the prevalence of a very pragmatic approach on the part of priest confessors and their bishop superiors on the question of American Catholics joining unions. They worried more about the secret character of the organizations than any other single factor in their programs. If a generalization might be risked it would be: the closer the spiritual leader or adviser was to the workingman's situation, the more he favored the union and the less concerned he was with its real or imagined radicalism. For example, it is impressive that confessional policy on union membership at the Baltimore cathedral, even before the mid-nineteenth century, was tolerant, and as early as the II Plenary Council in 1866, the American hierarchy in solemn panoply assembled approved of Catholics joining a bona fide organization for economic self-help.[6]

Several examples might illustrate this class-identity influence on churchmen. In the 1870s Bishop James Wood of Philadelphia allied himself with the powers that crushed the militant Mollies; many of their pastors were torn between knowledge of their miserable plight in the mines and rejection of their violence. Much more explicitly pro-worker was Father Cornelius O'Leary's defense of the Missouri railroad strikers in 1886. Before a congressional committee he blamed corporations for breeding radicalism and later, while in exile imposed by his archbishop, avowed he was a "socialist and rebel at heart as was every Irishman."[7] The passage of time brought class changes. In Lawrence, Massachusetts, in 1912 two Catholic working-class-community pastors of later ethnic arrivals (Italians and Syrians) were found endorsing the radical IWW textile workers strike in the face of the respectable clergy of the city led by the Irish Catholic pastor. At that same period Catholic clergy influence was alleged by the Socialist Party in New York City for the failure of its program to make any headway among Irish and Italian workers. Yet a recent scholar studying the case puts the religious factor secondary to political, economic, and social ones. These workers were getting their security and power elsewhere, including from the Church, Tammany Hall, and AF of L unionism, and did not need to turn to the despair of radical politics.[8]

It might be submitted that not only distance from the problems of the workers but also other class considerations such as educational and social background and connections had more influence than theological considerations or the hostile attitude of some American bishops toward the supposedly radical efforts of American workers. The late-nineteenth-century bishops outstanding for their fear of the menace of socialism working through unions were James Roosevelt Bayley of Baltimore, most certainly a social snob, and such European-connected types as Francis S. M. Chatard of Vincennes, John Dwenger of Fort Wayne, and John Baptist Salpointe of Santa Fe. The last of these, right after leaving his city torn by the strife of the rail strike in 1886, joined Archbishop Peter Richard Kenrick of St. Louis to make the two votes out of the twelve archbishops of the country against the Knights of Labor. Kenrick was reported to be close to railroad interests, as was Bishop Nicholas Matz of Denver said to have been friendly with mining powers during the troubles in that area in 1903. Matz denounced the socialist threat of the Federation of Miners and clubbed them with the anti-socialist defense of private property found in *Rerum novarum.* However, a recent study of Matz begs the question of his influence on the workers. For example, out of the approximately two hundred listed as deported by the occupying military out of the mining district almost 50 per cent seem to have Catholic ethnic names and so may be considered to have cordially ignored the bishop's pro-Establishment threats.[9] For further enlightenment it might be useful to trace the growth of the fear of socialism among American bishops, even such liberals as John Ireland of St. Paul, as they grew closer in friendship to such men as James Hill, the railroad magnate.[10]

The major trouble with the Saposs-Karson thesis is that it takes the word for the deed. The attitude of the organization and its official spokesmen is presumed unquestionably to motivate members to accept the body of approved doctrine. The Catholic fears of the danger of socialism expressed so vividly in *Quod apostolici muneris,* the encyclical of 1878, hardly call one today to holy warfare against its programs in the light of *Mater et magistra* and *Progressio populorum.* The question is whether the bugle sound was ever heard or acted upon that well by the ranks even a hundred years ago. It has been established, to the satisfaction of social science at least, that religion makes a difference in social and political attitudes. At the same time there is doubt about the authentic relationship between attitudes expressed and actual positions taken.[11] Philip Taft, for example, who was the first really to exploit in a scholarly way the archives of the American Federation of Labor, could not find any such distinctive reaction to questions relating to socialism in the votes of the Catholic members of the executive council of that organization. The conclusion of this study of the matter is worth quoting:

> The theory that Catholic influence prevented American labor from endorsing socialism and independent political action never gained a following outside of radical and anti-Catholic circles. The opposition

to socialism in the early years was led by men such as Gompers, and McGuire, who was not a practicing Catholic although he was of a Catholic family and died in the church. Lennon, Duncan, Kidd and McCraith, who carried the attack against the Socialists, were of Protestant origin, McCraith being a philosophical anarchist without much religion of any kind. Moreover, the A.F. of L.'s defense of revolutionaries and anarchists refutes the implication of domination by the Church.[12]

It should also be pointed out that Catholic spiritual leaders in the United States were not as often on the spot as their counterparts in Europe, since control of the American economy was not in Catholic hands, and hence the Church not as beholden to such anti-labor power. The esoteric social doctrine of the Church was far removed from the masses of its members. That is not to say that the American Catholic blue-collar worker did not in time of crisis seek and even have volunteered for him the aid of the intellectuals and pastors of his faith. This was certainly true of the organizing days of the CIO in the 1930s when clerics and organizers worked hand in hand.

Yet John Brophy, who was one of the great forces in that movement and who, owing to his fostering the industrial councils' plan, was considered the rare self-made Catholic intellectual in the labor movement, testified to the absence of ideological formation. His memoirs credit his rejection of Marxist materialism to what he calls vaguely his Christian humanism. He registered his agreement with most socialistic reforms and stressed the pro-labor rather than the pro-private property aspects of the papal encyclical of 1891. He then went on to recall:

> Had I known of the papal social encyclicals I could have saved much distress of mind. American churchmen were very slow about heeding the papal counsel on these important issues. I never read *Rerum Novarum* until a generation after it was issued. I heard of it only vaguely as an anti-Socialist tract, or even as an apology for capitalism. American churchmen seem not to have grasped the meaning of that great document for a long time; certainly I, like many others, was long left in ignorance of its criticism of capitalism and of its constructive counsel.[13]

American Catholic enthusiasm for such movements as New Deal reformism, industrial unionism, and even the Christian anarchy expounded in the *Catholic Worker,* not to mention the many other eddies of social change that flowed out of that movement of the thirties, may have abated during the last generation's flight to suburbia. Yet even if the "socializing," "cultural conformist," and "society sustaining" aspects of American Catholicism continue strong, it retains nonetheless room for even the revolutionary who may have caught some glimpse of the socialist dream. Peter McGuire, Terence Powderly, Fathers Thomas Haggerty and Thomas McGrady, the McNamara brothers, Tom Mooney, Elizabeth Gurley Flynn, and others like them gave up the Church as the defender of an unjust industrial status quo, and settled mostly for more radical doctrines of society. Today they might find themselves more at home in a loosened if not chastened Church on whose doctrine some of its members are now building programs of radical social change.[14]

The evidence at any rate leaves room to suspect that other factors—including the whole spirit of the country—were more potent than the religious in keeping organized labor from coming under the ideological dominion of socialism.[15] The claims even I made for the religious influence some twenty years ago have been tempered by a decade's efforts at moving people in social action and finding religion to be more a personal justification than a motivation to most men, whose concerns continue to be overwhelmingly bread-and-butter ones.

NOTES

1. Marc Karson, *American Labor Unions and Politics, 1900–1918* (Carbondale, 1958), pp. xi–xv.

2. Philip Taft, *The A.F. of L. in the Time of Gompers* (New York, 1957), p. 336, so characterized Dietz's efforts. This writer's agreement is found in "Roman Catholicism," *The Shaping of American Religion* (Princeton, 1961), p. 101. The opposite view is found in Mary Harrita Fox, *Peter E. Dietz, Labor Priest* (Notre Dame, 1953).

3. Philip Gleason, *The Conservative Reformers: German-American Catholics and the Social Order* (Notre Dame, 1968), pp. 69–143.

4. Robert Cross, *The Emergence of Liberal Catholicism in America* (Cambridge, 1958), pp. 119–24, gives a brief but balanced account of the New York scene, while the review of the 1900–17 developments is found in Aaron Abell, *American Catholicism and Social Action: A Search for Social Justice, 1865–1950* (Garden City, 1960), pp. 136–53.

5. Michael Harrington, "Catholics in the Labor Movement: A Case History," *Labor History,* I (Fall 1960), pp. 231–63.

6. Abell, op. cit., p. 47, in an ancient disagreement with this writer predicated hostility against unions on the part of bishops and priests up to the mid-1880s. Perhaps as a layman he was not as aware of how much pastoral counterforce it must have taken to get even a minimal statement of friendliness to unions in 1866. Henry J. Browne, *The Catholic Church and the Knights of Labor* (Washington, D.C., 1949), p. 16.

7. William B. Faherty, "The Clergy and Labor Progress: Cornelius O'Leary and the Knights of Labor," *Labor History,* XI (Spring 1970), p. 188. Cf. Wayne G. Broehl, *The Molly Maguires* (Cambridge, 1964), *passim.*

8. Philip S. Foner, *History of the Labor Movement in the United States,* IV (New York, 1965), pp. 333–34; Melvyn Dubofsky, "Success and Failure of Socialism in New York City, 1900–1918; a Case Study," *Labor History,* IX (Fall 1968), pp. 372–73.

9. George G. Suggs, "Religion and Labor in the Rocky Mountain West: Bishop Nicholas C. Matz and the Western Federation of Miners," *Labor History,* XI (Spring 1970), pp. 190–206; cf. "The List of Deported," in Emma F. Langdon, *The Cripple Creek Strike: A History of Industrial Wars in Colorado, 1903–4–5* (Denver, 1905), pp. 456–57.

10. It may be instructive that Liston Pope in his pioneer study of religious and economic factors in society found only two clergymen in Gaston County friendly to the labor organizer, two detached and non-influential Catholic monks. *Millhands and Preachers* (New Haven, 1942), p. 202.

11. Cf. Gerhard Lenski, *The Religious Factor: A Sociological Study of Religion's Impact on Politics, Economics and Family Life* (Garden City, 1961) and Irwin Deutscher, "Words and Deeds: Social Science and Social Policy," *Social Problems,* XIII (Winter 1966).

12. Taft, op. cit., p. 336.

13. John Brophy, *A Miner's Life* (Madison, 1964), p. 100. It may be interesting for comparative purposes to note that in 1969 a study in the diocese of Worcester, Massachusetts, indicated that 60 per cent of the Catholic laity were for all practical purposes unacquainted with the Second Vatican Council. Richard P. McBrien, *Church: the Continuing Quest* (New York, 1970), pp. 26–27.

14. Cf. Francine Gray, *Divine Disobedience: Profiles in Catholic Radicalism* (New York, 1970).

15. Sidney Hook, "The Philosophical Basis of Marxian Socialism in the United States," *Socialism and American Life,* I (Princeton, 1952), pp. 450–51.

REPLY

Marc Karson

Father Browne does not accept my analysis of his Church's role in the early-twentieth-century political development of American labor unions. I am criticized for being "essentially naïve and simplistic," and in the "ideological milieu" of anti-Catholic intellectuals like Paul Blanshard. I can understand that Father Browne is probably tired of the never-ending bigotry his Church encounters and has responded with an honest reaction to an article that has overtones of a stereotyped reaction to Catholicism. Priests have feelings, too. However, my article should be judged on the data it contains, not on my own particular views, and this data, which is repeated in a chapter of my book *American Labor Unions and Politics, 1900–1918,* received favorable reviews in such Catholic periodicals as *America* and *Social Order,* as well as being declared "admirably fair and objective" in a testimonial from Monsignor George Higgins printed on the jacket of the book.[1] I welcome Father Browne's criticism, however, because like that I received many years ago from Catholic clergy, it helps me examine my own motivation and increase my knowledge of Catholicism and priests, as well as of myself.[2]

It is tragically true that anti-Catholicism has been America's "most persistent non-racial phobia," a phobia not limited to Southern Baptists and Midwestern Republicans but which includes liberals, Unitarians, intellectuals, and socialists also. Paul Blanshard's *American Freedom and Catholic Power* well illustrates that anti-Catholicism can be the intellectual anti-Semitism of the Left. Father Browne is also correct in saying that there has been a "lore of the Left" which has seen "a deviously organized and Church-directed block in the labor movement." This view cuts across the Left from the *Miners' Magazine* of the militant Western Federation of Miners, the *International Socialist Review,* and Daniel De Leon's *The People* to the contemporary labor history volumes of Philip Foner.

It is also true that any implied criticism my article makes of the conservative influence of the Catholic Church as an institutional force in the early twentieth century certainly does not apply to today's Church. As Father Browne well puts it, today there is "a loosened if not chastened Church on whose doctrine some of its members are now building programs of radical social change." This remarkable reversal of a Church undergoing internal democratic transformation and crusading against war, racism, and poverty is one of the most hopeful and heartening political developments in my lifetime. Pope John's superb encyclicals, *Pacem in Terris* and *Mater et Magistra,* are a far cry from the war-on-socialism encyclicals that established political principles for Catholics during the period of my study.

From the hindsight of middle age, I can acquiesce in Father Browne's statement that "the major trouble with the Saposs-Karson thesis is that it takes the word for the deed." This is an unfortunate error that human beings are prone to make, "budding scholars" included. It is apparent to me now that in the late 1940s, when I was researching labor's early-twentieth-century political history, my motivation in pursuing leads on the role of the Catholic Church was not that of a disinterested academician, but rather of a left-wing partisan seeking material to document an a priori emotional conviction. In my political orbit, a class conflict existed and the Catholic Church was an ally of privilege far more concerned with the salvation of souls than with man's material suffering on earth. It was all very simple. Socialism declared it was for equality, human happiness, and the liberation of man; Catholicism was for obedience to authority, the acceptance of inequality, and preparation for the future life. Hence, socialism was right and Catholicism was wrong.

While I may have been guilty of overexaggerating the influence that the institutionalized anti-socialism of the Catholic Church had on Catholic workers, however, I never saw the Church as possessing the power unilaterally to account for the failure of socialism in the labor movement. Father Browne misinterprets the message in my article when he writes that I "blamed it [Catholicism] for stopping the advance of socialism in the American labor movement." I was blaming it for its compulsive anti-socialist role, which I saw as a negative kind of social action. At no point in my article did I assert that Catholicism was "more potent" than other factors in accounting for the weakness of socialism in the American labor movement. The contribution I hoped to make, as I stated in the "Conclusions" to my article, was that "the definite opposition of the Catholic Church should be added to the reasons usually advanced" for the failure of socialism to become the political creed of early-twentieth-century American unionism. My statements on the success of the anti-socialist role of Catholicism were always qualified ones which declared that the weakness of socialism in the union movement was "in part" and "in some measure" due to the Catholic Church and that "Catholicism could take partial credit" for this development.[3] As Father Browne has come around to recognize, I, too, see religion as a secondary, not primary, influence on men's motivation. As communist revolutions and socialist ballot box victories tell, bread-and-butter concerns and emotional needs move men more than encyclicals and priests' efforts.

There are a few areas in which I still would not share Father Browne's outlook. Father Dietz is downgraded as a "one-man paper show." I prefer to take the judgment of Sister Mary Harrita Fox, who did her Ph.D. dissertation and later a book on the life of Dietz. She writes that an evaluation of Dietz's Militia of Christ should go beyond its surface records of a four-year life, a peak membership of seven hundred, and a handful of functioning chapters and not "ignore the intangibles that are hard to evaluate." The Militia provided "Catholic solidarity" for its "individual members scattered throughout the various labor organizations" and gave them the conviction of its "founder, that Socialism, the insidious enemy of trade unionism, must be defeated at all costs."[4]

Most of Father Browne's comments on my paper do not focus exclusively on the period 1900–18. In touching on the influence of Catholicism on Catholic workers in the formative years of the labor movement, he cites the opinion of Philip Taft, who rejects the theory of Catholic influence within the early AF of L. While Taft is seen as the elder statesman among labor historians by the pragmatic school of labor philosophers and leadership, he is held in contempt by the Left as an apologist for the "Establishment" in the trade union world. Taft is so uncritical of the official line of labor that he can perpetuate the myth that the AF of L has acted in "defense of revolutionaries and anarchists."[5]

The difference, I think, between Father Browne and me is one of degree and not of kind with regard to the impact that the Church had on the political behavior of Catholic workers in the early twentieth century. Father Browne maintains that this impact cannot be determined objectively without utilizing the methodology of today's behavioral scientists. Some people, myself included, might not feel it necessary to give such weight to behavioral research. It does not take such empirical techniques, however, to recognize a lesser but vital fact which my article communicated—that no Catholic worker in early-twentieth-century America could be unaware that his Church was an adversary, not an ally, of socialism.

NOTES

1. Marc Karson, *American Labor Unions and Politics, 1900–1918* (Carbondale, Ill.: Southern Illinois University Press, 1958), 358 pp. (paperback: Beacon Press, Boston, 1965).

2. My review of Father Theodore Purcell's book *The Worker Speaks His Mind on Company and Union* in the *New Republic,* April 12, 1954, caused Monsignor George Higgins to voice his objections in his syndicated column, "The Yardstick." Father Purcell reacted with two letters in the *New Republic,* May 4 and August 2, 1954. I replied in the *New Republic,* June 21, 1954.

3. In the last chapter in my book I list the following characteristics of twentieth-century America as an explanation for the weakness of socialism within organized labor: (1) the vitality of American capitalism; (2) the middle-class psychology of American workers; (3) the American faith in individual rights; (4) the conservative features of the American political system; (5) the anti-socialist position of the Catholic Church; and (6) the anti-socialist leadership of Samuel Gompers.

4. Sister Mary Harrita Fox, "Peter E. Dietz: Pioneer in the Catholic Social Action Movement" (Ph.D. Dissertation, University of Notre Dame, 1950), p. 114.

5. There were instances when the AF of L supported efforts to free Leftists such as Tom Mooney and Joe Hill. Pressure from Leftist affiliates, however, was mostly responsible for such action. At other times the AF of L gave no major aid to imprisoned Charles Moyer and Bill Haywood or to imprisoned IWW leaders during and after World War I. Other myths relating to AF of L political ideas and policies that Taft repeats in his writings are that the Federation's political policy was non-partisan, that its support of Asiatic immigration exclusion contained no traces of racism, that it was opposed to discrimination against American blacks, and that it was a foe of American imperialism.

Chapter 4

SOCIALISM AND AMERICAN TRADE UNIONISM*

John H. M. Laslett

What were the reasons for the growth of socialist sentiment among a minority of American trade unionists during the crucial formative years of the American labor movement, between 1886 and 1917? Even more important, why did that sentiment remain a minority influence, instead of becoming a majority one as it did in the labor movements of several European countries during these years? Was it the case, as a number of historians have argued, that the hostility displayed by Samuel Gompers and other conservative leaders of the American Federation of Labor was primarily responsible for preventing the emergence of a widespread, grass roots radical movement which would, had it been allowed to develop, have transformed American labor into a revolutionary force? Or were other factors more important in precluding such a development?

In attempting to answer these questions, attention must also be paid to the tactics of the socialists themselves. It has been argued, by Philip Foner for example, that in the decade of the 1890s, when in relative terms the socialists were probably stronger in the American labor movement than they were at any other time, the dual unionist tactics of Daniel De Leon's Socialist Trades and Labor Alliance, followed in 1905 by the alleged impossibilism of the IWW, had a crucial effect in alienating moderate radicals who favored some form of independent radical coalition, but who stopped short of supporting the Socialist Party of America in part because of the divisive tactics of a minority of socialists. In particular, one might ask whether it would have made any difference during this period—when, for example, Thomas J. Morgan's 1894 Political Program, which included as Plank Ten "the collective

* Revised version of a paper delivered before the Organization of American Historians in Dallas, Texas, on April 19, 1968.

ownership by the people of all the means of production and distribution," came near to being adopted by the AFL–if the socialists, instead of dividing bitterly over tactics, had united in a common effort to secure the allegiance of the labor movement.[1] Or were external factors, deriving not so much from the character of the labor leadership or from the ideological positions adopted by the socialists, but from the more general characteristics of American political and industrial development during this period, primarily responsible both for the rise of socialist influence and for its limited appeal? Evidence drawn from six labor organizations, which included a large proportion of the radicals then active in the labor movement, suggests strongly that the second set of factors was more important than the first.[2]

I

It has long been established that Gompers personally, as well as several other national leaders of the labor movement, moved from a position of tolerance and even of limited support for certain socialist doctrines in the 1870s and 1880s to one of profound mistrust in subsequent years.[3] Inside the American Federation of Labor, this was evident in the failure to elect socialists to the Executive Council after 1889, despite their considerable strength in the organization;[4] in the dubious parliamentary tactics and the bitter speeches which Gompers and other AFL leaders employed against the socialists in the annual conventions of the Federation;[5] in the treatment meted out to Thomas J. Morgan's Political Program of 1894;[6] and in numerous other ways. Among the affiliates, it was apparent from such incidents as the Executive Council's offer of a charter to the racist International Association of Machinists, in preference to its already chartered (and both socialist and non-racist) affiliate, the International Machinists Union, in 1894–95.[7] It was clear from the AFL's post-1900 support for the conservative faction in the formerly socialist Boot and Shoe Workers Union;[8] and from Gompers' welcoming response to the increasing moderation of the Western Federation of Miners and other previously radical organizations in the period after 1912.[9]

Where the socialists were strong, the AFL would sometimes make exceptions to this policy, as in Gompers' unwillingness to expel the socialist Brewery Workers Union from the federation in 1907, despite the fact that it had violated the Executive Council's jurisdictional rulings; in the general support which the AFL gave to the ILGWU and other socialist garment unions in the early 1900s; or in Gompers' indirect endorsement of Socialist Party candidate Meyer London and other socialists in the congressional elections of 1912.[10] But these exceptions were made for tactical reasons, or for the sake of the unity of the labor movement in general. They were not made out of sympathy with socialism on ideological grounds. In general, Gompers' opposition to the socialists within the AFL, reinforced by the self-perpetuating and bureaucratic character of the Executive Council, as well as by Gompers' own personal prestige, almost certainly prevented them from being more successful in this period than they might otherwise have been. For instance, in terms of delegate support the socialists enjoyed their largest influence in the AFL in the 1890s, before the Gompers' regime had been thoroughly established; whereas their peak was not reached in the labor movement generally until the period immediately preceding and following the presidential election of 1912.

It is also true that the dual unionist tactics of the impossibilists to some extent diminished the appeal of moderate socialism within the labor movement, and were used by the conservatives as a means of deterring other trade unionists from supporting the socialist cause. De Leon and the SLP turned against the AFL in the 1890s just at the point when the socialists were gathering strength, and when they might conceivably have been able to turn the labor movement, if only temporarily, into more radical paths.[11] Similarly, the dual unionist tactics of the American Labor Union, the IWW, and the communists after the First World War undoubtedly did some harm to the cause of socialist influence in the labor movement in later years. Among the affiliates, the mid-1890s attacks of the dual unionist, a De Leonite Socialist Trades and Labor Alliance against the locals of such AFL affiliates as the Boot and Shoe Workers Union in Rochester, Buffalo, New York, Chicago, and St. Louis, as well as in Massachusetts, were bitterly resented. Moreover, in this case, they helped to turn the boot and shoe workers away from their former socialist position, and toward conformity with the conservative job-conscience philosophy of the craft unions as a whole.[12] In the Western Federation of Miners, the unremitting hostility of the IWW toward the union after it had broken with the Wobblies in 1906–8 helped to weaken it to such an extent that it had little choice but to fall back upon the AFL.[13] After the Bolshevik revolution of 1917, fear of communism was also used as a weapon against the more moderate socialists in the United Mine Workers, the International Association of Machinists, and elsewhere.

But despite the attention which has been given to it by labor historians, the impact of impossibilism upon the bulk of trade unions in the American labor movement during these years was in fact quite small. In the sample analyzed here it was only in the Boot and Shoe Workers Union and the Western Federation of Miners that it had more than a marginal effect in weakening the position of the socialists as a whole. In the United Mine Workers of America, fear of communism and the efforts of extremists to exploit the discontents of the coal miners were not enough to prevent the reemergence of a strong labor party movement in that industry after the First World War. Over fifty miners' delegates attended the National Labor Party convention held in Chicago in November 1919—more than from any other trade union—and resolutions favoring an independent labor party and mine nationalization were passed by several post-war UMW conventions.[14] Similarly, in the International Association of Machinists and the ILGWU, moderate socialist influences remained powerful despite the criticisms of the impossibilists on the extreme Left and the wholesale denunciation of radicals from the Right during the period of the Red Scare. In the ILGWU, the bitter struggle which took place between the socialists and communists after 1919 did not prevent many garment workers from remaining socialists until the 1930s and beyond. In the immediate post-World War One period, President William Johnston of the IAM became chairman, as well as a leading initial advocate of third-party action, in the Conference for Progressive Political Action in 1922–24.[15]

The periods of influence of dual unionists in the American socialist and labor movements were also quite short. De Leon only maintained effective control of the SLP between 1891 and 1896, after which the moderates revolted against his policy of opposition to the AFL. The American Labor Union and the IWW had little influence over most craft unions, and it was not until the 1920s that the communists took up dual unionism once more. In 1901 the Socialist Party of America, while remaining critical (albeit insufficiently so) of the AFL for its failure to organize unskilled and semi-skilled workers and its hostility toward industrial unionism, adopted a policy of cooperation toward the existing trade union movement which has maintained in effect, save for a minority on the extreme left of the party, throughout the whole of the twentieth century.[16] But this policy in itself appears to have had little to do with the reasons for either the growth or the decline of radical influences throughout the labor movement as a whole. For example the socialists received no spectacular increase in working-class votes because of the change in their trade union position. Nor were they able to prevent a rapid loss of influence in the labor movement in the period after 1912.

Hence the preoccupation of various scholars with changes in the ideological position of the labor and socialist leadership, although valuable up to a point, does not in my judgment provide an adequate causal explanation for the failure of socialism to take root in the American labor movement, unless one assumes the views of these leaders to be wholly representative of the rank and file. But without discounting the influence of Gompers and the AFL Executive Council, or of the National Executive Committee of the SLP or the Socialist Party of America, this is clearly to carry the manipulative abilities of both the socialist and the trade union leadership much too far. In practice, for example, although in its internal structure the AFL developed the characteristics of a bureaucratic and machine-led organization quite early in its career, in its relations to the affiliates in this early period it had little in the way of formal power. On matters of trade autonomy, jurisdictional disputes, and strike action—which at this time were its central concerns—the AFL was primarily a collection of sovereign, independent trade organizations, with Gompers and his colleagues serving mainly as a broker between them.[17] It is extremely unlikely, in other words, that the national leadership alone could have prevented the growth of a mass revolutionary movement, had the prevailing social and economic conditions been favorable for such a development.

II

To turn first to the reasons for the rise of socialist influence in the labor movement, a wide variety of factors determines the reasons for voting socialist, many of which of course are influenced by matters other than union membership and the experiences of work. Insofar as these are important considerations, however, I would argue that two sets of factors, one internal to the labor movement and one external, predominated over the particular tactics employed by the labor leadership in helping such revolutionary influence as did develop in the pre-World War American labor movement to grow. Within the labor movement, radical and in some cases socialist influence may be traced to the impact of an earlier tradition of Knights of Labor idealism, radicalized Populism, and strong dissatisfaction with the narrow craft unionism of the AFL. External or societal factors such as technological developments, a high degree of competition in several industries in the post-Civil War period followed by a period of rapid economic concentration, and the social and economic dislocation occasioned by the destruction of traditional crafts appear also to have played an extremely important role.

Taking the internal factors first, dissatisfaction with the AFL because of its political conservatism, its preference for craft unionism, its narrow view of the functions of trade unionism, and its voluntaristic attitude toward the state cannot be treated, except in an indirect way, as a cause of socialist sentiments as such. But taken together, these dissatisfactions undoubtedly served as a catalyst for more serious ideological conflicts which the socialists exploited to their advantage within the unions. It is no coincidence, for example, that several of the unions considered in our sample were industrial rather than craft organizations in their structure, and that at least two of them, the United Mine Workers of America and the Brewery Workers, were involved in severe jurisdictional conflicts with the dominant craft union majority in the AFL.

Industrial unionism as such is not necessarily a sign of socialist activism or militancy. But in the AFL in the 1890s, as in the English Trades Union Congress at a similar period, disappointment and irritation at the failure of the craft unionists to recognize the broader social philosophy which lay behind the demands of the industrial unionists certainly helped to create sympathy for socialism and the Socialist Party. For example, the withdrawal of the Western Federation of Miners from the AFL in 1897, and its decision to endorse the Socialist Party in 1902, in part resulted from frustration and anger at the refusal of the AFL to adopt a more radical course. Similarly, it was no coincidence that the International Association of Machinists coupled its 1903 questionnaire to union members concerning Gompers' continued leadership of the AFL with a request for the membership's views on political endorsement of the Socialist Party. The continued presence of conservative ex-president James O'Connell on the council of the AFL from 1912 to 1918, even though he was no longer president of the IAM, also created considerable bitterness among the machinists, and served to strengthen the hand of the union's socialist administration in the period after 1912.[18]

As to Knights of Labor idealism, it has, of course, long been established that this organization was considerably more radical than the AFL in its attitude toward industry-wide organization, third-party activity, and cooperation as a labor ideal. Less well remembered, however, is the fact that a significant proportion of the unions in the AFL had earlier been connected with the Knights of Labor, and that they retained considerable sympathy for that organization and what it stood for even after they had transferred their formal allegiance to the AFL.

At least four out of the six unions considered in the sample had strong ties with the Knights of Labor and its radical traditions, which persisted for years after the Knights had passed its peak. The Brewery Workers Union, for example, retained a joint affiliation with both the Knights of Labor and the AFL until 1896. In that year the AFL convention refused to endorse the union's label as long as it remained affiliated to the Knights, a matter which caused widespread bitterness within the union, especially in view of the important role which the label played in strengthening the brewery workmen through the selling of union beer. A similar dual affiliation also characterized the United Mine Workers of America for a time. The Boot and Shoe Workers Union developed originally out of the Knights of St. Crispin, a radical shoe workers' organization consisting largely of native-born workers which had much in common with the Knights of Labor, and which in 1869 helped to elect twenty-one independent labor representatives to the Massachusetts state legislature. In addition, the International Association of Machinists also had intimate connections with the Knights of Labor in the South. For some years it retained the secret ritual and fraternalistic nomenclature of the Knights, and even before it formally espoused socialism the *Machinists Monthly Journal* was imbued with the Knights' traditional commitment to moral improvement, third-party political action, and the hope for a regeneration of society along utopian and cooperative lines.[19]

Care must be exercised in dealing with the third source of radical influence listed under this head: namely, radical Populism. For it is still uncertain, pending the detailed study of voting returns, just how many urban workers voted Populist in the critical elections of the early 1890s.[20] And it is also unclear, save in the case of a few prominent men such as Debs, how many ex-Populists were dissatisfied with the petit bourgeois ideology of the Peoples Party and after the fusion of 1896 moved across into the socialist movement. Nevertheless, evidence from the International Association of Machinists, the United Mine Workers, and the Western Federation of Miners suggests strongly that those unions which had the strongest commitment to the ideals of Populism were also those in which socialist influence turned out to be considerable.

In the case of the UMW, Chester M. Destler demonstrated some years ago that a significant, albeit unsuccessful, labor-Populist-socialist alliance, which included a number of coal miners from the northern and southwestern portions of the state, was attempted in Illinois in the fall elections of 1894. My own research suggests that the Populists in Kansas and in West Virginia, because of their support for government ownership of the mines in those states, were also able to secure a number of coal miners' votes. An ambitious labor-Populist coalition, similar to that in Illinois, was also attempted in Ohio under the leadership of the president of the United Mine Workers, John McBride.[21]

A similar development occurred among the metal miners of the mountain West. In Colorado, Montana, Idaho, and elsewhere, partly because of the silver issue, Populism was a working-class rather than an agrarian movement, and after its collapse the metal miners in several of these states helped to develop the revolutionary, semi-syndicalist form of socialism which was later taken up by the WFM. Many of the radicals in the International Association of Machinists also moved into socialism via Populism, partly because the People's Party was strong in a number of the southern railroad towns in which the machinists were employed, and partly because of the antipathy and fear which many machinists, like many coal miners, felt toward the railroad corporations because of their dependence upon them for employment. For example,

Douglas Wilson, editor of the *Machinists Monthly Journal* from 1895 until 1915, ran unsuccessfully as a Populist for the Alabama legislature in 1894. Soon thereafter he became a socialist, developing a close personal friendship with Debs. Peter J. Conlon, a socialist member of the IAM's executive board, began his career as a Populist in Sioux City, Iowa. And the Machinists' conventions, which in the 1890s adopted numerous Populist resolutions in favor of the initiative and referendum and the democratization of the political process, as well as on other matters, in the early 1900s began to pass socialist ones which included much of the same kind of Populist rhetoric which had gone before.[22]

As to the external or second and more important set of factors which I have listed as causes of socialist influence in the labor movement, in the decades after the Civil War technological changes, changes in the nature of the market—both in the labor market and in the market for goods and services—and changes also in the relationship between employers and employees were proceeding rapidly throughout American industry as a whole. Nevertheless, they had a particularly severe impact upon several of the trades considered in our sample.

The shoe industry was one of the first American industries to suffer the effects of industrialization. Before 1850, the expansion of the market and the displacement of custom shops (in which a father and son worked together, with perhaps one apprentice or journeyman) by larger, competing retail or wholesale-order shops, had already begun to alter the traditional pattern of economic relationships in the industry, and had undermined, to some extent, the independence of the individual artisan. The possibility of a single journeyman attaining ownership and control of one of these larger shops still existed, and the handcraft of the shoemaker had not yet been undermined. But the pegging machine, introduced in 1857, the McKay sole-sewing machine, first used in 1862, and the Goodyear welt machine, introduced in 1875, quite rapidly destroyed the traditional craft skill of the journeyman shoemaker, and turned him into little more than a factory hand. By 1880 the factory system had already assumed much of its modern form in the shoe industry, and the journeyman or small master who had traditionally operated his own independent shop was increasingly forced to abandon his business and find employment in one of the new factories in Lynn, Haverhill, Brockton, or one of the other small shoe towns which grew up around the city of Boston.

In addition, the expanding post-Civil War shoe industry was going through an intensely competitive stage, so that in several cadres of employment the shoe worker's factory wages were for some years appreciably lower than the earnings of the labor force in the industry had previously been. In 1881, for example, in ten out of the fourteen major occupations associated with the industry in Massachusetts, average weekly wages had fallen to a level appreciably below what they had been in 1872, some by as much as 25 per cent. Those employed on the new machines suffered most: average weekly wages among the McKay sole operators, for example, which had been $22.22 in 1872, fell to $15.29 in 1897 (they had been even lower in the 1893–96 depression). It was not until 1903 that they returned to a level significantly higher than they had been thirty years before.[23]

There is quite a lot of evidence to suggest that it was these changes, with the loss of skill, of status, and of earning power which they (temporarily) entailed, which were primarily reponsible for the growth of socialist sentiment among the shoe workers. Frank Sieverman, a young shoe worker who became prominent in both the SLP and the Socialist Party, ascribed his socialist beliefs to the "disappointed aspirations and shattered ideals" which, he said, he experienced upon entering a shoe factory at the age of seventeen. President John F. Tobin of the Boot and Shoe Workers Union had undergone a similar experience as a young man. Thomas Philips, a leading advocate of producers' cooperation as the only effective means of restoring independent self-employment to the trade, declared in 1889 that he was continually "putting in more work than ever for less wage." And J. W. Sherman, the unsuccessful socialist candidate for mayor of Boston in 1899, attributed a significant proportion of the increased socialist vote in Massachusetts—which was the center of the shoemaking trade—to the discontented shoe worker, who today, "in a great shoe factory, . . . produces fully 20 times what he could do 40 years ago. Nobody thinks for an instant that he is getting 20 times as much in comfort from his labor as he did then. Looked at fairly it is at once seen that his present condition . . . grows from the fact that he is producing for somebody else, who takes for the service of furnishing him a machine to work with and a 'job', the slight toil of four-fifths of the product."

But it was Horace M. Eaton, the socialist general secretary of the Boot and Shoe Workers Union, who summed up perhaps best these economic discontents of the shoe workers in his report on behalf of the union membership to the BSWU convention of 1897. "So long as we allow the employer to traffic in human flesh," he said, "and to reduce wages simply on the ground that he must meet competition, so long as we submit to these brutal conditions without declaring and working for the abolition of such a brutal system of industry, so long have we, in greater or less degree, to endure the evils of which we now complain."[24]

A similar development took place in the machinists' trade. Until about 1870, the machinist resembled a carpenter who worked in metal instead of in wood. He worked at a bench, usually in quite a small shop, and used numerous small hand tools and lathes, which required great skill to operate. In the early years the capital outlay involved in such an enterprise was not so great as to prevent the individual journeyman from establishing a workshop of his own. For example, Grand Master Machinist Thomas W. Talbot, the first president of the International Association of Machinists, was one of many machinists who owned his own small machine shop in the period just after the Civil War. By the middle of the 1880s, however, this type of self-employment was increasingly difficult to achieve. John Morrison, for example, a New York machinist who gave evidence on behalf of his trade before a Senate committee in 1883, had this to say: "I understand that at this present day you could not start in the machinists' business to compete successfully with any of these large firms with a capital of less than $20,000 or $30,000. That is my own judgment. There have been cases known where men started ten or fifteen years ago on what they had earned themselves, and they had grown up gradually into a good business. . . . But since that time it appears that the larger ones are squeezing out the smaller, and forcing more of them into the ranks of labor, thus causing more competition among the workers."

In addition, the machinist's craft was revolutionized by the introduction of large and costly steam- or, later, electrically driven machinery, most of it automatic, which was set up in large machine shops very different from the workshops in which he had been traditionally employed. As in the shoe industry, these developments undoubtedly stimulated the development of radical discontent. In May 1898, for example, a correspondent in the *Machinists Monthly Journal* reported this about the condition of his fellow shopmates in Chicago: "The old feeling of mutual dependence between employers and men has disappeared under its blighting influences which have driven thousands of men into the streets of the cities and highways of the land as tramps and paupers without occupation for the present or hope and ambition for the future." The time had come, he said, for members of the union to face up to this problem if they hoped to live better than Chinese coolies.

Another rank-and-file member asserted in December 1898 that technological changes in the craft had destroyed the independence of the machinist and severely limited his opportunities for upward mobility. "The division and subdivision of work done by both man and machine," he wrote, "eliminates the skilled machinist, . . . and drives all skilled mechanics downwards to the level of all labor." The apprenticeship system, he went on, was out of date, and the machinist's job would soon be within the competence of any unskilled worker who chose to undertake it. Numerous other instances of this phenomenon could be cited also. The lesson was plain: the machinist could never hope to improve his condition so long as the machine, the great leveler, remained in private hands.[25]

In the coal mining industry the problem was not so much the development of the factory system or the destruction of a traditional craft, as it was depressed wage levels and chronic instability in employment resulting from the sudden incursion of cheap immigrant labor from eastern Europe and from a period of fierce competition followed by rapid trustification in the period following the Civil War. Before the Civil War, and for a brief period after it, coal mining was confined to a number of separate coal fields, such as those in Pennsylvania, Ohio, and Illinois, each of which served largely separate markets and each of which had a wage and price structure of its own. But the development of a sophisticated railroad system rapidly created a national market where earlier there had been a series of local ones, bringing fierce competition between individual coal operators, overinvestment, and strong pressure to reduce wages in the trade.

This was a tendency, it should again be noted, which was not simply dependent upon the severe depressions of the mid-1870s and mid-1890s, although it was accentuated by them. Coupled with this, there were the special hazards of the miner's task, almost total dependence on the company store, as well as, the brutal repression of both coal and metal miners' strikes by the militia and other agents of the civil state. The cumulative effect of these developments, as cheap immigrant labor flooded into the eastern mines, was to force the English-speaking miners in various parts of Pennsylvania, who had been accustomed to a relatively stable level of employment, westward into Indiana and Illinois. Partially as a result of this, there occurred the rapid growth of socialist sentiment among the coal miners of District 12 of the United Mine Workers in the southwestern counties of Illinois which has already been remarked upon.[26] Similar economic developments took place in the Rocky Mountain states, where the western metal mining industry was located.[27]

Even in the ILGWU and the Brewery Workers Union, which were dominated by foreign-born radicals, there is evidence to suggest that European socialist ideology was far from being the only source of revolutionary zeal. Among the brewery workers long hours, frequent beatings, the abuses of the boarding system (under which the workers were required to live with their masters), and the heavy drinking of beer—which was often given to the workers as a substitute for wages or as an inducement to work longer hours—were in themselves an independent source of radicalism. One group of immigrant brewery workers, for example, reminiscing in 1901, complained that "in the social life, the American brewery was just as much, if not more, depressed and disregarded as in South Germany." In the ILGWU, sweatshop conditions in themselves, in addition to the socialist influences brought over by Russian-born revolutionary intellectuals, have long been recognized as a contributing factor in the garment workers' socialism. However, it must also be remembered that in the crucial formative period of the New York Jewish labor movement, which lasted from approximately 1880 to 1910, there was a considerable initial gap between the philosophy and outlook of the atheistic, Russian-speaking socialists, who later rose to positions of leadership in the garment trades, and the orthodox, Yiddish-speaking, and often socially conservative small-town Jewish tailors and cloakmakers who made up part of the rank and file. It may be, therefore, that even more weight should be given to sweatshop conditions as a formative influence in the development of radicalism in the garment industry than has hitherto been allowed.[28]

English-speaking workers and northern Europeans generally, save to some extent the Irish, provided the main source of leadership and skill throughout American industry at this time. As such they usually rose fairly rapidly in the social and economic scale. It may be suggested from the preceding analysis, however, that in the four industries discussed in which these workers were extensively employed—coal mining, shoemaking, metal mining, and the machinist's trade—their progress was at least temporarily impeded by the processes of rapid industrial change. In each of them, the relative position of the English-speaking workers appears to have been undermined by technological changes, by rapid expansion and economic instability, by relatively static or falling wage levels, and by the threat posed (in imagination if not always in practice) by the incursion of cheap immigrant labor from eastern and southern Europe, and in some cases from the Orient. In these industries, it was ex-artisans and skilled or semi-skilled workers, not the recent immigrants or the poor, who tended to become radicals. In part this helps to confirm the hypothesis, which has been accepted by a number of labor historians, that it is from those with rising expectations, not the *Lumpenproletariat,* that we should expect radical tendencies. Even more interesting, however, is the future hypothesis that in an achievement-oriented society such as the United States the motivation for political radicalism may also have resulted partially from the frustrated aspirations of those bodies of workers whose expectations are traditionally supposed to have been high.[29]

III

Turning, lastly, to the decline of socialist influences in the pre-1930s American labor movement (which is of course to be kept separate from the period of the New Deal and the CIO, when radical influences revived under the quite different auspices of the Communist Party), the evidence from the six trade unions analyzed indicates less disagreement with previously held views. To the extent to which immigrant influences from continental Europe were responsible for the rise of socialism—and, of course, the main thrust of my argument has been to suggest that these influences were less influential than has hitherto been supposed—it is clearly important to reemphasize the consequences of the assimilation and Americanization of these groups, and their acceptance of the American political system and of American political values. The speed with which this assimilation took place depended in part upon the nature of the immigrant group involved, in part upon the strength of the immigrant culture, and in part upon the degree of ethnic concentration in particular cities. In Milwaukee, for example, where the Brewery Workers were powerful and the German socialist community quite large, the process of assimilation took longer than it did in smaller German communities. Equally, the size of the Jewish socialist community in New York City, and its initial concentration in the urban ghetto, undoubtedly helped to prolong its commitment to socialist ideals.

Nevertheless, over the long run this process of ethnic assimilation was one of the elements which were responsible for the decline of socialist loyalties. This is perhaps clearest in the case of the Brewery Workers Union, whose socialism may in large part be ascribed to the influence of socialists who came to this country after the abortive German revolution of 1848, and in greater numbers after Bismarck's anti-socialist legislation of 1878. The radicalism of the union noticeably declined as these older groups either died off, moved upward into the entrepreneurial or professional middle class, or were replaced by ethnic groups whose commitment to socialism was less intense.[30] A similar process occurred in the garment industry and in the ILGWU, although the tenacity with which the Jewish labor movement retained its socialist idealism even after several immigrant generations had been assimilated indicates that a high level of economic and status mobility is not in itself enough to put an end to political radicalism, once it has acquired the force of a tradition.[31]

But assimilation and Americanization also had an important meaning for those workingmen who were not immigrants. Pressure toward conformity was generated not so much by overt coercion from the AFL as by its acceptance in the eyes of public opinion generally as the proper model for an American labor movement. This made it harder for radical opponents of AFL political and economic policies to persist with their endeavors. In a society in which a high value was placed upon conformity, especially at a time when the labor movement was weak and under considerable pressure from outside, this was a matter of great importance. The response of the Irish in the Boot and Shoe Workers Union to organizing success or the results of the re-entry of the Western Federation of Miners into the AFL in 1911 illustrate this point very well.

More specifically, adaptation to prevailing American values had both an industrial and a political aspect. From the industrial point of view, there was an increasingly evident conflict between the logic of collective bargaining (which even the most radical trade unionists came in the end to accept) and the demands of the socialists for separate, revolutionary action on the part of a united working class. The most dramatic example of this was in the Boot and Shoe Workers Union, where acceptance by Massachusetts employers of the Union Stamp Contract (based upon the union label) in the period after 1898 helped to bring about a dramatic improvement in the union's membership which was reflected to some extent, also, in wage levels. As a result in 1904 President John F. Tobin, who in 1896 had been an orthodox De Leonite, went so far as to urge his fellow union members to take the profit margins of the shoe manufacturers into account before pressing for wage increases. "The employer gains an opportunity to adjust to a gradual change in wages," he argued, to the astonishment and anger of the remaining socialists in the union, "while propositions for a general advance . . . [have] resulted in failure."[32]

This change of heart might perhaps be attributed to the class-collaborationist tendencies of one particular union leader. But there are plenty of other examples of the same consequences occurring after similar developments in other formerly radical trade unions. For example, the adoption of time contracts by the Western Federation of Miners (which had earlier been bitterly resisted by most members of the union), the negotiation of the Protocol of Peace in 1910 in the ladies' garment industry by the ILGWU, and the increasing cooperation between management and labor in the brewing industry, over Prohibition, and over pension schemes for union members—all had similar effects. In the United Mine Workers the situation was more ambiguous, since acceptance of the principle of joint interstate agreements with the coal operators took place in 1898, *before* the most radical phase in the history of the union. But there too the checkoff system of paying dues, the need to abide by nationally negotiated contracts, and growing cooperation between the union and the coal operators in imposing order upon an anarchic coal market rapidly limited the union's potential for revolutionary change.[33]

In societies with more traditional class barriers, such as Great Britain or Germany, there was no necessary conflict between collective bargaining and the revolutionary assumptions of socialism, at least in the short run. But in the United States, where class lines were traditionally fluid and the pressure toward assimilation was strong, the adoption of collective bargaining techniques had profound and far-reaching implications for the relations between labor and management, especially where such cooperation (as in the garment and shoemaking industries) made a great difference to the worker's security of employment. As Paul Jacobs has pointed out, in a society dominated by the Lockeian tradition, the process of bargaining *within* the system inexorably endowed the contractual relationship with primary importance.[34]

In addition, the notion of time contracts implies a recognition by the union of its responsibilities for enforcement of a collective bargaining agreement, which sometimes placed radical union leadership in the seemingly anomalous position of having to act against the interests of its own membership when contracts were violated by members of the rank and file. Thus the price which the union had to pay for the benefits it received was to become part of the productive system itself, able to modify but not to change in any basic way the nature of that system. The most dramatic effects of this development, again, may be seen in the case of the Boot and Shoe Workers Union, where the Tobin administration felt itself obliged to break unofficial strikes by its own union members which were held in violation of the Union Stamp Contract.[35] But similar consequences occurred before 1914 in the coal industry, the garment industry, and in the western metal mines.

From the point of view of third-party politics, most historians of the Socialist Party are in agreement that it reached its peak either at or not long after the election of 1912, and that a series of subsequent events, most notably the Wilsonian reforms of 1913–16, the refusal of the Socialist Party to support American entry into the First World War, the socialist-communist split of 1919, the collapse of Wilsonian idealism, and the return to prosperity of the 1920s, were important factors in that decline. But there is considerable disagreement as to just which of these factors was the most important, and as to just when, in time, the main movement toward decline began. James Weinstein, in his book *The Decline of Socialism in America, 1912–1925,* takes the view that there was "no serious decline after 1912; the Party grew in strength and popularity during the war." "Socialist trade unionists," he argues, "played an increasingly prominent role in the Party during these years, and the Party seems to have developed greater solidarity with the labor movement. If one is to find a substantial decline of socialism in the trade unions, it must be after the United States entered the war, in April 1917."[36]

Weinstein bases this view upon limited and rather fragmented evidence. When one examines carefully the change of heart which took place between 1912 and 1916 in virtually all of the socialist trade unions examined in the sample under review, Weinstein's position is not borne out. Once President Wilson had been elected, and had begun to enact the series of social reforms for which his first administration became famous (the Clayton Act, the La Follette Seamen's Act, the establishment of a Department of Labor, and so on), virtually all of the unions considered in this sample began immediately to turn away from their earlier political support of the Socialist Party, and to align themselves with the Democrats. It is true that in some of the state federations of labor, notably those in Illinois and Pennsylvania under the direction of John H. Walker and James M. Maurer respectively, the socialists maintained, and in some cases increased, their influence for a time after America entered the First World War. But in this period the state federations of labor had very little influence within the trade union movement generally, either in terms of voting power at AFL conventions, or in terms of over-all labor policy. And in the case of the Illinois State Federation of Labor, at least, Walker from the first used his influence on behalf of the traditional "reward your friends, punish your enemies" philosophy of the AFL, not on behalf of socialist or labor party candidates.[37] For the socialist element in the trade union movement, in other words, American entry into the First World War simply served to confirm a trend toward the two major parties—and in particular, toward the Democratic Party—which had begun several years before.

Three examples of this development may be cited, although there were others also. The International Association of Machinists, which benefited particularly from President Woodrow Wilson's reforming legislation (notably from the Adamson Act of 1916, establishing an eight-hour day on the railroads), moved from open support for Debs in 1912 to almost equally open support for Woodrow Wilson in the election of 1916. "The time may come in this country when organized labor will have a party of its own," the *Machinists Monthly Journal* wrote in October 1916, "but until then labor will lend its sympathy to those in sympathy with its aims and objects." The Illinois miners, who had been strong supporters of the socialists up until 1912, began to move across into the Democratic camp very soon after that time; and the *United Mine Workers Journal* expressed open pleasure at President Wilson's narrow victory over the Republican candidate, Charles Evans Hughes.

A similar shift in allegiance can be seen even in the case of the Brewery Workers Union, which had hitherto been the most obviously Marxist of the radical trade unions. At the 1914 convention of this union, the national secretary asserted that there was no reason for the organization to change its support of the Socialist Party simply because of the progressive legislation which had been enacted in the past two years. But in 1916, when faced with the actual record of the first Wilson administration, an editorial in the *Brauer-Zeitung* admitted that the Democrats had done much for the organized labor movement; and it indirectly recommended the union membership to vote for Wilson.[38]

On this general point it seems clear as far as the socialists in the trade union movement were concerned that it was indeed the reforms enacted by the Democratic Party under Woodrow Wilson that were the decisive factors in undermining trade union support for the Socialist Party. Of course, the party included intellectuals, Negroes, middle-class reformers, and other elements in addition to trade unionists, and it does not follow, simply because of this, that the party went into an immediate decline. Nor is it suggested that the loss of support from the unions which the Socialist Party suffered brought to an end all radical political sentiment in the labor movement for the remainder of the period under review. Several of the unions described above played an important role in the Conference for Progressive Political Action, which nominated Senator Robert M. La Follette for the presidency on an independent party ticket in 1924, as well as in the labor party movement which emerged briefly in several states in the period immediately following the First World War. But as far as the Socialist

Party itself was concerned, with the single (and important) exception of the ILGWU, all of the unions in our sample had withdrawn at least their official support from the party by 1916. Although many other factors were involved in this changeabout—among them the fact that Allan Benson, the party's presidential candidate in that year, was virtually unknown compared to Debs, and he made a tactical error by concentrating on opposition to war preparedness in his campaign—this probably helped to account for the more than one-third drop which took place in the party's vote compared to 1912.

This disaffection of radical unionists was important, for if one accepts that strong trade union support is essential for a viable and successful independent political party of labor, then the loss of trade union support in the years after 1912 was in many ways an irremediable blow. On this point, I find myself in disagreement with Weinstein and in general agreement with earlier historians, such as Ira Kipnis, David Shannon, and, on this matter, also Daniel Bell.

Lastly, the effect of increasing economic affluence in undermining support for revolutionary behavior must be reemphasized. This has been remarked upon in general terms by a number of social scientists and historians,[39] but not in relation to specific industries and trade unions. The years between 1873–76 and 1893–97 were, with some exceptions, a period of depression in American industry, resulting in severe difficulties for the trade union movement. This helped to lay the foundations for a corresponding increase in third-party political activity.[40] As already indicated, in this period also money wages in several of the industries examined in this sample, notably in the garment industry, in the coal mining industry, and in shoemaking, were either static, or actively in decline. This was not necessarily the case with real wages, representing the purchasing power of the dollar, which in some cases rose rather than declined. But it is problematical whether a cut in money wages, which was overt and immediate in its impact, did not have a more important effect in inducing radical sentiments than a long-term, and often concealed, rise in purchasing power did in diminishing them.

At all events it seems clear that the return to prosperity in the years after 1900, coupled with the increasing economic success of trade unions, had an important long-term effect in undermining the militancy and radicalism of those who had formerly held socialist opinions. It is important to point out that the issue here was not only (perhaps not even primarily) one of rising wages.[41] It was also the fairly rapid, and in some cases quite sudden, increase in union membership which (although not nearly so large as that which occurred in the 1930s) brought collective bargaining and the other benefits of union membership to a significant proportion of the labor force in these industries for the first time. This appears to have had a particularly important impact in the case of the Boot and Shoe Workers Union, where the period of socialist influence coincided with a time of struggle and failure for the organization in the 1880s and 1890s, and the period of conservatism followed in subsequent prosperous years.[42]

Moreover, once trade unions had become successfully established as bargaining agents in these industries in the period after 1899, they were able to provide for their members not only a relatively high degree of economic security, but also—at least through the 1920s—the prospect of a continuing rise in their standard of living. The economic activities of the American trade union movement, the editor of the *Shoe Workers Journal* wrote in January 1919, citing numerous examples in support of his case, had helped to give American workers the highest standard of living in the world. "In our country not a few shoemakers working at the bench own automobiles, and this condition exists in other trades. Where else on earth can this be said of shopmen? It is not [a] labor party that we want, but more labor unionism."[43] In the 1930s, American industry went through a new crisis which was more severe than anything which had affected it in the 1870s or the 1890s, and which brought a new wave of labor radicalism, this time largely under the aegis of the Communist Party. But without passing judgment in detail upon the reasons for the failure of independent labor politics in that period, it is likely that the bonds between labor and the Democratic Party, which were finally cemented in 1936, were now so strong as to make it virtually impossible for a separate socialist party (whatever its label) to recover even the limited degree of strength which it had enjoyed before 1914.

In those unions in which the impetus for third-party activism was partially motivated by non-economic factors, socialist sentiment outlasted the improvements in labor's standards of living by a considerable number of years. The ILGWU obviously provides the best example of this kind of phenomenon. But even here, by the end of the period the effect of increasing complacency had begun to show its effect. "It should never be forgotten," Morris Hillquit reminded the delegates to the 1924 union convention, "that the labor movement and your movement are not based solely on material struggles and material conditions. Of course, we want better material conditions; but this is not the end. The labor movement is ever struggling for better and higher conditions of life, . . . for universal prosperity, and universal brotherhood, and for peace."[44] The ILGWU remained faithful to this vision of society longer than any of the other old socialist trade unions.

IV

This essay has attempted to argue that although many of the traditional arguments put forward to explain the weakness of socialism in the American labor movement may be valid, indigenous factors deriving from the effects of industrialization upon American society were more important than have hitherto been supposed. It has also suggested that both the rise and fall of socialist influence in the trade union movement were intimately affected by a wide variety of other factors, some of them internal to the labor movement at the time but some of them not, such as Populism, an earlier tradition of Knights of Labor idealism, the frustrated aspirations of northern European artisans, and the ideological flexibility of the American two-party system.

This suggests, further, that explanations based upon the particular policies pursued by the national leaders of the labor movement, whether in the trade unions or in the Socialist Party, are no longer adequate (if they ever were) to provide a general explanation for the relative weakness of socialism in the labor movement, even though they have often been used to do so. Throughout his work Philip Taft, for example, continuing to rely upon the conservative interpretation of the American labor movement initially put forward by Selig Perlman in his *Theory of the Labor Movement* in 1928 (which was in turn based upon the examination of a limited number of official trade union documents),[45] assumes the essential correctness of the AFL's position on industrial unionism, third-party politics, and other issues, without examining the relevance of job-conscious unionism to the affiliated membership in the already existing trade unions, still less to the great mass of unorganized unskilled and semi-skilled workers who remained outside.

At the other end of the ideological spectrum Philip Foner, from the Left, argues that the failure of socialism in the American labor movement was largely due, on the trade union side, to the bourgeois and "class collaborationist" character of the labor leadership. On the side of the socialists he argues that it was due, in the case of the SLP, to the "incorrect policies" of dual unionism; and in the case of the Socialist Party of America to the domination of "Center-Right" elements which Foner erroneously suggests "abandoned altogether the battle against the Federation's narrow, craft, pure and simple trade unionism."[46]

Without denying the importance of these factors, I would challenge the adequacy of both Marxist and (in the case of Taft) anti-Marxist interpretations of the American labor movement when they are based upon evidence drawn from the behavior of the national leadership of the labor movement alone, and suggest the importance of more general economic, political, and structural factors as well. I acknowledge that any analysis based primarily upon the internal activities of the radical trade unions, as this has largely been, cannot in itself fully answer the more general social and economic questions which have been raised, even though in my view they provide a broader basis for judgment than the limited type of evidence made use of by the Perlman school. But I hope that enough has been said to demonstrate the need for a much more sophisticated and comprehensive type of explanation, if we are to answer the questions raised by this essay satisfactorily, or in full.

NOTES

1. Philip S. Foner, *History of the Labor Movement in the United States* (New York: International Publishers, 1947–65), II, ch. 19, IV, ch. 3. See also Anthony Bimba, *The History of the American Working Class* (New York: International Publishers, 1927), pp. 199–208; David Herreshoff, *American Disciples of Marx: From the Age of Jackson to the Progressive Era* (Detroit: Wayne State University Press, 1967), p. 180.

2. These are the Brewery Workers Union, a Marxist industrial union consisting largely of German immigrants in the East and the Midwest; the Boot and Shoe Workers Union, a New England craft organization composed of Yankee and Irish artisans; the ILGWU, the most famous of the New York Jewish garment workers' unions; the International Association of Machinists, originating among native-born railroad machinists in the South; and the Western Federation of Miners and the United Mine Workers of America, which between them incorporated most of the militant, direct-action industrial workers then organized into trade unions. For a more detailed analysis of the rise and decline of socialist influence in these unions, see my book *Labor and the Left: A Study of Socialist and Radical Influences in the American Labor Movement, 1881–1924* (New York: Basic Books, 1970).

3. For Gompers, among other works see Bernard Mandel, *Samuel Gompers: A Biography* (Yellow Springs, Ohio: Antioch Press, 1963); Louis S. Reed, *The Labor Philosophy of Samuel Gompers* (New York: Columbia University Press, 1930); and *Samuel Gompers, Seventy Years of Life and Labor* (New York: E. P. Dutton & Co., 1925), I, pp. 69–105, 188–204, 381–427. It tends to be assumed that Gompers himself was largely responsible for the anti-socialist bias of the AFL. In fact, his views were shared by most other members of the Executive Council, including First Vice-President James Duncan, Second Vice-President John Mitchell, Treasurer John Lennon, and Secretary Frank Morrison. See *Proceedings, Twenty-Fourth Annual Convention of the A.F. of L.* (San Francisco, 1904), pp. 193–202; *Proceedings, Thirty-First Annual Convention of the A.F. of L.* (Atlanta, 1911), pp. 177–230, 255–57. See also Philip Taft, "Differences in the Executive Council of the American Federation of Labor," *Labor History,* V (Winter 1964), pp. 40–56; and H. M. Gitelman, "Adolph Strasser and the Origins of Pure and Simple Unionism," *Labor History,* VI (Winter 1965), pp. 71–83.

4. The 1885 convention elected two acknowledged socialists, Henry Emrich of the Furniture Workers and Hugo Miller of the German-American Typographia, to the Executive Council. But no socialist sat on the council after Emrich relinquished the treasurership in 1890, despite the fact that the socialists continued to poll more than one

third of the vote in convention debates for a number of years. See *Proceedings, Fifth Annual Convention of the Federation of Organized Trades and Labor Unions* (Washington, 1885), p. 19; Taft, op. cit.

5. In 1895 the AFL inserted into its constitution a provision that party politics of whatever kind "should have no place in the conventions of the A.F. of L." At later conventions Gompers frequently invoked this as a means of declaring even non-political socialist resolutions out of order. See, for example, *Proceedings, Twenty-Fifth Annual Convention of the A.F. of L.* (Pittsburgh, 1905), p. 230; *Proceedings, Twenty-Seventh Annual Convention of the A.F. of L.* (Norfolk, 1907), p. 219.

6. Probably a majority of unions endorsed this program calling for the establishment of an independent labor party either by referendum or by convention vote in the period between January and December 1894, and had all the delegates from those unions which had previously supported it voted in favor at the December 1894 AFL convention, it might well have passed. But Gompers openly campaigned against the program in the *American Federationist* and in his report to the convention; P. J. McGuire led a behind-the-scenes attempt to persuade the delegates to vote against it; and Adolph Strasser reduced Plank Ten to ridicule by suggesting that collective ownership be achieved by "confiscation without compensation." See Foner, op. cit., II, pp. 289–92; *American Federationist,* I (October 1894), p. 172; *Proceedings, Fourteenth Annual Convention of the A.F. of L.* (Denver, 1894), pp. 14, 36–40; Gerald N. Grob, *Workers and Utopia: A Study of Ideological Conflict in the American Labor Movement, 1865–1900* (Evanston: Northwestern University Press, 1961), pp. 176–79.

7. In 1891 the AFL issued a charter to the socialist International Machinists Union, refusing one to the then largely conservative International Association of Machinists because, as a southern organization, it refused to admit Negroes. However, in the summer of 1895 the Executive Council reversed its position, admitting the IAM into the AFL even though its local unions still refused to admit Negroes; and in December 1895 it withdrew its charter from the IMU. This incident is rightly taken by labor historians to be the first important case in which the AFL chartered a national union which pursued an openly racist policy. But it also indicates the growing anti-socialist bias of the organization, since the Executive Council chartered the IAM irrespective of the fact that the IMU was already an affiliate, and that its policy was to charter only one union in a given trade. Although negotiations for a merger between the two organizations were begun before the chartering of the IAM took place, they were never completed, as stated in the accounts given by Foner, and by Spero and Harris. The locals of the IMU either joined the IAM one by one or lost their separate identity. See Foner, op. cit., II, p. 348; Mark Perlman, *The Machinists: A New Study in American Trade Unionism* (Cambridge: Harvard University Press, 1961), pp. 7, 16–17; Sterling D. Spero and Abram L. Harris, *The Black Worker: The Negro and*

the Labor Movement (New York: Columbia University Press, 1931), p. 88; *Monthly Journal of the International Association of Machinists,* V (January 1894), pp. 525–27, VII (July 1895), p. 236, VII (January 1896), p. 528; John McBride to T. J. Morgan, May 16, 1895 (Letterbooks of Samuel Gompers, Library of Congress).

8. In 1907 the radical elements in the Boot and Shoe Workers Union broke away from the parent body to form their own organization, claiming that the contracts negotiated by the Boot and Shoe Workers Union gave too much away to the manufacturers. However, the AFL gave its full support to the Boot and Shoe Workers leadership, and commended the union administration for taking a strong line against the radicals. Augusta E. Galster, *The Labor Movement in the Shoe Industry, with Special Reference to Philadelphia* (New York: The Ronald Press Co., 1924), pp. 138–39; Brockton *Times,* IV (October 5, 1907), p. 1, VI (March 21, 1909), p. 1, VII (March 4, 1910), p. 2; Brockton *Searchlight,* VI (August 5, 1910), p. 1; Michael J. Tracey to Frank Morrison, October 11, 1909, Morrison to Tracey, October 14, 1909 (Gompers Correspondence with Affiliates, A.F.L.–C.I.O. Collection).

9. In July 1916 President Charles Moyer of the WFM, reflecting on the difficulties which his union had encountered because of employer hostility and the radical image which the organization had projected among the public at large, urged it to abandon its socialist policies and become "a business institution, directing its efforts to the object for which it was organized, namely to unite the various persons working in the mines . . . into a central body, to increase their wages and improve their conditions of employment." Gompers considered this statement so striking a reversal of the WFM's former radical policies that he sent a copy of it to President John P. White (a conservative) of the United Mine Workers of America. *Proceedings, Twenty-Second Consecutive and Second Biennial Convention of the W.F.M.* (Great Falls, 1916), pp. 40–41; Samuel Gompers to John P. White, March 7, 1917 (Gompers Correspondence with Affiliates, A.F.L.–C.I.O. Collection).

10. The Brewery Workers were in fact expelled from the AFL for a brief period between May 1907 and early 1908 for refusing to relinquish their firemen and brewery engineer members to the appropriate craft unions, but this was despite Gompers' personal opposition. Benjamin C. Roberts, "Jurisdiction Disputes Between the Brewery Workers and other A.F. of L. Affiliates" (Unpublished M.A. Thesis, University of Chicago, 1936); *Brauer-Zeitung,* XXII (November 1907), p. 1. For the support given to the ILGWU, and the endorsement of Meyer London, see Louis Levine, *The Women Garment Workers: A History of the International Ladies' Garment Workers Union* (New York: B. W. Huebsch, Inc., 1924), pp. 115–17, 136–39, 272, 292; M. Shamroth to Gompers, October 10, 1912, Gompers to M. Shamroth, October 25, 1912 (A.F.L. Collection, Wisconsin State Historical Society).

11. On August 13, 1893, De Leon's *The People* urged all socialists to leave the AFL, causing concern among moderate socialists, and leading Gompers to write H. D. Lloyd: "Until the advent of Prof. De Leon in the Socialist movement we managed matters so that we could at least work together. . . . He has simply widened the chasm between the different wings of the labor movement." On the other hand it must be remembered that the high vote which the Morgan Program received and the defeat of Gompers for the AFL presidency in 1894–95 were probably due as much to the prevailing depression, to the loss of the Pullman strike, to the inability of the larger unions to send a full complement of delegates to the 1894 convention, and to general dissatisfaction with Gompers' leadership, as they were to an increase in socialist sentiments as such. Grob, op. cit., pp. 176–82; Foner, op. cit., II, pp. 286–94; Gompers, op. cit., I, pp. 356–60, 391–94; clipping from Boston *Labor Leader,* December 22, 1894 (A.F.L. Collection, Wisconsin State Historical Society); Gompers to H. D. Lloyd, July 2, 1894 (Letterbooks of Samuel Gompers, Library of Congress).

12. "For years," President John F. Tobin of the Boot and Shoe Workers Union wrote in May 1898, he had considered De Leon "an able exponent of the doctrine of Socialism." But the deliberate efforts which the ST&LA had made to undermine the locals of his own union had destroyed that faith. De Leon had become nothing but an "unscrupulous falsifier." *Monthly Report* of the Boot and Shoe Workers Union (May 1898), pp. 20–21; "Transcript of debate between Tobin, De Leon, and others April 24, 1898," pp. 2, 4–5, 7, 9, 11, 15, 22 (Archives of the Boot and Shoe Workers Union).

13. For relations between the IWW and the Western Federation of Miners, see Vernon H. Jensen, *Heritage of Conflict, Labor Relations in the Non-ferrous Metals Industry up to 1930* (Ithaca: Cornell University Press, 1950), pp. 244–46, 272, 298–353ff.

14. *Proceedings, First Convention of the Labor Party of the United States* (Chicago, 1919), pp. 126–31; *Proceedings, Twenty-Seventh Consecutive and Fourth Biennial Convention of the U.M.W. of A.* (Cleveland, 1919), pp. 392–97, 631–32, 841–49, 867–70; *Proceedings, Twenty-Eighth Consecutive and Fifth Biennial Convention of U.M.W. of A.* (Indianapolis, 1921), p. 1137.

15. For a description of the socialist-communist conflict in the ILGWU, see David Schneider, *The Workers (Communist) Party and the American Trade Unions* (Baltimore: The Johns Hopkins Press, 1928), pp. 87–104. For Johnston's role in the CPPA see Kenneth C. McKay, *The Progressive Movement of 1924* (New York: Columbia University Press, 1947), pp. 60–70; *Machinists Monthly Journal,* XXXIII (March 1921), pp. 197–98, XXXIII (April 1921), pp. 293–95, XXXIV (April 1922), pp. 269–73.

16. The founding convention of the party, held in July 1901, specifically repudiated the tactics of the De Leonites, and urged all socialists to "join the unions of their respective trades." "We recognize," the party declared, "that trades unions are by historical necessity organized on

neutral ground, as far as political affiliation is concerned." See *Proceedings, Socialist Unity Convention* (Indianapolis, 1901), pp. 529–30. Similar resolutions were passed at the party conventions of 1904, 1908, and 1912.

17. Philip Taft, *The A.F. of L. in the Time of Gompers* (New York: Harper, 1957), pp. xii–xiv, 163–82ff.; Louis Lorwin, *The American Federation of Labor, History, Policies and Prospects* (Washington: The Brookings Institution, 1933), pp. 48–50.

18. For the WFM, see Jensen, op. cit., pp. 59–71. For the IAM, see *The Worker,* XII (June 7, 1903), p. 4; *International Socialist Review,* IV (January 1904), pp. 435–36; *Machinists Monthly Journal,* XXIV (September 1912), p. 851, XXVII (January 1915), pp. 82–83, XXVIII (May 1916), pp. 530–35; Taft, "Differences in the Executive Council," pp. 55–56.

19. Marion D. Savage, *Industrial Unionism in America* (New York: The Ronald Press Co., 1922), pp. 62–64, 82; Perlman, op. cit., p. 3; Commons, *History of Labour in the United States* (New York: Macmillan, 1936), II, pp. 138–44; Norman J. Ware, *The Labor Movement in the United States, 1860–1895* (New York: D. Appleton and Co., 1929), pp. 209–27. For the Knights of St. Crispin, see Don Lescohier, *The Knights of St. Crispin, 1867–1874; A Study in the Industrial Causes of Unionism* (Madison: University of Wisconsin Press, 1910).

20. For recent suggestive accounts of how rural (and some urban) workers may have voted in the South and the Southwest, however, see James R. Green, "Industrial Workers and Agrarian Socialism in the American Southwest, 1895–1915" (Unpublished Paper, American Historical Association, December 1971) and J. M. Kausser, "The Disenfranchisement Movement in the South, 1890–1910" (Unpublished Ph.D. Dissertation, Yale University, 1971).

21. Chester M. Destler, *American Radicalism, 1865–1901: Essays and Documents* (New London: Connecticut College, 1946), pp. 166–71, 175, 179, 207–8; *United Mine Workers Journal,* III (June 8, 1893), p. 1, III (March 22, 1894), p. 5, IV (August 9, 1894), pp. 4–5, IV (August 23, 1894), p. 4.

22. Melvyn Dubofsky, "The Origins of Western Working Class Radicalism, 1890–1905," *Labor History* (Spring 1966), pp. 140–41; *Machinists Monthly Journal,* VI (September 1894), p. 315, X (October 1898), pp. 594–95; Perlman, op. cit., pp. 8, 36; *Proceedings, Tenth Convention of the International Association of Machinists* (Milwaukee, 1903), p. 522. On the general issue of Populism and socialism, it may be suggested that it was not so much the case, as Norman Pollack argues, that the Populists were more radical in their ideology than agrarian historians have supposed. It was rather that in certain limited areas and on a certain limited range of issues (leaving aside ethnic and economic-interest differences between the two groups), such as control over the railroads, mine nationalization, and the threat which the growing power of the trusts presented to the bargaining position

of the trade unions, there was, temporarily, sufficient common ground between urban workers and farmers to make possible a political coalition between the two. See Norman Pollack, *The Populist Response to Industrial America, Midwestern Populist Thought* (Cambridge: Harvard University Press, 1962), pp. 1–24, 103–43ff.

23. Lescohier, op. cit., pp. 12–24; Galster, op. cit., pp. 3–8, 16–21, 30–37; John R. Commons, *Labor and Administration* (New York: Macmillan, 1913), pp. 255–66; *Twenty-Eighth Annual Report of the Massachusetts Bureau of Statistics of Labor* (Boston, 1898), pp. 12–13; *Labor Bulletin of the Commonwealth of Massachusetts,* Nos. 39–44 (Cincinnati, 1904), pp. 16–17.

24. *The Comrade,* III (November 1903), pp. 32–33; Haverhill *Social Democrat,* I (December 23, 1899), p. 1; *Proceedings, Third Convention of the Boot and Shoe Workers Union* (June 1897), pp. 34, 42; Thomas Philips to John C. Mulryan, March 30, 1890 (Thomas Philips Papers, Wisconsin State Historical Society). See also the testimony of Horace Eaton, George McNeill, Edward Cole, J. E. Tilt, I. B. Myers, and others before the Congressional Industrial Commission in 1899–1900. *Report of the Industrial Commission on the Relations and Conditions of Capital and Labor Employed in Manufactures and General Business,* 56th Cong., 2nd sess., House Doc. 495 (Washington, 1901), VII, pp. 119, 359–73, 684, 728–30ff.

25. Perlman, op. cit., p. 5; *Monthly Journal of the International Association of Machinists,* VII (April 1896), pp. 90–91, X (May 1898), p. 278, X (December 1898), pp. 722–24; Harold M. Groves, "The Machinist in Industry: A study of the History and Economics of His Craft" (Unpublished Ph.D. Dissertation, University of Wisconsin, 1927), pp. 75–85; William H. Buckler, "The Minimum Wage in the Machinists' Union," in J. H. Hollander and G. E. Barnett (eds.), *Studies in American Trade Unionism* (New York: H. Holt & Co., 1912), pp. 114–16, 136; U. S. Cong. Sen., *Report of the Committee of the Senate upon the Relations Between Labor and Capital* (Washington, 1885), I, pp. 755–59.

26. William A. McConagha, "The History and Progress of the United Mine Workers of America" (Unpublished Ph.D. Dissertation, University of Illinois, 1925), pp. 37, 40–48, 50–57; McAlister Coleman, *Men and Coal* (New York: Farrar and Rinehart, Inc., 1943), pp. 41–44; John Brophy, *A Miner's Life* (Madison: University of Wisconsin Press, 1964), pp. 38–46; Andrew Roy, *A History of the Coal Miners of the United States from the Development of the Mines to the Close of the Anthracite Strike of 1902* (Columbus: Trauger Printing Press, 1907), pp. 81–85, 186–214, 267–72, 281–89, 370–79, 427–40; Frank J. Warne, *The Slav Invasion and the Mine Workers: A Study in Immigration* (Philadelphia: J. B. Lippincott, 1904), pp. 65–83, 88–90. For a more detailed study of the impact of Slav immigration, see Peter Roberts, *Anthracite Coal Communities: A Study of the Demography, the Social, Educational and Moral Life of the Anthracite Regions* (New York: The Macmillan Co., 1904). For

the economic development of the industry, see Harold W. Aurand, *From the Molly Maguires to the United Mine Workers: The Social Ecology of an Industrial Union, 1869–1897* (Philadelphia: Temple University Press, 1971).

27. Dubofsky, op. cit., pp. 133–34; Jensen, op. cit., pp. 4–9; Rodman K. Paul, *The Mining Frontier of the Far West, 1848–1880* (New York: Holt, Rinehart & Winston, 1963), pp. 136–38, 143–44; *Report of the Industrial Commission on the Relations of Labor and Capital Employed in the Mining Industry* (Washington: G.P.O., 1901), pp. lxi–lxiv, lxxvii–lxxx, 191–618 *passim;* Edward Lord, *Comstock Mining and the Mines* (Washington: U. S. Government, 1883), p. 319, 397–99, 403.

28. *Brauer-Zeitung,* XVI (March 30, 1901), p. 4, XVIII (February 28, 1903), p. 1, XXV (January 29, 1910), p. 1; *Proceedings, Tenth Convention of the Brewery Workers Union* (Boston, 1897), pp. 5–6; Hermann Schlüter, *The Brewing Industry and the Brewery Workers' Movement in America* (Cincinnati: International Union of United Brewery Workmen of America, 1910), pp. 92–94, 123; Joel Seidman, *The Needle Trades* (New York: Farrar & Rinehart, Inc., 1942), pp. 55–56, 60–61ff.; Benjamin Stolberg, *Tailors Progress: The Story of a Famous Union and the Men Who Made It* (New York: Doubleday, Doran and Co., Inc., 1944), pp. 4–12; Aaron Antonovsky, *The Early Jewish Labor Movement in the United States* (New York: 1961), pp. 246–71.

29. Both of these hypotheses, however, must remain nothing more than that until detailed statistics have been undertaken into both occupational and geographical mobility rates among properly constructed local samples of the workers in these trades. In their researches into both volatility and occupational mobility in the American labor force Stephan Thernstrom, Clyde Griffen, and others have rightly pointed to the need to examine available sources of employment in alternative industries, as well as the opportunities for upward mobility among the sons of threatened artisans, before drawing any firm conclusions about the supposed consequences of "blocked mobility" resulting from the mechanization of the skilled trades. Pending the results of such detailed analysis, however, the economic history, at least of the shoemakers' and machinists' groups considered in this study, suggests that mechanization and the growth of large-scale production may have taken place so rapidly that they occurred within the working life of a single generation. The effect of this seems to have been that in the absence of alternative sources of employment (which were less likely to be available in depression years such as 1873–79, 1883–86, and 1893–97), technological developments may indeed have had a severe impact upon the established cadre of workers in a trade (who were those most likely to join a union), irrespective of the opportunities which were available to their sons. Secondly, it should be pointed out that we are dealing here not simply with the results of mechanization, but with the combined effect of a variety of complex and sometimes conflicting developments, including unstable industrial conditions resulting from

rapid economic expansion, the influx of unskilled and semi-skilled immigrant labor–which made unionization difficult and created a temporary oversupply of labor in certain trades, such as textiles and coal –and the effects of several prolonged periods of depression. None of this invalidates the need for detailed analysis of mobility rates among both organized and unorganized elements of the labor force. It does, however, suggest that the problem is more complicated than may at first be supposed. For Thernstrom's views, see his *Poverty and Progress: Social Mobility in a Nineteenth Century City* (Cambridge: Harvard University Press, 1964), especially Chapter 8; "Urbanization, Migration, and Social Mobility in Late Nineteenth Century America," in Barton J. Bernstein (ed.), *Towards a New Past, Dissenting Essays in American History* (New York: Pantheon Books, 1969, Vintage ed.), pp. 171–72; and Thernstrom and Knights, "Men in Motion: Some Data and Speculations about Urban Population Mobility in Nineteenth Century America," *Journal of Interdisciplinary History,* I (Autumn 1970), pp. 7–35. For those of Griffen, see his "Making It in America: Social Mobility in Mid-Nineteenth Century Poughkeepsie," in *New York History,* LI (October 1970), pp. 479–99; "Workers Divided: The Effect of Craft and Ethnic Differences in Poughkeepsie, New York, 1850–1880," in Stephan Thernstrom and Richard Sennett (eds.), *Nineteenth Century Cities* (New Haven: Yale University Press, 1969), pp. 49–93; and his very suggestive "Problems in the Study of Social Mobility" (Unpublished Paper).

30. Louis Kemper, the German-born national secretary of the Brewery Workers Union, died in 1914; Gustav Mostler, the editor of the *Brauer-Zeitung,* died in 1917. Julius Zorn, another German-born editor of the union journal who succeeded Mostler until his death in 1926, found that his socialist editorials became increasingly unpopular among the newer members of the union, who consisted largely of native-born yeast, vinegar, alcohol, wine, and cider workers with political backgrounds quite different from the initial core of German radicals. Savage, op. cit., p. 75; *Proceedings, Twenty-First Convention of the Brewery Workers Union* (Houston, 1917), pp. 13, 40–51, 60; *Brauer-Zeitung,* XXXVII (March 18, 1922), p. 1.

31. For an interesting discussion of the evolution of the political outlook of the urban Jewish community, see Nathan Glazer and Daniel P. Moynihan, *Beyond the Melting Pot: The Negroes, Puerto Ricans, Jews, Italians, and Irish of New York City* (Cambridge: M.I.T. Press, 1963), pp. 137–80.

32. *Proceedings, Sixth Convention of the Boot and Shoe Workers Union* (Cincinnati, 1904), pp. 16–17.

33. *Miners' Magazine,* XII (November 1912), pp. 4–6, XIII (January 1913), pp. 4–5; *Solidarity,* III (September 28, 1912), p. 3; *Proceedings, Twentieth Annual Convention of the W.F.M.* (Victor, 1912), pp. 191–213, 221–22; Levine, op. cit., pp. 249–72 *passim;* Hyman Berman, "Era of Protocol: A Chapter in the History of the International Ladies Garment Workers Union, 1910–1916" (Unpublished Ph.D.

Thesis, Columbia University, 1956), pp. 2–3; Savage, op. cit., p. 73; *Brewers Journal,* XXXIX (December 1914), pp. 71–74; *Proceedings, Twentieth Convention of the Brewery Workers Union* (Baltimore, 1914), pp. 131–34; McConagha, op. cit., pp. 79–380; *United Mine Workers Journal,* IX (November 3, 1898), p. 4.

34. Paul Jacobs, "What Can We Expect from the Unions?", in Irving Howe (ed.), *The Radical Papers* (New York: Doubleday, 1966), pp. 262–64.

35. Galster, op. cit., pp. 91, 106–10, 114; *Shoe Workers Journal,* XI (September 1910), p. 8; *Proceedings, Sixth Convention of the Boot and Shoe Workers Union* (Cincinnati, 1904), pp. 10–11.

36. James Weinstein, *The Decline of Socialism in America, 1912–1925* (New York: Monthly Review Press, 1967), pp. x, 45.

37. For this, see John H. M. Laslett, "End of an Alliance; Selected Correspondence Between Socialist Party Secretary Adolph Germer, and U.M.W. of A. Leaders in World War One," *Labor History,* XII, 4 (Fall 1971), pp. 567–77ff.

38. *Machinists Monthly Journal,* XXIV (October 1912), pp. 925–27, 942, 944, 950, XXV (November 1913), pp. 1203–5, XXVII (April 1915), pp. 296–300, XXVIII (October 1916), pp. 1026–29; *United Mine Workers Journal,* XXIII (October 24, 1912), p. 4, XXVII (November 16, 1916), p. 4; William Green, *Labor and Democracy* (Princeton: Princeton University Press, 1939), pp. 26–27; Roger W. Babson, *W. B. Wilson and the Department of Labor* (New York: Brentano's, 1919), pp. 122–26; *Proceedings, Twentieth Convention of the Brewery Workers Union* (Baltimore, 1914), p. 140; *Brauer-Zeitung,* XXXI (October 14, 1916), p. 2.

39. See, for example, David M. Potter, *People of Plenty, Economic Abundance and the American Character* (Chicago: University of Chicago Press, 1954), pp. 91–127; Charles A. Gulick and Melvin K. Bers, "Insight and Illusion in Perlman's Theory of the Labor Movement," *Industrial and Labor Relations Review,* VI (July 1953), pp. 528ff.

40. For graphs illustrating the relationship between third-party voting and changes in the business cycle, see Murray S. and Susan W. Stedman, *Discontent at the Polls: A Study of Farmer and Labor Parties, 1827–1948* (New York: Columbia University Press, 1950), pp. 79, 81, 84, 90.

41. The extent to which collective bargaining is able to raise wage levels above those prevailing throughout industry in general is still somewhat unclear. The consensus seems to be by some 10 to 15 per cent. See Albert Rees, *The Economics of Trade Unions* (Chicago: University of Chicago Press, 1962), pp. 75–80; Arthur M. Ross, "The Influence of Unionism upon Earnings," *Quarterly Journal of Economics,* XXXVIII (February 1948), pp. 241–59.

42. The membership of the Boot and Shoe Workers Union rose from 8966 in 1898 to 69,290 in 1904; that of the ILGWU from under 9000 in 1908 to over 90,000 in 1913; that of the IAM from 18,000

in 1899 to 75,000 in 1915; and that of the UMW of A from just over 8000 members in 1894 to over 30,000 in 1905.

43. *Shoe Workers Journal,* XXI (January 1919), p. 17.

44. *Proceedings, Seventeenth Convention of the International Ladies' Garment Workers Union* (Boston, 1924), pp. 115–16.

45. Selig Perlman, *A Theory of the Labor Movement* (New York: Macmillan, 1928), pp. 262–79.

46. Philip Taft, *A.F. of L. in the Time of Gompers,* pp. xii–xiv, 163–82ff.; Foner, op. cit., II, p. 280, III, p. 391.

COMMENT

Philip S. Foner

Dr. Laslett asserts that I have attributed "the failure of socialism in the American labor movement," so far as the trade unions are concerned, "to the bourgeois and 'class collaborationist' character of the labor leadership." So far as the socialists are concerned, he quotes me as having asserted that it was due, in the case of the SLP, to the "incorrect policies" of dual unionism; and, in the case of the Socialist Party, to the domination of the "Center-Right" elements which I have "erroneously" suggested "abandoned altogether the battle against the Federation's narrow, craft, pure and simple trade unionism." Laslett repeats this sweeping declaration in his book *Labor and the Left: A Study of Socialist and Radical Influences in the American Labor Movement, 1881–1924.*[1] In both cases, he cites as a source for this conclusion one page from the second and one from the third volume of my *History of the Labor Movement in the United States.*

A reading of these pages should convince any objective student that I certainly did not attempt to explain in such simplistic terms so complicated a problem as the "failure of socialism in the American labor movement." For one thing, though I have been criticized for using the words "correct" and "incorrect" in evaluating the policies of the AF of L leaders and the socialists—as though a labor historian, after an examination of the sources, has no right to pass judgment on the policies pursued in the past—I believe one should be careful in discussing "success" or "failure" in generalities. One must first clearly establish a criterion as to what constitutes "success" or "failure." I believe this to be one of the major weaknesses of Dr. Laslett's own writings on the subject. Neither in his article "Reflections on the Failure of Socialism in the American Federation of Labor," published in the *Mississippi Valley Historical Review,*[2] nor in his present paper or his recent book does

Dr. Laslett establish any criteria by which to measure success or failure. To be sure, there is little doubt as to which was the winning side between "pure and simple unionists" and the socialist-minded in the American labor movement. But is success to be measured by the number of socialist leaders in unions or by the adoption of resolutions at conventions favoring socialist candidates for office?

The fact that some unions had socialist leaders is no indication of the influence of socialism in these organizations. In his account of the Illinois Central and Harriman Lines strike of 1911, Carl E. Person describes a meeting with the leaders of the International Association of Machinists arising out of his charge that they had collaborated with the railroad companies to break the strike. Person describes how these union leaders set out to convince him that they could not possibly be guilty of his accusation:

> "Yes, I've been a comrade now for eighteen years," said Mr. Johnston [President William H. Johnston of the IA of M], and as he passed a small book over to Buckalew he added, "and I was the party's choice as candidate for governor of Massachusetts at one time."
>
> "I am proud of my red ticket," said Wharton [Arthur O. Wharton, General Executive Board member of the IA of M], as he started to pass his duesbook around for inspection.
>
> "We have a fine little movement in Topeka," said Buckalew as he started his book out for the once-over by the comrades.
>
> As I sat there perfectly injured over the cheapness of the situation, smiling Hugh Molly was introducing his ticket, after which a conversation was carried on for my benefit. They had, of course, agreed among themselves to put on this preliminary show for the purpose of persuading me to "come along," being fully aware of the fact that I had read Bellamy's *Looking Backward* with delight and considered Karl Marx one of the family.[3]

Other socialist trade union leaders, including those in the garment unions, proudly displayed their red cards and delivered lengthy speeches about the evils of capitalism. But in practice they often turned their membership against socialism by proving to be corrupt and despotic as many of the "pure and simple" trade union leaders.[4] For all his faults, De Leon had a point when he argued that many socialists changed their faces as soon as they became officeholders in a trade union and immediately began to pursue a policy of appeasing the conservatives. He warned that such conduct only brought inestimable harm to the prestige of socialism among workers.[5] He might have added that socialists did not lift the prestige of socialism among workers when, as mayors of cities, they discharged municipal workers seeking to organize and called in the police to break their strikes.[6] In short, one must certainly consider what was socialism and who were the socialists when one passes judgment on the "success" or "failure" of socialism. *The Independent* raised this point in 1912 in an editorial entitled "The Mystery of Socialism," and indicated that an answer to the question of "What is socialism?" was "confusing" because of the conduct of many who called themselves socialists.[7]

Dr. Laslett tends to dismiss my criticism of the dual unionist policies of De Leon and the SLP as an important factor in the waning influence of socialism in the AF of L. It is true that after 1900 Gompers became increasingly paranoid on the subject of socialism and insisted that there was a dichotomy between socialism and trade unionism which could not be resolved.[8] But Laslett concedes that the "socialists enjoyed their largest influence in the A.F.L. in the 1890's, before the Gompers regime had been thoroughly established. . . ." Yet it was precisely at this point that the dual unionist policies of De Leon and the SLP resulted in an exodus of the elements who should have influenced the course of the labor movement. It is significant that Gompers sought to obtain Frederick Engels' backing for his stand against the SLP and that Engels, while no admirer of Gompers, criticized the De Leonites for precipitating a conflict with the AF of L leadership which ended with their isolation from the main body of the American labor movement.[9] It is also significant that Lenin, whose *What Is to Be Done?* Dr. Laslett cites though without making the connection clear, repeatedly criticized the SLP and other dual unionists in this country for having weakened the struggle for socialism by refusing to work in the reactionary trade unions. As Lenin noted, this policy made it easier for the Gompers regime to become thoroughly established.[10]

As for the socialists who worked within the AF of L, it is becoming clearer, as new studies emerge, that the American Socialist Party never really defined a socialist policy for the American labor movement and had no well-developed trade union program. The trade union position of the Socialist Party emphasized the analogy of the two-armed labor movement—but with the two arms completely independent.[11] In practical terms, this meant a pro-AF of L policy regardless of the position the Gompers leadership took on fundamental issues. Algernon Lee maintained as early as 1904 that this pro-AF of L policy had shown such good results that the proposition to abandon it could be put aside as academic.[12] But then socialist unionists in the AF of L were easily satisfied. Resolutions favoring independent political action or even what Lewis Lorwin calls a "vague promise" to favor such action convinced them that they were making headway for socialism. Max S. Hayes, the chief socialist spokesman in the AF of L, regularly welcomed any departure from "pure and simple" trade unionism by the AF of L as bound to lead to the formation of a Labor Party like Great Britain's, or to the "endorsement" of the Socialist Party as the one party which would give unqualified support to labor's demands. The socialists, of course, were doomed to disappointment, but the fact remains that they concentrated most of their energies in this direction as the means of "making the socialist movement" felt inside the AF of L.[13]

As has been pointed out by a number of scholars, the factionalism between right and left wings which constantly plagued the Socialist Party during the first two decades of its existence revolved mainly around the question of trade unionism. The Left became increasingly alienated by the uncritical attitude of the socialist leadership toward the AF of L and complained repeatedly of the party's reluctance to offend influential leaders of the craft unions.[14] Even when the party's convention in 1912 conceded to the Left that more could be done to organize the unorganized, it claimed no desire to interfere in any union disputes. On the contrary, it declared the party duty was to support the unions morally and materially regardless of their policies.[15] Hence it is not surprising that when the AF of L was unwilling to move in the direction of organizing the unorganized, the socialists, fearing that relations with the Federation would deteriorate, did nothing on the issue. In his autobiography, socialist James H. Maurer, long-time president of the Pennsylvania State Federation of Labor, emphasized that organization of the unskilled was a key to the rise in socialist influence in this country, and that the failure of the socialists to press for this policy more actively in the AF of L was a serious weakness of the movement.[16]

This, of course, is linked to the whole issue of industrial unionism. It is true that in *Syndicalism, Industrial Unionism and Socialism,* published in 1913, John Spargo discussed the severe drawbacks of craft unionism. But the socialists did little to advance the cause of industrial unionism. With the IWW pressing from the Left, the socialists in the AF of L had until 1912 made a concerted attempt to push the issue of industrial unionism. But after the "cleansing" of the party in 1912 of the pro-IWW elements and the withdrawal of Haywood and his followers, the fight for industrial unionism diminished. At the AF of L conference in 1913 the motion for industrial unionism was defeated without a roll call vote and with no one speaking in favor of it. In 1914 the issue was taken up by the non-socialist Illinois Federation of Labor and again defeated. Militant socialists who were still in the party criticized the leadership for failing to conduct a campaign in behalf of "a thorough working knowledge of that powerful weapon—industrial unionism."[17] Probably the party was so weakened by the split that it could not have done much in this direction. In 1915, Hillquit admitted to Berger that the Socialist Party organization was "in an awful mess."[18]

Whatever the reason, the fact remains that the socialists in the AF of L had all but abandoned any real opposition to the Gompers policies. Like the Commons-Wisconsin school, many socialists in the Federation had reached the conclusion that the AF of L was the only labor organization which could have established a permanent foothold in the American environment and its continued existence was proof of the correctness of its policies and of its leadership. Saul Yanovsky, editor of *Justice,* official organ of the ILGWU and a leading socialist theoretician in the labor movement, revealed that the socialists had abandoned any pretense of combating the "pure and simple" craft unionism of the AF of L when he wrote in 1919:

> An organized labor body, millions strong, can surely not be spoken of as the labor aristocracy, we will go even further and say that in our opinion, these three and one quarter million workers represent not the cream, but indeed the body of American labor—whether they be conservative or radical. Its voice will be the voice of American labor and not that of a particular radical or conservative group or clique. . . .
>
> Gompers has been at the head of the labor movement for these many years because he knows best how to voice the true sentiments,

views, and aspirations of the workers of America. It is beside the question whether the aspirations of American labor are radical and wise enough . . . the fact is that the views of American workers are what they are, and that only the man who will truly reflect their views and give them voice will be acknowledged as their leader, even though it may seem to some that he rules them with an iron hand.

An Iron Hand! How ill-suited this phrase is to Samuel Gompers. . . .[19]

In his book, Laslett concedes that "the opposition of the Catholic leaders toward socialism did later help to prevent its further growth," but insists that Karson oversimplifies in asserting that the "opposition of the Catholic church precluded virtually all socialist influence among Irish workingmen." But this avoids the real issue. Certainly an increasing number of studies have demonstrated how important a force was the Catholic Church in offsetting socialist influence in the American labor movement. Mark Hanna may have exaggerated when he boasted that the Catholic Church was America's greatest bulwark against socialism in the opening decade of the twentieth century. But according to statistics drawn up by a competent labor commission and quoted in *The Nation* in 1909, "about one-half of those in trade unions are Roman Catholics, the rest Protestants or without religious differences." Peter Collins, Catholic trade union official and publicist in these years, estimated that 50 per cent of all delegates to AF of L conventions were Roman Catholics.[20] Equally important, Catholics occupied a proportionate number of seats in the Executive Council. The Church not only served a warning to the AF of L to avoid socialist tendencies, but as Edward G. Roddy points out: "By open and subtle warnings, the Church hierarchy threatened to forbid Catholic participation in any union that opted for socialism."[21] Certainly the socialists did not underestimate the importance of this influence; at the 1912 AF of L convention and again in 1913, socialist resolutions to "exclude fraternal delegates of church organizations from all future conventions of the A.F. of L." were introduced, but tabled.[22]

But while trade unionists were bombarded with anti-socialist propaganda from the Catholic Church and by groups like the Presbyterian Department of Church and Labor, headed by Charles Stelzle,[23] the party did little to try to impress the workers with its message. Morris Hillquit conceded, "We have often tried to coax, cajole and browbeat the trade unions into socialism, but we have made but little systematic effort to educate their members in the socialist philosophy." While organizing for the Socialist Party, White of the Molders Union was "surprised at times at the density of the ignorance as to the meaning of socialism, but found that they were willing to come and listen." He and other socialists noted that the party had never taken any efforts to introduce the rank-and-file members to socialist principles, and this despite the fact that "when they heard the position of socialism they stated they were glad to buy books and pamphlets, and learn more of the movement." In 1909 the Socialist Party did make a halfhearted effort to get a number of socialist trade unionists to conduct a general educational campaign among the local unions, but the attempt was soon abandoned. There remained, therefore, in the American labor movement a body of untapped support which the socialists failed to reach.[24]

In addition to paying little attention to the conversion of the already organized, the Socialist Party did precious little to reach the mass of the unorganized workers who, even the socialists admitted, were more apt to be influenced by a socialist message. For one thing, most of the unorganized workers were unskilled and their organization would have necessitated an all-out policy of industrial unionism, but this meant combating the policies of the AF of L. Moreover, to bring the message of socialism to the unorganized in many industrial centers where the companies completely dominated the economic, political, and social life required more courage than most socialist leaders possessed. Since the Socialist Party's approach to the Negro workers was similar in many respects to that of the AF of L, despite its nod to the principle of working-class solidarity, it could not accomplish much in influencing black workers in socialist principles.[25]

In his book Dr. Laslett also points out, as does David Shannon, that the Socialist Party "at its height contained more native-born Americans than it did immigrants," and that the "evidence from the trade union movement" sustains this conclusion. But he fails to see that this was precisely a reflection of the indifference of the Socialist Party to the unskilled workers in the mass production industries. Socialist trade unionists conceded that the IWW was able to succeed temporarily in organizing these workers, for they could "easily be got to participate in a strike." But these workers were actually of little value for a socialist movement since their ideas "of maintaining a permanent organization are very hazy and confused."[26] Yet these were the workers who made up the bulk of the American working class and it was among them that the socialist message could have received the greatest response. Given this approach, it is not surprising that, as one student of socialism and the American labor movement has pointed out, "socialism remained weakest where it probably had most to offer in the long run."[27]

To conclude: while Dr. Laslett has added new and interesting information about socialism and American labor, he has not, in my judgment, altered the fact that a decisive reason for the weakness of socialism in the American labor movement arose from the sectarian, dual unionism of De Leon and the SLP and others who followed this policy as well as the nature of the trade union program pursued by the Socialist Party of America.

NOTES

1. (New York, 1970), p. 290.
2. L (March 1964), pp. 634–51.
3. Carl E. Person, *The Lizard's Trail* (Chicago, 1918), p. 100.
4. Philip S. Foner, *The Fur and Leather Workers Union* (Newark, N.J., 1950), pp. 78–81. One writer in the *Bakers Journal* saw a correlation between a decline in socialist feeling in the union and an unwillingness of the socialist leadership to conduct a truly socialist policy and their tendency to "make disparaging remarks about the mob"—i.e., the rank and file. (*Bakers Journal,* March 13, 1909.)
5. *Proceedings,* Socialist Labor Party Convention, 1900, pp. 211–17.
6. Kenneth E. Hendrickson, Jr., "George R. Lunn and the Socialist Era in Schenectady, New York, 1909–1916," *New York History* (January 1936), pp. 23–40; Webb Waldron, "Jasper Goes to Town," *American Magazine,* April 1938.
7. *The Independent,* October 10, 1912, p. 850.
8. *American Federationist,* XXII (August 1915), p. 675, XIX (November 1912), p. 923, XVII (March 1910), p. 211. In his article "Reflections on the Failure of Socialism in the A.F. of L.," in op. cit., Laslett accepts Gompers' view that there was a basic incompatibility between trade unionism and socialism.
9. Philip S. Foner, "Samuel Gompers to Frederick Engels: A Letter," *Labor History* (Spring 1970), pp. 207–11; Frederick Engels to Hermann Schluter, January 29, 1891, and to F. A. Sorge, January 6, 1892, Alexander Trachtenberg (ed.), *Karl Marx and Frederick Engels: Letters to Americans, 1848–1895* (New York, 1953), pp. 233–34, 240. Gompers' high opinion of Engels at this time is evidenced by his concern over the fact that the co-father of scientific socialism believed that the Knights of Labor was the organization of the proletariat of America. (Gompers to Florence Kelley Wischnewetsky, October 17, 1888, Samuel Gompers Letterbooks, Library of Congress.)
10. V. I. Lenin, *Left-Wing Communism: An Infantile Disorder* (New York, 1934), pp. 36–38; Philip S. Foner, "Lenin and the American Working-Class Movement," in Daniel Mason and Jessica Smith (eds.), *Lenin's Impact on the United States* (New York, 1970), pp. 121–31. Even Carl Reeve, in his effort to refute the charge that De Leon's dual-unionist policies disastrously affected socialist influence in the AF of L, ends up his discussion of "Dual Unionism-Splits and Expulsions" by proving that "De Leon's entire program of dual unionism" had precisely this result. (*The Life and Times of Daniel De Leon,* New York, 1972, pp. 57–67.)
11. *Proceedings,* Socialist Party Convention, 1908, pp. 94–102.
12. *Proceedings,* Socialist Party Convention, 1904, pp. 123–24.
13. *International Socialist Review,* VII (August 1906), p. 112, VIII (March 1908), pp. 566–69; Lewis L. Lorwin, *The American Federa-*

tion of Labor: History, Policies, and Prospects (Washington, D.C., 1933), p. 416; *Proceedings,* AF of L Convention, 1913, pp. 314–15.

14. *International Socialist Review,* XIV (July 1913), p. 22.

15. *Proceedings,* Socialist Party Convention, 1912, p. 195.

16. James Hudson Maurer, *It Can Be Done* (New York, 1938), p. 244.

17. *International Socialist Review,* XIV (July 1913), p. 17; W. H. Kinger to Frans Bostrom, January 13, 1913, Socialist Party Collection, Duke University Library; Michael E. R. Bassett, "The Socialist Party of America, 1912–1919: Years of Decline" (Unpublished Ph.D. Thesis, Duke University, 1963), pp. 52–53.

18. Morris Hillquit to Victor Berger, September 25, 1915, Socialist Party Collection, County Historical Society, Milwaukee, Wisconsin. Weinstein concedes that the Socialist Party lost influence in the AF of L after 1912, but argues that it did increase its influence in certain specific unions as well as in the Pennsylvania State Federation of Labor. (James Weinstein, "The Socialist Party: Its Roots and Strength, 1912–1919," *Studies on the Left,* I [Winter 1960], pp. 15–18.) This is a subject that would require more space than is available to discuss in full, but it should be noted that for all his criticism of the tendency of labor historians to rivet their attention on the national federations of labor, Dr. Laslett ignores in his analysis the radicalization that took place in the local city central bodies and the state federations of labor. Under the AF of L constitution, to be sure, the role of city centrals and state federations was very much circumscribed, and efforts to change this in the interests of permitting them to play a more active part in the labor movement proved fruitless. Undoubtedly this was due to a fear of the traditional radicalism of the local federations. (See Lorwin, op. cit., pp. 348–49.)

19. *Justice,* I (June 14, 1919), p. 4. Norman H. Ware, historian of the Knights of Labor, saw nothing inevitable in the success of the American Federation of Labor, and James H. Maurer pointed out that the AF of L had still not accomplished in the 1930s what the Knights of Labor had attempted–organization of the unskilled. (Norman J. Ware, *The Labor Movement in the United States, 1860–1895* [New York, 1929], p. xiv; Maurer, op. cit., p. 244.) As for Gompers' "iron hand," Yanovsky could have profited from reading socialist Duncan McDonald's report on his experiences at the AF of L convention during which he noted: "If anybody can get a progressive idea through the A.F. of L., he deserves a monument bigger than that built to George Washington. . . ." (*Proceedings,* United Mine Workers Convention, 1912, pp. 310–12; 1914, pp. 353–61.)

20. *The Nation,* August 12, 1909; *Central-Blatt and Social Justice,* II (February 1910), p. 10.

21. Edward G. Roddy, "The Catholic Church and the A.F. of L., 1910–1920; A Study in Ambivalence" (Unpublished paper before the joint meeting of the Labor Historians and the American Catholic

Historical Association at the fifty-eighth annual meeting of the Mississippi Valley Historical Association, April 22, 1965), p. 13.

22. New York *Call,* November 19, 1912; November 20, 1913.

23. See William John Villaume, "The Federal Council of the Churches of Christ in America and Labor Problems in the United States" (Unpublished Ph.D. Thesis, Hartford Seminary Foundation, Hartford, Conn., May 1951); George H. Nash, III, "Charles Stelzle: Apostle to Labor," *Labor History* (Spring 1970), pp. 151–74.

24. New York *Call,* December 12, 1909; Socialist Party, Minutes of National Executive Committee Session, December 11–13, 1909 (Socialist Party Collection, Duke University Library); Socialist Party Press Release, May 28, July 2, 1913 (Socialist Party Collection, Duke University Library).

25. A recent study points out: "During the years under consideration the [Socialist] party failed to raise any significant protest against trade union discrimination unless one counts the labor organization resolution adopted at the 1912 convention. . . ." (R. Laurence Moore, "Flawed Fraternity–American Socialist Response to the Negro, 1901–1912," *Historian,* November 1969, pp. 13–14.) It is rather interesting that Dr. Laslett in discussing a number of unions in which socialists had influence, such as the Machinists, says nothing about the attitude toward black workers. The *Machinists Monthly Journal* may have been "imbued" with ideas stemming from the Knights of Labor, but organization of workers regardless of race and color was not one of them.

26. A. Rosebury in *Ladies' Garment Worker,* April 1914, pp. 12–14.

27. William Milner Dick, "Labor and Socialism in America: The Gompers Era" (Unpublished Ph.D. Thesis, University of Toronto), p. 304. In his Memoir, at the Columbia University Oral History Project, John Brophy concedes that the Socialist Party was always rather remote from the mass of the working class. (Columbia University Oral History Project, John Brophy Memoir, p. 315.)

REPLY

John H. M. Laslett

Despite protestations to the contrary, in his Comment on my essay Philip Foner has chosen to confine himself, as he has in his books on the subject, almost entirely to defects in the policies pursued by the leaders of the SLP and the Socialist Party of America as the major reasons for the weakness of socialism in the American labor movement, largely ignoring my efforts to demonstrate the limited value of this limited kind of explanation, and to draw attention to the relevance of other kinds of factors as well. In particular, he accuses me of oversimplifying the analysis of the problem which he presents in his own previous writings, of neglecting to define what is meant by "success" or "failure," in relation to the record of the socialists in the labor movement, and of failing to recognize that it was the indifference of the Socialist Party toward the mass of unorganized, unskilled, and immigrant workers that was a crucial reason for their inability to build up a strong third-party movement.

The question of how one measures socialist success or failure in the labor movement is certainly an important one, and I would agree that it is not resolved simply by pointing to the number of socialists elected to union office or the type of resolutions adopted by union conventions—although I believe Foner goes much too far in arguing that evidence of this kind "is no indication of the influence of socialism in these organizations." Although labor historians are now quite properly making use of a wide variety of new types of material to determine the potential for radical consciousness among various segments of the American working class, given the paucity of source material available it is sometimes the only major index that we have.

Even if one adopts a more sophisticated criterion of success or failure, however, such as the level of "socialist" rather than trade union consciousness achieved as the result of a strike or some other particular act—which is what Lenin took as his standard in the *What Is to Be Done?* essay to which Foner refers[1]—the record of the American labor movement in this period does not, unfortunately, appear to be a great deal more encouraging. The alleged sellout of the Illinois Central and Harriman Lines strike by the socialist leadership which Foner takes as his example (which did not take place until June 1915, incidentally, after the union's treasury had become exhausted with supporting the strike for more than four years[2]) is an example of the kind of tactical compromises which were—and still are—carried out by all types of labor unions, whether socialist or not; and the question which it raises is not whether President William H. Johnston of the IA of M or Saul Yanovsky of the ILGWU were not socialists for most of their union careers, which by a wide variety of measures they undoubtedly were. Rather, it is whether there was something peculiar about the American environment which made labor leaders succumb to this kind of behavior to an unusual degree.

The point is an important one, but it is not in the nature of things capable of solution simply by looking at the nature of socialist and trade union tactics, as Foner does, instead of at the reasons which lie behind them. As early as the 1850s both Marx and Engels noticed the particular difficulty which American working-class leaders seemed to experience in remaining faithful to their original beliefs once they had secured positions of power in the society.[3] I attempted to discuss the same problem (in connection with time contracts, relations with non-socialist union officials, and the rewards of union office) at various points in my own book.[4] What lies behind this problem, however, is the more general question—which Foner ignores—of whether the behavior of American labor leaders in this matter was simply a response to the corrupting and bureaucratizing effect which union office often has upon labor leaders of proletarian origin, or whether it is also attributable to something peculiar about the American environment and American business values, as Robert Michels argued in his *Political Parties* as long ago as 1911.[5]

On this matter, as in so many other areas of labor history, we need a thoroughgoing comparative analysis to settle the issue. But David Brody's 1968 essay on careerism in the American labor movement represents a most useful start. The higher ratio of full-time officials to union members in the United States compared to a number of European countries, he argues, suggests that American labor leaders may have placed a greater value than their European counterparts on advancing their own individual careers, rather than upon preserving their sense of solidarity with members of the rank and file.[6] This, in turn, takes us back to the need to examine problems of American individualism, assimilation, and business values, which point to characteristics of the society generally, not to problems of the labor movement as such.

More generally, we cannot know whether the particular policies pursued by the trade union and socialist leadership were the crucial determinant of success or failure until we examine much more carefully the political and economic environment in which they operated, as well as the particular characteristics of the labor force with which they had to deal. This does not mean that leadership is unimportant. It may well be that the quality of socialist and trade union leadership in America was lower than it was in a number of other countries due, perhaps, to higher rates of geographical and occupational mobility which siphoned off potential leaders from the radical movement, or to the availability of free public educational facilities for advancement into other fields. But just as not even a Lenin or a Rosa Luxemburg could have made a revolution in Russia or in Germany without the prior development of a revolutionary mentality among crucial sections of the working class, so we cannot know whether a mass working-class party could have grown up in this country simply by examining the policies of the party and trade union leadership alone.

The same remark can be made concerning Foner's argument, which given the assumptions of his analysis is well taken up to a point, that despite its initial efforts to secure the support of the existing trade unions, the Socialist Party of America made few really serious attempts to educate the workers generally into socialism, or to reach the mass of immigrant, unskilled, or black elements in the labor force. It may well be that this policy (or lack of a policy) helped contribute to the alienation of the left wing within the Socialist Party, to its lack of any really extensive ties with the proletariat, and hence to its excessively bourgeois character. The trouble is, however, that this kind of analysis only looks at one side of the coin. How do we know that it was among the immigrants, the unskilled, and the black elements "that the Socialist message could have received the greatest response"? (Foner, incidentally, misunderstands my remark that evidence from the trade union movement confirms Shannon's finding that the socialist movement at its height was more native-born than immigrant. The point there was simply to rebut the popular misconception that the pre-1914 Socialist Party was foreign-dominated, not to commend it for so being.)

On this general point, it is obvious that little can be done in the way of organizing a mass working-class party without securing a mass base within the labor movement from which to operate—as, for example, the British Labour Party had in the 1890s within the "new union" wing of the TUC, which may have been one of the crucial reasons for the difference in political outlook between the labor movements in the two countries. But even if we leave aside the thorny question—which a more extended analysis could not afford to do—of whether political radicalism is more likely to arise among the labor aristocracy, i.e., from among skilled craftsmen and artisans, rather than from among the poorer segments of the working class (an issue which I discussed indirectly in my book, and which has recently been the subject of an interesting academic debate among labor historians in England[7]), Foner's approach to the problem assumes that we know a great deal more about the political outlook—and hence about the potential for radicalization—among black, unskilled, and immigrant workers in this country in the early part of this century when the Socialist Party should have taken root than we in fact do.

So far, such research as has been carried out on blacks and socialism, for example, has been largely confined to criticizing the Socialist Party because of the racism of some of its spokesmen, and because it tolerated segregated locals in the South for fear of offending its white supporters in the South and elsewhere.[8] What is needed now is to look at the other half of the problem by seeking answers to a number of basic questions concerning black political attitudes to which we still do not have satisfactory replies. Among northern black workingmen who actually registered to vote, for example, how many were tied by reasons of tradition and political mythology to the Republican Party? Did disenfranchisement and the relatively small number of blacks in industrial jobs in the South mean that the Socialist Party made a realistic (if ideologically retrograde) choice in preferring to pursue the white voter rather than the black, if, indeed, such a conscious choice was made at all? Still more important, was the Socialist Party (and later the Communist Party too) hampered in its appeal to this section of the "absentee proletariat" by persistently treating the problem primarily as one not of race, but of class?

The same kind of basic research into the political orientation of the urban immigrant worker, who made up most of the unskilled element in the labor force in the late nineteenth century, is also needed before we can venture any kind of definitive judgment as to their potential for radicalism. It is now twenty years since Oscar Handlin (followed by Richard Hofstadter) offered the broad but largely unsubstantiated judgment that "the failure of the socialists and anarchists to win an important position in the associational life of the immigrants" was due largely to the "peasant's inherited distrust of radicalism," or to his supposed lack of the "faculty of abstraction"—as if all immigrants to the United States after the late 1880s were ex-peasants, and differences in generation or in place of origin were of no account.[9] And yet, although the Handlin-Hofstadter thesis has been effectively challenged concerning the ability of the Progressive movement to secure political support among immigrant workers, very little work has been done on the attitudes of the immigrants toward socialism. One of the few exceptions, Melvyn Dubofsky's article on the political appeal of the Socialist Party among ethnic voters in New York City between 1900 and 1918, tends to confirm the view that only the Jewish voters were drawn to the Socialist Party in any numbers: Irish and Italian workers remained largely indifferent. What is needed now is a detailed state-by-state analysis of the orientation of immigrant workingmen toward both reform and socialist politics (they may have been quite different), on the order of Joseph Huthmacher's studies of immigrant attitudes toward the Progressives in Massachusetts and New York.

It may turn out, as Victor Greene implies in his interesting study of strike solidarity among Slav coal miners in the anthracite district of Pennsylvania in the 1890s, that the relative indifference of the socialists toward unskilled and immigrant workers was indeed one reason for the weakness of the party—if, that is, the kind of evidence which Greene presents about class solidarity in strike situations can be shown to carry over into the realm of politics, which is in itself a large question.[10] But in order to demonstrate this it will be necessary to examine the whole complex of influences which helped to shape the political orientation of those workers themselves, instead of simply looking at the policies of the socialist and trade union leadership alone. The Marxist tendency to assume inherent, or at least latent, class consciousness among rank-and-file elements in the labor force, to which Foner subscribes, is at bottom just as deterministic and ahistorical as the earlier tendency of Perlman and the Wisconsin school of labor economists to assume American labor's inherently conservative or job-conscious orientation.

In saying this, I do not wish to suggest that I have myself escaped the historian's tendency to overgeneralize. As I acknowledged at the end of my initial essay—and as at least one reviewer of *Labor and the Left* has quite rightly pointed out[11]—evidence drawn even from a broad spectrum of opinion within the labor movement cannot, in itself, supply complete answers to the questions which I attempted to raise. I remain convinced, however, that only by examining the full range of influences which affected the American workingman's political behavior in this period, preferably in a comparative context, will we be able to judge whether sectarianism on the part of the socialist leadership or class collaboration on the part of the trade unions was more important than structural factors in contributing to the failure of socialism to secure the support of the American worker. At present, I do not believe they were.

NOTES

1. V. I. Lenin, *What Is to Be Done? Burning Questions of Our Movement* (New York: International Publishers Co., 1969), pp. 30–34ff.

2. John H. M. Laslett, *Labor and the Left: A Study of Socialist and Radical Influences in the American Labor Movement, 1881–1924* (New York: Basic Books, 1970), pp. 165–66.

3. R. Laurence Moore, *European Socialists and the American Promised Land* (New York: Oxford University Press, 1970), p. 5.

4. Laslett, op. cit., pp. 90, 135, 179–80ff.

5. "Whilst in Europe such corruption gives rise to censure and anger," Michels wrote, "in America it is treated with indifference or arouses no more than an indulgent smile. . . . We cannot wonder, then, that North America should be pre-eminently the country in which the aristocratic tendencies of the labour leaders, fostered by an environment often permeated . . . by a gross and unrefined materialism, should have developed freely and upon a gigantic scale." Robert Michels, *Political Parties* (New York: Dover, 1959), pp. 310–11.

6. David Brody, "Career Leadership and American Trade Unionism," in Frederick C. Jaher (ed.), *The Age of Industrialism in America: Essays in Social Structure and Cultural Values* (New York: Free Press, 1968).

7. See Eric Hobsbawm, *Labouring Men: Studies in the History of Labour* (New York, 1964), ch. 15, and Hobsbawm's review of Henry Pelling, *Popular Politics and Society in Late Victorian Britain* (London, 1968), in *Bulletin* No. 18 of the Society for the Study of Labour History (Spring 1969), pp. 49–54. The only two methodologically rigorous studies of the occupational background of sample elements within the American socialist movement which to my knowledge have so far been completed tend to confirm the view, which I put forward on the basis of very limited evidence in *Labor and the Left,* that it was from the more skilled elements in the American labor force, rather than from the unskilled and the more recent immigrants, that support for the Socialist Party came. One study, based upon a detailed statistical analysis of two nationally conducted samples of Socialist Party membership in 1908 and 1914, shows that socialists tended to be "more heavily concentrated among craftsmen, professionals, proprietors (in descending order)." The other, contained in an excellent recently completed statewide study of socialism in West Virginia, suggests that radical sentiments developed more readily among skilled iron molders, glass blowers, machinists, and painters than it did among unskilled miners and other "non labor aristocracy" workers in that state. See Shannon Ferguson, "American Social Reform; 1896–1912: The Grass-Roots of Socialism and Populism" (Unpublished Research Paper, Yale University, 1963), pp. 22–23; Frederick A. Barkey, "The Socialist

Party in West Virginia from 1898 to 1920: A Study in Working Class Radicalism" (Unpublished Ph.D. Thesis, University of Pittsburgh, 1971), pp. 89–93.

8. See, for example, Ira Kipnis, *The American Socialist Movement, 1897–1912* (New York: Columbia University Press, 1952), pp. 134ff.; James Weinstein, *The Decline of Socialism in America, 1912–1925* (New York: Monthly Review Press, 1967), pp. 63–74. Somewhat more illuminating is Sally Miller's article "The Socialist Party and the Negro, 1901–1920," in *Journal of Negro History,* LVI (July 1971), pp. 220–29, although her analysis is still almost wholly confined to the Socialist Party's own attitudes.

9. Oscar Handlin, *The Uprooted* (Boston: Little, Brown, 1951), pp. 217ff. See also Richard Hofstadter, *The Age of Reform* (New York: Knopf, 1955), pp. 180–84.

10. Melvyn Dubofsky, "Success and Failure of Socialism in New York City, 1900–1918: A Case Study," *Labor History* (Fall 1968), IX, pp. 361–75; Joseph Huthmacher, *Massachusetts People and Politics, 1919–1933* (Cambridge: Harvard University Press, 1959); Huthmacher, "Urban Liberalism and the Age of Reform," *Mississippi Valley Historical Review,* XLIX (September 1962), pp. 231–41; Victor R. Greene, *The Slavic Community on Strike: Immigrant Labor in Pennsylvania Anthracite* (Notre Dame: University of Notre Dame Press, 1968), *passim.*

11. See, for example, that by Frederick Olson in the *American Historical Review,* 76 (December 1971), pp. 1613–14.

Chapter 5

SOCIALISM AND SYNDICALISM*

Melvyn Dubofsky

From 1909 to 1919 a legend enveloped the IWW. Many Americans, especially during World War One and the postwar Red Scare, became convinced that the Wobblies were "cut-throat, pro-German, or . . . bolshevik, desperadoes who burn harvest-fields, drive iron spikes into fine timber and ruin sawmills, devise bomb plots, who obstruct the war and sabotage the manufacture of munitions—veritable supermen, with a superhuman power for evil, omnipresent and almost omnipotent."[1] The hobo Wobbly had replaced the bearded, bomb-carrying anarchist as a bogeyman in the middle-class American's fevered imagination. This version of the Wobblies died hard.

It died hard because violence and bloodshed *did* follow Wobblies wherever they fought for free speech or higher wages. It died hard because IWW rhetoric and songs fed the myth of the Wobbly as a wild and woolly warrior, a man who contemptuously scorned the conventional morality of what he characterized as a "bushwa" society. While organizers like James P. Thompson were boasting that only *"red-blooded"* revolutionaries belonged to the IWW, Wobbly bards like Joe Hill were deriding voting machines and suggesting that workers "may find out that the only 'machine' worth while is the one which the capitalists use on us when we ask for more bread for ourselves and our families. *The one that works with a trigger.*"[2]

With the IWW, as with other radical organizations that have been romanticized and mythologized, the legend is several removes from reality. Wobblies did not carry bombs, nor burn harvest fields,

* Taken from Chapters 7 and 19 of Melvyn Dubofsky, *We Shall Be All: A History of the Industrial Workers of the World* (Chicago: Quadrangle Books, 1969), pp. 146–70, 480–84. In the original the chapters are entitled "Ideology and Utopia: The Syndicalism of the IWW," and "Remembrance of Things Past: The IWW Legacy."

nor destroy timber, nor depend upon the machine that works with a trigger. Instead they tried in their own ways to comprehend the nature and dynamics of capitalist society, and through increased knowledge, as well as through revolutionary activism, to develop a better system for the organization and functioning of the American economy.

The IWW, it is true, produced no intellectual giants. It did not spawn a Karl Marx or a Georges Sorel, a Lenin or a Jean Jaurès, or even an Edward Bellamy or a Henry George. It offered no genuinely original ideas, no sweeping explanations of social change, no fundamental theories of revolution. Wobblies instead took their basic concepts from others: from Marx the concepts of labor value, commodity value, surplus value, and class struggle; from Darwin the idea of organic evolution and the struggle for survival as a paradigm for social evolution and the survival of the fittest class; from Bakunin and the anarchists the "propaganda of the deed" and the idea of "direct action"; and from Sorel the notion of the "militant minority." Hence, IWW beliefs became a peculiar amalgam of Marxism and Darwinism, anarchism and syndicalism—all overlaid with a singularly American patina.

True, they did read books—IWW libraries included works by Marx, Engels, Kautsky, Sorel, Jaurès, Bellamy, George, and others; IWW publications advertised complete bibliographies of socialist literature—but they read to understand better what they already knew from life. For above all else, Wobblies derived their beliefs from their own experiences in America. The Coeur d'Alenes, Leadville, and Cripple Creek taught them that society was divided into contending classes; that American business had evolved from small-scale endeavors to giant corporations; that labor was divided, not united; and that a "militant minority" could surmount the resistance of a complacent majority. In other words, European theoreticians explained in coherent, analytical, and learned terms what most Wobblies grasped instinctively.

As early as 1912 William E. Bohn, an astute journalist and observer of the American scene, could declare that the IWW "did not come into being as the result of any foreign influence. It is distinctly an American product." Ben Williams agreed. For seven years, as editor of *Solidarity,* he vigorously criticized those who associated the IWW with foreign ideologies. "Whatever it may have in common with European labor movements," he insisted, the IWW

> is a distinct product of America and American conditions. . . . Neither "in aim and methods" is the I.W.W. European. . . . Whatever terms or phrases we may borrow from the French or other language to denote our methods cut no figure: the methods conform to American conditions. . . . The form of structure of the I.W.W. is also distinctly American, and differs materially from the less developed forms of European labor organization . . .[3]

IWW beliefs must be understood in terms of those whom the organization tried to organize. After the defection of the Western Federation of Miners in 1907, Wobblies concentrated upon those workers neglected by the mainstream of the labor movement: timber beasts, hobo harvesters, itinerant construction workers, exploited eastern and southern European immigrants, racially excluded Negroes, Mexicans, and Asian Americans.

Contemporaries frequently remarked the IWW's unique following. Rexford Tugwell poignantly described the timber beast attracted to the IWW: "His eyes are dull and reddened; his joints are stiff with the rheumatism almost universal in the wettest climate in the world; his teeth are rotting; he is wracked with strange diseases and tortured by unrealized dreams that haunt his soul. . . . The blanket-stiff is a man without a home. . . . The void of his atrophied affections is filled with a resentful despair and a bitterness against the society that self-righteously cast him out." The same could be said of the IWW harvest worker and construction hand. After a careful study based upon personal interviews with West Coast Wobblies, Carleton Parker concluded that they were floaters, men without homes, wives, women, or "normal" sex; the men who appear in his case studies shared lives of brutality, degradation, and violence, "starting with the long hours and dreary winters of the farms they ran away from, or the sour-smelling bunkhouse in a coal village, through their character-debasing experience with the drifting 'hire and fire' life in the industries, on to the vicious social and economic life of the winter unemployed . . ."[4]

Wobbly recruits thus shared aspects of what cultural anthropologist Oscar Lewis has only recently labeled the "culture of poverty." Like Lewis' more recent case-study families in Mexico, Puerto Rico, and New York City, America's Wobblies had life histories revealing "family disruption, violence, brutality, cheapness of life, lack of love, lack of education, lack of medical facilities . . ."[5]

Lewis also contends that the "culture of poverty" emerges within a society that possesses the following dominant characteristics: (1) a cash economy, wage labor, and production for profit; (2) a persistently high rate of unemployment and underemployment for unskilled labor; (3) low wages; (4) a paucity of social, political, and economic organization, whether on a voluntary basis or by government imposition, for the low-income population; and (5) a pervasive set of values, imposed by the dominant class, which stresses the accumulation of wealth and property and the possibility of upward mobility through thrift, and explains low economic status as the result of personal inadequacy or inferiority.[6]

Although Lewis' loosely drawn characteristics might apply to almost any society in the process of industrialization, they are particularly relevant to the America of 1877–1917. Unencumbered by a feudal-aristocratic tradition and the paternalistic anti-capitalism associated with it, America's dominant business class could impose its values on society with relative ease. This was singularly true in the American West, where, in less than a generation, industrialization and urbanization tamed a wilderness. There, where social structure was fluid and government relatively weak, the spirit of rugged individualism reigned supreme and the strong prevailed. Those who failed to rise were pushed into society's backwaters to endure, as best they could, the stigmata associated with failure in a competitive industrial society.

Wobbly members, like Marx's proletariat and Lewis' poverty-stricken, were "people . . . from the lower strata of a rapidly changing society and . . . already partially alienated from it." The men who associated with the IWW in its heyday were largely first-generation citizens of an industrial society. As is frequently noted, immigrants from the south and east of Europe often first experienced urban-industrial life upon their arrival in the new world. But dispossessed native Americans were equally newcomers to industrial society; like E. J. Hobsbawm's first-generation English industrial workers, such native Americans may be considered internal immigrants who also made the frightening journey from a preindustrial to an industrial society.[7] Caught between two systems and two modes of existence, these immigrants–internal and external–were indeed uprooted. Torn from an old, ordered, and comprehensible way of life, they found themselves unable to replace it with an integrated and meaningful mode of existence, and soon became the human flotsam and jetsam of early industrial capitalism's frequent shipwrecks.

Feeling impotent and alienated, these men harbored deep grievances against the essential institutions of the ruling classes: police, government, and church. Hence, Wobblies, like Lewis' Latin Americans living in a "culture of poverty," exhibited a high susceptibility to unrest and to radical movements aimed at destroying the established social order.[8]

This is what IWW leaders sensed, though they themselves did not come out of the "culture of poverty." The leadership consisted largely of two types: skilled workers and formerly successful trade-union officials such as Haywood, St. John, Ettor, and Little; and restless intellectuals such as Williams, Ebert, and the Swedish immigrant syndicalist John Sandgren. These men shared a common desire to effect a nonpolitical revolution in America and a common alienation from the AFL and from reformist American socialists. Eager to make a revolution which would destroy the existing system root and branch, they naturally turned to those most alienated from the American dream—and located them in the lower strata of a rapidly changing society.

The IWW clearly shaped its doctrines and its tactics to attract such recruits. That is why it maintained low initiation fees and still lower dues, why it allowed universal transfer of union cards, why it belittled union leaders as the labor lieutenants of capitalism, and why, finally, it derogated business unionism as pork-chop unionism and trade-union welfare systems as "coffin benefits." IWW members simply could not afford the initiation fees and dues required to sustain business unionism; partly because of their feelings of impotence and partly because they moved from industry to industry, Wobblies also needed self-leadership and self-discipline more than the counsel of professional, bureaucratic union officials. Thus, only by implementing policies sure to keep its treasury bare and its bureaucracy immobilized could the IWW attract the followers it sought. Accordingly, the IWW's formal defense of its non-benefit system should be understood more as a rationalization of what existed than as a hard-core belief in what should exist. The same kind of rationalization, or ambivalence, as we shall see, permeated many other Wobbly beliefs and practices.

Basically, the IWW did what other American unions refused to do. It opened its doors to all: Negro and Asian, Jew and Catholic, immigrant and native. Wobbly locals had no closed membership rolls, no apprenticeship regulations. As West Coast organizer George Speed put it: ". . . One man is as good as another to me; I don't care whether he is black, blue, green, or yellow, as long as he acts the man and acts true to his economic interests as a worker."[9]

The disinherited joined the IWW by the thousands because it offered them "a ready made dream of a new world where there is a new touch with sweetness and light and where for a while they can escape the torture of forever being indecently kicked about." Or, as Carleton Parker discovered of his wandering rank and file, the IWW offered "the only social break in the harsh search for work that they have ever had; its headquarters the only competitor of the saloon in which they are welcome. They listen stolidly to their frequent lecturers with an obvious and sustained interest . . . the concrete details of industrial renovation find eager interest."[10]

Most important of all, the IWW promised its members a way out of their respective "cultures of poverty." "When the poor become class-conscious or active members of trade-union organizations," Lewis notes, "they are no longer part of the culture of poverty." He adds: "Any movement . . . which organizes and gives hope to the poor and effectively promotes solidarity and a sense of identification with larger groups, destroys the psychological and social core of the culture of poverty." That is just what the IWW attempted to do, as it sought to improve the self-image and self-respect of its members. Wobblies instilled among their alienated following what Lewis found Castro offering the Cuban peasants: ". . . a new sense of power and importance. They were armed and were given a doctrine which glorified the lower class as the hope of humanity."[11]

But, as Rexford Tugwell perceptively noted in 1920, the revolutionary potential of the poor in America is limited. "No world regenerating philosophy comes out of them and they are not going to inherit the earth. When we are a bit more orderly they will disappear."[12] When Tugwell wrote those lines, the IWW had been fatally weakened by federal and state repression. Yet for a time, from 1909 to 1917, the IWW seemed well on the way to organizing the revolutionary potential of the poor.

The IWW's ideologues, as suggested earlier, had few original thoughts about the nature of society, the place of workers within it, or the manner by which society changes. For social theory and its economic foundations they turned, as we have seen, to the writings of others, particularly Marx and Darwin. Yet they also drew upon an older American tradition, dating back to the era of Jefferson and Jackson, which divided society into producers and nonproducers, productive classes and parasites.

Wobblies never questioned the labor theory of value, or the other basic tenets of Marxian economics. Indeed, since labor created all value, the worker was robbed when (as under capitalism) he did not receive the money equivalent of his full product. Capitalism and thievery were thus synonymous: profits represented the capitalist's seizure of his worker's surplus value. This robbery could end only with the abolition of capitalism.[13]

Like Marx, the Wobblies also believed that the working class, or proletariat, would rise up in wrath and destroy the capitalists. Like Marx, they asserted that capitalism carried the seeds of its own destruction, and that workers would create "the new society within the shell of the old." Like Marx, again, they saw in the class struggle "the relentless logic of history," which would roll on until, as the IWW proclaimed in its preamble, ". . . the workers of the world organize as a class, take possession of the earth and the machinery of production and abolish the wage system."

The IWW was never precise in its definition of class. Sometimes Wobblies divided society into two classes: capitalists and workers; sometimes they perceived distinct and separate sub-classes within the two major categories; and sometimes they followed Haywood's example of dividing "all the world into three parts: the capitalists, who are the employing class that makes money out of money; the skilled laborers; and the masses."[14] The IWW, of course, represented the masses who would act as the agents of the new and better social order.

Wobblies also reversed common American assumptions about the applicability of Darwinian evolution to social change. Carrying the theory of biological evolution over into social analysis enabled many Americans to conclude that the wealthy had risen to the top of the economic heap solely as a result of their fitness in the struggle for business survival; conversely, failure, poverty, and dependence were signs of unfitness. Eric Goldman has called this ideology conservative Darwinism, in contradistinction to reform Darwinism, the ideology which used the theory of biological evolution to promote reform and attack the status quo.[15] If Goldman's concept of conservative versus reform Darwinism has any validity, then Wobblies may properly be termed radical, or revolutionary, Darwinists. For IWW ideology began with the belief that "social evolution differs in no essential respect from organic evolution." "The central fact or principle which we cannot ignore except at our own peril," wrote Ben Williams, "is the fact of social evolution, which is not always a direct or simple process, but often a slow, painful, and tortuous course of human development with the wrecks of social experiments scattered along the way." Whatever the perils along the way, the IWW sought to ride the evolutionary wave of the future. In the IWW's amalgam of Marxism and Darwinism, capitalism was the stage preceding the establishment of the workers' paradise. As Ben Williams expressed it: "Trustified American Capital leads the world. The I.W.W. aims to trustify American labor." In the IWW's view, since the working class was most fit, its mode of organization would be superior to that of the capitalists, and thus would enable the IWW to build its new order within the shell of the old.[16] Thus was social Darwinism stood on its head; thus would the beaten become the fit; thus would the slaves become the masters.

Wobblies glorified themselves as the saviors of society. The IWW perceived in America's disinherited the raw material for the transformation of a basically sick society. Writing to the *Industrial Worker* from a Louisiana jail, the organizer E. F. Doree was moved to poetry: "Arise like lions after slumber / In unvanquishable number. / Shake your chains to earth like dew / Which in sleep have falled on you. / Ye are many, they are few." John Sandgren added: "The world is gone mad. We are the only sane people on earth. The future belongs to us."[17] IWW ideology, in essence, saw America's downtrodden masses, no longer satisfied with mere crumbs from their masters' abundant tables, emerging from the abyss of society to seize for themselves the world of industry. "We are many," proclaimed *Solidarity*. "We are resourceful; we are animated by the most glorious vision of the ages; we cannot be conquered, and *we shall conquer the world for the working class.*" Listen to our song, urged the paper, printing the IWW's own version of the "Internationale":

> Arise, ye prisoners of starvation!
> Arise, ye wretched of the earth!
> For Justice thunders condemnation.
> A better world's in birth.
> No more tradition's chains shall bind us;
> Arise, ye slaves! No more in thrall!
> The earth shall stand on new foundations;
> We have been *naught*—We shall be *All!*
> 'Tis the final conflict!
> Let each stand in his place.
> The Industrial Union
> Shall be the Human Race.[18]

The song epitomizes the IWW's ultimate objectives: a combination of primitive millennarianism and modern revolutionary goals. "The essence of millennarianism," Eric Hobsbawm writes, "is the hope of a complete and radical change in the world which will be reflected in the millennium, a world shorn of all its present deficiencies . . ."[19] It seems clear that the IWW shared with primitive millennarians an instinctive distaste for the world as it was, as well as hope for the creation of a completely new world. But the Wobblies had rejected the apocalyptic Judeo-Christian vision of the way in which the millennial society would be established. In its place they substituted more earth-bound ideas about how to topple the old order and create the new one. Modern revolutionary movements—Marxism and syndicalism especially—would be the means to achieve what Hobsbawm calls "the transfer of power." Yet Wobblies always remained more vague about the processes of revolution than the Marxists, and never abandoned primitive millennarian dreams of a final conflict, a Judgment Day when the exploiters would be turned out and the banner of Industrial Freedom raised over the workshops of the world "in a free society of men and women . . ."[20]

Notwithstanding this belief in ultimate revolution, the IWW constantly sought opportunities to improve the immediate circumstances of its members. Speakers and publications emphasized a twofold purpose: "First, to improve conditions for the working class day by day. Second, to build up an organization that can take possession of the industries and run them for the benefit of the workers when capitalism shall have been overthrown." Or as William D. Haywood phrased it in testimony before the Commission on Industrial Relations: "I don't think that I presented any Utopian ideas. I talked for the necessities of life, food, clothing, shelter, and amusement. We can talk of Utopia afterwards."[21] For, as St. John insisted, before it could have utopia the IWW must necessarily handle the workers' everyday problems: shorter hours, better wages, and improved shop conditions. A Wobbly organizer said simply: "The final aim . . . is revolution. But for the present *let's see if we can get a bed to sleep in, water enough to take a bath and decent food to eat . . .*"[22]

But utopia and revolution always lurked just beneath the surface. To the convinced Wobbly, each battle, whether for higher wages or shorter hours, better food or better bedding, prepared the participant for the final struggle with the master class. Only by daily fights with the employer could a strong revolutionary organization be formed. ". . . The very fights themselves, like the drill of an army, prepare the workers for ever greater tasks and victories."[23]

IWW leaders made no bones about their quarrel with other labor leaders who contented themselves with wringing short-term concessions from employers. Joe Ettor proudly proclaimed the IWW's unwillingness to subvert its ideas, make peace with employers, or sign protocols and contracts. Like Marx, he said, "we disdain to conceal our views, we openly declare that our ends can be attained only by the forcible overthrow of all existing conditions." "Big Jim" Larkin, émigré Irish labor leader and in 1914 a new recruit to the IWW, gloried in the IWW's refusal to endorse the palliatives and outworn nostrums (arbitration, time agreements, and protocols) proposed by the "sycophants masquerading as labor leaders, whose sole purpose in life seems to be apologizing for and defending the capitalist system of exploitation." The IWW, Larkin averred, "true to its mission as the pioneer movement of the newer time . . . advocates perpetual war, and the total abolition of wage slavery that blights humanity." Organizer James Thompson reminded government investigators that "the I.W.W. is aiming not only to better our condition now but to prepare for the revolution." He warned businessmen: "You are doomed. The best thing you can do is to look for a soft place to fall."[24]

Only the revolution could produce the dream which inspired Haywood:

> . . . I have had a dream that I have in the morning and at night and during the day, that is that there will be a new society sometime in which there will be no battle between capitalist and wage earner . . . there will be no political government . . . but . . . experts will come together for the purpose of discussing the welfare of all the people and discussing the means by which the machinery can be made the slave of the people instead of a part of the people being made the slave of machinery . . .

Haywood's dream also included a day when no child would labor, when all men would work—either with brain or with muscle—when women would be fully emancipated from bondage to men, and when every aged man and woman would have at least the assurance of dying in peace.[25]

Unlike primitive millennarians, Wobblies did not expect their revolution to come about through "a divine revelation . . . an announcement from on high [or] . . . a miracle." Furthermore, they expected neither the inevitable Marxist class struggle nor the ineluctible Darwinian evolution of society alone to make their revolution. Inevitable it was, but they could assist the course of history. "Our organization is not content with merely making the prophecy," asserted *Solidarity,* "but acts upon industrial and social conditions with a view to shaping them in accord with the general tendency."[26]

To make history, as Marx advised all good radicals to do, the Wobblies followed the pattern of modern revolutionaries: they proposed a program, developed a doctrine concerning the transfer of power, and elaborated a system of organization. But unlike most other modern revolutionaries, with the exception of the anarcho-syndicalists whom they resembled, Wobblies excluded politics from any role in their struggle for utopia.

The Wobblies believed they could best make history by seizing power. He who held power ruled society. The IWW proposed to transfer power from the capitalists, who used it for anti-social purposes, to the proletariat, who, they fondly believed, would exercise it for the benefit of humanity.

In *The Iron Heel,* a novel well known to Wobblies, Jack London expressed better than any IWW pamphlet the organization's notions about power. Ernest Everhardt, London's fictional Haywood, responds to a capitalist adversary who has just given him a lesson in *realpolitik:* "Power. It is what we of the working class preach. We know and well we know by bitter experience, that no appeal for the right, for justice, can ever touch you. . . . So we have preached power." "Power will be the arbiter," Everhardt proceeds, "as it has always been the arbiter. . . . We of the labor hosts have conned that word over till our minds are all a-tingle with it. Power. It is a kingly word."[27]

The IWW's gospelers with their doctrine of power made a great deal of sense to men in the social jungle who saw naked force—by employers, police, and courts—constantly used against them. When an IWW pamphlet proclaimed, "It is the law of nature that the strong rule and the weak are enslaved," Wobblies simply recognized the reality of their own lives writ large. George Speed, an admired IWW organizer, expressed their emotions tersely. "Power," he said, "is the thing that determines everything today . . . it stands to reason that the fellow that has got the big club swings it over the balance. That is life as it exists today." When Speed asserted that neither socialism nor politics nor legislation could aid the Wobblies, and that they would suffer until they learned the uses of power, he made sense to those he represented.[28]

The IWW's antipathy toward political action also made sense to its members. Migratory workers moved too often to establish legal voting residences. Millions of immigrants lacked the franchise, as did the Negroes, the women, and the child workers to whom the IWW appealed. Even those immigrants and natives in the IWW ranks who had the right to vote nourished a deep suspicion of government. To them the policeman's club and the magistrate's edict symbolized the state's alliance with entrenched privilege. Who knew the injustices of the state better than a Wobbly imprisoned for exercising his right of free speech, or clubbed by bullying policemen while picketing peacefully for higher wages? Daily experience demonstrated the truth of Elizabeth Gurley Flynn's comment that the state was simply the slugging agency of the capitalists. Or, as *Solidarity* phrased it: all governments in history "have become cruel, corrupt, decayed and perished by reason of their own internal defects. To this rule the government of the United States is no exception."[29] Hence, Wobblies refused to believe that stuffing pieces of paper—even socialist ones—into a box would transform the basically repressive institution of the state into a humane one.

Even the wonderful list of reform legislation enacted during the Progressive years did not impress Wobblies. When IWW members were reminded of marvelous labor reforms newly placed on the statute books, their reply was: "How are they *enforced?*" To Wobblies, as to most other trade unionists, labor legislation was worthless without the organized power to enforce it on the job. Wobblies were as perceptive as AFL members in realizing that American workers were more concerned with what went on at the plant than with what transpired in the state capitol, that they cared more about a higher wage and a more secure job than about a Democratic or a Republican—or even a Socialist—victory.

By thus refusing to endorse political parties, the IWW did not, as Philip Foner asserts, divorce itself from the mainstream of the American labor movement. Quite the contrary. The IWW's political position brought the organization closer to the masses to whom it appealed and more in harmony with the attitude of AFL members—those to whom the political party and the state always remained a distant and fearful enemy.

Representing workers who could not conceive of political power as a means to alter the rules of the game, Wobblies had to offer an alternative. This they discovered in economic power. Naively believing themselves better Marxists than their socialist critics, Wobblies insisted that political power was but a reflex of economic power, and that without economic organization behind it, labor politics was "like a house without a foundation or a dream without substance."[30] IWW leaders concentrated on teaching their followers how to obtain economic power. To quote some of their favorite aphorisms: "Get it through industrial organization"; "Organize the workers to control the use of their labor power"; "The secret of power is organization"; "The only force that can break . . . tyrannical rule . . . is the one big union of all the workers."[31]

From the IWW point of view, direct action was the essential means for bringing its new society into existence. As defined by Wobblies, direct action included any step taken by workers at the point of production which improved wages, reduced hours, and bettered conditions. It encompassed conventional strikes, intermittent strikes, silent strikes, passive resistance, sabotage, and the ultimate direct-action measure: the general strike which would displace the capitalists from power and place the means of production in working-class hands.[32] "Shall I tell you what direct action really means?" an IWW manifesto asked. "The worker on the job shall tell the boss when and where he shall work, how long, and for what wages and under what conditions." Direct action, according to Haywood, would eventually reach the point at which workers would be strong enough to say: "Here, Mr. Stockholder, we won't work for you any longer. You have drawn dividends out of our hides long enough; we propose that you shall go to work now and under the same opportunities that we have had."[33]

The emphasis on direct action in preference to parliamentary politics or socialist dialectics represented a profound insight by IWW leaders into the minds of industrial workers and inhabitants of the "culture of poverty." Abstract doctrine meant nothing to the disinherited; specific grievances meant everything! Justus Ebert expressed this idea for the IWW:

> Workingmen on the job don't care a whoop in hell for free love . . . they are not interested in why Bakunin was fired from the International by Marx . . . nor do they care about the co-operative commonwealth; they want practical organization first, all else after. They want to know how they can win out against the trusts and the bosses. . . . Give us specific shop methods. We plead for them.[34]

Richard Brazier on the West Coast echoed Ebert's plea. He asked fellow Wobblies to stop telling men to stay away from bum jobs; instead, Brazier urged workers to take such jobs and fight. The Philadelphia Longshoremen, an IWW affiliate which successfully used direct action and actually controlled job conditions, urged: "We have work to do. We function as a job organization and have no time to split hairs. Job control is the thing."[35] How much like the AFL!

But while the IWW's emphasis on direct action, job control, and economic power resembled the AFL's line, the Wobblies' rhetoric was of an entirely different order. Restrained in action, Wobblies were considerably less restrained in utterance. Where the

AFL spoke cautiously of law and order, the IWW exuberantly discussed the law of the jungle. Where the AFL pleaded for contracts and protocols, the IWW hymned clubs and brute force. Where the AFL sought industrial harmony, the IWW praised perpetual industrial war.

Consequently, it became easy for critics of the IWW, whether on the right or the left, to listen to Wobbly speakers, to read Wobbly propaganda, and to conclude that the IWW actually *preferred* bullets to ballots, dynamite to mediation. After all, Wobblies constantly announced that their organization respected neither the property rights of capitalists nor the laws they made. *"I despise the law,"* Haywood defiantly informed a Socialist party audience, "and I am not a law-abiding citizen. And more than that, no Socialist *can* be a law-abiding citizen." Equally defiant, he told the Commission on Industrial Relations: ". . . I have been plastered up with injunctions until I do not need a suit of clothes, and I have treated them with contempt." He warned Socialist party members fearful of breaking the law and going to prison: "Those of us who are in jail—those of us who have been in jail—all of us who are willing to go to jail care not what you say or what you do! We despise your hypocrisy. . . . We are the Revolution!"[36]

Wobblies even enjoyed comparing themselves to antebellum abolitionists, who also had defied laws which sanctioned human bondage, and who had publicly burned the Constitution. As James Thompson boasted: "We are the modern abolitionists fighting against wage slavery."[37] Some Wobblies may indeed have considered unsheathing the Lord's terrible swift sword. St. John, for one, admitted under questioning that he would counsel destruction of property and violence against persons if it accomplished improvement for the workers and brought the revolution closer. Other IWW leaders conceded they would be willing to dynamite factories and mills in order to win a strike. All of them hurled their defiance at "bushwa" law.[38]

Such talk led most Americans to conclude, as did Harris Weinstock of the Federal Commission on Industrial Relations, that "it is the organized and deliberate purpose of the I.W.W. to teach and preach and to burn into the hearts and minds of its followers that they are justified in lying; that they are justified in stealing and in trampling under foot their own agreements and in confiscating the property of others . . . that it would make a Nation of thieves and liars and scoundrels."[39]

Having created this image of itself, the IWW simultaneously tried to dispel it. To the convinced Wobbly, Weinstock's words better described the practices and attitudes of the American capitalist. Although the IWW employed the vocabulary of violence, more often than not it practiced passive resistance, and was itself the victim of violence instigated by law-enforcement officials and condoned by the law-abiding. In fact, even the Wobblies' vocabulary was ambivalent, the language of nonviolence being employed at least as frequently as that of violence. Big Bill Haywood, for example, whose career with the WFM had been associated with labor violence, told a reporter during the 1912 Lawrence textile strike: "I should never think of conducting a strike in the old way. . . . I, for one, have turned my back on violence. It wins nothing. When we strike now, we strike with our hands in our pockets. We have a new kind of violence—the havoc we raise with money by laying down our tools. Pure strength lies in the overwhelming power of numbers."[40]

Any careful investigator of the IWW soon becomes aware that the organization regularly proclaimed the superiority of passive resistance over the use of dynamite or guns. Vincent St. John, while conceding the possible usefulness of violence under certain circumstances, nevertheless insisted: "We do not . . . want to be understood as saying that we expect to achieve our aims through violence and through the destruction of human life, because in my judgment, that is impossible." Joe Ettor similarly commented: ". . . We are organized against violence and our war cry is 'War against war.' " Haywood remarked in 1912 that he regarded hunger strikes as "action more violent than the discharge of bombs in St. Patrick's Cathedral."[41] Big Bill now looked forward to a "bloodless revolution."

Solidarity, the *Industrial Worker,* and IWW pamphlets all preached the same nonviolent message. The *Industrial Worker* cautioned members against being misled by *agents provocateurs* into resorting to violent means of economic action. *Solidarity* noted: "The revolutionary industrial union promises the only possible safeguard against violence in industrial warfare." Sometimes it puts its position another way: "Our dynamite is mental and our force is in organization at the point of production." Again and again IWW publications advised members: *"We do not advocate violence;* it is to be discouraged."[42]

In actuality, Wobblies looked to *non*violent tactics in order to throw into sharper relief the brutality of their enemy, and to win sympathy for their sufferings. Passive resistance, *Solidarity* editorialized, "has a tremendous moral effect; it puts the enemy on record; it exposes the police and city authorities as a bunch of law breakers; it drives the masters to the last ditch of resistance. 'Passive resistance' by the workers results in laying bare the inner workings and purposes of the capitalist mind. It also reveals the self-control, the fortitude, the courage, the inherent sense of order, of the workers' mind. As such, 'passive resistance' is of immense educational value."[43]

But IWW passive resistance should not be confused with pacifism. Nonviolence was only a means, never an end. If passive resistance resulted only in beatings and deaths, then the IWW threatened to respond in kind. Arturo Giovannitti, sometime poet and Wobbly, put the IWW's position bluntly: "The generally accepted notion seems to be that to kill is a great crime, but to be killed is the greatest." Haywood cited Abraham Lincoln's alleged advice to citizens suffering from hunger as a result of wartime food speculation: "Take your pickaxes and crowbars and go to the granaries and warehouses and help yourselves . . ." That, said Haywood, "is good I.W.W. doctrine."[44]

In most cases the IWW hoped to gain its ends through nonviolent measures, through what it described as "Force of education, force of organization, force of a growing class-consciousness and force of working class aspirations for freedom."[45] One forceful method explicitly advocated by the Wobblies—indeed, the tactic with which they are most indelibly associated—was sabotage. To most Americans, sabotage implied the needless destruction of property, the senseless adulteration of products, and, possibly, the inexcusable injuring of persons. Wobblies did not always dispel such images. The *Industrial Worker* suggested to harvest hands in 1910: "Grain sacks come loose and rip, nuts come off wagon wheels and loads are dumped on the way to the barn, machinery breaks down, nobody to blame, everybody innocent . . . boss decides to furnish a little inspiration in the shape of more money and shorter hours . . . just try a little sabotage on the kind hearted, benevolent boss . . . and see how it works." For the next three years the paper continued to urge this method upon its readers, telling them: "Sabotage is an awakening of labor. It is the spirit of revolt." This campaign culminated in 1913 with a series of twelve editorials fully explaining the methods of sabotage and when they should be utilized.[46]

Eastern Wobblies proved no less restrained in their emphasis on sabotage. Haywood informed the same Socialist party audience mentioned above, which he had encouraged to break the law: "I don't know of anything that can be applied that will bring as much anguish to the boss as a little sabotage in the right place at the proper time. Find out what it means. It won't hurt you, and it will cripple the boss." To help Wobblies find out what sabotage meant, Elizabeth Gurley Flynn prepared a new translation of Emile Pouget's classic, *Sabotage,* which the IWW published and distributed in 1915. Even Ben Williams, generally unenthusiastic about the effectiveness of sabotage, felt constrained to recommend its use. "Sabotage has great possibilities as a means of defense and aggression," he explained. "It is useless to try to argue it out of existence. We need not 'advocate it,' we need only explain it. The organized workers will do the acting."[47]

What was actually meant by all this talk? Some Wobblies might have agreed with James Thompson, who said, ". . . I not only believe in destruction of property, but I believe in the destruction of human life if it will save human life." But most stressed sabotage's nonviolent characteristics. Repeatedly, IWW speakers asserted that sabotage simply implied soldiering on the job, playing dumb, tampering with machines without destroying them—in short, simply harassing the employer to the point of granting his workers' demands. Sometimes, it was claimed, the workers could even effect sabotage through exceptional obedience: Williams and Haywood were fond of noting that Italian and French workers had on occasion tied up the national railroads simply by observing every operating rule in their work regulations. They suggested that laborers refuse to cooperate in the adulteration of products, and that labor unions warn consumers against purchasing inferior goods. That, the Wobblies argued, was benevolent sabotage: *"sabotage not aimed at the consumer but at the heart and soul of the employing class—the pocketbook."*[48]

One might scarcely expect the typical Wobbly to comprehend the subtleties of nonviolent as compared to violent sabotage. Sabotage, after all, is a weapon of the disorganized, the defeated, the dejected, and, as such, it must have had great appeal to workers drawn from the "culture of poverty." What better way to strike back against one's enemy than to destroy what he most worships —in this case, private property! Yet, hard as they tried, state and federal authorities could never establish legal proof of IWW-instigated sabotage. Rudolph Katz, a De Leonite who had followed his leader out of the St. John IWW in 1908, was perhaps close to the truth when he informed federal investigators: ". . . The American Federation of Labor does not preach sabotage, but it practices sabotage; and the . . . I.W.W. preaches sabotage, but does not practice it."[49]

Wobbly ideology and tactics explained why Katz was right. In revealing testimony before the Commission on Industrial Relations, Jim Thompson declared: "The greatest weapon in the hands of the working class is economic power. . . . All we have to do is fold our arms and industry is paralyzed. . . . I would much prefer as a lesson to . . . other workers . . . instead of destroying the street car in times of a street car strike that they should stop that car by shutting off the juice at the power house. That would be a lesson." Ben Williams phrased this attitude simply: "Organized a little we control a little; organized more we control more; organized as a class we control everything."[50]

Until the IWW succeeded in organizing all workers into industrial unions which combined to form the celebrated "One Big Union" which would eventually seize control of industry, it had to employ practices and tactics much like those of any labor union. Accordingly, the IWW encouraged strikes to win immediate improvements in working conditions, for such strikes served a dual purpose: they offered the men involved valuable experience in the class struggle and developed their sense of *power,* and they weakened the capitalist's power. When conventional strikes failed, the IWW recommended the on-the-job strike—essentially a form of nonviolent sabotage—and the intermittent or short strike begun when the boss least expected it and ended before the strikers could be starved or beaten.[51]

The IWW never lost its vision of the ultimate revolution. Thus, many demands associated with AFL industrial conflicts were absent from those of the IWW. With improvements in working conditions, the AFL unions demanded recognition and ironclad contracts. The IWW spurned both. It would achieve its closed shop "by having an 'open union' for everybody who toils." In other words, collective action and voluntary cooperation by the exploited, not capitalist concessions, would bring the true closed shop. Wobblies were convinced that employer benevolence only lessened working-class solidarity. For somewhat similar reasons, the IWW refused to sign contracts which restricted the right to strike for stated periods of time. All workers had to retain the right to strike simultaneously, the IWW reasoned, or employers could play one group of workers off against another, as had happened time and again in the AFL's history. No agreement could be allowed to impinge upon the IWW's governing principle: "An injury to one is the concern of all." Workers, moreover, had to be free to strike when employers were weakest, but time contracts provided employers with the option to choose the moment of conflict and to prepare for it in advance. Finally, without the unreserved right to strike, the IWW could not wage the class war, and without the ongoing class struggle there could be no revolution and no cooperative commonwealth.[52]

But even on the issue of time contracts the IWW could be ambivalent, conceding the possibility that it might sign agreements which concerned only wages, hours, and conditions of work. Nevertheless, it regularly reiterated its belief that employers had no rights that workers were obliged to respect. "The contract between an employer and a workman is no more binding than the title deed to a negro slave is just."[53]

The organization's refusal to sign contracts raised problems that the IWW never resolved. American employers were never particularly happy dealing with labor unions, and certainly under no circumstances would they negotiate with a labor organization that refused to sign contracts and insisted that capitalists had no rights worthy of respect. Hence, employers constantly used the IWW's no-contract principle to rationalize their own resistance to any form of collective bargaining. If the IWW could not negotiate with employers, how could it raise wages or improve working conditions? If it could offer its members nothing but perpetual industrial warfare, how could it maintain its membership, let alone increase its ranks? On the other hand, if the IWW did sanction contracts, win recognition, and improve its members' lives, what would keep them from forsaking revolutionary goals and adhering to the well-established AFL pattern? If the IWW began to declare truces in the class war, how could it bring about the ultimate revolution? In the end, IWW leaders usually subordinated reform opportunities to revolutionary necessities, while the rank and file, when it could, took the reforms and neglected the revolution.

Even for those Wobblies who cherished the hope of revolution, the means of achieving their dream remained vague. Politics or working-class violence would not accomplish it. What, then, remained? "In a word," wrote Haywood and Ettor, "the general strike is the measure by which the capitalistic system will be overthrown."[54]

Neither Haywood nor any other Wobbly ever precisely defined the general strike. Haywood described it as the stoppage of all work and the destruction of the capitalists through a peaceful paralysis of industry. Ben Williams insisted that it was not a strike at all, simply "a 'general lockout of the employing class' leaving the workers in possession of the machinery of distribution and production." Whatever the exact definition of the general strike, Haywood wrote, when its day comes ". . . control of industry will pass from the capitalists to the masses and capitalists will vanish from the face of the earth."[55] That utopian day would come peaceably if workers had their way, violently if capitalists attempted to postpone it with "roar of shell and whine of machine-guns."

The precise date of the general strike which would usher in the arrival of the IWW's utopia remained as vague for Wobblies as the millennium, or Judgment Day, does for Christians. But the *prospect* of such a Judgment Day was intended to stir among the toiling masses the same ecstatic belief and fanaticism that anticipation of the Second Coming arouses among evangelical Christians. Only with such true believers could the IWW build its One Big Union which would, when fully organized, ring the death knell for American capitalism. In other words, in IWW ideology workers represented a chosen people who, through faith and works—faith in the One Big Union and such works as peaceful sabotage—would attain salvation and enter the Kingdom of Heaven here on earth.

In a jail cell in Aberdeen, Washington, John Pancner dreamed the pleasures of an IWW utopia, where there would be no poverty, jails, police, army, or marines; no Christians, no churches, no heaven or hell. The cities would be clean and beautiful, filled with wide streets, parks, flowers, and fine homes; the workers would be "no longer stoop shouldered and consumptive looking . . ." Prudery would have vanished, and naked children would frisk on the grass and bask in the sun. Economic freedom, plus an abundance of food, shelter, clothing, leisure, and education, would lead "all hearts and minds . . . [to] turn . . . towards solving the mysteries of the Universe."[56]

Wobblies never quite explained how their terrestrial paradise would be governed. They did agree that the state, as most Americans knew it, would be nonexistent. "There will be no such thing as the State or States," Haywood said. "The industries will take the place of what are now existing States." "Whenever the workers are organized in the industry, whenever they have a sufficient organization in the industry," added St. John, "they will have all the government they need right there." Somehow each industrial union would possess and manage its own industry. Union members would elect superintendents, foremen, secretaries, and all the managers of modern industry. The separate industrial unions would also meet jointly to plan for the welfare of the entire society. This system, "in which each worker will have a share in the ownership and a voice in the control of industry, and in which each shall receive the full product of his labor," was variously called the "Cooperative Commonwealth," the "Workers' Commonwealth," the "Industrial Commonwealth," "Industrial Democracy," and "Industrial Communism."[57] Unsure of what their system was, the Wobblies could not label it.

Perhaps Ben Williams came closest to describing how the IWW commonwealth would function. Writing primarily about city government, Williams suggested that every aspect of urban life would be managed by different groups of municipal workers, "their efforts being correlated by whatever central body they may find necessary. The members of that central body will not be 'placemen' or 'politicians,' but *technical experts,* trained for that special service" [italics added]. Haywood also foresaw a future society molded and managed by experts in the different branches of industry, "brain workers" who directed the activities of scientifically organized laborers.[58]

A future society based upon "brain workers," technical experts, and scientific controls resembled St. Simon's ideal state or Bellamy's society of the year 2000 more than it did the Marxian "dictatorship of the proletariat," or the revisionist socialist's equalitarian parliamentary society. It was this aspect of the IWW, combined with its abiding distrust of political parties and the state, which made the American Industrial Workers so much like the continental European syndicalists of the same era.

It was in their views about the general strike and the governance of utopia that Wobblies diverged farthest from the modern revolutionary spirit, for these two vital matters were indeed left as vague as the primitive millennarians' eschatology. How the IWW expected to displace capitalism from power peaceably, when the masters of "The Iron Heel" couched their answer in "roar of shell and whine of machine-guns," advocates of the general strike failed to explain. How the IWW would defend its utopia from counterrevolutionary terror, supporters of its syndicalist commonwealth never clarified. Like primitive millennarians, but unlike modern revolutionaries, Wobblies almost expected their revolution to make itself, if not by divine revelation, at least by a miracle (secular, of course). Some Wobblies even saw the roots of their doctrine in the works of the "Hobo Carpenter from Nazareth," whose call, "stripped of the mystical and mythical veil of Constantine and his successors, and clothed in the original garb of communism and brotherhood, continues to sound intermittently across the ages."[59]

While IWW ideology derived much of its spirit from Socialist party doctrine, the two maintained only an uneasy harmony. Both Wobblies and Socialists drew their inspiration from similar ideological sources, both opposed the capitalist order, and both demanded the establishment of a just and equalitarian new order. Beyond that, they conflicted more often than they agreed.

Industrial unionism, Haywood once said, was socialism with its working clothes on. But after 1913, when Haywood was recalled from the Socialist party's National Executive Committee, IWW industrial unionists and American Socialists had little in common. When Socialists talked of capturing control of existing government through the ballot box and transforming the capitalist state into the Cooperative Commonwealth, the IWW responded with a proverb: "A wise tailor does not put stitches into rotten cloth."

To American Socialists who prided themselves on their intellectual abilities, Haywood asserted: "Socialism is so plain, so clear, so simple that when a person becomes an intellectual he doesn't understand socialism."[60]

In short, American Socialists, optimistic about their future prospects and eager to widen the popular base of their party, subordinated revolutionary fervor to the cause of immediate reform and popular acceptance. Wobblies, more pessimistic about the future and more respectful of capitalism's staying power, tried to instill revolutionary fervor in their adherents. The Socialist party, unlike the IWW, had no room for men who counseled defiance of the law, neglect of the ballot box, and "real" revolution. Hence Haywood's recall from the National Executive Committee in 1913. After that date, though some "left-wing" Socialists still looked to the IWW as the hope of the working class and the vanguard of revolution, most Socialists and Wobblies went their own separate ways—ideologically as well as organizationally.[61]

Actually, as Will Herberg perceptively pointed out more than fifteen years ago, the IWW was much more the left wing of the American labor movement than of the socialist movement. Herberg emphasized that the AFL's early approach, "with its stress on proletarian direct action and its marked distrust of government and politics, shows definite affinity to basic syndicalism. It differs from the more familiar radical variety of syndicalism in very much the same way as the gradualistic socialism of Eduard Bernstein differed from the revolutionary socialism of his orthodox opponents."[62] What Bernstein and evolutionary socialism were to Marx and revolutionary socialism, Gompers and the AFL were to St. John, Haywood, and radical syndicalism.

Indeed, the IWW *was* the American variety of the syndicalism which at that time was sweeping across the Italian, French, and Scandinavian labor movements. There is no escaping the similarities. Even when the IWW denied its syndicalist nature, it would simultaneously counsel syndicalist principles. One editorialist, for example, while maintaining that the IWW was not a syndicalist organization but an industrial union, went on to assert: "Industrial unionism accepts all of the syndicalist tactics that experience has shown to be available for present purposes." Despite the fuzzy-mindedness of some Wobbly thinkers, there was absolutely no incompatibility between industrial unionism and syndicalism. The

IWW even took over George Sorel's syndicalist concept of the militant minority, claiming in the words of the *Industrial Worker:* "Our task is to develop the conscious, intelligent minority to the point where they will be capable of carrying out the imperfectly expressed desires of the toiling millions," who were still "hopelessly stupid and stupidly hopeless."[63] Whenever some Wobblies attempted to dispute their organization's syndicalist tendencies, other more perceptive members stressed the IWW's basic similarity to European syndicalism. John Sandgren, a Swedish immigrant and IWW theorist who maintained close contact with the labor movement of his native land, tried to impress upon Wobblies their obvious likeness to Scandinavian syndicalists. The Socialist Robert Rives LaMonte, while acknowledging that "because Revolutionary Unionism is the child of economic and political conditions, it differs in different countries," nevertheless firmly asserted: "In spite of superficial differences this living spirit of revolutionary purpose unifies French and British syndicalism and American Industrial Unionism. To forget or even make light of this underlying identity can but substitute muddle-headed confusion for clear thinking."[64] Finally, John Spargo's 1913 definition of syndicalism clearly encompasses the IWW's mode of operation. Syndicalism, he wrote,

> is a form of labor unionism which aims at the abolition of the capitalist system. . . . Its distinctive principle as a practical movement is that these ends are to be attained by the direct action of the unions, without parliamentary action or the intervention of the State. The distinctive feature of its ideal is that in the new social order the political state will not exist, the only form of government being the administration of industry directly by the workers themselves.[65]

Certainly nobody should expect American syndicalism to be precisely like that of France or Italy; also, nobody should seek to explain the emergence of syndicalism in America, as does Philip Foner, by tracing its roots to Europe and then treating it as a foreign import transplanted to fertile native soil.

In the final analysis, ideological disputation remained a form of academic nitpicking to most Wobblies, for the organization always appealed to the activist rather than the intellectual. It sought to motivate the disinherited, not to satisfy the ideologue. As an

IWW member, reviewing John Graham Brooks's *American Syndicalism,* noted: "It is not the Sorels . . . the Wallings, LaMontes and such figures who count the most—it is the obscure Bill Jones on the firing line, with stink in his clothes, rebellion in his brain, hope in his heart, determination in his eye and direct action in his gnarled fist."[66] To such as "Bill Jones" the IWW carried its gospel from 1909 to 1917.

In their analyses of the IWW's eventful history, several scholars have concluded that had it not been for America's entry into World War I and the repression of the organization that ensued, the IWW might well have usurped the CIO's subsequent role in organizing mass-production workers. These scholars believe that the base established by the IWW among harvesters, loggers, and copper miners would have become sufficiently stable, had war not intervened, for the Wobblies later to have penetrated other unorganized sectors of the economy.[67] This rendering of history leads one to conclude that the IWW's ultimate failure was more a result of external repression than of internal inadequacies.

Nothing, of course, need be inevitable. Yet given the internal deficiencies of the IWW, the aspirations of most of its members during the organization's heyday, and the dynamics of American capitalism—what might better be called the "American system"—the Wobblies' attempt to transform American workers into a revolutionary vanguard was doomed to failure. Wobbly doctrine taught workers how to gain short-range goals indistinguishable from those sought by ordinary, non-revolutionary trade unions. Able to rally exploited workers behind crusades to abolish specific grievances, the IWW failed to transform its followers' concrete grievances into a higher consciousness of class, ultimate purpose, and necessary revolution; to create, in short, a revolutionary working class in the Marxist sense. This was so because the IWW never explained precisely how it would achieve its new society—apart from vague allusions to the social general strike and to "building the new society within the shell of the old"—or how, once established, it would be governed. Wobblies simply suggested that the state, at least as most Americans knew it, would disappear. Hence, at their best IWW ideologues offered only warmed-over versions of St. Simon's technocratic society, with gleanings from Edward Bellamy's *Looking Backward*—scarcely a workable prescription for revolution in the modern world. In their imprecise ideology and vague doctrine, the Wobblies too often substituted romantic anarcho-utopianism for hard analysis of social and economic realities.

Even had the IWW had a more palatable prescription for revolution, it is far from likely that its followers would have taken it. In fact, IWW members had limited revolutionary potential. At the IWW's founding convention Haywood had alluded to lifting impoverished Americans up from the gutter. But those lying in Haywood's metaphorical gutters thought only of rising to the sidewalk, and once there of entering the house. Individuals locked in the subculture of poverty share narrow perspectives on life and society; as Oscar Lewis has observed, the main blight of the "culture of poverty is the poverty of its culture."[68] Struggling just to maintain body, such men lacked the time or comfort to worry much about their souls; they could think only of the moment, not the future, only of a better job or more food, not of a distant utopian society.

This placed the IWW in an impossible dilemma. On the one hand, it was committed to ultimate revolution; on the other, it sought immediate improvements for its members. Like all men who truly care about humanity, the Wobblies always accepted betterment for their members today at the expense of achieving utopia tomorrow. This had been true at Lawrence, McKees Rocks, and Paterson, among other places, where the IWW allowed workers to fight for immediate improvements, a result which, if achieved, inevitably diminished their discontent and hence their revolutionary potential. Even at Paterson, where IWW-led strikers failed to win concessions, some Wobblies discerned the dilemma of their position —the leaders' desire for revolution coming up against their members' desire for palpable gains.

Internally, the Wobblies never made up their minds about precisely what kind of structure their organization should adopt. By far the most capable IWW leaders favored an industrial union structure under which largely independent, though not entirely autonomous, affiliates organized by specific industry would cooperate closely with each other under the supervision of an active general executive board. But many lesser leaders, and more among the rank and file, were captivated with the concept of the One Big Union (the mythical OBU) in which workers, regardless of skill, industry, nationality, or color, would be amalgamated into a single unit. Incapable of negotiating union-management agreements owing to its protean character, the OBU would be solely the vessel of revolution. Considering the inherent difficulties involved in organizing unskilled workers on a stable basis, organizational form and structure was an issue of the utmost importance. Yet it remained a problem that the Wobblies never resolved satisfactorily.

This was not the only issue the IWW failed to resolve. Operating in industries traditionally hostile to unionism, Wobblies aggravated hard-core employer prejudices. To employers who rejected negotiations with AFL affiliates that offered to sign and to respect binding legal contracts, the IWW offered unremitting industrial war, for it refused to sign time agreements reached through collective bargaining, and declined to respect labor-management contracts. Hesitant to recognize unions on any basis, management thus had less reason to acknowledge the IWW. If the IWW had had the raw economic power to win concessions without time agreements and written contracts, its policies might have made some sense. But time and again it challenged powerful employers from behind union fortifications erected on sand.

Its mythology concerning rank-and-file democracy—comprising what today is known as "participatory democracy"—further compounded the IWW's internal deficiencies. The IWW had been most successful when led by strong individuals like Haywood, who centralized general headquarters in 1916, or Walter Nef, who constructed a tightly knit and carefully administered Agricultural Workers' Organization. Too often, however, jealous and frustrated Wobblies, lacking the abilities of a Haywood or a Nef, but desiring their power and positions, used the concept of "participatory democracy" to snipe at the IWW's leaders on behalf of an idealized rank and file. And without firm leadership the organization drifted aimlessly.

Even had the IWW combined the necessary structure, the proper tactics, and experienced, capable leaders, as it did for a time from 1915 to 1917, its difficulties might still have proved insurmountable. There is no reason to believe that before the 1930's any of America's basic mass-production industries could have been organized. Not until World War II was the CIO, an organization with immense financial resources, millions of members, and federal encouragement, able to solidify its hold on the nation's mass-production industries. And even then the CIO made no headway among migratory workers or Southern mill hands.[69] What reason, then, is there to think that the IWW could have succeeded in the 1920's or earlier, when it lacked funds, counted its members by the thousands, not the millions, and could scarcely expect government assistance? To ask the question is to answer it.

Yet had the IWW done everything its academic critics ask of it—established true industrial unions, accepted long-term officials and a permanent union bureaucracy, signed collective agreements with employers and agreed to respect them—done, in other words, what the CIO did, what would have remained of its original purpose?[70] Had the founders of the IWW been interested in simply constructing industrial unions on the model of the CIO, the advice of their scholarly critics would be well taken. But the IWW was created by radicals eager to revolutionize American society, and to have asked them to deny their primary values and goals would have been to ask too much.

Whatever the IWW's internal dilemmas, the dynamics of American history unquestionably compounded them. Unlike radicals in other societies who contended with established orders unresponsive to lower-class discontent and impervious to change from within, the Wobblies struggled against flexible and sophisticated adversaries. The years of IWW growth and success coincided with the era when welfare capitalism spread among American businesses, when all levels of government began to exhibit solicitude for the workingman, and when the catalyst of reform altered all aspects of national society. This process became even more pronounced during World War I, when the federal government used its vast power and influence to hasten the growth of welfare capitalism and conservative unionism. Whatever success the Wobblies achieved only stimulated the reform process, for employers who were threatened by the IWW paid greater attention to labor relations, and government agencies, initially called upon to repress labor strife, encouraged employers to improve working conditions. While IWW leaders felt federal repression during World War I, their followers enjoyed eight-hour days, grievance boards, and company unions. Put more simply, reform finally proved a better method than repression for weakening the IWW's appeal to workers.

Although the IWW ultimately failed to achieve its major objectives, it nevertheless bequeathed Americans an invaluable legacy. Those young Americans who practice direct action, passive resistance, and civil disobedience, and who seek an authentic "radical tradition," should find much to ponder in the Wobblies' past. Those who distrust establishment politics, deride bureaucracies, favor community action, and preach "participatory democracy" would also do well to remember the history of the IWW. Indeed, all who prefer a society based upon community to one founded on coercion cannot afford to neglect the tragic history of the IWW.

In this history, two lessons stand out. The first underscores the harsh truth of Antonio Gramsci's comment, quoted earlier, that in advanced industrial nations revolutionaries should take as their slogan: "Pessimism of the Intelligence; Optimism of the Will." The second lesson emphasizes the irony of the radical experience in America, and elsewhere in the Western industrial world. As a result of their commitment to ultimate revolution as well as to immediate improvements in the existence of the working class, radicals the world over quickened the emergence of strong labor unions and acted as midwives at the birth of the "welfare state." But success, instead of breeding more success, only produced a new working class enthralled with a consumer society and only too willing, even eager, to trade working-class consciousness for a middle-class style of life. The ultimate tragedy, then, for all radicals, the American Wobblies included, has been that the brighter they have helped make life for the masses, the dimmer has grown the prospect for revolution in the advanced societies.

Yet no better epitaph could be written for the American Wobbly than A. S. Embree's comment from his prison cell in 1917: "The end in view is well worth striving for, but in the struggle itself lies the happiness of the fighter."

NOTES

1. Lewis S. Gannett, "The I.W.W.," *Nation*, CXI (October 20, 1920), p. 448.

2. Joe Hill to Editor, *Industrial Worker*, May 25, 1911, p. 3; *Final Report and Testimony of the United States Commission on Industrial Relations* (Washington, D.C., 1915), V, pp. 4234–35 (hereafter cited as CIR).

3. B. H. Williams in *Solidarity*, September 14, 1912, p. 2; William E. Bohn, "The I.W.W.," *Survey*, XXVIII (May 4, 1912), p. 221.

4. Rexford G. Tugwell, "The Casual of the Woods," *Survey*, XLIV (July 3, 1920), p. 472; Carleton Parker, "The I.W.W.," *Atlantic Monthly*, CXX (November 1917), pp. 651–62.

5. Oscar Lewis, *La Vida* (New York, 1966), p. xlv.

6. Ibid., p. xliii.

7. E. J. Hobsbawm, *Primitive Rebels and Social Bandits* (New York, 1963), p. 108.

8. Lewis, op. cit., pp. xiv, xlv–xlvi.

9. CIR, V, p. 4947; W. D. Haywood, "To Colored Working Men and Women," *Solidarity*, March 10, 1917, p. 2; *Industrial Worker*, April 29, 1909, p. 4, June 17, 1909, p. 2.

10. R. G. Tugwell to Editor, *Survey*, XLIV (August 16, 1920), pp. 641–42; Parker, op. cit., p. 656.

11. Lewis, op. cit., pp. xlviii–xlix.

12. Tugwell to Editor, *Survey*, XLIV (August 16, 1920), pp. 641–42.

13. *Solidarity*, July 1, 1911, p. 2.

14. Quoted in Arno Dosch, "What the IWW Is," *World's Work*, XXVI (August 1913), p. 417.

15. Eric Goldman, *Rendezvous with Destiny* (New York, 1952), pp. 90–97.

16. Ben H. Williams, "Trends Toward Industrial Freedom," *American Journal of Sociology*, XX (March 1915), p. 627; Williams also in *Solidarity*, April 15, 1911, p. 2, and September 14, 1912, p. 2; John Sandgren, "Industrial Communism," ibid., July 31, 1915, p. 12.

17. E. F. Doree to Fellow Workers, *Industrial Worker*, November 7, 1912, p. 4; Sandgren, op. cit., p. 12.

18. *Solidarity*, March 22, 1913, p. 2.

19. Hobsbawm, op. cit., p. 57.

20. Ibid., p. 60.

21. *Solidarity*, February 19, 1910, p. 2; CIR, II, pp. 1446, 1449, XI, p. 10,598.

22. *Industrial Worker*, July 1, 1909, p. 3.

23. Ibid., June 3, 1909, p. 2; Ben Williams to Editor, August 20, 1907, *Industrial Union Bulletin*, September 7, 1907, p. 2.

24. J. J. Ettor, "A Retrospect on Ten Years of the IWW," *Solidarity,* August 14, 1915, p. 2; James Larkin in *International Socialist Review,* XVI (December 1915), pp. 330–31; CIR, V, pp. 4234–35, 4239.

25. CIR, XI, pp. 10,574, 10,579.

26. Ibid., V, p. 4239; *Solidarity,* March 14, 1914, p. 2; cf. Hobsbawm, op. cit., pp. 58–59.

27. Jack London, *The Iron Heel* (New York, 1924), pp. 96–99.

28. CIR, V, pp. 4940, 4946–47; *The Lumber Industry and Its Workers* (Chicago, n.d.), p. 59.

29. *Solidarity,* April 2, 1910, p. 2; CIR, XI, p. 10,574.

30. CIR, V, p. 4942; *Solidarity,* July 9, 1910, p. 3.

31. V. St. John, "Political Parties Not Endorsed by Us," *Industrial Worker,* August 12, 1909, p. 3; Vincent St. John, *The I.W.W.: Its History, Structure, and Methods* (Chicago, 1919 ed.), pp. 40–45; CIR, II, p. 1449, XI, p. 10,575; *Lumber Industry and Its Workers,* p. 59.

32. *Industrial Worker,* June 6, 1912, p. 2.

33. *Lumber Industry and Its Workers,* p. 73; CIR, XI, p. 10,575.

34. J. Ebert, "Suppressing the IWW in New York," *Solidarity,* February 14, 1914, p. 20.

35. R. Brazier to Editor, *Industrial Worker,* February 2, 1911, p. 3; *Solidarity,* May 30, 1914, p. 2.

36. *International Socialist Review,* XII (February 1912), p. 467, XIII (September 1912), pp. 246–47; CIR, XI, p. 15,580.

37. CIR, V, p. 4237.

38. Ibid., II, pp. 1451, 1555, V, pp. 4947–48; Frank Bohn and W. D. Haywood, *Industrial Socialism* (Chicago, 1911), p. 57.

39. CIR, XI, p. 10,581.

40. Quoted in Dosch, op. cit., p. 417.

41. CIR, II, pp. 1452, 1456, XI, p. 10,592.

42. *Industrial Worker,* I (June 1906), p. 8; *Industrial Union Bulletin,* June 29, 1907, p. 2, April 4, 1908, p. 2; *Industrial Worker,* May 8, 1913, p. 2, August 12, 1909, p. 2; *Solidarity,* June 8, 1912, p. 2.

43. *Solidarity,* December 24, 1910, p. 2.

44. *Industrial Worker,* October 8, 1910, p. 2; Arturo Giovannitti, "Syndicalism: The Creed of Force," *The Independent,* LXXVI (October 30, 1913), p. 210; CIR, XI, p. 10,578.

45. *Industrial Union Bulletin,* April 6, 1907, p. 2.

46. *Industrial Worker,* May 28, 1910, p. 1, February 23, 1911, p. 2, July 1912–January 1913.

47. *International Socialist Review,* XIII (February 1912), p. 469; *Solidarity,* February 25, 1911, p. 4.

48. J. Thompson quote from CIR, V, pp. 4240–41; Haywood in ibid., XI, pp. 10,578–79; *Solidarity,* February 25, 1911, p. 4; *Industrial Worker,* March 13, 1913, p. 2.

49. CIR, III, p. 2482.

50. Ibid., V, pp. 4240–41; B. H. Williams, *American Labor in the Jungle: The Saga of the One Big Union* (microfilm copy, Wayne State University Labor Archives), p. 45.

51. *Industrial Worker,* May 23, 1912, p. 2; *Industrial Union Bulletin,* September 7, 1907, p. 2.

52. *Industrial Worker,* I (May 1906), p. 1; W. E. Trautmann, *Industrial Unionism* (Chicago, 1908), pp. 16–18; *Industrial Worker,* May 6, 1909, p. 2; *Solidarity,* June 4, 1910, p. 2; CIR, II, pp. 1450–51, III, p. 2598.

53. *Industrial Worker,* May 6, 1909, p. 2; *Solidarity,* June 4, 1910, p. 2.

54. Haywood and Ettor, "What the IWW Intends to Do to the USA," reprinted from the New York *World* in *Solidarity,* June 27, 1914, p. 3.

55. Haywood quoted in Dosch, op. cit., p. 417; Williams, *One Big Union,* p. 45.

56. *Solidarity,* August 24, 1912, p. 2.

57. CIR, II, pp. 1449, 1455, 1459, XI, pp. 10,574, 10,588; *Industrial Worker,* October 3, 1912, p. 2, October 13, 1910, p. 3; *Lumber Industry and Its Workers,* p. 73.

58. CIR, XI, p. 10,584; *Solidarity,* November 1, 1913, p. 2.

59. *Solidarity,* December 28, 1912, p. 3.

60. For the working-class definition of socialism, see WFM, *Proceedings of 1905 Convention* (Denver, 1905), p. 304; CIR, XI, p. 10,583; W. D. Haywood, "Socialism: The Hope of the Working Class," *International Socialist Review,* XII (February 1912), pp. 461–71.

61. See Philip S. Foner, *History of the Labor Movement in the United States,* Vol. 4: *Industrial Workers of the World, 1905–1917* (New York, 1965), ch. 17.

62. Will Herberg, "American Marxist Political Theory," in Donald D. Egbert and Stow Persons (eds.), *Socialism and American Life* (Princeton, 1952), I, pp. 491–92.

63. *Industrial Worker,* November 2, 1910, p. 2, October 3, 1912, p. 2, January 9, 1913, p. 2; CIR, XI, p. 10,587.

64. John Sandgren, "The Syndicalist Movement in Norway," *Solidarity,* February 14, 1914, p. 3; Robert R. LaMonte, "Industrial Unionism and Syndicalism," *New Review,* I (May 1913), p. 527.

65. John Spargo, *Syndicalism, Industrial Unionism and Socialism* (New York, 1913), pp. 13–15.

66. *Industrial Worker,* May 8, 1913, p. 3.

67. Philip Taft, "The I.W.W. in the Grain Belt," *Labor History,* I (Winter 1960), p. 67; Michael L. Johnson, "The I.W.W. and Wilsonian Democracy," *Science and Society,* XXVIII (Summer 1964), p. 274; William Preston, Jr., *Aliens and Dissenters* (Cambridge, Mass., 1963), pp. 150–51.

68. Oscar Lewis, op. cit., p. 1. Cf. Seymour Martin Lipset, *Political Man: The Social Bases of Politics* (New York, 1960), pp. 115–22.

69. For employer resistance to the IWW, see Selig Perlman and Philip Taft, *A History of Trade Unionism in the United States, 1896–1932* (New York, 1935), pp. 280–81. Cf. Walter Galenson, *The C.I.O. Challenge to the A.F.L.* (Cambridge, Mass., 1960); and David Brody, "The Emergence of Mass Production Unionism," in John Braeman et al., *Change and Continuity in Twentieth Century America* (Columbus, Ohio, 1966), pp. 221–62.

70. Ray Ginger, *The Bending Cross* (New Brunswick, N.J., 1949), p. 257; Bert Cochran, "Debs," in Harvey Goldberg (ed.), *American Radicals* (New York, 1957), p. 173; Robert F. Tyler, "Rebels of the Woods and Fields: A Study of the I.W.W. in the Pacific Northwest" (Unpublished Ph.D. Dissertation, University of Oregon, 1953), pp. 2, 21, 204–6; Paul F. Brissenden, *The I.W.W.* (New York, 1919 ed.), pp. xx–xxi, among numerous other works.

COMMENT

Robert L. Tyler

However American cultural "exceptionalism" has operated in the past to soften the class struggle and to frustrate hopes of socialist revolutionaries, the same forces, whatever they are precisely, must also account for the failure of the Industrial Workers of the World. At the outset one might quibble at such an assessment of failure, finding evidences all around one today that the IWW, like "Bird" Parker or the late James Dean, still "lives." Joan Baez sings "I Dreamed I Saw Joe Hill Last Night" at Woodstock and on a recent phonograph record for a younger generation of dissidents; East Village boutiques sell Joe Hill buttons advising that same younger generation not to mourn but to organize; Joseph Robert Conlin in a recent book describes an IWW commune of a hippie character in Chicago's Bohemian Near North Side, which somewhat disconcerts the Wobblies of an older generation still surviving at their moth-eaten headquarters on Halsted Street;[1] and Melvyn Dubofsky, as well as this writer, adds to the new flood of books and monographs on the IWW. But, of course, it would be only a quibble. The IWW did indubitably die. It did not bring off the apocalyptic "general strike" it preached. It did not bring in the age of "Industrial Democracy" or of the "Cooperative Commonwealth" it also preached. It did not even succeed, at least for very long, in organizing industrial workers into viable labor unions to work practically for such less ultimate objectives as higher wages or better working conditions.

The IWW arrived on the American scene in 1905, not even on center stage, and by 1920 it was in disarray and retiring to the wings. Its *floruit* thus coincides with that of the Socialist Party, and it is probably safe to assume that the same social forces explain the waxing and waning of both movements. The Socialist Party reached its greatest strength in the presidential election of 1912.

The peak of the IWW, in the Lawrence, Massachusetts, strike, came early in the same year.

This symposium as a whole is addressed to that larger question of why socialism found America inhospitable. Any answers to the question would cover the IWW because the IWW was rather like the fundamentalist wing of the socialist church, or like that purist proletarianism which Lenin was in a few years to castigate as "left-wing communism," or an "infantile disorder." In 1912 and 1913 the Socialist Party purged the IWW and its leaders from the party, ridding itself of a public liability in those days of its rapid growth. The IWW had a decidedly bad press, rather like that of the Black Panthers or the Weatherman faction of the Students for a Democratic Society. After attracting almost a million votes for Eugene V. Debs in the 1912 election, the Socialist Party "politicos" —as the IWW came to call them disparagingly—had reasons to want to be "practical." The IWW, in or out of the Socialist Party, preached and acted out a reductivist version of Marxist doctrine, urging the primacy of the "class war," the futility of bourgeois politics, the state as an ultimately otiose institution. As one IWW spokesman put it: "Revolutions do not come through politics or politicians. . . . To think that by electing a Socialist President we can hasten the dawn of the Cooperative Commonwealth is to imagine that we can veer the wind around by sheering the weather vane."[2] The young Walter Lippmann, in his socialist phase, complained that the IWW mistook a means or a tactic for the end.[3]

The first historians and journalistic analysts of the IWW—Paul F. Brissenden,[4] John Graham Brooks,[5] Andre Tridon,[6] Louis Levine[7]—seem to have agreed, if on nothing else, that the IWW was the American reflection of the international syndicalist movement. Indeed, Robert Hunter, in an early study of violence and the labor movement, dismissed the IWW in a footnote as a rather disorganized and ineffectual appendage to the labor movement whose only significance was as a peddler of "French ideas."[8] Syndicalism—in large part a "French idea"—was that modish revolutionary ism of the early twentieth century, influential in the French labor movement and attaching itself to the Bakunin anarchist tradition in Spain and elsewhere. Syndicalists, like the IWW we have characterized, plucked the leading idea of class warfare from the Marxist socialists, distilled it to high-proof purity, and used it as a heady apolitical, or even anti-political, revolutionary tactic. The working-class revolution would be accomplished through the agency of the labor movement, through the tactic of the general strike. All that history required of the class-conscious and revolutionary proletariat was that it stop work, "fold its hands," and watch capitalism crumble. Workers' organizations would then pick up the pieces, administer things rather than people, and thus establish the post-revolutionary socialist society of equality and justice. Intellectuals and activists from both the labor movement and the socialist movement came to advance such an ideology out of disillusion with the political "game" of bourgeois democracy which was seen as a preemptive trick being played on the workers. The very rules of that "game" were, of course, laid down by the bourgeois enemy.

However accurately this thumbnail sketch may fit the Sorels and Pougets of the French syndicalist movement, newer American scholars and historians have tended to question any easy association of the IWW with the European counterpart. Dubofsky and others have found few transatlantic ties between the IWW and, let us say, Georges Sorel. They prefer to locate the sources of the IWW in the American grass roots. But they then finally agree—as does Dubofsky[9]—that the IWW can be considered America's syndicalism, as if there is no great harm in the linguistic usage.

In a way it is curious that Dubofsky, and this writer, and Conlin, and others have felt obliged to go through this somewhat elaborate examination of the "syndicalism" of the IWW. It is probably an idle effort, an argument at bottom over definitions. The method seems to be to try to find whether certain IWW pamphlets were written under the influence of some Frenchman, whether the author could have read Pouget on sabotage, or whether he knew of Sorel. The solution to such a question proposed by John Spargo back in 1913—and requoted by Dubofsky[10]—settles the matter quite sensibly by merely proposing an adequate definition of syndicalism to cover both the French and the American phenomena. Thus, by agreeing on a definition, the IWW becomes America's syndicalism. Dubofsky, for example, finds no way "to escape," as he puts it, the similarities between the IWW and its European contemporaries.[11]

Such a question of social taxonomy, of "influence" in almost the literary historian's sense, is the kind of question to which historians are given professionally. They are not necessarily idle questions. Such a question as the "syndicalism" of the IWW does relate, in its way, to the more substantial question under examination in this symposium: why did socialism fail in America? The indigenousness of the IWW—or its foreignness—is obviously pertinent to any examination of the reasons for its failure. The missing premise in this enthymematic explanation would be: cultures tend to reject any too exotic influences, rather like organ rejection in transplant surgery. If the IWW did indeed lack roots in American culture, if it were only a curiosity imported from France by bemused intellectuals and radical dreamers, then its failure is rather simply explained. But rather too simply.

Dubofsky argues, as has this writer in his own proffered explanations of the failure of the IWW, that it was a peculiar and paradoxical conflict of practice and purpose *within* the IWW which accounts, at least in part, for its demise.[12] This debilitating conflict at the core of the IWW was suddenly exposed when the organization was attacked and checked violently during the First World War. The enthusiasm and *élan* of the IWW before the war, and its sometimes successful but temporary representation of the grievances of unskilled immigrant workers in the East and of migratory workers in the West, bore it along with an illusion of success until it ran into the cruel brick wall of reality during the war. What was the integral confusion or contradiction within the IWW? It was a failure to realize that its two simultaneous goals, effective bread-and-butter unionism and revolution, were in reality contradictory.

Most of the well-known, half-legendary exploits of the IWW, upon close examination, reveal this confusion of purpose, this masking of reality temporarily with a splendid activism and a wonderful revolutionary style. The twice- or thrice-told tale of the Lawrence, Massachusetts, strike of 1912, for example, reveals the problem. But two much lesser-known IWW episodes might better show the typicalness of the problem.

In December 1912 IWW railroad workers on a grade outside Eugene, Oregon, walked off the job in a spontaneous protest against low wages and abusive foremen. They marched into town singing revolutionary songs. The following day they apparently decided that their protest was a strike, and from the local IWW hall they issued a series of demands including the nine-hour day, reinstatement on the job, and an end to bullying by the foremen. The strikers and hangers-on at the hall then tried to induce all other workers on the project to join the strike. They met the railroad work car as it left the town in the morning and as it returned to town in the evening, and, amid scenes of near riot, tried to persuade the workers to stop scabbing. Every evening of the strike, forty or fifty Wobblies paraded down Willamette Street, the main street of Eugene, carrying placards, singing irreverent songs, shouting their grievances. They also picketed the Quick Lunch restaurant on lower Willamette Street because the restaurant catered to scabs and because it supplied free eggs to spectators who wished to pelt Wobblies during the evening parades. The leader of the strike, James Morgan, was thrown in jail for assaulting one of the non-strikers at the nightly proselytizing at the work train. The Wobblies began to drift away to other casual laboring jobs in the region. From his jail cell, Morgan promised a resumption of the "strike" in the spring, and he evinced no remorse for having beaten up the non-striker, an ignoramus who was just walking around "to save funeral expenses" in any case.[13]

A local strike of loggers in the Coos Bay region of Oregon in May 1913 set off another medley of troubles. The strike began, as usual, in a spontaneous protest over a particular grievance, the laying-off of a number of IWW agitators. The following day, for good measure, the IWW designated their protest a strike and listed a number of demands such as higher wages and better living conditions in the logging camps. By June the strike had died out, but the local burghers had been roused by it to take radical action of their own. A group of Marshfield citizens—six hundred in all—deported W. J. Edgworth of the local IWW hall. They marched the IWW leader out of town and gave him a boat ride eight miles down the coast. The vigilantes, however, let two Wobblies slip through their net, and while they deported Edgworth, the two Wobblies, with splendid effrontery, mounted soapboxes in Marshfield to harangue the few lethargic citizens remaining in town. The returning vigilantes discovered them and deported them on a second boat, first marching them through the streets and forcing them periodically to kneel and kiss an American flag.[14]

From such episodes as these—which could be multiplied almost indefinitely—it is obvious that the IWW was often more sinned against than sinning. But apportioning justice was not the lesson intended in these brief illustrations of IWW methods and style. In the harsh circumstances of their lives Wobblies could not decide

—or even distinguish—between the demands of labor unionism and a kind of quixotic revolutionary vanguardism. As Dubofsky describes this conflict of purpose, the IWW failed to transform its occasional and local organizational successes into any effective "higher consciousness," i.e., revolutionary consciousness and discipline.[15] Or, we might add, into effective labor unions.

In this respect Dubofsky assumes with most historians of the IWW, early or late, the peculiar lack of hospitality of American culture to class-conscious movements. Americans have viewed their society as idyllically classless. But the IWW stubbornly acted out its dilemma, insisting on simultaneous unionism and revolution. Of course, it failed to achieve either objective. But analyzing these peculiarities of the IWW as it struggled with its own problem in the matrix of American culture only partly explains its failure. It is really the hostility of American culture that is the basic cause of the failure. And that is assumed, not explained, in emphasizing the idiosyncrasies of the IWW.

It is clear that any explanation of failure and decline specific to the IWW must be but a variant or special case of the explanation for the failure of socialism in general. Any hypothesis seeking causes in the peculiarities of the IWW only seems to beg the larger question. Therefore, Dubofsky—as well as this writer and most other historians of the IWW—has not really shed much light on this underlying question, however admirable and definitive is his new narrative history.

It seems to this critic—however against the grain of the newest revisionism it may seem—that such "consensus" historians as Louis Hartz may have proposed the most persuasive explanations of this indubitable hostility of America toward socialism and all its class-conscious relatives, including the early labor movement itself. Even radicals themselves, late or soon, come to be overpowered by the reality of this bourgeois consensus at the heart of the American culture. Dubofsky has cited—in the quotation from Ben Williams, for example[16]—a recurring IWW protestation of its essential "Americanism," a protestation appearing even more unabashedly in the IWW's rejection of the Comintern in 1919 and after. Perhaps Earl Browder's equation of communism with "twentieth-century Americanism" during the Popular Front era of the mid-1930s is an even more obvious, if not embarrassing, instance. The New Left, of more contemporary experience, can be observed doing the same thing, as in Staughton Lynd's recent quest for a usable American past, accommodating Tom Paines, abolitionists, and Vietniks into his party and earning the charge of unhistorical behavior from Eugene D. Genovese in a hostile review of the book.[17] I do not imply that such efforts—by Wobblies, Earl Browder, or Staughton Lynd—to "Americanize" their radicalisms are capitulations or disingenuous. But the phenomenon is interesting. The radical assumes the role of suppliant, a petitioning outsider, knocking on historical doors to be let in. To plead and argue one's essential Americanism is a tactic, of course, in practical politics, but it also is an obvious admission of both alienation and of the ubiquity of the consensus which triggers the supplication. The radical is proffering a wistful code word which seems to say, "Look, I am a real American too. And, moreover, I am not *really* dangerous because my people are your people." That such a state of affairs holds in the history of American radicalism only confirms that already recognized hostility of American culture to socialism, the problem to which this book addresses itself. It again reveals the cogency of the question, but does not answer it.

If the methods of historical research and narrative can answer the question—certainly an arguable proposition—the answer may not lie in more and better histories of the radical movements themselves, such as Dubofsky's generally excellent history of the IWW, but rather in putting different and more clever questions to the surrounding culture, perhaps in the directions established in Louis Hartz's study. The answer to the question of the failure of socialism in America may lie not in histories of the Socialist Party and its satellites but in better historical anatomies of American culture.

Also, Dubofsky's history of the IWW illuminates another more general problem in the uses of history, and points to a radical skepticism that is a possible response to the central question of this symposium. Dubofsky makes a heroic effort, for which he is to be commended, to connect his story of the IWW to contemporary social problems and thus, hopefully, to improve our understanding of both the past and the present, to make his work "relevant" in the newest cant meaning of the term. By trying to relate the story of the IWW to the "culture of poverty," discussed by Oscar Lewis and other contemporary social critics and observers, and to the situation of the dispossessed, exploited, or economically redundant, then or now, he only brings into sharp focus those debated problems of the very uses of history.[18] This critic, for one, thinks he has not improved our understanding of either the IWW or the contemporary poor in the "culture of poverty." But he has done a service nonetheless by trying. All historical investigation designed, as Dubofsky apparently designed this part of his work, to improve our understanding of the present rests on a logic of analogy, loose and amateurish as in the case of, say, Harry Truman in some of his historical justifications, or tight and professional as in the case of a research historian seeking the "roots" of some present situation. The "lessons" of history, if there be any, are necessarily analogies. Because social change has been so precipitate, radical, and dizzying over the last several generations we can reasonably ask whether such a logic of analogy has become unworkable, whether there is sufficient continuity to justify comparisons. If we are really sailing in new seas, then old navigational experience may be useless, and we may be in regions of dreadful freedom indeed. It may be useless to study the Socialist Party, the IWW, or whatever, except for their own sakes, as exercises in literary re-creation. History as explanation may be in greater logical difficulties than it has been before. Perhaps socialism as a lost option in America is simply unexplainable, or open only to speculative answers. Or, in a world of radical discontinuity, it may be coming tomorrow, a possible scenario that can be extrapolated from a pastless present.

NOTES

1. Joseph Robert Conlin, *Bread and Roses Too: Studies of the Wobblies,* Greenwood Contributions in American History (Westport, Conn.: Greenwood Publishing Corp., 1969), pp. 136–40.

2. Robin Ernest Dunbar, "A Conflict Among Leaders," *International Socialist Review,* X (August 1909), p. 151.

3. Walter Lippmann, "The IWW–Insurrection or Revolution?" *New Review,* I (August 1913), p. 705.

4. Paul F. Brissenden, *The IWW: A Study of American Syndicalism* (New York: Columbia University Press, 1919).

5. John Graham Brooks, *American Syndicalism: The IWW* (New York: Macmillan, 1913).

6. Andre Tridon, *The New Unionism* (New York: B. W. Huebsch, 1913).

7. Louis Levine, "Development of Syndicalism in America," *Political Science Quarterly,* XXXVIII (September 1913), pp. 451–79.

8. Robert Hunter, *Violence and the Labor Movement* (New York: Macmillan, 1914), p. 247.

9. Melvyn Dubofsky, *We Shall Be All: A History of the IWW* (Chicago: Quadrangle Books, 1969), p. 169.

10. Ibid., p. 170.

11. Ibid., p. 169.

12. Ibid., p. 449. Dubofsky refers to this problem as "internal inadequacies." Robert L. Tyler, *Rebels of the Woods: The IWW in the Pacific Northwest* (Eugene, Ore.: University of Oregon Books, 1967), ch. 1.

13. This episode can be traced in issues of the Eugene, Oregon, *Guard,* between December 2, 1912, and December 13, 1912.

14. This episode can be traced in the Coos Bay, Oregon, *News* for May 13, 1913, and in the Portland *Oregonian* for June 26, 1913.

15. Dubofsky, op. cit., pp. 480–81.

16. Ibid., p. 148.

17. Staughton Lynd, *Intellectual Origins of American Radicalism* (New York: Pantheon, 1968). Eugene D. Genovese's review appeared in *The New York Review of Books,* XI (September 26, 1968), p. 69.

18. Dubofsky, op. cit., pp. 149–51.

REPLY

Melvyn Dubofsky

Robert L. Tyler's Comment raises two points fundamental to any sound interpretation of the role of radicalism and socialism in American society. One question involves the essential dilemma, or dichotomy, between reform and revolution confronting *all* radicals, and the second concerns the alleged "exceptionalism" of American history. According to Tyler's formulation—which might be considered the conventional academic wisdom—a combination of piecemeal reforms and American uniqueness rendered ineffectual political socialism and IWW-style syndicalism. In my book I dissented from the conventional wisdom in several basic particulars, and at great length. Here, however, I can only present a bare-bones outline of my disagreement with Tyler's version of the quandary of the radical in American history, and trust that the reader will tolerate some of my bald assertions, necessitated as they are by the brief compass of this response.

With Tyler's assertion that the Wobblies (also the socialists) faced a problem in the intrinsic contradiction between bread-and-butter unionism (political reforms) and ultimate revolution, I take no exception. That, after all, is the predicament of all revolutionaries in periods of non-crisis. Certainly, today, we realize that societies simply do not exist in a state of permanent crisis, and that a revolutionary situation is a rare moment indeed in history. In the absence of what for want of a better term might be labeled a "revolutionary situation," radicals, no matter how dedicated to their cause, make no revolutions. Moreover, most radical political and social movements, particularly those with a mass base, are led by a vanguard which maintains its influence and power by winning immediate demands for its constituents. It was the French Communist Party, functioning in a society with a living revolutionary tradition, which chose during the May days of 1968 to spurn the possibility of immediate revolution in preference to tangible economic and political gains. The history of Western European radical movements suggests that Tyler's dilemma is common to all revolutionaries, *not* unique to American socialists or Wobblies.

But to go further and to allege that "Wobblies could not decide —or even distinguish—between the demands of labor unionism and a kind of quixotic revolutionary vanguardism" is to engage in self-delusion and, perhaps, falsification of historical reality. From the first, as I thought my book made clear, IWW leaders perceived the distinction between the "demands of labor unionism" and the imperatives of revolution, which was why they broke with the AF of L. The IWW's difficulty was not to distinguish between reform and revolution; rather it was to bring the two into harmony. Wobblies fought to improve conditions today, while struggling consistently toward revolutionary goals. Awareness of the distinction between reform and revolution and of the gap in consciousness between vanguard and mass was made evident in Elizabeth Gurley Flynn's analysis of the strike defeat in Paterson (1913), in which she acknowledged: "We are dealing with human beings and not with chemicals. People are not material, you can't lay them down on the table and cut them according to pattern. You may have the best principles, but you can't always fit the people to the best principles."[1] That Miss Flynn and other Wobblies failed ultimately to permeate the masses with a higher, or Marxian, consciousness of class was unique neither to the IWW nor to American society. A similar failure has vitiated the endeavors of socialists and labor radicals in Western Europe. Which brings us now to the notion of American exceptionalism.

Both in my book on the IWW and elsewhere I have argued that to view American society as unique is to mystify history. Still, I would be among the first to concede that no two societies are precisely alike. That point conceded, it must be added, however, that much of our perception of contemporary and historical reality is relative, or as a sociologist might say, *situational.* An individual from one society is usually most aware of differences in another society; hence contrasts become magnified and similarities fade from view. Frenchmen remark on the bourgeois, shopkeeper mentality of Englishmen; Englishmen on the open, middle-class nature of American society; and Americans on the more closed, class-bound structure of British society. Yet, as a colleague of mine in Asian history has observed: as the Chinese came increasingly into contact with the Western world in the nineteenth and twentieth centuries, they were impressed more by resemblances among Westerners of diverse nationalities than by disparities. And who is to say that the Chinese perception is not more accurate than various Westerners' self-images?

Tyler's references to Louis Hartz and to the concept of a "bourgeois consensus" throughout American history as the principal explanation for the failure of American socialism also rest more on faith than on evidence.[2] The consensus that Tyler, Hartz, and others maintain was at the heart of American life was an import from England, the society, after all, which produced John Locke, Hartz's putative creator of the "bourgeois consensus." Asa Briggs in a remarkably insightful essay on "The Language of 'Class' in Early Nineteenth-Century England" describes an ideology that in its particulars resembles Hartz's and also Seymour Martin Lipset's model of an American ideal-type, middle-class consensus.[3] In Great Britain this consensus prevailed as long as the ruling class remained confident, united, and able to satisfy the ruled with minimal reforms. This was particularly true of English history from the end of the Chartist era to the last decade of the nineteenth century, c. 1850–90. From 1890 on, and especially after the blows inflicted by World Wars One and Two, the English ruling class lost part of its confidence and some of its ability to retain the acquiescence of the ruled. As a result, the consensus version of society weakened.

In the United States over the same period of time, that is since 1890, the ruling class grew more confident, more united, and much more able to pay off the lower classes with political reforms and material gains.[4] Recently, however, under the strains of the war in Southeast Asia and challenges from long-oppressed minority groups at home, the American ruling class has met its own crisis of confidence. Today the Hartz-Lipset version of the basic American consensus seems less convincing and resembles more in fact what it always was: an attempt to mystify the reality of class relationships in American society by lumping all citizens together in an amorphous, middle-class mass. This was something Robert and Helen Lynd realized back in the 1920s when they wrote their classic sociological analysis of industrial society, *Middletown,* and consciously refused to use the rubric "middle class," because the term cloaked more about society than it revealed.[5] What I am suggesting is this: the Wobblies and socialists failed not because American society was exceptional, but because they reached their respective peaks when the nation's rulers were most confident, united, and propagated an illusion with a basis in reality.

Finally, Tyler's claim that American radicals have been singular in seeking to "Americanize" their movements also collapses under close scrutiny. What Tyler considers the Wobblies' attempt to Americanize their organization is a phenomenon common to radicals in other societies who ordinarily seek to sanction their programs on the basis of a real or an imagined national past. Such was the case of E. P. Thompson's radical English workers of the late eighteenth and early nineteenth centuries who strove to reassert the rights of freeborn Englishmen; of generations of French radicals who have revived the tradition of the "revolution of '89"; of E. J. Hobsbawm's "primitive rebels" who used the past as their constant bench mark; and even of a Communist Party-endorsed biography of the radical English labor leader Tom Mann, which devotes nearly half its pages to reviving the hallowed English tradition of liberty and freedom.[6] In other words, American radicals, searching for indigenous roots, have behaved in much the same manner as revolutionaries in other societies and other times.

Rather than end by discussing the IWW's relevance—need it be said that relevance is an illusive quality in the mind of the reader—I would like to suggest that the time has passed for further analyses of the failure of American socialism. To me it appears evident that the uniqueness of American society lies not in its exceptional middle-class bourgeois structure and mentality, but rather in the enormous success of the owners and managers of our industrial capitalist society. It is high time we scholars discovered why and how, since the decline of what Herb Gutman has called the era of American Chartism (1873–97),[7] corporate leaders and their political allies have successfully extended their hegemony into the values, attitudes, and actions of the working-class masses—that is, why American culture has been, as remarked by Thomas Cochran, a preeminently business culture.[8]

NOTES

1. Melvyn Dubofsky, *We Shall Be All* (Chicago, 1969), p. 284.

2. Louis Hartz, *The Liberal Tradition in America* (New York, 1955), and *The Founding of New Societies* (New York, 1964), pp. 69–122. Cf. Seymour Martin Lipset, *The First New Nation: The United States in Historical and Comparative Perspective* (New York, 1963), *passim* and esp. p. 175. For other examples of this same thesis see David Shannon, "Socialism and Labor," in C. Vann Woodward, *The Comparative Approach to American History* (New York, 1968), p. 249; Kent and Gretchen Kreuter, *An American Dissenter: The Life of Algie Martin Simons* (Lexington, Ky., 1969), p. 220; John H. M. Laslett, *Labor and the Left* (New York, 1970), p. 304.

3. Asa Briggs, "The Language of 'Class' in Early Nineteenth-Century England," in Asa Briggs and John Saville, *Essays in Labour History* (London, 1967 ed.), pp. 43–73, esp. pp. 70–71.

4. The most complete, though tendentious, analyses of this development can be found in Gabriel Kolko, *The Triumph of Conservatism* (Glencoe, Ill., 1963) and James Weinstein, *The Corporate Ideal in the Liberal State, 1900–1918* (Boston, 1968). A more subtle and believable version of this period in American history is offered in Robert H. Wiebe, *The Search for Order, 1877–1920* (New York, 1967), esp. chs. 5, 7–8, 11.

5. Robert S. and Helen M. Lynd, *Middletown* (New York, 1929), pp. 22–24.

6. E. P. Thompson, *The Making of the English Working Class* (London, 1965), chs. 4–5, 12, 16; E. J. Hobsbawm, *Primitive Rebels* (New York, 1965 ed.), and also the same author's *Labouring Men* (London, 1964), chs. 17–18; Dona Torr, *Tom Mann and His Times: Volume One: 1856–1890* (London, 1956). For a similar analysis of the sources of violence in society see Charles Tilly's essay "Collective Violence in European Perspective," in Hugh D. Graham and Ted R. Gurr (eds.), *Violence in America* (New York, 1969), pp. 4–42.

7. Herbert Gutman, "Culture, Conflict, and Discontinuity in American Labor History: Some Comments and Some Evidence" (Unpublished Paper, 1968).

8. Thomas C. Cochran, "The History of a Business Society," *Journal of American History,* LIV (June 1967), pp. 5–18.

Chapter 6

SOCIALISM AND RACE*

Sally Miller

The Socialist Party of America occupies an interesting position in American historiography. While much has been written about its history, many party policies and viewpoints have been misunderstood or distorted. The attitude and program of the Socialist Party toward the black American has not been assessed by scholars independently of its threatening offspring, the American Communist Party. The Communist Party, following its organization in 1919 as the Socialists split into three groups, has been studied by scholars of the various disciplines and scrutinized by the press and public; its attitudes have been explored and distorted, but most especially publicized. Thus, whether or not accurate, judgments on its positions and activities are felt to be common knowledge, whereas by comparison its predecessor, the Socialist Party, remains in the dimly perceived background.[1]

The Communist focus on the status of the Negro in America in the 1930s is well known, but in contrast the attitudes and programs of the Socialist Party toward the black American have not been assessed by scholars in terms other than generalities, and the public, as in all matters relating to this once prominent party, remains unaware of the party's early notoriety and its specific programs. Among historians of the Socialist Party, there has been a tendency to impose sweeping statements on the organization despite its constant divisions into separate factions, and this has served to distort understanding of the party in its relationship with the Negro as well as in other matters. It is unenlightening to learn from Ira Kipnis in 1952, a time when the Negro's subordinate position was

* Sally Miller, "The Socialist Party and the Negro, 1901–1920," *Journal of Negro History,* 56, no. 3 (July 1971), pp. 220–29.

starting to attract attention, that the old Socialist Party was increasingly racist; it is no more edifying to be informed by James Weinstein in 1967, a year in which New Left historians attempted to find their own past, that the party grew to recognize the Negro's plight.[2] Each of these historians has allowed the concerns of the present to shape his writing of history to the extent that the subject becomes disfigured rather than clarified. Both men, molded by their intellectual environment, have manipulated the Socialist Party of the early twentieth century in accord with their own visions formed in the latter half of the century.

It should be noted, however, that historians, creatures of the American experience, were molded by forces in society, as was the Socialist Party. It, too, was shaped and formed by the attitudes of the nation despite its generally critical posture. And, thus, the Socialist Party in the Progressive Era failed, as did the country at large, to view the Negro as an individual, as a distinct human being in a unique dilemma. The Socialist, concerned as he might be with the downtrodden, the impoverished, the underrepresented, nevertheless did not see the Negro. The American Negro for the Socialist Party was, as aptly described by Ralph Ellison, "the invisible man." The party did not reject Negro membership—it stood for Negro suffrage when the issue arose—yet with the exception of a vocal minority, it doubted Negro equality and undertook no meaningful struggles against second-class citizenship. The Negro might be noticed by the party in his economic role as a worker, but he was not seen to be a worker with peculiar difficulties imposed by the existing semi-caste system. Marxist ideology, instead of leading Socialists to seek out the Negro as the worker with absolutely nothing to lose but his chains, reinforced the existing national tendency to overlook his comprehensive exploitation. In an era dominated by distorted Darwinist views of competing species and nations with different degrees of adaptability, not even a socialist party based on international brotherhood and anticolonialism—in theory, at least—endorsed the concerns of the Negro. The reform movements of the times rested, among other elements, on a comfortable assumption of Anglo-Saxon superiority. A paternalism toward the non-Anglo-Saxon, reflected in an imperialist phrase such as "the little brown brother," and supported by the uncertain social sciences of the day, pervaded the general climate. Rare was the organization opposed to the prevailing ethos.

The Socialist Party was never a monolithic organization imposing decrees upon its membership. Moreover, its genuine fragmentation meant that always there were at least three opinions on any subject, that of the Marxist or revolutionist left, the revisionist or reformist right, and the amorphous middle or center that might agree with one of the extremes or hold to a distinctive view. The party's view of the Negro must be examined in light of this division.

The dominant reformist wing of the party was closely tied to conservative organized labor. Some reformist leaders were trade unionists themselves, and all of them were anxious to cement a firm alliance with the American Federation of Labor that might lead to its ideological capture. Courting the federation as they did, it was logical for reformists to support increasingly segregationist labor's contention that the Negro was unorganizable and to be ignored except for condemnation as a scab. Therefore, the reformist orientation to the trade union movement reinforced whatever racist tendencies were present.[3]

As an example, reformist leader Victor L. Berger was a trade unionist as well as the dominant voice in the dynamic socialist movement in German Milwaukee. All contemporary strains leading toward racism coalesced in the European-born Berger. As a unionist he saw the Negro as unorganizable, as a Socialist he thought him irrelevant, and as a German he believed the Negro, and indeed all others, to be inferior. In a debate before the party's National Congress in 1910, Berger acknowledged that the recent electoral success of the Milwaukee Socialists was due to trade unionist support and insisted that support must be rewarded. "If we are a party of workingmen," he told the congress, "we must stand for what will help them." He referred to the existence of a race problem but one that was to be shunned rather than rectified: inferior races ought to be kept out of the United States for, with the Negro presence, "we have troubles enough. . . ." The Negro was a burden whose weight the party, in partnership with labor, must wear as lightly as possible. To Berger's mind a Negro problem existed rather than a dilemma created by the inequities of American life. Berger held a pronounced vision of a natural inequality of peoples. In an almost pyramidal view he spelled out distinctly superior and inferior racial and ethnic classes. White was at the top of the color pyramid, yellow below, and black at the bottom, and potential for education, unionization, and even morality declined progressively. When dealing with numbers of yellows or blacks, this Socialist Party leader was capable of telling his comrades in convention that "this is a question of civilization mainly. I believe that our civilization, the European or Caucasian or whatever name you choose to call it, I believe that our civilization is in question."[4] He was not able to transcend the existing contrast in standards of living or life styles to analyze the forces extant.

Such blatant racism, however, was voiced publicly by few of the party's leaders. Some, unlike Berger, were so appalled by the inequities, Jim Crowism, and violence to which the Negro was subjected that they welcomed the first moves in the Negro community away from Booker T. Washington's Atlanta Exposition philosophy, enunciated in 1895, of narrow economic advancement at the price of social inequality, limited vocational education, and subordinate political status. They applauded and cooperated with the Niagara Movement of W. E. B. DuBois and others after 1905, and helped organize the National Association for the Advancement of Colored People at the end of the decade.

Mary White Ovington, a young settlement-house worker descended from Massachusetts abolitionists, had immersed herself in the social problems of the northern Negro after the turn of the century. As a socialist, she was convinced that the major problem facing civilization was economic. While her life's work was to help the Negro obtain his constitutional rights, it was her hope that subsequently he might choose to join with white workers in the promotion of the collective ownership of the means of production and distribution. But she did not think her task should be proselytizing the Negro; he must make his own decisions.[5]

Mary White Ovington's efforts, perhaps more than those of any other individual, provided the impetus for the formation of the NAACP. She, like other sympathetic northerners, was aghast at the violence that swept Lincoln's Springfield, Illinois, for two days in August of 1908, resulting in lynchings and other less deadly but forceful pressures upon Negroes to flee the city. She read an analysis of the riots by a fellow socialist, William English Walling, which concluded with an open-ended plea: "What large and powerful body of citizens is ready to come to their aid?" Miss Ovington responded to his hope for an organization of black and white Americans that would secure the rights still remaining to the Negro and would reclaim those lost or never obtained.[6]

Walling was the son of a wealthy Kentucky family. He had moved beyond his narrow elitist background to embrace causes as diverse as factory inspection, settlement house social service, the National Women's Trade Union League, and the Socialist Party. Although he did not become a member of the party until the next year, in 1908 he was a leading propagandist for the uncompromising, revolutionist wing. In that capacity he and Victor Berger became involved in a bitter quarrel over his assertion that the reformists who controlled party machinery were deflecting the movement toward progressivism.[7] The two men were as acrimonious in their charges over policy as they were distant in their assumptions about the Negro.

For Walling the trauma of race riots in Lincoln country was magnified because he had just returned from a visit to Czarist Russia with his wife, Anna Strunsky, and there the government at least had to stoke fires to create a pogrom. In Springfield, however, spontaneous violence had erupted, and Walling clearly found that while mob action was frowned upon by the respectable citizens, public opinion in the North nonetheless endorsed race hatred. In order that the "southification" of the country be countered, political democracy saved, and the Negro reach "a plane of absolute political and social equality . . . ," the next year Walling and Miss Ovington, along with Socialist friends such as the muckraker Charles Edward Russell and the non-socialist, abolitionist-descended publisher, Oswald Garrison Villard, organized the National Negro Committee, soon to be known as the NAACP. While Villard in his personal correspondence could write that the "most ardent workers who are really accomplishing something . . . are all Socialists . . . ," none attempted to exploit the Negro for the advancement of the Socialist Party.[8] It is apparent that all of them held an underlying belief in the efficacy of a coalition of the downtrodden—workers both white and black, the unemancipated woman, defenseless consumers, and the like—but through the NAACP they simply began at the beginning and attempted to end legal barriers obstructing the Negro's path to where he might want to go.[9]

The Socialist Party, encompassing attitudes toward the Negro as different as Berger's was from Walling's, moved through its first two decades acknowledging the Negro in a rather absent-minded fashion. A few Negroes were present at the Unity Convention of 1901 in Indianapolis, where some feuding factions came together to form a Socialist Party in which they could quarrel at closer range. The gathering put together a constitution that contained a clause pertinent to the Negro. Article II, Section I of the Socialist Party's constitution spoke out against discrimination in American life.[10] The party even went so far as to recognize the Negro's unique experience in the United States but nevertheless declared his position and his interests to be identical to those of the white worker.

In its daily functioning the party did not concern itself with the Negro's economic and political problems. Only when it became necessary to assume a formal posture, as above, did the party comment on the Negro directly. For example, the first Socialist Congressman supported Negro suffrage when the issue was before the House of Representatives. Ironically, this Congressman was the racist Berger, elected in 1910 by the voters of the Fifth Congressional District of Wisconsin; but nevertheless when a stand had to be taken, he endorsed a bill for federal supervision of primaries in the South. Berger's committee assignment was to that of the District of Columbia, and he introduced various measures for the benefit of District residents, measures that, had they passed, would have aided the large Negro population of Washington. Berger sponsored home rule, a cooperative store for the civil servants of Washington, and limitations on women's hours of employment. In his various speeches to his colleagues, he condemned what he called the starvation wages prevalent in the District. In all of these efforts, he was representing the interests of the Negro, but that was beside the point for him. Berger, in this term and in his later service from 1922 to 1926, was not thinking particularly of the Negro's plight.[11] The only other Socialist ever elected to the House of Representatives was Meyer London of the Twelfth Congressional District of New York, the Jewish ghetto. He served from 1914 to 1918 and was elected again in 1920; he, like Berger, attempted to represent the American worker without regard to the gradations of problems that color imposed.[12] Thus, the only representatives in Congress of the workers of the world were not representing those most oppressed.

In the South, however, Socialist locals in some areas demonstrated direct interest in attracting the black man. While historians have generalized mistakenly on the racism of southern Socialists, the party in the South offered a varied picture.[13] In 1913 the party, prodded by a request for membership information, circulated a questionnaire to determine the number of Negroes in the party and the number of integrated locals. The survey, handled by the party's information department, revealed that northern locals had no special provisions pertaining to race, while in the South a color curtain divided the party between integrated practices of locals in the upper South and segregated procedures of those in the deep South. South Carolina, Georgia, Mississippi, and Florida all were recorded as practicing segregation within locals. In cases where there were insufficient numbers of Negro members for a black local, Negroes were enrolled as members-at-large in the state organization. On the other hand, state secretaries from the upper South, such as the District of Columbia, Maryland, Kentucky, and Tennessee, reported that Negroes were enrolled automatically in the local nearest to their home. The state secretary for Kentucky, Walter Lanferseik, within a few months of assuming the role of Executive Secretary of the party, reported that an important factor in the easy relationship between white and black members was their mutual participation in the integrated United Mine Workers. The state secretary for Tennessee wrote simply, "If a negro [*sic*] signs our application cards [*sic*] . . . we give him a membership card." But he added sadly that most Negroes were stand-pat Republicans.[14] The survey thus demonstrated that regional ideology and habit tended to overwhelm Marxist colorblindness.

The national office did not use the knowledge it gained from the survey to interfere with segregationist practices, although had it chosen to do so, the party tradition of local autonomy would have prevented any such manipulation. The leadership refrained from initiating measures on behalf of its now formally recognized Negro membership or from seeking to alter the status quo in any way. The Socialist Party had been led to its inquiry, but it had no interest in exploring the ramifications further.

During and immediately after World War One, the Socialist Party took a few tentative steps toward the Negro, but none of these efforts was either imaginatively conceived or vigorously implemented. That the party recognized the Negro to any extent may have been due to the simple fact of increasing migration of the Negro to the North, where he became somewhat more visible to the public in general. In addition, as Harlem became the black mecca during the war, it began to contain different strains of cultural and political ferment, including a few radical notes.[15]

One of those who evinced interest in the Socialist Party was W. E. B. DuBois. As early as 1907, only four years after he broke with Washington's limiting vision, DuBois gravitated toward the party. Influenced by some of his colleagues in the NAACP, he joined the movement briefly to embrace its gospel of collectivist advancement and brotherhood. His commitment to socialism in the Progressive Era was not so much ideological as humanistic. While he called some socialists fanatics, he nonetheless believed they promoted the public good and gave the Negro hope that was lacking elsewhere. Moreover, he wished to see a linking of various reform movements that would inevitably strengthen all forces for change. He left the Socialist Party to support Woodrow Wilson in 1912, although with considerable ambivalence; he felt impelled to contribute to the defeat of Theodore Roosevelt's blatantly lily-white Progressive Party while nevertheless harboring skepticism about the Democratic Party.[16]

A. Philip Randolph and Chandler Owen, both with backgrounds in organized labor, became members of the Socialist Party and in 1917 transformed a black unionist monthly into the *Messenger*, whose masthead proudly proclaimed itself "the only radical Negro magazine in America." The *Messenger* advised its readers to vote Socialist because the party represented all working men. It reproduced the usual arguments on the advantages of socialism over capitalism, but in most cases an emphasis was provided to appeal specifically to a Negro audience. One of Randolph's editorials offered the Marxist analogy of chattel-slavery and so-called wage-slavery with great pointedness. The People's Council of America, which arose in conjunction with the Socialist Party as a response to events in Russia, was held by the *Messenger* to be a force that would democratize labor and deprive the racist American Federation of Labor of its monolithic position. Negroes were also advised to join the Wobblies as "the labor organization which draws no race or color line."[17]

The *Messenger* supported Socialist Morris Hillquit in the mayoralty election in New York in November 1917. The magazine exulted over his strong showing and most especially over the 25 percent of the Negro vote he had won. The hope was expressed that in the next election 50 percent of Negro voters would cast ballots for Socialists.[18] Six months later, the *Messenger* rejoiced again as a heavily Negro local was organized in New York's Twenty-first Assembly District.[19] Randolph himself campaigned in 1920 for public office on a Socialist ticket, and while he won over 200,000 votes, the party by then had split and his performance was not a harbinger of future electoral successes by Socialists of any color.[20]

The *Messenger* not only advised its readers to turn to the Socialist Party, but also steered them toward the party-related Rand School of Social Science as one of the few institutions where Negroes might obtain an equal education. Some enrolled there, such as Lovett Fort-Whiteman, later to join the Communist Party and settle in Soviet Russia, and editors Randolph and Owen taught a course at the Rand School entitled "Economics and Sociology of the Negro Question."[21]

The magazine and its promotion of black radicalism suffered a blow in the postwar era as the Socialist Party divided. The *Messenger* shied away from the more revolutionary Communists and continued to support the reformist Socialists, but with the competition between the separate parties and the attraction for the dissatisfied of the Garvey movement, then peaking in Harlem, there was less chance than ever to create a radical movement among mass numbers of Negroes.[22]

The party's interest in the Negro as radical during the war was demonstrated by an invitation to Randolph and Owen to address the People's Council on the problems of the Negro. In 1918 it planned to send organizers into the black community, even into the South. The ramifications of its program implied conflict with the trade unions; they are indicative of the radicalization of the party as the war progressed and an increasing criticism of and distance from organized labor.[23]

More instructive, however, than announced intentions and formal gestures of reaching out to the Negro was the actual performance of the Socialist Party, which was to view the Negro traditionally. Following the split in 1919, the shrunken remnant of the party issued a pamphlet entitled *Why Negroes Should Be Socialists.* Negroes were asked to join the party in their capacity as workers since the party was the only political reflection of the American worker. The pamphlet maintained that race was not the issue and gave examples of white employers exploiting white workers:

> Were not the steel and coal strikers beaten down by white soldiers and policemen when they committed the crime of striking for a living wage? Both the strikers were white men and the employers were white men, yet their interests were opposed and they fought. . . . Is not white Ireland oppressed by white England?[24]

Therefore, it was maintained, the oppression of the Negro was due to class rather than to race, and the remedy was prescribed to be working-class solidarity. That the Socialist Party could issue such a pamphlet in the aftermath of World War One, a time when the Negro was threatened with violence throughout the country on a level not seen in decades, must be taken as a comment on the near-sightedness of the party. It could not be denied that the Negro was of the working class, the most insecure element within that class, and in need of representation. But more fundamentally, the menaced position of the Negro—the violence meted out to returning black veterans, the race riots promoted against ghetto dwellers, the increased rate of lynchings, and the revival of the Ku Klux Klan—surpassed the economic exploitation cited.[25]

The Negro's position in America was far more complex than the Socialist Party seemed willing to realize. The party's belated appeal to the Negro in 1920 was couched in unrealistic terms that refused to recognize the dimensions of the inequities he faced. Socialists attempting to respond to the American environment had themselves been shaped by it, even members who were of alien backgrounds. Thus, they dealt with the issue of race, never of great interest to them, within the existing restrictive context. They lacked the desire, vision, and imagination to discern or to strive for a wholly equitable social, as well as political, situation. The Socialists, like many other Americans of relative good will toward the Negro, were captives of the intellectual climate of their time.

However, had the Socialist Party as an organization in opposition to many existing injustices been able to reach out to the Negro in a more realistic fashion, it is unlikely that a fruitful relationship would have evolved. With American workers as a whole slow to respond to an ideology that appeared alien to them, there is no reason to think that Negroes would have reacted in mass numbers had a more pertinent argument been presented. They, too, despite the failure of the country to apportion to them a fair share of its goods and services, were shaped by the American mind.

In the first decades of this century, the Negro demonstrated very little interest in the abolition of capitalism. What he wanted was his opportunity to prosper within that system. As much as other more favored Americans, he was taught the American mystique of individual initiative. Few of his leaders pointed to other vistas. And while his willingness to accept the legend of Horatio Alger and its various implications may appear improbable, no evidence indicates otherwise. The Negro, too, was shaped by the intellectual environment of his country and absorbed its teachings as did the American Socialists. As a result, the Socialist Party remained as invisible to the Negro as the Negro was invisible to the party.

NOTES

1. Manuscript sources for this paper are found in the Socialist Party Collection, Duke University; the William English Walling Collection, Wisconsin State Historical Society; the Victor Berger Collection, Milwaukee County Historical Society. In 1912 Debs captured 901,062 votes, almost 6 percent of the ballots cast, while the party occupied the office of mayor in seventy-four cities in states as disparate as Pennsylvania, North Dakota, Arkansas, and California. In addition, it elected a member to the House of Representatives in every election between 1910 and 1926, with the exception of 1912. Standard works on the Socialist Party are Daniel Bell, *Marxian Socialism in the United States* (New York, 1967), Ira Kipnis, *The American Socialist Movement* (New York, 1952), David A. Shannon, *The Socialist Party of America* (New York, 1955) and, most recently, James Weinstein, *The Decline of Socialism in America, 1912–1925* (New York, 1967).

2. Kipnis, p. 134; Weinstein, pp. 67, 75. For a critique of the New Leftist historians and American socialism, see Irwin Unger, "The 'New Left' and American History: Some Recent Trends in United States Historiography," *American Historical Review,* 72 (July 1967), pp. 1250–51.

3. On labor and the Negro, see Gerald N. Grob, "Organized Labor and the Negro, 1865–1900," *Labor History,* 1 (Spring 1960), p. 174; Herbert Hall, "In the Age of Gompers and After—The Racial Practices of Organized Labor," *New Politics,* 4 (Spring 1965), p. 39; August Meier and Elliot Rudwick, "Attitudes of Negro Leaders Toward the American Labor Movement from the Civil War to World War I," *The Negro and the Labor Movement,* ed. Julius Jacobson (New York, 1968), p. 27.

4. Socialist Party, *Proceedings* of the National Congress, 1910, pp. 119–21.

5. Mary White Ovington, *The Walls Came Tumbling Down* (New York, 1947), pp. 47–48; Gilbert Osofsky, "Progressivism and the Negro: New York, 1900–1915," *American Quarterly,* 16, pt. I (Summer 1964), pp. 159–61. Osofsky remarks that Ovington's optimism in the face of overwhelming obstacles marked her as a product of the confident era in which she lived.

6. William English Walling, "The Race War in the North," *Independent,* 65 (September 3, 1908), p. 534; Walling, "The Founding of the NAACP," *Crisis,* 36 (July 1929), p. 226.

7. William English Walling to Eugene V. Debs, December 14, 1909, William English Walling Collection, Wisconsin State Historical Society; Walling, *Socialism as It Is: A Survey of the Worldwide Revolutionary Movement* (New York, 1912), pp. 179–80; Victor Berger to

Algie M. Simons, December 6, 1909, Socialist Party Collection, Duke University.

8. Ovington, p. 102; Ovington, "William English Walling," *Crisis*, 43 (November 1936), p. 335; Walling, *Independent*, 65, p. 530.

9. Walling, *Independent*, 65, p. 543; *Negro Year Book*, 1 (1912), pp. 134–35; Villard as quoted from his papers in Charles Flint Kellogg, *National Association for the Advancement of Colored People*, Vol. 1: 1909–1920 (Baltimore, 1967), p. 45. Years later Walling maintained that he specifically wished the new organization to embrace people of all political persuasions and to avoid any descent to sectarianism. Walling, *Crisis*, 36, p. 226. See also Charles Edward Russell, *Bare Hands and Stone Walls: Some Recollections of a Side-line Reformer* (New York, 1933), pp. 224–26; Oswald Garrison Villard, *Fighting Years: Memoirs of a Liberal Editor* (New York, 1939), pp. 192–94.

10. The constitution of the Socialist Party is most readily found with its convention proceedings. See, for example, Socialist Party, *Proceedings* of the 1908 National Convention, pp. 324–28. The measure, however, was introduced by a Negro delegate; see R. Laurence Moore, "Flawed Fraternity—American Socialist Response to the Negro, 1901–1912," *Historian*, 22 (November 1969), p. 17.

11. Victor Berger note of April 17, 1911, Victor Berger Collection, Milwaukee County Historical Society; Berger's record in the Sixty-second Congress is summarized in Milwaukee Social Democratic Party, *Campaign Manual*, 1912, pp. 17–26.

12. Meyer London's congressional record is found in typescript in Box D50 of the Meyer London Collection, Tamiment Institute, New York City.

13. See, for example, Dewey W. Grantham, Jr., "The Progressive Movement and the Negro," *South Atlantic Quarterly*, 54 (October 1955), pp. 461–77. Grantham holds that "the Socialists of the South proved no more tolerant on the race question than non-Socialists." He offers no distinctions among party practices in the different areas of the South, p. 472. The same faulty overview characterizes Sterling D. Spero and Abram L. Harris, *The Black Worker* (New York, 1968), p. 407. These historians echo mildly a contemporary charge levelled at the party by one of its antagonists, the anarchist Emma Goldman. Her periodical claimed that Socialists treated blacks "like dogs" and that "the party consists chiefly of national and racist philistines, moral eunuchs, and religious soul savers." *Mother Earth*, 6 (October 1911), p. 198.

14. Carl D. Thompson to State Secretaries and replies, May 1913, Socialist Party Collection, Duke University. There are no extant figures on Negro membership in the party as a whole.

15. Harold Cruse, *The Crisis of the Negro Intellectual* (New York, 1967), pp. 11–63. Chapter 2 contains a comprehensive analysis of Harlem's cultural and political evolution at this time.

16. W. E. B. DuBois, *The Autobiography of W. E. B. DuBois* (New York, 1968), p. 289; DuBois, *Dusk of Dawn: An Essay Toward an Autobiography of a Race Concept* (New York, 1940), pp. 234–35; DuBois, "Socialist of the Path," *Horizon*, 1 (1907), p. 7; DuBois, "Negro and Socialism," ibid.

17. *Messenger,* November 1917, p. 19, March 1919, p. 12, July 1919, p. 8; Spero and Harris, pp. 389–90. On the relationship to the Industrial Workers of the World, see Philip S. Foner, "The IWW and the Black Worker," *Journal of American History,* 55 (January 1970).

18. *Messenger,* November 1917, p. 10; May-June 1919, p. 14.

19. Ibid., November 1917, p. 11; January 1918, p. 23; July 1918, p. 27.

20. Ibid., January 1918, p. 11; July 1918, p. 8; November 1920, p. 135.

21. Ibid., January 1918, p. 22; August 1919, p. 6; and Cruse, p. 118.

22. Cruse, pp. 40, 118. Christopher Lasch, echoing DuBois, comments that had black radicals and the Socialist Party fully coalesced each would have been immeasurably strengthened; the former inevitably would have weaned the party from its overdependence on European political and economic frames of reference, while the latter would have taught the need for self-determination for the ghetto within a collectivist orientation. Christopher Lasch, *The Agony of the American Left* (New York, 1969), p. 41.

23. *Messenger,* November 1917, p. 10; *Eye Opener,* August 1918. This issue of the party newspaper contains the Socialists' congressional platform for the November elections and includes for the first time since the party's formative years fresh recognition of the Negro.

24. *Why Negroes Should Be Socialists* (Chicago). Internal evidence suggests this publication appeared in 1920.

25. See *Negro Year Book,* 5 (1918–1919), especially pp. 67–71, for a record of the terror to which the minority was subject.

COMMENT

Theodore Kornweibel

To understand Socialist Party ideology and programs as they addressed or, more commonly, failed to address the realities of black America, one must begin with Sally Miller's caveat that the party was no monolithic organization. Indeed, her division of membership into three categories—the Marxist or revolutionary left, the AFL-oriented "reformist" right, and a loosely defined center—does not go far enough. Variations in racial perceptions and attitudes occurred at each point on the ideological spectrum. Focusing on leadership leads to a myopic view, for if one reads widely in the Socialist press, as Philip S. Foner has done, one unearths blatant racism expressed by both leadership and rank and file in all sections of the country, among Marxists as well as "reformists." Some Socialists, including a few southerners, were freeing themselves from racist stereotypes by the early twentieth century.

But rarely did a relative absence of bias lead to the next, and ultimately more important, step: a perception that blacks suffered an alienation far deeper than industrial discontent and that the party must offer a realistic political program against disenfranchisement, Jim Crow, lynching, and agricultural peonage, not merely the promise of industrial equality in the future cooperative commonwealth. The Oklahoma party, alone among state branches, mounted a sustained and moderately successful defense of black voting rights. This was closer to meeting black needs than the politically unfocused progressivism of white socialists of undoubted good will like Mary White Ovington and William English Walling. Aside from the Oklahoma example, however, the party's record in recruiting black members in the South, much less sponsoring change that would benefit the masses of the race, was dismal. Miller states that in parts of the South locals were interested in attracting black membership, but even taking into account "integrated" mining camp locals in Kentucky, Foner counts no more than two or three hundred black party members in the South in 1913.[1] Such membership is historically significant only for its minuteness; at a time when nearly 90 percent of the black population resided in the South, this ostensibly "national" political party had almost nonexistent roots among Afro-Americans.

To limit one's vision to the Socialist Party, however, is to ignore other, more committed attempts to address black needs from a socialist perspective. Much more positive efforts were initiated by the Industrial Workers of the World, founded in 1905 by socialists and radical dissidents from the AFL. Taking an industrial unionism approach, the IWW actively recruited black members, not on the basis of humanitarianism, but on the basis of practicality: "Leaving the Negro outside of your union makes him a potential, if not actual scab, dangerous to the organized worker, to say nothing of his own interests as a worker."[2] Despite this stance, the Wobblies, like the Socialist Party, failed to recognize fully that racism was equal in importance to the wage problem. Here the IWW's socialist ancestry is clear. Yet despite such ideological shortcomings, the IWW accomplished what the Socialist Party never would have attempted, organizing East Coast and Gulf port longshoremen and southern timber workers into integrated locals that pursued meaningful economic objectives while also addressing the role of racism in economic exploitation. That greater bread-and-butter benefits were gained for the dockers than for the lumber workers, who suffered under brutal feudal conditions, was due more to the tremendous social and economic power of capitalist interests in the South than to IWW weakness.

As Miller notes, Socialist interest in the black population increased during and after World War I, although this resulted only in efforts to gain members, not the creation of new programs focused on black grievances. The activities of A. Philip Randolph and Chandler Owen, the antiwar editors of the *Messenger* magazine, are duly noted and have more recently been accorded book-length treatment.[3] But there were other significant black socialists in this time period, whose history Miller slights. The *Messenger* was more than a magazine—it was an intellectual circle. Many of its early contributors and associates were socialists, and a study of the class and national backgrounds and subsequent political activities of men like the Rev. George Franzier Miller, Wilfred A. Domingo, and George S. Schuyler illuminates the attraction of socialism as well as its very limited appeal to blacks. Other militant black socialists outside the *Messenger* orbit were the Rev. George Washington Woodbey and Hubert H. Harrison. The African Blood Brotherhood, a "secret revolutionary" organization founded by Harlem socialists, saw World War I as an imperialist struggle for what we would today call the Third World. Its domestic goals called for armed resistance where necessary in the United States and self-determination in those states where blacks comprised the majority. After 1919 much of the ABB leadership turned to communism.[4] The World War I era, then, marks the height of black involvement in both the Socialist Party and the wider socialist movement. The importance of these Afro-American socialists lies in their linkage of racial nationalism to collectivism, the implications of which will be discussed shortly.

Few scholars would disagree with Miller that the Socialist Party (as a national entity) "undertook no meaningful struggle against second-class citizenship" in the early twentieth century, but her assertion that no "fruitful relationship" would or could have evolved between the party and black Americans can be challenged. Was it possible for the Afro-American population to be receptive to socialism, and were there individuals who could have led their race in the direction of an unfamiliar political and social ideology? Were there issues and strategies that the Socialist Party could realistically have employed? Positive hypotheses can be constructed for both questions.

Prior to 1910, nearly 90 percent of the country's black population resided in the South, the large majority in rural areas. Stimulated by unique economic opportunities in the North, frustrated by continuing political and economic discrimination and increasing crop failures in the South, nearly 1.5 million Afro-Americans moved to northern and midwestern cities between 1916 and 1929, by which date about 75 percent of the black population still lived in the South. This was the "Great Migration." Both southern and northern blacks had grievances aplenty, and there were ways in which the socialist movement could have addressed them, as well as tactical routes through which socialist approaches to the black minority could have been made.

The most pressing problems of blacks in the South included a denial of political rights, overt racism expressed in Jim Crow laws and lynchings, and economic exploitation through the noose of peonage and sharecropping. That an attack on disfranchisement was politically possible, under the banner of socialism, is demonstrated in the history of the Oklahoma Socialist Party. White socialists there did not oppose the grandfather clause, poll tax, and literacy test out of a widespread sense of racial egalitarianism, but from the recognition that when black workers lost their rights, those of white workers were similarly in jeopardy. Here was the best, and perhaps the only, basis for political progress in the South in this era: a class unity that would override racial antagonism and draw together poor whites and poor blacks in mutual cause. The party did not go further, however, and attack Jim Crow or lynching.[5] But despite the limited goals, this campaign clearly demonstrates that white southerners could be convinced to support the protection of black votes; it is thus all the greater pity that the national party failed to perceive the possibilities for working-class unity on the basis of a struggle for black rights.

More than the issue of voting rights, the need to escape economic exploitation was uppermost in the minds of rural southern blacks. Was there any possibility that an attack on peonage and sharecropping could form the basis for a vigorous radical movement? Miller asserts that blacks had little interest in abolishing capitalism and would have responded only feebly to "an ideology that appeared alien to them." But the possibility of mass organization on economic issues existed with no ideological base other than that which already existed, viz., the multiple economic grievances. The best proof of this likelihood lies in the history of agricultural militancy in the 1930s, with particular reference to the Sharecropper's Union in Alabama. In the early years of that decade, Communist Party workers entered rural east-central Alabama and began to organize sharecroppers. Significant numbers responded, although not out of any concrete knowledge of or adherence to communist goals; they responded simply because, for the first time in two generations, someone on the outside was taking a positive interest in their welfare, someone understood their oppression, and someone promised them the mechanism—mass organization—with which to try to deal with these realities. Nor were the aroused 'croppers overtly anticapitalistic. A reading of both historical accounts and the memoirs of one of the leading participants, "Nate Shaw" (Ned Cobb), makes clear that communist ideology played a negligible role in sharecropper militancy. The important points here are the willingness of the masses to respond to the promise of economic improvement through political cooperation and the rapidity with which indigenous, total leadership emerged. That the white Establishment also perceived these phenomena is seen in its brutal suppression of the Sharecroppers' Union.[6]

A similar scenario, with slightly different results, was played out in Arkansas and neighboring areas beginning in 1934, when the interracial Southern Tenant Farmers Union organized to fight landlessness, sharecropper exploitation, and peonage. In this case the Socialist Party lent organizational experience and support. As with the Alabama sharecroppers, the response was not to ideology—few were overtly anticapitalist—but rather to oppressive local conditions. Again, the population was ripe for organized mass action, and capable local leaders emerged.[7] What is the relevance of these Arkansas and Alabama examples? Similar conditions prevailed in the rural South in the first two decades of the present century, at a time when the Socialist Party was far stronger than in the 1930s. Political disfranchisement and social segregation were flowering while lynching was only slowly tapering off from its peak in the 1890s. There would have been no more necessity for a prior anticapitalist mentality among black and white rural laborers at that time than there was during the Great Depression; injustice and oppression were sufficient ideological foundations for the successful mass organization of workers on either an all-black or integrated basis. Certainly there would have been difficulties, but as one surveys the period 1900–1920 perhaps the greatest obstacle was the timidity of the Socialist Party itself.

Possibilities also existed for effective socialist mobilization of blacks in the growing ghettoes of northern cities, again without the necessity for an explicitly anticapitalist outlook. Blacks in the cities lacked an effective political voice, even though the right to vote was not commonly restricted on a *de jure* basis. In Harlem,

Chicago, and several other cities, the Afro-American population was sufficiently concentrated by the teens to form the mass base for a political movement. And neglect by the Republican and Democratic Parties both increased discontent and underlined the unfulfilled expectations of migrants who expected a brighter political future outside the South. In addition to political grievances, the growing urban population desperately needed industrial union protection such as the IWW was then attempting to forge and the CIO would begin to provide two decades later. Industrial jobs in significant numbers first opened up for blacks during World War I, yet many of these positions were lost in the postwar cutbacks and recession. If alienation is necessary to spawn a radical political movement, then northern black ghettoes indeed presented many opportunities. Here, conditions were ripe for a well-organized, adequately financed, and goal-oriented mass movement. But that movement belonged to Marcus Garvey, not to socialism.

The factors that made possible Garvey's success were the same ones that could have been capitalized on by a committed nonracist Socialist Party. A mass movement benefits from a closely packed city population; rallies, soapbox orations, printed propaganda, and parades are especially effective in such an environment. Moreover, the northern urban black population was rooted, albeit precariously, in a money economy, in contrast to the many southern blacks who still lived largely in a barter economy. So a city-based movement could more likely pay for itself, as Garvey's did. Add to these ecological factors a growing alienation—the realization that the Promised Land had not been found by moving North—and one sees the circumstances that enabled Garvey's brief star to rise so high so quickly. The Socialist Party, with goals far more tangible than Garvey's, ought to have taken advantage of these same circumstances in the late teens. The tragedy of the party was its failure to perceive this new opportunity and then to alter the traditional Debsian formula that the party had nothing special to offer minority groups. Certainly this would have been no simple task, even for a party purged of racism, for white socialists would have had to face squarely a deeply uncomfortable issue: black nationalism. Whether they could have accepted the necessity for racial self-assertion and self-definition concomitant with an integrated working-class program is open to some question.

The importance of this point lies in the fact that black socialists of the World War I era, like A. Philip Randolph, Chandler Owen, Wilfred A. Domingo, and Hubert H. Harrison, were racial nationalists at the same time that they were socialists. In fact, they had been nationalists before they acquired a socialist vision. They were not darker duplicates of the "progressive" white socialists. Their radicalism *began* on a racial basis, and they embraced collectivism as a means of elaborating or fulfilling racial goals. Ironically, the existence of black nationalists-socialists would have disturbed white party members in the South less than those in the North, at least initially, for in this era mature black militancy was confined almost exclusively to the North; in the South socialist programs could have been pursued largely without nationalist ideological encumbrance. But in the Harlems of the North one could not preach pure socialism and hope to be persuasive; an integration of socialism with what the *Messenger* termed "New Crowd Negro radicalism" would have been necessary. But the Socialist Party never fully had its heart in the task, even during the brief period of financial support for Randolph and Owen's magazine and the nomination of black socialists to the party ticket.

In the end, the socialist movement failed itself—it did not clearly perceive either the winds of change in the North or the fertile conditions in the South. From this perspective several conclusions outlined in the last two paragraphs of Miller's essay are open to debate and revision. A fruitful relationship between the black community and the Socialist Party would have been possible had more direct actions been taken in the South, as were attempted in the 1930s in Alabama and Arkansas and the teens in Oklahoma. Blacks could have responded to concrete socialist-led programs without having to accept or understand fully party ideology, at least in the early stages of activity. Blacks would not have had to be specifically interested in the abolition of capitalism to welcome socialist aid. An artful exposition of socialist principles could have conveyed, moreover, not a stereotypical and abstract anticapitalism, but, as was articulated in the 1930s, the more immediate possibility of freedom from economic exploitation. This is hardly alien to the experience and values of the large majority of Afro-Americans, for whom group action to achieve communal goals was essential for survival during and after slavery. Miller is correct in asserting that blacks wanted their opportunity to prosper in America, but the question of whether prosperity lay within the current system or in some alternative would have been distinctly secondary to them. She errs in assuming that the allegiance of many black leaders to industrial capitalism, Social Darwinist progress, and the myth of Horatio Alger was shared on a committed level by the masses. An analogy may be drawn to black loyalty and patriotism during World War I; a majority of leaders supported the war openly and vocally, but despite this support a deep vein of apathy to the war and its professed aims ran through the minds of the black masses. Miller asserts, again correctly, that few black leaders were inclined to lead their fellows into socialism. But an important perspective is missed in this statement, and again the analogy to World War I is helpful. A. Philip Randolph, in a recent interview, concluded that many blacks were willing to listen to and agree with opposition to the war, but they had only a handful of figures who could articulate these feelings for them. What was lacking was leadership, not a willingness to consider and perhaps embrace a radical perspective.[8] The same was true for socialism; the black masses were ripe for change, but there were only a handful of effective socialist leaders, men like Harrison, Randolph, and Woodbey, and they could not rely on a committed, nonracist party to support them with tangible programs directed toward racial improvement. Had white socialists embarked on such a program, the incentive for wider black leadership would have been present. The fault lies in the party. Blacks were ready to be included in and even lead a progressive mass movement, but only Marcus Garvey offered such an opportunity.

The irony of this chapter in black history and the history of socialism is that the Socialist Party was only successful in reaching a segment of the black masses when it was a far weaker entity, in the mid-1930s in Arkansas. Here black and white sharecroppers organized not on an ideological basis but around concrete political and economic needs. These were not new grievances; they had existed two and three decades earlier, between 1900 and 1920, when the party was far stronger in both numbers and national influence. On the basis of this evidence, then, it is incorrect to assume that socialism was irrelevant to black America in the early twentieth century. There simply was no adequate trial.

NOTES

1. Philip S. Foner, *American Socialism and Black Americans From the Age of Jackson to World War II* (Westport, Conn., 1977), p. 252. This volume offers the most detailed study of the Socialist Party's activities on behalf of and among blacks. Scholars owe Foner a considerable debt for his diligent research into party newspapers.

2. Quoted in Philip S. Foner, "The IWW and the Black Worker," *Journal of Negro History*, 55 (January 1970), p. 47. This article provides the best analysis of the IWW's efforts to organize blacks between 1905 and 1920.

3. Theodore Kornweibel, Jr., *No Crystal Stair: Black Life and the MESSENGER, 1917–1928* (Westport, Conn., 1975).

4. The most complete biographical data on World War I–era black socialists can be found in Foner, *American Socialism and Black Americans*; Kornweibel, *No Crystal Stair*; and Jervis Anderson, *A. Philip Randolph: A Biographical Portrait* (New York, 1973). Only one member of this group has written autobiographically. Schuyler, who died in 1977, viewed his socialist days through right-wing spectacles in *Black and Conservative: The Autobiography of George S. Schuyler* (New Rochelle, N.Y., 1966).

5. Foner, *American Socialism and Black Americans,* ch. 10.

6. John Beecher, "The Sharecroppers' Union in Alabama," *Social Forces,* 13 (1934–35), pp. 124–32; Theodore Rosengarten, *All God's Dangers: The Life of Nate Shaw* (New York, 1974).

7. Jerold S. Auerbach, "Southern Tenant Farmers: Socialist Critics of the New Deal," *Labor History*, 7 (Winter 1966), pp. 3–18.

8. Theodore Kornweibel, Jr., "Apathy and Dissent: Black America's Negative Responses to World War I," *South Atlantic Quarterly,* 80 (Summer 1981), pp. 322–28.

REPLY

Sally Miller

My essay entitled "The Socialist Party and the Negro, 1901–1920" attempts to highlight the relationship between the pre-World War One Socialist Party of America and black Americans.[1] The essay argues that the Socialist Party's treatment of the actual plight and exploitation of American blacks was marked, at best, by indifference, even though it must be acknowledged that a number of individual Socialists clearly sought to commit the party to a serious struggle on behalf of black liberation.

Theodore Kornweibel, Jr., and I agree that the prewar Socialist Party failed to address the problems of black America. Not only was the racism manifested by many American socialists a factor in that failure but, it should be noted, additionally important was the fact that the party's class perspective precluded a consensus emerging on support for liberation struggles for any groups other than the working class as a whole. Distinguishable groups, whether racial, religious, ethnic, or sexual, could not easily persuade the Socialist Party that a struggle on their behalf would not dilute party energies needed for the class struggle. No less a party leader than Morris Hillquit argued in 1903, in the deliberations of the International Socialist Bureau, against the principle of recognition of distinctive groups. While Hillquit was at the time opposing separate representation for Jewish socialists in the Russian delegations to the Second International, he also opposed, and thus succeeded in delaying, ethnic representation within the Socialist Party of America. Not until 1910, at least half a dozen years after the issue was raised, did socialist foreign-language federations in the United States win the right to affiliate with the Socialist Party. Thus, the party's failure to undertake an overt struggle for black equality was entirely consistent with its general emphasis on class to the exclusion of any other identification.

Kornweibel correctly notes that one state branch of the party, Oklahoma's, was an exception to the pattern of obtuseness on racial issues and, had he considered the recently published *Grass-Roots Socialism: Radical Movements in the Southwest* by James R. Green,[2] he could have fully amplified the picture of this one branch of the party recognizing the special aspects of black workers' exploitation. Indeed, numbers of Oklahoma-based Socialists, such as Oscar Ameringer, opposed segregation.

The bulk of the Kornweibel rejoinder is conjectural and, therefore, impossible to disprove. Kornweibel cites examples of interracial radical alliances in Alabama and Arkansas during the Great Depression involving communists and socialists as suggestive that at least the possibility existed of mass interracial organization based on economic concerns in the prewar period as well. If only the Socialist Party, in this its most vibrant era, had been willing to take up that challenge, he implies, but Green already has traced the existence of a few such relatively successful efforts in prewar Oklahoma.[3] Although Kornweibel alters my statement that a fruitful relationship could not or would not have evolved, nevertheless his argument for the fundamental possibility of mass militancy cannot be denied. But when he suggests that World War One apathy of the black masses in the face of the war patriotism of black leaders might mean that a mass radicalism could have occurred had a large number of radical black leaders emerged, he is far from convincing. Kornweibel points out Philip Foner's "discovery" of a group of historically neglected black socialist preachers,[4] but the degree of the influence wielded by these few men is yet to be clarified. Clearly, the number of black leaders committed to socialism was always slim, and the black masses did not choose socialism. Had community leaders in great numbers done so, the masses may or may not have followed. We simply do not know. In essence, Kornweibel believes that it is incorrect to assume that the socialist message, if projected to black America, would have been perceived as irrelevant; while in my view, it is incorrect to assume that a black radical leadership and a Socialist Party commitment to black liberation would have met with a positive response in the black community.

NOTES

1. For a fuller treatment of this matter, see Philip S. Foner, *American Socialism and Black Americans: From the Age of Jackson to World War II* (Westport, Conn., 1977).

2. James R. Green, *Grass-Roots Socialism: Radical Movements in the Southwest, 1895–1943* (Baton Rouge, La., 1978).

3. Ibid., p. 108.

4. Foner, pp. 151–81.

Chapter 7

SOCIALISM AND ETHNICITY*

Charles Leinenweber

The failure of the American Socialist Party to develop, in its early years, into a viable working-class movement is as much due to its own shortcomings as to the material conditions of American capitalist society. From the time of its formation in 1901 to the time of its disastrous split in 1919, the party faced several critical political decisions. One of the most important of these was how to relate to the vast numbers of "new" immigrant workers in the United States—southern and eastern Europeans by birth. These new immigrants found work in the nation's industrial centers, primarily as unskilled laborers. By 1909, they made up the majority of the industrial working class.[1] At the same time—and until shortly before the split—the ethnic composition of the party differed remarkably. In 1908, when it had some forty thousand members, 71 percent were native Americans, while 17.5 percent were "old" immigrants from northern and western Europe.[2]

Throughout its formative years—the only period when it represented a possible threat to American capitalism—the Socialist Party failed to attract substantial numbers of new immigrant workers. Historian Marcus Hansen comments, "Probably more immigrant Socialists were lost to the cause in the United States than were won from the ranks of the newcomers."[3] One major reason for this failure is that the party chose *not* to relate to the new immigrants. Instead, it chose to relate—indecisively, but almost exclusively—to the AFL-organized workers and their leaders, and independently organized "old" immigrant workers. As a consequence of this exclusive focus, the Socialist Party remained out of touch with large segments of the American working class.

* Charles Leinenweber, "The American Socialist Party and 'New' Immigrants," *Science and Society*, 32, no. 1 (Winter 1968), pp. 2–25.

The attitude of the Socialist Party toward immigrant workers is most clearly reflected in its attitude toward immigration. For as one of the leading historians of immigration, Oscar Handlin, points out, the future immigrants are judged by those already present, and the decision concerning who shall be admitted is based upon an image of those already here.[4] The party had a definite image of those already here, but it was developed more within the narrow perspective of American craft unionism than the broad perspective of international socialism.

Around the turn of the century, nativism became a potent force in American politics.[5] Partly as a result of the massive increase in immigration from southern and eastern Europe, and partly as a result of American imperialist ambitions, this period gave rise to "scientific" theories of racism. Among the early proponents of American nativism were the craft unions.[6] The AFL almost from its inception favored restricting immigration,[7] and its leaders were given to increasingly nativist notions about foreign workers. In 1906, the AFL presented its famous "'Bill of Grievances" to President Theodore Roosevelt and leaders of the House and Senate. A key proposal—and one of the few Roosevelt liked—was a bill to restrict immigration.[8] The AFL continued to seek restriction until its proposals were enacted.

The AFL listed a number of economic reasons for restricting immigration. The new immigrants, the AFL felt, threatened the standard of living of American workers. They came as cheap labor reconciled to lower standards of living, were willing to work for less pay, and thus drove the native workers and older immigrants out of their jobs. Moreover, the AFL said, they were incapable of organization, and they scabbed.

Beyond this, the AFL was outspokenly nativist. Samuel Gompers upheld the principle that "the maintenance of the nation depended upon the maintenance of racial purity" and suggested that immigrant workers "could not be Americanized and could not be taught to render the same intelligent service as was supplied by American workers."[9] Gompers felt the AFL was striving for "the maintenance of American institutions as they are and only immigrant restriction could make this possible."[10]

In an exhaustively documented study of immigration and labor published in 1912, labor economist Isaac Hourwich stripped away the specious economic arguments of the AFL.[11] Immigrants, he said, were attracted by expanding industries that needed labor far beyond the resources of the labor market. They did not drive out the old work force; either they supplemented it or it moved upward, out of the ranks of the unskilled. Despite the rapid influx of new immigrants, the proportion of surplus labor available to capitalists remained the same. Generally, Hourwich said, the new immigrants were paid *more* than the native and old immigrant workers preceding them and *more* than the native workers in similar jobs in regions where there were no immigrants.[12] While it was true that immigrants were frequently used as strikebreakers, this was also true of native workers—including those in AFL unions. Finally, the new immigrants were fully capable of organization—there were many instances of militant and cohesive strikes by them. However, the AFL was unwilling to touch them so long as they remained unskilled. Oscar Handlin comments,

> The A.F. of L. . . . focused its attention entirely upon the skilled workers enlisted in craft unions which abjured any general reforms and concerned themselves entirely with improving the status of their own members. These associations had long regarded the newcomer with distrust; the addition of every new hand to the labor force was an unsettling element that threatened their own established position.[13]

In proposing restrictions on immigration, the AFL was fighting a rearguard action against mechanization. The unions as a whole were protecting their positions as an aristocracy of labor, while the leaders were protecting their own offices.[14]

During the period of the new immigration, American skilled workers formed an aristocracy of labor. Southern and eastern Europeans replaced native Americans and old immigrants in unskilled jobs and also became unskilled laborers in expanding and new industries. Meanwhile, native American and old immigrant workers took virtually all the skilled jobs in the new industry.[15] The net result of this process was that the line between skilled and unskilled workers became very clear: skilled workers were native Americans and old immigrants; unskilled workers were new immigrants. Thus added to the usual differences between skilled and unskilled workers were language and culture. At the same time,

American society as a whole was becoming more and more nativistic. The new immigrant workers were greeted with contempt by the native and old immigrant workers.[16] The refusal of the AFL to organize unskilled workers made the distinction ever more clear, and its frequent discrimination against new immigrants erected a real barrier between unskilled and skilled workers. AFL and other skilled workers were not only protecting their jobs and wages, but they were withholding their gains from foreigners. It was this action that made skilled workers an aristocracy of labor.

Besides wanting to protect the aristocracy of labor, the AFL demanded restrictions because it feared the radicalism of the immigrant worker. Handlin says the AFL felt that "restriction would bar entirely those who might listen to the blandishments of the revolutionaries."[17] The leadership was aware of the deep hostility of immigrants toward the AFL and witnessed the success of the IWW in organizing them. William Leiserson, writing for the well-known Carnegie-sponsored Americanization Studies, took up this question. He says that the president of a national union

> explained that his union ceased trying to organize immigrants because he found they were only recruiting for the I.W.W. Still another official, when asked as to the advisability of issuing foreign language literature explaining trade union principles, replied that this would only give the agitators among the immigrants better opportunities to make the American Federation of Labor ridiculous in the eyes of their countrymen. . . . And the representative of the Federation in a large industrial state frankly declared he did not want to organize too many foreigners as there were so many radicals among them.[18]

Leiserson also tells of an interview with leaders of the AFL United Textile Workers who characterized the "foreign elements" as "Socialists and radicals. . . . It was easy enough to organize them, but generally the I.W.W. reaped the harvest. . . . Even those foreigners who do not come here as radicals are carried away by the flighty ideals."[19] These AFL leaders were not simply operating on the stereotype of the immigrant as an anarchist. They knew firsthand the militancy of the immigrants and their unions.

It is only within the broader context of the attitude of organized labor toward immigration that the Socialist Party position makes sense. Of course, the party could not possibly share the AFL's fear of the spread of socialism among workers—even though many did share its fear of syndicalism. Still—if only to gain influence—the party could share the AFL's nativism and racism and its desire to protect the aristocracy of labor.

One of the major questions raised at the 1910 Party Congress concerned the new immigration.[20] The party was faced with a dilemma: should it reaffirm the principle of international working class solidarity—so strong an element in the Marxist tradition—and welcome immigrants? Or should it call for restricting immigration in line with the AFL policy?[21]

For several years prior to the 1910 Congress, immigration had been a hotly debated question throughout the party. The Stuttgart International Socialist Congress of 1907 passed a resolution condemning restrictions based on race or nationality and calling for organizing immigrants for political and economic rights.[22] The Party National Executive Committee and later the National Committee rejected the Stuttgart resolution and came out for the exclusion of workers from oriental and other "backward" countries.[23] In 1908, the question was put before the party convention in the form of a resolution, which was reported and defended by John Spargo. In part, it said:

> To deny the right of workers to protect themselves against injury to their interests, caused by the competition of imported foreign laborers, whose standards of living are materially lower than their own, is to set a bourgeois Utopian ideal above the class struggle.[24]

The resolution went on to specify Socialist opposition to "all immigration which is subsidized or stimulated by the capitalist class, and all contract labor immigration. . . ."[25] It proposed that the question of exclusion based on race—primarily Asian—be left to the next convention, with a committee elected to study it in the meantime.[26]

In the debate that followed, no really clear divisions emerged based on the resolution. Its wording was so vague that it could be supported or opposed by supporters and opponents of exclusion alike. One delegate, a militant opponent of exclusion, began his statement, "I am in favor of the resolution," and ended, "so far as I am concerned, my yellow working wage slaves and comrades, we will stand or fall together."[27] He was followed by Ernest Untermann, a militant racist, who concluded his statement, "I am determined that my race shall be supreme in this country and the world. For this reason I am in favor of the report adopted by the committee. . . ."[28] Sol Fieldman opposed it because the workers of the world are equal, and socialists should not believe "that the American workingman needs to make a study of the yellow workingman."[29] Max Hayes opposed it because he wanted "immediate action here and now in favor of the exclusion of the coolies from Japan and China."[30]

But even though the nature of the resolution was elusive, the debate itself began to touch on the fundamental question of nativism and racism versus internationalism. Victor Berger, a racist speaking for exclusion, made the homey suggestion, "Because your neighbor's house is burning, shall you set your own house on fire? No, say I. Defend your own house and then help your neighbor, that is the way."[31] Untermann—one of the leading Marxist theoreticians in America—agreed: "I believe in the international solidarity of the working class. . . . But I do not believe in international solidarity to the point of cutting my own throat."[32] The most eloquent defender of internationalism in the debate, Barney Berlyn, said, "If we permit ourselves to go to work and tack on amendments to the proposition of 'Workingmen of all countries, unite'—if you tack on amendments to that, then tack a clause to the name of the Socialist Party, the words, 'A damn lie.' "[33] (The minutes record "A d--- lie.") The nativists replied that the famous Marxist slogan did not mean that workers should all come to America. It did not mean "workingmen of the world rotate."[34] Max Hayes explained that had he investigated conditions on the Pacific Coast, "Karl Marx would be likely to change his tactics on the question. . . ."[35]

The Spargo resolution was adopted by voice vote. The convention elected four racists—Ernest Untermann, Victor Berger, Joseph Wanhope, and Guy Miller—and the equivocal John Spargo to the permanent committee on immigration.[36]

At the 1910 Party Congress, the division between the racists and nativists, on the one hand, and the internationalists, on the other, became more clear. The committee report and the statements supporting it are prime examples of racism and nativism couched in left-wing rhetoric. Orientals should be excluded, the report stated, because their "backwardness" makes them "a menace to the progress of the most aggressive, militant and intelligent elements of our working class population."[37] Oriental immigration would relegate "the class war to the rear . . ." by weakening labor organizations and increasing race conflict.[38] The report made no specific mention of European immigration.

John Spargo submitted his own minority report, which quoted the entire Stuttgart resolution and went on to call for breaking down the racial barriers that divided the working class. But once again he equivocated. Toward the end, the resolution specifically disagreed with the Stuttgart position that exclusion based on race is necessarily "in conflict with the principle of proletarian solidarity." It stated that if a race "menaces our standard of living, or our democratic institutions," then the Socialist Party "would be compelled, however regretfully," to stand for total exclusion.[39] Spargo felt that current Asian immigration was too low to warrant exclusion—but the Chinese Exclusion Act was in effect!

Although the reports and debate focused primarily on oriental exclusion, there were references to southern and eastern European workers. One delegate reminded the Congress of the ignorant protests of Italian and Sicilian immigrants and their divisive influence in the trade unions.[40] A spokesman for the Polish organization warned, "This talk about America for the Americans is simply proving to the Americans that you are determined to fight the foreign elements of this country and exclude them from the shores of America."[41] Other representatives from foreign-language federations feared that restrictions might be extended to people from their homelands.[42] John Spargo explained that "if today you vote Asiatic exclusion, next time you will be voting Italian exclusion or Hebrew exclusion."[43]

Several of the militant racists, however, had friendly remarks for the new immigrants. Ernest Untermann contrasted the relative ease with which Sicilians, Italians, and Greeks were organized with the difficulties encountered with Orientals.[44] But in the same speech—meticulously woven into an anticapitalist context—he sounded the universal, nativist slogan "Get out of America and give it back to the Americans."[45] Victor Berger stressed that all European immigrants could be assimilated over time and were welcome. He mentioned the opposition of German social democracy to coolie labor and attacked the notion that "we should have the coolies."[46] But while Berger limited himself to denouncing Asian coolies at the 1910 Congress, elsewhere he was more inclusive. In June 1911, before the House of Representatives, he referred to "Slavonians, Italians, Greeks, Russians, and Armenians" as the "modern white coolies" of the steel industry, who had "crowded out the Americans, Germans, Englishmen, and Irishmen."[47]

Early in the debate over the resolution, Morris Hillquit introduced a substitute. He correctly pointed out that both reports agreed in principle to the exclusion of races as such. "To that," he said, "I am opposed."[48] His resolution was brief. It began:

> The Socialist Party of the United States favors all legislative measures tending to prevent the immigration of strike-breakers and contract laborers, and the mass importation of workers from foreign countries, brought about by the employing classes for the purpose of weakening the organization of American labor, and of lowering the standard of life of American workers.[49]

David Shannon accurately comments that this "might have been written by an AFL convention."[50] But Hillquit's resolution went on to say:

> The party is opposed to the exclusion of any immigrants on account of their race or nationality, and demands that the United States be at all times maintained as a free asylum for all men and women persecuted by the governments of their countries on account of their politics, religion or race.[51]

Just as they had in 1908, the resolutions drew confused support. The majority report attracted only racists. But Spargo presented a solidly internationalist defense of his resolution, and it drew support and fire from both sides. The same was true of Hillquit's substitute, which eventually the congress adopted by a narrow margin.

Seen in the context of AFL policy, the Hillquit resolution could have meant no less than restrictions on southern and eastern European immigration. As one delegate pointed out, the resolution "will save the face of the majority report in this congress."[52] The first half was strictly AFL. Of the second half, only the phrase pertaining to exclusion based on race or nationality was uniquely internationalist. Yet even the original committee report claimed to advocate "unconditional exclusion" of Asians, "not as races per se," but rather because they came from backward places.[53] (It is interesting to note that these backward places included Japan.) The AFL view was that virtually *all* immigration was brought about for the purposes of weakening organized labor and lowering the standard of living. It followed that all immigration must be limited or stopped. That Hillquit felt himself in general agreement with the AFL policy is beyond dispute. In an article on immigration—written in 1907, *after* the Stuttgart Conference[54]—Hillquit praised the AFL leadership for its policy[55] while criticizing indifference to the problems of immigrants:

> And finally the majority of American socialists side with the trade unions in their demand for the exclusion of workingmen of such races and nations as have not yet been drawn into the sphere of modern production, and who are incapable of assimilation with the workingmen of the country of their adoption, and of joining the organization and struggles of their class. . . . Just what races are to be included in this category is a question that can only be decided from time to time with reference to the particular circumstances and conditions of each class.

Many years later, Hillquit could look back and say of the participants in the cloak-makers strike of 1910, "Like most Jewish workers they were long-suffering, meek, and submissive. But every once in a while they would flare up in an outburst of despair and revolt, and go on strike."[57] Prior to 1910, he said, "They seemed hopelessly unorganizable on a permanent basis."[58] In other words, they were incapable of joining the organization and struggles of their class.

Eugene Debs was outraged by the party's debate on immigration. His views were published in the *International Socialist Review* shortly after the congress—which, typically, he did not attend. Debs felt that the majority report represented a thorough capitulation to the AFL—"civic federation unionism."[59] He called it "utterly unsocialistic, reactionary, and in truth outrageous" and warned, "If Socialism, international revolutionary Socialism, does not stand staunchly, unflinchingly, and uncompromisingly for the working class and for the oppressed masses of all lands, then it stands for none and its claim is a false pretense and its profession a delusion and a snare."[60] The charge that the opponents of free immigration were simply capitulators to the AFL was a common one during the congress itself. One delegate saw "some sort of effort to sweeten our program for the A.F. of L."[61] Another claimed, "It is the beginning of catering to the demands of the A.F. of L. . . ."[62] Frank Cassidy said, "We are posing as the champions of the working class. But you are kowtowing to the American Federation of Labor. . . ." He asked, "Why must we crawl on our bellies to Sam Gompers?"[63] Ernest Untermann replied to these charges in his summary:

> We are not toadying to the American Federation of Labor. We are scientific investigators charged by the Socialist Party with the analysis of a certain problem. . . . If Gompers or the American Federation of Labor adopts a policy which is in the interests of the working class, then the Socialist Party will work with them no matter if we are charged with toadying to them. . . .[64]

Untermann went on to say that if the AFL advocated a policy that was in the interest of the capitalist class, the party would "oppose them uncompromisingly."[65]

Whatever the motivations, the lines of division between racists and nativists, on the one hand, and internationalists, on the other, were becoming clear. The division did not follow regional lines, even though frequent reference was made to the Pacific Coast. The Washington state organization instructed its delegates to vote for exclusion,[66] but the Portland local opposed it.[67] Nor was it based on native American versus immigrants. Berger and Untermann, for example, were immigrants, although Berger came to this country, he pointed out, "imbued not only with Socialism but also with the right kind of Americanism."[68] Nor was it based on a rural-urban split. Surprisingly, some of the most militant opponents of exclusion came from farm areas. Perhaps the most moving speech for international brotherhood came from a Missouri delegate, W. W. McAllister, who said,

When I sat down on my plow beam and studied this thing over, there was a mental picture that came to me, and the Chinese came to me and the Japanese came to me, and the nationalities all came around me in that old field on the Ozark Mountains, and I said, "We are all of one blood." I went back home and told the folks, and for twenty years I have been preaching the doctrine of human solidarity of the laboring class of people all around the globe; not here in Chicago, not down in Missouri, not here in Illinois, but as far as the sin of capitalism extends, the solidarity of every man, woman and child.[69]

Nor was the division based on class. Both sides were supported by "blanket stiffs," trade unionists, editors, and lawyers.

The lines of division followed the left-right split in the party. On the right were municipal socialists, on the whole friendly or at least neutral toward the AFL. Among them were the racists. The municipal socialists favored an end to free immigration. On the left were industrial socialists, generally hostile toward the AFL but friendly toward the IWW and revolutionary industrial unionism. They favored free immigration.

During the debate on immigration, Ernest Untermann charged that "the comrades allied with the IWW" led the opposition to the majority report.[70] He was certainly close. At the 1910 Congress, the party debated its traditional "no interference" attitude toward the AFL. Frank Cassidy introduced a militant resolution calling for Socialist endorsement of industrial unionism.[71] Of those voting, every one of the delegates who had spoken out for restricted immigration voted against Cassidy's resolution. They numbered fifteen in all. Of the ten delegates who had spoken out against restricted immigration, seven voted for the Cassidy resolution. The voting was essentially the same on a milder resolution endorsing industrial unionism.[72] Both were defeated overwhelmingly as the party reasserted its "no interference" attitude.[73]

One reason the industrial socialists were hostile toward the AFL was that they wanted to unify the working class. They were determined to erase lines of division and sectional interests within the working class. One such line was craft. Another very important one was nationality. Their appeal had to transcend nationality, and it did. If the immigrant workers couldn't be a part of American society, they could be a part of something much greater: the international working class.

The industrial socialists entered the field with a broad, internationalist perspective. They saw the working class as world-wide, and their brotherly contact with so many different nationalities reinforced this belief. To the industrial socialists there were, as Bill Haywood put it, "no foreigners in the working class." They saw the restriction policies of the AFL as an attempt to bolster the privileged position of craft unions and thus strengthen the aristocracy of labor and working-class divisions. The industrial socialists reaffirmed proletarian internationalism by demanding that the gates be kept open.

The workers who interested the industrial socialists most were unskilled and unorganized. This meant that they were overwhelmingly new immigrants, and so the industrial socialists became linked to them. The link was usually forged in the following way: unskilled immigrant workers would strike spontaneously, without leadership or organization. The only experienced, militant organizers who were willing to work with them were the industrial socialists—especially the IWW—and the immigrant workers would invite them to lead the strike. The biggest IWW victories in the East followed this pattern.

In the big strikes, the politics and actions of the immigrant workers coincided with those of the industrial socialists, bringing them ever more closely together. The immigrants were very hostile toward the AFL, which ignored and even scabbed on them. They were engaged in a naked struggle—the local law and citizenry were always against them; they were not voters. The immigrant workers fought courageously and with deep solidarity. Their entire communities threw themselves into the battles. It is no wonder that the industrial socialists felt so close to them, no wonder that they wanted no restrictions on immigration.

Municipal socialists, on the other hand, tried to develop close ties to the trade unions, such as the highly successful Social-Democratic Party of Milwaukee had. Most could only wish they had them, but even so they began to absorb the limited perspective of trade unionism, at least in anticipation; wherever socialists are linked to trade unions, they must share at least part of the perspective of the unions. For the municipal socialists, this sharing was especially important: even where they had the opportunity, as in Milwaukee, they were unwilling to *broaden* that perspective through aggressive leadership. Instead, they chose to relegate it to the economic dimension of a dichotomy, economic versus political struggle—an approach similar to the German social democrats' "twin pillars." Thus aside from effecting a few reforms, the municipal socialists never did anything extraordinary in the AFL other than challenge its conservative leadership.[74] They remained officially neutral on the question of how to organize the unskilled (mainly immigrant) workers. That was part of the economic struggle, the job of the trade unions alone.

Similarly, the question of immigration manifested itself in economic terms. The trade unions saw immigration as an economic threat and so, then, did the municipal socialists. When Ernest Untermann told the 1910 Socialist Party Congress that the pro-restrictive forces were not selling out to Gompers, but their positions merely coincided, he was probably telling the truth. The municipal socialists felt they were expressing the genuine economic interests of trade unionists. They were in profound agreement with those interests and were incapable of viewing immigration in any way distinct from the AFL.

Their preoccupation with the political dimension of the dichotomy meant that the political struggle came to be everything for the party. Thus they organized to get out the vote more than anything else. In New York, municipal socialists chased votes.[75] In Milwaukee, they built a machine, and Victor Berger was its boss. The municipal socialists then looked upon the new immigrant merely as voting-booth fodder. Winfield Gaylord, a former Congregationalist minister and one of Berger's right-hand men, told the 1910 Socialist Party Congress this revealing story about the social democratic engineering:

> I went down to the Italian ward and spent the whole of election day there watching to see that those crooked Irishmen did not lead the Italians around by the nose. Victor Berger took an automobile and went from one Polish precinct to another to see to it that those same Irish politicians did not lead the Poles around by the nose.[76]

By 1916, after working with Berger for several years, A. M. Simons could complain that the Socialist Party was "today little more than an organized appetite for office—a Socialist Tammany, exploiting the devotion of its members instead of the funds of corporations, for the benefit of a little circle of perfectly honest, but perfectly incompetent and selfish politicians."[77] Like any political machine, the Socialist Tammany looked on its immigrant supporters with disdain.

The municipal socialists became so caught up with local campaigns and problems that the notion of an international movement began to fade. As their focus narrowed, they reflected more and more the sentiments and interest of their local constituencies. Further, they sacrificed principles and diluted their programs and thereby decreased their independence even more. The municipal socialists continued to look to European parties as models but rejected their internationalist proposals, such as the one on immigration at the Stuttgart Conference. They emphasized the immediate, sectional interests of the people at home before all else and thus enhanced the growth of working-class nationalism. From where they stood, immigration seemed an invasion from foreign soil, and they wanted it stopped.

Until the 1910 Congress, the Socialist Party failed to take an official position on organizing immigrants for socialist ends. Amazingly, even immigrant socialists had remained virtually invisible to them despite the emergence of numerous, unaffiliated socialist foreign-language groups and newspapers throughout the nation.

In 1904, several of these groups sent fraternal representatives to the Socialist Party convention. They asked to affiliate, and the convention referred the problem to the National Committee, which in turn passed it on to the National Executive Committee.[78] The NEC suggested a peculiar arrangement that involved a choice between high dues or disbanding and hence was unacceptable to the immigrant socialist groups.[79] In 1906, the NEC allowed a Finnish group of over two thousand members to affiliate with no vote in exchange for dues to the national. The Finnish locals then affiliated with their respective state Socialist parties to gain the vote indirectly, while maintaining their distinctive national organization. Numerous other immigrant groups affiliated their locals with state parties, but only the Lettish affiliated with the national party.[80]

This kind of arrangement did not satisfy the immigrant socialists. They felt that the problems they faced were unusual enough to warrant separate organizations within the party, yet they wanted equal rights. These included separate representation at conventions and the right to be elected to party committees. They wanted to be able to work among their own people in the name of the Socialist Party, to recruit them to an organization in which they both felt comfortable and played an active role. Immigrant socialists who made their way to the party individually soon dropped away because they and their comrades could not understand each other. The futility of this sort of encounter was unintentionally dramatized before the 1910 Party Congress. Party Secretary J. Mahlon Barnes was confronted by two sets of delegates claiming to represent the Hungarian Socialist Society. He was unable to choose between them and explained to the congress, "I do not understand Hungarian. I wish the chairman or someone who understands the language would inquire into the facts."[81]

The immigrant socialists were offended by the party's refusal to recognize their unusual problems and to give them a fair chance to resolve them. A Polish representative told the 1910 Congress,

> . . . a good many foreign organizations being affiliated with the Socialist Party do not participate in the votes . . . for the simple reason that you send out the referendum of the party in the English language. . . . And even suppose they were participating and were voting for our candidates, don't you know that we are in a hopeless minority so that we can not elect a single member to this body, to represent our interests?[82]

The opponents of separate organizations replied that the immigrant socialists must be integrated into the American movement immediately: "You are in America now; get into the American movement."[83] The immigrants countered that it was impossible for the party to hold them unless foreign-language affiliates were set up. Therefore, they were proposing the only effective way of integrating the immigrants into the American movement.

> They don't want to separate; they don't want to withdraw from the party; they want to join in the party. . . . When you go to one of the Italians or Poles and talk to him in English about the party, he does not understand. This is all the privilege we ask; to conduct our work in our own tongue until we learn the American tongue.[84]

The Party Congress recognized the tremendous potential for growth the immigrant groups offered and so passed a constitutional amendment providing for fairly autonomous foreign-language federations. The terms still included a somewhat heavy dues load for the federations and refused them a vote at the national convention,[85] but they were acceptable to the immigrants.

Between 1910 and 1912, five foreign-language federations—South Slavic, Italian, Scandinavian, Hungarian, and Bohemian—affiliated with the party, bringing the total to seven.[86] Altogether, they accounted for 16,000 of the party's 118,000 members.[87] The federations had varying success. The Finns showed the same rapid rate of growth and remarkable stability they had in previous years. They were by far the biggest of the federations with more than 11,000 members and 223 locals, and also the wealthiest, doing an annual "business" of two hundred thousand dollars and owning property worth over half a million dollars.[88] The Italian federation showed rapid turnover. From December 1910 to October 1911, twenty-two branches joined, but fourteen disbanded.[89] No reasons are given in their report to the 1912 party convention, but an accurate guess can be made. The southern and eastern European socialist groups were proletarian and therefore highly susceptible to fluctuations in the labor market. The South Slavic section reports eight discontinued locals: one because of merger, two "on account of the neglect of the Secretary," one because the members left town, one "on account of closing of mine," and three "on account of unemployment."[90]

Despite turnover, all the federations grew fairly rapidly. Most of their growth came from organizing new locals, but of course much came from recruiting previously established groups. A number of the old party foreign-language locals did not join the new federations.[91] The foreign-language socialist press grew considerably, but not nearly so rapidly as the English. In 1910, the party reported 3 English dailies and 33 weeklies, and 6 foreign-language dailies and 22 weeklies.[92] By 1912, there were 5 English and 8 foreign-language dailies, and 262 English and 36 foreign-language weeklies.

By 1916, the English dailies had decreased to 2 and the foreign-language increased to 13; the English weeklies had dropped from 262 to 42, and the foreign-language from 36 to 22.[93]

The 1912 party convention was pleased with the successes of the foreign-language federations. But at the same time, a few—mostly of the left wing—felt that the federations were not integrating immigrant socialists into the party. The reports of the federations indicate that they spent a significant portion of their energy supporting movements in the old country. The Finnish comrades explained,

> This has not been done for the love of the "fatherland," nor for the purpose of keeping our nationality alive, or to simply save the so-called state autonomy of Finland. At least a great majority of us have had a deeper interest in the matter—have had the aim of international socialism in mind and have given help to that part of the globe where suppression is more felt and where . . . our cause at present has a considerably strong foothold.[94]

Whatever their motives, it is clear that some of the socialist immigrants were at heart political emigrés trying primarily to build a base for supporting their European movements. Still, the socialist movement among new immigrants on the whole was a product of American conditions, not a "foreign import."[95] The problem was that the immigrant socialists were not taking advantage of the relevant American theory on conditions in the United States, and they were not joining directly with their American comrades to fight these conditions. The 1910 Congress provided that foreign-language locals would be linked closely to the state parties, but this turned out not to be the case. Instead, they were linked rather loosely through national federations to the party national office. Thus the foreign-language locals rarely came in contact with neighboring English-speaking locals and were ignorant about the party and its propaganda. Furthermore, the erection of foreign-language locals sometimes drew members out of integrated locals, thus increasing the distance between foreign and English-speaking comrades.[96]

Charles Ruthenberg of the left-wing Ohio party told the 1912 convention that foreign-language locals affiliated with the party only through the national office "never come near our central organization, are not in touch with the central organization, and take no part whatsoever in the business of the local."[97]

The left-wing critics did not want to disband the foreign-language groups but simply wanted to draw them into the activities of the local and state parties. Most federation delegates agreed with their general criticisms.[98]

The 1912 convention altered the section of the constitution pertaining to the federations, but not seriously.[99] They were required henceforth to pay dues to the state and city parties, but only through the national office.[100] The federations continued to grow, and seven more affiliated with the party by 1915. In the meantime party membership declined, so that of the 80,000 members in 1915, about a third were in the federations.[101] By 1919, party membership had climbed to 109,000, over half in the federations.[102]

However, the immigrant socialists were never integrated into the party. From the very beginning they stood to the left of the party leadership, and this was undoubtedly a major factor in their isolation. The vast majority joined after the right wing had taken a firm grip on the controls, and they were never able to exert influence in proportion to their numbers. David Shannon suggests that the leadership probably would have brought the federations closer to the party had it not been for the following incident, which occurred in 1914: A Michigan copper strike precipitated a growth of syndicalism among Finnish federation locals in the area. The federation expelled the syndicalist locals, but they retained their state and national Socialist Party affiliations. The right-wing party leadership decided,

> If autonomous foreign groups are permitted to join the party like an English local, it becomes possible to annul and wreck the work of the regular foreign-speaking federations. Any kind of syndicalist or impossibilist propaganda can be carried on, and there can be no local control, because the language becomes a barrier.[103]

Therefore, the leadership resolved to give the federations "full charge and jurisdiction in the organization of the language locals, and of all propaganda in the particular language."[104]

As it turned out, however, the right-wing leadership was willing to grant autonomy only when it served their own interests. In 1919, under fire from the left, Morris Hillquit sounded the call, "Let us clear the decks."[105] They then proceeded to expel seven Eastern European federations—Hungarian, Lithuanian, Lettish,

Russian, Polish, South Slav, and Ukrainian—with some 30,000 members. In his memoirs Hillquit explains, "These new recruits were Bolsheviks to the core."[106] Within six months, the leadership expelled or suspended two-thirds of the membership, including the seven federations and the Michigan, Ohio, Massachusetts, and Chicago parties.[107]

By 1912, the party position on immigration had fully crystallized. The municipal socialists were in control of the national organization and used it to their advantage. The 1912 party convention heard a report by the Committee on Immigration that, as Ira Kipnis says, "made the 1910 majority report seem pro-Asiatic in comparison."[108] They also heard a one-sentence minority report that simply endorsed the Stuttgart resolution.[109] But there was no debate, and the convention accepted both reports by voice vote.[110] The 1910 Hillquit resolution remained official party policy.[111] Nevertheless, the 1912 *Socialist Campaign Book*—distributed to party workers throughout the country—gave no hint of this position. Edited by municipal socialist theoretician Carl Thompson, the campaign book instead filled its section on immigration with relevant excerpts from Robert Hunter's writings on poverty. Hunter was also of the right wing, and his campaign book excerpts advance the proposal that immigration is a product of two forces: employers seeking cheap labor and steamship companies seeking passengers. Hunter told of agencies established in Europe "for the purpose of making the ignorant peasantry believe fabulous stories of wealth to be had in America."[112] Then he warned that "unskilled labor is already too plentiful"[113] and concluded,

> Immigration presents for our serious consideration a formidable array of dangers. It is unnecessary to summarize the facts and the arguments which have been given. These are the two things which, of all that have been stated, seem the most important: the likelihood of race annihilation and the possible degeneration of even the succeeding American type.[114]

With this, the Socialist Party drew past the Republican Party of William Howard Taft, which stated in its 1912 platform:

> We pledge the Republican party to the enactment of appropriate laws to give relief from the constantly growing evil of induced or undesir-

able immigration, which is inimical to the progress and welfare of the people of the United States.[115]

But the Socialist Party was running Eugene Debs! This ludicrous paradox—of party workers explaining their opposition to immigration while campaigning for their most prominent internationalist—highlights the power of the right wing. But it also highlights the fact that in 1912—the year of its greatest vote—the party was in shambles. Debs was by far the best-known and most popular socialist in America. He was especially loved in the Midwest and among new immigrant socialists. Yet he was increasingly unpopular with the right-wing leaders in the party, and they were anxious to wipe out his influence—however rarely exercised. As a national spokesman, he was much too far to the left for them. The syndicalist elements in the left wing also worried them, and so 1912 saw the party adopt a constitutional amendment outlawing "direct action" and sabotage. Using this as a lever, they pried Bill Haywood from his position on the National Executive Committee. Haywood left the party, and with him went thousands of Wobblies and sympathizers.

Still the sources of strain remained. The municipal socialists were intent on building a massive, amorphous labor-reform party through increasingly large showings at the polls. The industrial socialists were intent on building a fairly homogeneous revolutionary proletarian party through industrial organization plus educational and some electoral activities. They were willing to sacrifice numbers for the sake of principles. These two opposing forces—municipal and industrial socialism—often pulled the party into warring camps engaged in ongoing, bitter factional fights. Each side saw the other as blocking its way to the ideal party—and to socialism. Occasionally the fights grew so severe that one side would attempt to eliminate the other. In the American Socialist Party, it was always the right wing that took the step. In 1912, the municipal socialists eliminated the syndicalists. In 1919, the municipal socialists again transformed their vision of the party as amorphous into a homogeneous one and eliminated two-thirds of the membership. This transformation was made easy because, despite their party intentions, the right wing was always relatively tight-knit. The left wing, on the other hand, was relatively loose.

Of those expelled in 1919, most dropped out of sight and were probably never recovered by the socialist movement. The rest formed *two* communist parties.

If the multitudes of new immigrants were at all touched by American socialism, they were merely grazed. Of the opposing forces of municipal and industrial socialism, only industrial socialism approached them in the spirit of brotherhood. But the IWW was unable to concern itself with day-to-day union issues and routine demands, and lost immigrant workers almost as quickly as they were recruited. The socialist unions that often followed up the IWW soon became bureaucratic and—especially when the communists started threatening—made their peace with Gompers and craft unionism. The appeal of municipal socialism could hardly have been more impressive to the new immigrants than the appeal of progressivism. Yet progressivism was repulsive to the immigrants. When municipal socialists built Tammany machines, they were successful with immigrants, but only in getting their votes. They did not make socialists out of them.

So long as the party was controlled by the right wing, it was incapable of molding a socialist army out of the new immigrants. The party's attitude toward immigration, its neutrality with regard to exclusive craft unionism, its municipal reform campaigns, its inability to counteract the Church—these factors combined to make the party impotent with respect to immigrants. Had the left wing been in control, the result may have been the same.

Within the party, the new immigrants added to the force of industrial unionism. But they lay outside the center of conflict between municipal and industrial socialism because they were on the periphery of the party. Thus they added more numbers than weight to their political tendency.

The immigrant socialists were the party's transmission belt to the new immigrant workers. But the party never set this transmission belt in motion. Instead, partly motivated by nativism and racism and worried by their politics, it kept these immigrant socialists adrift, failing to integrate them. As a consequence, the immigrant socialists and their audience were denied an adequate socialist comprehension of the United States. Likewise, the Socialist Party failed to gain insight into the conditions of life of immigrant workers.

NOTES

1. In 1909, the U.S. Immigration Commission made a study of wage workers in twenty principal mining and manufacturing industries. They found that 60 percent of the men and 47 percent of the women were immigrants. The percentage was only slightly less in sixteen minor industries. See William M. Leiserson, *Adjusting Immigrant and Industry* (New York, 1924), pp. 12–13.

2. Nathan Fine, *Labor and Farmer Parties in the United States, 1828–1928* (New York, 1928), p. 324.

3. Marcus Hansen, *The Immigrant in American History* (Cambridge, 1940), p. 9.

4. Oscar Handlin, *The Uprooted* (Boston, 1951), p. 294.

5. Ibid., p. 286.

6. William S. Bernard, *American Immigration Policy* (New York, 1950), p. 10.

7. Marc Karson, *American Labor Unions and Politics* (Carbondale, Ill., 1958), p. 136.

8. Ibid., pp. 42–43.

9. Quoted in Karson, op. cit., p. 137.

10. Ibid.

11. Isaac A. Hourwich, *Immigration and Labor—The Economic Aspects of European Immigration to the United States* (New York, 1912); see his summary review, pp. 1–39, and relevant chapters.

12. Ibid., pp. 401ff.

13. Handlin, op. cit., p. 289.

14. See Hourwich, op. cit., p. 414.

15. See Hourwich, op. cit., pp. 148–76.

16. When the United Mine Workers began organizing immigrant workers, their first task was to overcome the prejudice of native miners. They were asked not to call the foreigners "Hunky" or "Dago" but to use their Christian names. Leiserson, op. cit., p. 187.

17. Handlin, op. cit., p. 289.

18. Leiserson, op. cit., p. 182.

19. Ibid., pp. 202–03.

20. Fine, op. cit., p. 268; David A. Shannon, *The Socialist Party of America* (New York, 1955), p. 47.

21. Shannon, op. cit., p. 47.

22. Ira Kipnis, *The American Socialist Movement, 1897–1912* (New York, 1952), pp. 277–78.

23. Ibid., p. 279.

24. *Proceedings,* National Convention of the Socialist Party, 1908, p. 105.

25. Ibid.

26. Ibid.
27. Arthur M. Lewis, ibid., p. 110.
28. Ibid., p. 111.
29. Ibid., p. 119.
30. Ibid., p. 120.
31. Ibid., p. 111.
32. Ibid., p. 110.
33. Ibid., p. 114.
34. Ibid., p. 117.
35. Ibid., p. 121.
36. Ibid., p. 312.
37. *Proceedings,* National Congress of the Socialist Party, May 15 to 21, 1910, p. 76.
38. Ibid., p. 77.
39. Ibid., p. 80.
40. Adolph Germer, ibid., p. 134.
41. I. Kawier, ibid., p. 153.
42. Fine, op. cit., p. 271.
43. Quoted in ibid, p. 270.
44. *Proceedings,* 1910, pp. 165–66.
45. Ibid., p. 164.
46. Ibid., pp. 118–19.
47. Speech of the Hon. Victor I. Berger of Wisconsin in the House of Representatives, June 14, 1911, *Congressional Record,* pp. 2026–30, quoted in Hourwich, op. cit., p. 394.
48. *Proceedings,* 1910, p. 99.
49. Ibid., p. 98.
50. Shannon, op. cit., p. 50.
51. *Proceedings,* 1910, p. 98.
52. Ibid., p. 103.
53. Ibid., p. 76.
54. Hillquit claimed at the 1910 Congress that he had been for restriction prior to the Stuttgart Conference but against it afterward. *Proceedings,* 1910, p. 158.
55. Morris Hillquit, "Immigration in the United States," *International Socialist Review* (July 1907), p. 71.
56. Ibid., pp. 74–75.
57. Morris Hillquit, *Loose Leaves from a Busy Life* (New York, 1934), p. 180.
58. Ibid., p. 131.
59. Letter from Eugene Debs to George D. Brewer, *International Socialist Review* (July 1910), pp. 16–17.
60. Ibid.
61. Thomas M. Kennedy, *Proceedings,* 1910, p. 123.
62. Fred H. Merrick, ibid., p. 104.
63. Ibid., p. 126.
64. Ibid., p. 163.

65. Ibid.
66. Mrs. E. D. Cory (Washington), ibid., p. 122.
67. Tom Lewis (Oregon), ibid., p. 142.
68. Ibid., p. 110.
69. Ibid., p. 106.
70. Ibid., p. 162.
71. Ibid., pp. 278–79.
72. Based on analysis of voting, ibid., pp. 288–89.
73. Ibid.
74. David J. Saposs, *Left Wing Unionism: A Study of Radical Policies and Tactics* (New York, 1926), p. 35.
75. Shannon, op. cit., p. 11.
76. *Proceedings,* 1910, p. 132.
77. Shannon, op. cit., pp. 79–80.
78. National Secretary J. Mahlon Barnes, *Proceedings,* 1910, p. 267.
79. Kipnis, op. cit., p. 273.
80. Fine, op. cit., p. 325.
81. *Proceedings,* 1910, p. 16.
82. Ibid., p. 18.
83. Ibid., p. 261.
84. Ibid., p. 264.
85. Ibid., p. 260.
86. Fine, op. cit., p. 325.
87. Ibid., p. 326.
88. Report of the Finnish Section, *Proceedings,* National Convention of the Socialist Party, 1912, pp. 236–39.
89. Report of the Italian Section, *Proceedings,* 1912, p. 241.
90. *Proceedings,* 1912, p. 239.
91. Ibid., p. 241.
92. Report of the National Secretary, *Proceedings,* 1910, pp. 32–33.
93. Fine, op. cit., p. 232.
94. *Proceedings,* 1912, p. 238.
95. See Julius Faulk, "The Origins of the American Communist Movement," parts 1 and 2, *New International* (Fall 1955 and Winter 1955–1956), pp. 140–44, 152–53.
96. *Proceedings,* 1912, p. 88.
97. Ibid., p. 86.
98. Ibid., p. 89.
99. Compare *Proceedings,* 1910, pp. 259–60, with *Proceedings,* 1912, p. 20.
100. *Proceedings,* 1912, p. 203.
101. Fine, op. cit., p. 326.
102. Ibid.
103. Shannon, op. cit., p. 46.
104. Ibid., p. 47.
105. Theodore Draper, *The Roots of American Communism* (New York, 1957), p. 158.

106. Hillquit, *Loose Leaves,* p. 291.
107. Draper, op. cit., p. 158.
108. Kipnis, op. cit., p. 288. The Report is in *Proceedings,* 1912, pp. 209–11.
109. *Proceedings,* 1912, p. 211.
110. Ibid., p. 167.
111. Kipnis, op. cit., p. 288.
112. *Socialist Campaign Book,* 1912, p. 233.
113. Ibid., p. 234.
114. Ibid.
115. Kirk H. Porter and Donald Bruce Johnson, eds., *National Party Platforms, 1840–1960* (Urbana, Ill., 1963), p. 187.

COMMENT

Rudolph J. Vecoli

Why did not the new immigrants rally to the red flag of socialism in America? Leinenweber's answer is that the Socialist Party, pervaded by nativism and racism, was unable to gather the eastern and southern Europeans in a fraternal embrace. Retracing ground covered some fifteen years earlier by Ira Kipnis,[1] Leinenweber assesses the party's stance with respect to the foreign-born and concludes that it failed "to relate to the new immigrants." A partisan of the left wing, he charges the municipal socialists with selling out the ideal of internationalism in their eagerness to accommodate the AFL. A reading of the proceedings of the party conclaves, however, leads me to these contrary conclusions: (1) the party majority consistently upheld the principle of international solidarity by opposing immigration restriction on the basis of race or nationality; (2) it sought earnestly to incorporate the foreign-speaking socialists within the American movement; and (3) the opposing positions on the immigration issue cannot be neatly identified with the right-left split within the party.

The immigration debate that occupied the better part of three days at the party's National Congress of 1912 reflected a wide range of opinions and concerns.[2] The arguments *against* Asian exclusion in particular and restrictions based on race and nationality in general clearly expressed the sentiments of the majority. The committee report advocating Asian exclusion was so unpopular it did not even come to a vote. Morris Hillquit's substitute, which placed the party on record as favoring legislation prohibiting the immigration of strikebreakers and contract laborers, but opposing "the exclusion of any immigrants on account of their race or nationality," was finally endorsed. This position was consonant with the resolution adopted by the International Socialist Congress at

Stuttgart in 1907. True, as Leinenweber observes, the Hillquit substitute carried by a narrow margin, but it is important to note that among those voting against it were antirestrictionists like Tommy Morgan, Tom Lewis, and Frank Cassidy, who felt it was not liberal enough to suit them. More revealing is the vote on Algernon Lee's amendment, which would have explicitly identified Asians as contract labor and hence subject to exclusion. It was defeated by a vote of 6 yeas to 99 nays. Grasping for straws, Leinenweber cites "racist passages" from Robert Hunter's *Poverty* (quoted in the *Socialist Campaign Book* for 1912) as evidence of the party's nativism, but fails to note that the party took a formal stand in opposition to the Dillingham bill while affirming the role of the United States as a political asylum for political refugees from all countries.[3] To equate the position of the Socialist Party with that of the AFL, which was contemporaneously lobbying for the literacy test, as does Leinenweber, is sheer historical distortion.

The 1910 Party Congress also adopted a constitutional amendment providing for foreign-language federations to be affiliated with the national Socialist Party. This action was in direct response to the demands of the immigrant socialist organizations as well as to self-criticisms of the failure to bring the foreign-born into the party. Clearly, the American Socialists were trying to "relate" to the new immigrants, and the rapid growth of the foreign-language federations over the next few years suggests that they were at least partially successful in doing so. Leinenweber recognizes this development without, however, reconciling it with his thesis, but he then identifies himself with the left critics of the immigrant socialists who attacked the federations for their ethnic exclusiveness and failure to integrate themselves into the American party at the state and local levels. Ironically, he does not seem to appreciate that this was a socialist version of the drive for Americanization of the foreign-born.[4]

No doubt nativist and racist prejudices infected the ranks of American socialists, and we are indebted to Leinenweber for exposing the inroads of such attitudes within the party. Yet despite the rhetoric of a Victor Berger, one is finally impressed by the vitality of the socialist ideals of international solidarity and fraternity. N. F. Holm, delegate of the Scandinavian American socialists, expressed this credo:

> Sentences like the "universal brotherhood of man," or the "rights of man," may be mere phrases, but I must say that for me they have a very deep meaning, and I am not yet ready to sacrifice my principles in order to gain the favor of some labor leader, or to gain a few votes. It was love of those principles that brought me into this party.[5]

Such appeared to be the majority, not minority, sentiment within the party.

Beyond its ideological implications, the phenomenon of immigration was extraordinarily complex in terms of its practical consequences. The continuing mass influx of ethnically diverse peoples *did* pose enormous obstacles to the effective organization of the workers. From the debates one gets a sense of men wrestling with this recalcitrant reality in a way that appears to escape Leinenweber. He seems to derive more satisfaction from using the label "racist" (shades of the sixties!) as a club against right-wing socialists than from seeking to understand the range of plausible responses to the immigration issue. Nor is his effort to assign all virtue to the left persuasive. Questions relating to the foreign-born and the Negro cut across the spectrum of ideological factions within the party. While there were blatant nativists on the right, as R. Laurence Moore has noted, "the left wing of the party harbored several of the most virulently racist socialists."[6] The leading advocate of Asian exclusion was Ernest Untermann, a proponent of Marxist orthodoxy and industrial unionism.

If one were to pursue the question of why socialism failed to attract substantial numbers of new immigrants, a more profitable line of inquiry might be to study the immigrants themselves rather than the Socialist Party.[7] An unspoken assumption underlying Leinenweber's thesis appears to be that the new immigrants *ought* to have been prime recruits for socialism. Few today presumably would find such a vulgar Marxist equation tenable: new immigrants = industrial workers = class-conscious proletarians = potential socialists. Rather, we might ask were or were not the new immigrants receptive to the socialist message? Or perhaps, were some receptive and others not? And if the latter were the case, what determined their degree of receptivity?

Theories of modernization have provided a fashionable conceptual framework for recent interpretations of the immigrant experience. Migrations of peasant folk are, in this perspective, depicted as passages from traditional to modern society with all the trauma and transformation that entailed. Oscar Handlin has contended that this uprooting made the peasant more rather than less conservative. Alienated and isolated, the immigrants spurned the radical appeal for the security to be found within the ethnic group and particularly the church.[8] The thesis of immigrant conservatism has been rendered in its most dogmatic form by Gerald Rosenblum. The absence of a class-conscious, militant labor movement in the United States he attributes to the new immigration that absorbed the shock of industrialization without becoming radicalized.[9] Modernization theory, however, is a two-edged sword. Adam Ulam has, to the contrary, emphasized the disorientation, bitterness, and class hatreds resulting from the clash of peasant values with industrial realities. The response of the emerging proletariat took the form of anarchism and syndicalism.[10] This conflict model has been applied by Herbert Gutman in his interpretation of the making of the American working class. A succession of pre-modern artisans and peasants carrying their traditional values and work habits into the factory precipitated recurring periods of labor conflict and violence.[11]

Whether predicting conservative or radical responses, all of the above interpretations posit a deterministic and universal law of social evolution. In a brilliant critique of modernization theory, Daniel T. Rodgers has cautioned that "tradition and modernity are too homogenizing of the intractable variety of both past and present to serve historians well."[12] Rodgers further observed "that what shaped those who moved across the boundaries of industrial society was neither culture nor economic conditions but the highly specific interaction of the two—the ways in which expectation, memory, and habit met with the force of circumstance. *The process contained not one, but a wide variety of potential outcomes*" (my italics). Such an open-ended approach to the study of the immigrant response to industrial America seems to be the better part of wisdom.

The political acculturation of the new immigrants is a subject of much greater importance than simply their relationship to the American Socialist Party, for it has to do with the shaping of the consciousness of the industrial working class in the United States.

In this process the immigrants are not to be viewed as so much plastic material to be molded by the American environment, but rather as active participants in the creation of their own American identities. Ethnicity and social class are the stuff out of which they fashioned "their sense of self and place in society." E. P. Thompson's remarks are particularly relevant to the experience of the foreign-born workers:

> The class experience is largely determined by the productive relations into which men are born—or enter involuntarily. Class-consciousness is the way in which these experiences are handled in cultural terms: embodied in traditions, value-systems, ideas, and institutional forms. If the experience appears as determined, class consciousness does not.[13]

The cultural terms in which the immigrants handled their industrial experiences were essentially the ethnic heritage they brought with them to America. Yet labor historians have consistently ignored these "cultural terms" in interpreting the behavior of foreign-born (and native, for that matter) workers.

Immigrant radicalism, for example, has been most often described as a direct and spontaneous response to exploitation. Leinenweber asserts that socialism among the new immigrants was a product of American conditions and not a "foreign import." Such an interpretation divests the immigrants of their cultural substance and portrays them as purely economic creatures. In their cultural repertoire, the southern and eastern Europeans had a broad range of ideas, experiences, and commitments derived from their participation in the class wars of Europe. It was from these resources that they created the ethnic socialist movements that flourished in early twentieth-century America.

The radical heritage of Germans and eastern European Jews and their role in the American left have long been recognized. Otherwise, the immigrants, especially those from southern and eastern Europe (with the possible exception of the Finns), have been regarded as relatively innocent of socialist ideas. We are only now coming to recognize that each of these ethnic communities, to be sure in varying degree, contained elements imbued with radical ideologies. The upheavals of the nineteenth century altered the consciousness of vast segments of the European population.

From a traditional and religious world view, they turned to a secular, materialist, and sometimes socialist conception of life. Beginning in the west and gradually moving east across the Continent, such ideas were first embraced by the aristocratic and bourgeois intelligensia, but gradually spread among artisans, industrial workers, and even the peasantry. Recurring periods of repression drove many leading theorists and agitators of the radical persuasion into exile, some to America. Following the abortive revolutions of 1905 in Tsarist Russia, for example, there was an exodus of Estonian, Finnish, Lithuanian, and Polish, as well as Jewish, socialists. But in addition to the ideologues, many thousands of immigrants had participated in socialist parties, syndicalist organizations, and peasants' leagues. Regrouped on American soil, these veterans of the class struggle in Europe formed the cadres of the ethnic socialist movements. By the outbreak of World War I, the spectrum of European radicalism from social democracy through anarcho-syndicalism to individualistic anarchism had been transplanted in microcosm to the United States.[14] Perhaps we may find in the history of these ethnic movements an answer to the question of why the new immigrants did not flock to the socialist banner.

Leinenweber and others have recognized the existence of these ethnic socialist groupings but have regarded them as of interest only in terms of their relationship to the American movements, not as important in their own right. Daniel Bell, for example, has commented: "In actual practice the [foreign language] federations were really small nationalist socialist parties attached to the American organization but responsive largely to the passions and concerns of the land of their origin."[15] Leinenweber also chides the immigrant socialists for being too intensely involved in Old World politics instead of joining the American comrades in their fight against capitalism. The foreign radicals did regard themselves as engaged in a world-wide struggle without respect to geography or political boundaries. Their organizations were extensions of the socialist and anarchist movements of Europe. Agitators, journalists, and organizers moved back and forth across the ocean as did a steady stream of publications and correspondence. The immigrant socialists were often much more cosmopolitan than their American colleagues and possessed an international comprehension of the class struggle that the American party largely lacked.

But the foreign radicals were also fully engaged in the battle against the exploitation and abuse that was often the immigrants' lot in the Promised Land. Their newspapers, for example, were primarily devoted to the American scene. Alongside ideological treatises and party polemics were reports on labor conditions and politics in the United States as well as articles on science, literature, the arts. From his study of immigrant journalism, Robert Ezra Park concluded: "Gradually and largely through the efforts of the Socialist press, the reading habit establishes the thinking habit. The net result has been to raise the intellectual level of the immigrant body."[16] True, the immigrant left contained widely differing and conflicting elements. To take the membership of the foreign-language federations of the Socialist Party as a true measure of radical influence among the ethnic groups would be grossly misleading. The 800 dues-paying members of the Italian Language Federation reported in 1917 were far outnumbered by the adherents to the syndicalist *Federazione Socialista Italiana* and the followers of Carlo Tresca and Luigi Galleani.[17]

While the social democrats urged their fellow immigrants to become citizens and vote for Socialist candidates, the syndicalists favored the strike over the ballot as a weapon in the class war. For some ethnic groups, behavior at the workplace may be a better index of political commitments than behavior at the polls. Yet the mass strikes of the early twentieth century have often been described in the terms used by Leinenweber: "Unskilled immigrant workers would strike spontaneously, without leadership or organization."[18] The impression is of Jacqueries, uprisings of "primitive rebels," without preparation or direction. This scenario omits the role of the immigrant radicals who laid the groundwork for strikes through long periods of propaganda and organization. How else to explain the appearance almost overnight of picket lines, strike bulletins, soup kitchens, and other manifestations of solidarity and discipline? If the headlines were captured by "Big Bill" Haywood or Elizabeth Gurley Flynn, the local cadre of radicals, often veterans of labor struggles in Europe, provided the leadership in the shop and on the street.[19]

These immigrant radical movements can be understood only as integral parts of the "working-class ethnic subcultures in industrializing America," to use Gutman's phrase. The ethnic settlements in the industrial cities, factory towns, and mining camps provided the cultural milieu for the work of proselytization and organization. Here the radicals published their newspapers and pamphlets; orated in halls, saloons, and on streetcorners; sponsored plays, picnics, and dances; established study groups, libraries, schools, and cooperatives. However, such efforts to radicalize the immigrants encountered stiff opposition from the conservative elements within the ethnic communities. An embryonic middle class providing a range of services to the workers became the exponents of bourgeois values and ethnic nationalisms. Meanwhile, an immigrant clergy gathering their scattered flocks discovered that nationalism reinforced religious faith. Thus a clerical-business elite came to dominate many settlements through the parish, the mutual aid society, and the patriotic organization. Between the radicals and this elite was a bitter enmity expressed in endless polemics and occasional violence. The socialists correctly perceived that the *prominenti* (the derisive Italian term for the colonial bigshots) were the proximate enemy in the class struggle. The anticlerical and antimonarchical propaganda of the immigrant radicals appeared to the uncomprehending native socialists as quixotic, irrelevant, and un-American. Yet at stake was nothing less than the redefinition of the consciousness of the immigrant workers: would they become ethnic Americans imbued with nationalism and middle-class values or class-conscious adherents to a radical movement?[20]

Because of the ideological polarization within the ethnic groups, radicalism for its followers became a way of life. Ostracized by the conservatives, the socialists had to create counter-cultures to satisfy their need for community. The "Finn Hall" perhaps best embodied this holistic radical culture. Found in isolated mining locations and at rural crossroads, the Finn Hall offered a full array of cultural, social, and political activities: lectures, musicals, theatre, athletics, classes; in short, instruction and entertainment for all ages, conditions, and sexes. Together with the cooperative store, the Finn Hall offered the Finnish leftists a high degree of "institutional completeness." Other ethnic radical movements also sought to free the immigrants from dependence upon the clerical-business elite. However, in the process, the socialists themselves became more and more engaged in ethnic and language maintenance.[21]

More important than the "material conditions of American capitalism" in determining the politics of ethnic groups appears to have been a calculus of cultural influences. Religion, nationalism, and radicalism competed for the loyalty of the immigrants. The Roman Catholic Church in and of itself was not an insuperable obstacle to the radicalization of the foreign-born. If a nationality had a tradition of anticlericalism as did the Italians or of rationalism as did the Czechs, the hold of the church upon the people was often tenuous. But when the Catholic (or as among the Greeks, the Orthodox) faith merged with a spirit of patriotism, the resulting religio-nationalistic identity proved to be highly resistant to the radical virus. Among the Catholic and Slavic immigrants, such as the Poles and Slovaks, the socialist appeal, regardless of the horrors of the steel mills and the packing houses, went largely unheeded.[22]

Even among the radicals, the predominance of patriotism over internationalism was conclusively demonstrated during the First World War. Following the outbreak of hostilities, many socialists, especially those from the subject nationalities of eastern Europe, rallied to the cause of national independence. The uncompromising stand against the war taken by the Socialist Party in its St. Louis Manifesto of April 1917 alienated a substantial segment of its immigrant membership. Several of the foreign-language federations split on the war issue, while others seceded from the party. This large-scale disaffection was obscured by the mass influx of eastern Europeans following the Bolshevik Revolution and has been overlooked by historians of American socialism. Yet it illustrates how the flood of nationalist feeling during the war eroded the support for the ethnic socialist movements.[23]

The radical appeal also ran into the pragmatic goals of the immigrants. Most came to America intent upon improving their condition here and now, while all the socialists had to offer was a vision of a better life in the "sweet by-and-by." An Hungarian socialist described the consequences of such motives: "Everybody who arrived here came for money, everybody is alien and feels no solidarity with others. The selfishness of the Americans is the product not only of capitalism but also of immigration itself."[24] Allowing for hyperbole, there was still truth in this observation. Leinenweber scorns such "compromised" institutions as trade unions and political machines and attributes similar feelings to the immigrants. Daily bread, not ideological purity, however, was the newcomers' primary concern. They were willing to trade allegiance and votes for jobs, favors, and assistance. Not surprisingly, the major parties had little difficulty integrating the southern and eastern Europeans into their organizations. Where the socialists played the political game successfully, as in Berger's Milwaukee, even Polish Catholics voted the Socialist ticket.[25] Obviously, immigrants did not find progressives like Robert F. Wagner, Al Smith, and Fiorello La Guardia "repulsive." In fact, urban liberalism in twentieth-century America, it is now generally recognized, has been based on the ethnic vote.[26]

Leinenweber also exaggerates the hostility of the new immigrants toward the AFL unions. Certainly ethnic and skill distinctions often did pit American and old stock workers against these latecomers, but this was not the permanent and impassable barrier that he makes it out to be. Faced with the competition of unorganized workers or the threat of dual unionism, trade unionists tended to swallow their prejudices and take in the "greenhorns." As Leinenweber well knows, the Slavic, Italian, and Jewish immigrants formed the backbone of such early industrial unions as the United Mine Workers of America, the International Ladies' Garment Workers Union, and the Amalgamated Clothing Workers of America. The immigrant radicals played a vital role in the organization of their countrymen into these and other AFL-affiliated unions. Recognizing their effectiveness, conservative labor leaders like John Mitchell had no hesitancy in utilizing the services of foreign socialists. "The ultimate irony," as Robert Asher has commented, "is that by securing entry into the mainstream of the labor movement for the 'new immigrants' the left facilitated their Americanization and insured their ultimate loyalty to the free enterprise system."[27] In labor, politics, and religion, the bulk of the new immigrants were in time integrated into American institutions from which they received satisfactions sufficient to nullify the appeal of radicalism. If instead they had confronted a system of permanent exclusion, of apartheid, socialism might have found more recruits among them.

What then can one conclude regarding the success or failure of the ethnic movements? Should one accept Marcus Lee Hansen's oft-quoted statement as the last word on the subject—"Probably more immigrant Socialists were lost to the cause in the United States than were won from the ranks of the newcomers"?[28] The question remains to be studied systematically, but on the basis of impressionistic evidence, I would argue that the radicals made substantial numbers of converts among previously apolitical immigrants. And for a generation the socialists kept the faith, not without defections, but with single-minded devotion to their ideals. Although they bore the brunt of the Red Scare when many of their leaders were deported, the ethnic movements appear to have been more resilient to the adversities of war and its aftermath than the American party. Labor history gives the impression that after the dramatic IWW strikes the immigrant agitators faded away. In fact, they figured prominently in the radical labor and politics of the 1920s and 1930s. The immigrant radicals dominated the leadership of the Communist Party until its "Americanization" in the 1930s, were in the forefront of the antifascist resistance, and participated in the CIO organizing drives in the mass-production industries.[29]

Today the ethnic movements exist only in the memories of a rapidly dwindling group of survivors who sometimes gather to reminisce and rekindle the aspirations of their youth. Immigrant socialism was a one-generation phenomenon. As Paul Buhle put it, the radicals' children tended "to join the consensual modes of the large society."[30] Through the schools, the mass media, and their peer cultures, they absorbed the dominant values of middle-class America. They learned that to be radical was to be un-American. Thus assimilation meant not only de-ethnicization but also de-radicalization. This may be the most revealing feature of the history of ethnic socialist movements. Transplanted as sturdy saplings from Europe, they could not take root in the inhospitable soil of America. Lacking a sturdy trunk of native American socialism onto which they might have been grafted, they flourished for a time but were destined finally to languish and die.

NOTES

1. Ira Kipnis, *The American Socialist Movement 1897–1912* (New York: Columbia University Press, 1952), pp. 272–88. Leinenweber also espouses the pro-left-wing interpretation that characterizes the Kipnis volume.

2. Socialist Party, *National Congress,* 1910 (Chicago: Socialist Party, 1910), pp. 75–168.

3. Socialist Party, National Campaign Committee, 1912, *Socialist Campaign Book* (Chicago: Socialist Party, 1912), pp. 1–5. Leinenweber equates Hillquit's position on immigration with that of the AFL, intimating that his nativism extended even to his fellow eastern European Jews. However, his quotation from Hillquit's autobiography, which Leinenweber interprets to the effect that the Jewish workers were "incapable of joining the organization and struggles of their class," fails to take into account Hillquit's following comment regarding the cloak workers' strike of 1910: "It was a crusade that brought out what was best and noblest in a mass of fifty thousand oppressed and abused workers and united them all in a new spirit of faith, hope, and solidarity reminiscent of the great popular movements for liberation in all ages." *Loose Leaves from a Busy Life* (New York: Rand School Press, 1934), p. 137.

4. Socialist Party, *National Congress,* 1910, pp. 259–67. It is worth noting that Charles Ruthenberg, a critic of the foreign-language socialists in 1912, was the leader of the Workers Communist Party in 1925, when its foreign-language federations were abolished. The immediate result of this policy of Bolshevization (or Americanization) was a drop in membership from 14,037 in September 1925 to 7,215 in October 1925. Nathan Glazer, *The Social Basis of American Communism* (New York: Harcourt, Brace & World, 1961), pp. 40–56; Harvey Klehr, "Immigrant Leadership in the Communist Party of the United States of America," *Ethnicity,* 6 (March 1979), pp. 29–44.

5. Socialist Party, *National Congress,* 1910, p. 138. Such expressions of international brotherhood are more impressive when viewed against the prevalence of racist attitudes as documented by John Higham, *Strangers in the Land: Patterns of American Nativism 1860–1925* (New Brunswick, N. J.: Rutgers University Press, 1955). But Higham himself is misled by Kipnis to make the following statement: "After 1908 . . . the national Socialist Party abandoned a cosmopolitan immigration policy under the racist urgings of one of its western leaders." Ibid., p. 173.

6. R. Laurence Moore, "Flawed Fraternity—American Socialist Response to the Negro, 1901–1912," *The Historian,* 32 (November 1969), p. 16; Kipnis, op. cit., pp. 186, 278–83.

7. Leinenweber has anticipated this approach in his more recent

work, "Socialists in the Streets: The New York City Socialist Party in Working Class Neighborhoods, 1908–1918," *Science and Society,* 41 (Summer 1977), pp. 152–71. In this article, he speaks of the need to address "socialism as a movement from below" but appears not to take ethnicity seriously as a component of working-class culture. Thus the conclusion: "Socialism in New York was a movement of industrial militancy which transcended the limitations of workplace and ethnicity to proclaim the solidarity of all working people." Ibid., p. 170.

8. *The Uprooted* (Boston: Little, Brown, 1951), pp. 217–18.

9. *Immigrant Workers: Their Impact on American Labor Radicalism* (New York: Basic Books, 1973).

10. "The Historical Role of Marxism," in James J. Sheehan, ed., *Industrialization and Industrial Labor in Nineteenth-Century Europe* (New York: John Wiley, 1973).

11. "Work, Culture, and Society in Industrializing America, 1815–1919," *The American Historical Review,* 78 (June 1973), pp. 531–88.

12. "Tradition, Modernity, and the American Industrial Worker: Reflections and Critique," *The Journal of Interdisciplinary History,* 8 (Spring 1977), pp. 655–81.

13. *The Making of the English Working Class* (Penguin Books, 1974), p. 10.

14. On the European backgrounds, see Peter N. Stearns, *European Society in Upheaval* (New York: Macmillan, 1967), and his essay, "The European Labor Movement and the Working Classes, 1890–1914," in Stearns and Harvey Mitchell, *The European Labor Movement, the Working Classes and the Origins of Social Democracy 1890–1914* (Itasca, Ill.: F. E. Peacock, 1971), pp. 118–221. Histories of the ethnic radicalisms among the new immigrants remain for the most part to be written. The labor movements of the eastern European Jews have been most thoroughly studied; key works are Melech Epstein, *Jewish Labor in U.S.A. 1882–1952,* 2 vols. (New York: Trade Union Sponsoring Committee, 1950–1953); Moses Rischin, *The Promised City: New York's Jews, 1870–1914* (Cambridge, Mass.: Harvard University Press, 1977); Elias Tcherikower, *The Early Jewish Labor Movement in the United States,* trans. and rev. by Aaron Antonovsky (New York: Yivo Institute for Jewish Research, 1961); Irving Howe, *World of Our Fathers* (New York: Simon and Schuster, 1976). Finnish American radicalism has also received considerable attention, particularly of late: A. William Hoglund, *Finnish Immigrants in America 1880–1920* (Madison: University of Wisconsin Press, 1960); Michael G. Karni et al., eds., *The Finnish Experience in the Western Great Lakes Region: New Perspectives* (Vammala, Finland: Institute for Migration, 1975); Karni, "YHTEISHYVA—or, For the Common Good: Finnish Radicalism in the Western Great Lakes Region, 1900–1940," unpub. Ph.D. diss., University of Minnesota, 1975; Auvo Kostiainen, *The Forging of Finnish-American Communism, 1917–1924: A Study in Ethnic Radicalism* (Turku, Finland: Migration Institute, 1978);

Michael M. Passi et al., *For the Common Good: Finnish Immigrants and the Radical Response to Industrial America* (Superior, Wisc.: Tyomies Society, 1977); Carl Ross, *The Finn Factor in American Labor, Culture and Society* (New York Mills, Minn.: Parta Printers, 1977). On Italian American radicalism relatively little has been published: Edwin Fenton, *Immigrants and Unions, A Case Study: Italians and American Labor, 1870–1920* (New York: Arno Press, 1975); and Fenton's articles, "Italians in the Labor Movement," *Pennsylvania History,* 26 (April 1959), pp. 133–43, and "Italian Immigrants in the Stone-Workers' Union," *Labor History,* 3 (Spring 1962), pp. 188–207; Rudolph J. Vecoli, ed., *Italian American Radicalism: Old World Origins and New World Developments* (New York: American Italian Historical Association, 1973); and Vecoli's articles, "Pane e Giustizia," *La Parola del Populo,* 68 (Sept.-Oct. 1976), pp. 55–61 (in English), and "Italian American Workers, 1880–1920: Padrone Slaves or Primitive Rebels?" in S. M. Tomasi, ed., *Perspectives in Italian Immigration and Ethnicity* (New York: Center for Migration Studies, 1977). For the other eastern and southern European ethnic groups, there are only a few scattered, and for the most part unpublished, studies. Although considerably broader in scope, the following two works contain much information regarding radical activities among Poles and Ukrainians respectively: Jözek Miaso, *The History of the Education of Polish Immigrants in the United States* (New York: The Kosciuszko Foundation, 1977), and Myron B. Kuropas, "The Making of the Ukrainian American, 1884–1939: A Study in Ethno-National Education," unpub. Ph.D. diss., University of Chicago, 1974. Useful unpublished papers include Joseph Cada, "A Survey of Radicalism in the Bohemian-American Community" (1954), Tõnu Parming, "The Estonian-American Workers Movement: 1906–1919," and Donald E. Pienkos, "Progressives, Socialists and the Milwaukee Poles." A recent unpublished dissertation is " 'In Unity is Strength': Immigrant Workers and Immigrant Intellectuals in Progressive America: A History of the South Slav Social Democratic Movement, 1900–1918," University of Minnesota, 1978, by Joseph Stipanovich.

15. "The Background and Development of Marxian Socialism in the United States," in Donald Drew Egbert and Stow Persons, eds., *Socialism and American Life* (Princeton: Princeton University Press, 1952), vol. 1, p. 311. Focusing upon the growth spurt following the Bolshevik Revolution, Bell also interprets this increase in the federation's membership as "less a product of conditions in America than of enthusiasm for events in Europe." This inference fails to explain the growth of the foreign-language federations prior to November 1917. It is also worth noting that the monumental Egbert and Persons two-volume work contains very little on the ethnic socialistic movements.

16. *The Immigrant Press and Its Control* (Westport, Conn.: Greenwood Press, 1970, 1922), p. 79.

17. Vecoli, "Italian American Workers": the discussion that follows is based upon the literature cited in n. 14.

18. Charles Leinenweber, "The American Socialist and 'New' Immigrants," *Science and Society,* 32, no. 1 (Winter 1968), pp. 2–25.

19. Among labor historians, Philip S. Foner has given the fullest recognition to the role played by immigrant radicals in the organizing drives and strikes; *History of the Labor Movement in the United States,* vol. 4: *The Industrial Workers of the World 1905–1917* (New York: International Publishers, 1965). But see also Melvyn Dubofsky, *We Shall Be All: A History of the Industrial Workers of the World* (New York: Quadrangle, 1969).

20. In addition to the works cited in n. 14, other relevant writings are John Bodnar, *Immigration and Industrialization: Ethnicity in an American Mill Town, 1870–1940* (Pittsburgh, Pa.: University of Pittsburgh Press, 1977); Virginia Yans-McLaughlin, *Family and Community: Italian Immigrants in Buffalo, 1880–1930* (Ithaca, N.Y.: Cornell University Press, 1977); John W. Briggs, *An Italian Passage: Immigrants to Three American Cities, 1890–1930* (New Haven, Conn.: Yale University Press, 1978); Caroline Golab, *Immigrant Destinations* (Philadelphia, Pa.: Temple University Press, 1977); and several articles of Robert F. Harney, "The Padrone and the Immigrant," *The Canadian Review of American Studies,* 5 (Fall 1974), pp. 101–13, and "Ambiente and Social Class in North American Little Italies," *Canadian Review of Studies in Nationalism,* 2 (Spring 1975), pp. 203–24.

21. On the "Finn Hall," see Ross, op. cit., pp. 169–70; Douglas Ollila, Jr., "From Socialism to Industrial Unionism (IWW)," in Karni, *The Finnish Experience,* pp. 156–57; and Sirkka Tuomi Lee, "The Finns," in *The Origins of Left Culture in the U.S.: 1880–1940, Cultural Correspondence* (Providence, R.I.: Dorrwar Bookstore, 1978), pp. 41–49.

22. On the role of religion and nationalism in the immigrant communities, see Victor Greene, *For God and Country: The Rise of Polish and Lithuanian Ethnic Consciousness in America, 1861–1910* (Madison: Wisconsin Historial Society, 1975); Rudolph J. Vecoli, "Prelates and Peasants: Italian Immigrants and the Catholic Church," *Journal of Social History,* 2 (Spring 1969), pp. 216–68; also the essays in Randall M. Miller and Thomas D. Marzik, eds., *Immigrants and Religion in Urban America* (Philadelphia, Pa.: Temple University Press, 1977), and Keith Dyrud et al., eds., *The Other Catholics* (New York: Arno Press, 1978).

23. For the impact of the war on the Czechs and South Slavs respectively see Cada, op. cit., pp. 19–29; Stipanovich, op. cit., pp. 17–27. On the response of Polish socialists see William I. Thomas and Florian Znaniecki, *The Polish Peasant in Europe and America* (New York: Dover Publications, 1958), vol. 2, pp. 1609–10.

24. Imre Basch to Ervin Szabo, New York, April 18, 1909, in J.

Jemnitz, "The Relations of the American and the Americo-Hungarian Labour Movements as revealed in the Correspondence of Ervin Szabo," *Acta Historica* (Budapest), 9 (1963), p. 209. The article contains extracts from letters written by Hungarian socialists from the United States with interesting and often critical comments on the American labor and socialist movements. Ibid., pp. 179–214.

25. Pienkos, loc. cit., pp. 10, 18–20. Socialist candidates in the presidential elections ran more strongly in the Polish wards than in Milwaukee as a whole. In 1912, Debs received a plurality of the vote in four Polish wards. But Socialist candidates also received as many as 10 to 15 percent of the Polish votes in Chicago; Edward R. Kantowicz, *Polish-American Politics in Chicago* (Chicago: University of Chicago Press, 1975), pp. 29, 95, 102–7.

26. John D. Buenker, *Union Liberalism and Progressive Reform* (New York: W. W. Norton, 1978); J. Joseph Huthmacher, "Urban Liberalism and the Age of Reform," *Mississippi Valley Historical Review,* 44 (September 1962), pp. 231–41, and *Senator Robert F. Wagner and the Rise of Urban Liberalism* (New York: Atheneum, 1971); Arthur Mann, *La Guardia: A Fighter Against His Times 1882–1933* (Chicago: University of Chicago Press, 1969).

27. "Union Nativism and the Immigrant Response," unpub. paper, p. 17; William M. Leiserson, *Adjusting Immigrant and Industry* (New York: Harper & Brothers, 1924); writings by Fenton cited in n. 14.

28. *The Immigrant in American History* (New York: Harper & Row, 1964), p. 95.

29. Glazer, op. cit., pp. 38–89; Klehr, loc. cit.; Ross, op. cit., pp. 172–73; Alice and Staughton Lynd, *Rank and File: Personal Histories by Working Class Organizers* (Boston: Beacon Press, 1973); Peter Friedlander, *The Emergence of a UAW Local, 1936–1939: A Study in Class and Culture* (Pittsburgh, Pa.: University of Pittsburgh Press, 1975); Roger R. Keeran, "Communist Influence in the Automobile Industry, 1920–33: Paving the Way for an Industrial Union," *Labor History,* 20 (Spring 1979), pp. 189–225; John P. Diggins, "The Italo-American Antifascist Opposition," *The Journal of American History,* 54 (December 1967), pp. 579–98.

30. "Debsian Socialism and the 'New Immigrant' Worker," in William L. O'Neill, ed., *Insights and Parallels* (Minneapolis, Minn.: Burgess Pub. Co., 1973), p. 276. This perceptive essay is marred by an uncritical acceptance of "Old Immigration" and "New Immigration" as descriptive of objective realities. Buhle concludes, "In the long view, the Socialist problem with the immigrant worker was for that time and place insoluble." Ibid., pp. 250, 276.

REPLY

Charles Leinenweber

"The American Socialist Party and 'New' Immigrants" was written early in 1967 in Berkeley, California, during the building of the antiwar and black power movements. On the one hand, it was intended as a contribution to the ongoing debate "Why no socialism in America?" On the other, it was intended to address implicitly the practical matter of creating a new socialist movement. The old socialists, the article implied, went wrong in frittering away their natural and presumably responsive base among new immigrant industrial workers and courting instead the aristocracy of labor. What we must do in our time is seek and hold the proper social base. The article's practical aspect is less interesting to us now, since the movements of the 1960s have long subsided and no new ones have arisen to take their place, at least by this writing (1979). I mention it only because it informs the article's methodology.

We may well estimate the article's weaknesses and strengths by reopening the questions central to it. First, was the Socialist Party really shot through with nativism? Second, if so, did it matter much for the party's numerical growth and decline?

This is a different order of questions than that posed by Vecoli, whose critique ranges far beyond the intent and even the possibilities of the original article. Vecoli basically contends that the study ought to have been of "the immigrants themselves rather than the Socialist Party" and goes on to cite roughly thirty studies of the immigrants themselves, few of them about the matter in hand, politics—nearly all appeared after 1973, and the balance had been hard to come by in 1967. The literature on the American working class has increased enormously over the recent decade not simply in quantity but in richness and sophistication. All our earlier work of course would have been very much different had we been able to take the latter into account. But things can't happen that way.

Was the Socialist Party nativist? From our present vantage point I would say that the answer is more complicated than the original article makes out. Among the leadership—which consisted mainly of local leaders, some of national prominence among socialists, and included regular convention delegates—the general inclination certainly was to support restrictions, often with a nativist rationale. Again, just as in the original article, I would argue that this inclination derived not from, as Vecoli suggests, a "wrestling with a recalcitrant reality," but rather from the party's real or hoped-for attachment to an AFL busy defending its craft unions. As John Spargo argued in 1916, "Sentiment in favor of a general restriction of immigration . . . is very widespread in our party. This is very largely due, I think, to the preponderance of trade union members and those who believe that the party must always unite with the unions or be lost."[1] We need not pass judgment on Socialist and AFL positions but only note their similarities and common origin. Wherever the party succeeded locally, it was rooted in the trade union movement, and party leaders assimilated and incorporated that movement's outlook. Not all unions supported restrictions and, I would argue, the differences among leaders on the matter varied according to what unions they sought or found their bases in.

The debate over immigration, the one for which a record remains, occurred among the leadership, a fairly stable and distinct entity. Yet the Socialist Party and certainly the socialist movement, which extended well beyond the party's formal membership, consisted also of a more fluid and elusive entity, the rank and file, for which records are scarce. The article's methodology—although it could hardly have been otherwise—is too limited to pick up and reflect much about the ranks. What I did was to study and join in the leadership's debate over immigration and seek the origins of the various positions.

But viewing the party from the perspective of the ranks results in quite a different picture from that gained solely by examining the leadership's record. I am now fairly familiar with the ranks in one of the most important Socialist strongholds, New York, and feel safe in saying that no debate over immigration occurred there, for there was nothing to debate. The ranks consisted overwhelmingly of immigrants, the majority of them recent, who universally favored free immigration and who also were organized into unions that likewise supported free immigration, at least from Europe. My impression is that Socialist ranks across the nation favored free immigration and that Vecoli is right in saying that a majority did, although that cannot be gauged by looking at the leadership. In New York the attitude of the ranks contrasted with that of the leadership, whose "significant others" seemed to be more the AFL, and some of whom, such as Morris Hillquit, occasionally found themselves brought to task for it.

Was the Socialist Party nativist? The leaders generally were, or at least, generally supported restricting immigration. Did this matter much for the party's numerical growth and decline? No. Party leaders made all sorts of outrageous blunders—including in this regard, once running two nativist snobs for Congress in the Lower East Side—but these usually were corrected over time or simply weren't important in a movement that in some cities achieved mass proportions anyway, including among new immigrants, and soon was to shrink violently for other reasons.

The article far too much sees the Socialist Party as an external force that imposes itself upon and recruits from the working class, rather than as an organizational and political expression of a movement created by the working class. (Vecoli's approach, despite its language of cultural self-determination, also sees the working class as a passive shopper for political goods brought to it by outside merchants.) The article's perspective may be understood as a concomitant of the 1960s' radical student movement, which was isolated from the working class but which many of us hoped by our efforts could become connected to it. Whatever the merits of this perspective in the 1960s—too "voluntaristic," I would now say—it does not accurately reflect the reality of the socialist movement where it achieved mass dimensions. That movement grew out of rather than attached itself to the working class.[2]

Let me note in passing a small but annoying matter: Vecoli's statement that "Leinenweber is a partisan of the party's left wing." How he divined this is beyond me, as is his reason for claiming it. Had he read my very next article, "American Socialist Opposition to World War I," he would have discovered me to be a "partisan of the Right," for there I attacked the Left and defended the Right. The fact is that I am a partisan of certain principles, such as internationalism and democracy, and I feel critical toward movements or parts of movements that ought to uphold them but do not. The American Socialist Left was more consistently internationalist than the Right on the matter of immigration, and less so on the war.[3]

Some brief space remains for us to consider Vecoli's own arguments about, as he puts it, the receptivity of immigrants to the socialist message. Vecoli seems to feel that cultural influences are more important determinants of ethnic group politics than are "material conditions." These cultural influences consist essentially of the ethnic heritage that immigrants bring with them to America: their particular group's traditions, value systems, ideas, and institutions.

There are serious problems with this cultural approach, which by now dominates historical thinking on the working class. One is that it attempts to leap past the tedious nuts-and-bolts work of building a literature on the material conditions surrounding American working-class development simply by asserting that they aren't very important. This forgets that E. P. Thompson was able to make his claim for class-consciousness or culture only because the material conditions of class in Britain—including such matters as standard of living—already had been well studied. Not so in America. How may we assert, for example, that Catholicism kept Irish-Americans from socialism when we know so little of material factors in Irish working-class organization and disorganization, which may instead have been sufficient? Or how may we claim, as Vecoli does, that children of immigrant radicals became conservative because they "absorbed the dominant values of middle-class America" through "schools, the mass media [vaudeville, maybe?], and their peer cultures"? Certainly we should not make that claim before we have investigated the importance of such material factors as shifts in the occupational structure that created a huge, new white-collar grouping and separated immigrant and American-born generations by class.

Yet even as this approach claims a distinction between culture and material conditions, it smuggles material factors back in as cultural. Thus when Vecoli describes the actual substance of the "ethnic heritage" of immigrant socialists, it is that they were "veterans of the class struggle in Europe." That experience is not exactly ethnic heritage—although it may combine with national or ethnic experience—nor is it exactly cultural, unless by culture one means the totality of human experience and institutions. Practically speaking, culture and material conditions don't separate, for the very good reason that values, traditions, and institutions depend on certain material circumstances for their flourishing. Industrialization and in recent decades de-industrialization still hold as the governing factors in the immensely complicated world processes of the formation of "the working class."

Surely the cultural investigations of class formation stand as our greatest achievement so far in developing a social history of twentieth-century working-class America. Yet the invocation of culture as a nondetermined (or self-determined) determining factor in history results in the creation of an enormous "residual category" that swallows up all explanation, leaving us farther and farther from achieving social science.

NOTES

1. *New York Call,* September 24, 1916, magazine section, p. 7.

2. For a detailed class analysis of the Socialist rank and file, see Charles Leinenweber, "The Class and Ethnic Bases of New York City Socialism, 1904–1915," *Labor History,* 22, no. 1 (Winter, 1981), pp. 31–56. See also the author's "Socialists in the Streets: The New York City Socialist Party in Working Class Neighborhoods, 1908–1918," *Science and Society,* 41, no. 2 (Summer 1977), pp. 152–71.

3. *Radical America,* 2, no. 2 (March–April 1968), pp. 29–49.

Chapter 8

SOCIALISM AND WOMEN*

Sally Miller

In recent years, the bibliography on women and socialism has begun to grow. Studies on the Socialist Party of America have appeared focusing on the era of World War I, the party's most expansive period. Biographical articles on women organizers and intellectuals have provided additional data but have not fully illuminated basic questions about the role of women in radical politics, or, that is, radical politics and woman's "place." This essay is an institutional study of the Socialist Party and its women members, their role in its power structure, their views on policy, their activities, and their priorities.[1]

The Socialist Party of America at its founding convention in 1901 included in its platform a commitment to "equal civil and political rights for men and women." Indeed, following the position taken in the late nineteenth century by European socialism, the party was virtually obligated to support such a position. Moreover, influential socialists abroad, such as August Bebel of the German Social Democratic party, Paul Lafargue of the French socialists and the son-in-law of Marx, and Frederich Engels himself, had acknowledged the exploitation of women in a special guise and had written on behalf of sexual equality.

Women were perhaps one-tenth of the membership of the Socialist Party and played a visible role in its internal affairs. In national conventions between 1904 and 1912, women were conspicuous, serving on subcommittees, leading floor fights, and lobbying for resolutions. Unlike the dominant political parties where women were almost never convention delegates (from 0 to under

* Sally M. Miller, "Women in the Party Bureaucracy: Subservient Functionaries," in Sally M. Miller, ed., *Flawed Liberation: Socialism and Feminism* (Westport, Conn.: Greenwood Press, 1981), pp. 13–35.

1 percent in these years), the Socialists had relatively large female contingents. In 1904, 6 percent of the delegates were women, in 1908, 10 percent, and in 1912, again 10 percent.[2]

Women served the party as organizers, propagandists, pamphleteers, and candidates for public office. In 1912, the party sent sixty speakers throughout North America on a lyceum circuit, and over one-fifth of these were women. Party journalists were women almost as often as men, with copy editors and staff people tending to be women. Autonomous women's socialist study groups, organized in most of the states and also in Ontario, Manitoba, Alberta, and British Columbia, coordinated their programs and their lobbying around party initiatives. Women party members raised funds for strike benefits and campaign expenses, distributed propaganda, served as poll watchers, established and taught in socialist Sunday schools and, in general, built bridges to nonsocialist women and women's organizations. In 1908, responding to the possibility of an autonomous national organization of socialist women, the party convention established a Woman's National Committee as a clearinghouse and focus for women's party activities. A salaried woman national organizer was assigned specifically to seek out women for membership, and each state organization and every local was urged to utilize women organizers and to form a woman's committee. The Woman's National Committee raised funds, commissioned leaflets, and otherwise sought to increase party strength by appealing to women's interests and needs.[3]

However, party treatment of the so-called Woman Question and of women members often seemed perfunctory, more lip service than genuine commitment. The platform demand of 1901 for equal rights was virtually a dead letter. The platform plank of 1904 supporting equal suffrage for men and women seemed an absent-minded acknowledgment. No literature was commissioned for women in these early years, no organizers assigned. It was not until the convention of 1908 when women delegates forcefully acted as a special interest group that the party pledged an active campaign for unrestricted and equal suffrage.[4]

Through those first half-dozen years prior to the appearance of a cohesive women's bloc, the Socialist Party had expended no energy in organizing women or appealing to their needs. As a leading male Socialist, John Spargo complained that not only did the party fail to seek out women but it often held its meetings in the locker-room atmosphere of neighborhood saloons. Such locations were clearly unattractive to women, who might often be circumspect about venturing into politics. When women joined the party on their own initiative, no effort was made to fit proceedings into a framework understandable to political novices. Moreover, propaganda and arguments were always expressed in terms of the male identity, concerns, and life style. No campaign was initiated to reach women in their dual capacities as wage workers by day and housewives by night, nor was any real attempt made to penetrate the ignorance in which it was believed organized religion had trapped women. Women's role in the party, some women noted, was to be no more than cake bakers and tea pourers. "Women are tired of being 'included,' " one wrote, "but not really recognized." As to party politics, women could be seen, possibly, but not heard in the locals.[5]

In addition to such institutional sins of omission, male party leaders informally revealed strong reservations about women activists. When a woman was first elected in 1909 to the party executive, Victor Berger, a dominant force in the party right wing, commented to a colleague, Morris Hillquit, that having a woman on the National Executive Committee was "by no means necessary for a political party at this stage of the game and under the present conditions." In 1913 when Kate Richards O'Hare was elected as a representative to the International Socialist Bureau in Brussels, the same two leaders feared that she would make the Socialist Party look ridiculous abroad. Berger as a congressman fulfilled his obligation to introduce a bill for woman suffrage, only to find such efforts suspect. A woman's socialist group complained that the two Socialists elected to Congress, Berger of Milwaukee and Meyer London of the Lower East Side, minimized the suffrage issue, and Florence Kelley of the Henry Street Settlement House, and a sometime socialist, questioned the sincerity of their commitment to protective legislation for women. To reassure doubters, male party leaders emphasized the pioneering commitment of socialists everywhere to woman suffrage, but some admitted a belief that votes for women would delay the advent of socialism since women were presumed to be dominated by reactionary priests and ministers.[6]

Patronizing of women was rampant in the party. A leading journal, the *International Socialist Review,* described women delegates as "on all questions . . . acquit[ting] themselves nobly." The socialist press was also capable of referring to one woman convention delegate as having "her feathers all ruffled," and Eugene V. Debs, the party's perennial candidate for the presidency, generously commented on the value of women speakers who always attracted a crowd.[7]

In short, women were not taken seriously by a political party theoretically committed to equality. "How bitter is our disappointment," one woman wrote, "whenever we come to look upon matters as they really are." Women were not welcome in the party's power structure. They were clustered in the lower levels of the party hierarchy, far from positions of authority. Women members were relegated to precinct work and thus were effectively segregated from responsibility. At best, women played roles at conventions, although even there resentments surfaced over all-male state delegations. The National Office of the party and its National Executive Committee (N.E.C.), the decision-making body between conventions, were masculine provinces. Even the day-to-day decisions on fiscal matters, policy determinations, and organizational campaigns were prerogatives of the professional functionaries and the most prominent party politicians. With women effectively barred from this segment of the party arena, a pattern of institutional discrimination prevailed; only upon occasion were women allowed other than marginal roles. Prejudicial attitudes and institutional arrangements meant that hers were party bazaars but not party power.[8]

The identity of the women activists was remarkably homogeneous. The background of most of these women was middle class and native American. In fact, the pattern was predominantly bourgeois WASP. Of two dozen women who served on the Woman's National Committee, three-fourths were American-born, perhaps reflecting the fact that the socialist movement itself had shrugged off its nineteenth-century domination by European immigrants. Among seventeen other women featured in cover stories by the only national woman's socialist monthly, the same percentage prevailed. Among these forty-one prominent women socialists, only four could claim working-class backgrounds: Rose Pastor

Stokes, Kate Richards O'Hare, Elizabeth Gurley Flynn, and Theresa Malkiel. The typical profile was of a college-educated woman, often a teacher, often with formative experiences in evangelical or suffrage movements.[9] These women were relatively youthful, in their thirties and forties, with only an occasional older activist who had participated in abolitionist struggles. A few were offspring of activist mothers. Most of these women were married, usually to men who were also socialists. In instances where couples shared a party prominence—Algie and May Wood Simons, J. G. Phelps and Rose Pastor Stokes, Victor and Meta Berger—the wife generally worked in the shadow of the husband's more important position. But whether married, divorced, or single, most appeared to live independent lives that were not male dominated.[10]

Geographically, an overwhelming proportion of these women came from the rural Middle West and the Far West, with a few hailing from the South. Illustrative of that pattern, more than 50 percent of women convention delegates from 1904 to 1912 represented areas west of the Mississippi River, and 25 percent the Great Lakes. Most of the autonomous women's socialist organizations, except for a number headquartered in New York, were established in the western half of the continent. This pattern may be explained by the fact that many western women had won the franchise a generation earlier, and therefore the political process was not alien to them. Thus, socialist women helped underline the party's own western tilt.[11]

In 1908, soon after the establishment of the Woman's National Committee (W.N.C.), a Woman's General Correspondent was appointed, and her office became the keystone of a vertical organization which extended increasingly deep and independent roots. A distinct separatism that almost no one wanted developed. Although all W.N.C. decisions had to be endorsed by the party's executive and the committee lacked budgetary authority, nevertheless its network spread throughout the country. An office of Woman's State Correspondent was also established at this time to serve as liaison among local, state, and national woman's committees. This office, set up immediately in four midwestern and western states, was always held by women, although not so legislated, and was closely tied to a woman's state committee. In the next eighteen months ten additional states (two-thirds west of the

Mississippi River) established the same offices. When other states did not follow suit, the W.N.C., after some prodding, considered submitting its own nominations for the unfilled posts, an action sure to be perceived as a threat to local autonomy. However, by 1915 such an edifice for women's activities existed in thirty-seven states.[12]

On the local level, wide discrepancies existed in practice. Party policy provided that each local organize a woman's committee, but in some locals apparently the only action was the posting of a "Ladies Invited" sign. By 1911 the woman's committees were said to have been established in 69 percent of reporting locals, but this fact was based on a questionnaire to which only 7 percent of the locals responded. Regional differences were pronounced. The Mississippi State Correspondent reported that she found that southern notions of woman's "place" and of male chivalry adversely affected party efforts toward organizing women, and the New Mexico State Correspondent reported that her state's poverty and sparse population hindered organizational drives. But the California State Correspondent wrote that 13 percent of her state's membership was female, and the New York State Correspondent estimated 10 percent. Throughout the country, areas of party strength were often reflected in an expanding women's sphere, and party weaknesses were usually paralleled by a low level of such activity.[13]

However, data indicate that there was greater willingness in certain areas than others to include women in the regular party apparatus. Women still served infrequently on the party's National Committee (never more than six women at a time, with fluctuations from 1910 to 1914 of 3.5 percent to 8.5 percent of the committee), and seldom were they elected by eastern states, despite the fact that a state like New York had many prominent women members. The all-important N.E.C., to which five to seven members were elected annually between 1901 and 1917, had only a total of three women. All three were exceedingly prominent party organizers: Lena Morrow Lewis, elected in 1909; Kate Richards O'Hare in 1911; and Anna A. Maley in 1916. Among state secretaries, women held a maximum of 16 percent of the positions. The official delegates to the International were almost entirely male in 1904 and 1907, but in 1910 three of the party's eight mandated delegates to the Congress of the Second International at Copenhagen were women, and in 1913, as mentioned above, O'Hare was elected as one of the few women ever to sit on the International Socialist Bureau in Brussels.

Ad hoc party committees tended to be exclusively male. The only type of position for which the Socialist Party turned regularly to women nominees was in the field of education. In 1909 Milwaukee elected the first Socialist woman to a public post in the United States when the party ran Meta Berger for the Milwaukee School Board, a position she held for over two decades. The party's National Education Committee in 1913 was chaired by May Wood Simons and consisted of three women and four men. In 1908, the Socialists named thirteen women among their 271 candidates in state races (4.7 percent), and of that number, eight were candidates for superintendencies of public instruction or for regents of state universities. In 1910, of 255 candidates for state level public offices sixteen were women (6.2 percent), half of whom ran for educational posts.[14]

Clearly, then, woman's sphere was carefully defined; in effect the party had made room for women in a hierarchy of their own. Their socialist activity was confined to their own structure, reported in their own separate newspaper columns, and it was their energy alone that would determine how widely their sector of the party might grow. The Woman's National Committee developed a "Plan for Work in Socialist Locals" which established guidelines for attracting women to membership. The plan was based on the stated assumption of "the need to make distinct efforts to reach women. . . ." Separate woman's locals were officially eschewed in favor of mixed locals although a few women favored separatism temporarily in order to establish a relaxed environment in which to raise consciousness. But woman's committees were elected by locals from their entire membership, and each chose a correspondent to maintain contact with other woman's committees. The committees distributed party publications, promoted specific issues, sought out new members, and sponsored entertainments and social events. Increasingly, emphasis was placed upon combining serious study with social events or traditional woman's activities such as sewing bees in order to attract potential converts.[15]

After a few years, the W.N.C.'s Plan for Work became quite refined. The pioneering day of general organizing had ended, as one woman declared, and organizers had to respond to varieties of life styles among women. The woman's committees, now called Local Committees on Propaganda among Women in order to minimize implications of auxiliary functions, were to be integrated into the general work of the locals, sharing responsibilities on all issues. The members were to canvass house-to-house, in shops, and wherever women congregated. Special distributions and demonstrations occurred on the annual Woman's Day, May Day, the Fourth of July, and Labor Day. The W.N.C. published monthly programs for the guidance of local committees and routinely sent appropriate articles to the labor and socialist press. The local committees formed strike subcommittees and suffrage campaign groups. In some large cities, a Central Woman's Committee, composed of delegates from each ward branch, was organized, and innercity Socialist locals were provided with special guidelines to transcend the suspicions of tenement women. The W.N.C. also offered suggestions for reaching women on farms and in prairie hamlets, emphasizing the ways in which the party could serve a poignant human need by alleviating the loneliness of such isolated women.[16]

The W.N.C. issued approximately two dozen leaflets of interest to women. The leaflets appealed to women in their various working capacities and dealt with issues such as suffrage, social problems, socialism and the home, the boy scout movement, and the cost of living, the most widely distributed leaflet. The party executive, bearing veto power over publications, occasionally requested revisions for stylistic reasons and sometimes for matters of substance. One leaflet was criticized for using the expression, "the sex struggle."[17]

Each year the W.N.C. focused on a few specific lines of activity. In 1913, for example, the emphasis was on promoting suffrage, winning new members, and cooperating with immigrant women's organizations. Depending on the thrust, the W.N.C. tried to route organizers on various issues and in specific regions of the country. It considered placing organizers in an area for three days instead of the party's usual practice of one-day whirlwind visits since feeling was widespread that a more comprehensive type of barnstorming was necessary to break through the barriers surrounding women. Organizing methods were modified in favor of meetings in private homes, congenial environments where the uncommitted would feel comfortable. The Woman's National Committee established a Socialist Teachers' Placement Bureau and a Children's Strike Fund and explored the idea of "family dues" instead of the humiliating lower dues for women. It encouraged using women on the party's major committees, on delegations, and as national organizers, filled requests for women speakers, and tried to arrange national tours for European socialist women. Throughout all the W.N.C.'s efforts to involve women in routine party work and to encourage the cooperation of locals, it sought to minimize any suggestion of separatism. Lena Morrow Lewis, arguing unsuccessfully against a national conference of socialist women, cautioned that their work must always illustrate the fact that the Socialist Party was not a men's club: "We must never allow our woman's committees or conferences to be the means of eliminating [the] women from the regular party."[18]

The Socialist women succeeded in forging an institutional structure in over three dozen states, some of which became vigorous pockets of party activity. However, despite their wide-ranging efforts, although women joined the party, they did not flock to it. Fragmentary evidence clearly indicates a rise in women members. Just prior to the founding of the Woman's National Committee, a survey of 15 percent of the locals suggested that women were 4.9 percent of the membership. In 1912, the general correspondent, Winnie E. Branstetter, estimated—based on returns from only thirty-five locals—that 10 percent of the membership was female. The next year the reports of the state correspondents suggested 15 percent, and in 1915 May Wood Simons guessed that women made up 17 percent of the party. The dimension of the struggle to increase the female contingent can be gleaned from the fact that even membership data by sex remained elusive. The W.N.C. was obviously envious when it noted that the Young People's Socialist League claimed a membership that was one-third female.[19]

The Woman's National Committee sought to develop dialogues with several peer groups external to the party proper: women in the socialist movement overseas, immigrant women, and the bourgeois suffrage movement. The American women who attended the Congress of the Second International in Copenhagen in 1910, Luella Twining, May Wood Simons, and Lena Morrow Lewis, eagerly participated in the Second International Conference of Socialist Women, which preceded the Congress. German women had raised the Woman Question years before at the founding of the Second International in 1889, and by 1907 they had won an endorsement of universal suffrage and had organized an international conference of socialist women. American women, an ocean away, could not play a full role, yet the infrequent gatherings were inspirational to them. They enjoyed the collegial environment at the 1910 conference but nevertheless did not hesitate to oppose Clara Zetkin and other leaders who eschewed reforms such as protective legislation for women. The W.N.C. studied the European women's methods of propaganda and data collection and created a position of International Correspondent to systematize their contacts. The correspondent, Meta Stern Lilienthal of New York, monitored European publications and translated pertinent articles into English. The W.N.C. regularly sent reports of its work to Zetkin in Germany and to Annie Grundy in London and saw its own annual Woman's Day adopted by some of the European socialists. In 1914 the W.N.C. elected its own representative to the anticipated Third International Conference of Socialist Women scheduled for August in Vienna prior to the opening of the Congress of the International, and it also prepared a report for presentation there on the woman suffrage movement in the United States.[20]

The W.N.C., whose own membership sometimes included women of European background, was somewhat slow to recognize the potential for socialism among immigrant women, but eventually the committee sought to mine that resource. At the 1912 party convention, Caroline A. Lowe, a midwesterner, pleaded for funding for translators so that W.N.C. leaflets could reach the foreign-speaking. In 1913 the W.N.C. tried to forge links with the occasional woman serving on the executives of the party's foreign-language federations and with their few woman's branches. The federations, clearly male in leadership and, among certain nationalities, in membership as well, were asked by the W.N.C. to translate its woman's publications into their own languages. Translations appeared in Finnish, Slovak, Polish, Bohemian, Hungarian, German, and Yiddish, with only the South Slavic and the Italian federations lacking leaflets. The W.N.C. debated whether perhaps a "cultural problem" existed which might preclude verbatim translations into Eastern European languages and considered preparing a "simpler" literature for immigrant working-class women. A new leaflet was issued for such women on the importance of naturalization.[21]

A subcommittee was established to formalize a link between the W.N.C. and the party's foreign-language federation women. This move made feasible a survey of ethnic women's attitudes and situations. The survey, limited to women members of the foreign-language federations, showed that the Finnish federation led all wings of the party; with its family-based party activities, one-third of its membership was female. The Scandinavian and German federations were 15 percent women, the Bohemian, Polish, and Jewish were 10 percent female, and the South Slav and Italian—immigrant groups in which men often came without their families—only 1 percent female. Valuable data were assembled on the occupational status of women by ethnic group, putting the W.N.C. in a position to make knowledgeable appeals to each language group.[22]

The Woman's National Committee maintained an ambivalent relationship with the woman's suffrage movement. The W.N.C. found it necessary to justify any collaboration with the National American Woman's Suffrage Association because both the Second International and the Socialist Party opposed cooperation with middle-class suffrage efforts. But the W.N.C. spoke of capturing and radicalizing the suffrage movement; it maintained that its propaganda was always based on class consciousness, emphasizing that the ballot was only one means toward the goal of social transformation. Despite the fact that the Socialist Party never resolved the suffrage issue, the W.N.C. always assisted suffrage campaigns in every municipality and every state; it cooperated with the nonsocialist suffragists, and even joined them in testifying before the House Judiciary Committee in its hearings on several woman suffrage bills, one of which had been introduced by Socialist Congressman Berger. The W.N.C. sent observers to the conventions of the N.A.W.S.A. and shared credit with the suffragists when a state enacted woman suffrage.[23]

Most Socialist women believed that the suffragists were shortsighted; they reasoned inadequately on the basis of natural, that is, political, rights, whereas Socialist women stressed economic and social questions and realized that the ballot was not an end in itself. Still, some Socialist women considered suffrage a major goal, calling it as important as the demands of labor, whereas others stressed woman suffrage as a step toward socialism, and a number noted that to delay woman suffrage until the revolution would be as unreasonable as delaying the eight-hour day. To those who argued that women themselves had to energize their cause outside of the socialist movement, party feminists asked if worker propaganda should be set aside until the workers awoke.[24]

The issue crystallized at the party congress in 1910. By then, the Woman's National Committee under Simons had embarked on a sweeping educational campaign to convince women that the suffrage struggle should not be "a pure and simple feminine affair" but, rather, a class-conscious movement. Nonetheless, the debate demonstrated that a large number of women delegates favored cooperation with suffrage groups. An emotional discussion culminated in the defeat of a resolution to support the suffrage movement. Thus party doctrine still sought to restrict suffrage activity to internal efforts, and the Woman's National Committee's main thrust continued to be encouraging every local and state organization to establish a woman's committee which, in turn, would push suffrage. And yet at the next convention, when the feminist movement within the party was still at its height, a delegate questioned whether or not a belief in woman suffrage was necessary to a commitment to socialism.[25]

Aside from the Woman's National Committee and the woman's columns in the various socialist newspapers, socialist activity within the party structure was limited to the party's Information Department. In 1914 this party clearinghouse contacted the state secretaries of seven states with full or partial woman suffrage and determined that, despite voiced fears, women voters were not adversely affecting the movement. The department examined the historical experiences of states with woman suffrage and also surveyed the effect of minimum wage laws for women across the country. The efforts of the Information Department, like the W.N.C. itself, were focused on social reforms rather than the theoretical impossibility of emancipation within the capitalist structure.[26]

Socialist state legislators introduced a great number of bills and resolutions that either directly related to women or were thought to appeal to them. In addition to measures on behalf of woman suffrage, legislators introduced bills for women to serve as jurors, for free school lunches and textbooks, child labor legislation and protection for the rights of illegitimate children, minimum wage laws, Mothers' and Widows' Pensions, and various other protective measures such as maximum hours and rest periods. In contrast, the national platform of the Socialist Party in 1916 offered women only the equal franchise and the Mothers' Pension. Aside from those commitments, the national party apparatus was likely to turn to women only when policy required demonstrations and petitions against militarism, conscription, or war itself. Such appeals to socialist women were issued during the mobilization of American troops on the Mexican border and during World War I. Thus, women were still channeled into innocuous and undemanding areas without real responsibility. As mothers, women could always be counted on to provide antimilitary troops.[27]

But in several of the states and in various locales, the socialist woman's movement was growing into an energetic and imaginative, expansive focus for party activity. Based on their earlier socialization, many Socialist women sought to tap segments of what could be termed a woman's network. Many turned to lyceums and chatauquas to interest women who might have been intimidated by direct socialist approaches. In California, for example, a socialist chatauqua was held in 1909. Elsewhere in the West, women sponsored party booths at state and county fairs; they pioneered weekly or monthly party suppers in Pennsylvania, Washington, D.C., and elsewhere; and they arranged for entertainments and speakers as they caravaned out to workers in lonely mining camps in Kansas. Various approaches were used in order to transform public schools into community centers so that party activities could encompass the entire family. Plays were presented during strikes to raise funds and to lift morale.

Monthly reports of the state correspondents recorded new party members, listed sympathizers, and informed the general correspondent of the names of local women organizers and speakers. Newly organized woman's committees sometimes revived an entire area. In Nevada in the summer of 1913, for example, ten new locals were 50 percent female in membership. In Utah, it was reported, women of the Mormon faith who were hesitant to join the party nevertheless participated in party activities. Women even held statewide socialist conferences in New York, Massachusetts, and Kansas. The woman's effort, thus, was developing grassroots and a responsiveness to local conditions and emerging needs. The socialist woman's movement, in but not of the party through its separate bureaucracy, was succeeding in minimizing isolation, providing role models and opportunities for leadership, stimulating awareness and organization, and apparently spreading socialism.[28]

In regard to policy, most Socialist women accepted the revisionist and gradualist direction of the party. With a few exceptions, Socialist women by their votes, statements, and writings supported the reformist wing of the party, which controlled the bureaucracy and policy. But while most of the women activists agreed with mainstream party thinking, their distance from party responsibilities granted them some independence in policy formulation,[29] including the paramount issues of these years, which revolved around the party's relationship with organized labor. In the winter of 1909–1910 a party crisis erupted stemming from failure to attract large numbers of working people. Eventually all party leaders polled by the *International Socialist Review* disavowed the idea of forming a separate labor party. Not one of the two dozen polled was a woman, as only candidates for the National Executive Committee were interviewed, and thus women played no part in the discussion.[30]

The Wobblies, too radical a group for the tastes of most party officials, enjoyed the support of some women Socialists. A woman organizer, Ida Crouch-Hazlett of Montana, argued unsuccessfully against party discouragement of any evidence of worker solidarity. When the Industrial Workers of the World (IWW) led so-called free speech fights on the West Coast, using civil disobedience to publicize the closing of street corners to their soapbox speakers, Kate Sadler of Washington and Marguerite Prevey of

Ohio joined a minority effort to force the party to give moral support to the Wobblies' struggle. In 1912, the party in convention amended its constitution to make an endorsement of sabotage, considered an IWW tactic, grounds for expulsion from the Socialist Party. Prevey argued that such a move could only assist capitalists in the protection of private property. Women delegates divided over the amendment, fifteen supporting it and nine opposing. As a postscript, the IWW leader, Big Bill Haywood, was soon manipulated out of the party and recalled from the N.E.C. in an extraordinary procedure. Thirteen of the three-dozen activists writing to condemn the railroading tactics were women.[31]

Another issue concerned a party compromise on the subject of immigration restriction. Despite its avowed internationalism, the Socialist Party did not wish to contravene the restrictionist policy of the American Federation of Labor (A.F. of L.). Socialist women, however, had little difficulty supporting internationalist principles. They tended not to be linked to the A.F. of L. as were many of their male counterparts, and thus some women freely acknowledged that exclusion was a pseudo-issue, merely a bone thrown to satisfy West Coast trade unionists. Josephine R. Cole, a California journalist, argued that labor had not reached an anti-immigrant consensus, and she maintained that the Socialist Party had to assume the lead in uniting all races [*sic*] against capitalism. A Washington state woman, however, at the 1910 party congress, vilified Chinese workers. Although such remarks were not extraordinary, one woman, a Finnish delegate from Minnesota, cited the absurdity of the pluralistic United States excluding nationality groups and took the unusual step of forthrightly denigrating A.F. of L. restrictionism on the grounds of its minority status in the labor movement. But as in various party debates, the voices of the women members tended to be muted, at best. Since they were absent from policy-making positions, intraparty controversies lay in the male domain. Women activists were left to "woman's issues," that is, issues that fell "naturally" to their "place."[32]

Women's concerns as reflected in their writings and speeches related especially to family fragmentation and social problems under capitalism. Not only did the male-dominated party generally reserve these issues for women members, but the life experiences of these women shaped them toward such concerns which then were reinforced by the party. A consensus among Socialist women appeared to exist over some issues: the importance of progressive education and the evils of child labor, the capitalist foundation of alcoholism, divorce, and white slavery. Marriage itself was likened to prostitution because some women had to sell their bodies for economic security. On many matters, however, Socialist women disagreed. Most stressed the equality of the sexes while a few implied female superiority. A majority appeared to support birth control as a necessary factor in the emancipation of human beings, while a minority—perhaps influenced by Clara Zetkin—viewed increasing numbers of workers' children as assets in the class struggle. Most Socialist women welcomed protective legislation for working women, but a vocal handful considered it patronizing and empty reformism. As to the future of the family, a common view held that socialism would emancipate wives from domestic drudgery; under the socialist system, readily available appliances would simplify household chores. But a few stressed the importance of women having an opportunity to be individuals, in addition to being mothers and wives, and theorized that perhaps marriage would become a relic of the capitalist past. Viewing marriage as an economic institution, some suggested that the independence inherent in the new system would drastically alter the marital relationship. Often on such basic questions a Marxist-feminist split was evident. The most radical women in terms of Marxist ideology tended to lack a feminist consciousness.[33]

On the fundamental issue, the Woman Question itself, the division among Socialist women was searing. They never reached a solid consensus on the emancipation of women as a legitimate issue for the Socialist Party. Those who opposed the Woman Question as an issue maintained that the socialization of property was the only means to insure economic independence for all, and, therefore, overt concern for a specific group would simply waste energy. The struggle to raise class consciousness must be waged without regard to sex or color. It was argued that even a direct attack on beliefs in female inferiority would be a tactical error, resulting in a monolithic alliance of men against women. In contrast, the avowedly feminist position emphasized that the unique political and economic tyranny to which women were subject required a special campaign within the class struggle. Women, especially working women, were not only oppressed by capitalism but were also oppressed as the proletariat of the family, as Engels had noted. Many socialist feminists wrote of the double enslavement of women—bearing the burden of class and sex—and the need for double emancipation. Women's economic exploitation was more complex than that of workingmen, as a realistic appraisal of conditions would indicate.[34]

Ironically, many vigorous arguments on behalf of the Woman Question were home-centered, focusing on women's special biological nature and their greater spirituality and sensitivity, and thus were ultimately traditionalist in their thrust. American women were advised by Socialist women to join the party because of their unique concerns as mothers, and they "should throw . . . [the] strength of maternal altruism into the only cause that can give equal opportunity for children of the human race." Modern women, editorialized the *Socialist Woman,* have to be taught that socialism is the only way to solve the increasing problems of the family and the home. While often Socialist women objected to the view that socialism would permit women to be home full time without social responsibility, nevertheless a consistent theme placed the emancipated woman in that setting. Women party leaders were often praised as model homemakers, examples that socialism would not destroy domesticity. And, indeed, their pride as homemakers and their marital life styles, other than the not uncommon use of the hyphenated name, demonstrated little that set them apart from their bourgeois counterparts. As one woman wrote, "The genuine good old standards need never be lost in gaining the genuine goal of new freedom. . . ."[35]

The vision of Socialist women was neither cohesive, incisive, nor innovative. Those who saw women's liberation as a distinct part of the class struggle often did not transcend traditional role assignments and family structure. They, like most sexist male comrades, ultimately viewed the sexes and the family according to standards which the male-dominated institutions of western society had shaped. One socialist feminist might argue that society must be organized so that women, like men, were seen as bearing potential beyond the reproductive. Another might stress that marriage must mean more for women than the termination of their personal aspirations. But no one designed a new family structure to facilitate full female liberation. A basic social transformation was never conceptualized.[36]

The Woman's National Committee, after six years of intense activity, was undercut by forces in the party that either considered the Woman Question irrelevant trimmings or a divisive threat. Thus, in 1914, work on behalf of the socialist woman's movement halted without the resolution of the internal tensions or the further development of programs then maturing. But, logically, if there were no real Woman Question, there was no need for a woman's sector. The aftermath of the national campaign of 1912 witnessed party retrenchment due to membership slippage, a type of leveling off of activity familiar to all political parties following elections. The National Executive Committee embarked on a cost-cutting crusade, involving the cancellation of meetings, publications, and any efforts thought to be unessential. Accordingly, the N.E.C. "withdrew all support from the W.N.C."

The W.N.C. could no longer publish leaflets, field organizers, effect policy decisions, or even maintain its correspondence. No money was budgeted for W.N.C. operations, and its meetings were discouraged. Some of the women concluded bitterly that totally eliminating possibly flawed machinery clearly demonstrated that women's organized activities were no more than ornamental to the male hierarchy. May Wood Simons, the dominant figure in the establishment of the Woman's National Committee and the only person to have served on it since its founding, resigned in protest. In 1914 the National Committee discussed the abolition of the W.N.C., and in 1915 such a motion was passed and sustained in referendum. With that stroke of a pen, as it were, the entire structure in which the socialist woman's movement was concentrated dissolved. In the aftermath, a number of women spontaneously demonstrated against the dissolution of their party machinery, while a few women registered their approval, arguing that that mechanism had served to shunt them off to a corner of the party. Most of the protesters emphasized that women would again be invisible in the party and might once more work outside it. A few affirmative action resolutions by men and women were submitted in favor of proportional representation for women on major committees in lieu of a special hierarchy. As a probably not unconnected development, a woman did win election to the N.E.C. for the first time in four years.[37]

In the subsequent years of war and strife, culminating in the party schism of 1919, women resumed the peripheral role they had played earlier, as some had predicted. Only a few of the "exceptional" continued to be prominent, and women made up nearly 6 percent (a loss of 4 percent) of the delegates to the Emergency Convention of 1917 at the start of war intervention. Such an unimpressive figure, as well as the infrequency with which women members were nominated for public office, suggests as little visibility as before. Wartime resolutions for reestablishing a woman's sector were tabled.[38]

The unwanted party-within-a-party that had provided the movement with new sources of energy was ironically snuffed out arbitrarily in the midst of its most dynamic and vital period, just as the Socialist Party itself was to be cut down in World War I by forces external to it. No evidence exists to prove a thesis that the woman's movement within the party peaked in 1912 and then declined.[39] Rather, that movement continued to sink roots and to establish an increasingly comprehensive network, which, however, was handicapped by its lack of autonomy and by the constant need to fight a rearguard action to convince both men and women of the seriousness and the legitimacy of its effort. In the final analysis, the woman's movement proved a fragile structure because of the lack of a powerful base in the national bureaucracy. Tensions and ambivalence destroyed the separate and parallel movement.

NOTES

1. See, e.g., "Women and Socialism," in James Weinstein, *The Decline of Socialism in America, 1912–1925* (New York: Monthly Review Press, 1967), pp. 53–63. He does not systematically explore the extent of female integration into the party structure and, moreover, takes individuals' statements and party pronouncements concerning women's rights at face value. Also see Ira Kipnis, *The American Socialist Movement, 1897–1912* (New York: Monthly Review Press, 1972), pp. 260–65, for the only historical consideration of this question prior to the mid-1960s.

2. Edgard Milhaud, "Socialist Propaganda Among Women in Germany," *International Socialist Review,* 1 (May 1901), pp. 713–18; Paul Lafargue, "The Woman Question," ibid., 5 (March 1905), pp. 547–59. See lists of delegates, Socialist Party, *Proceedings of the 1904 National Convention* (Chicago: Socialist Party, 1904), p. 16; S.P., *Proceedings . . . 1908,* pp. 16–18; S.P., *Proceedings . . . 1912,* pp. 83–85, 204–08.

3. For a general overview of women's socialist activities, see the *Socialist Woman 1907–1913* (renamed the *Progressive Woman,* and then the *Coming Nation;* each name change was symbolic of a search for wider support). Arthur Brooks Baker, "Be a Party Builder," *International Socialist Review,* 13 (September 1912), pp. 259–62; *Socialist Woman,* 2 (August 1908), p. 16; *Socialist Woman,* 3 (September 1909), p. 15; *Socialist Woman,* 2 (April 1909), p. 8; Socialist Party, *Proceedings . . . 1904,* p. 326; S.P., *Proceedings . . . 1908,* pp. 10–11; S.P., *Proceedings . . . 1912,* pp. 205–06; "Plan of Work for Women in Socialist Locals," Woman's National Committee, Socialist Party, 1913. For the autonomous socialist woman's clubs, see Bruce Dancis, "Socialism and Women in the United States, 1900–1917," *Socialist Revolution,* 6 (January–March 1976), pp. 109–10.

4. Socialist Party, *Proceedings . . . 1912,* p. 204. See, e.g., the instructions of Oklahoma Assistant State Secretary Winnie E. Branstetter that all speakers work for woman suffrage, in *Socialist Woman,* 1 (February 1908), p. 5.

5. John Spargo, "Woman and the Socialist Movement," *International Socialist Review,* 8 (February 1908), pp. 449–55; Theresa Malkiel, "Where Do We Stand on the Woman Question?," ibid., 10 (August 1909), pp. 159–62; Lida Parce, "The Relation of Socialism to the Woman Question," ibid., 10 (November 1909), p. 442; Josephine Conger-Kaneko, "Are the Interests of Men and Women Identical? A Suggestion to the National Convention," *Socialist Woman,* 1 (May 1908), p. 5. Those women arguing for separate locals actually favored mixed locals but thought they were feasible only where the

men were responsive to women's needs and where the women were sufficiently enlightened. Separate locals, never effected, were expected to raise women's consciousness, educate them, and give them the confidence for an active role in mixed locals. But such views led to the necessity of a public denial by the head of the Woman's National Committee that a separate women's organization was their goal. See Josephine Conger-Kaneko, "Separate Organizations," *Socialist Woman,* 1 (April 1908), p. 5; "Socialist Women Hold Meetings During Convention Week," ibid., 2 (June 1908), pp. 9–10; Theresa Malkiel, "Some Impressions of the New York State Women's Conference," ibid., 2 (August 1908), pp. 12–13; May Wood Simons, "Origin and Purpose of the Woman's Committee," ibid., 5 (July 1911), p. 6; Josephine Conger-Kaneko, "Why the Movement Has a Woman's Paper," ibid., 5 (July 1911), p. 15.

6. Spargo, "Woman and the Socialist Movement," p. 450; Parce, "The Relation of Socialism," p. 442. See also Victor Berger to Morris Hillquit, February 13, 1910, Morris Hillquit Collection, State Historical Society of Wisconsin; Morris Hillquit to Victor Berger, October 16, 1913, Berger to Hillquit, October 23, 1913, Berger to William James Ghent, November 13, 1911, Bronx Socialist Women's Society to Berger, March 8, 1915, Florence Kelley to Berger, May 15, 1911, and also Berger note, July 1912, Socialist Party Collection, Milwaukee County Historical Society; Josephine R. Cole, "The International and Woman Suffrage," *Socialist Woman*, 1 (November 1907), p. 3. Mary White Ovington, a socialist more active in the National Association for the Advancement of Colored People than in the Socialist Party, echoed these concerns and noted that many writings by socialists featured "not a word . . . on woman and her disabilities . . ." (Mary White Ovington, "Socialism and the Feminist Movement," *New Review,* 2 (March 1914), pp. 114–15). John Spargo and John Work seemed to be the only male party leaders to have believed genuinely in sexual equality. Work argued for a fuller recognition of women within the party in his "The Party Machinery," *Socialist Woman,* 5 (July 1911), p. 10. One male state secretary maintained that perhaps only 10 percent of the men in the party actually believed in sexual equality, and he said that the Woman's National Committee ought to make the elevation of men's consciousness a top priority. See *Party Builder,* August 9, 1913, p. 5.

7. Editorial, "Sparks from the Convention," *International Socialist Review,* 10 (June 1910), pp. 1127–29; Henry C. Slobodin, "The National Socialist Convention of 1912," ibid., 12 (June 1912), p. 824; Eugene V. Debs, "Women Needed in Campaign," *Socialist Woman,* 2 (August 1908), p. 4.

8. Malkiel, "Where Do We Stand?" p. 161. On the manifestation of oligarchic tendencies in the bureaucracy of a radical political party, see Carl Schorske, *German Social Democracy, 1905–1917: The Develop-*

ment of the Great Schism (Cambridge, Mass.: Harvard University Press, 1955), pp. 116–45.

9. See the monthly profiles in the *Socialist Woman, 1907–1909.* This composite is based on that important primary documentation, a crucial source since the *American Labor's Who's Who* (1925), the best source for biographies of radicals, lists very few women. Flynn, of course, was closely associated with the IWW rather than the Socialist Party. There are few collections of the correspondence of these women; the papers of only those women whose husbands' letters have been saved tend to be extant.

10. Ages are deduced from the internal evidence in the monthly biographies. The women biographers in the *Socialist Woman* politely omitted the birthdates of their subjects. While Rose Pastor Stokes was more famous than her husband, he rather than she served on the National Executive Committee.

11. See list of delegates, as cited in note 2, for the geographic breakdown.

12. Socialist Party, *Official Bulletin,* 4 (June 1908), p. 1; ibid., 5 (May 1909), p. 1; ibid., 6 (May 1910), p. 4; ibid., 7 (October 1910), p. 1; ibid., 8 (August 1911), p. 5; *Party Builder,* January 23, 1914, p. 5. Two women of the Plains States, Caroline A. Lowe of Kansas and Winnie E. Branstetter of Oklahoma, served as the general correspondent.

13. Prizes were given to locals for attracting women members as part of the campaign of the Woman's National Committee, but whatever its efforts or a state's conditions, an individual official could discourage women from joining the party. Socialist Party, *Official Bulletin,* 5 (June 1909), p. 4; ibid., 7 (October 1910), p. 1; ibid., 7 (December 1910), p. 2; ibid., 9 (February 1913), p. 2; *Party Builder,* October 2, 1912, p. 2; October 16, 1912, p. 2; October 23, 1912, p. 2; October 30, 1912, p. 2; January 25, 1913, p. 2; July 12, 1913, p. 4; August 9, 1913, p. 5; August 23, 1913, p. 5.

14. For representative National Committee membership data, see Socialist Party, *Official Bulletin,* 6 (January 1910), p. 4; ibid., 8 (August 1912), p. 8; *Party Builder,* March 7, 1914, p. 5. The Woman's Department Report in S.P., *Proceedings* of the 1912 National Convention, pp. 204–05, provides information on convention delegations. For other data, see S.P., *Official Bulletin,* 5 (July 1909), p. 4; ibid., 5 (September 1908), p. 1; ibid., 7 (September 1910), p. 3.

15. A letter to the editor summarized these views by stating that unfortunately a special appeal to women was necessary due to their capitalist-induced conservatism. See *Socialist Woman,* 1 (July 1907), p. 8, and also, "Grace D. Brewer" (a biographical study), ibid., 1 (January 1908), p. 2; Josephine Conger-Kaneko, "Separate Organizations," ibid., 1 (April 1908), p. 5; Ida Crouch-Hazlett, "Women's Organizations," ibid., 2 (September 1908), p. 11. One woman argued

that any desire for separate locals was an unfortunate indication of social norms; see Mila Tupper Maynard, "Woman Suffrage as Observed by a Socialist," *International Socialist Review,* 5 (January 1905). W.N.C., "Plan of Work for Women in Socialist Locals," Chicago, 1913; *Party Builder*, August 28, 1912, p. 3; May 31, 1913, p. 2; September 13, 1913, p. 5; September 20, 1913, p. 5; March 7, 1914, p. 5. Informal talks on the cost of living and on shoddy consumer goods were considered especially good openers when approaching potential women members. *Party Builder*, December 25, 1912, p. 2.

16. S.P., *Official Bulletin*, 7 (October 1910), p. 1; ibid., 8 (June 1912), pp. 3, 4; *Party Builder*, October 30, 1912, p. 2; November 20, 1912, p. 2; December 25, 1912, p. 2; March 26, 1913, p. 2; July 19, 1913, p. 4; October 18, 1913, p. 5; February 14, 1914, p. 5; March 7, 1914, p. 5.

17. Copies of the various Woman's National Committee leaflets can be found in the files of the Socialist Party, National Office Papers, Duke University. A discussion on possible leaflet topics can be traced in the *Minutes* of the Woman's National Committee meeting of May 20, 1910, which appears in S.P., *Official Bulletin*, 6 (May 1910), p. 4. See also ibid., 5 (November 1908), p. 2, and ibid., 5 (August 1909), p. 3, and *Party Builder*, May 10, 1914, p. 5.

18. Winnie E. Branstetter, "Woman's National Committee Enters a New Field of Activity," May 28, 1913, Socialist Party, National Office Files, Duke University; S.P., *Official Bulletin*, 4 (May 1908), p. 2; ibid., 5 (May 1909), p. 2; ibid., 7 (August 1911), p. 5; ibid., 8 (November 1911), p. 2; ibid., 8 (March 1912), p. 2; ibid., 8 (June 1912), p. 4; *Party Builder*, May 31, 1913, p. 2, July 19, 1913, p. 4, July 26, 1913, p. 5, November 15, 1913, p. 5. The independent *Socialist Woman* editorialized on the need to elect a woman or several women to the party executive, arguing that women knew their own condition best. See *Socialist Woman,* 1 (January 1908), p. 6. The *International Socialist Review* editorialized in the same vein in its issue of January 1909 (vol. 9, p. 535).

19. A 1908 survey of the membership showed that of 325 women members responding, 177 were housewives; one-third were in the 30–45 age bracket, with the rest evenly divided between younger and older women. S.P., *Official Bulletin,* 5 (April 1909), p. 2; ibid., 8 (June 1912), p. 4; Socialist Party, *Proceedings* of the 1912 National Convention, p. 205; *Party Builder,* May 31, 1913, pp. 3–4; May 16, 1914, p. 5; *American Socialist,* January 1915, p. 4.

20. S.P., *Official Bulletin,* 4 (May 1908), p. 2; ibid., 6 (August 1910), p. 5; ibid., 8 (July 1912), p. 4; ibid., 9 (October 1912), p. 8; *Party Builder,* May 31, 1913, p. 2; January 10, 1914, p. 5; March 14, 1914, p. 5; June 6, 1914, p. 3; "From the International Congress," *Socialist Woman,* 4 (October 1910), pp. 2–3. See also Second International Conference of Socialist Women, *Program,* 1910, Copenhagen

(bound with *Report* of the Socialist Party Delegation to the International Socialist Congress, 1910, at International Institute of Social History, Amsterdam) and Socialist Labor Party, *Report* of the Socialist Women of Greater New York to the International Socialist Congress, 1910, Copenhagen.

21. Socialist Party, *Proceedings . . . 1912*, pp. 88, 207; *Party Builder,* October 11, 1913, p. 5; S.P., *Official Bulletin,* 8 (September-October 1911), p. 3; ibid., 6 (May 1910), p. 4; ibid., 8 (September 1912), p. 7. The issues of the *Party Builder* in 1913 and 1914 provide a good overview of the W.N.C.'s growing relationship with the foreign-language contingent. Apparently the first W.N.C. formal consideration of immigrant women occurred in 1911. See S.P., *Official Bulletin,* 8 (July 1911), p. 1.

22. Contradictory data exist on the percentage of women in the foreign-language federations; the percentages used in the text seem the most reasonable (an unlikely listing of the Hungarian federation as 20 percent female was dismissed as suspect). Centers of activity for foreign-speaking socialist women were clearly New York City, Chicago, and some Finnish-dominated rural areas. *Party Builder,* May 31, 1913, pp. 3–4; July 5, 1913, p. 5; November 1, 1913, p. 4; February 7, 1914, p. 3; February 21, 1914, p. 5; May 23, 1914, p. 5; S.P., *Official Bulletin,* 7 (August 1911), p. 5; ibid., 8 (June 1912), p. 4.

23. Corinne S. Brown, "Votes for Women," *Socialist Woman,* 1 (February 1908), p. 4, criticizes the International's 1907 position at Stuttgart against collaboration with the suffrage movement. The Socialist Party debate on this point is summarized in "Sparks from the Convention," *International Socialist Review,* 9 (June 1910), pp. 1126–27. See also Ida Crouch-Hazlett, "The Socialist Movement and Woman Suffrage," *Socialist Woman,* 2 (June 1908), p. 5. A letter from M. J. Scanlon to Winnie E. Branstetter, Carson City, Nevada, February 22, 1915, indicates that the Nevada state suffrage movement credited local socialist help for its triumph at the polls the previous November. See letter in S.P., National Office Files, Duke University. S.P., *Official Bulletin,* 6 (April 1910), p. 2; ibid., 8 (November 1911), p. 7; ibid., 8 (April 1912), p. 4; ibid., 8 (May 1912), p. 3; ibid., 9 (December 1912), p. 1; *Party Builder,* May 31, 1913, p. 2.

24. Cole, "The International and Woman Suffrage," pp. 1, 3; Lena Morrow Lewis, "Woman Suffragists and Woman Suffragists," *Socialist Woman,* 1 (February 1908), p. 3; Brown, "Votes for Women," p. 4; Winnie E. Branstetter, "Socialist Party Should Make a More Active Propaganda for Female Suffrage," ibid., p. 5; Anna A. Maley, "The Suffrage and Freedom," ibid., p. 10; Crouch-Hazlett, "The Socialist Movement," p. 5; "'First State Conference of Woman's Socialist Union of California," ibid., 3 (June 1909), p. 9; "Women at the Convention," *International Socialist Review,* 7 (June 1908), p. 782; Parce, "The Relation of Socialism," p. 443.

25. "Open Letter to Socialists from Woman's National Committee," *Socialist Woman,* 3 (September 1909), pp. 15–16; May Wood Simons, "Aims and Purposes of Women's [sic] Committee," ibid., 3 (October 1909), p. 2; E.C.U., "The Suffrage Question and the Congress," ibid., 4 (June 1910), p. 5; "Sparks from the Convention," pp. 1126–27; Socialist Party, *Proceedings* of the 1912 National Convention, p. 119; Ira Kipnis, *The American Socialist Movement,* p. 264. E.C.U. was no doubt the party theoretician, Ernest Untermann.

26. See the records of the Information Department of the Socialist Party in the S.P., National Office Files, 1914–1915, Duke University, for correspondence with party officials in states with woman suffrage, for a study of minimum wage laws, and for surveys of states' suffrage patterns.

27. Ethelwyn Mills, ed., *Legislative Program of the Socialist Party: Record of the Work of the Socialist Representatives in State Legislatures, 1899–1913* (Chicago: Socialist Party, 1914), pp. 13–14, 18, 20, 24, 25–26, 33, 38–39; "Massachusetts Socialist Bills," January 15, 1913, listed in Information Department Files in S.P., National Office Files, Duke University; George W. Downing to Winnie E. Branstetter, Sacramento, February 21, 1915, S.P. National Office Files, Duke University; *Official Bulletin,* 8 (January 1912), p. 3; ibid., 8 (June 1912), p. 4; *Party Builder,* May 2, 1914, p. 2; *American Socialist,* September 5, 1914, p. 3; "Socialist Party Platform," in S.P., *Socialist Handbook* (Chicago: Socialist Party, 1916). As late as fall, 1914, May Wood Simons argued that it was necessary to prod Socialist state legislators to introduce woman suffrage bills. See *American Socialist,* January 2, 1915, p. 4.

28. See, e.g., S.P., Grand Rapids, "Suggestions for Social Center Work," S.P., National Office Files, Duke University; "News of Organizations," *Socialist Woman,* 3 (September 1909), pp. 13, 15; "Conference of Socialist Woman's Committees of Kansas," ibid. (July 1909), p. 9; *Party Builder,* July 12, 1913, p. 4; August 23, 1913, pp. 1, 5; September 6, 1913, p. 4; November 11, 1913, p. 4; January 7, 1914, p. 5; March 7, 1914, p. 5. S.P., *Official Bulletin,* 4 (June 1908), p. 1; ibid., 9 (March-April 1913), p. 2. For examples of the extensiveness of the reports of the state correspondents, see S.P., *Official Bulletin,* 9 (January 1913), p. 2.

29. Examples of women leaders' endorsements of reformism are Mila Tupper Maynard, "The Socialist Program," *Socialist Woman,* 3 (October 1909), p. 12; "Hurrah for Milwaukee," ibid., 4 (May 1910), p. 8; S.P., *Proceedings* of the 1904 National Convention, pp. 244–63. For an overview on party policy, see Sally M. Miller, *Victor Berger and the Promise of Constructive Socialism, 1910–1920* (Westport, Conn.: Greenwood Press, 1973), pp. 6–14.

30. See *International Socialist Review,* 10 (January 1910), pp. 594–606.

31. Ida Crouch-Hazlett, "The Other Side," *International Socialist Review*, 5 (March 1905), pp. 86–91; Slobodin, "The National Socialist Convention of 1912," pp. 817, 825–27; for a list of Haywood supporters, see ibid., 13, p. 623; Socialist Party, *Proceedings* of the 1912 National Convention, pp. 61–62, 70–71, 135–37, 127.

32. S.P., *Proceedings* of the 1908 National Convention, pp. 114–15, 120; Josephine Conger-Kaneko, "Notes on the National Congress," *Socialist Woman,* 3 (June 1910), pp. 4–5. S.P., *Proceedings* of the 1910 National Congress, pp. 121, 140.

33. "Rose Pastor Stokes," *Socialist Woman,* 1 (October 1907), p. 2; Robin E. Dunbar, "Girls and Bourgeois Philosophy," ibid., p. 5; May Walden, "True Home Under Socialism," ibid., 1 (January 1908), p. 5; Walden, "Party Politics and Prostitution," ibid., 1 (February 1908), p. 2; Mary S. Oppenheimer, "Is It a Handicap?" ibid., 2 (October 1908), pp. 13–14; Josephine Conger-Kaneko, editorial, ibid., 4 (October 1910), p. 12; William J. Robinson, "The Birth Strike," *International Socialist Review,* 14 (January 1914), pp. 404–06; Caroline Nelson, "The Control of Child Bearing," ibid., 14 (March 1914), pp. 547–48.

34. S.P., *Proceedings* of the 1908 National Convention, pp. 302–05; Charles Kerr, "Socialist National Convention," *International Socialist Review*, 8 (June 1908), pp. 736–37; Malkiel, "Where Do We Stand?" pp. 159–61; "News and Views," ibid., 9 (February 1909), p. 630; 'Hebe,' "Message to Socialist Party Convention," *Socialist Woman,* 1 (May 1908), p. 3; "The National Convention on the Woman Question," ibid., 2 (June 1908), pp. 3–4; "Woman's Socialist League of Chicago Meeting," ibid., 2 (June 1908), p. 10.

35. Georgia Kotsch, "The Mother's Future," *International Socialist Review,* 10 (June 1910), p. 1099; Spargo, "Woman and the Socialist Movement," p. 453; Elizabeth H. Thomas, "Why Women Should Be Socialists," *Socialist Woman,* 1 (June 1907), p. 2; Mila Tupper Maynard, "Our Women Delegates to the International—May Wood Simons," ibid., 4 (August 1910), p. 10; "May Wood Simons," ibid., 1 (June 1907), p. 3; Lena Morrow Lewis, "Letter," ibid., 4 (October 1910), p. 3.

36. Grace C. Brown, "Why Women Should Organize," *Socialist Woman,* 1 (July 1907), p. 2; Lida Parce, "What Is the Woman Question," ibid., 2 (March 1909), pp. 3–5.

37. See the weekly issues of the *American Socialist* from January 1915 to September 1915, especially the letters to the editor for discussion of the dissolution of the Woman's Department. Sophia Salkova of Cincinnati angrily wrote that the party pattern showed that women were seen as "the rear end of the movement." Replying to the comment by a sympathetic John Work that the loss of the Woman's Department reflected an attempt at a unifying effort, she said that by the same logic the foreign-language federations should be abandoned. See *American Socialist,* September 25, 1915, p. 3. For the decision of

the Social Democratic Party in Germany to provide proportional representation for women members on its various executive bodies, see Werner Thönnessen, *The Emancipation of Women: The Rise and Decline of the Women's Movement in German Social Democracy, 1863–1933* (London: Pluto Press, 1969), p. 129.

38. Kate Richards O'Hare and Kate Sadler played possibly the most significant roles at the Emergency Convention where the party hammered out its antiwar position, as suggested in a summary of the proceedings of the secret sessions of the Committee on War and Militarism. See S.P., *Emergency Convention, Minutes* (summary of), Fifth Day, April 11, 1917, n.p., Second Day, April 8, 1917, p. 16; S.P., National Executive Committee-State Secretaries, *Minutes* of the Joint Conference, August 1918, pp. 256–59. At the assembling of what turned out to be the schismatic convention, August 30, 1919, 10 of 137 (or 7.2 percent) of the uncontested delegates were women. See list in S.P., National Office Files, Duke University.

39. This position is argued in Mari Jo Buhle, "Women and the Socialist Party," *Radical America*, 4 (February 1970), p. 51; Dancis, "Socialism and Women in the United States," pp. 126–30.

COMMENT

Mari Jo Buhle

Sally Miller presents a concise summary of women's experiences within the Socialist Party of America at its peak, during the first two decades of the twentieth century. She estimates fairly their disproportionately small membership, between 10 and 20 percent nationwide, and records in unprecedented detail women's truly marginal status within state, national, and international delegations. Both sexes shared the responsibility for this poor record, Miller intimates. The male leaders espoused at best a luke-warm advocacy of women's emancipation whereas the few women who achieved prominence failed to develop a clear and forceful perspective on the Woman Question and ultimately limited their appeals to a white, native-born, and mostly middle-class constituency. Even the Socialist Party's much-touted endorsement of equal rights, a plank in its original platform, seemed merely a perfunctory accordance with the European dictates of Second International policy. What emerges from Miller's description, then, is a gloomy profile of a socialist women's movement lacking in the necessary theoretical as well as tactical resources to counteract the rampant sexism that pervaded the party.

I do not wish to quibble with Miller's data or to impugn her overall assessment of women's fate within the Socialist Party. I agree wholeheartedly with her assertion that the majority of men merely tolerated the interjection of the Woman Question into political discussions and remained single-mindedly devoted to the time-honored strategic questions concerning the primacy of trade union or electoral struggle. The debates at the 1908 and 1910 party conventions, wherein delegates expressed their opinions on the Woman Question at unusual lengths, revealed mainly their reticence to take up the cause. Most socialists, despite official pronouncements to the contrary, adhered to the era's prevailing notions about woman's place. They did not welcome the ideologically heterodox or strong-minded woman.

Although I admire Miller's rigorous research into the records of the Socialist Party and affirm her assessment of women's status within its ranks, I disagree with some of her conclusions, especially with regard to the essay's larger claims. Miller states that she aims to address "basic questions about the role of women in radical politics, or, that is, radical politics and woman's 'place.' " Although I too deem essential this type of exploration, I mistrust Miller's particular approach, *an institutional study* of the Socialist Party and its women members. An examination of socialist women bound by their experiences within the party bureaucracy is very valuable, but in my opinion it is too limited to address effectively those weighty, basic questions that frame Miller's essay. Especially for assessing the major strategic issues of the period, namely, methods or modes of organization and the theory of women's liberation, an institutional study of socialist women exclusively within the party, however finely drawn, provides only partial evidence and thereby underestimates the breadth of their activities and the range of their political choices. By confining her analysis to women's status within the Socialist Party proper, Miller tends to distort in several ways the significance of their endeavors. Her gauge is too narrow, I believe. As a result, her study abstracts its subjects from the larger political and, equally important, social context.

This limitation shows itself primarily in the way Miller analyzes the organizational history of socialist women. She focuses almost exclusively on the role of the Woman's National Committee in creating a distinct women's sector within the party. Established in 1908 at the party's national convention, the W.N.C. worked with minimal funds and personnel to expand a network of women's committees across thirty-seven states. Although regional differences precluded a uniformity of experience, by 1915 women enjoyed a viable organizational structure that served at times and in places, according to Miller, as "vigorous pockets of party activity." Miller thus acknowledges the significance of this feat as one far in advance of women's accomplishments within other contemporary national political parties. She nevertheless concludes that the W.N.C. failed on strategic grounds.

Key to Miller's evaluation of the W.N.C.'s role is her assessment of female separatism and its impact on the organizational trajectory of socialist women. As she points out, the W.N.C. never achieved the integration of women into the bureaucratic structure of the party on an equal basis with men and instead allowed, however reluctantly, its constituents to cluster in their own special committees. Miller writes: "A distinct separatism that almost no one wanted developed"; the women's sector became the "unwanted party-within-a-party," and lacking "a powerful base in the national bureaucracy," this "fragile structure" succumbed to disarray during World War I. Relegated to separate organizations, women could neither participate fully in the party's governing bodies nor challenge effectively male prerogatives. As a consequence, Miller concludes, the women's sector of the Socialist Party suffered fatally from political isolation, caused in effect by its unwanted separatism.

Certainly, the issue of female separatism is central to the history of socialist women and any assessment of their role. Nevertheless, I believe that Miller misrepresents its significance. First, socialist women did not drift unwittingly into separate organizations; nor did they group together primarily because the party allowed no other option. Rather, socialist women wrestled long and hard with the poignant questions concerning the form of women's organization. Especially during the century's first decade, that is, before the establishment of the W.N.C., the majority of socialist women had gathered purposefully into separate clubs or associations precisely because they valued their independence from the party. Moreover, in promoting separate organizations as a strategic priority, these women constituted a sizable faction within the socialist movement, although not, of course, within the party. Second, female separatism, although historically rooted in the nineteenth century, represented a meaningful political strategy to socialist women in the twentieth; indeed, it has continuing relevance to radical women today.

To appreciate the meaning of female separatism and its place in radical politics, one must trace the organizational history of socialist women prior to the 1908 convention. By the time the party moved to establish a women's department, socialist women had organized a network of independent clubs, with functioning statewide federations in Kansas and California. Since the founding of the Socialist Party in 1901, and actively at its 1904 convention, the leaders of this movement had attempted to gather women into a national organization that would be loyal to the goals but distinct bureaucratically from the party. Seasoned activists, like Marion Dunham of Burlington, Iowa, and Wenonah Stevens Abbott in Southern California, maintained a public correspondence and attempted to coordinate efforts to organize women in the Midwest and West, the heart of the socialist movement during the party's formative years, as Miller points out. They found a strong voice in the socialist movement's most important woman journalist and publisher, Josephine Conger-Kaneko, who regularly recorded their activities, first in her column in the *Appeal to Reason* and later in her own magazine, the *Socialist Woman.* Although the projected Woman's National Socialist Union or League enjoyed only a fleeting existence and tapped the energies of a small portion of the women drawn to the socialist milieu, nevertheless, it embodied the aspirations of a distinct and important sector.

Although the firm advocacy of independent organizations represented the desires of thousands of rank-and-file activists, it generated harsh criticism from others. In the major urban areas and industrial centers where the party gained members mainly among German-Americans and new immigrants, an oppositional tendency surfaced and became especially pronounced after 1904. Although relegated primarily to the patently secondary role of the service auxiliary, first- and second-generation immigrant women looked askance upon the network of autonomous women's clubs created by their native-born sisters. Especially in places like Milwaukee, Chicago, and New York, where German-American women had gathered in auxiliaries since the 1870s, strong cries for party loyalty resounded. They found allies in yet a third type of socialist woman, a younger, better-educated, and more worldly activist, who affirmed their judgment of independent organizations. These women saw in the women's club not the political renegade their foreign-born allies imagined but, rather, the cultural remnant of a bygone era, a stigma of women's inferiority. Instead of preferring the company of their sex, they eagerly sought equality with men as well as immediate admission to the chambers of power. These women managed, sometimes at great personal price, to eke out a place for themselves within the party's governing structure.

They also came to dominate its Woman's National Committee.[1]

By 1908, then, when the party finally took up the question of women's status, socialist women had been energetically discussing among themselves the issues concerning organizational form and affiliation. Strong differences of opinion marked their deliberations.

At the 1908 party convention, the forces against separate organization acted to settle the matter and won support from the majority of delegates. The presence of large numbers of women at the party's periphery but beyond its organizational reach tantalized a few astute observers, who moved to place the issue on the agenda of the national meetings. As John Spargo remarked in an open letter to members, women had organized themselves into their own autonomous movement, and the party stood only to lose ground unless it incorporated these numerous activists into its structure. Spargo suggested the creation of an office for women's affairs within the party. Although many delegates balked at the notion of a distinct department for women—some because they refused blanketly to entertain any discussions of women's role or status, others because they feared the long-range implications of special treatment—the majority agreed to sponsor the Woman's National Committee. They carefully designated its purpose: to act as an expedient and temporary mechanism to assist the integration of women into the regular party locals and, in effect, to discredit independent clubs.[2]

Although the W.N.C. lacked the full support of the membership, it forcefully voiced the party's newly instituted and official policy and challenged the legitimacy of the independent clubs. The majority of socialist women assented to its directive. With many reservations but nonetheless willing to test the party's good will, most clubs simply reconstituted themselves as committees of the local and recognized the W.N.C.—and therefore the party—as their leader. They also acknowledged that their own efforts to create an autonomous national movement had reached a dead end. Like native-born socialists in general, their chief activists, many quite advanced in years and failing in health and energy, seemed distant from the shifting centers of socialist activity and changing constituency. In good faith, they passed the mantle to the younger generation of women that officiated within the W.N.C.

Although the W.N.C. claimed to represent the interests of all socialist women, it never completely resolved the dilemma of organizational form. Between 1908 and 1914 the W.N.C. countered successfully the formation of independent clubs, but it nevertheless fell short of its stated goal, the integration of women into the regular party locals. Affiliated through the committee form, socialist women nevertheless continued to conduct their affairs separately from men. They performed the time-honored services essential to the movement, such as the fund-raising bazaars, the bakefests, and entertainments, ran the socialist Sunday schools, and conducted the choir and children's debating societies. They met by themselves in study clubs and at forums on women's issues such as the efficacy of woman suffrage or birth control. The W.N.C. succeeded most when it gave the party's official stamp of approval to these affairs and when it secured funds to finance such activities.

Nor could the W.N.C. eliminate the principled advocacy of female separatism. In 1914, when the party dismantled its women's department and threw its women's sector into organizational disarray, heated discussions once more surfaced over this matter. Josephine Conger-Kaneko, who had served the W.N.C. as its chief publicist, announced that she had nurtured suspicions that the party's move to establish the W.N.C. had been primarily an effort to undercut women's autonomy. Rather than giving credence to the Woman Question, the party bureaucracy and its women lackeys, according to Conger-Kaneko, played a major role in destroying the independent clubs, thereby rendering women powerless to resist party dictates and unable to determine their own course.[3] In the minds of veterans like Conger-Kaneko, the W.N.C. had drawn its authority from a male-dominated party that wished to subordinate women's needs to its own. The lesson seemed clear: women should have retained their own independent clubs, however weak or marginal. Although women retained a place within the Socialist Party after the dissolution of the W.N.C., as Miller contends, they no longer represented a discernible sector, and their movement fell apart.

The above narrative of the organizational history of socialist women is different from Miller's because it relies upon evidence from sources outside the party mainstream. Miller, in overlooking the record of separatist activities, discounts the preferences of those socialist women who valued independent organizations. She thereby reduces the complexity of their history as well as the significance of a major political issue. In her rendition, the central dynamic is between men and women, and women appear relatively passive victims of the party's alleged desire to relegate women to separate and therefore powerless enclaves. Miller downplays women's own efforts to determine their course, their differing opinions on forms of organization, and the discussions focused precisely on this issue. In sum, she misses a crucial dynamic within women's own sector.

Miller's framework, in my opinion, does not encompass the larger history of socialist women. Miller draws her evidence principally from the records of the party, especially its official bulletins, which gave little space to dissenting opinions. Equally important, Miller focuses chiefly on the role of the W.N.C. and the positions of its members. As a result, she further minimizes the contributions of independent-minded women during the party's formative years, that is, before the establishment of the W.N.C. In picking up the story only in 1908, Miller misses a crucial stage in the development of the socialist women's movement. In effect, she begins at mid-point and therefore assigns female separatism an important yet ambiguous part in her analysis. Although she acknowledges that the W.N.C. never advocated separate organizations for women, Miller contends that it nevertheless fostered a distinct women's sector and thereby doomed itself to failure. Because Miller does not note how the W.N.C. actually abetted the decline of the autonomous women's sector and acted self-consciously to discredit the principle of female separatism, she fails, in my estimation, to appreciate how much this issue was a point of contention among women themselves. It was not merely, as she seems to indicate, a question of women versus the (male-dominated) party and the failure of women to overcome sexism and integrate themselves into the party bureaucracy, but an issue at the forefront of women's own and varied understanding of political strategy.

The political significance of female separatism extends beyond the particular history of the American Socialist Party to the contemporary women's movement. As Estelle Freedman has argued, a separatist strategy predominated within the women's movement in general during this era and maintained strong roots in middle-class women's culture and gender roles. Freedman has traced the origins of this phenomenon to the sharp sexual division of labor accompanying the Industrial Revolution and the historic disjuncture between the spheres of men and women. The emergence of a distinct realm of experience for women, shaped by familial and domestic concerns and cemented by strong friendships, marked a major historic development. Moreover, these informal associations—what historian Carroll Smith-Rosenberg has termed "homosocial networks"—helped women rise above the limitations of their prescribed sphere. The informal networks cast by mid-nineteenth-century women served as the basis for increasingly large-scale activities outside the home as women created separate yet influential organizations in the public sphere. By the century's close, a virtual efflorescence of women's organizations had taken hold across the country. Clubs for cultural uplift and practical social reform, a suffrage movement officiated by women and freed from the male influence of antebellum times, a pioneering group of women's colleges nurturing a generation of inordinately high achievers, and the mammoth Woman's Christian Temperance Union—all marked what Freedman termed the era of "female institution building."[4]

The institutional development of female separatism was not only a logical structural by-product of woman's sphere but a self-conscious and well-articulated strategy for social change. Frances Willard, the era's most powerful woman, expressed herself forcefully and repeatedly on the efficacy of female autonomy. Within the WCTU and the women's movement generally, women were training, Willard believed, to wield political power. That men would endanger their progress seemed apparent to anyone who understood the nature of contemporary gender relations. More important, women had distinctive interests to promote and impulses to develop. Willard, in her most fanciful flights of political imagination, envisioned an ideal government as one that ensured the dual representation of the sexes. Rather than the integration of women into the existing structures, she advocated a "republic of women," wherein women would sit, figuratively speaking, alongside men to direct the affairs of the state, but they would maintain their integrity by drawing authority from a well-defined representative assembly of women, organized down to the congressional districts of the states. A wild dream, of course. Willard nevertheless touched the sensibilities of a generation of women activists who believed they had been empowered politically by their special identities as women.[5]

This legacy inspired the socialist women's movement after the turn of the century. The native-born women who formed the first independent organizations and who fostered the idea of a Woman's National Socialist Union had political roots in one or another component of the late nineteenth-century women's movement. Literary, temperance, and suffrage organizations, or women's labor unions stood prominently on their lists of associational work; the principles they espoused in the mainstream women's movement played important roles in their socialist organizations. Some women, of course, like Lena Morrow Lewis, severed ties with "bourgeois" women's groups upon converting to socialism. But the majority, especially those who never strayed far from their small town or Midwestern homes or who in their declining years drew upon a political sensibility decades in the making, maintained loyalty to the women's movement and its operational modes. The enormous popularity of Frances Willard among these socialist women, especially in the century's first decade, is a testimony to the strength of this historically determined preference for female separatism.

Despite its tenacity, female separatism was a strategy waning in popularity. As Freedman explains, once women achieved a modicum of influence within the public sphere and once the sexual division of labor became less pronounced as more and more women took their places in the marketplace, many activists adopted an integrationist approach and the rhetoric of equality. By the early 1900s, when the relationships between men and women had clearly departed from nineteenth-century norms, the separatist course seemed strategically archaic. Its disavowal marked the end of an epoch in women's political history.[6]

The socialist women's movement might serve as a case study of this shift, which affected virtually all organized women's groups. The W.N.C., its members young women in their thirties, as Miller points out, voiced the increasingly popular alternative to female separatism. Capable of acting upon the prerogatives of a new generation of womanhood, they eschewed the politics of a seemingly bygone era and struggled instead to secure places and power within the party bureaucracy. That they failed to do so, that they failed to make their goals acceptable to all socialist women, is a fate they shared with many activists outside their movement.

Despite its historical limitations, female separatism is nevertheless a strategy not easily dismissed on political grounds. As Freedman writes:

> The strength of female institutions in the late nineteenth century and the weaknesses of women's politics after the passage of the Suffrage Amendment suggest to me that the decline of feminism in the 1920s can be attributed in part to the devaluation of women's culture in general and of separate female institutions in particular. When women tried to assimilate into male-dominated institutions, without securing feminist social, economic, or political bases, they lost the momentum and the networks which had made the suffrage movement possible. Women gave up many of the strengths of the female sphere without gaining equally from the man's world they entered.[7]

In contrast, Miller dismisses separate organizations among socialist women as either unimportant or retrograde and emphasizes only the discriminatory practices fostering the "unwanted party-within-a-party."

Here is the crux of my disagreement with Miller: I believe she minimizes both the historical context and political significance of female separatism within the Socialist Party. Especially in taking up the difficult task of assessing women's place within radical politics, Miller reduces the complexity of the matter and assumes the efficacy of an integrationist strategy. Indeed, the recent history of women within the civil rights movement and New Left affirms the continuing relevance of the sticky question: how do women best represent their interests and ensure equal participation within a party or movement necessarily limited by the constraints of prevailing gender roles and sex relations?[8]

NOTES

1. For a more detailed narrative and fuller analysis, see ch. 3 of my study, *Women and American Socialism, 1870–1920* (Urbana, Ill.: University of Illinois Press, 1981).

2. John Spargo, "Woman and the Socialist Movement," *International Socialist Review*, 8 (February 1908), pp. 449–55; *Proceedings of the National Convention of the Socialist Party, May 10–17, 1908* (Chicago: Socialist Party, 1908), pp. 303–06.

3. *American Socialist* (Chicago), July 10, 1915.

4. Estelle Freedman, "Separatism as Strategy: Female Institution Building and American Feminism, 1870–1930," *Feminist Studies*, 5 (Fall 1979), pp. 512–29; Carroll Smith-Rosenberg, "The Female World of Love and Ritual: Relations Between Women in Nineteenth-Century America," *SIGNS*, 1 (Autumn 1975), pp. 1–29. For the organizational roots within woman's culture, see Nancy F. Cott, *The Bonds of Womanhood: "Women's Sphere" in New England, 1780–1835* (New Haven: Yale University Press, 1977). For the extension of similar forms into early twentieth-century radical activities, see Blanche Wiesen Cook, "Female Support Networks and Political Activism: Lillian Wald, Crystal Eastman, Emma Goldman," *Chrysalis*, no. 3 (1977), pp. 43–61. For an extended discussion of this relationship, see "Politics and Culture in Women's History: A Symposium," *Feminist Studies*, 6 (Spring 1980), pp. 26–64.

5. "President's Address," *Transactions of the National Council of Women of the United States, 1891*, ed. Rachel Foster Avery (Farmingdale, N.Y.: Dabor Social Science Publications, 1978), pp. 26–31. Willard's influence is ascertained in three excellent and essential studies: Mary Earhart, *Frances Willard: From Prayers to Politics* (Chicago: University of Chicago Press, 1944); Ruth Bordin, *Woman and Temperance: The Quest for Power and Liberty, 1873–1900* (Philadelphia, Pa.: Temple University Press, 1981); and Barbara Leslie Epstein, *The Politics of Domesticity: Women, Evangelism, and Temperance in Nineteenth-Century America* (Middletown, Conn.: Wesleyan University Press, 1981).

6. Buhle, *Women and American Socialism*, ch. 2 and 3.

7. Freedman, "Separatism as Strategy," p. 524.

8. Sara Evans, *Personal Politics: The Roots of Women's Liberation in the Civil Rights Movement and the New Left* (New York: Knopf, 1979).

REPLY

Sally Miller

My essay entitled "Women in the Party Bureaucracy: Subservient Functionaries" is a case study of the way in which women functioned in a particular radical context. It explores the choices that these women made and the institutional constraints upon them. It also considers how that particular early twentieth-century organization, the Socialist Party of America, operated at a distance from the life styles and concerns of many of those women who nevertheless opted to commit their energies, talents, and hopes to that political party. Thus, the essay examines the experiences of radicalized women who, it may be argued, chose to join a men's club. In contrast, Mari Jo Buhle in her comments on my essay and in her own publications, focuses on late nineteenth- and early twentieth-century women's networks, especially in their radical manifestations. She seeks to unravel and explore the development of autonomous radical women's organizations. Her emphasis, thus, is different, and the writings of each author complement one another. This is especially apparent in regard to the consensus on the outline, at least, of the history of women in the Socialist Party from 1908 to 1915.

In Buhle's recent monograph, *Women and American Socialism*, on which she draws here, she explores the social context and cultural milieu that led a number of native-born and foreign-born American women to become socialists. In so doing, she cast a wide net and provides valuable environmental insights into their activities. But because hers was not an institutional study, she was not obligated to search internal Socialist Party records, which she therefore used somewhat sporadically. But her thrust in no way should be construed by a reader to mean that the experience of women within the party was of little significance. Similarly, this author's effort to explore the work of women whose radical ideologies made it seem worthwhile to them to enter the Socialist Party should not permit a reader to misconstrue that approach to mean an author's assumption that separate organizations were "either unimportant or retrograde" or an assumption of "the efficacy of an integrationist strategy."

Buhle cannot safely conclude that before 1908, and the establishment of the woman's sector, the many radical women who worked outside the party in autonomous groups did so because of a preference for an independent female base. For some, the reason they organized separately may have been that the Socialist Party did not offer them a familiar and comfortable environment as it tried to do for men. Buhle's assumption simply cannot be proven, and quotations suggesting that preference for one or another famous woman do not demonstrate that numbers of women made that same choice for the same reason. That after 1908 they decided to join the Socialist Party implies that its nod toward women by the decision to permit the election of a Woman's National Committee made it seem a more logical headquarters for radical, activist women than were their autonomous organizations.

Women in the Socialist Party certainly debated heatedly the separatist issue, as Buhle correctly states. Among others (as indicated in my footnote 15 above), Josephine Conger-Kaneko, Ida Crouch-Hazlett, and Mila Tupper Maynard, prior to and after the formation of the women's sector, argued about the value of gender separatism, but as party members they accepted the prevailing integrationist policy. That policy did indeed undermine the autonomous women's groups and ultimately undercut a collective female role in the socialist movement, and, thus, the W.N.C. bore responsibility. But its members did not seek that goal or foresee that development. Unlike women such as Lena Morrow Lewis and Laura B. Payne, who held themselves aloof from the women's sector which they opposed, May Wood Simons and others who served on the W.N.C. wanted women to have a collective presence in policy making. For a historian to use hindsight to argue otherwise is to distort their basic goals. Their experience did in fact foreshadow the fate of women decades later in the Communist Party, the New Left, the civil rights movement, and a variety of "mainstream" campaigns, but to blame them now for their failure to recognize the dimensions of the issue more clearly is a gross injustice.

Part Two

External Problems: American Society and American Socialism

Chapter 9

THE LIBERAL TRADITION*

Louis Hartz

1. *Liberal Reform in America*

One can use the term "Liberal Reform" to describe the Western movement which emerged toward the end of the nineteenth century to adapt classical liberalism to the purposes of small propertied interests and the laboring class and at the same time which rejected socialism. Nor is this movement without its ties to the earlier era. If there is a link between Progressivism and the Jacksonian movement, there is a link also between the Jacobinism of 1848 and that of the French Radicals. The socially conscious English Liberals at the turn of the nineteenth century had their progenitors even during the age of the First Reform Act. But the American movement, now as during that age itself, was in a unique position. For swallowing up both peasantry and proletariat into the "petit-bourgeois" scheme, America created two unusual effects. It prevented socialism from challenging its Liberal Reform in any effective way, and at the same time it enslaved its Liberal Reform to the Alger dream of democratic capitalism.

The fate of America's socialism was thus deeply interconnected with the fate of its Liberal Reform, as both were involved in the triumph of its reconstructed Whiggery: we are dealing with an equation of interdependent terms. Because the Progressives confronted no serious challenge on the left, they were saved from a defensive appearance, were able to emerge as pure crusaders. And yet this very release from the tension of the European Liberal reformers was reflected in a peculiar weakness on the part of the Progressives themselves, which was their psychic susceptibility to the charm and terror of the new Whiggery. America's "petit-

* Chapter 9 from *The Liberal Tradition in America: An Interpretation of American Political Thought Since the Revolution* (New York: Harcourt, Brace, 1955), originally entitled "Progressives and Socialists."

bourgeois" giant, in other words, if he would not flirt with Marx, was in constant danger of falling into the hands of Elbert Hubbard. And who can deny that the Progressive movement has a spottier history than anything to be found in the Liberal Reform of Europe? During the dizzy decade of the 'twenties, when Alger and the American Legion locked hands against the background of Bolshevism, Republican Presidents were not only elected but even the Democratic party reshaped itself in their image. If the Catholic Church was a refuge for Brownson after 1840, the left bank of Paris provided a refuge for many of his successors during the age of the stockmarket boom. Flight from the American liberal world itself, the technique of the "frustrated aristocrat," became the technique as well of the "frustrated radical."

But moments of utter collapse are not all that we have to consider. What sort of program did the American Progressive advance even during the vivid days of the New Freedom and the Bull Moose? The answer in general is obvious enough. He advanced a version of the national Alger theme itself, based on trust-busting and boss-busting, which sounded as if he were smashing the national idols but which actually meant that he was bowing before them on a different plane. Wilson, crusading Wilson, reveals even more vividly than Al Smith the pathetic enslavement of the Progressive tradition to the "Americanism" that Whiggery had uncovered. To be sure, there is a quaint academic touch in Wilson's Algerism, which inspired him to depict "what it means to rise" by reference to Princeton freshmen and priests in the Catholic Church during the middle ages, but in essence he is as sound as a Chamber of Commerce orator. So is Teddy Roosevelt, although here we find, if not the atypical atmosphere of the classroom, the rather unusual bombast of a frustrated Nietzschean in the American setting. Certainly the contention of Croly that there was a great and "fundamental difference" between the New Freedom and the New Nationalism can hardly be defended, when we consider their common allegiance to democratic capitalism, and William Allen White had one of his keenest insights when he described the chasm between them as the chasm between Tweedledum and Tweedledee. One need not deny, of course, that both movements called for social measures such as hours legislation and workmen's compensation which were not entirely within the ambit of "Americanism" and which in their own small way offered a hint of the European Liberal reformers. But these were loose marginalia, lacking a definite rationalization other than that which the Alger scheme afforded, and certainly without the concept of a permanent "working class" or a permanent "social debt" such as the English Liberals and the French Radicals hurled against reactionary capitalism and Toryism.†

Which brings us again to the crucial significance of ideology: the Algerism of the Progressives was no more due in the last analysis to the boom of the time than was the Algerism of Whiggery. Boom sustained it, as it did the other, but after the crash of 1929 it would not disappear but would go underground to serve as the secret moral cosmos on the basis of which New Deal pragmatism moved. It was an expression of the dogmatic Lockianism of the nation, which is why it has a very peculiar pathos. Essentially, though of course in modified form, the American Progressive confronted the same realities as confronted the European Liberal reformers: the irreversible rise of a proletariat, the irreversible inequity of the capitalist race. But in the irrational grip of "Americanism," and not yet having learned through the agony of the crash the New Deal technique of burying ethics and "solving problems," he could not look these frightening facts in the face. He could not speak of "proletarians" or "capitalists" or even "classes." He could not see what every Western Liberal reformer saw with ease. Come what may, he had to insist that the Alger formula would work if only given a chance.

Here we have the clue to the whole trust obsession of the time. We think of the trust as an economic creation of American history, and we fail to see that it was just as much a psychological creation of the American Progressive mind. Granted that America now superseded England as the home of the "great industry," to use the words of Ashley,[1] it is still a fact that the relative concentration

† European Liberal Reform was not, of course, all of a doctrinal piece, and one can refer to it as a whole only in the sense that it sought generally to transcend the earlier individualism. There is a world of difference between Mazzini's nationalist idealism, influenced by the utopian socialists, and Bourgeois' theory of solidarity, influenced by French sociology. And there is a lot of difference between both and the collective idealism of T. H. Green and his liberal followers. What is involved in all cases of the "New Liberalism" is a frank recognition of the need for collective action to solve the class problem (though in fact this action was not always taken on a comprehensive scale). The image of Horatio Alger, for all of the effort of the movement to retain the core of individualism, was alien to it.

of economic power was greater in almost any part of Europe than it was in America. And yet the European Liberal reformers, though they blasted "monopoly"–the English in the case of the tariff and land, the French in the case of large business in general–did not make the same fetish of the symbol that the American Progressives did. They spoke of other things, the large alignment of classes. The truth is, the trust in America was in significant part an intellectual technique for defining economic problems in terms of a Locke no one dared to transcend. If the trust were at the heart of all evil, then Locke could be kept intact simply by smashing it. It was a technique by which a compulsive "Americanism" was projected upon the real economic world.

But this technique, simple as it seems, was not without its problems. As time went on more and more of economic fact had to be obscured in order to make it work. Representative minds like Lloyd and Brandeis were fairly good at this, which is why the surface of their thought does not show the problem clearly. It is in figures apparently more complicated, men like Croly and Ward, where the tension between reality and projection suddenly explodes to the surface, that we see the agony it involved. These were the courageous minds of the Progressive era, Comtians indeed, men who dared to think of "planning." But put their Comtism alongside Comte himself, and what do you find? A pathetic clinging to "Americanism" which in the case of Croly led to practically unintelligible rhetoric when the crucial questions were posed, and in the case of Ward led to a queer "sociocracy" half based on the very Lockian animism that Comte so vigorously assailed. Granted that the European Liberal reformers, even in France, did not advance the Comtian state, still they were a good deal closer to it than anything we find in these American iconoclasts. Is it any wonder then, if these intellectual heroes suffered so, that the common man should flee in his leisure hours to the fantasy Bellamy offered? It is only a superficial paradox that a utopia based on perfect planning should sell so widely in an age that struggled for perfect individualism. The dream is the subconscious wish: utopias are mechanisms of escape. Could there be any sweeter release for the tormented trustbuster than to dream of a perfect trust, a trust so big that it absorbed all other trusts, so big that the single act of its nationalization collectivized all America? Moreover notice this: there was nothing "un-American," "socialistic," or "alien" about this vision. "On the precise contrary," as the good Dr. Leete himself said, "it was an assertion and vindication of the right of property on a scale never before dreamed of."[2]

Surely it is not accidental in the light of this that American socialism was isolated. Actually, though the whole of the national liberal community sent the Marxists into the wilderness, the final step in the process which did so was the nature of American Liberal Reform. For what is the hidden meaning of all this compulsive "Americanism," with its rejection of the class and social language of the European Liberal reformers, if not precisely the burning of every conceivable bridge between Progressivism and the socialist movement? A man could move from Lloyd George's defense of the working class to socialism, as many Englishmen in fact did. A man could move from Bourgeois's theory of solidarity to socialism, as many Frenchmen did. But how could a man move to Marx from a Progressivism which even in its midnight dreams ruled out the concepts of socialism? Here we see why the American socialist movement could not cut into the Progressive vote appreciably, save in areas like the German-populated Wisconsin, for it was the drift of disenchanted Liberal reformers into the socialist camp which accomplished this process in Europe. It was the discovery by labor that Liberal Reform did not go far enough which produced the Labor party in England and the rise of Socialism in France. To be sure, there was in one sense less objective ground for such a drift in America, since it cannot be said that Progressivism permitted vestiges of the feudal order and feudal ethos to survive as European Liberal Reform did, since such vestiges were not here to begin with. Everywhere in Europe, in MacDonald's England hardly less than in Kautsky's Germany, socialism was inspired considerably by the class spirit that hung over not from capitalism but from the feudal system itself. On the other hand, since we are dealing with mythological assets and liabilities, we can also note that Progressivism paid for this advantage by an inability to dominate the socialists in a campaign against the old feudal institutions, a technique which European Liberal Reform took over from European Whiggery. The real issue remains, however, that the vital point at which the American world isolated socialism was the point at which Progressivism compulsively embraced the Alger ethos.

And yet we must not dismiss this irrelevant European analysis too easily, since it was soberly reflected in the American socialist literature, which suggests that if the socialists were isolated by the mechanism of the national life they did little enough to sweeten their lot. Of course, their persistent use of the European concepts of Marxism when the nation was frantically ruling them out of its mind displays their behavior in the broadest way. But when we consider their own internal struggles, the battles over which they expended the colossal energies dammed up by political failure, we see how completely they were dominated by the European patterns of thought. For if the whole issue of collaboration with the "bourgeois reformers" took a unique shape in America, this did not prevent them from fighting, line by line and issue by issue, the European battle over the question. Even before the formation of the Socialist party in 1900 the struggle between Guesde and Jaurès arising out of a Dreyfus affair America never saw was dutifully fought out by the American Marxists, with De Leon, the eccentric half-genius of the movement, emerging as the leading "impossibiliste" of the New World. And, of course, when around 1910 the Socialist party split into two wings over the reform question, Victor Berger and the Milwaukee socialists, followers of Bernstein in a world Bernstein never knew, emerged as the leading "bourgeois collaborators." If the American socialists were determined not merely to advance the basic "un-Americanism" of the socialist scheme but also its secondary, interstitial, and post-Marxian "un-Americanism," is it surprising that their fate was even worse than that of the Southern "feudalists"? . . .

The attitude toward socialism remains, therefore, the final test of Progressive "Americanism." Here we need not expect an inner tension, since it is the indomitable drive to stick to a nationalistic Locke which inspires the peculiar pathos of the Progressive mind. What we ought to expect, and what indeed we find, is a rejection of the Marxian creed no less fanatical than the one in Whiggery itself. When W. D. Howells said that socialism "smells to the average American of petroleum, suggests the red flag, and all manner of sexual novelties, and an abusive tone about God and religion,"[3] he had in mind, with good reason as we have seen, even his fellow Bellamy enthusiasts. The issue, of course, is this matter of the "petroleum" odor, for the European Liberals opposed socialism as well, only with much the same concepts that socialism itself used, which meant that, instead of being horrified by the atmosphere of Marx, they could easily drift into it. We are brought directly to the isolation of socialism.

2. *Socialism in the Wilderness*

It is good for the analyst of the American liberal world, if not for the socialists themselves, that they were men of such fine European courage. Of course, they compromised a bit: they would be inhuman if this were not the case. When for a moment some of them dissolved and joined the "nationalist" movement of Bellamy, were they not compromising pathetically, as if the American fantasy, which as we know was American enough, could ever be the same as the European theory of Marx? Even within the context of socialism, moreover, and even in De Leon the revolutionary, we occasionally find a curious twisting of Marxian doctrine in order to satisfy the Alger ethos. But by and large the sins were remarkably few, and Spargo noticed the charge against even reform socialism that it sought "to apply to American life judgments based on European facts and conditions."[4] All in all the movement went doggedly ahead, even without feudal remnants, even without the power to make a serious impact on Liberal Reform. So that one might say it has the same relationship to the general pattern of Western Marxism that a postage stamp has to a life-size portrait: all the lines are there, all the features, but the size is very small.

It is not surprising that when the American socialists did begin to twist their Marxism a bit they did it with reference to the great American fetishes of the trust and direct democracy. Needless to say, Marxism, even of the Kautsky-Bernstein variety, which stressed the educational impact of the democratic process on the proletariat, did not yearn for anything like the long ballot, and yet the Socialist party again and again made it a crucial part of the Marxian scheme. One might call this, if he were in a satirical mood, "Jacksonian socialism," and ask how direct democracy would work under socialism when it could hardly work under capitalism where the business of government was comparatively small. But it was the trust issue which really played havoc with the American socialists, not because socialism did not blast monopoly but because its approach to it was radically different from anything the Progressives advanced. First of all, it did not blast monopoly in order to establish individualism, but rather to establish collectivism, so that when Atkinson spoke of creating "opportunities" by smashing trusts he was really being the worst thing in the socialist book: "petit-bourgeois." Even Jaurès, when he modified French socialism to satisfy the peasant, did not go as far as this. Ironically enough, moreover, it was the "impossibiliste" De Leon who integrated Atkinson's trustism into the Marxian historical theory. He said that he agreed with Bryan and Roosevelt that America had once been a land of freedom and that trusts had changed it when of course Marxism held that no capitalist society at any time, even in its early fluid stages, was ever really free.

But these sell-outs to "Americanism," considering its devastating impact upon the socialists, can easily be excused. Certainly they did not—by means of borrowing from Liberal Reform rather than challenging it, a kind of inversion of the European process—lead to any serious socialist inroad into the Progressive vote. To be sure, they helped the socialists in 1912, but this triumph could not last and even then it was minor compared to the Progressive enthusiasm on which it so obviously fed. The idea that Wilson could have been driven out of New Jersey by Debs as Clemenceau was driven out of Paris by Guesde and Lafargue is of course fantastic. Even the pressure that the Independent Labor party in England put on the liberals before the World War was out of the question. Even after Bellamy wrote his American introduction to the *Fabian Essays,* the average American still, as he said there, "conceived of a socialist, when he considered him at all, as a mysterious type of desperado, reputed to infest the dark places of continental Europe and engaged with his fellows in a conspiracy as monstrous as it was futile, against civilization and all that it implied."[5] Nor was this the sort of hatred of "the continental agitators" that the English Marxist Hyndman used to entertain. That was a natural British distaste, as with Mill, for the Blanquist, putschist nature of radicalism across the channel, not a dislike of the socialist scheme itself. The American view involved the very foundations of socialist thought.

The fact that Progressivism could not be accused of compromising with an original feudal ethos, of failing to complete the original liberal campaign, was of course critical in the socialist fiasco. If Helen Lynd can list as one of the sources of the incipient English socialism of the eighties the "leaders and followers" pattern of British life, and if Adam Ulam can list it as one of the sources of the rise of the Labor Party itself, pointing out that labor could have bargained with the Liberals for specific policy measures,[6] is not the lesson for America clear? Could Debs argue that socialism was essential to abolish the class spirit emanating from Henry Adams? If the socialists were not lured in the direction of Progressivism by the desire for a united front against Adams, and thus avoided one of the significant European sources of internal factionalism, this was small consolation. In the long run Jaurès and Briand, as well as Guesde and Sembat, gained more than they lost from the Millerand question at the time of the Dreyfus affair. Without the *ancien régime,* the issue of collaborating with the Radicals against it would not to be sure have split French Marxism, but French Marxism would not have existed either.

In any case, the question of collaborating with the Radicals, so to speak, was fought out by the American socialists as well, thus sending them even farther into the wilderness they occupied in a liberal society. Of course the matter of "bourgeois collaboration" extended much beyond the issue of a united front against reaction. There were aspects of it, indeed, which were given a peculiar vividness by the nature of American liberal society. In a land where labor was truly bourgeois, the issue of what Lenin called "trade union consciousness" was indeed interesting: witness De Leon's battle against Gompers. In a land where democracy had been established early, the issue of what Bernstein called the "partnership" of liberalism was also vivid: witness Berger's plea for peaceful change. But these interesting intellectual twists were purchased at the price of isolation, so that if "parliamentary idiocy" was fascinating in a very parliamentary country, the term was also meaningless there.

There is this parallel between the problem of Progressivism and the problem of socialism: both were in the grip of fetishes, "Americanism" on the one hand, Marxism, or "Europeanism" if such a term exists, on the other. But if these are in some sense similar psychological experiences, "word-worship," to use a term of Henry Carey's, they were antagonistic in a profound way. The word of Alger excluded the word of Marx, so that in a community of the blind and half-blind a significant logic was in play. Word-worship is peculiarly bad for scholarship, which is why the social science both of Progressivism and American socialism failed in its analysis of America. And that is our next problem. . . .

3. *The Problem of Historical Analysis*

There can be no doubt that there were other reasons, apart from activism, which prevented American Marxists from exploring the implications for America of the absence of the feudal factor in the Marxian scheme. Concentrating on labor and capital within the bourgeois order, for one thing, meant that the Marxist necessarily viewed feudalism as an antique phenomenon. This orientation was even true of Marx and Engels themselves who predicted socialism in America and yet explicitly noted the fact that America had skipped the feudal stage of Western development. Moreover the instinctive tendency of all Marxists to discredit ideological factors as such blinded them to many of the consequences, purely psychological in nature, flowing from the nonfeudal issue. Was not the whole complex of "Americanism" an ideological question? But after all of this has been said, the simple refusal to face unpleasant facts stands out as crucial. Let us recall again that a law of combined development did appear in Russia when the facts it seemed to produce were pleasant.

To be sure, however blind he was about history, it was not always easy for the American socialist to whistle in the American dark. Usually he conceded that he was in the poorest position of any Western socialist, holding that this was due to transient material prosperity, in line with the Marxian materialist emphasis. Noting that "until quite recently" it was easy for the worker to become a capitalist in America, and that land had been abundant, Spargo traced the whole of the socialist isolation to passing economic circumstances. The fact that a thousand strikes a year were taking place showed that the circumstances were passing.[7] De Leon, possibly because being more revolutionary he was more impatient, could not always tolerate even this analysis. Pointing out that capitalism was "full-orbed" in America, he argued that the revolution would come most quickly here, avoiding the unpleasant fact that where capitalism is "full-orbed" even the people who are supposed to make the revolution are inveterate capitalists. "Plutocracy," another point made by practically all socialists, did not prove anything. So long as the American millionaire stood at the apex of the Alger scheme he did not symbolize the fulfillment of the Marxian hope.

The historical insight lost by this frenzied optimism is clearly revealed in the familiar socialist effort to root socialism in the American past. When De Leon cites Jefferson as the "great confiscator,"[8] how can he grasp the nonrevolutionary nature of American life? Even Veblen, outside the strategic compulsion of Marxism, was forever making the same mistake. Though an acute observer of the capitalist spirit in America, he lumped the "American Declaration of Independence, the French Declaration of the Rights of Man, and the American Constitution" in the same liberal category.[9] But the eighteenth century was of course not the only thing at stake. Given this orientation, which obscured the relevance of the nonfeudal issue, how could American socialism understand anything about its fate? How could it understand the crucial importance of the absence of surviving feudal elements? How could it understand the nature of its failure to make an impact on Progressivism? How could it understand its odd link with the fate of the Southern "feudalists"? In the end Marxist theory paved the way for socialist disappointments as Progressive theory paved the way for Progressive disappointments, which is another way that the two "radicalisms," one nativistic and the other alien, seemed to blend together. A valuable historical analysis, which might have laid bare much concerning the American liberal world, went unused.‡

‡ The question is bound to be raised: In terms of the whole concept of a liberal society, what is the general estimate of Marxism? On the one hand there is a negative view of Marxism stemming from the fact that socialism is traced ultimately to the *ancien régime* as well as to capitalist growth. On the other there is an affirmative view of Marxism stemming from the breadth of its categories as compared with those of the Progressives. These two views are not incompatible, even if the first has implications for economics and ideology which, when carried to their logical conclusion, are damaging to the basic metaphysics of the Marxian scheme. Categories can still be useful even if they are misapplied. However one may legitimately ask, after all of this watering down has taken place, whether there is much more of Marx left than the Western concepts of class which one can find practically everywhere in the Western literature. I would not deny this. The only reason for insisting on the peculiar utility of Marxism here is that it happened to be the one manifestation of the European viewpoint which had followers in America.

NOTES

1. W. Ashley, *Surveys Historic and Economic* (New York, 1900), p. 385.

2. E. Bellamy, *Equality* (New York, 1913), p. 12.

3. Quoted, J. Dorfman, *The Economic Mind in American Civilization* (New York, 1949), vol. iii, p. 152.

4. J. Spargo, *Socialism* (New York, 1906), p. 139.

5. G. Shaw et al., *Socialism; the Fabian Essays,* with introduction by E. Bellamy (Boston, c. 1894), p. ix.

6. H. Lynd, *England in the Eighteen Eighties* (New York, 1945), p. 110; A. Ulam, *Philosophical Foundations of British Socialism* (Cambridge, Mass., 1951).

7. Spargo, op. cit., pp. 143, 144.

8. Quoted, Olive M. Johnson, *Daniel De Leon* (New York, 1935), p. 24.

9. T. Veblen, *The Vested Interests* (New York, 1920), p. 20.

COMMENT

Kenneth McNaught

Now that we are all beyond consensus we can see that consensus history has been, like Progressive history before it, markedly influenced by the political climate of the years in which it flourished. In this light we may find it ironical that Louis Hartz chose the term "liberal" to define the theme of a book which became at once central to an essentially conservative passage in American historiography. Professor David Donald has pointed out that the exponents of consensus have been, by and large, the historical Establishment—an Establishment which now finds itself under surprisingly fierce and un-consensual attack by younger historians of both the Old and New Left.[1] It further strikes a non-American historian that a principal feature of consensus history is one inherited, not surprisingly, from mainstream American historical writing. That is a trait which Hartz recognizes implicitly and which he exhibits explicitly. It is a proclivity, far more pronounced than in the historiographical traditions of other nations, to employ the causal notion of inevitability. But Hartz reinforces this inevitabilism with the insights of intellectual history and the goals of sociological history to produce a basically conservative account of how-it-had-to-be.

The brilliance of Hartz's argumentation and his frequently startling perceptions—reminiscent of those of a Veblen or a McLuhan—guaranteed *The Liberal Tradition in America* immediate and widespread acclaim. The need, now that the Hartzian analysis has been so broadly incorporated in consensus explanations of American history, is not to identify its points of strength. Rather, as the consensus shows signs of weakening both in the field of historical interpretation and on the battlegrounds of contemporary society, it is reasonable to speculate about the weaknesses in Hartz's Locke/Alger Law. And since it is the Left that is tugging most fiercely at the rents in the consensual fabric the Hartzian explanation of how such criticism cannot produce serious results may most properly be examined.

I should like to look at three aspects of *The Liberal Tradition:* the nature of Hartzian comparative history, the problem of definitions, and Hartz's application of his absence-of-feudalism law to the history of American socialism.

Throughout *The Liberal Tradition* Hartz employs a heady mixture of comparison, analogy, and allusion. While the allusions and the analogies raise specific problems of definition for other historians the comparisons lie at the very heart of the method and the thesis. The only way, Hartz argues, to grasp fully the uniqueness of American history, is by comparison with other national histories. The uniqueness which such comparison will reveal lies in the definitive role played by liberalism. Belief in the tenets of John Locke, later popularized in the mythology of Horatio Alger, has dictated the course followed by American political, economic, and social growth. The reason for the strength of this liberal tradition in America is that Americans have enjoyed the Tocquevillian condition of being "born equal." They broke cleanly from their European parent stem, leaving behind the feudal tradition and retaining only the Lockian premises of a contractual, market-oriented society.[2] The validity of this conception depends, of course, not only upon its self-evident truth, but also upon the accuracy of Hartz's historical comparisons and analogies.

A historian who is at all skeptical of "inevitability" is particularly apt to take exception to the specific points of comparison in the Hartzian edifice. Such a historian is likely to conclude that the parts do not add up to the whole and even that many of the parts are not historically valid at all. He will be very tempted to say that, having decided to prove American liberal uniqueness, Professor Hartz has gone abroad in search only of differences and has thus blinded himself to similarities. In effect, it might be argued, Hartz seeks the lawmaking results of the quantitative method without actually using that method. This line of criticism leads quickly to the problem of definitions and thus to a selective examination of the Hartzian method.

When Hartz asserts that socialism could never have succeeded (or even have taken firm root) in America because America lacks a feudal tradition, a critic can only argue with him on the basis of his definitions and imprecisions. Hartz himself tries to disarm in advance such a critic by observing that his use of the word "feudal" is not only imprecise but that "its technical meaning is stretched when one applies it in the modern era."[3] Having entered this apology, however, he goes on throughout his book to use "feudal" just as if its "stretched meaning" were clearly understood. Well, the meaning to a historian is not clearly understood. Moreover, if Hartz means by "feudal tradition" and "feudal institutions" what one might reasonably expect (a tendency toward legal enforcement of class privilege, various forms of latter-day latifundia, corporate concepts of society, landholding in return for payment in kind, etc.), the historian is bound to say either that Hartz misunderstands his own "stretched meaning" or else that he does not prove his case.

Whatever feudalism as a legacy or tradition may mean, it is clear that as a set of institutions and laws England and Europe were free of it at least as soon as was the United States (or the American colonies). If it means huge landed estates, established churches, class privilege legally enforced, and an organic view of society, then all of these things have been present to the American experience. No American colony was without its land question, most had some experience with established churches, in some the concept of entailed inheritance had to be beaten down, and the "habit of authority" was scarcely unknown throughout one of Hartz's great "exceptions," the American South. Again, if America was born equal because it accepted John Locke, then we must presume that England was born equal somewhat sooner.[4] One might well follow up this logic by recalling that the illiberal institutions of imprisonment for debt and slavery were both abolished in England before they were ended in the United States—and with somewhat less difficulty.

These preliminary remarks about Hartzian comparisons and definitions suggest that there is a basic flaw in his schema. That flaw may now be identified more precisely. It is Hartz's requirement of his readers that they accept, first, his use of terms which are either not defined or whose meanings appear to change in the course of the argument and, second, that they accept comparisons and analogies based upon this impressionistic device. Some further specific illustrations must stand for many that could be given. At the outset Hartz argues that American history *is* the escape from Europe—feudalism and all—and that not until recently has America had to confront Europe. Here, of course, the historian simply cannot agree. How, he must ask, can one explain the origins of American party divisions without taking account of America's reaction to French revolutionary doctrines and Napoleonic (let alone British) policies?[5] What Hartz says of twentieth-century communism is, in fact, just as true of earlier French and English influences on America, namely that they "redefined . . . the issue of our internal freedom in terms of our external life." Again, when Hartz employs Tocqueville's aphorism that Americans are "born equal" he ignores the need to deal with what is plainly another big exception to his format. Tocqueville, after all, was describing Jackson's America rather than the political battles by which Jacksonian "equality" had been achieved—battles which *had* conjoined the forces of liberalism and radicalism in the very manner which Hartz argues cannot happen in non-feudal America. To admit this, of course, would be to concede either a) that such political combination does not require a "conservative" target or b) that there was a conservative target.

Part of the confusion lies in Hartz's equating of liberalism and democracy, and part lies in his cavalier attitude to the sequences of American history. At one point Locke seems to stand for liberty against the tyranny of the majority; at another we hear of the "hidden conformitarian germ" in Lockianism which "transforms eccentricity into a sin."[6] The point which Hartz misses here seems to be that Jacksonian democracy is not implicit in Locke, let alone in Alger; and that liberalism is more usually antipathetic to democracy than otherwise. Perhaps the signal of warning for this misconception was the erratum slip in the first edition of *The Liberal Tradition* which corrected the Tocquevillian misquotation about Americans being "born free." Which is different from being "born equal." The confusion in definitions is the symptom of Hartz's necessity to skirt the obvious conclusion from much of his own evidence that the real spirit of Locke *is* conservative—and thus that the ubiquitous Whigs in the Hartzian system are in fact conservatives. Recent writing by Gabriel Kolko, James Weinstein, Martin Sklar, and others seriously undermines Hartz's argument that Lockians (or Whigs) cannot be conservatives. Theodore Roosevelt and Woodrow Wilson were as thoroughgoing conservatives, by any other standard than that of livery and maintenance, as one can well imagine. Thus the historian is not likely to be much impressed by the Hartzian implication that to be a real conservative in, say, the period 1876–1920, you had to have a title or perhaps what H. G. Wells called Disraeli's "oriental imagination." Indeed, when Hartz chooses Disraeli as a principal example of the kind of Tory democrat that America could never produce he gives the whole game away—for Disraeli himself was an outstanding example (a kind of British Alexander Hamilton) of how an aristocratic cast of mind can be voluntarily adopted without benefit of birth or determining historical laws.

What thus emerges as Hartz's crucial obfuscation is his recurrent assumption that because America had no hereditary titles it had no real class system and therefore no defenders of that system against whom liberals, democrats, and socialists could ally themselves. Thus he declares, for example, that the southern "feudalists" failed inevitably and, like "the modern socialists," made no "dent in the American liberal intelligence." Well, the historian can only reflect that the southern "failure" was made "inevitable" only by means of horrendous civil warfare (which itself is an interesting comment on being "born equal") and that the present condition of American political life strongly suggests that socialism left something more than a dent. Moreover, if Lockianism means, as Hartz says, a curious combination of equality, classlessness, liberty, and democracy, how does one adjust this conception of Americanism to the consistently neo-mercantilist (and triumphant) drive of the Whigs, the political capitalists, and the "national class" discerned so effectively by William A. Williams, Gabriel Kolko, et al.? And, to pursue further this problem of categories or definition, one must ask (ignoring the internal contradictions): is Alger really a symbol of Lockian, egalitarian, liberal democracy? The fact is that the Alger whom Hartz selects as symbol is redolent of class feeling. His theme is always how to get to the top, which is scarcely a classless concept. Indeed, Alger's tiresomely repeated accounts of how one gets to the top are a compound of good fortune, loyalty, and acceptance of what Veblen called the business discipline of the High Command. The fact that Veblen's instinct of emulation led most Americans to hope for a summer palace at Newport, unquestioned credit at Delmonico's, and a gingerbread monstrosity on any town's highest elevation does not suggest that Americans believed America was classless—especially if they read Alger. Rather, it is to say that American commoners (how did Bryan cut so much ice with such a phrase?) have envied the class above them just as much and just as consciously as have the commoners of "feudal" states. They have believed in Alger, Daddy Warbucks, and any other agent of an illiberal fate just as others have believed in the "guv'nor" or the football pools. One might plausibly argue that Alger's great contribution was to Americanize the classic "feudal" fairy tale of the suitor, the princess, and the king.

At one point Hartz suggests that no effort has been made to pursue the comparative analysis suggested by the fact that Hamiltonianism has been called by the English term "Whiggery." It is particularly unfortunate, surely, that he himself did not pursue such an analysis. For it would then be made clear that the elitism of Hamilton did not die in America and was, in fact, the dominant intellectual component of Progressivism—which in turn found so much inspiration (from Lippmann and Croly to Wilson) in English thought. It is this failure to keep an eye out for similarities that leads Hartz into a whole series of misconceptions. Only by using evidence selectively and by looking exclusively for differences can he argue that socialism in America could not find allies among liberals for an attack on anti-democratic "feudal remnants." There were, he argues, no such remnants (and by remnants Hartz means conservative ideology and interest as well as institutions—such as the ideas of the "Southern Filmerians") and this robbed socialism of "a normal ground for growth." But this crucially important point is "proven" by allusion and a rhetorical question: "Could De Leon take over the liberal goal of extended suffrage as Lassalle did in Germany or the crusade against the House of Lords as the Labor Party did in England?"[7] Well, De Leon did not stand in the United States for "American socialism"—certainly not for the socialism of Debs, of Berger, or of Hillquit.

But there is a still more insidious error in the Hartzian rhetoric. That is the assumption that Americans believed that democracy had been won (or received as a gift). This assumption, if we take Populist-Progressive platforms, speeches, and tactics at all seriously, does not flow from the facts. The fact is that most Americans of the Progressive era felt they were engaged in a battle *for* democracy. That battle required and received the full cooperation of socialists and liberals. The point here, surely, is that the British Lib-Lab assault on the House of Lords was for exactly the same purposes and employed the same arguments as the American battle for direct democracy (especially for direct election of the Senate). That the Lords had "feudal" titles should not be allowed to obscure the fact (well known to liberal-socialists on both sides of the Atlantic) that they were defending the same capitalism that was defended by American senators. The undemocratic Lords were leashed in the same democratic interest that required the senators to submit to the elective process—and with much the same result.

It is because of this basic confusion in definitions and comparisons that Hartz's chapter on Progressives and Socialists is so unconvincing among its illuminations. This chapter brings to a focus the inevitabilist argument that runs through the whole of *The Liberal Tradition:* socialism failed because America was non-feudal in origin and experience and thus had no feudal-conservative targets which would compel liberals to cooperate with (and thus eventually be absorbed by) socialism. Ambiguity of definition, frailty of allusion, and disregard of similarities here reach a crescendo. Yet the key to this interlocking fallacy Hartz himself provides when he earlier writes that "socialism arises not *only* to fight capitalism but remnants of feudalism itself. . . ."[8] For this reveals that he will take surface differences (e.g., between a House of Lords and an undemocratic Senate) and treat them as absolutes. Thus he rejects the obvious similarities between the Hobhouse-Green-Mill liberals (who could slide into socialism) and the Lippmann-Croly-Weyl-Dewey liberals for whom the socialist option is denied by Hartz and yet who could and did slide into various kinds of socialism. Moreover, avoidance of such obvious similarities leads Hartz to miss other, more subtle similarities altogether. The most important of these is that the liberal-socialists of American Progressivism faced the same basic problem of "socializing" the labor unions as was faced by their British counterparts with whom they often corresponded on the subject.

These similarities which emerge in any comprehensive comparison lead again to the principal criticism of the Hartz schema: socialism is demonstrably not a *natural* working-class growth in "feudal" societies but is, rather, a response to the particular power structure and inequities fostered by capitalism. Feudal or aristocratic traditions, in other words (and quite apart from Hartz's shaky analysis of the non-feudal background of America), are largely irrelevant to the reasons for socialist growth. With one exception. In a society which enters the age of democracy with a strong anti-aristocratic bias liberals are more likely to find it dangerous to offer basic criticisms and alternatives, let alone effective reform leadership. Thus the American Progressives on the Left, just at the point when American social democracy was becoming respectable, abandoned the leadership role which they had vociferously prescribed, and which their British Fabian counterparts were bringing to a fruitful outcome in the Labour Party—abandoned it in the face of patriotic preparedness and a carefully conducted campaign of calumny. Their socialism had proved *too* ready to accommodate itself to the American context, to cooperate with Progressives, and to undermine the goals of the National Civic Federation—goals which were, incidentally, neo-mercantilistic and therefore un-Lockian in all respects (at least as Hartz uses "Lockian"). Socialism was, in fact, proclaimed un-American because it had become too American.

To prove his point Hartz has further to ignore the fact that the voluminous Progressive and muckraking literature (indeed the entire American press) was alive with the terminology of class—from workingmen to bosses, magnates, and barons. He has further to overlook the plain evidence that socialists in a "feudal" or deferential society such as England had their own special difficulties in converting the trade unionists to socialism and, in fact, never did succeed entirely. In short, Hartz fails to prove that socialism was in a fundamentally different position in the United States and therefore that it never did (and never could have) become a legitimate or indigenous part of American political life. The failure results from the transparency of the veil he draws across the face of reality. Not only is this made clear by the work of Kolko and Weinstein, and by numerous unpublished theses, it is crashingly evident to any historian who has measured the concern expressed by Theodore Roosevelt, Woodrow Wilson, S. S. McClure, Ralph Easley, et al. in the face of socialist growth. Indeed, the debates within the SPA itself show that the "Marxist" minority were as uneasy about the roots being struck by democratic socialism as was the High Command of American capitalism. Conversely the practical and intensely American socialist leaders such as Debs, Hillquit, and Berger regularly displayed the power of class analysis and the strength to be gained by working, like Fabians, at the grass roots and on particular issues of general progressive concern. One American of the kind that Hartz does not much like to quote put this whole matter very well in 1916. Commenting on a labor union-socialist municipal victory in Minneapolis, the socialist lawyer G. B. Leonard wrote:

> Is it not possible that we have been too much carried away with the deductive methods of thought of the German Socialists? After all, the German mind, as indicated by its history and literature, proceeds from the general to the specific, while we have not developed that train of mind. We are rather an empirical people. . . . We proceed from the practical to the theoretical. Even the general propositions laid down in the Declaration of Independence have lost their significance. Maybe we are on the wrong track [in Minneapolis]. But in this campaign the reason for our success lies in the fact that we dealt with concrete things and fought shy of general theories. We chose our battle cry and battle ground for the purpose of this campaign—qualifications of the respective candidates and the stand they respectively took on what we call the main issue in this campaign, the streetcar franchise. The opposition tried to force upon us everything else. We refused, and they were beaten. This is political tactics, but if it accomplishes the result of solidifying the elements that ought to be with us, it must be the proper procedure. . . .[9]

Well, one can debate forever the relative merits of doctrinaire purity vs. pragmatic adjustment, of programmatic politics vs. single-issue politics. What is now really beyond debate is that socialism, particularly in its progressive-intellectual and local-machine aspects, did strike roots in America—and that its ideas and methods, while clearly subject to international cross-fertilization, were no *more* derivative than were those of Lockianism, social Darwinism, sea power, or a lot of other pretty central currents of American thought. Socialist fortunes in America were decided not by abstract and congealed ideological determinants but by policies selected by both socialists and anti-socialists in an American and worldwide context. The line dividing liberal progressives from socialists was frequently just as fine as the similar line in England and elsewhere. Insofar as a feudal-aristocratic tradition existed in England and Europe, but not in America, this fact seems to have strengthened conservatism (Whiggery in Hartzian terminology) in America and liberalism in Europe and England. What Hartzian analysis most inhibits is recognition of the fact that democracy is not a synonym for liberalism—a Tocquevillian point that surely should not have been missed. Conversely, and equally from Tocqueville, democracy can be the most conservative of all political systems. Hartz's juggling of the definitions only obscures the fact that American democracy ("born equal"), when manipulated by genuine conservatives, is an anti-liberal force which is neither Lockian nor socialist–but nationalist and conservative. It is a force which could, perfectly conceivably, *become* socialist just as it has been persuaded to become mercantilist and imperialist. If one policy does not seem to work Americans will choose another policy–and their choice will not be predetermined either by John Locke or Horatio Alger, although it would undoubtedly be explained in terms of the Declaration of Independence as modified by the *Federalist Papers*.

The Hartzian tradition, then, seems open to some pretty basic questions. While such questions often apply equally to the whole conception of consensus history they apply with particular force to Hartz's comparative method and to his erratic use of terms such as "liberalism," "democracy," "Lockian," and "Algerism." Pursuit of such questions is unlikely to lead us to identify liberalism with Americanism, socialism with conservatism, or American history with inevitability.

NOTES

1. New York *Times Book Review*, July 19, 1970.

2. I here anticipate Hartz's later book, *The Founding of New Societies*, in which he and others develop the "congealment" thesis and extend the comparative method to countries such as Canada, Australia, and South Africa. Contributors to *The Founding* underline and elaborate Hartz's assumption that new nations cast off from European societies find their political-economic beliefs congealed in the mold of their founding years—except when they are directly confronted by the impact of external ideologies-cum-power. As applied to Canada this thesis is spectacularly unimpressive. Indeed its weakness is made manifest in the work of a protégé of Professor Hartz's: *Canadian Labour and Politics* by Gad Horowitz (Toronto, 1968). In an introductory chapter Horowitz compares the history and fates of socialism in the United States and socialism in Canada. In the course of his review he confesses the impossibility of determining any point at which political ideology in Canada may be said to have congealed. While the Horowitz chapter does not necessarily affect the argument about American exceptionalism it directly refutes the case put in *The Founding* and certainly raises some nagging questions about the congealment of ideology in the United States.

3. Louis Hartz, *The Liberal Tradition in America* (New York, 1955), p. 4.

4. For a persuasive argument that in England capitalism had replaced feudalism by the time that either Hobbes or Locke wrote, see C. B. Macpherson, *The Political Theory of Possessive Individualism* (Oxford, 1962).

5. Post-Hartzian analysis of the extent to which American expansionism shared many features in common with "feudal" European nations suggests that "confrontation" and its resulting influences have been coterminous with American history. Mahan does not appear in *The Liberal Tradition* nor does Hartz discuss Woodrow Wilson's debt to Burke and Bagehot.

6. *The Liberal Tradition*, pp. 11–12.

7. *The Liberal Tradition*, p. 9. Throughout the book Hartz hangs his argument on the De Leon peg. Like Daniel Bell he would have us believe that only "Marxian Socialism" is at issue, and thus both analysts stack the deck in their own favor; e.g., p. 205: Because "the language of De Leon was just about as different from the language of Wilson as it was from the language of McKinley" therefore "while it was possible for a European liberal reformer to drift into socialism . . . it was extremely difficult for a Wilsonian Progressive to do the same thing." Or again, at p. 237, impossibilism is directly imputed to Victor Berger (!) by referring to his "messianic world." One could,

by such means, construct a Hartzian analysis of England, identifying English socialism only with Hyndman and calling Ramsay MacDonald "messianic."

8. *The Liberal Tradition,* p. 9. Italics added.

9. G. B. Leonard to Algernon Lee, November 14, 1916 (Lee Papers, Tamiment Institute, New York). As a postscript to this reasoning (and a tangential reflection on inevitability) one might also refer to Karl Kautsky's letter to Lee (September 18, 1932): "I am very happy to hear from you on the new spirit in the A.F. of L . . . we may be sure that this is no passing whim, but a permanent current in the ranks of American trade unions for state intervention. . . . The only way in the Anglosaxon world to create a powerful Socialist party is to interest the trade unions for interference of the state for the working class to such a degree that only a separate working class party can satisfy them. That [party] may not be a Socialist one in the beginning, but the logic of events will propel them inevitably in the direction of Socialism. That was the way in England and will be the way in America."

REPLY

Louis Hartz

Professor McNaught maintains a logical position in his criticism of my work: having asserted the presence in the United States of the elements yielding a powerful socialist movement, he goes on to imply that such a movement in fact existed. However, I am afraid that I must disagree with him on both counts.

At various points I have isolated three factors stemming from the European feudal inheritance the absence of which in the United States precluded the possibility of a major socialist experience. One is a sense of class which an aristocratic culture communicates to the bourgeoisie and which both communicate to the proletariat. Another is the experience of social revolution implemented by the middle class which the proletariat also inherits, as when Babeuf arises out of the French upheaval of the eighteenth century. Finally, I have cited the memory of the medieval corporate spirit which, after liberal assault, the socialist movement seeks to re-create in the form of modern collectivism. It has been my contention that when the great migration which created American history left these factors behind in the Old World, it left behind also the seeds of European socialism.

Professor McNaught seeks to undermine my first point in two ways. He argues that American colonial culture and southern slave culture were truly aristocratic and that the liberal culture of Hamilton and Alger were at any rate aristocratic enough. However, it is stretching the empirical data much too far to hold that colonial elitism, which fell so rapidly in the Revolution, amounted to the elitism of Europe and it is also torturing the facts to make out of the southern slaveholder, the heir of Jefferson and in many ways a classic capitalist, a symbol of Western feudal culture. Certainly it is to obscure the issue almost completely to stress the "class" component in Whiggery or Alger. In earliest times the elitism of the

American Whig did not match that of the English Whigs and the French Liberals, themselves apostles of capitalism, and the very absence of the class passion induced by the aristocratic encounter is what stands out even in the case of a man like Hamilton when we compare him with Brougham. Professor McNaught says that I have not followed up the comparative analysis involved in this transatlantic correlation but I believe I have done precisely that. And what the analysis suggests is not merely the looser elitism of the Americans but the much more crucial fact that in a liberal society even that elitism could not survive long and had to redefine itself, under the Jacksonian impact, into the democratic capitalist ideology of Alger. As for the effort to extract from Alger himself the class spirit of socialism, I must say that I find it to be an unusually dramatic misconception of the data. I would not deny that there was in the Alger cosmos a very exclusive position for millionaires, the significance of which may in fact have been overlooked in terms of the national discipline required for industrialization. But that position was associated precisely with the idea that access to it was universally available, down to the personage of Ragged Dick, an idea which notoriously undermined the crystallization of class feeling in America.

My second point, that the basic experience of social revolution is missing in America, Professor McNaught scarcely deals with at all. If he intends to do so by his remark that America reacted to French revolutionary doctrines and that this was reflected in American party divisions, surely we have here slight evidence of an authentic domestic experience of social upheaval. Of course the inheritance of the experience of social revolution involves to some extent also the carrying forward of anti-aristocratic goals by the working class itself, and Professor McNaught's identification of Senate reform with the Lib-Lab assault on the House of Lords is relevant in this connection. But he is right to say that what relates the two movements is an attack on financial power. The passionate revolt against sheer snobbishness which motivates British Labour is not part of the American movement of political reform. The truth is, Professor McNaught adduces practically nothing to demonstrate that the American worker had historic contact with one of the factors which Marx himself recognized as crucial to the making of the socialist movement: the precedent of the middle class in assailing an aristocratic order arising out of the Middle Ages.

Even less is said by Professor McNaught concerning my third argument: that there could not in the United States be a working-class movement motivated by the desire to reconstitute medieval collectivism. The reference to an "organic view of society" in the colonial era or, again, to the Southerners has precious little to do with the affirmative ambitions of the American labor movement or the central drift of Progressivism. The whole meaning of the Alger syndrome, and the reason why it flourished in the United States as it did not in Europe, is to be found in the compulsiveness of an individualist ethic coeval with the national culture. There was some organicism in Puritanism, to be sure, some persistence of the medieval world, but its great contribution to Western culture was individualism, and by the time Alger appeared on the scene that contribution had in America, Puritan from the outset, reached a blazing national climax. The "memory" of the American laborer went back to the *Mayflower* but not to the medieval corporation.

When in line with his historical analysis Professor McNaught seeks to prove that there was a socialist movement in America comparable to the European, he becomes very vague indeed. His central point seems to be that socialism "was, in fact, proclaimed un-American because it had become too American." But it is hard to know what this means. The fact that "the American Progressives on the Left" did not behave like "their British Fabian counterparts" cannot really be explained by the fact that socialism had become overwhelmingly accepted in the United States. What Professor McNaught calls their compromise with the "Progressives," presumably the normal Alger Left, suggests this clearly enough. So in fact the failure of Fabianism in the United States is proof of the power of the liberal tradition. Indeed, toward the close of his paper Professor McNaught makes some rather startling concessions to my general position. After saying that feudal traditions are irrelevant to socialism, he mentions "one exception." This is that "(i)n a society which enters the age of democracy with a strong anti-aristocratic bias liberals are more likely to find it dangerous to offer basic criticisms and alternatives, let alone effective reform leadership." But why does a society enter the democratic age with such a bias? It can only be because it has somewhere along the line left the feudal world behind. And why should such a bias militate against "basic criticisms and alternatives?" It can only be because the society is not split apart in terms of class and because, lacking contact with the experience of social revolution, liberalism has become a moral absolute. I am afraid that Professor McNaught comes close to restating my own argument here but in terms rather vaguer than the ones I have employed.

Let me say a final word concerning my use of the comparative method to which Professor McNaught often alludes. I have tried to vindicate my interpretation of socialism in terms of a number of other "fragment" cultures derived from Europe like the American: Professor McNaught refers to this work but curiously in connection with the technical issue of the congealment of the fragment rather than the evidence which concerns socialism itself. Yet that evidence everywhere, whether in Canada, South Africa, or Australia, not only demonstrates a sufficient amount of congealment to produce an American "liberal tradition" but also emphasizes the significance of the very factors affiliated with socialism that I have been discussing here. The volume published by Professor Horowitz[1] further confirms the importance of these factors, even though Professor Horowitz and I might not be in complete agreement on the precise characterization of Canadian history in comparative terms. Professor McNaught says that I do not stress "similarities" with Europe. There are indeed critical similarities between America and Europe derived from a common heritage of Western culture, and when world history has come into its own we will understand them much better than we do now. But these are not the similarities of a common socialist experience within the Western framework. Here the United States is distinctive as against Europe, and its distinctiveness derives from the fact that the *Mayflower* left behind in Europe the experiences of class, revolution, and collectivism out of which the European socialist movement arose.

NOTE

1. Gad Horowitz, *Canadian Labour in Politics* (Toronto, 1968).

Chapter 10

THE RELEVANCE OF MARXISM*

Clinton Rossiter

1. *Marxist and American Views of Human Nature, and of Liberty and Equality*

When I wrote [earlier on] . . . of the essential pluralism of the American tradition, I had our view of the behavior and capacities of man uppermost in mind. To say the very best we can about it, this view is pleasantly clouded. Few American political thinkers have moved more than a step or two into the trackless field of psychology, and among these men there have always been serious disagreements. Thanks to the stern Calvinists among us, we have never been able to laugh off entirely the Augustinian warning that all men are miserable sinners; thanks to our happy liberals, we are still tempted by the Pelagian (if not Marxist) dream that all men can be made perfect. We are distinctly more sanguine about the nature of man in explicit words with which we exhort one another than in the implicit assumptions that account for our laws and institutions.

Yet having taken note of both the inadequacies and the contradictions in the view of man professed in the American tradition, I am prepared to draw at least the outlines of a consensus. We seem to have operated through most of our history in response to a mixed view of man's nature and capacities; yet, except for a deep suspicion we entertain of man in power, the mixture is still made up largely of the ingredients of hope. If the American tradition is not perfectibilist, it is certainly meliorist. It makes more of man's benevolence than of his wickedness, more of his educability than of

* Taken from Chapters 3, 4, 6, and 8 of Clinton Rossiter, *Marxism: The View from America* (New York: Harcourt, Brace, 1960), pp. 74–78, 81–82, 85–92, 110–14, 184–92, 237–43. In the original the chapters are entitled "Marxist Man," "Marxist Society: The Classes," "The Marxist State," and "America and Marx."

his perversity, more of his urge to be free than of his need to submit, more of his sense of justice than of his capacity for injustice; and it plainly lacks any secular counterpart to the doctrine of Original Sin. It assumes that the forces of good, if nurtured carefully by education and supported by a favorable environment, can generally hold the upper hand; at the same time, it insists that the forces of evil may be checked but never completely driven from the field, neither from the conduct of any one man nor from the behavior-patterns of the race. If we have been entertained but not impressed by the old line of revivalists, we have been excited but not convinced by the new breed of psychologists. The man of the American tradition is a rational man, one who, when given half a chance, will make political decisions calmly and thoughtfully with the aid of Aristotelian reason—reason tempered by experience. What we mean by "half a chance" is a decent environment and a system of constitutional restraints that can hold his ineradicable love of power in fairly close check. No matter, then, how we look at man, we see him as a jumble of cross-cutting tensions between good and evil; and no matter how far we look ahead, we see no final resolution of any of the tensions, especially of the tension between his sense of justice and capacity for injustice. The nature of man is changeable only slowly and within limits ordained by God and nature.

To men who stand on this ground the Marxist psychology presents a mixed picture of appealing insight and distressing prescription. We may be happy to find support for our own long-standing confidence in the power of human reason, but we are obviously not as prepared as Marx—certainly not in our political and social calculations—to give it first place among the forces that direct men's minds. We may rouse to his proclamation of human perfectibility, but in this instance, too, the sober side of our tradition forbids us to act too impetuously on such an assumption. The new man of Marxism, we are bound to say, is a dream in which a line of tough-minded thinkers from John Adams to Reinhold Niebuhr has forbidden us steadily to indulge at all purposefully.

Where we begin to part company decidedly is with Marx's view of man as "the *ensemble* of the social relations,"[1] as the exclusive creation of labor, class, and the system of production; for this, we think, is to see man as a collectivized and abstracted image of his unique and robust self. We give much credit to social and economic environment, but certainly not half so much as does Marx. We are far more skeptical than he in our evaluation of its role in the development of the species in history and its influence on the behavior of each individual in his own time. As to history, the American tradition teaches that forces deeply implanted in human nature had a great deal to do with the making of modern man; as to the individual, it assumes that he can rise above or fall below his alleged destiny, and that his class and occupation may often have little to do with his behavior. Our tradition asks us to believe that there is such a thing as a good man, and not just a good member of an economic class. The notion of proletarian man and bourgeois man as two different species is one that we cannot accept on proof or principle. The American tradition insists that there are some things common to all men, at all times, and in all classes, and that men can transcend society, as they have transcended nature, by virtue of their spirit, self-reliance, and desire for freedom. Many things have made each man what he is, and one of these has been the man himself.

We are not totally deaf to the argument for the plasticity of human nature, yet we are bound to say that Marx carries it much too far for our tastes with his call for "the alteration of men on a mass scale."[2] Man's nature is malleable, yes, but even continuously favorable circumstances existing over a long period of time can do little to erase or even recast those traits in his make-up which have set him eternally far below the angels. What Marx calls "vicious tendencies" are not wholly a product of present environment or a relic of past environment; rather they are a burden that man is destined to carry with him on his pilgrimage as far as the eye of sober imagination can see. The doctrine of plasticity, to tell the truth, is doubly unacceptable from the American point of view, for it appears politically dangerous as well as psychologically unsound. If we were to concede the point that a new race of men can be created by conscious manipulation of the social environment, what power could we then properly withhold from those in whose hands have been placed the levers of political control? The assumption of the infinite plasticity of human nature is a major intellectual support of the total state, and for this reason, if for no other, we cannot admit its validity.

The concept of alienation touches upon matters about which we have begun to think seriously only recently, and Marx deserves much credit for having made us think about them. Americans, I trust, cry out as loudly as do the Marxists at the sight of fragmented, depersonalized, dehumanized men, but we deny that such men exist in very large numbers, and deny further that capitalism or any other merely economic arrangement is the sole cause of their estrangement. We are not ignorant of the particular dangers to a healthy mind and spirit that flow from overspecialization and "fetishism," but we consider these the price of industrialism rather than of capitalism (a price, incidentally, which the whole world seems willing to pay). To the extent that men in Western society are alienated, the fault lies with them as much as it does with their surroundings. Life without anxiety, which appears to be the essence of the Marxist promise, is a will-o'-the-wisp, a Utopian dream that can never be made reality. Life without anxiety, I am tempted to add, would not be life at all, and it might well be argued that the elimination of all the tensions and frustrations that we label collectively as "alienation" would be undesirable as well as unattainable. The perfectly integrated mass-society would very likely be a sink of boredom and mediocrity in which creativity would be lost without a trace. Man, in any case, will always be alienated, troubled within and estranged without, simply because he is trapped in the paradox of human existence that we see fuzzily and the Marxists simply ignore: that he is always one alone and yet one among many.[3] The American tradition assumes that man has his best chance of self-fulfillment in a system that cuts him loose from the state and puts a large part of the responsibility for his conduct on his own will and capacities. If there is perhaps a little too much naiveté in this assumption, surely we can correct that without going outside the bounds of the tradition. This is one of those points at which we can learn from Marx's insights without embracing his prescriptions. . . .

The liberty of any man, Marx insisted, was determined by his membership in a class, just as were his nature, conduct, and morality. Each man was free to the extent that his class was free, and no man, therefore, was free at all. Even the vaunted liberty of the English and Americans was a weak, stunted, imperfect abstraction. Marx surveyed with arrogance what he liked to call "the narrow horizon of bourgeois right."[4] He had withering contempt both for the philosophical foundation on which Western man has grounded his claims to personal liberty, the concept of natural and inalienable rights, and for the practical machinery through which he has exercised his claims, the "pompous catalogue" of laws and customs that guarantee the freedoms of speech, press, worship, suffrage, assembly, petition, association, and fair trial.[5] The foundation of Western liberty was the rankest sort of idealism, the machinery was a legal cloak for the exploitation of the working class. As for constitutions and bills of rights, Engels had this to say of the most famous one:

> It is significant of the specifically bourgeois character of these human rights that the American constitution, the first to recognize the rights of man, in the same breath confirms the slavery of the colored races existing in America: class privileges are proscribed, race privileges sanctioned.[6]

In this context Marx made his famous distinction between "formal" and "effective" freedom.[7] Formal freedom is the kind that exists under capitalism and bourgeois democracy. In theory, it is the freedom to pursue one's ends in the absence of legal restraints; in fact, it is the harsh mixture of privilege and bondage that is guaranteed—privilege to the few, bondage to the many—by the complicated legal structure of "bourgeois right." Effective freedom is the kind that Marx promised in the future. In theory, it is the power to realize the ends one has chosen to pursue; in fact, it will be the happy condition of life for the proletariat under socialism and for all men under Communism. Formal freedom, Marx warned, will never become effective until private property in the means of production is rooted out and destroyed. The unequal distribution of control of property leaves most men in a state of subjection—as commodities to be bought and sold—and no amount of "prattle" about freedom of speech or the right to vote can mask this cruel fact from the honest eye. Marx was never more certain of the truth of his analysis of contemporary society than when he looked upon its painfully wrought structure of political rights and judicial safeguards, and pronounced it an extravagant fraud from top to bottom. And the most fraudulent part of the whole formal structure, in his opinion, was the boasted "freedom of contract." No one who studied the history of this "right" so precious to the bourgeoisie could fail to grasp the essential connection between freedom and exploitation in even the most "democratic" bourgeois societies. The "free" labor market, he wrote with savage irony in *Capital,* "is in fact a very Eden of the innate rights of man. . . ."[8]

It hardly seems necessary to make an elaborate statement of the meaning of liberty in the American tradition. There are a dozen ways of making such a statement, and no one who reads these pages will fail to have his own version of American liberty in mind. It will be enough, I think, to move directly into a critique of the Marxist theory of liberty, in the course of which the essentials of the American tradition should emerge into sufficiently clear view. In making this critique I will refrain from beating Marx over the head with the fact of the Soviet Union. Let us once again concentrate on Marx himself.

The first thing to be noted is that any meaningful debate with Marx and the Marxists on liberty is quite impossible to conduct.[9] This is not so much because our approach to liberty, which concerns itself largely with the relation of man to authority and is therefore concrete, contrasts so sharply with that of Marx, which concerns itself largely with the relation of man to history and is therefore metaphysical—although this difference in approaches does raise at least one insoluble problem. It is, rather, because our definitions and assumptions are so radically at odds with those of all the Marxists who have ever lived. We and they seem truly to live in two different worlds. What they call freedom, we call either airy fancy or real bondage; what they scorn as "formal," we cherish as real. They, too, as we know to our despair, define our freedom as bondage, and they do it so confidently that we cannot deny their sincerity.[10] Yet even if we were to accept their definitions, how could we then take the next step, which is to agree that the minimum price of genuine freedom is the root-and-branch destruction of our entire social, economic, and political system? And even if we were to agree to that—for the sake of the argument, I hasten to add—what concrete things can they tell us about freedom in the Communist society of the future, a society about which Marx and Engels were never more vague than when they spun their fine words about the "kingdom of freedom"? At no point is the gulf between Marxism and the American tradition so impossible to bridge, even for the sake of a verbal duel.

There are a few adverse comments, however, that we can make about Marx's view of liberty in language that Marxists can understand. No matter how his words are twisted and turned, he cannot escape these criticisms:

1) that he never came to grips with the paradox of freedom, the pattern of unceasing tension between liberty and authority, which he may have thought he had resolved by prophesying the "withering away of the state," but which, as the Soviets have proved,[11] he had not resolved at all;

2) that, as a result, he had nothing to say about political power, at once a mighty threat to, and stout guardian of, personal liberty;

3) that he failed to understand the importance of the instruments of "mere formal freedom," of laws and charters and elections, in protecting men against the abuses of public authority and the exploitations of private power;[12]

4) that in grounding the case for human rights exclusively on the fact of human needs, he did a serious disservice to the concept —so necessary to liberty as either fact or aspiration—of human dignity;

5) that in denouncing the distinction between public and private man he passed a sentence of death upon privacy, one of the most cherished of our legacies from the past and one of the saving refuges of our present;

6) that in this, as in all matters of importance to mankind, he put too much stress on economics, and thus refused to tell us how men might move beyond the negative if essential freedom from exploitation to the positive and creative practice of liberty;

7) that in this, as in all matters, he put too much stress on class, and thus failed to place the chief responsibility for the day-to-day practice of liberty, now or in the future, where it surely belongs: on man himself;

8) that in concentrating his attention on the element of effective power in personal freedom, he ignored the central question of who was to hold control of this power—the individual or some authority outside him? Few Americans will now deny a place to power in the formula of liberty, but not at the expense of independence and privacy.

Marx and Engels were most remiss, I think, in making so absolute a connection between liberty and necessity, and in making it

—how else can we put it?—in so offhand a manner. Since the time of the Flood we have told ourselves, and have been told, that liberty is obedience to necessity, that (to state this principle in the Scholastic version) it is the freedom to do that which is right and good. Now most of us have no quarrel with the argument, in either its metaphysical or practical form, that the freedom to do wrong is less sacred than the freedom to do right, and that those who do wrong will suffer sooner or later for having ignored the dictates of necessity. But the question we go on to ask is: Who is to say in fact, in the real world of laws and penalties, what is right and what is wrong? Who is to judge what is necessary and therefore proper? John Winthrop's answer was the Word of God, to be spoken by the Puritan elect; Rousseau's was the General Will, to be interpreted by the people massed in the public square; Hegel's was the Absolute Idea, to be brought to earth by the rulers of Prussia; and Marx's was the Laws of History, to be proclaimed by those who understand them best, by "the most advanced and resolute" of the Communists. With none of these solutions, all of which put final authority in the hands of supposedly infallible men, can we have anything to do. Law, popular will, tradition, and custom must all have a hand in deciding what is right and what is wrong, and a way out must be left to men who cannot agree with the definitions operative at any particular time. . . .

The appeal of Communism to millions of . . . people all over the world lies chiefly in its promise of an end to unjust privilege and degrading discrimination. It is therefore essential for us to learn what Marx and his followers have had to say about equality. The first and most surprising thing to learn is that they have had very little to say, that no leading Marxist, from Marx himself to Mao, has given himself over to long or searching thoughts about the matter.[13] For a man who is celebrated for having made equality the essence of justice, Marx was amazingly reticent in dealing with its philosophical supports or practical applications. This, in any case, is the sum of his ideas about equality; if the sum be trifling, let the blame fall on Marx himself:

To begin with, as we have learned to expect of Marx, he branded all other affirmations of equality, even those of the radicals who had gone before him, as nothing more than "obsolete rubbishy phrases."[14] The "equality" for which men had struggled in the

French and American Revolutions was, in Engels' words, simply a "bourgeois demand for the abolition of class privileges."[15] The political and judicial "equality" guaranteed in the laws of the bourgeois democracies was, like the "liberty" they also proclaimed, "mere formal" equality that masked the most shocking of all inequalities: the division of men into exploiters and exploited.

Marx and Engels refused to be lured into any rhetoric about the brotherhood of man. They recognized that men are not created equal and cannot be made equal; they even went so far in the *Manifesto* as to charge the Utopian socialists with preaching "universal asceticism and social leveling in its crudest form."[16] The Marxists of the Soviet Union, who gave up on equality long ago in the face of human nature and in the interests of an advanced technology,[17] have even less patience with those who insist on being naive about social and economic equality. "It is time it was understood," Stalin told the Seventeenth Party Congress in 1934, "that Marxism is opposed to leveling."[18] It is opposed, moreover, during the long period of socialist transition to anything resembling equality of income—to what Vyshinsky castigated as "petty bourgeois wage-leveling."[19] Marx himself made the great and careful distinction in his *Critique of the Gotha Programme* between the lot of men under socialism, who would continue to be rewarded on the basis of their contributions to society, and of men under communism, who would be satisfied, like the members of a family, on the basis of their needs.[20] Thus the Communists are able to rest their present case against the "left-egalitarian" call for equality of income—"a petty bourgeois deviation"—directly on scripture.[21]

What, then, we may ask, is equality in Marxism? And the answer comes in two parts: first, in words of Engels that are held sacred by the orthodox:

> The demand for equality in the mouth of the proletariat has . . . a double meaning. It is either . . . the spontaneous reaction against the crying social inequalities, against the contrast between rich and poor, the feudal lords and their serfs, the surfeiters and the starving; as such it is simply an expression of the revolutionary instinct, and finds its justification in that, and in that only. Or, on the other hand, this demand has arisen as a reaction against the bourgeois demand for equality, . . . and in this case it stands or falls with bourgeois equality itself. In both cases the real content of the proletarian demand

for equality is the demand for the *abolition of classes.* Any demand for equality which goes beyond that, of necessity passes into absurdity.[22]

And second, in words of Marx that are even more sacred:

In a higher phase of communist society, after the enslaving subordination of individuals under division of labour, and therewith also the antithesis between mental and physical labour, has vanished, after labour has become not merely a means to live but has become itself the primary necessity of life, after the productive forces have also increased with the all-round development of the individual, and all the springs of co-operative wealth flow more abundantly—only then can the narrow horizon of bourgeois right be fully left behind and society inscribe on its banners: *from each according to his ability, to each according to his needs.*[23]

Abolition of classes in the socialist future, equal satisfaction of human needs in the communist future beyond: this is the Marxist promise of equality. This promise has obviously been of little value in preventing the resurgence in the Soviet Union of the sharpest disparities in rank, privilege, and income. Yet in fairness to Marx it should be said that his own impatience with easy egalitarianism never blinded him, as it has blinded the Communists, to this great hope and truth: that while society must take the differences among men into honest account, it must not exploit these differences to the illicit advantage of the naturally superior and unseemly degradation of the naturally inferior. Most important of all, it must be careful always not to confuse artificial with natural inequalities.

The American tradition of equality is also, in essence, a protest against the existence of unjust, unnecessary, unnatural privileges. But it looks beyond the limited horizon of class determinism to account for the origin and persistence of such privileges. As a result, it prescribes quite different methods for achieving meaningful equality among the American people. Instead of concentrating passionately on one kind of equality, it proclaims the excellence and necessity of many: moral equality, the right of each man to be treated as end and not means; judicial equality, the right of each man to justice on the same terms as other men; political equality, the right of each man to a vote that counts no more and no less than any other man's vote; legal equality, the right to be exempt from class legislation; and, at the heart of the tradition, equality of opportunity, the right of each man to exploit his own talents to their natural limits. No American with a conscience can deny the existence of a grim wall between the ideal and the reality of equality in our way of life. Every American with a conscience is anxious for the wall to be torn down stone by stone, especially to demolish the crazy-quilt structure of privilege and exploitation that sits upon the treacherous foundation of racial discrimination. But we are determined, thanks to our tradition, that the struggle for equality be carried on through constitutional and customary processes, that it be directed exclusively toward the reduction of illicit privilege, and that it not sacrifice genuine liberty to spurious equality.

I think it useful to close on this very last point, for it represents one of the most serious breaks between Marxism and the American tradition. There can be no doubt that in a showdown between liberty and equality, which must often take place in both theory and practice, the Marxist chooses for equality and the American for liberty. There are many reasons for the choice that each of them makes, but the most important, I think, is the two different views they have of man. Marxism, by its own admission, is interested primarily in the "toiling masses" and therefore treats any one man as an abstraction of millions of men. Whenever it may be necessary for revolutionary purposes, Marxists have not the slightest trouble voicing the slogans of equality. The American tradition is more concerned with "self-reliant individuals." It therefore treats any one man as just that—one man—and even when we talk of equality, as we do with feeling, we tend to emphasize equality of rights rather than of goods or position. . . .

2. *Marxist and American Views of Social Class*

America has spawned some notable sociologists—Lester Frank Ward, William Graham Sumner, E. A. Ross, Thorstein Veblen, Arthur F. Bentley, W. Lloyd Warner, C. Wright Mills, and David Riesman, to mention a few of the best known—but as yet they have had little success in shaping our ideas about society to their findings or insights. The American social tradition is a kaleidoscope of contradictions. We talk a great deal about the classless society, yet we must admit under close questioning that such a society has never existed in America. We still love to toss about the slogans of rugged individualism, yet we know that the practice of such individualism by more than a few well-placed persons is disruptive of social stability. And certainly we manage to keep an uncomfortable distance between the way we preach and the way we practice the principle of equality. More disturbing than that, the kaleidoscope is only half-assembled. Our thoughts about society have been few and casual, as befits a people that has made a fetish of individualism. There are many questions about America that we have not even asked, much less answered, and this is one of those points at which the man who seeks to describe the American tradition must draw on the implicit workings of our customs and institutions rather than on the explicit words with which we are fond of praising them. What I am trying to say is that the real American social tradition is a benign reflection of the real American social structure. Its essence, which is Madisonian rather than Marxist, is roughly this:

Society is the sum of all the social units, and nothing more. From one point of view, it appears as a loose heap of freewheeling individuals; from a second, as a pattern of natural and voluntary groups; from a third, as a rough pyramid of social classes. Although no one of these views is any more "real" than the others (and all must be taken in order to get a clear picture of society), let us, out of deference to Marx, take the third, and so come up with these further observations:

Classes are an inevitable fact of social life, and what is inevitable is probably also necessary, not only for maintaining social stability but also for insuring social progress.

Classes in America are stages rather than castes. Our class system is a ladder, with at least six or eight rungs, up and down which heavy traffic moves constantly. (Here we have always been more sanguine than the statistics entitle us to be.)

Not only is there a vast amount of vertical movement between the classes, but the whole society is moving steadily upward in the scale of human existence. In specific terms, this means the steady growth, relative to all other classes, of an ever more prosperous and secure middle class.

The chief criterion of class distinction is achievement, especially economic achievement, although birth, wealth, taste, manners, power, and awareness all play their part.

The natural relationship of classes is a mixture of dependence and antagonism. There is friction in the joints, but not nearly enough to force us to talk of a "class struggle."

The best of all classes—in many ways, the only class that counts—is the middle class. The performance of any institution is to be judged finally in terms of how well it serves to expand or strengthen or reward this class.

A few additional details will emerge in the critique of Marxism to follow, but these, I think, are the basic points in the American social tradition. It would be hard to imagine a sharper confrontation between Marxism and the American tradition than exists in this field. Not even in the clash of materialism and idealism are the lines of battle more clearly drawn. These would seem to be the most compelling reasons for our inability to accept the lessons and exhortations of Marxist sociology:

First, Marx places far too much stress on economics as the decisive force in shaping social groups and patterns. It is simply not true that the institutions and tastes and habits and taboos of the American people are what they are and could be no different because of our mode of production. It is simply an exercise in definition, and not a very clever one at that, to say that a social class is fundamentally an aggregate of persons who perform the same broad function in the economy. History, psychology, cultural anthropology, and sociology all unite to affirm that both the origin and persistence of social classes can be understood only in terms of a plurality of causes, many of which defy economic determinism. Long before Marx, at least as early as James Madison, Americans knew well that men divided socially and politically on economic grounds, and certainly we should be the last people on earth to deny the power of production to influence our lives. But once again Marx has made one of the great determinants of social behavior the only determinant, and common sense bids us demur.

Second, we must demur, too, from the analysis of the class structure in Western society upon which he bases his revolutionary call to arms and his confident promise of a new society. When he talks of several kinds of bourgeois, several kinds of workingman, and of peasants and landlords and "third persons," we listen with interest and respect. When he insists that all these groupings are resolving inexorably into two, those who own and those who labor, interest turns to amusement, and respect to exasperation. There is no place in our thinking for this dialectical mania for shuffling all the complexities of social existence into a pattern of polar contradictions.

Third, even if we were to assume that his diagnosis was essentially correct, we could not take seriously his description of either of the two great classes. As the land of the bourgeoisie, a fact that Marx and Engels both acknowledged, what are we to say of the contempt he heaps upon us, our institutions, and our ideals? As the land with no proletariat (or so we like to think), what can we do but gasp when we hear of the role assigned to it? The fact is, as a hundred learned critics of Marx have pointed out, that the proletariat as Marx described it is a colossal myth, one of the most absurd if compelling in the Marxist armory (or whatever place it is in which men store myths). The Marxists themselves have never acted as if the proletariat were more than a useful abstraction, for always and everywhere it has been a select few—before the revolution a handful of intellectuals, after it a handful of bureaucrats—who have acted for and as the proletariat. The proletariat described by Marx does not and cannot exist; even if it did we would hardly care to put our destiny in its keeping.

Fourth, our history and tradition protest in unison against Marx's assertion that the class struggle is the normal condition of society and the motive power of history.[24] To the contrary, the pattern of class relationships in this country, as in many countries that come to mind, has been one of collaboration as well as of conflict. The advances of one class have brought benefits as well as injuries to other classes. We have long since abandoned the happy view of perfect harmony among classes, but this does not mean that we must now rush to the other end of the spectrum and embrace the bitter view of total war. One may find evidence of class antagonisms at many points in our history, but rarely has there been an antagonism that was not dampened eventually by the democratic process of give and take, if not dampened sooner by the flow of men from class to class. There is a wide gulf between the tensions and envies that can be found in even the healthiest society and the kind of "war to the knife" in which Marx saw the promise of revolution.

3. *Marxist and American Views of the Role of Power and the State*

The structure of government is grounded on certain manifest truths about the mixed nature of men. The fact that men can be wise and just, that they can govern themselves and other men fairly, is reflected in provisions for popular elections and for popular participation in the decision-making process. The fact that they can be unwise and unjust, that they can be hurried into rash decisions and corrupted by the taste of power, is reflected in arrangements that divide and check the total authority of government. Of these the most important are: the *separation of powers,* the distribution of political authority horizontally among a series of independent offices and agencies; *federalism,* the distribution of authority vertically among two or three levels of government; *checks and balances,* the provisions that guarantee mutual restraint among all these centers of power; *constitutional restraints,* the written laws and unwritten customs that reduce the discretion of public servants to the lowest level consistent with the effective operation of the political machinery; and *representative government,* the system under which the laws are made at a level once removed from the people, that is, by representatives elected to serve a limited period and held directly responsible by their electors.

The great services of all these arrangements, which bear the generic label of *constitutionalism,* are that they force men to think, talk, and bargain before they act, and that they institutionalize the processes through which public policy is made, administered, and enforced. The rule of the majority is the essence of democracy, but the majority must be coolheaded, persistent, and overwhelming, and it must be forced to recognize those things it cannot do by right or might. Without limitations there can be no constitutionalism; without constitutionalism, no democracy.

Finally, democracy flourishes strongly only when social and spiritual conditions are favorable. Some of these conditions are a healthy political system, in which two or more parties contest seriously but not savagely for power, and thus provide both a spur (the majority party) and a check (the opposition) to the process of government; a network of associations not beholden to the state, through which the legitimate interests of society may express and defend themselves; a productive economy, which guarantees a broad distribution of property and gives most men a "stake in society"; a sound pattern of morality, under which men may put trust in other men; a sound system of education, which raises men who can live decent lives and make prudent decisions; and, most essential, a faith in the rightness and fairness and competence of democracy, a faith that spreads wide and deep among the people.

I have made this statement of our political tradition in a "characteristically American" vein, that is, in ideal terms. I am aware of the gap between ideal and reality in our application of many of these principles. I am aware, too, that our political history has been a long battle to suppress our own urges toward Jacobin democracy. And I suspect that several principles of our tradition may need extensive reshaping in response to the pressures of an advanced industrial civilization. Yet I consider this a fair statement of the principles of good government to which we will be giving our allegiance for a long time to come, one that presents the American tradition in a light neither brighter nor darker than it deserves. Viewed in this light, most of the points at which Marxism and the American political tradition are in opposition are so visible to the naked eye that it would be a waste of time, not to say an insult to intelligence, to tick them off one by one. If ever there was a system of political institutions designed to exasperate the Marxists of this world, it is the "smokescreen for the dictatorship of capital" that operates in Washington and all over America through "ideological fictions" like the separation of powers and "Babbitt ideals" like federalism.[25] If ever there was a set of political ideas calculated to quicken the Marxist talent for abusive ridicule, it is the "apology for decay and oppression" I have just done my best to present. Marxism has no respect at all for our constitutional democracy, and I feel sure that my readers can be counted on to understand the reasons why. For my own part, I should like to single out the fundamental reasons for the inability of any constitutional democrat to accept the teachings of Marxism about politics and government, to list the points at which Marx and Engels and all their followers left the path of political reality to go astray in the fields of error.

The first of these points I discussed at some length earlier, the flaw in the Marxist view of the realities and potentialities of human behavior. No orthodox Marxist, from Marx himself through the latest apologist for the Soviet state, has ever grasped the implications of the universality of man's desire for power, nor ever stopped to observe or imagine the changes that can come over even the noblest members of the race when power without restraint or responsibility is placed in their hands. Marx's prescription for the dictatorship of the proletariat, like the dictatorship that has actually emerged in one Communist country after another, is based on the assumption that some men can be trusted to wield absolute power over other men without succumbing to the corruptions of greed or ambition or pride or even spite. To us this assumption, whether it be made out of indifference or conviction, appears absurd and dangerous. We are not yet prepared to base our own prescriptions for good government on the notion that all men are perfectible and a few men, whether Communists or Republicans or professors of political science or graduates of West Point, already perfect.

The second point is a corollary of the first. In failing to make room in his system for the psychology of power, Marx also fails to grasp the essentials of what we may call its sociology, that is, the way in which political power is structured and manipulated in society. We have already noted how strangely blind he is to the realities and ambiguities and perils of economic power, at least under socialism; and he is, if anything, even less conscious of the play of forces in the political arena. The most unacceptable result of this indifference, certainly from our point of view, is the gaping absence in his thought of any appreciation of the uses and merits of constitutionalism, a gap that has been filled by the Bolsheviks with their autocratic doctrine of "democratic centralism."[26] What we think is the first prerequisite of a sound system of government—the diffusion and restraint of authority through the techniques of constitutionalism—Marx and the Marxists consider either counterfeit or irrelevant. We may shudder at what we hear from Hobbes or Machiavelli about the uses of power, but at least we hear something. We may squirm when we read Madison or John Adams on the abuses of power, but we know that they are grappling honestly with a universal problem of government. It would be hard to find a figure in the whole history of political thought who has less to say than Marx on either aspect of the problem of power, indeed who gives less appearance of knowing that the problem even exists. Our aim has always been to *institutionalize* the uses of political power, that of the Marxists to *personalize* it, and their aim is a direct legacy from Marx and Engels. Marx or no Marx, it continues to amaze us that the repeated purges of Soviet officials for "abuses of authority" has never led to even a whispered reconsideration of the necessity of constitutionalism.

It is no wonder, then, that we fall out with the Marxists irreconcilably over the importance to human liberty of the instruments of "mere formal freedom." As Karl Popper writes, "This 'mere formal freedom,' i.e., democracy, the right of the people to judge and to dismiss their government, is the only known device by which we can try to protect ourselves against the misuse of political power; it is the control of the rulers by the ruled."[27] And since it is admitted today, in both the Soviet Union and the United States, that political power can go far to control economic power, "political democracy is also the only means for the control of economic power by the ruled." In our opinion, the Marxists have grossly undervalued the efficacy of what Lenin called the "hackneyed forms of routine parliamentary democracy"[28] as the means of making the state the servant and guardian of the entire people. No small part of the world's present grief may be traced to the distressing truth that Marx never understood what institutions and rules were essential to the proper conduct of popular government. He was altogether right in pointing out that the trappings of democracy can be used to serve the selfish interests of a ruling class, altogether wrong to insist that they can never be used to serve the common interests of an entire society.

The truth is that Marxism has never been able to get the role of political authority in proper perspective. It has never really attempted to answer the question posed by Edmund Burke, whom Marx saluted as that "celebrated sophist and sycophant,"[29] of "what the state ought to take upon itself to direct by the public wisdom, and what it ought to leave, with as little interference as possible, to individual discretion."[30] This, needless to say, is a central question of politics, and we condemn the Marxists for their refusal even to think about it. Marx himself errs in the direction of granting the state too little competence; the latter-day Marxists, who share his sentiments on the futility of bourgeois politics, err in the direction of granting it too much. Marx was a peculiar sort of anarchist, the Marxists are straight-out statists; and for neither of these polar positions can we have respect. We can show sympathy for the old Marxism, since we, too, were once classical Liberals who suspected that the power of government was both evil and useless. We were, to be sure, far better Liberals in theory than we were in practice, yet it cannot be denied that we now give a larger assignment and thus a larger measure of respect to government than we did twenty-five or fifty or a hundred years ago, and that anarchy is no more than a fleeting thought in which Americans indulge once a year when they file their income tax returns. Marx himself, we feel, is never more mistaken than when he derides the capacity of government to serve the general welfare —to humanize industrialism, to reduce class and group tensions, and generally to improve the lot of all men. We think we have proved what he denies: that government can manage efficiently and direct equitably the pursuit of at least some of the common interests of society. . . .

4. *America and Marx*

"I hope," Marx once wrote in a mixed mood of jest and spite, "that the bourgeoisie as long as they live will have cause to remember my carbuncles." I expect that we will have cause, as long as we live; and we may give thanks that only rarely has he proved so keen a prophet. Marx is a giant who reigns in awe over the world—even over those parts that deny his sovereignty—as no man of ideas has reigned in all history. He is, in his own words, a "specter . . . haunting" every country, every party, every interest, indeed every thinking man in the world, and not just because he is the father of Communism. Marx the thinker may be a man to reckon with long after Communism has joined the other legendary tyrannies in "the dustbin of history." For all his trespasses against reason, science, history, and common sense, he owned one of the mighty minds of the human race, and we may be prisoners of his words and categories and eccentricities as long as we were of Aristotle's. The prospect is appalling, but it lies before us, and we had better learn to live with it bravely.

We in the West, especially in America, have most to learn, for upon us Marx unleashed the brunt of his attack, and upon us the attack continues in undiminished violence. Indeed, it almost seems as if he were as vibrantly and censoriously alive today as he was in 1848. We have no social arrangement—our welfare capitalism, the ascendancy of our middle class, the variety of our groups and interests—for which he can say one kind or even understanding word. We have no institution—church, family, property, school, corporation, trade union, and all the agencies of constitutional democracy—that he does not wish either to destroy or to transform beyond recognition. We have no ideals or ideas—from the Christian ethic through patriotism to individualism—that he does not condemn out of hand. The essence of Marx's message is a prediction of doom for the Western, liberal, democratic way of life. He announces that prediction not sadly but gladly, not timidly but furiously, not contingently but dogmatically; and so, of course, do his heirs. Lenin was once again a faithful child of Marx when he wrote, "In the end one or the other will triumph—a funeral requiem will be sung over the Soviet Republic or over world capitalism," and Khrushchev a faithful grandchild when he laid to rest all doubts about our future by promising happily, "We will bury you." He will bury us, he thinks, because we deserve to be buried, and because Marx promised that we will get what we deserve. Khrushchev harbored a quasi-religious conviction of the overpowering rightness of Communism and the overweening wrongness of Western democracy. He made the sharpest possible confrontation of his system and ours, and he makes it, let us not forget, apocalyptically—that is, by predicting the total victory of the one and the total defeat of the other, whether the game be played on the battlefield, in the laboratory, or in the heavens.

It is time that we, too, made this confrontation far more sharply than we have made it in the past generation. Whether we, too, must come to an apocalyptic conclusion I am not yet ready to say, but I am certain that we must not fear to look orthodox Marxism straight in the face. That is why I have attempted this small beginning by looking into the assumptions and motives which make that face so grim as it stares back at us and so hopeful as it scans the future. Let me collect and restate the many points of confrontation we have discovered, in the form of three deep-cutting, irreconcilable conflicts:

The first arises primarily in the realm of ideas: the head-on collision of monism and pluralism. Marxism is, as Engels said jokingly, "an all-comprising system" constructed by men of a "terribly ponderous *Gründlichkeit*"; it is, as Lenin said solemnly, a "solid block of steel," a "prolific, true, powerful, omnipotent, objective, and absolute human knowledge." Marxism is the latest and greatest (and easily the most presumptuous) of all those celebrated systems of thought with which learned men, moved by the doubts and fears of the unlearned, have sought to interpret the world in terms of a single principle. It has an explanation of everything, and to everything it grants one explanation. The whole range of man's behavior is explained in terms of the business of making a living, the whole configuration of society in terms of the class structure, the whole sweep of history in terms of the class struggle, the whole phenomenon of classes in terms of private property; and all these primary forces, most notably property, are hung upon a hook fashioned from the "solid block of steel": dialectical materialism. The dialectic of Hegel and the materialism of Hobbes and Holbach are clamped together, if never really consolidated, to account for all things from "the dance of the electrons" to "the conflicts in human society."[31] Marxism, at least as theory, is a closed system in which all new facts and ideas are made to conform to the original pattern, which is itself a thing of breathtaking simplicity.[32]

The American tradition, to the contrary, is consciously pluralistic. Its unity is the result of a process through which unnumbered diversities of faith and intellect seek to live together in accommodation, if not always in harmony. Man, history, society, politics, nature—all are explained, to the extent that they can be explained, in terms of multiple causation. Our system of ideas is open to new thoughts and fresh evidence. It has its bedrock beliefs in the dignity of man, the excellence of liberty, the limits of politics, and the presence of God; but on these beliefs, even in defiance of the last, men are free to build almost every conceivable type of intellectual and spiritual mansion. For this reason, we find it hard to grant much respect to Marxism, a system that presumes to relate all thoughts and all wonders to a single determining principle. More to the point, we find it increasingly hard to grant it license, for too much evidence is now before our eyes that monism in the world of ideas leads to absolutism in the world of events. In order to survive, a truly monistic system must put an end to the great debates that have gone on for thousands of years,[33] give dogmatic answers to questions that men can never answer finally, and destroy all other systems, closed or open, that seek to understand something of the mysteries of life. The monism of Marxism makes it the ideology of ideologies, and we can never make peace with it. Those Americans who have themselves succumbed to monism are in palpable violation of one of our most cherished principles, and they could profit a great deal from the Communist example.

The second conflict arises primarily in the realm of institutions: the head-on collision of collectivism and individualism. Marx, we have learned, seems more concerned with abstract men in the real mass rather than with real men in the abstract mass. He talks of classes rather than of individuals, of systems rather than of persons; he seems to have no respect at all for private man. His prescriptions are based on an honest assumption that all conflicts between the interests of any one man and the interests of all society, between what a man owes himself and what he owes his fellows, can be eliminated by social reconstruction. On both "the individual withdrawn into his private interests" and the family with even a symbolic fence between itself and the community he pronounces a sentence of doom; and he does it in the best of faith because he cannot believe that any man or family will feel the need to hold something of value aloof from the proletarian or classless community. His prescriptions are therefore, as we have seen, thoroughly collectivistic. No man, no group, no interest, no center of power is to defy the dictatorship of the proletariat in the period of socialist transition or to remain outside the harmonious community in the endless age of Communism. That age would surely be marked, as I wrote earlier, by a state of "togetherness" that would obliterate every barrier between man and mankind. Collectivism is Marx's means, and it is also his end. It may be gentle, comforting, and unforced—once the dictatorship has passed—but it is still collectivism with a vengeance.

The American tradition is doggedly individualistic. It makes room for the state, for society, and for natural and voluntary groups; and only a few men on the fringes of the tradition have ever denied the intensely social nature of man. Yet it leaves a wide sphere to private man, the private family, and private groups even in its most socially conscious moments, and it insists on a meaningful, lasting contradiction between the interests of this sphere and those of the common weal. Lacking the monistic urge to have all things in order, it understands that freedom is an eternal paradox. It is prepared to live indefinitely with the division of each person into an "individual" and a "citizen." If this leaves all thinking men in a state of ceaseless tension, the tension must nonetheless be borne as part of the human condition.[34] Marx tries to resolve it, and that is where he goes off the track, or rather down the wrong track. We try to live with it, and that is why we go bumping along on the right track. There have been times, to be sure, when we hurried down it much too blithely. We have lost sight of the free group in our anxiety to celebrate the free individual; we have made too much of competition and too little of co-operation as engines of social progress. But fundamentally our tradition is a challenge to collectivism at both levels; a challenge in behalf of the free individual, a challenge in behalf of the free group. The full measure of this giant confrontation should be understood as a collision of collectivism with both individualism and social pluralism.

The last confrontation is both ideological and institutional: the not quite head-on, yet resounding enough collision of radicalism with conservatism and liberalism. Marxism is, by almost any standard, the supreme radicalism of all time. It is radical in every sense of that sticky word: because it is revolutionary, because it is extremist, because it proposes to dig down to the roots of all things. It insists that the political and social institutions of the West are oppressive and diseased, the values that support them rotten and dishonest; it bids us supplant them with an infinitely more just and benign way of life. So complete is its commitment to the future, so unwilling is it to suffer delay, that it is prepared to force entry into this future by subversion and violence. Its attitude toward the social process is simple and savage: it means to disrupt it as thoroughly as possible in defiance of all rules of the game. The rules, in any case, are monstrous cheats, which may be ignored, manipulated, or turned against their makers—whatever course seems most likely to serve the cause of revolutionary radicalism. The Marxist is a man with a blueprint for rebuilding society, and the first three items on the sheet of instructions that goes with it read: smash the foundations of the old society into rubble; cart the rubble away; start to build a new foundation with new materials that have never been used before.

The American tradition, like most successful traditions with a broad appeal, is a casual blend of conservatism and liberalism. It is conservative in all the useful senses of that sticky word: because it is cautious and moderate, because it is disposed to preserve what it has inherited, because it puts a high value on tradition as a social force and prudence as an individual virtue. It does not encourage, to put it mildly, an attitude of bitter criticism among its children; it is committed to a discriminating but dogged defense of the American system against radical change. Yet it is liberal, too, in most senses of that stickiest word of all: because it is open-handed and open-minded, because it really expects the future to be better than the past, because it is interested first of all in the development of free men. Product of a history of ceaseless change and growth, it makes a large place for progress through conscious reform and prescriptive innovation. It breeds optimism rather than pessimism about the next hundred years, even in the teeth of the Marxist challenge. Some Americans interpret their tradition as a stamp of approval on things as they are, others interpret it as a summons to restless experiment; but all (or almost all, because the tradition also makes room for the men on the fringes) have little use for the kind of radicalism Marx proclaims. While there is still room for Utopia in the American dream, short cuts to it are looked upon as roads to ruin. The American mind has been sold some amazing prescriptions for specific ills; it has never been sold a panacea, and probably could not be.

NOTES

1. Sixth "Thesis on Feuerbach," Karl Marx, *Selected Works* (New York, n.d.), vol. I, p. 473.

2. Karl Marx, *German Ideology* (New York, 1947), p. 69.

3. On this point, see M. Watnick, "Georg Lukacs," *Soviet Survey,* January–March 1958, pp. 60, 65, and works there cited.

4. Karl Marx, *Critique of the Gotha Programme,* in *Selected Works,* vol. II, p. 566.

5. *Capital* (Chicago, 1906–9), vol. I, p. 330.

6. Friedrich Engels, *Anti-Dühring* (Moscow, 1954), pp. 147–48.

7. A. L. Harris, "Utopian Elements in Marx's Thought," *Ethics,* vol. LX (1949), pp. 79, 87–89.

8. *Capital,* vol. I, p. 195. See Engels' strictures on this "freedom" in his *Condition of the Working Class in England* (New York, 1887), pp. 51–52.

9. Even, I fear, with so reasonable a Marxist as John Lewis. See his contribution to the UNESCO symposium on human rights in his *Marxism and the Open Mind* (London, 1957), pp. 53–76, and also 77–93. And note Stalin's insistence, in his famous interview with Roy Howard in 1937, that "we have not built this society in order to cramp individual freedom." A. Vyshinsky, *The Law of the Soviet State* (New York, 1954), p. 539. For an excellent critique of Marxist ideas about freedom, see H. B. Parkes, *Marxism: An Autopsy* (New York, 1939), ch. 4.

10. I know of no book that gives a more completely orthodox statement of the Marxist concept of liberty than Roger Garaudy, *La liberté* (Paris, 1955), esp. pts. II, IV. Christopher Caudwell, *Studies in a Dying Culture* (London, 1938), ch. 8, is an eloquent Marxist statement of the irreconcilability of the two liberties, one a "bourgeois illusion," the other the "social consciousness of necessity."

11. Note Vyshinsky's comment, so much at odds with our way of thinking, that "any contrasting of civil rights with the state is alien to socialist public law." *Law of the Soviet State,* pp. 562–63.

12. This is why, as an English Marxist points out, a "higher synthesis" of the "earlier inherent individual rights" and communist "social and economic rights" is an impossible dream. Lewis, *Marxism and the Open Mind,* p. 58.

13. For a useful bibliography on this subject, see D. D. Egbert and Stow Persons, eds., *Socialism and American Life* (Princeton, 1952), vol. II, pp. 340–42. Werner Sombart, *Der proletarische Sozialismus* (Vena, 1924), vol. I, ch. 9, is an excellent introduction.

14. *Critique of the Gotha Programme,* in *Selected Works,* vol. II, p. 567.

15. *Anti-Dühring,* p. 148.

16. *Selected Works,* vol. I, p. 237.

17. John Strachey, *The Theory and Practice of Socialism* (New York, 1936), p. 117. Barrington Moore, Jr., *Soviet Politics—The Dilemma of Power* (Cambridge, 1956), pp. 405ff., puts the necessary connection between industrialism and a "system of organized social inequality" with particular conviction. So, in his own way, does Milovan Djilas, *The New Class* (New York, 1958), esp. pp. 37ff. Engels beat them both to the draw by pointing out in *Anti-Dühring,* p. 193, that "each new advance of civilization is at the same time a new advance of inequality."

18. Marguerite Fisher, *Communist Doctrine and the Free World* (Syracuse, 1952), p. 216. See R. N. Carew Hunt, *A Guide to Communist Jargon* (London, 1957), pp. 69–73; B. Moore, *Soviet Politics,* pp. 182–88, 236–46, 404.

19. *Law of the Soviet State,* p. 209. For the sad story of Lenin's doctrine of "maximum income," see E. H. Carr, *The Bolshevik Revolution* (New York, 1951–53), vol. II, pp. 112–15. See his orthodox comments on equality in *State and Revolution* (New York, 1932), pp. 76–82.

20. *Selected Works,* vol. II, pp. 560–68; Lenin, *State and Revolution,* pp. 75–85.

21. Joseph Stalin, *Leninism* (New York, n.d.), vol. II, pp. 373–77.

22. *Anti-Dühring,* pp. 148–49. The italics are Engels'.

23. *Critique of the Gotha Programme,* in *Selected Works,* vol. II, p. 566. The italics are mine.

24. On the difficulties inherent in this concept, see Alexander Gray, *Socialist Tradition* (London, 1946), pp. 499–504. G. H. Sabine, *Marxism* (Ithaca, N.Y., 1958), ch. 3, is a powerful indictment from the democratic point of view.

25. Vyshinsky, *Law of the Soviet State,* pp. 166, 220, 312ff. See Julian Towster, *Political Power in the U.S.S.R.* (New York, 1948), pp. 52, 61–62, 184–86, for typical Marxist statements on federalism and the separation of powers. On Soviet federalism, see John N. Hazard, *The Soviet System of Government* (Chicago, 1957), ch. 6; Richard Pipes, *The Formation of the Soviet Union: Communism and Nationalism, 1917–1922* (Cambridge, 1955). Lenin sealed the theoretical doom of federalism in *State and Revolution,* pp. 46, 60–62.

26. On this concept, see R. N. Carew Hunt, *A Guide to Communist Jargon* (London, 1957), pp. 53–56; B. Moore, *Soviet Politics,* pp. 64ff., 81, 139, 232; Towster, *Political Power in the U.S.S.R.*, pp. 186, 207–8; Merle Fainsod, *How Russia Is Ruled* (Cambridge, Mass., 1953), pp. 180–81. This is an essentially party concept now transferred in application to the whole state.

27. There are other known devices, but the hyperbole serves its purpose. K. R. Popper, *The Open Society and Its Enemies* (Princeton, 1950), p. 316.

28. Marguerite Fisher, *Communist Doctrine and the Free World* (Syracuse, 1952), p. 166.

29. *Capital,* vol. I, p. 354.

30. *Works* (9th ed.; Boston, 1889), vol. V, p. 166.

31. J. M. Cameron, *Scrutiny of Marxism* (London, 1948), p. 25.

32. On the intellectual dangers of working within such a system, see Arthur Koestler, *Arrow in the Blue* (New York, 1952), pp. 260–61, and for an intelligent Marxist's warning of the sorrowful consequences of intellectual monism, see Pierre Hervé, *La révolution et les fétiches* (Paris, 1956).

33. The course of events in Red China over the past few years is a fascinating case study in the inevitable results of monism. In February 1957, Mao Tse-tung made his famous appeal to the Supreme State Conference in Peiping: "Let a hundred flowers bloom, let a hundred schools of thought contend." No sooner had Mao's garden begun to grow, however, than most of the new flowers were identified as "poisonous weeds," and rooted out savagely. As the New York *Times* said editorially, any flower may grow in Chinese soil if it meets these conditions: "First, views expressed must serve to unite and not divide the people. Second, they must benefit socialist transformation and construction. Third, they must help to consolidate the 'people's democratic dictatorship.' Fourth, they must help to consolidate 'democratic centralism.' Fifth, they must strengthen the leadership of the Communist party. Sixth, they must benefit international Communist solidarity and that of 'peace-loving peoples.'" This hardly leaves much room in the garden for even slightly mutant blooms. The text of Mao's speech is printed in the New York *Times,* June 19, 1957. An interesting commentary is Michael Walzer, "When the Hundred Flowers Withered," *Dissent,* vol. V (1958), p. 360.

34. H. M. Roelofs, *The Tension of Citizenship* (New York, 1957).

COMMENT 1

Tom Bottomore

Clinton Rossiter's study of Marxism in an American context is disappointing in several respects. It deals with a rather simplified version of Marxism, which verges at times upon the crudities of the political doctrine once known as Marxism-Leninism-Stalinism. Represented in this fashion Marxism is then contrasted with an "American tradition," which is portrayed in a very abstract way and not subjected to any critical examination. Finally, Rossiter explains the lack of appeal which Marxism has had in America entirely in terms of a conflict of ideas, without reference to the institutions and conditions of American society which provided the framework and material of this conflict.

Let me comment first, very briefly, upon Rossiter's view of Marxism. He concentrates his attention on two themes: one, the question of individual liberty in relation to Marx's conceptions of human nature and of social classes; the other, Marx's idea of government, or political power, in present-day and future society. In a number of different contexts Rossiter argues that the tendency of Marxist thought is to deny or devalue the autonomy and freedom of the individual. Thus he writes: "we begin to part company decidedly . . . with Marx's view of man as 'the *ensemble* of the social relations' "; and in another passage: "The liberty of any man, Marx insisted, was determined by his membership in a class, just as were his nature, conduct, and morality." But this is to disregard the complexity of Marx's thought, and in particular the tension in it between the idea of the determining influences of the economy, property relations, and social classes on one side, and on the other side the idea of men's ability to grasp their situation rationally and to act in such a way as to change it. Rossiter himself, in other passages, attributes to Marx an excessive confidence in the power of human reason, but he does not see that this is an element which modifies profoundly Marx's "determinism."

The phrase which Rossiter quotes from the *Theses on Feuerbach* to the effect that man's "real nature" is the "*ensemble* of social relations" itself needs to be interpreted in the light of Marx's thought at that time; his argument is directed against Feuerbach's conception of man as an abstract, isolated, unhistorical individual, and asserts that what is needed is a critical examination of man's "real nature" as it is revealed in the historical development of societies. Only by looking at Marx's early writings, and especially his *Economic and Philosophical Manuscripts* (which were less well known when Rossiter published his study than they are today), can we see clearly his intention to lay the basis of a doctrine of human emancipation which would be historical and realistic, taking into account both men's ideal strivings, the product of their reason and imagination, and also (against the utopians) the actual social conditions in which men live, struggle, and form their ideals. This intention was less prominent in Marx's later writings, when he was preoccupied with the analysis of the economic structure of capitalism, but it was always present in some form, whether in his discussion in *Capital,* vol. III, of the "true realm of freedom" as the "development of human potentiality for its own sake," which requires as an essential precondition the shortening of the hours of work, or in his judgment of the Paris Commune as "the political form, at last discovered, under which to work out the emancipation of labour."

Marx's analysis of the experience of the Commune also helps to elucidate his ideas on political power and the manner in which it might be transformed in a future type of society. What Marx criticized in the bourgeois state was that it organized political power as a separate and limited sphere of activity, detached from civil society and claiming to be independent of it, although in fact it had its basis in the social structure inasmuch as it upheld and consolidated the interests of an economically dominant class. The bourgeois state is an alien force, beyond the control of the great majority of individuals; and the "general interest" of the whole community which it claims to represent is illusory so long as there is a real conflict of interests in civil society, between classes, and among individuals themselves as a consequence of the fact that civil society is organized on the principle of a war of all against all in the pursuit of particular interests. When Marx referred to the supersession (*Aufhebung*) of the state in a socialist society he meant that political power would become truly universal; all men would participate in its exercise (thus taking back the powers which they had alienated), and political power would be used to regulate all the conditions of men's collective existence, so that there would no longer be a contradiction between the state as representative of a general interest and civil society as the arena of antagonistic private interests. Marx saw in the Commune a first, tentative realization of this new political form, the principal features of which were that it was based upon universal suffrage, that its elected representatives were well known and trusted by the people, and were subject to recall, and that they were not separated from the rest of the population by differences in their wealth, income, or style of life. In Marx's words, the Commune would bring about "in place of the old centralized government the self-government of the producers." The Commune thus provided an occasion for Marx to elaborate, in terms of a practical experience, the political ideas formulated early in his life in his *Critique of Hegel's Philosophy of the State* (1842–43), which were directed against the centralized autocratic state. There is no justification, if Marx's political theory is systematically examined as a whole, for Rossiter's exclusive concentration upon the "dictatorship of the proletariat," or for his claim that Stalinism is a direct legacy from Marx's theory. On the contrary, it is all too evident that the theory and practice of the Bolsheviks diverged widely from Marx's own theoretical and practical aims: it was Lenin, not Marx, who formulated the doctrine of the leading role of the party, and thus prepared the way for a political dictatorship; it was Lenin who suppressed, after the Revolution, the workers' and soldiers' councils which embodied the same political principles that Marx had praised in the Commune.

To say this is not to deny in any way that the process in which Marx's theory was transformed into the Bolshevik ideology constitutes an important social and intellectual problem; or that this historical metamorphosis may provoke (as it has indeed done) new critical reflections upon Marx's own conception of the transition to socialism and of the institutional framework of a socialist society. But Rossiter has a curious way of proceeding. He expounds Marx's ideas in a form which makes them appear wholly consistent with Soviet reality, and then condemns them by reference to that reality; yet when he discusses the "American tradition" he presents it only in an ideal form, and does not confront it at all with the reality of American society. (At most he makes a formal acknowledgment, from time to time, that there is a gap between ideal and reality.) It is evident, in any case, that a "tradition" constitutes a body of ideas considerably less precise, articulated, and homogeneous than a systematic theory such as Marxism; it may include divergent or even contradictory elements, and what is referred to as *the* tradition (or in sociological language, the "central value system") is unlikely to be more than a dominant ideology, interpreted from a particular point of view. As an ideology it needs to be critically examined, in terms of the ideas which it chooses to emphasize, the interests which it sanctions, its relationship with opposing doctrines, and its degree of correspondence with the actual processes and development of social life.

Rossiter singles out, as vital elements in this American tradition, liberty and pluralism. The idea of liberty which he propounds may be summed up in his own phrase as that of the "self-reliant individual." Undoubtedly this notion has had great historical importance in America, but it corresponds much more with the conditions of early American society than with the state of affairs which has come to exist in the twentieth century. As Wright Mills observed in *White Collar* (1951): "Over the last hundred years, the United States has been transformed from a nation of small capitalists into a nation of hired employees, but the ideology suitable for the nation of small capitalists persists, as if that small-propertied world were still a going concern." Today this ideology, which Rossiter merely reasserts, is much less widely accepted; more and more people seem to feel trapped and powerless in a society dominated by large business corporations, large military establishments, and inaccessible party machines, and they are seeking changes in society which would allow them to restore and develop their freedom, not so much as "self-reliant," but as "self-directing" and "self-governing" individuals. This is the sense which is to be found in one of the most widespread radical conceptions of the 1960s—"participatory democracy"—and it leads necessarily to a reconsideration of Marx's fundamental ideas about the ending of class domination and the introduction of "self-government of the producers" as essential conditions for personal freedom.

The notion of "pluralism" which Rossiter outlines is equally open to criticism. American pluralism has always been confined within a limited sphere, in this century especially by the powerful ideology of "100 per cent Americanism" (and its counterpart, "un-American activities"). In practice, pluralism has meant on one side the acceptance of a laissez-faire market economy with minimum government interference (as Charles Beard put it in describing conditions at the end of the nineteenth century, political leaders believed in "the widest possible extension of the principle of private property, and the narrowest possible restriction of state interference, except to aid private property to increase its gains"), and on the other side diversity of political views and organizations so long as they did not challenge in any fundamental way the capitalist market economy. Those political movements which presented, or seemed to present, such a challenge—from Populism to the socialist movement of the first two decades of this century—were either absorbed by the existing parties or if necessary repressed. Thus American pluralism can be defined broadly as "right-wing pluralism." Even this kind of pluralism has tended to decline during the twentieth century, according to the critics of "mass society," with the disappearance or assimilation of those autonomous groups which could have an influence upon public policy in particular areas of social life. From this aspect the radical movements of the 1960s can be seen in part as attempts to re-create such autonomous groups, and to enhance their influence, in such diverse fields as civil rights, education, poverty programs, consumer protection, and women's rights. But in this case too Rossiter shows a lack of concern for the trends in practical social life, and confines his attention to the ideal of pluralism.

The radicalism of the 1960s is only the latest manifestation of a long-established alternative tradition in America which has many affinities, even where it does not have direct connections, with Marxism. From the 1880s onward the development of large-scale capitalism and the consolidation of the class structure in American society brought into existence opposing forces in the shape of new political and industrial organizations and a wave of social criticism. These diverse groups of intellectuals and activists engendered, in the first decade of the present century, a rapidly growing socialist movement through which, despite many differences of ideology and political practice, the essential ideas of Marxism about the conflict of class interests and the opposition between capitalism and socialism as forms of society began to be clearly expressed. At this time it seemed possible, and even likely, that the divisions in American society would result in the formation of a political labor movement on a scale similar to that which already existed in many of the European countries. This sense of a new direction in politics found its intellectual expression in various attempts to introduce Marxist methods and ideas in the study of American society, and to expound and assess the Marxist theory or defend it against its critics; for example, in the work of the historians, Beard and Robinson, in E. R. A. Seligman's *The Economic Interpretation of History* (1902, rev. ed. 1907), in Louis Boudin's *The Theoretical System of Karl Marx* (1907), in Veblen's *The Socialist Economics of Karl Marx and His Followers* (1906–7), and somewhat later in the writings of Randolph Bourne, who concluded that ". . . the three cardinal propositions of Marx–the economic interpretation of history, the class struggle, and the exploitation of the workers by the capitalistic private ownership of the means of production–if interpreted progressively are the *sine qua non* of Socialism."[1]

The development of Marxist and socialist thought was interrupted by the entry of America into the war, which provided an occasion for extreme repressive measures against radicalism; and after the war the socialist movement failed to regain its momentum. This failure has only recently begun to be systematically investigated,[2] but the studies so far undertaken already lead toward a reinterpretation of the history of ideas and political movements in America. It is clear that socialism became for a time a significant force in American life, and that large sections of the population were far from being as unresponsive to Marxism as the exponents of a unique "American tradition" have claimed. The decline of socialism in the 1920s needs to be explained in terms of specific features of American society and particular historical events; it cannot be taken simply as the continuation of a natural state of affairs, attributable to the overwhelming strength of an established tradition, when it is seen that this tradition was seriously and extensively questioned, or in some cases rejected, during the first decade of this century. One reason for the post-war decline may be found in the fact that the socialist movement, in spite of its successes, had not yet acquired the mass character which would have provided it with the strength to survive both the repressive actions of the government and internal dissension on the scale which followed the Russian Revolution, the organization of the Third International, and the creation of new doctrinaire parties, based upon the Bolshevik model, in the United States.[3] This relatively slow development in the pre-war period can itself be explained, in part, as a consequence of mass immigration, ethnic diversity, and the particular form which American trade unionism had assumed. These factors need to be considered just as much as the possible influence of an ideology which proclaimed, against the experiences of everyday life, the values of equality, mobility, and individual success.

From the mid-1920s, under Bolshevik influence, Marxism became the affair of small political sects, and it retained this character through the economic and social crisis of the following decade. In the 1930s Marxism attracted many literary intellectuals, who debated the "proletarian novel" and later on gave their support to the Republican government in the Spanish Civil War, but most of them were quickly disillusioned. By contrast, the influence of Marxism as a social theory was slight and its impact upon the American working class negligible; despite the extent of the economic crisis no broad socialist movement developed and popular discontent was channeled into the limited reforms of the New Deal. In this period Marxism actually took on the character of an alien doctrine which Rossiter implicitly attributes to it.

Only since the end of the 1950s has Marxism again found a large audience in America, its intellectual revival coinciding, here as elsewhere, with the decay of the Bolshevik ideology. Marxist ideas have reappeared in the social sciences, from which they had been largely absent for three or four decades, and Marx's writings are probably more widely known and more thoroughly studied than ever before. Thus at the very moment when Rossiter was asserting the incompatibility between Marxism and the "American tradition" there was in fact beginning a renewal of Marxist thought, marked by a more direct relevance to American society than at any time since the early years of this century.

It is, however, a different style of Marxism, not tied to any political orthodoxy, and diversely interpreted as one element in a tradition of socialist thought and practice. The variety of interpretations, and the numerous attempts to amend and supplement previously accepted versions of the Marxist theory, may of course signify that Marxism is beginning to lose its distinctive character and will eventually be absorbed into a new radical or socialist theory of society. I think this is a plausible view of what is now happening. But such a development would not involve any *rap-*

prochement with the ideas of the "liberal-pluralist" theory. Any radical theory which advanced beyond Marxism would still include among its major preoccupations the class inequalities in American society; the conflicts which arise, sometimes in curious forms, from these inequalities; the widespread sentiments of dissatisfaction and disenchantment with the present organization of society; and the possibility of creating a classless society in which individuals would experience a genuine liberation insofar as they ceased to be dominated by other men through the instrumentalities of wealth, political power, or social privilege.

These conceptions of conflict, liberation, and a radical transformation of society are quite foreign to "liberal-pluralist" theory, which is characterized above all by an acceptance (and sometimes idealization) of the present social order. It assumes, in Rossiter's notion of a single American "tradition," or in conceptions of American democracy as the final attainment of the "good society," the fundamental unchangeability of American institutions. Reforms and improvements are possible, economic growth is taken for granted, a decline in social antagonisms is assumed; but all this is regarded as no more than the unfolding of what has always been implicit, and partially realized, in the established framework of society. The possibility of any radical change to a new form of society—a change from the dominance of private corporations to industrial democracy within a system of public ownership, from competitive and acquisitive individualism to public service and cooperation, from the present organization of political parties and the state to a less centralized system without party bosses and political elites—is simply not conceived.

The intellectual predominance of this liberal theory is the result, certainly, of some particular features in the development of American society, and especially the failure of socialism to become established as a major political force. It does not correspond, however, with any factual existence of a single American "tradition," or "political culture," or "way of life," for there has often been, as I have indicated, widespread dissent and acceptance of alternative political ideas. There is very plainly a radical tradition in America, though it has never become predominant. Least of all can one speak of a single tradition at the present time, when dissatisfaction and opposition have grown rapidly, and there exists, throughout a large part of society, a profound sense of the need for fundamental social change.

NOTES

1. Randolph Bourne, "The Next Revolution," *Columbia Monthly* (May 1913).

2. Notably in James Weinstein, *The Decline of Socialism in America, 1912–1925* (New York, 1967).

3. See Weinstein, op. cit., ch. 4.

COMMENT 2

Ann J. Lane

The selections from the late Clinton Rossiter's *Marxism: The View from America* suggest the aura—I cannot say charm—of a period piece, the quality of another era, not so long gone but hopefully in our past permanently. The specter that was haunting Rossiter surely could not be as simple-minded as he would have it, else how explain the seriousness of its threat or the seduction of its appeal. To account for the tone and substance of the comments excerpted here, in the context of a life's work of otherwise impressive and significant stature, one must point to the heavy hand of the 1950s and sadly recognize the enormous price extracted, although voluntarily, from the intellectual community during those grim years.

The important body of Marxist thought does not end with Marx, in spite of Rossiter's implication to the contrary. In a general way Marx himself foresaw the limitations of his own analysis; he recognized in advance that social relations would undoubtedly alter in important ways that were not predictable. Since his day, and especially in the last generation, there have been sustained and valuable efforts to extend the essentials of his argument to contemporary experiences. Although the Marxist intellectual community is somewhat less developed in the United States than elsewhere, the increasing number of sophisticated and competent scholars in this country too, respectably established in universities, will make difficult a recurrence on that level of the charges directed at what purports to be Marxism. The list of contributors in the table of contents of this volume alone attests to the existence of an ongoing debate. To refuse to recognize, as Rossiter seems to, the extended body of Marxist thought as encompassing an entire intellectual community is to distort and deny the value of its total contribution and to reduce markedly the value of his criticisms.

What can one say in response to Rossiter's description of the American tradition as rooted "in the dignity of man, the excellence of liberty, the limits of politics and the presence of God"? (And note that it is soon followed by an assertion, made in the name of liberty, that Marxism is so inherently authoritarian that it is "hard to grant it license.") In a few pages Marx is ridiculed for giving "first place" to the power of human reason and then denounced for locking man permanently as a "good member of an economic class," which is the way Rossiter erroneously interprets Marx's view of man as the ensemble of social relations. At the same time Rossiter denies that man is as plastic as Marx suggests, or as Rossiter says Marx suggests. Rossiter too would like man to be capable of perfection, but he is burdened with "vicious tendencies" (Marx's phrase which Rossiter misuses) that are "deeply implanted in human nature." As if to compensate for this tragic failing, Rossiter asserts that man is also imbued with a "spirit of self-reliance and desire for freedom" that transcend any given society. We are then informed that Marx believed a new race of men will be derived by "conscious manipulation of the social environment." Marx's extraordinary and complex views of alienation are reduced to "anxiety," which, Rossiter tells us, is a permanent condition because humanity "is trapped by the paradox of human existence." Freedom becomes to Rossiter "an eternal paradox" that leaves all men in a state of tension "as part of the human condition."

Setting aside, for the moment, what Marx meant, or at least what I think Marx meant, the contradiction that spills out of Rossiter (and represents one element in American conservative thought in general) is what fascinates. On the one hand there is the "human condition" and "the paradox of human existence"—a secularized original sin. On the other hand, Rossiter is committed to the American myth. If radicals have failed to untangle their view of mankind from the American dream machine, conservatives such as Rossiter are no further along. (There are other conservatives who offer a more serious challenge to the traditional radical view, or views, of mankind, but it is not possible to confront their analysis here.)

Rossiter also presents the reader with a difficult methodological problem. His conclusion, that the Marxist critique, as he re-creates it, is invalid because the American experience disproves it, is built into the method. He presents a tautology that cannot be criticized but only accepted or rejected. He takes as given that which must be tested and then, not surprisingly, proudly proclaims he has proved his case.

In the process of redesigning Marx to fit a Cold War mold, Rossiter ignores several painful historical and contemporary social problems; the evolution of political theory from John Locke and John Stuart Mill to the present suggests some of the reasons for Rossiter's neglect.[1] Seventeenth- and eighteenth-century liberal democratic theory developed as a way of enlisting support from the whole of society against the common enemy; at the same time it wished to protect itself from increasingly radical pressures. Its definitions of liberty, equality, and fraternity as the formal protection of law, minimal state power, and economic struggle independent of others—all conformed to the needs of an emerging market economy. Liberal democratic theory, in an effort to generalize its appeal, went on to argue that these procedural protections ultimately led to substantive ones. Rossiter simply proclaims the truth of that proposition and offers no demonstration of its validity, despite overwhelming evidence in recent years to the contrary from liberals as well as radicals.

Locke and Mill, in an effort to defend their position, resorted to some ambivalent conceptions, of which they were at least dimly aware. Locke begins with the assumption of equality of men in a state of nature (even as a theoretical model Marx rejected the possibility of man outside of society, but saw society as a force for defining humanity) and ends up with a political and economic system that protects unequal property, without providing a satisfactory explanation of how the first led to the second and without being content with the inequities. C. B. MacPherson in his extended essay on Locke brilliantly locates the source of the contradiction in Locke's ambivalent views of human nature. While MacPherson emphasizes the logical evolution of Locke's thought, rather than a struggle between conflicting elements within it, he concludes by exposing those confusions, which he describes as the "result of honest deduction from a postulate of equal natural rights which contained its own contradiction."[2] John Stuart Mill too struggled, unsuccessfully but nobly, to explain how the human values he cherished could flourish in an inhuman society he defended. Forced to choose, because he forced himself to examine honestly, he chose the system over the values. In Mill's words:

> In all human affairs, every person directly interested . . . has an admitted claim to a voice. . . . But though everyone ought to have a voice—that everyone should have an equal voice is a totally different proposition. When two persons who have a joint interest in any business differ in opinion, does justice require that both opinions should be held of exactly equal voice?[3]

It is, as one critic said, "the equal right of all to participate in an unequal . . . system,"[4] and while Locke and Mill were concerned with establishing a political structure in which different interests would be protected from each other, they recognized and did not challenge the desirability of those different interests. The very existence of a political system based upon checks and balances and the division of power, a system Rossiter endorses, suggests a social order built on inequality, a conception Rossiter denies but early political theorists reluctantly admitted. At least they, and many others, including Adam Smith, who struggled to understand the origin of profit, confronted the problems directly and maintained and endorsed commitments to democracy if they could not convincingly reconcile all disparate aspects of their thought. Most twentieth-century theorists deny the problem and reject the ideal, Rossiter placing himself in the first category but not having the consistency to recognize that he also belongs in the second. Contemporary spokesmen for the "American way of life" no longer are concerned with the roots of social inequality but rather accept it as given and speak instead to the existence of mass manipulation and "the human condition." If it is "realistic" in relation to current conditions, it also illustrates the degeneration of the democratic doctrine. The freedom for which Locke and Mill spoke denied dependence on others and repudiated social obligations. In the seventeenth and eighteenth centuries these weaknesses were balanced by the strength of the vision they endorsed, for if their notion of freedom inherently denied freedom to many it did provide it for many others. By the twentieth century the social good to be gleaned from their propositions has worn bare and we are left with only the inhuman and antisocial elements. It becomes less painful simply to proclaim an end to ideology than to confront its bankruptcy.

If Rossiter's answers are disappointing, the kinds of questions to which he addressed himself are provocative and important. Marx's work is not without error, limitation, or incompleteness. Capitalism has obviously proved more flexible than he anticipated. Indeed, much of the ambivalence with which later supporters have had to contend is inherent in the body of Marx's writings, though not in the way it is represented by Rossiter. Although the world has much changed, Marx's analysis remains in its essentials valid. Despite the many differences among Marxists, there is a large body of thought, from Marx and Engels to the present, whose fundamentals are shared. To paraphrase one contemporary analyst, if we must go beyond Marx to understand the present world we cannot go without him.[5] Advances made in socialist theory in years past can be dramatically compared to the increasing impoverishment of liberal democratic theory. One thinks immediately of André Gorz, George Lukács, Antonio Gramsci, and Louis Althusser, among many others, without easily discovering liberal counterparts.

Rossiter's critique challenges many of Marx's basic conceptions such as the source of state power, class structure, and class struggle but I would like to single out for brief comment Marx's and Marxist views of individualism, political democracy, and ideology.

Rossiter's claim that Marx was uninterested in individuals, a traditional complaint, misrepresents Marx, who saw the reality of the individual in the totality of his social relations. Man's individuality, to Marx, is a product of his relationships; it has no meaning beyond them. Marx believed with Rossiter that man has an "essence," but not one that is eternal and permanent. Not only is man always in the process of change but that change is the core of the process of development. Man, not raw economic fact, as Antonio Gramsci said, is the center of Marx's thought. Rossiter may insist that man can transcend his social relations, but Gramsci's observation that man "is a conformist to some conformity" is considerably more perceptive.[6]

The political rights that the individual in this society enjoys are to Marx the rights of persons in civil society, of the individual separated from his fellows and from his community. Under this social order political rights are the rights of self-interest. "As a result every man finds in other men not the realization but rather the limitation of his freedom," said Marx. By defining freedom as a private matter, freedom under capitalism is what one obtains by depriving others. While Marx paid great attention to the achievements of capitalist society, total human freedom, as Marx defined it, must come in the realm of social relations.

Marx's balance of choice and determinism is complicated and not entirely satisfactory. "Man makes his own history, but he does not make it out of whole cloth, he does not make it out of conditions chosen by himself but only of such as he finds at hand." The difficulties that are inherent in such a proposition, that indeed can be traced to Marx's work—where does choice end and determinism begin?—have been commented on by many, perhaps most brilliantly by André Gorz, who examines the idea of man as "half-victim, half accomplice," or as "involuntarily accomplice," who, "having produced an involuntary order [is] led to will that order."[7]

On the matter of political power as defined by the franchise, Marx, frequently impatient, probably was, as Rossiter said, "contemptuous"; his critique, nevertheless, goes beyond ill temper. The counting of votes, while undeniably an important ingredient in legitimate democratic process, is hardly by itself a measure of democracy. Voting itself is the last phase of a long process; that process, which includes all levels and qualities of a society's "ability to . . . persuade,"[8] demonstrates that voting may be a necessary part of a democratic society but it is not a sufficient one.

The "ability to . . . persuade"—the realm of ideology—leads to one of Marx's most significant contributions. Representing the way a given epoch looks at the world, any ideology distorts and imposes its distortions on reality, at the same time that it reflects a certain degree of reality, without which it could not adequately function. What is crucial, this total world view is accepted voluntarily by those living under it. It is easier to see the ideological force of societies other than one's own, but the capitalist vision is as subject to examination as any other, particularly for those, like Rossiter, to whom the world of ideas is familiar. Capitalism has created a world view in which the pursuit of material wealth is glorified, a view that maintains that material progress is an important ingredient of human happiness and one in which individual effort, multiplied many times, results in the general good. It is a world view that defends and claims to be based, as to an extent it is, upon reason, law, and efficiency. Marx saw his role as critic to remove the ideological façade and expose the social mechanisms that underlie it. Rossiter offers the façade as real.

The world being much more complicated than it was, revolutionary critiques will in the future have to confront the problems of two world views: capitalism and socialism. If Marxism is to be a critique of all existing societies we need "a relentless Marxist critique of Marxism"[9] and a careful examination of those societies that claim to operate under its principles.

Rossiter, after asserting that he does not fault Marx for the failures of the Soviet Union—a concession he ought not to have made in the first place—then faults Marx for the failures of the Soviet Union. Where he might have examined the development of that nation in its relationship to Marxism and thereby deepened our understanding of both, he instead relied on invective. "All history is but the continuous transformation of human nature," Marx wrote. In the course of the many centuries that capitalism struggled within the existing feudal order "bourgeois man" was born and matured slowly. By the time capitalism emerged as the victor, those qualities associated with bourgeois man—rationalism, competitiveness, individualism—had been long developed and refined. The "transformation of human nature" had already occurred in the process of the struggle between two competing social orders.[10] The transition to socialism did not and probably cannot occur as the result of that kind of slow process. "Socialist man"—one whose ideology should encompass a commitment to cooperation, equalitarianism, community—does not develop in the process of capitalist growth and decay. The establishment of socialism requires not simply a new set of social relations but a changed consciousness. Without engaging in dispute over the "real" nature of Soviet society it is now clear that the construction of socialism there is at best incomplete and unsatisfactory. The Russian experience provides "devastating proof of the impossibility of infusing seemingly socialist forms—such as nationalized means of production and comprehensive economic planning—with genuine socialist content unless the process goes hand-in-hand with the formation of social human beings." The limited information from China suggests that there for the first time the significance of this problem is recognized. Whatever failures occur in the coming years in China, much has apparently been learned from the Russian catastrophe.[11]

In addition to a Marxist critique of Marxism, the traditional Marxist critique of world capitalism requires extension, refinement, and revision. Socialism has failed in the United States because it has not convinced the American community that it is preferable. There are many and serious reasons in this century for the disinterest that Americans have shown to socialism, beyond the obvious one of affluence. Socialist doctrine has been too long burdened by its inability to offer a reasoned and reasonable analysis of Soviet, Chinese, and Cuban experiences. At the same time, and connected to that failure, has been the inability to examine judiciously and intelligently "bourgeois rights" in a way that recognizes their limitation and their historic role but also their immense value for human development. Marx's criticism of bourgeois rights, when seen as part of the specific political struggle in which he was actively engaged, and not as justification for denial of those rights in communist countries, has an entirely different significance from that attributed to it by Rossiter. If bourgeois rights are a fraud, they are also real. If they are limited they must be extended, not denounced for being limited and then denied. Marxism attempts to offer an explanation of the origin and function of liberal democratic social order but it does not follow that the gains made by it are insignificant or undesirable.

The struggle in the West is, in Gramsci's words, not in "pitched battles between classes: the class struggle becomes a 'war of position,' and the 'cultural front' the principal area of conflict."[12] The difficulties facing any socialist movement become enormous when one recognizes the overwhelming strength of the dominant ideology and the success with which the ruling class has been able to persuade the mass of the population that its interests represent those of the society at large. Thus it is the "totality of the bourgeois world view," as one contemporary Marxist said, "—the enormous complex of prejudices, assumptions, half-thought-out notions and so small number of profound ideas—that infects the victims of bourgeois rule, and it is the totality of an alternative world view that alone can challenge it for supremacy."[13]

The socialist movement in this country has traditionally tried to work within the trade union movement in an effort to demonstrate that capitalism has been unable to satisfy the needs it created and provide the kind of life it promised, not an easy or wise task to set for itself in the face of the material progress many Americans have enjoyed. Radical movements in our past have trapped themselves into accepting the definition of those needs and satisfactions as created by the capitalist vision: essentially more and better commodities. The very instrument for evaluating the "good life" in twentieth-century America—the statistic that can tell us how many people own automobiles—is itself an ideological tool and ideological concept that parades as an objective measure of an objective world. Only recently has the notion that well-being is identified with the accumulation of commodities been challenged. American society is torn by what seems to be disparate elements demanding entirely different satisfactions. There are, first, the poor, whose existence we can no longer explain away as a product of individual weakness or temporary social maladjustment but have come to recognize, reluctantly, as a permanent and organic part of the system. They see the wealth all around and most still maintain the hope that someday they will share in it. Then there are those, small in number but vocal, who, having grown with the affluence, reject it. They recognize, as earlier radicals did not, that this kind of abundance is insufficient and inhuman. Those who are poor and demand equity and those who have certain material comforts but reject them are largely unaware that their dissatisfactions derive from the same social process. Most Americans, who fall into neither of those categories, do share a sense of unease about the malfunctioning of their society: problems of air, water, food, the aged, the young, war, racism, crime, violence, drugs, but see these difficulties as part of the "human condition," or the process of industrialization, which to some extent they are, amenable to amelioration but not elimination. Industrialization, regardless of social system, generates great problems: the possibility of a solution to those problems resides in another realm.

We have yet to forge a critique that connects this social malaise with what is known as the "consumer society," with the phenomenon of men as owners of the machine, not the machines of production, but the machines of consumption, which give an unreal sense of power and provide the façade of control. The acquisition of things provides us as consumers, one analyst asserts, the power to make "technical choices in the service of inhuman needs, a passive 'freedom,' in which our choice is limited to which form of passivity we wish," increased physical comfort that leads to a "reduction of our *being* to the dimension of *having*."[14] Unfortunately, Rossiter's critique does not get us on our way.

NOTES

1. For a useful critique, upon which my remarks are based, see Richard Lichtman, "The Facade of Equality in Liberal Democratic Theory," *Socialist Revolution,* vol. I, no. 1 (January–February 1970), pp. 85–126.

2. *The Political Theory of Progressive Individualism: Hobbes to Locke* (London: Oxford University Press, 1962), p. 251.

3. *Considerations on Representative Government* (Indianapolis: Bobbs-Merrill, 1958), p. 24, as quoted in Lichtman, op. cit., p. 106.

4. Lichtman, op. cit., p. 106.

5. Svetozar Stokanovic, "Marxism and Socialism Now," *New York Review of Books,* July 1, 1971, p. 16.

6. *The Modern Prince and Other Writings* (New York: International Publishers, 1959), p. 58.

7. *The Traitor* (New York: Simon & Schuster, 1959), p. 46.

8. In discussing the importance of the franchise, Gramsci said: an "instrumental value, which offers a measure and a relationship and nothing more. . . . What is measured is precisely the effectiveness and ability to expand and persuade." Op. cit., p. 183.

9. Stokanovic, op. cit., p. 16.

10. See discussion by Paul Sweezy, *Monthly Review: An Independent Socialist Magazine,* vol. 23, no. 1 (May 1971), pp. 1–16.

11. Ibid., p. 12.

12. John Cammett, *Antonio Gramsci and the Origins of Italian Communism* (Stanford: Stanford University Press, 1967), p. 190.

13. Eugene D. Genovese, *In Red and Black: Marxian Explorations in Southern and Afro-American History* (New York: Pantheon, 1971), p. 408.

14. Richard Lichtman, "Capitalism and Consumption," *Socialist Revolution,* vol. 1, no. 3 (May–June 1970), p. 92.

Chapter 11

SOCIALISM AND SOCIAL MOBILITY*

Stephan Thernstrom

Few clichés are more venerable than that which holds that the more fluid the composition of the working class of a given society and the greater the opportunity to climb from lower to higher rungs of the class ladder, the less the likelihood of sharply class-conscious collective working-class protest. Marx, of course, assumed this in his well-known remark about mid-nineteenth-century America, where, "though classes, indeed, already exist, they have not yet become fixed, but continually change and interchange their elements in a constant state of flux," and American public figures from the Age of Jackson to the Age of Johnson have devoted much rhetoric to the same alleged phenomenon, though disagreeing with Marx, I need hardly say, about both its permanence and its desirability.[1]

It is the fate of clichés, however, to escape serious critical scrutiny. So at least in this instance. It is impossible to write about a social group—the working class, the bourgeoisie, or whatever—without making assumptions about the extent to which its composition is stable or in flux, without making assumptions about patterns of social recruitment and social mobility. And yet few students of working-class history have made systematic—in this case, I believe, systematic is synonymous with quantitative—attempts to measure the social mobility of ordinary working people in the past. Thus we have an excellent and generally well-documented survey of the American laboring man in the 1920's baldly asserting, without supporting evidence, that "the worker was seldom afforded the opportunity to rise in the social scale. He lacked the qualifications for the professions and the capital for business."[2] More surprising and amusing is a major historical study of the American

* Chapter 8 from Melvin Richter (ed.), *Essays in Theory and History* (Cambridge: Harvard University Press, 1970), originally entitled "Working-Class Social Mobility in Industrial America."

labor force by one of the "new" economic historians, who prefaces some ingenious new statistical estimates of unemployment rates in nineteenth-century depressions with the sound remark that the traditional historian's tendency to rely upon the impressions of contemporary observers yields a better measure of variations in the prose styles of those observers than of variations in actual unemployment; he then blithely proceeds to explain America's rapid economic development as the consequence of the country's exceptionally fluid social system, with nary a hard fact to support the claim that American society was less rigidly stratified than any other.[8] The need for careful empirical examination of propositions such as these should be self-evident.

This paper reports on some of the recent work which is beginning to provide something more than an impressionistic outline of working-class social mobility patterns in the United States in the past century or so, drawing heavily on my own work on Boston in the period 1880–1963. Research of this kind, I believe, can take us one small step toward a better understanding of the vast question of the relationship between social mobility and class solidarity, and the slightly less vast related question of the sources of American exceptionalism. Studies of American materials alone, of course, can take us but a limited distance, for these questions demand comparisons between nations. The absence of an American labor party cannot be explained in terms of the uniquely high level of mobility opportunities open to the American worker without demonstrating that the composition of the working class in the United States has been highly volatile not in some absolute sense, but volatile relative to other societies in which a strong labor or socialist party has emerged.

As yet there has been very little historical research on social mobility in other societies, though there has been a good deal of contemporary work by sociologists, so that for the present we must settle for the unsatisfactory tactic of evaluating the American findings largely in isolation. It should be noted, however, that the two major efforts at comparative analysis of national differences in mobility rates and patterns since World War II, those by Lipset and Bendix and S. M. Miller, pose a powerful challenge to the assumption that American society has been uniquely open and that its relatively classless politics may be attributed to that circumstance. Lipset and Bendix argue that "widespread social mobility has been a concomitant of industrialization and a basic characteristic of modern industrial society, and though Miller is somewhat more impressed with differences between nations, his analysis too has a basically revisionist thrust.[4] There are a good many technical objections which might be raised against these studies—most important, that their measure of mobility, the rate of intergeneration movement between blue-collar and white-collar occupations, is much too narrow, that major differences between national social structures cannot be captured in so crude a sieve. And there is the obvious objection that occurs to the historian: that whatever similarities there may be between mobility rates in various industrialized countries since World War II, it is by no means evident that we may safely extrapolate these findings backward to the time, probably somewhere in the nineteenth century, at which the political role of the working class was initially defined. The as-yet unpublished research of William H. Sewell, Jr. on the working class of nineteenth-century Marseille, coupled with my own work on Boston, suggests that such extrapolation may be quite unfounded. The two of us are presently collaborating on a paper which will argue that the sons of Marseille workers escaped into nonmanual occupations with far less frequency than was the case in Boston.

Nevertheless, we must be prepared for the possibility that further mobility research, which should some day permit elaborate and systematic comparative historical analysis, will yield the conclusion that variations in objective mobility opportunities, between nations or over time within a nation, do not in themselves explain very much, that mobility data are meaningless except within a context of well-defined attitudes and expectations about the class system, and that these attitudes and expectations may be most unstable and susceptible to change. Thus, as I have argued elsewhere, the current complaints of American Negroes about their constricted opportunities are the result not of any real deterioration of the position of blacks, but rather of the fact that blacks today are no longer comparing their achievements with those of blacks yesterday, but with those of previous white immigrants and indeed with a romanticized stereotype of the immigrant experience, a stereotype drawn more from the experience of the Jews than that of the Irish or Italians.[5] Similarly, in a fascinating recent paper on social mobility in France on the eve of the explosion of 1789, Philip Dawson and Gilbert Shapiro have shown paradoxically that in those areas where the institutional structure of the ancient regime "made it possible for a bourgeois to improve his social position in a most significant way—by becoming legally a noble— . . . disapproval of the existing system, particularly the details of class and status, was most vigorously manifested. And conversely, where the bourgeois was denied the right to improve his social position in this way . . . demands for change in general and for reform of the system of rewards for achievement in particular were neither powerful nor widespread."[6] This too should remind us that there is no simple mechanical relationship among social mobility, class solidarity, and political radicalism that holds for all classes, societies, and historical epochs, and that the austerely objective facts uncovered by empirical social research influence the course of history only as they are mediated through the consciousness of obstinately subjective human beings. Though in the body of this paper I largely confine myself to some conveniently measurable aspects of the historical experience of the American working class, I would agree with Edward Thompson that the development of the working class "is a fact of political and cultural, as much as of economic, history."[7] The political and cultural dimensions get short shrift in what follows, not because I think them unimportant but because space is limited and I think it appropriate to concentrate on the least well-known aspects of American working-class history.

I

The first phenomenon which demands attention—geographical mobility, or population turnover—is not normally considered an aspect of social mobility, but I suggest that movement through space, movement into and out of communities, may retard the development of class consciousness in a manner somewhat analogous to movement into a higher social stratum. In his suggestive paper on interindustry differences in the propensity of workers to strike, Clark Kerr proposes that varying degrees of social integration or isolation of the labor force account for the tendency of workers in certain industries to be exceptionally strike-prone and in others to be exceptionally quiescent.[8] In some industrial environments—most notoriously the logging camp, the mining town, the ship, the docks—laboring men form what Kerr calls "an isolated mass." One element making for isolation in these cases is the absence of a complex occupational hierarchy—the absence of a labor aristocracy, really—and minimal opportunities for upward social mobility. This is the venerable assumption mentioned at the outset of this paper, and I will present some data pertaining to it at a later point. But Kerr also alludes to the related variable which is of immediate concern when he remarks that men in the "isolated mass" not only "have the same grievances, but they have them at the same time, at the same place, and against the same people." Conversely, it is well known that certain occupations are inordinately resistant to efforts at trade union organization because they have spectacularly high rates of job turnover. When only 5 percent of the men working at a particular job in a given city at the start of a year are still employed there twelve months later (as is the case in the United States today with short-order cooks and menial hospital employees, for instance), how do you build a stable disciplined organization? An adequate model of the conditions which promote working-class solidarity must presume not only relative permanence of membership in the class—that is, low levels of upward occupational mobility—but also some continuity of class membership *in one setting,* so that workers come to know one another and to develop bonds of solidarity and common opposition to the class above them. This might require a stable labor force in a given place of work; data on labor turnover at the plant level are important if this be the case. But I will give "continuity of class membership in one setting" a looser definition and use it to mean considerable stability of the working class at least within a given city, which would seem to be a minimal necessity if mere complaints are to be translated effectively into class grievances and to inspire collective protest.

Such is the model suggested by Kerr, but he regrettably did nothing to *test* his assumptions about rates of labor turnover, or for that matter rates of occupational mobility, in relatively strike-prone and relatively strike-free industries. Kerr's article provides a persuasive theoretical rationale for systematic scrutiny of labor turnover and occupational mobility; we will have to look elsewhere for solid evidence bearing on these two subjects.

As to the first—geographical mobility—it has long been assumed that the American population has been exceptionally volatile, that Americans have been a uniquely restless, wandering breed. Not until 1940, however, did the Census Bureau include a census question asking where respondents had lived five years previously. Before 1935, population mobility from place to place can be studied in only two ways. One can examine the Census Bureau's tabulations of state of birth data and discover in any census year what fraction of the American population was living in a state other than their state of birth, a useful but exceedingly crude index of internal migration patterns.[9] The other method is what I and a few others have begun to do–to take manuscript census schedules or some other lists of a city's inhabitants at two points in time, and to compute rates of persistence and turnover for the intervening period. This is slow, tedious, and expensive, but it gives a far more accurate sense of the degree to which past Americans–and in particular, working-class Americans–have characteristically remained long within the boundaries of a unit more meaningful than an entire state.

All of the work which has been done–and it is admittedly exceedingly fragmentary–tends to support the stereotype of American rootlessness and to suggest that an "isolated mass" whose members have grievances "at the same time, at the same place, and against the same people" has been a rare species in the United States. The first study of this kind was James C. Malin's classic article "The Turnover of the Farm Population in Kansas," written thirty-three years ago and little noticed.[10] Both Malin's article and the later inquiry which stimulated much of the current American interest in quantitative social history–Merle Curti's 1959 book on a Wisconsin frontier county in the 1850–1880 period–seemed for a time to be of doubtful relevance to the larger question, since the staggeringly fluid and shifting population they described was on the booming agricultural frontier.[11] It was entirely possible that Americans were more settled in more settled regions of the country, perhaps especially within the cities. And there was the further possibility that figures registering high turnover rates for the population as a whole concealed large deviations from the mean by particular groups–that, for example, there was a majority of ambitious, rising men incessantly on the move, but a substantial minority of low-skilled laborers trapped in urban ghettos.

Both of these possibilities may now be dismissed. Blake McKelvey's examination of Rochester, New York, in the middle of the nineteenth century, my Newburyport inquiry for the same period, and Doherty's research in progress on Northampton, Massachusetts, suggest that the urban population was highly volatile, with half or more of the adult population disappearing from the community in the course of only a decade.[12] Nor is it the case that men on the bottom were immobilized by their poverty, an isolated mass, unlike their restless superiors. To the contrary. In Newburyport and Northampton the working class was more volatile than the middle class, with the least skilled and least well-paid workers most volatile of all. Ray Ginger's analysis of the turnover of textile workers in Holyoke, Massachusetts, in the 1850's points to the same conclusion.[13]

When I began my Boston study, however, I was still a little uneasy about how far this argument could be pressed. Newburyport, after all, was a way station in the orbit of a major metropolis—many of the Irish laborers there had landed in Canada and were in fact slowly working their way down the coast to Boston. Rochester was similarly a stepping stone to the West. Thus these cities might have an unusually large transient population, and there was the more general consideration that relatively small cities might well differ from big cities in this respect. It seemed reasonable to assume that the laborers who drifted out of Newburyport so quickly after their arrival must eventually have settled down somewhere else and that a great metropolis would have offered a more inviting haven than a small community, where anonymity was impossible and institutions of social control pervasive, as contrasted with the classic big-city lower-class ghetto, in which the down-and-out might huddle together in an enduring, protective "culture of poverty." In a major metropolis like Boston, if anywhere in the United States, one might expect to find a stable lower-class population, an isolated mass, a permanent proletariat.

This expectation proved false. If Boston was at all typical, and I believe that it was, in no American city has there been a large lower-class element with continuity of membership. More or less continuously lower-class *areas* can be identified, but *the same individuals do not live in them very long.* As in Newburyport and other small nineteenth-century cities which have been studied, the chance that a worker appearing in a Boston census would be in the community to be counted at the next one a decade later was roughly fifty-fifty throughout the period from 1880 to the present. It is possible that these men in motion typically went to find better jobs, if not fame and fortune, elsewhere. American folklore has always held that migration and upward social mobility go hand in hand, but the point has never been demonstrated with historical evidence; given the sources, it is virtually impossible to explore the issue before the age of modern survey research. In any event it is clear that the bottom layer of the social order of the American city in the past century has included large numbers of permanent transients, unable to sink roots and to form organizations. So rapid was the turnover at this level that the seemingly innocuous residency requirements for voting—typically requiring a year's residence prior to the election—must have disenfranchised a sizable fraction of the working-class population. If the population turnover for Boston is computed on an annual rather than a decennial basis, as I have been able to do using the city directories for the period 1837–1921, it can be determined that roughly a quarter of the population at any one date had not been living in the community 365 days before! This figure is for the entire population, not simply the working class, and the volatility of the working class, especially the unskilled and semiskilled portion of the working class, was even greater. A great many workers, therefore, were legally barred from political participation because they were birds of passage; a great many more, though they remained in Boston long enough to meet the legal residency requirement, were doubtless sufficiently transient in psychology to be politically and socially inert.

These findings are very suggestive, even in the absence of comparable information about working-class-population turnover rates in other societies. The absolute figures themselves are so dramatic as to give considerable credence to the interpretation I put upon them. But it is, of course, important to know if the American experience is at all special in this respect, or if we are instead confronted with a phenomenon common to all industrial societies—or indeed all societies. We know pathetically little about this aspect of demographic history. There are some recently published fragments which raise questions about the assumption of American uniqueness—the remarkable volatility disclosed by the Laslett and Wrigley studies of two seventeenth-century English villages and Lawrence Wylie's demonstration that the population of the seemingly placid, sleepy rural commune of Rousillon today is strikingly unstable.[14] Some fascinating research in progress on late nineteenth-century France, however, squares nicely with the argument advanced here. Joan Scott's study of the glassblowers of Carmaux and Albi links the sharp rise in labor militancy that occurred in the 1890's to the sudden settling down of formerly itinerant artisans.[15] With the French glassblowers as well as Eric Hobsbawm's "tramping artisans" and the sheep shearers of Australia and the United States, of course, a high degree of solidarity and craft identification was possible even in the itinerant phase; the distinction between labor turnover of this type and what I have been describing in the American city should be obvious. But that the disappearance of the itinerant pattern should heighten solidarity and militancy as it did in Carmaux and Albi helps to confirm the general hypothesis I have drawn from Clark Kerr's paper. Clearly it will take a good deal of European work comparable to that now going on in the United States to further clarify the relationship between physical mobility and class identification, but pending that I think there is a prima facie case for the view that remarkable volatility of the American working class, past and present, has been an important influence retarding the development and expression of distinctive class loyalties.

II

Let me now turn to the question of occupational mobility. Sometimes it is mistakenly taken to be the only dimension of social mobility worthy of close study, but that it is an important one goes without saying.

Enormous gaps exist in our knowledge about occupational mobility patterns in nineteenth and early twentieth-century America. A good deal is known about patterns of recruitment into the national business and political elite, but this tells us very little indeed about the range of opportunity at the lower and middle levels.[16] There is Curti's study of Trempeaulau County in the 1850–1880 period, but it would obviously be perilous to generalize from the Wisconsin frontier to the urban frontier. There is my work on the unskilled laborers of Newburyport in the same years. But my attempt at the end of that book to argue that Newburyport was America in microcosm was more open to questions than I realized at the time. I had found little movement from working-class to middle-class occupations in my samples, though there was considerable upgrading within the manual category; the major achievement of the typical laborer in the community was to become a homeowner. At least four questions about the generalizability of this finding remained open:

1) Was it possible that the social structure of the large cities of this era was notably different—either more or less fluid?

2) Was Newburyport atypical even for small cities, in that its rate of population growth and economic expansion in the years I treated was unusually low?

3) I examined the career patterns of unskilled workmen and their children. Might not a study of the skilled craftsmen have yielded much greater evidence of interclass mobility?

4) A large majority of the unskilled laborers in Newburyport were recently arrived Irish immigrants. To what extent would mobility patterns have differed in a community in which the working class was less heavily immigrant, or immigrant but not Irish?

It was in hopes of clearing up some of these uncertainties that some years ago I began work on a large-scale statistical study of the career patterns of some 6,500 ordinary residents of Boston in the years 1880–1963. The analysis is not yet complete, but the main outlines of the argument are fairly clear.

It does appear either that Newburyport was an unusually sluggish place for aspiring laborers, or that small cities in general offer fewer opportunities; rates of movement from blue-collar to white-collar posts, both in the course of a career and between generations, were much higher in Boston throughout the entire period. If an individual's first job was in a blue-collar calling, the odds were that at the end of his career he would still be in the working class. But a substantial minority of men climbed to a middle-class post, usually in small business or in minor clerical and sales positions, and remained there—25 to 30 percent in the five cohorts I traced. There were, in addition, others who began in the blue-collar world, worked for a period in a nonmanual position, and fell back into a manual job later in life. Very little of this upward mobility involved penetration into the upper reaches of the middle class, to be sure; these men did not become professionals, corporation managers, or the heads of large business operations. But certainly here was evidence which challenged the socialist critic's assumption that the dream of individual mobility was illusory and that collective advance was the only realistic hope for the worker.

Even more impressive was the opportunity to escape the class into which one was born—the class of one's father. Fully 40 percent of the working-class sons in Boston held middle-class jobs of some kind by the end of their own careers. The comparable figure for mid-nineteenth-century Marseille, William H. Sewell, Jr., has found, was a mere 11 percent. And if there was any rationality in the system by which the 40 percent who climbed were selected from the entire pool of working-class sons, they must have included much of the leadership potential which would have accrued to the working-class cause in a more rigidly stratified society.

Both types of mobility—career and intergenerational—occurred at a relatively constant rate over this entire eighty-year period. There were some minor temporal fluctuations, with the Great Depression of the 1930's showing diminished opportunities, as we would expect, but the overall similarity of the figures is very striking. To lament the creeping arteriosclerosis of the class system has been a popular American pastime for many a year, but the facts do not sustain this diagnosis.[17] The economy, the political structure, and a good many other aspects of Boston changed dramatically over this long span of time, but whatever governs the rate of circulation between occupations seems to have been highly resistant to change.

It is also noteworthy, and not a little surprising, that the sons of the least advantaged members of the working class—the sons of the unskilled and semiskilled—fared just as well in the competition for middle-class jobs as did the children of the labor aristocracy. That my Newburyport study dealt only with unskilled laboring families was therefore not as limiting as I had feared. The average rate of penetration into the middle-class world by the sons of unskilled and semiskilled workmen in Boston was actually a little above the 40 percent figure for the entire working class, with the figure for the children of skilled craftsmen a little below 40 percent. Similarly with respect to intragenerational, or career mobility, the 25 to 30 percent rate of ascent into the middle class for men who began their careers in a working-class job held for all grades of manual jobs—the lowest as well as the highest.

This is striking in light of the observation of Eric Hobsbawm and Royden Harrison that in nineteenth-century Britain perhaps the greatest break in the class hierarchy was between the labor aristocrat and the less skilled men below him. "The boundaries of the labor aristocracy were fluid on one side of its territory," the upper side, where it "merged with" the lower middle class, but "they were precise on the other." This is in part, though only in part, a judgment about mobility opportunities; the English labor aristocrat's "prospects of future advancement and those of his children" were allegedly much better than the prospects of ordinary workingmen.[18] That does not seem to have been the case in Boston. Now it is possible that Hobsbawm and Harrison are mistaken in their claim; the most judicious observers can go astray when they attempt to gauge mobility rates on the basis of qualitative rather than quantitative evidence. It should also be noted that we are not talking about precisely the same group; my working-class elite is simply all men in recognized skilled trades, whereas Hobsbawm and Harrison have in mind a much more select group, at most the top 15 percent of wage earners. For a variety of reasons I was unable to isolate a small element within the skilled category that would be exactly comparable to what they mean by "the labor aristocracy." Nevertheless, it is quite possible that we are dealing here with a genuine historical difference between the social structures of the two societies, with the imperceptible blending of the British labor aristocracy into the lower middle class taking in the United States the form of a blending of the entire urban working class into the lower middle class. Sewell's work in Marseille suggests that there was indeed a labor aristocracy there; the sons of skilled craftsmen rose into middle-class callings at three times the rate of sons of unskilled workers.

The work of Hobsbawm and Harrison is also helpful in suggesting the desirability of examining occupational advance within the working class, as well as from the working class to the middle class. The mobility of a common laborer's son into the skilled category as I have defined it was less of an achievement than the presumably rare entry of a laborer's son into the labor aristocracy of nineteenth-century Britain, but it was surely a clear-cut advance with respect to wages, vulnerability to unemployment, and so forth. If we consider the total movement of sons of unskilled or semiskilled workmen into skilled or white-collar occupations in Boston, we find that somewhat more than 60 percent of the sons of the semiskilled and slightly less than 60 percent of the sons of the unskilled were upwardly mobile. (The comparable figure for the sons of skilled craftsmen—the percentage who reached either skilled or nonmanual occupations—was 75 percent.) If this is at all valid as a measure of opportunity for working-class children—if entry into a skilled trade is a significant accomplishment, as I think it was—a distinct minority of the sons of Boston workers had grounds for doubting that the United States was the land of opportunity, where classes "have not yet become fixed, but continually change and interchange their elements in a constant state of flux."

I should hasten to say that these figures are, in one significant way, inflated. They sum up the mobility experiences not of all of the hundreds of thousands of workingmen who lived in Boston at some time in the 1800–1963 period, but rather of those who settled down in the community long enough to have careers which might be measured. I have already stressed the remarkable volatility of the American population, and here I should point out that this fact must be taken into account in interpreting findings based on the study of people who were sufficiently settled to remain under the investigator's microscope long enough to be examined. This would pose no great difficulty if it could be assumed that disappearance from the universe of the study was more or less random, but the problem is that migration and occupational mobility were intimately and intricately related, that those men most likely to leave the community and to go uncounted probably had different occupational mobility prospects than those who remained. Different types of people left the city for a host of different reasons, and I wouldn't dare attempt to generalize about them all. But I would suggest that though much of the movement of men with skills or capital was in response to new opportunities elsewhere, much of the movement of relatively unskilled and uneducated working-class people was of a very different kind—it was helpless drifting rather than rational pursuit of more favorable circumstances elsewhere. I strongly suspect, therefore, that if it were possible for me to track down all of the laboring men who appeared in one of my Boston samples but migrated elsewhere—most likely several elsewheres—and worked the rest of their lives outside of Boston, the net effect of including them would be to depress somewhat the mobility rates I have reported. Some of these working-class migrants were doubtless highly successful elsewhere, but my guess is that most were not and that indeed their departure from Boston was a symptom of failure and an omen of future failure.

This is speculative—necessarily speculative, I fear, in that there is no way of systematically tracing migrants from an American community in the past. But it does appear from my data that the American city—perhaps the European city too, but it remains to be seen—is a kind of Darwinian jungle into which vast numbers of low-status migrants pour. Most of them do not flourish, most of them do not stay very long; a process of selection, of unnatural selection if you like, takes place. Those who do manage to make a go of it economically are not as likely to depart physically, which is why any collection of individuals who simply survive ten years to be counted in the next census have an average occupational rank higher than a sample of newcomers in the intervening decade. . . .

If the Boston data on working-class occupational mobility is any guide, [therefore] most American workers in the past eighty years who were in a position to make themselves heard had good reason to think that they were edging their way up the social scale, that there was no impassable gulf which separated the exploited masses from the privileged class which lived on the fruits of their labor. Many workers did not make it in Boston, but they did not remain on the scene long enough to make their weight felt and were tossed helplessly about from city to city, alienated but invisible and impotent. . . .

III

The final question on which I wish to comment briefly involves another discrepancy between the Newburyport and Boston studies. Perhaps the most striking finding of the former inquiry was that despite wage levels hovering close to what middle-class observers thought bare subsistence, recurring unemployment, and slight opportunities for occupational advance, the laborers of Newburyport (especially the Irish) were remarkably successful in accumulating substantial property holdings, largely in the form of small homes and plots of land. I argued that such property mobility—movement not into the middle class but from the floating lower class into the stable working class—was of great significance in minimizing discontent and tying these men into the prevailing order.

Herbert Gutman has quite properly taken me to task for my somewhat vulgar assumption that homeownership is an inherently conservatizing influence, and I am happy to retreat from my exposed position and concede that it all depends—upon the social setting, the expectations of the group in question, and perhaps other things as well.[19] What I would insist upon is only that possession of property is an important determinant of a man's social position and social allegiances, and that students of working-class history have been insufficiently diligent about investigating this aspect of their subject. Royden Harrison notes that at one point in *Order and Progress* (1875) Frederic Harrison wrote that "there is no greater break in our class hierarchy than that between the lowest of the propertied classes and the highest of the non-propertied classes" and at another place that "throughout all English society there is no break more marked than that which in cities divided the skilled from the unskilled workmen" without detecting the inconsistency.[20] One appreciates Frederic Harrison's confusion, for it is a neat question whether occupational rank or property position is the more powerful influence. Not enough thought has been given to this question, partly because we have too readily assumed that the latter can safely be inferred from the former—that few workmen, except for the highly skilled, were able to save significant amounts. Doubtless this has been true of many societies, and it may well explain Frederic Harrison's seeming inconsistency; the distinction between the unskilled and the nonpropertied may have been a distinction without a difference in the England of the 1870's. It was, however, an important distinction in the United States, if the Newburyport experience is any guide. The Newburyport evidence suggests that a substantial fraction of the American working class, including many unskilled and semiskilled workers, stood on the propertied rather than the nonpropertied side of the break in the class hierarchy.

I had hoped to be able to illuminate this matter further with my Boston materials, but that hope was disappointed. The only records available for the period since 1880 disclose real-property but not personal-property holdings, and it happens that Boston was a city with very few single-family dwellings; the $1,000 which purchased a small dwelling in Newburyport had to be increased several-fold to buy a triple-decker tenement. The very inadequate measure I have of working-class property holdings—a measure of real estate holdings only—thus drastically underestimates total wealth of the group. At the last date at which the sources include information about personal as well as real property, 1870, real estate owners were only 41 percent of the total group of Boston workers holding some property. I therefore can say with confidence that the true incidence of property ownership in the Boston working class since 1870 was much higher than the real estate tax records suggest, but since I don't know which individuals in my samples had large savings accounts and which didn't, I cannot analyze the characteristics of the propertied as opposed to the unpropertied worker. For a variety of reasons I was unable to fill this gap by consulting the savings bank depositor's records that I found so helpful in Newburyport.

Future investigators who are fortunate enough to have more adequate sources of information about personal savings, however, will still face difficult problems of interpretation, for it is evident that American working-class attitudes toward saving, investment, and consumption have shifted dramatically in this century. Whether today's automobiles and appliances, often purchased on the installment plan, are in any way equivalent to the nineteenth-century home—which is not to imply that working-class homeownership is a vanishing phenomenon, quite the contrary—is a knotty question I can't attempt to answer here, except to suggest that it seems important that becoming a homeowner in nineteenth-century Newburyport required prolonged disciplined behavior long before the goal could be attained, whereas today even the poor have become accustomed to flying now and paying later. This makes them highly vulnerable to economic vicissitudes, because many have made long-term financial commitments based on the most optimistic assumptions about future income and few have developed the remarkable penny-pinching facility of the laborers of Newburyport. They have more possessions, certainly, but perhaps less security comes with the possessions.

Systematic knowledge about working-class social mobility in industrial America, in sum, is scanty and spotty, but what little there is does seem to square with the age-old belief that social classes in the United States "continually change and interchange their elements in a constant state of flux." High rates of occupational and property mobility and selective patterns of urban migration which weeded out the unsuccessful and constantly reshuffled them together produced a social context in which a unified "isolated mass" of dispossessed, disaffected workmen could not develop. It would be valuable to be more certain that these generalizations do indeed apply throughout industrial America in the past century. It would be interesting to see if deviations from what I take to be the national pattern could help explain these instances in which groups of American workmen acted in a more militantly class-conscious manner than has generally been the case; studies of population turnover and social mobility in such settings as mining towns organized by the Western Federation of Miners and the I.W.W. could be very revealing. It would also be helpful to discover whether these forms of working-class mobility were equally available in societies in which class solidarity was a more conspicuous fact of national life—Britain, France, Germany, and so forth. The answers to these questions are by no means obvious. I am certain only that they are worth asking and exploring if the social history of the common people is to advance beyond mere impressionism.

NOTES

1. Karl Marx, *The Eighteenth Brumaire of Louis Bonaparte* (New York, n.d.), p. 22.

2. Irving Bernstein, *The Lean Years: A History of the American Worker, 1920–1933* (Boston, 1966), p. 58.

3. Stanley Lebergott, *Manpower in Economic Growth: The United States Record Since 1800* (New York, 1964), pp. 187, 227–28.

4. S. M. Lipset and Reinhard Bendix, *Social Mobility in Industrial Society* (Berkeley, Cal., 1959); S. M. Miller, "Comparative Social Mobility: A Trend Report and Bibliography," *Current Sociology*, IX (1960).

5. Stephan Thernstrom, "Poverty in Historical Perspective," in Daniel P. Moynihan (ed.), *On Understanding Poverty: Perspectives from the Social Sciences* (New York, 1959); Thernstrom, "On Black Power," *Partisan Review*, XXXV (1968), pp. 225–28. For a fascinating discussion of changing English attitudes toward social inequality since 1918 and their failure to correspond to changes in social reality, see W. G. Runciman, *Relative Deprivation and Social Injustice* (London, 1966).

6. Philip Dawson and Gilbert Shapiro, "Social Mobility and Political Radicalism: The Case of the French Revolution of 1789" (Unpublished paper delivered at the American Sociological Association meetings, August 1967).

7. E. P. Thompson, *The Making of the English Working Class* (London, 1964), p. 194.

8. Clark Kerr and A. J. Siegel, "The Interindustry Propensity to Strike–An International Comparison," in Kerr, *Labor and Management in Industrial Society* (Anchor paperback edition, Garden City, N.Y., 1964), pp. 105–47.

9. This material is exhaustively analyzed in Simon Kuznets, Dorothy S. Thomas, et al., *Population Redistribution and Economic Growth in the United States, 1870–1950*, 3 vols. (Philadelphia, 1957–64).

10. James C. Malin, "The Turnover of the Farm Population in Kansas," *Kansas Historical Quarterly*, IV (1935), pp. 339–71.

11. Merle Curti, et al., *The Making of an American Community: A Case Study of Democracy in a Frontier County* (Stanford, Cal., 1959). For comparable data on an Iowa farming county in the same period, see Mildred Throne, "A Population Study of an Iowa County in 1850," *Iowa Journal of History*, LVII (1959), pp. 306–30.

12. Blake McKelvey, *Rochester, The Flower City, 1855–1890* (Cambridge, Mass., 1949), p. 3; Stephan Thernstrom, *Poverty and Progress: Social Mobility in a Nineteenth Century City* (Cambridge, Mass., 1964), pp. 84–90, 167–68; Robert Doherty, "Social Change in Northampton, Massachusetts 1800–1850" (Unpublished paper for the Yale Conference on Nineteenth Century Cities, 1968).

13. Ray Ginger, "Labor in a Massachusetts Cotton Mill, 1853–1860," *The Business History Review*, XXVIII (1954), pp. 67–91.

14. E. A. Wrigley (ed.), *An Introduction to English Historical Demography* (London, 1966), pp. 165–66; Lawrence Wylie, "Demographic Change in Rousillon," in Julian Pitt-Rivers (ed.), *Mediterranean Countrymen* (Paris, 1963), pp. 215–36.

15. Joan W. Scott, "Les Verriers de Carmaux," in Thernstrom and Sennett, *Nineteenth Century Cities*. Cf. the observations on itinerant English workingmen of the same period in Eric Hobsbawm's "The Tramping Artisan," in *Labouring Men: Studies in the History of Labor* (London, 1964), pp. 34–63.

16. The literature on the American business elite is conveniently reviewed in Lipset and Bendix, op. cit., ch. iv.

17. For a lengthy critique of the view that the opportunity structure in the United States today is less favorable than in the past and that poverty is accordingly "a permanent way of life" for the so-called "new poor," see my "Poverty in Historical Perspective," in Moynihan, op. cit.

18. Hobsbawm, "The Labour Aristocracy in Nineteenth Century Britain," in *Labouring Men*, pp. 272–315; Royden Harrison, *Before the Socialists: Studies in Labour and Politics, 1861 to 1881* (London, 1965), pp. 26–33.

19. Herbert G. Gutman, "Labor in the Land of Lincoln: Coal Miners on the Prairie" (Unpublished manuscript, 1967), p. 39.

20. Harrison, op. cit., p. 30.

COMMENT

Seymour Martin Lipset

As Stephan Thernstrom notes, many of the efforts to account for the lower level of working-class political consciousness in America as compared with much of Europe have stressed the supposed effect of a high American rate of social mobility in defusing class resentments. The emergence of a class political culture is presumably related to generational class continuity, i.e., limited opportunity to move up the occupational ladder. And the argument went, and is still reiterated, socialist and other efforts at working-class politics have suffered from the fact that American workers could realistically hope and work to improve their circumstances, to get out of their class, while European workers living in societies which offered much less opportunity were more likely to support socialist efforts to change the distribution of reward and opportunity. Those socialists, from Marx on, who made these assumptions anticipated the emergence of working-class consciousness and radical political movements in a future period when changes in the economic system would sharply reduce upward mobility.

These interpretations have been subject to two kinds of empirical challenge. First, a number of students of social mobility in comparative perspective (Sorokin, Glass, Lipset and Bendix, Miller, Blau and Duncan, and Boudon) have concluded from an examination of mobility data collected in various countries that the American rate of mass social mobility is not uniquely high, that a number of European countries have had comparable rates; and second, that with increasing industrialization and urbanization, rates of social mobility have not declined.

These observations, if valid, cast some doubt as to the value of emphasizing differences in patterns of opportunity comparatively and historically as a major structural explanation for variations in the political response of social classes in different countries.

In attempting to report and evaluate the implications of this literature, it is important to acknowledge that, as Thernstrom indicates, most such efforts at comparability are inadequate since they are often dependent on quite forced comparisons; many restrict their definition to shifts between manual and non-manual categories of occupations.[1] It may be noted, however, that the earliest such effort at broad international comparisons, that of Sorokin in 1927, reported on literally hundreds of limited studies of social mobility in various countries, some dating back to the late nineteenth century. While these data did not permit any systematic statistical evaluation of variations in rates, they did suggest that none of the societies or structures reported on could be described as "closed" or "non-mobile" systems. That is, all studies located substantial minorities who rose or fell in occupational status as contrasted with that of their fathers or their first jobs.[2]

These findings detailed by Sorokin, as well as the many subsequent results from national surveys in many countries, do not imply identical rates of social mobility. There are a number of relatively minor differences among the various countries, with the United States having a "slightly higher" rate, according to Blau and Duncan, the authors of the most comprehensive extant survey in the United States. They conclude that "there is indeed little difference among various industrialized nations in the rates of occupational mobility between the blue-collar and the white-collar class."[3] A more recent effort at a systematic quantitative comparison of data from thirteen countries by Philips Cutright does suggest that countries with a higher industrial level (and lower proportion of the work force in agriculture) do have higher rates of social mobility for the population as a whole. The differences, however, are considerably reduced when comparisons are limited to the non-farm population.[4] In any case, the variations are not great, and still serve to confirm Joseph Schumpeter's insistence that "class barriers are always, without exception, surmountable, and are in fact surmounted. . . ."[5]

In recent years, the Sorokin thesis which suggests that forces making both for the hereditary transmission of advantages and for considerable mobility occur in varying types of social systems has received additional striking confirmation in the rapidly growing number of empirical surveys of social mobility in different Communist countries. This is apparent, for example, in the findings of highly comprehensive and sophisticated surveys of rates and patterns of social mobility in the United States and in the most industrialized Communist country, Czechoslovakia. Czech sociologists systematically compared their 1967 data with those gathered by Blau and Duncan in 1962. Zdaněk Šafěř, a Czech scholar, concludes that the "openness of both systems . . . is surprisingly great." He stresses this finding in the context of refuting "the hypotheses frequently presented in the Western sociological literature concerning the 'mobility blockade' of the socialist countries."[6] That is, Šafěř argues it is not true that socialism means a lower rate of social mobility, that in fact their rate is as high as that under capitalism.

It may be worth noting that, as far as I am aware, no Western sociologist has suggested the existence of a "mobility blockade" in Communist countries. It may be, however, that such a hypothesis is current among internal critics of the system. For example, the Soviet dissident author Andrei Amalrik, after discussing the sharp differences in the standard of living of ordinary people and the elites in the Soviet Union, argues that the country has an "upper class which is trying to avoid any change and to prevent society from having any mobility, and . . . make permanent the breakup of our society into tightly closed castes."[7] The report of a conference on the social structure of Communist countries held in Moscow in the mid-1960s indicates that scholars also point to restrictions on opportunity.

> "Social mobility of young people in Poland is still very much dependent upon social origin" declared S. I. Wilderspil [a Polish sociologist]. . . . N. M. Blinov of the sociological laboratory at Moscow University supported him at the same conference, basing himself upon research made among employees of the First Ballbearing Factory in Moscow and at Moscow University itself. His conclusion was that "class differences still have a bright imprint (strong influence) upon social advancement of the individual. . . ."[8]

In reporting on the results of research in Hungary, Sandor Ferge notes the existence of a "vicious circle" inhibiting social mobility in her country and calls for "building security measures into the new economic mechanism as to prevent rigidity in the *already existing* or *newly developed social differences*. . . ."[9] Some statistical support for the thesis that Communist countries have lower rates of mobility than non-Communist ones is also suggested in the thirteen-nation comparison by Philips Cutright, which found that Hungary had the lowest rate of all, and that Yugoslavia was fourth lowest, following Finland and Italy.[10]

In spite of these analyses, however, the fairly comprehensive evidence from Communist countries, some like Šafěř's report more recent than those used by Cutright, would seem to support the theoretical analysis of the prospects for mobility in Communist societies by the Polish sociologist Stanislaus Ossowski, who argued persuasively that the basic processes which affect rates of social mobility are structural, are linked to the pace of economic development rather than to political or economic systems, and should, therefore, be comparable in socialist and capitalist countries. Writing in the mid-1950s, he observed:

> A socialist system needs economic development even more than a capitalist one . . . such development is a necessary condition of its success and even of its existence. Therefore one of the immediate aims of the leaders of the socialist states was to reach the level of more advanced capitalist countries in industrialization, urbanization, development of communications, and mass education. *All these processes imply an increase in social mobility in socialist countries as well as elsewhere,* and since they were induced by social revolutions we can therefore postulate a plain causal relation between social revolution and this increase of social mobility. *But it is the "social-economic expansion" and not the revolutionary introduction of a socialist order which can be considered a necessary condition of this increase.* Increased mobility of this type could have been accomplished also if the capitalist system had persisted; it could have been done, e.g., with the help of schemes like the Marshall plan.[11]

A recent Hungarian study of social mobility presented in a comparative context in an explicit effort to test Ossowski's thesis indicates that the results correspond to the expectations of the Polish scholar. In two separate sets of comparisons, first using the simple manual-non-manual dichotomy for five non-Communist countries and Hungary, and second measuring mobility among a much wider set of occupational class categories in Britain, the United States, and Hungary, Adorka found that when comparing outflow rates, i.e., the percentage shift from fathers' generation to sons, the Hungarian rates are more or less similar with those of other countries. When contrasting inflow rates, the proportion of sons in a given stratum who come from a parental class, a larger proportion of Hungarians in higher positions came from manual or peasant background than did those in the non-Communist countries. But he notes that as Ossowski had suggested this was *"a consequence of structural factors and ultimately of the rate of economic development."* That is, it reflected the fact that during the period of the comparison, Hungary's "occupational structure was at the lower level of development than that of the United States and England . . . the change of occupational structure was probably faster in Hungary than in the United States and England." Clearly, as Adorka states, the "doubling in one generation of the percentage of intellectuals [professionals] with university qualifications and of top executives implies an inflow of 50 per cent of persons originating from other social strata even in the case of the total occupational inheritance of the children of intellectuals."[12]

Hungarian research based on a sample of 15,000 looking at three-generational mobility illustrates Adorka's thesis. "In 71% of families where parents and grand-parents were in intellectual [requiring higher education] professions, all the employed children are in an intellectual [professional] career. Where the head of the family was an intellectual, but the grand-parents were still manual workers, the proportion falls to 57%, and drops to 41% if the grand-parents worked on the land." For those whose fathers and grandfathers were manual workers, over two thirds of the employed young were in manual employment.[13]

The comparability thesis is also strongly supported by an earlier comparison of mobility rates in seven countries, one Communist, Poland, and six non-Communist, by a Polish sociologist who found slightly lower rates of upward mobility in Poland than in the United States, West Germany, Sweden, Japan, France, and Switzerland. The author, however, drew no general conclusions concerning the mobility propensities of different systems. In any case, his estimates of the proportion of city populations of urban origin who were upwardly or downwardly mobile did not vary greatly among the seven countries, although Poland remained toward the lower end (24 per cent mobile as contrasted with 30 per cent in the United States).[14] Vojin Milić, the author of a Yugoslav study based on 1960 data which shows patterns similar to other countries, rejects making international comparisons of changes between manual and non-manual strata on the grounds that Yugoslav manual workers do not conceive of white-collar jobs as socially higher. He does, however, report that "the children of [white-collar] employees were relatively about ten times more heavily represented among [university] students than the children of workers, and even more [heavily] than the children of peasants." In a more comprehensive analysis of intergenerational mobility using multi-class (occupations) categories, Milić secured results similar to those found in studies in Sweden and Denmark.[15]

There is a growing body of literature in the field of social stratification and social mobility in the Soviet Union itself. Sociologists now begin to speak openly of "social differentiation" as involving different qualities of labor, related to "complexity and social significance."[16] Unfortunately, there are no published studies of mobility based on national samples. The available research, however, does point to pressures making for upward occupational mobility, inherent in the differential prestige, income, and skill associated with occupations which make Russian youth regard manual and peasant work as jobs to be avoided. Following the publication of a recent survey of the occupational preferences of a sample of Russian youth, the manager of an industrial plant wrote to a newspaper asking "where am I to find my turners and milling machine operators," occupations which placed seventy-fifth and seventy-sixth out of eighty occupations in one community. Two articles in *Pravda* by Georgi Kulagin, the manager of a Leningrad factory, complain that the emphasis on classes for "gifted children" and the rewards for higher education serve to denigrate manual occupations. As he notes:

> Families and children fight for admittance to such courses, because otherwise they would feel "inferior." Naturally not all are of a high enough standard, and many who could be excellent workers become very bad technicians and functionaries, thus providing a loss to society twice over. "Enough of the classes for the elite," appeals Kulagin. "The school must ensure a more realistic preparation for a working life. And we must remember that we need engineers, but we need workers too."[17]

The phenomenon seems to be a general one in the Soviet Union (as it is in other countries). M. Dobrynin, the author of a sociological study based on a sample of 25 per cent of the high school graduates in Vilnius, the capital of Lithuania, states: "The graduates dream of becoming medical doctors, scientists and artists, geologists and jurists, fliers and sailors. . . . The question, however, arises: 'who, after all, will build houses?' "[18]

The assorted surveys of the relationship between family occupational position and educational attainments indicate, however, that the concern of these Soviet factory managers for a supply of workers is somewhat exaggerated, though they may be right that young workers and peasants feel unhappy in their jobs because these are deemed lowly. At the same time there are strong forces pressing for hereditary transmission of privileged position, inherent in the considerable advantage which the children of the educated and cultured members of the class of intelligentsia have in obtaining the kinds of education which are necessary to secure the more interesting and better-rewarded work.

Mobility in Historical Perspective

If the patterns and rates of social mobility are relatively comparable in industrialized societies, whether Communist or non-Communist, the logic which suggests that economic growth, industrialization, should result in higher rates of mobility (rural to urban migration apart) would imply an increase in mobility during periods of rapid expansion, and a decline whenever economic stagnation occurred. Even more surprising, therefore, than the comparative findings are the results of historical studies, a field in which Thernstrom has played an initiating and major role, which also emphasize similarity rather than differences over time.[19] As Thernstrom notes in this book and in various others of his writings, quantitative research by himself and other American historians suggests the continuation of a high rate of social mobility over an eighty-year period, from the 1880s on. The most comprehensive effort to measure change by a sociologist, that of Natalie Rogoff, which compared mobility rates in Indianapolis in 1910 and again in 1940, holding constant changes in the occupational structure, made the same case for a shorter span.[20] Seeking to locate trends, Blau and Duncan analyzed the mobility patterns of different generations of Americans by relating family occupational background to first job (thus permitting a comparison of the very young still on their first job with the experience of the very old when they were young). They report, congruent with the findings of Thernstrom and Rogoff, that ". . . the influence of social origins has remained constant since World War I. There is absolutely no evidence of 'rigidification.'"[21] In his essay here, Thernstrom suggests that the high rates of social mobility in the United States may help to explain the lower level of class consciousness in this country in the nineteenth century as compared to Europe, since the research of William H. Sewell, Jr., on the working class of Marseille in the nineteenth century indicates that "the sons of Marseille workers escaped into non-manual occupations with far less frequency than was the case in Boston." The generality of the Marseille findings for European cities, however, is thrown into doubt by a recent comprehensive analysis of social mobility in Copenhagen from 1850–1950. Tom Rishøj found to his surprise that mid-nineteenth-century Copenhagen had an extremely high rate of social mobility, one which corresponded to 80 per cent of the maximum possible in a totally egalitarian society, i.e., roughly equal to that found by Natalie Rogoff for Indianapolis in 1910 and 1940.[22] And Rishøj was forced to conclude that there had been no change in the rate of social mobility (using a nine-class scale, not simply two) over a hundred-year period, "that in a preindustrial or early industrial community of Copenhagen we find the same rate of mobility as in the modern industrialized Copenhagen. This finding is in contrast to most of the expectations held by researchers and theorists in the field."[23] It corresponds, however, to the assumptions posited by Sorokin in his classic early work that there is no trend in the rise or fall of rates of vertical social mobility, that at most there may be short-run cyclical changes.

Elsewhere, Thernstrom has written eloquently concerning the doubt which these historical findings raise for the often voiced beliefs that changes in American capitalism and industrial society have created a permanent and growing class of the "poor" or the poverty-stricken. As he notes, there simply is no evidence in support of this argument; all the available data point in the opposite direction.[24] It may be noted that studies of the social background of the business elite also do not sustain the image that this stratum has become more restrictive, particularly to those of poor background. The most recent survey of the backgrounds of big business executives (president and chairman or principal vice-presidents of the six hundred largest U.S. non-financial corporations) found that the bureaucratization of American corporate life, the growth of the public corporation replacing the family-owned concern, had seemingly opened the business elite to entry from below in a way that had never before been true in American history. Since this study has never been widely disseminated, it may be worthwhile reproducing some of its salient results here:

> Only 10.5 percent of the current generation of big business executives . . . identify themselves as sons of wealthy families; as recently as 1950 the corresponding figure was 36.1 percent, and at the turn of the century, 45.6 percent. . . . The [subjective] finding is sustained . . . by quite objective data on the occupations of the fathers of the executives: two-thirds of the 1900 generation had fathers who were heads of the same corporation or were independent businessmen; less than half of the current generation had fathers so placed in American society. On the other hand, less than 10 percent of the 1900 generation had fathers who were employees; by 1964 this percentage had increased to nearly 30 percent.[25]

Surprisingly both to scholars in the field and to those radicals convinced that a mature capitalism would become increasingly immobile, particularly with respect to sharp jumps into the elite, the evidence indicates that the post-World War II period brought with it the greatest increase in the proportion of those from economically "poor" backgrounds (from 12.1 per cent in 1950 to 23.3 per cent in 1964) who entered the top echelons of American business, and a corresponding great decline in the percentage from wealthy families (from 36.1 per cent in 1950 to 10.5 per cent in 1964).[26] The underlying structural trend which made these figures possible is the fact that large corporations increasingly have drawn their top management from the ranks of college graduates, that men enter these firms in various junior managerial and professional capacities from the university, and that higher posts are secured through a competitive promotion process, much as in government bureaucracy. Privileged family and class background obviously continue to be an enormous advantage here as in the Soviet Union, but training and talent can make up for them in an increasing number of cases.

Although the increase in opportunity to move to the very top clearly does not affect the life chances of most people, it reflects the tail end of a process which is a mass phenomenon, namely the spreading out of higher education into the ranks of the working class. Studies of parental aspirations for children indicate that the vast majority of American workers desire higher education for their children, and today, in spite of the continued inequality noted earlier, close to half of them can see this aspiration become a reality. And seeing their children enter on this first step of the competitive ladder to bureaucratic success may serve to reinforce further the belief that opportunity exists even among those frustrated by their own minimal occupational achievements and work experiences.

The fact that the business elite include so many who have demonstrated the Horatio Alger story of the poor hard-working boy who becomes wealthy may also have political consequences in strengthening the conviction of the upper class that an important part of the ideology of the system, the idea of equality of opportunity, corresponds to reality. The more convinced a ruling elite is of the validity of its title to rule, of its social legitimacy, the better able it is to resist attacks on its power. One of the conditions for successful revolution is a "failure of nerve" of the elite, a loss in its confidence that it deserves to govern. Since the legitimating dogma of the American system has always included as a major component the notion that those at the top are there because they have won a race, the continued presence within the elite of large numbers of sharply upwardly mobile people is important for the system.

Two Mobility Systems

If differences in rates of mobility among countries and over time are not sufficient to account for the continued belief in opportunity, there is an aspect of American development which must be seen as part of the picture, the fact that class position has been differentially distributed among ethnic and racial groups.[27] For much of its history, the United States has been divided between "majority" and "minority" ethnic groups. The latter have, in effect, repeatedly provided new sets of recruits for the lowly paid, low-status positions, thus enabling others of less recent settlement to rise. An analysis of census data reported that in 1870 and 1880, "the foreign-born were most typically employed in the factories, in heavy industry, as manual laborers and domestic servants. Clerical, managerial and official positions remained largely inaccessible to them."[28] The census of 1890 gathered information for the first time on the occupations of the native-born children of immigrants, thus permitting a comparison of the two generations. They varied considerably. "Unlike the immigrant males who were in highest proportion among domestic and personal service workers, the second generation males were most numerous relatively among workers in trade and transportation and in manufacturing. It is also notable that those in the second generation were more successful in entering the professions, even though not as successful as members of the native stock (the native born of native parents). . . . Altogether, the second generation conformed more closely to the occupational distribution of the entire white labor force than did the foreign born."[29] This pattern in which the second generation, the children of immigrants, was as a group in much better positions than the immigrant generation continued for the duration of mass immigration. Thus, in 1900, "the data indicate that the foreign born were no more widely distributed by occupation . . . than in 1890, but that the second generation became more widely distributed and moved closer to the occupational distribution of the entire labor force in 1900."[30] The census was not as comprehensive in gathering comparable occupational data from 1910 on, but the evidence clearly indicates comparable patterns to those summarized above for the remaining period of mass immigration, i.e., prior to passage of restrictive legislation in 1924.

More recently, particularly since the economy began a prolonged period of relatively full employment in the 1940s, migrants from various parts of North America, blacks, Puerto Ricans, Mexicans, and to a small extent French Canadians, have furnished the bulk of the less skilled underprivileged labor force. As Reinhard Bendix and I wrote in our analysis of mobility processes in the late 1950s:

> Now, as before, there is a close relationship between low income and membership in segregated groups. A large proportion of seasonal farm laborers and sharecroppers in the South and Southwest come from them. In the cities, Negroes, Mexicans and Puerto Ricans predominate in the unskilled, dirty, and badly paid occupations. These twenty million people earn a disproportionately low share of the national income; they have little political power and no social prestige; they live in ethnic ghettos, in rural and urban areas alike, and they have little social contact with white Americans. Indeed, today there are

two working classes in America, a white one and a Negro, Mexican, and Puerto Rican one. A real social and economic cleavage is created by widespread discrimination against these minority groups, and this diminishes the chances for the development of solidarity along class lines. In effect, the overwhelming majority of whites, both in the working class and in the middle and upper classes, benefit economically and socially from the existence of these "lower classes" within their midst. This continued splintering of the working class is a major element in the preservation of the stability of the class structure.[31]

The assumptions made in that analysis concerning the relative difference between the situations of initially underprivileged whites and blacks have recently been given more elaborate statistical confirmation in the largest and methodologically most sophisticated study of American social mobility, that of Blau and Duncan. These authors found that lowly social origin *had little negative effect on the chances of whites, including the children of white immigrants, to advance economically*. The mobility picture for the whites is such that Blau and Duncan reject the idea that a "vicious cycle" perpetuating inequality exists "for the population at large." But if whites, including working-class whites, have experienced a fluid occupational class system, in which the able and ambitious can rise, the reverse is true for the blacks. Their data confirm the impression "that Negroes are handicapped at every step in their attempts to achieve economic success, and these cumulative disadvantages are what produces the great inequalities of opportunities under which the Negro American suffers. . . . The multiple handicaps associated with being an American Negro are cumulative in their deleterious consequences for a man's career."

Education, which we have seen opens all sorts of doors to whites, even to those of quite low social origin, does not work the same way for blacks.

The difference in occupational status between Negroes and whites is twice as great for men who have graduated from high school or gone to college as for those who have completed no more than eight years of schooling. In short the careers of well-educated Negroes lag even further behind those of comparable whites than do the careers of poorly educated Negroes. . . . Negroes, as an underprivileged group, must make greater sacrifices to remain in school, but they have less incentive than whites to make these sacrifices, which may well be a major reason why Negroes often exhibit little motivation to continue in school and advance their education.[32]

Given the fact that no European country has had to absorb as large an immigrant population into the lower echelons of an expanding economy, and that none of them have ethnic, racial, religious cleavages, which separate the distribution of occupational advantages along racial lines, as widely and as long as the United States has had, it should be clear that the fact (if it is a fact) of roughly comparable rates of mass social mobility among many different countries should have sharply different consequences on the possibilities for working-class consciousness or political solidarity. For as the data reported here, both for the past and the present, suggest, the opportunities and economic advantages available to the less privileged sectors of the native white population have been much greater than for comparable groups in Europe. Unskilled American blacks have a much lower rate of upward social mobility than Europeans, while when "the upward mobility rate of unskilled [American] white workers is considered separately, it is appreciably higher than the upward mobility rate for the total unskilled group. The assumption that the United States has higher mobility rates than European countries may, then, rest in part on a disregard of a sizeable sector of the society."[33]

Conclusion

Historians such as Thernstrom who have been willing to dig beneath the impressionistic consensus concerning American society by quantifying who did what, who got what, and the like, have severely upset many of our cherished beliefs about the American past. Not only have they challenged the conventional wisdom about mobility rates which assumed that we have moved from greater to lesser equality, but a related group of quantitatively oriented historians have examined the distribution of income and of variations in social class behavior from early times on. And the tentative conclusion which may be reached from a number of these studies is that Jacksonian America, described by Tocqueville and others as an egalitarian social system (which, compared to Europe, it undoubtedly was), was probably characterized by much more severe forms of social and economic inequality, of variations in standards of living among the classes than the society of the 1970s. The assumption that the growth of an industrialized urban society broke up an egalitarian one is simply contrary to the available evidence about Tocqueville's America, including even "agricultural areas and small towns."

> The explanation, popular since Karl Marx's time, that it was industrialization that pauperized the masses, in the process transforming a relatively egalitarian social order, appears wanting. Vast disparities between urban rich and poor antedated industrialization [in America].[34]

The evidence concerning the existence of extremely wide disparities in income, property, and consumption styles in pre-Civil War America puts into question the assumptions that industrialization has led to greater inequality, particularly in urban areas. Without entering into the issue of trends in the distribution of income in this century, it is obvious that economic growth has brought with it an almost constant increase in the Gross National Income, that the average per capita income has increased close to six times during this century. And as Bendix and I noted in our earlier work on social mobility, this dramatic growth in income necessarily has meant a wider distribution of various consumption goods, usually more general than in any other country. Thus, a much larger percentage of Americans (over 80) graduate from high school or enter college (close to 50) than is true in any other nation. Almost 80 per cent of the black population now finishes twelve years of school, and over 40 per cent of those of college age enters higher education. The greater wealth of the United States also means that consumer goods such as automobiles, telephones, and the like are more equitably distributed here than elsewhere. A recent effort, using twelve social indicators, at a comparative evaluation of the relative advantages of different countries as places to live by *The* (London) *Economist* placed the United States far in the lead of eight other major non-Communist industrialized states.[35] The wider distribution of consumers' goods that inevitably accompanies greater wealth means that the gap in standards of living between social classes, particularly among the white community, is relatively low by comparative world standards. And as income, as style of life, increases, even men who remain in the same occupational position may experience a sense of gain.

The discussion of rates of social mobility and related aspects of social stratification by Thernstrom and others is clearly premised on the oft repeated suggestion that societies characterized by high rates of social mobility are much less likely to be affected by intense class conflict, by polarized politics, than those in which little opportunity exists. This thesis has been enunciated by Karl Marx seeking to account for weak working-class consciousness in the United States and by a variety of contemporary sociological observers.[36] The most detailed effort to test some of the implications of these assumptions in the context of examining the differences between the mobile, upward and downward, and the non-mobile in different classes in the context of their opinion and voting choices in recent years tends to validate the proposition that mobile individuals are less likely to take strong class positions than the non-mobile. James Barber concludes his study with the assertion: "The influence of mobility on the political system would seem . . . to be a moderating one: lending flexibility to the electoral process, reducing the stakes involved in elections, and diluting the class content of politics."[37]

As a reading of the essays in this volume indicates, there are many factors and social processes which have determined the character of political conflict in America, particularly the weakness of socialist class-based politics. The emphasis here on the possible effects of social mobility is not meant to suggest a belief that the opportunity structure of the society is the main determinant of the state of class consciousness. Elsewhere, in the context of comparing various aspects of the United States and Canada, I have suggested that historical experiences which have sustained more "conservative," traditional, and hierarchical status structures north of the border, reflecting the fact that Canada came into existence as the country of the "counterrevolution," facilitated the emergence of more particularistic (group- and class-related) politics there than in the United States.[38]

Strong socialist movements exist in countries with high rates of mobility and strong emphases on equalitarianism (e.g., Australia and New Zealand). A radical movement may emerge in this country, as it briefly appeared to do in the late 1960s, though rates of mobility had not changed. That movement, however, was almost totally based on the liberal segment of the intelligentsia and the college student population. It had little or no appeal to white workers. Its momentary existence, therefore, does not challenge the contention that the high rate of social mobility existing among native working-class white Americans has adversely affected efforts to foster radical class politics in the United States. Hence, the kind of studies discussed here is of more than academic interest. And thus far, no available data indicate any sign of a decline in the rate of social mobility; if they suggest any trend, it is an opposite one, toward enlargement of opportunity through the combination of increased bureaucratization and a widening of educational facilities.

NOTES

1. A detailed, highly sophisticated methodological critique with references to much of the methodological literature is Karl Ulrich Mayer and Walter Müller, "Progress in Social Mobility Research?" *Quality and Quantity,* 5 (June 1971), pp. 141–77. For discussions of various methodological and theoretical issues in mobility research see the articles in Neil Smelser and S. M. Lipset (eds.), *Social Structure and Mobility in Economic Development* (Chicago: Aldine, 1966), esp. those by O. D. Duncan, H. L. Wilensky, W. E. Moore, and N. R. Ramsøy and the introductory chapter by the editors.

2. P. A. Sorokin, *Social and Cultural Mobility* (New York: The Free Press, 1959). This book was first published in 1927. David V. Glass (ed.), *Social Mobility in Britain* (London: Routledge, 1954); S. M. Lipset and Reinhard Bendix, *Social Mobility in Industrial Society* (Berkeley: University of California Press, 1959); S. M. Miller, "Comparative Social Mobility: A Trend Report and Bibliography," *Current Sociology,* 9, no. 1 (1960), pp. 1–89; Thomas G. Fox and S. M. Miller, "Economic, Political and Social Determinants of Mobility," *Acta Sociologica,* 9 (1965), pp. 76–93; Thomas G. Fox and S. M. Miller, "Intra-Country Variations: Occupational Stratification and Mobility," in Reinhard Bendix and S. M. Lipset (eds.), *Class, Status, and Power: Social Stratification in Comparative Perspective* (New York: The Free Press, 1966), pp. 574–81; Philips Cutright, "Occupational Inheritance: A Cross-national Analysis," *American Journal of Sociology,* 73 (1968), pp. 400–16.

3. Peter M. Blau and Otis Dudley Duncan, *The American Occupational Structure* (New York: John Wiley, 1967), p. 433.

4. Cutright, op. cit. A similar conclusion was reached by K. Svalastoga, *Social Differentiation* (New York: David McKay, 1965), pp. 123–26. He also points to "The pervasiveness of mobility. Even crude measurements produce the finding that in any industrial society the majority is mobile" (p. 141).

5. Joseph Schumpeter, "The Problem of Classes," in Bendix and Lipset (eds.), *Class, Status, and Power,* p. 45.

6. Zdaněk Šafěř, "Different Approaches to the Measurement of Social Differentiation of the Czechoslovak Socialist Society," *Quality and Quantity,* 5 (June 1971), pp. 205–6. See also P. Machonin, "Social Stratification in Contemporary Czechoslovakia," *American Journal of Sociology,* 75 (1970), pp. 725–41. For a detailed report of the large body of empirical research on social mobility and stratification in the Soviet Union, see S. M. Lipset and Richard Dobson, "Social Stratification and Sociology in the Soviet Union," *Survey,* 19 (Summer 1973), pp. 114–85.

7. As cited in I. F. Stone, "Can Russia Change?" *New York Review of Books,* 18 (February 24, 1972), p. 22.

8. From summary of the published Russian report in Z. Katz, *Hereditary Elements in Education and Social Structure in the USSR* (Glascow: Institute of Soviet and East-European Studies, University of Glascow, 1969), p. 4. I am very indebted to Professor Katz for references and comments.

9. As cited in ibid., p. 6 (emphases are by Z. Katz).

10. Cutright, op. cit.

11. Stanislaus Ossowski, "Social Mobility Brought About by Social Revolution" (Paper presented at the Fourth Working Conference on Social Stratification and Social Mobility, International Sociological Association, Geneva, December 1957). (Emphases mine—S.M.L.) This paper is discussed in Lipset and Bendix, *Social Mobility*, pp. 281–82.

12. R. Adorka, "Social Mobility and Economic Development in Hungary," *Acta Oeconomica*, 7, no. 1 (1971), pp. 40–41.

13. Maria Markus, "Quelques problèmes sociologiques du choix de la profession et de son pretige," in Andreas Hegedus (ed.), *Études recherches. sociologues hongrois* (Paris: Éditions Anthropos, 1969), pp. 198–99.

14. Adam Sarapata, "Distance et mobilité sociale dans la société polonaise contemporaine," *Sociologie du travail*, 8 (January–March 1966), p. 19. Joseph R. Fiszman, "Education and Social Mobility in People's Poland," *The Polish Review*, 16 (Summer 1971), pp. 5–31.

15. See Vojin Milić, "General Trends in Social Mobility in Yugoslavia," *Acta Sociologica*, 9, nos. 1–2 (1966), see p. 133, and notes 10 and 12 on p. 135.

16. For a review of the discussion of Soviet sociologists on social stratification, see Z. Katz, "The Soviet Sociologists' Debate on Social Structure in the USSR" (Draft prepared for the Center for International Studies, MIT; Russian Research Center, Harvard University, July 30, 1971), pp. 49–56.

17. "Young Soviet Citizens No Longer Wish to Be Workers" (a summary of an article by the Moscow correspondent of the *Corriere della Sera* [Milan], Giuseppe Josca), *SIPE* (International Student Press Service, Rome), 3 (October–November 1971), pp. 12–14.

18. As cited in Katz, *Hereditary Elements*, p. 41.

19. For a critique of historians, just ten years old, for ignoring the area, see Oscar and Mary Handlin, "Mobility," in Edward Saveth (ed.), *American History and the Social Sciences* (New York: The Free Press, 1964), pp. 215–30.

20. Natalie Rogoff, *Recent Trends in Occupational Mobility* (Glencoe: The Free Press, 1963).

21. Blau and Duncan, op. cit., p. 111.

22. Tom Rishøj, "Metropolitan Social Mobility 1850–1950: The Case of Copenhagen," *Quality and Quantity*, 5 (June 1971), pp. 131–40.

23. Ibid., p. 139.

24. Stephan Thernstrom, "Poverty in Historical Perspective," in D.

P. Moynihan (ed.), *On Understanding Poverty* (New York: Basic Books, 1969), pp. 160–86.

25. *The Big Business Executive/1964 A Study of His Social and Educational Background* (A study sponsored by *The Scientific American,* conducted by Market Statistics Inc. of New York City, in collaboration with Dr. Mabel Newcomer), p. 2. The study was designed to update Mabel Newcomer, *The Big Business Executive–The Factors That Made Him: 1900–1950* (New York: Columbia University Press, 1950). All the comparisons in it are with materials reported in Dr. Newcomer's published work.

26. Ibid., p. 33.

27. For a recent discussion of this factor in the context of American mobility, see Anselm Strauss, *The Contexts of Social Mobility: Ideology and Theory* (Chicago: Aldine, 1971), pp. 79–104.

28. E. P. Hutchinson, *Immigrants and Their Children* (New York: John Wiley, 1956), p. 114.

29. Ibid., pp. 138–39.

30. Ibid., p. 171.

31. Lipset and Bendix, *Social Mobility,* pp. 105–6.

32. Blau and Duncan, op. cit., pp. 404–7. Otis Dudley Duncan, "Inheritance of Poverty or Inheritance of Race," in Moynihan (ed.), op. cit., pp. 103–9.

33. Herbert Goldhammer, "Social Mobility," *International Encyclopedia of the Social Sciences,* vol. 14 (New York: Macmillan and The Free Press, 1968), pp. 434–35.

34. Edward Pessen, "The Egalitarian Myth and the American Social Reality: Wealth, Mobility, and Equality in the 'Era of the Common Man,'" *The American Historical Review,* 76 (October 1971), pp. 1027–28, 1030. Pessen cites many relevant recent historical works bearing on the intense forms of inequality in this period.

35. "Where the Grass Is Greener," *The Economist,* December 25, 1971, p. 15.

36. For a review of some of the literature on this subject see James Alden Barber, Jr., *Social Mobility and Voting Behavior* (Chicago: Rand McNally, 1950), pp. 9–12, 264–66. With respect to problems of developing countries, see Gino Germani, "Social and Political Consequences of Mobility," in Smelser and Lipset (eds.), op. cit., pp. 364–94.

37. Barber, op. cit., p. 267. See also Lipset and Bendix, *Social Mobility,* pp. 261–65, 66–71, 73–74, 268–69; Blau and Duncan, op. cit., pp. 436–41. For citation to the literature of specific studies, see Mayer and Müller, op. cit., p. 148, n. 16.

38. S. M. Lipset, *Revolution and Counterrevolution* (Garden City, N.Y.: Doubleday, Anchor Books, rev. ed., 1970), pp. 37–75; and S. M. Lipset, *Agrarian Socialism: The Cooperative Commonwealth Federation in Saskatchewan* (Berkeley: University of California paperback, rev. ed., 1971), pp. xiv–xv.

REPLY

Stephan Thernstrom

My essay attempted to shed a little light on a large problem—the failure of the American socialist movement. The explanations that can be offered for that failure are of two broad types. Some observers have placed heavy stress upon factors internal to the movement itself—tactical blunders, failures of leadership, and the like. About the precise nature of these internal weaknesses there has been disagreement, with some writers denouncing leaders of the radical movement as unduly opportunistic, and others maintaining that the chief problem was just the opposite—excessive ideological rigidity, sectarianism, an inability to grasp American realities. Both groups assume, however, that better leadership, pursuing a more "correct" strategy, could have brought masses of voters into the socialist camp.

Such internal explanations strike me as dubious on two grounds. First, it has yet to be demonstrated that the tactics of American socialists actually differed dramatically from those of their more successful brethren in other countries like France, Germany, and Britain. The problem, after all, is a problem in comparative history, and the necessary comparative analysis of socialist leadership and socialist tactics has yet to be done.

Second, even if it could be shown that American socialists were indeed distinctively deficient on this count, I would want to ask *why* that was the case. This kind of explanation is all too reminiscent of the now discredited view that the American Civil War erupted because of the mistakes of a "blundering generation" of inept politicians. Possibly Lincoln, Douglas, and other leaders of the 1850s were less talented politicians than the Founding Fathers or even Clay and Calhoun—though it seems doubtful—but the further question is whether this may be taken as an uncaused cause, i.e., a truly independent variable. My prejudice would be that the quality of political leadership available in a given historical context is largely determined by the context. It was the clash of the radically divergent social systems that had developed in the northern and southern states by the 1850s that brought the men of the "blundering generation" to the fore and pushed them toward the actions (and inactions) that led finally to war. Likewise, I would urge, the successes of Samuel Gompers and the failures of Gene Debs and Big Bill Haywood stemmed largely from fundamental features of the social context in which they operated. The failure of American socialism, I believe, was attributable not so much to internal as to external circumstances. Socialism foundered because certain basic structural features of American society were antithetical to the socialist impulse.

The task of defining those features is too large to attempt here. A full answer would certainly take cognizance of Louis Hartz's brilliant discussion of the role of feudalism in creating a politics of class. The absence of a feudal aristocracy in the American past inhibited the formation of a class-conscious bourgeoisie, which in turn dampened the degree of proletarian identification and solidarity. Lipset's comment on my initial essay properly emphasizes another factor—ethnic, racial, and religious cleavages within the American working class, and differentials in access to opportunity for different groups. One obviously must look too at the nature of the American political system itself, which has institutional features (such as the single-member electoral district) that tend to foster the dominance of two centrist parties.

My essay, of course, did not purport to offer a comprehensive discussion of the structural factors that impeded the rise of a socialist movement in the United States. Instead I concentrated on the possible relevance of four closely related circumstances: that American workers were exceptionally mobile geographically; that levels of occupational career mobility were high; that levels of intergenerational occupational mobility were also high; and that strikingly large numbers of American laborers were able to accumulate significant property holdings.

My view at the time the essay was written was that there was dismayingly little in the way of solid comparative evidence concerning levels of mobility of these four kinds in other societies in the nineteenth and early twentieth centuries, but that there were fragments of data pointing to the conclusion that the American social system was more fluid than those of other countries at comparable levels of economic development.

That still seems to me the best generalization that can be made on the basis of the information currently available. In his Comment Lipset has, rather surprisingly, failed to mention three of the four types of mobility I discussed; about them I will say only that the few fragments of new evidence that have come to my attention since my paper was written are consistent with my suggestion that the American social system was unusually fluid in these important respects.[1] Lipset draws bold conclusions about "social mobility" on the basis of evidence that bears upon only one kind of mobility –intergenerational occupational mobility.

On that one issue, I find his contribution provocative. The bulk of his material, of course, refers to the contemporary scene, not to the past. But his data from Eastern Europe does serve to strengthen the conclusion he and Bendix advanced earlier in *Social Mobility in Industrial Society*–that rates of intergenerational mobility display rather striking uniformities in all advanced industrial societies.

The one new long-term historical study he cites, however, Rishøj's *Quality and Quantity* paper on Copenhagen from 1850 to 1950, does not seem to me to provide persuasive support for his position. Rishøj asserts that there was no significant change in the Copenhagen mobility pattern in the course of a century on the basis of summary tables that show that the *total* amount of upward and downward mobility in the community remained roughly constant over the entire period. But the significant question is whether the rate of upward mobility for working-class sons remained similarly constant, and it appears that in Copenhagen it did not.

There was little upward mobility among workers' sons in his 1853–55 sample, and a good deal of downward mobility on the part of men born into the middle class. In 1901 and 1953 samples the reverse was the case.[2] It is not the constancy of over-all mobility ratio but the shift in the opportunity levels for particular social classes that seems most striking and important to me. The mid-nineteenth-century Copenhagen figures for youths of working-class origins do not diverge widely from Sewell's findings for Marseille at about the same time, and they contrast very sharply with the pattern of opportunity in several nineteenth-century American cities. Later, with advancing urbanization and industrialization, the gap between the American and European scene doubtless narrowed, but the common nineteenth-century belief that the social system of the New World offered unique opportunities for upward mobility had some foundation in fact.

It should also be pointed out that there is a serious question whether intergenerational mobility can legitimately be separated from the measurement of career mobility without producing misleading conclusions. Suppose that I am correct in my contention—ignored by Lipset—that there was a uniquely high rate of career mobility in the United States. Suppose, for instance, that 30 per cent of the Americans who began work in blue-collar jobs moved up into white-collar occupations by the time they started to rear children, and that in Denmark the comparable figure was only 10 per cent. In these circumstances, a finding that there were similar rates of upward and downward intergenerational mobility in the United States and Denmark could be quite misleading, for the base line from which intergenerational mobility is normally computed is the occupational rank of the father at some point subsequent to the birth of his son. A larger fraction of the sons of American white-collar workers *should* have been downwardly mobile, because fewer of their fathers were solidly established in the white-collar world for their full careers. Conversely, we would expect to find less upward intergenerational mobility on the part of the sons of American workers, because many of the more ambitious and intelligent workers would have been removed from the working class and drawn up into the middle class, leaving a diminished pool of talent at the working-class level. Identical rates of intergenerational mobility would in this instance obscure very real differences in the fluidity of the two social systems being compared.

Whether or not this hypothetical example corresponds to historical reality, of course, is unknown at present. The work of Lipset has been of immense value in challenging the easy assumptions that have so often been made about the unique fluidity of the American social system. It is not impossible that a wave of future historical mobility studies of a highly refined kind, studies that treat the full range of phenomena that are embraced in a comprehensive conception of social mobility, will show that his skepticism is well founded. But the issue is certainly open at present. I am still inclined to believe that American mobility patterns were in some ways distinctive, and that this distinctiveness did have a good deal to do with another fairly distinctive aspect of the American historical record—the failure of working-class-based protest movements to attract a mass following.

NOTES

1. I have in mind particularly the forthcoming study of the glassblowers of Carmaux by Jean W. Scott of Northwestern University, and the comparative analysis of mobility in Amsterdam, Frankfurt, and San Francisco being undertaken by Allen Emrich, Jr., of Temple University.

2. So it appears, at least, from Rishøj's Table 5. My own attempt to verify these figures by recomputing the raw data in Tables 1–4, however, shows a different pattern. A more detailed report on this study is badly needed. See Tom Rishøj, "Metropolitan Social Mobility 1850–1950: The Case of Copenhagen," *Quality and Quantity,* 5 (June 1971), pp. 131–40.

Chapter 12

AMERICAN CAPITALISM'S ECONOMIC REWARDS*

Werner Sombart

How the Worker Lives

If the American worker receives a money wage two to three times as high as that of the German, but obtains the necessaries of life at no significantly greater cost than with us [i.e., in Germany], then what does the living standard of the American worker actually consist of—what use does he make of his "surplus" income? Does he save more? Does he spend more on essentials, such as food, housing, or clothing? Or does he spend more on luxury items? For certainly these are the three possibilities which are open to him. As far as I can see—and the evidence presented here appears to confirm it—he does all three of these things, perhaps most of all the second.

Here the household budgets come into their own as the most important source. . . . For America we possess the frequently cited enquiry of the Washington Bureau [of Labor Statistics], which compiled its figures from 25,440 workers' budgets. The investigations of the Massachusetts Bureau of Labor [Statistics] in 1902, which covered 152 workers' families, serve to supplement the federal enquiry, and to act as a control on its results. The average [yearly] income of the families investigated by the Washington office was $749.50—that of the 2,567 families for which especially detailed information is available being $827.19. The comparable figures for the 152 families from Massachusetts was $863.37. [For Germany, we have] . . . the following, which I regard as the most valuable among the more recent compilations, and the most

* Taken from Section Two, Parts Four and Five, and Section Three, Parts One, Two, and Three, of Werner Sombart, *Warum gibt es in den Vereinigten Staaten keinen Sozialismus?* (Tübingen, 1906), pp. 112–42. Translated by Howard A. Fleming, Jr. Selected, edited, and revised by John H. M. Laslett.

useful for the purposes of this investigation. [Sombart here cites four German surveys of workers' budgets, the first a general survey of twenty urban and rural household budgets from a variety of areas; the second a survey of budgets in the city of Nuremberg; the third a survey of budgets drawn from seventeen rural communities near Karlsruhe; and the fourth from Berlin. For the full reference, see below.†]

Let us examine first of all how income and expenditure relate to each other in the budgets which are available for comparison, and what the chances of saving [money] are, in one case compared to another:

May [general German survey]: Out of 20 families, 5 save an average of 92 marks [$22] each.

Nuremberg [city]: 32 families have a surplus of 125 marks [$30] each on an average, 12 a deficit of 82 marks [$20] each.

Berlin [city]: 399 budgets have an average surplus of 53 marks [$13] each; 464 a deficit of 79 marks [$19] each.

Massachusetts [state]: For 96 families income exceeds expenditure on an average by $85. For nine they are in balance, so that here forty-seven [families] end up with an average deficit of $77

† 1. *How the Worker Lives: (Twenty) Urban and Rural Workers' Household Budgets* (Collected, Reported in Extracts, and with Comments by Max May, Berlin, 1897). Cited as May. The incomes vary between 647 and 1,957 marks [from $154 to $466], the average income totaling 1,222 marks [$291]. That of the big-city worker varies from 1,445 to 1,957 marks [from $344 to $466]. 2. *Household Budgets of Nuremberg Workers: A Contribution Toward Illuminating the Living Conditions of the Nuremberg Proletariat* (Edited in the Nuremberg Workers' Secretariat, Adolph Braun, ed. November 1901). Cited as Nuremberg. 3. *The Circumstances of Industrial Workers in Seventeen Rural Communities near Karlsruhe* (Presented by Dr. Fuchs, Grand Ducal Factory Inspector, Karlsruhe, 1904). Cited as Karlsruhe. The money incomes in the fourteen workers' budgets investigated vary between 1,065 and 2,285 marks [from $254 to $544]. The average totals 1,762 marks [$420]. 4. *Wage Investigations and Household Budgets of the Less Well-Off Population of Berlin in 1904* (Berlin Statistics, Issued by the Statistical Office of the City of Berlin, Professor Dr. E. Hirschberg, ed., vol. 3, Berlin, 1904). Cited as Berlin. Deals with 908 budgets, the total incomes in which averaged out at 1,751 marks each [$417]. In 221 cases the income was between 1,200 and 1,500 marks [$286 and $357]; in 303 cases, between 1,500 and 1,800 marks [$357 and $429]; in 169 cases, between 1,800 and 2,100 marks [$429 and $500]; and in 693 cases, between 1,200 and 2,100 marks [$285 and $500]. Note that the dollar equivalents for mark values are given to the nearest dollar, at the then current rate of exchange. (Ed.)

each. However, it should be noted in relation to this that two of the deficits alone total $710.85.

Washington [general U.S. survey]: 12,816 families have a surplus of $120.84 each on an average; 4,117 a deficit (averaging $65.58). The remaining 8,507 families have a balance between income and expenditure.

The Americans thus are in a somewhat more favorable position, but not as much by far as one would expect. The number of families that have something left over from their yearly income is not significantly greater than with us [i.e., in Germany]. . . . The American worker also as frequently spends everything that he takes in, and more. Therefore he must live significantly better than the German worker. And that he does so cannot be doubted. . . .

One can assume, [for example], that the American worker's dwelling has an average of four rooms each, whereas the German's does not even have two. After all, the 908 Berlin households, which more likely than not represent an above-average type, had on the average a dwelling area of about 1.4 rooms, while the 25,440 American families [of the general U.S. survey] averaged 4.67 rooms [per family] if they lived in rented houses, and 5.12 rooms if they lived in their own houses. But the interior furnishings of the dwellings are also incomparably more comfortable in America. . . . The better sort of workers' dwellings [in America] resemble those of the middle-class German: they are abundantly furnished with good beds, comfortable chairs, carpets, etc.

We can best measure the differences in *diet* if we know the amounts of food consumed and thus can compare the total consumption. The longer [American, i.e., Washington] inquiry contains useful data on this topic, and of the German investigations two, the Karlsruhe [rural] and the Nuremberg [city] ones, include at least partially comparable figures.

It should be noted that in all cases the size of the families is almost exactly the same: 5.31 members per family in America, 5.36 in Karlsruhe, and 5 in Nuremberg. I have converted the American measurements (bushels, quarts, pounds, and loaves) into kilograms in order to make them comparable to the German figures. For the food items missing no comparable figures were to be found.

On an average, a worker's family consumes yearly:

		In the U.S.	*Around Karlsruhe*	*In Nuremberg*
Black bread	kg.	113.2	582	—
White bread	"		132	—
Meat (for Germany, meat and sausage together; for the United States, fresh and salt meat, fish, and poultry together)	"	381.7	112	95 (without
Potatoes	"	376.1	647	267 sausage)
Flour	"	306.4	91	55
Butter	"	52.7	20	5.3
Other fats (for Germany, including chicken fat and edible oils; in the United States, including lard)	"	38.0	32	22.6
Cheese	"	7.2	12	—
Milk	Liters	333.2	737	—
Eggs	"	1,022.0	612	—
Sugar	kg.	120.6	31	—
Rice	"	11.3	—	5.5

According to this, the American worker eats almost three times as much meat, three times as much flour, and four times as much sugar as the German—the high consumption of flour, eggs, and sugar showing ample enjoyment of baked goods such as pies and puddings. . . . To sum it up, the diet of the American worker is much closer to that of our better-off middle-class circles than to that of our class of wage laborers: the American worker dines already, he no longer just eats.

The fact that the American worker ranks much more nearly with our bourgeois middle class than with our working class as far as standard of living is concerned is shown perhaps most clearly in his *clothing.* This strikes everyone who comes to America for the first time. Kolb, for example, noted the following: "Many [workers] even wore starched shirts there (i.e., in the bicycle factory); the collars were unbuttoned during work and the cuffs—all sewed on, without exception, by the way—were rolled back to the elbows. Then, when the whistle blew and the people peeled off their overalls, one could scarcely see that they were workers. Many used their bicycles for the ride home, and several rode off wearing elegant hats, yellow laced boots, and fashionably colored gloves—dressed fit to kill, [and they were] unskilled manual laborers with a daily wage of $1.25." And then the working women! —the "ladies," as they are generally called. Here the clothing is often downright elegant, particularly in the case of the young girls. In more than one factory I have seen working women in brightly colored, even in white silk blouses. A hat is almost never lacking on the way to the factory.

Mrs. [John] Van Vorst reports of a working girls' ball that "white gloves were compulsory," and describes the attire of the "ladies" in the restaurant where they lunch . . . as follows: "They arrived in groups, elegant in a rustle of silk skirts" (just think of that!), "under hats loaded with feathers, garlands of flowers, and a whole mountain of ornaments; with artificial flowers, kid gloves, silver sash purses, embroidered blouses, and embossed belt buckles—completely attired, with everything designed for effect."

The question arises of whether this luxury in clothing may be enumerated statistically, in order to be able to compare it, say, with that of other countries. Peter Roberts, who looks at the modern luxury of the working-class population with a petty and jaundiced eye, to be sure, nonetheless makes some very interesting observations on precisely [this question of comparative] expenditures for clothing, in his investigations into the condition of the coal miners of Pennsylvania. [According to him], while the newly arrived "Slav" woman satisfies her demand for clothing on $25 a year, the average American woman requires $50 to $60, and some up to $100 or $150. He reports as follows on the men: The "Hun" pays $5 for a suit, the "Pole" $10, and the "Lett" $15. The Anglo-Saxon pays $15 to $25, and many wear tailored suits. They [the Anglo-Saxons] never go without a collar and a tie, cuffs and a white shirt, tie pins, buttons, and a gold watch with a chain, and they are seldom without a gold ring. They pay $2 to $3 for a pair of shoes and approximately the same price for their hats. They never shop in a used clothing store. Each has a comfortable topcoat for cold weather. Many of them have two such coats: one for the early part of the year and the autumn, the other for winter. In contrast to recently arrived immigrants—and probably also to the older generation of the native-born—young America changes clothes mighty often. If a suit is somewhat worn, it is discarded. Collars and ties are changed according to the demands of fashion. Much is spent also for linen and underwear. So the average young man of native birth, married or single, must need about $40 to $50 [a year] (or 168 to 210 marks) for clothing.

These assertions are confirmed in the figures of our household budgets. [American] expenditures for clothing, both in absolute and in relative terms [i.e., relative to total income], are high throughout, and significantly higher than in Germany. The Washington [sample of] 2,567 [families] shows the following average expenditures per year:

Husband's clothing	142	marks	[$34] =	4.39%	of total income	
Wife's clothing	109	"	[$26] =	3.39%	" "	"
Children's clothing	202	"	[$48] =	6.26%	" "	"
Total clothing	453	"	[$108] =	14.04%	" "	"

On an average, the Massachusetts families spend annually, for clothing, 456 marks [$109], i.e., 12.81% of their total income.

In contrast now, the German surveys show the following average expenditure for clothing:

Mays' families	163	marks	[$39] =	13 %	of total expenditure	
Karlsruhe families	218	"	[$52] =	12.5%	" "	"
Nuremberg families	117	"	[$28] =	8.5%	" "	"
Berlin families	144	"	[$34] =	8.5%	" "	"

Living Standard and World View

It would be risky to attempt to demonstrate in detail the effect which such a different standard of living has upon the American worker. . . .

This much is certain, however: the American worker lives in comfortable circumstances. By and large he does not know the oppression of miserable housing. He is not driven out of his house into the saloon, because his home is not simply a "room," like that of the big-city worker in continental Europe; on the contrary, he can to a considerable degree indulge the "egotistical feelings" which a comfortable domestic life tends to develop. He is well nourished, and he does not know the miseries which necessarily result in the long run from a diet of potatoes and alcohol. He dresses like a gentleman, and the working woman like a lady, so that his outward appearance tends to make him unaware of the distance which separates him from the ruling class.

Small wonder if, in these circumstances, dissatisfaction with the existing social order is only established with difficulty in the mind of the [American] worker—particularly if his tolerable, even comfortable, standard of living appears safe over the long run. And up to this point in time [Sombart is writing in 1906 (Ed.)] he could be certain that it would remain safe. For we must never forget what steady progress, save for short periods, the "economic upswing" in the United States has made during the last two generations—during which socialism should actually have taken root—and this obviously not in spite of capitalism, but because of it.

A glance at the most general statistics is enough to dispel any doubt as to the reality of this "upswing." . . . And as the material condition of the wage worker has improved—and the increasing comfort of his way of life has enabled him to savor the corrupting effects of material wealth—so he has been impelled to love the economic system which has shaped his fate, and to adapt his spirit to the characteristic operations of the capitalist economy. He has fallen under the spell which rapid change and the increasing scale of modern production exert irresistibly on almost everybody in this wondrous age. A dose of patriotism—of the proud consciousness that the United States has led all other peoples along the high road of capitalist "progress"—has confirmed the businesslike character of his mind, and has made him into the sober, calculating, down-to-earth "businessman" that we know today. All socialist utopias have come to grief on roast beef and apple pie.

The Social Position of the Worker

I. THE DEMOCRATIC STYLE OF PUBLIC LIFE IN AMERICA

Not only is the position of the American worker in relation to the world of material goods, his standard of living, more favorable by far than that of his European counterpart. His relationship to other people and to social institutions, and his position both in society and in relation to it—in short what I would call his social position as a whole—is also advantageous compared to the situation [of his counterpart] in Europe. For him "freedom" and "equality" (not only in the legal and political sense, but also in the material and social sense) are not empty concepts, or vague dreams, as they are for the proletariat in Europe. To a great extent they are realities.

The American worker's superior social position results from his political and economic situation: namely from a radical-democratic Constitution, and from a comfortable standard of living, both of them present among rapidly developing population without a separate history, which basically consisted (and still consists) entirely of "immigrants," where the traditions of feudalism—with the exception of some southern states—are lacking. . . .

In his external appearance, the worker does not bear those signs of belonging to a separate class which almost all European workers have. In his approach, in his demeanor, and in his manner of conversation the American worker contrasts strikingly with the European worker. . . . He seems neither oppressed, nor submissive. He treats everyone as "his equal," not just in theory, but in practice. The union leader who goes to a formal banquet handles himself as well on the dance floor as any person of high rank in Germany. In addition, he wears a well-fitting dress suit, patent leather boots, and elegant linen in the latest fashion, so that here again no one can distinguish him outwardly from the President of the Republic.

Cringing and crawling before the "upper classes," which makes such an unpleasant impression in Europe, is absolutely unknown. It would never occur to any waiter, to any streetcar conductor, or to any policeman [in America] to behave any differently toward an "ordinary worker" than he would toward the governor of Pennsylvania. Being able to behave like that gives confidence to these kinds of people, especially if they belong to the poorer segment of the population, just as it does to those who are treated that way. . . .

Snobbery concerning one's social position is also probably less widespread in the United States than it is in Germany. The individual is not valued for what he *is,* still less for what his parents *were;* he is valued for what he *accomplishes.* Hence it is easy to make "work" in its abstract form into something honorable, and thereby also to treat the "worker" respectfully because of rather than in spite of the fact that he is simply a worker. As a result of this, of course, the workingman *feels* differently than his counterpart does in a country where "man" [properly so-called] first begins, if not with the baron, then with the reserve officer, the doctor, or the government official. Due to the factors described above, social distance between individual levels of the population—already smaller in reality as a result of the democratic Constitution, the general diffusion of education, and the workers' higher standard of living—becomes even smaller in the minds of the various classes than it actually is.

II. EMPLOYEES AND WORKERS

This tone of "equal treatment," to which social and public life in the United States is attuned, is also dominant within the capitalist enterprise itself. Here, too, the employer does not treat the worker as if he [the employer] were a "lord" who demands obedience, as the employer did, and still generally does, in "old" Europe, with its feudal traditions. From the beginning a purely business approach became the dominant one in dealing with wage contracts. Formal "equalization" of employers and workers did not have to be won first in a long struggle. Just as the American woman was given special consideration because she was few in numbers, so the employer of labor took care to adopt a polite, obliging attitude toward his workers—who were initially also in short supply—an attitude which naturally found strong support in the democratic atmosphere of the country. Even today, even English workers are astonished at the respectful tone which [American] employers and foremen adopt toward their workers; at the lack of restraints placed on the American worker even at his place of work; and at the "absence of what one might call annoying supervision." . . .

It is also a peculiarity of American factory owners that while on the one hand they do not introduce even the simplest safety precautions into their plants and do not worry in the least about the proper layout of their workshops—which on the contrary are often overcrowded, etc.—on the other hand they are most willing to do everything they can to provide what the workers regard as comforts, such as bathtubs, showers, lockers, and temperature controls in the workrooms, which are cooled by ventilators in the summer and heated in the winter. The English workers of the Mosely Commission could not marvel enough over this arrangement, in particular, which one finds fairly generally in American factories. "You imagine the answer of an English industrialist you asked to take such measures for the well-being of his personnel," said the iron founder Mr. Madison; and all the others were "impressed by the exceptional care taken to assure the comfort and well-being of the personnel."

Certainly these are minor things, but it is true here too that "it's the little things that count." I will try to show later that, seen objectively, in no other country in the world is the worker so exploited by capitalism as in the United States—in no other country is he "rubbed so bloody by the harness of capitalism," or works himself to death as quickly as there. But that is not the important thing when it comes to explaining the feelings of the proletariat. For the only thing which really determines these feelings is what the individual worker does or does not value, or likes or does not like for himself. And it is one of the most brilliant diplomatic feats of the American employer (just like the professional politician in his way) that he understands how to keep the worker in a contented mood in spite of all the actual exploitation, so that workers never become conscious of their actual situation. And being generous in little things has significantly contributed to that.

There is yet another circumstance which works in the same direction, and influences the worker psychologically so that he becomes not an opponent, but even an active supporter of the capitalist system. American employers understand brilliantly how to interest the worker in the success of their enterprise, how to identify his interests—up to a point at least—with their own. This is done not so much through profit sharing (although this does occur in the United States in all its various forms), but rather by means of a small, interrelated series of measures which, taken together, achieve marvelous results. In the first place, all American employers are praised—again, for example, by the people on the Mosely Commission—for not attempting to cut back on the exceptionally high wages which workers occasionally earn as a result of previously agreed-on piece rates, as European employers usually do. As a result of this liberal practice the [American] worker constantly remains in a fever of activity, and is, moreover, kept in a good mood by the possibility of *very* high gains.

A second widespread custom of the American employer is that of directly interesting the worker in technical progress by gladly entertaining every suggestion [his employees make] for improving the machinery, etc., and by letting the worker profit directly or indirectly from the suggestion if it is adopted and proves successful. Thus the organization of which the worker is a member becomes *his* plant, in the fortunes of which he has an interest. This habit of accepting "suggestions" and "complaints" from the workers and always taking them seriously is found in all branches of American industry: in steel production and in shipbuilding, in knife manufacture and in spinning, in leatherwork and in bookbinding, in paper manufacture and in the chemical or optical industry. In most factories there is a so-called "suggestion box," into which the workers put their "proposals" or "suggestions." This system is particularly well developed, like all such methods, in the well-known model works of the [National] Cash Register Co., of Dayton, Ohio. . . . Honorary diplomas and money prizes are distributed semi-annually for noteworthy suggestions. The amount of the prizes is based upon the value of the innovation, the company spending several thousand marks [at that time 4.20 = $1.00] on them annually. All the workers—over 2,000 people—are invited to a meeting for the distribution of the prizes, and the occasion is accompanied by music and speeches. In 1897, 4,000 "suggestions" were received, of which 1,078 were implemented; in 1898 2,500 more; and in 1901 2,000, of which one third were introduced into the plant either wholly or partially.

Finally, capitalists seek to attract the interest of their workers by profit-sharing schemes, through offering them stocks at advantageous rates. In this way the capitalists sometimes kill two birds with one stone. In the first place they draw the worker into the business operations of the company, awakening his lower instincts —his speculative fever, and his striving for gain—thereby attaching him to the system of production they represent. Secondly, though, this also enables them to dispose of their bad stocks, to prevent a threatened fall in prices, or perhaps to influence momentarily the stock market so as to get an extra something for themselves.

This system has been brought into widespread use by the steel trust [i.e., United States Steel]. In 1903 the company first used $2,000,000 of its profits from the previous year in order to buy 25,000 of its own preferred stock. It offered these to its 168,000 employees at $82.50 a share, payable within three years. To induce the workers to hold on to the stocks, an extra dividend of $5 per share per year was promised in the event that the stocks remained in the hands of the original purchaser for longer than five years. The offer found general approval: 48,983 shares were bought by employees of the company. . . . It is clear what at least is the temporary result of such a policy. [As one observer puts it]: "Partners in a great enterprise, the mass of petty shareholders are led more and more to consider economic questions from the employers' standpoint." "The chances of collision [with the employers] . . . will disappear . . ." [writes another observer], "when their differences are merged in a sense of common ownership. . . ." Above all, the worker is permeated with the ethos of capitalism: "The present ambition of the higher wage-earner" [writes a third observer], "seems to incline more to the pecuniary rewards of his work than to the work itself. Doubtless this tendency is due in no small measure to the fact that the wage earner is brought into constant and immediate contact with the money-making class. He sees that the value of the industry is measured chiefly by its profits. Sometimes the profit is flaunted in his face. At all times the thing most in evidence to him is money."

The Escape of the Worker into Freedom

However enticing these temptations may be . . .—and however successfully they may operate on the "weaker souls" among the workers—one may still doubt whether they would have been enough in themselves to turn the worker into the peaceful citizen he is, at almost every level, if he had not been induced in still another way to reconcile himself to the dominant economic system, or at least not to take up a hostile attitude toward it. For American capitalism, too, puts tight chains on a man; it, too, cannot wholly conceal the condition of slavery in which it holds its workers. It, too, has had periods of stagnation with all their ruinous consequences for the worker: unemployment, pressure on wages, etc. With the passage of time a spirit of opposition would almost certainly have developed at least among the best workers, had not an avenue of escape from the capitalist system—or at least from the tight circle of wage labor—been open to the leading elements among them, to those upon whom the fetters [of capitalism] had begun to chafe: to those, in other words, who were the most rebellious, defiant, and troublesome, and to those who were the most enterprising and farsighted.

With this I come to that peculiarity of the American economy which has been of the utmost significance for the development of the proletarian psyche. For there is a kernel of truth in all the chatter of the Carnegies and their clique, who want to lull the rabble to sleep by telling miraculous tales of themselves and others who began as newspaper boys and ended as billionaires: namely, that the chances of the worker rising out of his class were indeed greater than they were in "old" Europe. Anglo-Saxon purposefulness, the newness of the society and its democratic character, the smaller class barriers between employers and employees, the colonial vigor of many of the immigrants—all these and many other factors not infrequently operated to allow the ordinary worker to climb up the ladder of capitalism to the top, or almost to the top. The much greater extent of their savings—at least by European standards—enabled still other workers to become independent as *petits bourgeois,* i.e., shopkeepers, saloonkeepers, etc.

But yet another goal, bringing liberation in the fullest sense of the word, has beckoned the great mass of dissatisfied wage workers—and one which hundreds of thousands, in fact millions of workers have striven for and reached in the course of the past century, freeing them wholly from the burden of capitalism: namely, a free homestead in the unsettled West. In fact, I believe that the explanation for the peculiarly peaceful mood of the American worker lies above all in this fact, that practically any number of people of sound body could make themselves into independent farmers without—or almost without—any capital, by settling on free land. . . .

By means of the Homestead Laws of 1860 [sic] and subsequent years, every person over twenty-one years old who is a citizen, or who declares his intention of becoming one, secures the right to take possession of 80 acres of public land located between reserved railway lands, or 160 acres of public land located elsewhere, if he declares under oath that he actually intends to inhabit and cultivate the site exclusively for his own use, and not use it to bestow any advantage on anyone else, directly or indirectly. Only an insignificant fee has to be paid for this right. The right to [actual] ownership of this "homestead" is granted to the settler after five years, under certain conditions which are easily fulfilled.

It is a universally known fact, for which no proof need be given, that millions of people have settled as farmers in the United States [in this manner] during the last half century. I only cite the number of farms, as determined in each census year, in order to establish the real significance of the figures involved:

1850	1,449,073
1860	2,044,077
1870	2,659,985
1880	4,008,907
1890	4,564,641
1900	5,737,372

And these are all new farms, which have been developed on virgin soil, [shown by the fact that in] the same period of time the area of land under cultivation grew at almost the same rate as the number of farms.

1850	113,032,614 acres
1860	163,110,720
1870	183,921,099
1880	284,771,042
1890	357,616,755
1900	418,498,487

That is to say, in the two decades from 1870 to 1890 an area twice the size of the German Reich was brought under cultivation for the first time.

Americans themselves play the most prominent part in this process of new settlement. That is to say, the free land of the West is as much the goal of residents in other American states, which send their "surplus" population there, as it is of foreign immigrants, if not more so. Internal migration takes on greater dimensions in the United States than it does in any other country, and its character is totally different from the internal migration in European states. With us [i.e., in Germany] it is basically a desire to move out of predominantly agrarian areas into the cities and the industrial districts that sets the population in motion. This trend is by no means lacking in the United States now, particularly in the East, and it becomes stronger from year to year. But next to it, and far surpassing it in strength, there is an opposite movement out of the more densely settled, more industrial areas into non-populated areas with free land. . . .

But other figures, namely the statistics on the number of homesteads distributed each year, show us that these migrations are also to a large degree connected with developments in the capitalist system itself, i.e., that they indicate an escape from the nexus of capitalist organization. For we can clearly trace how the number of homesteads increases rapidly in times of economic depression, without this being explained by rising immigration. This means that it is the "industrial reserve army" which pours out of the industrial districts onto the land and settles there in these [depression] years. This applies especially to the earlier periods in which settlement was easier. Thus, for example, the number of acres given out under the Homestead Act, and since 1875 under the Timber Act as well, rose from 2,698,770 acres in 1877 to 6,288,779 and 8,026,685 in the following two years, respectively—when the industrial crisis reached its high point—while immigration was less in 1878 than in any year since 1863.

The economic depression continued throughout the 1880s. As a result immigration fell by one half, from 669,000 [immigrants] in 1882 and 789,000 in 1883, to 395,000 in 1885 and 334,000 in 1886. But despite this the number of acres given out rose from between seven and eight million at the beginning of the 1880s to over twelve million in the second half of the 1880s. In the middle of the 1880s an upheaval threatened to take place within the American working class due to the continuing depression. In Chicago and other cities anarchism raised its head and the Knights of Labor, which had originally been strongly socialistic, grew from a membership of 52,000 in 1883 to 703,000 in 1886, only to sink to almost one half of that number in 1888, when the force of the storm had been broken. [By this time] the rebellious unemployed population had begun to leave in ever larger numbers for the West, for the areas of *terra libera.*

The importance for the development of the proletarian psyche of the fact that American capitalism has developed in a land with enormous stretches of *terra libera* is by no means exhausted by indicating the number of settlers who have actually ceased being "servants of capitalism" over the years. In addition, one must take into account the fact that the mere awareness that at any time he *could* become an independent farmer must have given the American worker a feeling of security and ease which is foreign to the European worker. One can tolerate any unpleasant situation better if one at least lives under the illusion of being able to escape from it in the event of extreme necessity!

As a result of this, it is clear that the attitude of the proletariat toward future economic developments has of necessity become something very special: the possibility of choosing between capitalism and non-capitalism transforms every budding [movement of] opposition to the economic system from an active to a passive role, and takes the sting out of all anti-capitalist agitation.

COMMENT 1

Adolph Sturmthal

Werner Sombart's case rests, first of all, on the American worker's higher standard of living. Given the exchange rates then and now, and taking account of devaluation and revaluation, we may assert that money wages in the United States, on the average, are undoubtedly and substantially higher than in any other country. International comparisons of real wages—considering, as does Sombart, the relative prices of consumer goods bought by workers—are notoriously difficult, in view of the vast differences in consumption habits from country to country. In principle, such differences exist even within a given country, particularly one as large as the United States, containing various climatic and cultural zones. Still, in a rough estimate most observers agree that average real per capita incomes are, and were for more than a century, significantly higher in the United States than anywhere else.

This is Sombart's main argument. "Socialist utopias," he says, "have been defeated by roast beef and apple pie." As a first approximation, this proposition seems to be true enough. The attractiveness of socialist ideas is, in general, in inverse proportion to living standards. This, however, does not mean that there is a more or less straight monotonic functional relationship between the two.

In the first place, at the lower end of the income scale, the curve seems to reverse itself, flatten out, or become meaningless. At very low living standards, radicalism does not seem to flourish; lethargy prevails. Radical movements, including the early socialist and trade union organizations, have rarely been started by the lowest income group living in misery. The pioneers of such movements were either students and other members of the intelligentsia joining the cause of the workers, or skilled artisans threatened by a more modern industrial technology, or finally, men simply moved by a sense of solidarity with the poorest of the poor.

Second, the degree of inequality of the distribution of incomes can be of vital significance. Given a certain level of the per capita gross national product, the lowest-income groups may be living in misery or not, according to the degree of inequality of the distribution of the GNP. Was—or is—inequality greater in the United States than, say, in Western or Central Europe?[1] It would seem probable, although statistical evidence could hardly be conclusive, that once the social reforms of Bismarck and Lloyd George in Germany and Britain were accomplished, inequality in the United States—at least in the urban areas—was greater than in Europe. As against this, the "frontier" may have put a fairly high floor under wages in this country, even though the impact of this factor may have been less than Sombart assumed. A further complication is introduced by ethnic and racial divisions among the population. The sense of solidarity that caused intellectuals and skilled workers on the Continent and—in a different way—those in Great Britain to take the side of the uneducated and helpless poorest social groups and to organize them failed to operate with similar strength in the United States toward whichever was the most recent ethnic groups of immigrants. Hence the ease with which the skilled workers in the AFL separated themselves from the bulk of the immigrants and the blacks. We shall come back to this topic in due course.

Sombart's general proposition needs further qualification by reference to the rate of economic growth in this country as compared to that of most of Western Europe. There are two aspects to this issue. One is of lesser relevance today in a comparison between the United States and other industrial nations, but matters a good deal when we think of the newly industrializing nations. The first impact of modernization on pre-industrial nations is frequently powerful and revolutionizing. Radicalism has its strongest appeal—and meets its strongest resistance—when the pre-industrial social forms are in acute danger of being ousted. Once these early battles have been fought and the forces of modernization are victorious, the rate of economic growth—the second issue—becomes a primary factor determining the political and social climate. While the industrial revolution destroys the privileges of various social groups, it tends to advance the GNP and personal incomes after a more or less short interval. The fact that in the United States industrial output increased four times between 1870 and 1900 and again more than four times between 1900 and 1940, a period that included the Great Depression of the thirties, created that atmosphere of social optimism in which Marxian socialism had little appeal. Real wages in manufacturing in the United States rose by a yearly average of 1.6 per cent, a rate of advance that contrasted sharply with the almost total stagnation in the British workers' living standard during the quarter century before World War I,[2] and that of France during the period between 1929 and 1950 when the GNP did not grow at all. Even though the benefits of the expansion in the United States were highly unevenly distributed, economic growth was rapid and substantial enough to satisfy the bulk of the working class—by actual achievement or at least by arousing their hopes. The chances of social or economic advancement in an economy expanding in breadth as well as in depth were obviously more substantial than in the older and established countries of Western and Central Europe. Thus opportunities were available for a rapid improvement in working-class living standards without radical institutional reforms.[3]

The Role of Collective Bargaining

If rapid economic growth made rising living standards possible for large numbers of workers, the scarce labor supply in relation to land and other resources, to which Sombart refers only in passing, provided the necessary leverage for the American workers to share in prosperity. In countries with large excess labor supplies, strikes are a weapon of doubtful effectiveness for most workers; indeed, few of those lucky enough to have found a job would be willing to engage in strikes unless driven by despair. True, skilled workers may be successful in using collective action, even if total labor supply is excessive, because their skill may be rare. It is no accident that the separation of the skilled workers from the broad-based organization of the Knights of Labor occurred when it did, i.e., in a period of mass immigration of common labor which coincided with the relatively less prosperous era of the eighties and early nineties of the last century.[4] Once the unions of skilled workers had abandoned their alliance with the unskilled, the economic power which relative scarcity provided for the skilled workers became fully effective.

Collective bargaining was thus a convenient and powerful instrument to let the organized skilled workers share in prosperity. Economic expansion provided the means by which the standard of living of the workers could be raised without radical social change. In very much the same way, the long period of economic growth in Western and Central Europe following the reconstruction period after World War II, accompanied by a labor shortage unequaled in recorded European history, brought collective bargaining to the fore in countries—e.g., France—where earlier it had played only a secondary role even for skilled workers.[5]

Not every one, of course, shared equally in the results of economic progress and collective bargaining. While in the United States large numbers of semi-skilled workers, by way of the CIO, joined the organized labor movement in due course and benefited from its advance, substantial parts of the working population shared only little in economic progress. This was the case of the overwhelming majority of the blacks and Mexicans in the United States, of migratory workers in general, and of large numbers of sharecroppers and agricultural workers. Neither the great majority of the organized trade unions nor the new labor laws concerned themselves at first with the fate of these millions of workers. The gap between the more or less privileged members of the bulk of the trade unions and the poor—including the working poor—became one of the dominant features of the American social scene. On the one hand, a substantial number of workers approached the middle classes in their standard of living, though not in their style of life—in their outlook they had long before done so. On the other hand, large parts of the population continued to live on the fringes of society, separated not only from the upper and middle classes, but also from a large fraction of the working class. Indeed, the very term "working class" became meaningless, if it ever had any meaning in American society. For the gap—in standard of living, in outlook on economic and social problems, though perhaps not in cultural matters—separating the upper working class from the poor became greater than the distance between the bulk of the unionized workers and most of the middle- and higher-income groups, a tiny minority of semi-aristocrats perhaps excepted. While rapid economic growth and long-term labor shortages channeled the main effort of organized labor into collective bargaining, the "liberal"—in the European meaning of the term—industrial relations system had little to offer to a large number of people outside union ranks.

To this internal division of the working population in economic and social status corresponds the lack of class consciousness and class solidarity among American workers. Apart perhaps from brief episodes, the AFL was never a movement expressing common class interests, opposed to those of other classes in society, and it relied only infrequently upon means of action expressing a communality of interests transcending those of individual groups within the working class. Indeed, from its beginnings the AFL was a protest against, or at least a departure from, the vague social reform movement of the Knights of Labor. The craft unions defended the idea that each group best take care of itself without any ambition to change the fate of "the working class." Competitive sectional bargaining was the expression of this state of mind which corresponded to the social situation in the country. By contrast, even during the fifties and sixties of this century when vast labor shortages offered unequaled opportunities for collective bargaining successes to the European workers, interconfederal agreements, concluded by the trade union confederation and the organization of all employers, rather than individual unions and their industry counterparts, and covering all the members of all unions, were a frequent instrument of economic and social advance for French and Italian workers. While this may have been one step away from the traditional class consciousness that had contributed to working-class reliance on uniform law and administrative regulation in the past, the legacy of class solidarity was still strong enough to prevent competitive sectional advances. Occupational, industrial, and even ideological divisions were still secondary to the feeling of solidarity among organized workers. Indeed, in principle, most of these agreements covered all workers, whether unionized or not.

Lack of Class Consciousness

Most of the factors that prevented the development or at least the perpetuation of class consciousness among American workers have already been mentioned. Yet one of the fundamentals must still be added: the absence of a feudal tradition in the United States, i.e., of a social system which ordered life in all its aspects according to the social status of each individual. To rise above one's origins—

the American call to action—is the opposite of the European tradition of "living according to one's station in life," or of the "ridiculous" posture of anyone who pretends to be "better" than he is—both expressions of the ascriptive social order of feudalism. The lack of this tradition is at the root of the informal relationship between employer and workers in the United States which Sombart noticed with considerable surprise.

Further evidence for the importance of the feudal traditions (or of their absence), sometimes long after the feudal institutions themselves had withered away, is the "heroic" age of the European labor movements when they fought for political and social equality, and increased educational opportunities for the members of the working class. Class consciousness thus formed the firm basis for the growth of a socialist movement in all of its ramifications. While the struggle for equal suffrage and free secular primary school education for members of the working class was the most spectacular aspect of this movement, one should not overlook the extent to which socialist-inspired organizations endeavored to meet all the needs of their members which the existing society left unfulfilled—from education to sports and the upbringing of small children. This special class culture which the European—particularly the Continental—radical labor movements developed for their members provides a key for an understanding of the sources of strength of these movements and their appeal to the working class which Sombart unfortunately failed to discern, perhaps because in his days this subculture was still in its infancy.

In current terminology these ideas could be summarized as follows: Marx and following him Sombart put too much emphasis on the economic exploitation of the workers alone and expected the revolutionary movement to arise from increasing misery. They neglected to put equal emphasis on the exclusion of the workers from the political community. This exclusion manifested itself most clearly, though not alone, in the refusal to grant the franchise or equal franchise to the workers. This fact was as important for the appeal of revolutionary class consciousness to the workers on the Continent as the economic distress of the workers. The fact that the issue of equal suffrage was more or less settled in the United States when the modern labor movement arose and this symbol of class discrimination was eliminated made possible an early integration of the workers in the national community. Instead of class divisions, racial, ethnic, and religious issues proved of greater relevance in the consciousness of American workers. In England, too, the gradual extension of the right to vote to the workers during the nineteenth century at least weakened, if not prevented, the development of revolutionary class consciousness.[6]

In the United States social mobility, connected with the rapid economic expansion of the country, also helped prevent the development of a separate class culture. Some of the energies which in Europe found their expression in the organization and the leadership of movements of social protest and emancipation were diverted in the United States into the channels of personal advancement. Neither feudal tradition, nor a powerful sense of class solidarity, nor, finally, an overwhelming sense of scarcity of opportunity stood in the way of a search for individual success.

I am aware that the last remark is in open contradiction to Perlman's well-known theory. According to him, workers have a sense of a scarcity of opportunity, as distinguished from entrepreneurs, for whom the world is full of opportunities. There is little evidence to support this assertion unless his theory is interpreted to apply only to opportunities of a particular occupational kind, i.e., to jobs for carpenters or workers of a particular skill. In the light of technological change and of potentially competitive immigrants, the wish of the skilled trades to restrict access to their occupation is understandable. Yet mass immigration of people of foreign languages and little education provided many opportunities for the social advancement of those who had a higher level of education and were familiar with the language and the institutions of this country. Many a radical of leadership potential has ended up in the United States as a business magnate or at least a successful businessman.

It is in line with the absence of a sense of class belonging and class solidarity that labor organizations have consistently played a far smaller role in the lives of their members than in the European countries of the same period. There is little to be found in American labor of that sense of dedication, that call to achieve the millennium which animated, until fairly recently, the radical leaders of the European working class. Whether the impetus for this missionary sense came out of religious conviction, Marxian philosophy, or an anarchist sense of total rejection of what there is, few counterparts to such men as James Keir Hardie, Wilhelm

Liebknecht, Jean Jaurès, Émile Vandervelde, Anton Hueber, Hjalmar Branting can be found in the United States. And the few that did exist—Eugene Debs, Norman Thomas—rarely if ever succeeded in gaining lasting influence upon the bulk of the organized workers. Walter Reuther, who came closer to this goal than anyone else since Eugene Debs, could only do so by fitting himself within the existing structures in the very attempt to change them. Even so, he failed to achieve that leadership position to which his qualifications would have entitled him. The fact that not even John L. Lewis could "deliver the vote" of union members, while his counterparts in Europe control solid voting blocs is a measure of the more modest role which American labor organizations play in the lives of their members. Moreover, the marriage between radicalism and labor which formed the basis upon which the European socialist organizations were built was never consummated in the United States. There were a few moments when at long last an engagement seemed in sight—the nineties of the last and the thirties of this century—but in fact not even the engagement was ever formalized. And in the sixties, the role of the hardhats in combating the anti-war movement indicated the wide gap that separated at least a significant part of organized labor from the radicals.

NOTES

1. We are speaking, of course, of income after taxes and taking into account various social security measures.

2. Phelps Brown, *The Growth of British Industrial Relations* (London, 1959).

3. Except those required to make collective bargaining possible. Insofar as the latter necessitated governmental intervention to remove legal and other impediments for effective bargaining, the labor movement was compelled to rely upon the government and thus to turn toward political action. In France this involved the sit-down strikes and semi-revolutionary advent to power of the Popular Front government in 1936. In the United States the labor-supported New Deal may have appeared no less revolutionary to tradition-minded contemporaries, but in the end, both events proved evolutionary steps in the modernization of the capitalistic system in the two countries.

4. A declining branch of the Kondratieff cycle. "Less prosperous" means primarily a predominance of recession periods over boom periods. The general trend of production in the United States was of course still upward.

5. It will be noted below that even then collective bargaining largely took forms different from the sectional competitive bargaining of the Anglo-American variety.

6. Harold Wilensky, "Class, Class Consciousness, and American Workers," in William Haber (ed.), *Labor in a Changing America* (New York: Basic Books, 1966); Reinhard Bendix, "The Lower Classes and the 'Democratic Revolution,'" *Industrial Relations,* 1 (October 1961).

COMMENT 2

Iring Fetscher

A close rereading of Werner Sombart's famous book suggests that he was much less pessimistic as to the future of socialism in the United States than one would expect. At the end of his book, in fact, he forecast (wrongly as it turned out) the end of class harmony in the United States, and the coming of a strong socialist movement.[1] I think it is necessary to begin by reminding the reader of this, for Sombart's reputation–owing to his later alignment with the anti-socialist tendencies of the 1920s, and with Nazism–has by now sunk almost so low, in Europe at least, as to do him an injustice. It should also be remembered that earlier in his career he had been one of the first pro-socialist professors in imperial Germany.

I cannot and will not discuss Sombart's statistics, but assume that on the whole they are accurate. Nevertheless I think something should be said about the theoretical framework of his essay. Sombart bases his argument on three specific characteristics of American life: the political position of the worker and the two-party system; the economic situation of the worker, as compared with his position in European countries; and the social status of the worker. We are here concerned only with the economic and social aspects of his argument, which can be summarized in the following manner. First, that the economic situation of the American worker was superior to that of his European counterpart in respect of his money wages as well as in his general living conditions, particularly as to housing, food, and clothing. Second, the social position of the American worker was less clearly separated from that of the middle classes than it was in Europe, the worker being treated virtually as an equal by both entrepreneurs and business managers. And thirdly, Sombart argues that every American worker has (or at least had, in the 1890s) theoretically (and this is important for his level of consciousness) the possibility of becoming a free settler in the new territories with the help of state grants of land and public loans. According to Sombart, this permits the worker to "cease being a 'servant of capitalism.'" Leaving aside the question of whether or not the western frontier was indeed a "safety valve" for labor during this period—about which there is in America considerable academic debate[2]—I shall come back to this rather peculiar argument, which seems to assume that the settler-farmer drops out of the market society altogether, and becomes a self-supporting non-specialized farmer who thereby ceases to be a member of capitalist society.

Even though some of the statistics which Sombart gives in his general picture of the relative life-styles of the German and American worker might be criticized, I think on the whole the picture he gives is right. But it is not complete and it is therefore theoretically misleading. The principal omissions which I think should not have been made are as follows:

Sombart treats the American working class as a single unity. But in fact this has never been the case, and in the U.S.A. less so than in any other capitalist country. Not only does he not mention the Negro, but he also overlooks the importance of the constant inflow of immigrants and the marked distinctions between immigrants from different parts of Europe and Asia. These national and ethnic distinctions among the working class and their combination with specific strata within that class prevented (and still prevent to a large extent) the creation of a genuine sense of class consciousness and class solidarity. The "poor whites" psychology has many times been examined as a factor in separating the white working class from the black, but the mentality of the English, Dutch, Scandinavian, and German immigrants and the differences between these and the southern and western European immigrants have probably played a somewhat similar role. Another no less important division within the working class was the split between citizens or older immigrants on the one hand, and the most recent generation of newcomers on the other. The newcomers were not allowed to play a leading part in politics and as soon as they had become "citizens," they tended to distinguish themselves as much as they could from the next generation of newcomers "below them," as well as from the Establishment above.

Hand in hand with the integration of the immigrant into American society went his climbing (at least a few steps) up the social ladder, and this experience might well have played a role in the forming of his social consciousness as well. But it should be noted that the lack of class solidarity among workingmen has been a serious obstacle to class consciousness in England as well. In his letter to S. Meyer and A. Vogt in New York[3] of April 9, 1870, for example, Karl Marx wrote: "and what is most important: in all the industrial and commercial centers of England the working-class is now divided into two antagonistic camps: English and Irish proletarians. The average English worker hates the Irish worker as a competitor who depresses his standard of living. He feels himself compared to him [i.e., to the average Irishman] as a member of the ruling nation, and consequently becomes an instrument in the hands of his own aristocrats and capitalists against Ireland—in this way consolidating their rule over himself. He has religious, social and national prejudices against the Irish, and behaves about the same way as the poor white does towards the 'niggers' in the former slave-holding states of the American Union. The Irish 'pays him back,' with interest, in kind. He sees in the English worker someone who is both responsible for, as well as being a stupid instrument of, British dominion over Ireland."[4] So much was Marx convinced of the importance of this question that he even thought that "the decisive blow against the ruling classes in England (and this would be decisive for the labour movement all over the world) could not be made in England, but only in Ireland."[5]

A second omission in Sombart's essay is of lesser practical but of greater theoretical relevance. He writes about high wages and about the possibility of free settlement in the new western territories, but he does not comment on the close link between the two phenomena. The employers had to pay relatively high wages because the possibility of settlement—and of setting oneself up as an independent businessman, such as a small-shop keeper or a bar owner—deprived them of the benefit of an "industrial reserve army." One should perhaps add that at the time of the disappearance of the frontier American craft unions had already won such a strong bargaining position that they could—at least in times of "normal business"—maintain a high level of wages. On the other hand the very high level of wages had been (and is) a strong stimulus to mechanization and automation in industry, which gave some

American industrial products in the long run (i.e., for a period in the twentieth century) predominance on the world market. The reality of high wages was certainly due to the expansion of the American home market which allowed mass production to a much greater extent than in Europe and to the strength of American industry on the world market later on.

A third weak point in Sombart's argument has already been mentioned, namely his contention that the settlers "ceased to be servants of capitalism." I have not the statistical material on hand to prove it, but I am convinced that the settler movement not only served as a safety valve for the American proletariat but also as a means of increasing food production for the market, and of developing agricultural techniques that made food relatively cheap. It is possible that this economic consequence of increased agricultural production was—later on, when the farmers had to fight for their survival—balanced by their political influence, at least in some states. But it would be strange if increased farming should not have made for cheaper products at least in the earlier period. People coming from the cities certainly did not abandon all their habits, and it seems to me quite obvious that the new farmers from the very beginning had to produce for the market in order to get all the consumer goods they needed and were accustomed to. The necessary specialization of the farms certainly further increased this trend. As dairy farmers, crop farmers, or whatever (chicken farmers), the settlers did not "drop out" of capitalist society, but simply served it in another function, i.e., as commodity producers. It may be that in many instances their real income as new farmers did not surpass but even fell below the level which they had reached as industrial workers. The all-prevailing worship of "property" and the presumed "independence" of a "free settler" may have been a myth, but it was a myth which as such was at the same time a social reality.

A fourth point which is not completely overlooked by Sombart, but is not sufficiently stressed, is the size of American territory, with its enormously varied geographical, climatic, social, and cultural conditions. The enormous differences between—let us say Texas and New York, Montana and California—were another strong obstacle against nationwide class solidarity, an obstacle which was aggravated by the federal character of the American Constitution and of its political life.

A last point which should not have been overlooked even in 1906 is the international position of the United States. Sombart passes over the impact of the American position in Asia and Latin America, which began to be built up at the end of the nineteenth century. The role of American nationalism (jingoism) in preventing an internationalist socialist movement from developing into a powerful political force cannot easily be underestimated. (This connection could by the way be established indirectly if one looks at the combination of anti-Vietnam war feelings and growing criticism of American capitalism in the last few years. With the disappearance of pride in national achievements overseas, the possibility of radical social criticism in the United States has been opened once again.) But American imperialist policies overseas did not only have an impact on working-class ideologies (as they have up to our own day). They may also have played a role in the economic prosperity of the country, thus permitting the American entrepreneur to pay the high wages on which Sombart—in somewhat too superficial a manner—bases most of his argument.[6] This imperialistic aspect of American scenery corresponds again to the analogous phenomenon which Karl Marx earlier observed in England. In his address to the General Council of the International Workingmen's Association on January 1, 1870, Marx said: Ireland "is the only pretext the British government has for maintaining a large standing army, which—when necessary, as has been shown—can be used against British workers after having been trained in Ireland. . . ."[7] It would surely not be too difficult to find contemporary parallels to this argument now. And Marx adds: "Finally in England is repeated what we have seen in ancient Rome on a large scale. That people which enslaves another people is forging its own chains."[8] When Martin Luther King, Jr., discovered the connection between the Vietnamese war and the civil rights movement he had rediscovered—probably without knowing it—this century-old observation of Marx.

Sombart's book is—to a European reader—interesting for other reasons as well. Western European societies—above all England, West Germany, Scandinavia, the Netherlands, and Switzerland—are today in very much the same position that the U.S.A. was in in 1906. They are highly industrialized countries with objective antagonistic class structures, but they have no revolutionary socialist movement of any important size. The reason for this absence or weakness of revolutionary socialism may be to a certain extent the same as in the United States at an earlier period: a relatively high standard of living (together with social security measures which were largely absent from the United States in 1906), a new "underproletariat" in the form of foreign workers (from southern Europe above all), ethnic prejudices against these workers among the domestic proletariat, and a privileged international market position which allows for high profits and increased real wages at the same time; and finally also a growing domestic market (the European Economic Community) which may become analogous to the great American market. The differences which seemed so striking to Werner Sombart in 1906 are less prominent in our day. The problems confronting socialism are more and more the same.

NOTES

1. This assertion was not included in the excerpts translated here, but it is worth quoting: "My opinion," says Sombart, "is, however, the following: all these factors which up to now have prevented the development of socialism in the United States will soon disappear, or change into their opposite, so that in the next generation socialism has a very good chance of flourishing." *Warum gibt es in den Vereinigten Staaten keinen Sozialismus?*, pp. 141 et seq.

2. See, for example, Richard Hofstadter and Seymour M. Lipset, *Turner and the Sociology of the Frontier* (New York: Basic Books, 1968), *passim.*

3. Siegfried Meyer (about 1840 to 1872), a co-founder of the Berlin section of the International Workingmen's Association, emigrated in 1866 to the U.S.A., where he was a member of the German Communist Club in New York and one of the organizers of the American section of the IWA. August Vogt (about 1830 to about 1883), shoemaker and member of the League of Communists, participated in the revolution of 1848, emigrated in 1867 to the U.S.A., and became corresponding secretary of the International Workingmen's Association for the U.S.A.

4. Marx-Engels, *Werke,* vol. 32, pp. 668 et seq.

5. Ibid., p. 667.

6. American history—it is true—has only recently been analyzed in the light of economic imperialism. See, among others, the collection by Barton J. Bernstein, *Towards a New Past: Dissenting Essays in American History* (New York: Vintage Books, 1967).

7. Marx-Engels, *Werke,* vol. 16, p. 388.

8. Ibid., p. 389.

Chapter 13

THE ROLE OF INTELLECTUALS*

Adolph Sturmthal

In his *A Theory of the Labor Movement,* published in 1928, Selig Perlman attempted to demonstrate that "job consciousness" was labor's "home-grown philosophy" everywhere; the ideological and political elements in the European labor movement were the results of indoctrination by intellectuals. Having made a not too friendly attempt at classifying the intellectuals operating in and on the labor movement, Perlman ascribes to them the responsibility for having led labor in directions which do not correspond to the inborn trends of the workingmen, nor–it would seem–to their real interests. But, the *Theory* concludes on an optimistic note: European labor is in the process of freeing itself from intellectual leadership. It is particularly the German labor movement on which Perlman bases his main hopes for the delivery of labor from the "intellectual scourge." It was there that the trade union movement during the 1920's "delivered a critical blow to the leadership of the labor movement by the revolutionary intellectual."[1]

This raises a number of questions: Was it, indeed, the intellectual who carried the ideological and political germ into European labor's home-grown philosophy? What is the role of the intellectual in the labor movement? Does the emancipation of labor from intellectual leadership change the ideological and political character of European labor?

An attempt will be made to answer these questions in the light of the experience of the first half of this century and then to proceed to a brief examination of the present relationship between American and European labor.

* Adolph Sturmthal, "Comments on Selig Perlman's *A Theory of the Labor Movement,*" reprinted from the *Industrial and Labor Relations Review,* vol. 4, no. 4, July 1951.

Perlman's Precursors

Discussions about the proper role of the intellectual in the labor movement have been frequent in European labor history. No less a man than Lenin was greatly concerned with the question. It is important to understand the circumstances which led him to examine it.

In the early 1890's the Russian Social Democratic Party consisted of small groups of intellectuals and students who had few contacts with the industrial workers; most of the workers were completely untrained in trade union methods and unfamiliar with even the most primitive forms of organized action. In the middle of the 1890's a wave of prosperity led to an upsurge of working class activity. It concerned purely economic demands, mainly for higher wages and shorter hours. This gave the social democratic organizations an opportunity to establish closer contacts with the workers. The Socialists set up "associations for the struggle," to which workers in the factories reported. On the basis of these reports the associations wrote and published leaflets denouncing the employers. These leaflets were distributed in the factories by the workers who co-operated with the associations. The associations helped to formulate the workers' demands to be addressed to the employers. When strikes broke out, the associations supported the strikers morally and intellectually. In this way the social-democratic groups succeeded in gaining influence over larger numbers of workers. The large strike movements in Moscow and St. Petersburg in 1895 and the textile workers' strikes of the following year were led by social democrats.[2]

As a result, a movement arose within the Russian Social Democratic Party which corresponded in some ways to the contemporary "revisionist" movement of Eduard Bernstein in Germany. The struggles for the economic demands of the workers took precedence over the political struggle against Czarism and capitalism. This movement was labeled "economism." Lenin was its bitterest enemy. It is undeniable, however, that it was the activity of the "economists" which first established close co-operation between the social democratic intelligentsia and the workers. In this way, industrial workers in larger numbers were for the first time exposed to the Marxian propaganda of the "associations," while the Party was given its first opportunity to leave the ivory tower of its endless debates and to enter into action.

"Economism," however, was destined to be a brief, though vital, phase in the evolution of the Russian labor movement. The great strike wave petered out at the turn of the century and political issues took first place. It was this evolution which culminated in the revolution of 1905. The Social Democratic Party changed its strategy according to the new circumstances. For this change to succeed it was essential that the influence of the "economists" be overcome. The paper *Iskra,* published by Martov and Lenin—later the leaders of the Menshevik and Bolshevik wings of the Social Democratic Party, respectively, but at this stage still united—was devoted to the struggle against the influence of the "economists." To the same task Lenin dedicated his famous pamphlet "What Is to Be Done."[3] In this work, which is very important for an understanding of the principles of Leninism, Lenin wrote: . . .

> The history of all countries shows that the working class, exclusively by its own effort, is able to develop only trade-union consciousness; i.e., it may itself realize the necessity for combining in unions, for fighting against the employers, and for striving to compel the government to press necessary labor legislation, etc. The theory of Socialism, however, grew out of the philosophic, historical and economic theories that were elaborated by the educated representatives of the propertied classes, the intellectuals. According to their social status, the founders of modern scientific Socialism, Marx and Engels, themselves belonged to the bourgeois intelligentsia. Similarly, in Russia, the theoretical doctrine of Social Democracy arose quite independently of the spontaneous growth of the labor movement; it arose as a natural and inevitable outcome of the development of ideas among the revolutionary socialist intelligentsia. . . .

This statement—with one significant difference—could have been written by Professor Perlman. This is essentially the approach of the *Theory* to the problem of the relationship between the workers and the intelligentsia. The difference between the *Theory* and "What Is to Be Done" is, of course, that Lenin used the very same approach for a criticism of the "economists" which Perlman, in the same situation, would have used to support them. . . .

However, the difference does not stop at this point; for Lenin soon recanted. He found himself sharply opposed by the famous Marxian theoretician Plekhanoff. Lenin's views, he said,[4] were a throwback to long-surpassed "idealistic" views about the functions of the party. The opposition between the workers and the capitalistic society is not carried into the working class from the outside, Plekhanoff said. It is rather the result of the workers' experience under capitalism. Plekhanoff admitted that the theory of Socialism had been developed by members of the "bourgeois intelligentsia." But they can only clarify and give a "scientific basis" to what the workers themselves feel and experience.

Lenin answered[5] that Plekhanoff had attacked "sentences torn out of their context or individual expressions which I had not formulated well or carefully enough." The references to the spontaneity of the workers and their trade union consciousness ought to have been read in connection with the attack upon "economism." The "economists" had bent the stick in one direction. To make it straight, he bent it in the other direction.[6]

European Labor and Politics

These excursions into literary history do not have the purpose of branding Perlman a "Leninist" but rather of pointing out that this problem has been dealt with at some length in the Marxian literature. For quite clearly, the relationship between the intelligentsia and the labor movement represented a major question in Europe[7] far more than in the United States. But this difference is not due to the relative superiority of European intellectuals over their American colleagues, which enabled the first to succeed where the latter failed; the reason is a far more profound one; it has its roots in the political and social history of Europe.

Stated with extreme brevity, the salient fact is the legacy of feudalism and enlightened absolutism in Europe. The first has left behind it the tradition of a carefully and strictly stratified society, with a hierarchy whose remnants are still one of the basic elements in the organization of European society. The ranking of men according to social status has expressed itself most obviously in the survival into this century of electoral restrictions, such as the class suffrage system in Prussia (until 1918), in Italy (until 1918), in Austria-Hungary (where the first elections under universal and equal suffrage were held in 1907), in Belgium (where only the great revolutionary general strike at the beginning of this century achieved universal and equal suffrage), and so on. But the absence of equal and universal suffrage was only an expression of a far more deeply seated class consciousness on the part of all or most Europeans which permeated (and to a large extent still permeates) their lives. That far into the nineteenth century a German party of great significance refused membership to workers was as much expressive of this class consciousness as the fact pointed out by Michels that Italian workers, confronted with the choice of voting for a fellow worker or an intellectual as representatives of the same party, consistently preferred the latter to the former. The social hierarchy was not only a self-evident fact, but for many—the "good citizens"—a desirable state of affairs. It did not require Socialist propaganda to bring class consciousness into being; on the contrary, the feeling of social inferiority was so strong and widespread that it offered Marxian propaganda fertile soil. Indeed, roughly speaking, the success of Marxian Socialism in European labor has been closely related to the strength of the feudal tradition.[8]

The legacy of enlightened absolutism was the belief in the all-powerful state. The peculiar tendency of European labor to settle by law problems of labor relations that American unions traditionally solve by way of collective agreements fits clearly into the spirit of this legacy. It is significant that in this respect the labor movement of Great Britain is closer to American than to Continental practice—Great Britain being the only major European country in which the tradition of enlightened absolutism was broken, thanks to the Puritan and Glorious revolutions.[9]

Feudalism determined the class consciousness of the European worker—at least in the sense of making him ready to accept a social philosophy based upon the existence and the conflict of clearly determined social classes. It also aroused in him the desire to change the order of hierarchy—*"Mêler les fortunes!"* Enlightened absolutism convinced the Continental European that political power was the key instrument of social transformation. The combination of these two elements led to European political unionism.

European Labor and Education

The problem of the role of the intellectual in the labor movement is not fully understood unless one takes into account the low level of education of the workers in the early stages of the labor movement and their inherited attitude toward education, widely at variance with American attitudes.

Up to the middle and far into the second half of the nineteenth century an aristocratic view of education dominated in Europe. Its main tenets were that higher education was to be reserved to the children of the upper classes and that education for the children of the poor, if provided at all, ought to be restricted to those skills which would improve their value in work. This spirit was expressed in the famous words of Governor Berkeley of Virginia in the 1670's: "I thank God there are no free schools, and I hope we shall not have them these hundred years; for learning has brought disobedience and heresy and sects into the world."[10] While the "great educational awakening" during the period 1835–1860 brought the common school and the high school to many parts of the United States, educational progress in Europe was slow in developing. Thus in regard to France we are told that "during the eighteenth and early nineteenth century the different monarchic powers were not at all favorable to training the masses, and popular education was badly neglected. It required several revolutions in government and the establishment of a permanent republic, to break the old traditions completely, and to make it evident that universal suffrage should be accompanied by universal education."[11] Free elementary education was introduced only in 1881 and made compulsory the following year. In England, the "nationalization and universalizing of education were delayed even longer than in France," partly because "the House of Lords . . . strove to keep the poor in ignorance and to maintain the authority of the established church."[12] Compulsory attendance laws were enacted in 1876 and 1880.

Thus, at the time of the Chartist movement large parts of the British working class were still illiterate.[13] But there was gradual progress, there were substantial local differences, and some working class groups were far ahead of the great mass. Thus Lovett, writing to his fellow Chartist, Francis Place, in 1834, said: "If I now enter a mixed assembly of workingmen, I find twenty where I formerly met with one who knew anything of society, politics or government. . . ."[14] It was particularly the skilled craftsmen in London who were well educated. "Their influence gave an element of stability to the trade union movement."[15]

Needless to say, universal education was far more backward still in Belgium, Italy, Austria-Hungary, and, of course, Russia. Where —as in Prussia—universal education came at a fairly early date (1808 to 1817), it was accompanied by a class division which kept the children of the lower classes apart from those of the upper classes and reserved to the latter not only higher, but also secondary education and a whole series of privileges attached to graduation from the "reserved" schools.

What this brief survey may indicate is, in the first place, that intellectuals were, under the given conditions, indispensable for the labor movement in its first steps. Without their assistance even the list of demands to be presented to the employers might not have been drawn up in the Russian strikes of the 1890's; nor would it have been possible without their teaching for the Belgian unions to find the required number of workers who—by being able to read and write—had the legally necessary qualifications to become members of the labor courts (*conseils des prud'hommes*), since free universal compulsory education became a fact in Belgium as late as 1919.[16]

Furthermore, the aristocratic view of education has impressed the workers of Europe with a respect for higher education which has no counterpart in the United States. To be sure, there was a good deal of distrust, often enough not without justification, for the intellectual who "offered his services" to the labor movement.[17] But when it came, for instance, to elections, time and again the workers preferred to nominate members of the intelligentsia rather than workers as their candidates, or, given the choice among several candidates of the Socialist Party, voted for the intellectuals. As Michels points out: "The peculiar reluctance of the proletarian to give his vote to his equals, a reluctance which has its origin in his lack of confidence in himself, in his capacities and perhaps also in the strength of his own character has greatly contributed to cause . . . the Party of the Workers to be consistently and for a long time led almost entirely by intellectuals."[18]

From this would follow two important inferences: (1) that the influence of the intellectual on the labor movement in Europe is part and parcel of the very same legacy of feudalism which has given European labor so much of its general outlook on life; and (2) that with the progress of democracy, and particularly of democratic education, the influence of the intellectuals may be expected to diminish. Undoubtedly, this has happened, at least in the form that more and more workers and workers' children themselves turn "intellectual" and that unions develop in professional fields. Surely, the dependency of the workers on intellectuals who can read or write for them has greatly decreased, if not altogether disappeared.

But this evolution has not been accompanied by a turn of European labor away from politics and the reform ideas by which, according to Perlman, the intellectuals "corrupted" the "home-grown" philosophy of labor.[19] Indeed, . . . attempts to lead labor into new ways after World War II have failed, although by now quite clearly the influence of the intellectuals ought to be weakened as a result of the progress of working class education.

Have the intellectuals consistently led European labor into "leftist" ways? It is conceivable that on this point Perlman has been the victim of personal experience. In the United States the intellectual who has approached labor has been typically a radical who has criticized it, from a leftist point of view, as too conservative, as insufficiently ambitious, as showing only a limited interest in wider issues. Perlman's discussion of the role of the intellectuals in European labor[20] gives the impression that he judges the European intellectual in the light of his American counterpart.

The fact is, however, that in Europe intellectuals have been found at least as often on the "right" of the large mass of workers as on their "left." It is true that many trade union leaders supported the revisionists in Germany against the radicals, and even more so against the extreme left which advocated the revolutionary general strike; but many trade union leaders found themselves among the radical majority which defeated the revisionists, and the latter were quite typically led by intellectuals rather than by workers.[21] In other words: *the radical-revisionist division cut across the unions as well as the party, and the most articulate moderates were intellectuals rather than workers.* Indeed, the main trend of the discussions at the decisive Party Conference (Dresden, 1903) leaves no room for doubt that the German workers regarded the conflict as a revolt of moderate intellectuals against radical workers. The belief that the intellectuals were trying to lead the workers into "weak compromises" with capitalism has been at least as widespread in Europe as Perlman's view that intellectuals are attempting to force the workers into radical views and methods. Perlman's attempt to establish a division between the radical intellectuals and the moderate trade unionists clearly does not fit this situation. As I have attempted to show,[22] it was precisely the victory of the radical which for many years blocked the way for effective political action on the part of German labor.

Another example of the inappropriateness of Perlman's analysis as applied to European labor is his discussion of the French labor movement. Perlman's own explanation is limited to a footnote. He writes:

> Working-class anarchism, like French Syndicalism, has been a clever working-class stratagem to get rid of the hegemony of the intellectual. The intellectual was eliminated from the trade union movement in the name of the very revolutionary class-consciousness which he himself had helped to evoke in labor. But observe how naturally the Confédération Générale du Travail had slipped during the War into a position of opportunistic unionism. On the whole, the disappointing weakness of French unionism after 1921 exposing a deplorable instability in the movement, goes back to its constant absorption in mere matters of abstract ideology—syndicalism, reformist socialism and communism—largely the result of an earlier indoctrination, directly and indirectly, by intellectuals. Lacking a safe psychic anchorage in a body of "job control" practices, the French labor movement has proved an easy plaything for the gusts of wind blowing from Soviet Russia, until the frail bark has been broken on the rocks of an exceptionally entrenched capitalism.[23]

The phenomenon to be explained is the fact that the most anti-intellectual labor movement of Europe has been far more absorbed by ideological issues than, e.g., the labor movements of Germany and Britain, both of which are Perlman's own examples for move-

ments "infected" by intellectual leadership. By any yardstick the French unions have been (and continue to be) more interested in discussions of social philosophies than their far more practical brethren in Great Britain or Germany.[24] But to attempt to explain this by the intellectual influence to which the movement was exposed in the 1880's and 1890's, while intellectuals have been at work in the far more practical British and German movements up to this day, is obviously difficult. Perlman's thesis would lead us to expect that the British and the German unions are the most "ideological," the French the most "practical"; in actual fact, the situation is the exact reverse.[25]

In a certain sense Perlman's thesis might be compared with the theory underlying the War Labor Disputes Act of 1943, which provided that no strike could be called in an industry producing war materials until after the NLRB had taken a secret vote of the union members. The theory behind this was "that the policies of union leaders do not represent the wishes of the rank and file union members."[26] But for the union leaders, the workers would be reasonable and modest. Everyone knows that "the result in almost every case was an overwhelming majority vote in favor of a strike."[27] In somewhat the same way Perlman believes that "the intellectuals" have smuggled ideology as contraband into a labor movement which otherwise would have been eminently "practical" and merely job-conscious. The evidence contradicts this thesis as powerfully as the strike votes during the war were in opposition to the assumptions underlying the War Labor Disputes Act. Thus I doubt whether it could be shown that the demand for the nationalization of industry has been imposed upon the British and French workers by the intellectuals; indeed, in a few specific cases the exactly opposite view could be more readily defended. Similarly the demand for workers' control of industry in France has had its chief protagonists in the unions, while the intellectuals in the Socialist Party reluctantly accepted and modified what they regarded as inevitable.[28] It is quite true that one of the powerful forces behind these demands was the workers' belief—whether an illusion or not—that the attainment of these objectives would be followed by higher wages and better working conditions. But this was, according to all accounts, not the only motivating force, nor can we disregard the "political" and ideological character of the demand itself. It may well be that it was "bad" for the workers to embark upon these policies or that they failed ultimately to implement them; but this is immaterial in our context. What matters is that these demands were carried forward by the workers, often against the doubts of the intellectuals.

NOTES

1. *A Theory of the Labor Movement* (New York, 1949), p. 303.
2. See Isaac Deutscher, *Soviet Trade Unions: Their Place in Soviet Labor Policy* (London; New York, 1950), pp. 2–8. Otto Bauer, *Die illegale Partei* (Paris, 1939), passim.
3. Lenin, *Collected Works,* 1929, vol. IV. The quotation cited is on p. 114. Part of this is quoted by Perlman himself (p. 8, note) but not the subsequent Lenin-Plekhanoff discussion.
4. No. 70 and 71 of Iskra, reprinted in Lenin, *Collected Works* (Russian), vol. XIII.
5. In the Preface to the volume "Zwölf Jahre," Lenin, *Collected Works* (in German) (Vienna; Berlin, 1933), XII, p. 79.
6. Strangely enough, this part of the discussion is rarely, if ever, referred to in the U.S. literature.
7. It has provided Robert Michels with a good deal of material for his own writings, among others: *Le Proletariat et la Bourgeoisie dans le Mouvement Socialiste Italien (Paris,* 1921).
8. Far more than to the degree of "exploitation" or to living standards. This is in line with the well-known fact that, historically, unionization begins typically not with the working class groups whose living standards are lowest, but rather with those just in the process of losing or gaining social status.
9. At the Trades Union Congress of Southport, 1943, Ernest Bevin, then Minister of Labor, made a characteristic remark. Referring to the "guaranteed work week" for which the unions were then striving, he said: "Do not rely on the Government only to maintain it. Why not weave it into your collective agreements at the earliest opportunity: we are not anxious to have the duty of enforcing it by law. Do not turn the rising generation too much to the law and not enough to you. One principle in this connection we have tried to maintain is self-government in industry." This sounds familiar to American students of labor, but it would come as a surprise to most Continental laborites.
10. F. P. Graves, *A History of Education in Modern Times* (New York, 1928), p. 84.
11. Ibid., p. 292.
12. Ibid., pp. 301–2.
13. "Of a group who were tried in connection with a Chartist outbreak in the manufacturing districts, a large proportion could scarcely read or write." A. E. Dobbs, *Education and Social Movements, 1700–1850* (London, 1919), p. 213.
14. Quoted by Dobbs, op. cit., p. 215.
15. Ibid., p. 216. "Elementary education was aimed not at producing democratic citizens but at fitting the ordinary people for the state in life to which they were called, whereas secondary education was con-

ceived as fitting the potential rulers of the nation to take their rightful places in the state, church, or business world. Whenever American education is compared with European education, this essential difference in social structure and purpose of education should be taken into account." R. Freeman Butts, *A Cultural History of Education* (New York and London, 1947), p. 422. "Whereas most European countries maintained a dual system of schools frankly designed to separate the upper classes from the lower classes, the United States launched a democratic system designed to provide equality of opportunity for everyone to go as far upward as his talents and abilities would take him." Ibid., p. 486.

16. The law was passed in 1913, but implemented only after World War I. I have known personally a senator of Belgium who, for the reason stated above, learned how to read and write as an adult in a school run by the unions.

17. After Lassalle's death his followers, in their struggle against the rival Eisenacher group, boasted that they did not accept intellectuals as members, and above all not Jews. R. Meyer, *Der Emancipationskampf des vierten Standes in Deutschland*" (Berlin, 1874), p. 57. The Workers' Party of Milan declared in its Manifesto of May 17, 1882, that it accepted only manual workers as members; by 1890, however, it welcomed in fact the affiliation of intellectuals. Robert Michels, *Political Parties* (New York, 1915), p. 266.

18. Michels, op. cit., p. 311. This book contains (pp.87ff.) significant statistics about the proportions of intellectuals in the parliamentary group of Socialist parties of a number of European countries between 1903 and 1905.

19. This overstates Perlman's case, but only very little. In his contribution to H. A. Marquand's *Organized Labor in Four Continents* (Longmans: New York, Toronto, 1939) Perlman regretfully speaks of American labor's lack of "class consciousness"; and in his *Theory* (p. 33) he ascribes to the intellectual the virtue of having left "upon the labor movement an indelible imprint of idealism and of an unquestioned solidarity . . . which has survived, to the great advantage of the movement." But these are exceptions in a long list of "sins" enumerated by Perlman.

20. *Theory,* pp. 280–303.

21. Charles A. Gulick, *Austria from Habsburg to Hitler,* vol. I: *Labor's Workshop of Democracy* (Berkeley and Los Angeles, 1948), pp. 293–308.

22. In my *The Tragedy of European Labor 1918–1939* (New York, 1943), pp. 18ff.

23. *Theory,* pp. 288–89, note.

24. As one piece of evidence among many: At the founding congress of C.G.T.-F.O. in April 1948 the recorded votes, by name and organization, concerned the following four issues: Preamble of the Statutes, structure of organization, name of organization, affiliation (or

disaffiliation) with the World Federation of Trade Unions. None of the votes on labor issues in the accepted meaning of the term was found worthy of being recorded. Of 142 pages of the printed report on the congress proceedings roughly 25 are devoted to labor problems, 117 to "philosophical" questions. This seems to have upset even some of the delegates, for Albert Thomas, delegate of the metal workers of the Paris region, complained: "We hoped that in a trade union congress, the direction the union is to take, the purchasing power of the workers would interest the Congress at least as much as the conflict between two currents about the name of our Confederation. Well, I have discovered . . . that the Congress listened with attention when the 'stars' engaged in speech-making; everyone hung on their lips; but since we started talking about the purchasing power of the worker, the room has become almost empty and our comrades carry on little conversations aside. . . ."

25. An attempt to offer an alternative explanation would clearly far exceed the limits set to this essay, but as a working hypothesis the idea might be put forth that the problem might be connected with the traditional weakness of French unions. This in turn might well be related to the arrested economic development of the country, the relative weakness of its capitalistic spirit, the survival of feudal concepts, etc.; in other words, to national behavior patterns.

26. Lloyd G. Reynolds, *Labor Economics and Labor Relations* (New York, 1949), p. 268.

27. Ibid.

28. Perlman's statement (*Theory,* pp. 246–47) apparently refers to British experience. It surely does not apply to France.

COMMENT

Paul Buhle

The theoretical underpinning of Selig Perlman's *Theory of the Labor Movement* was, as Adolph Sturmthal perceptively noted, polemically misposed. Perlman believed that, in setting out a conception of worker "job consciousness" dominating over political concerns, he was implicitly denying the conclusions of Lenin's *What Is to Be Done?*, the foremost revolutionary political statement of the period. In fact, Perlman had merely agreed with Lenin that workers left to themselves would not create a revolution, and that therefore intellectuals would necessarily have to introduce socialist consciousness "from the outside." Sturmthal might have added that Lenin's view was by no means unique or philosophically original. In the words of situationist theoretician Guy Debord, Lenin was in this respect "a faithful and consistent Kautskyist who applied the revolutionary ideology of this 'orthodox Marxism' to Russian conditions, conditions which did not allow the reformist practice of the Second International."[1] Perlman had, in effect, taken on the central premises of the Second and Third Internationals' "orthodox Marxist" theory and practice. The larger theses of *Theory of the Labor Movement* reveal a similar impreciseness when measured against the subsequent historical experience of working-class movements. In Perlman's view, a matured working class would refuse to be led off to ideological utopias by left-wing intellectuals and politicians. Certainly, Perlman has in this narrow sense been vindicated: in recent decades there has been a widespread disaffection among the Western working classes toward the "parties of labor," self-avowedly revolutionary or reformist. However, what Perlman's central prophecy gains in form, it loses in content, for in throwing off the "ideologists" the workers have not returned to the passivity of mere wages-and-hours bargaining. Rather, while party and union bureaucracies have sought to limit the industrial struggle to wages and hours, workers have frequently demanded changes in the work process itself and occasionally—as in the case of many workers during the May–June 1968 events in France—striven for the transformation of the economic system.[2] Between the working class and the powers who own the machines of production, no new stratum of successful reform politicians or "social-minded" labor leaders of note has arisen. Indeed, Sturmthal's cautious prediction of reformers rising out of labor, such as Walter Reuther or James Carey in the United States, has proved as illusory as Perlman's view of worker pacification. In truth, no economic or political force—above all in the United States—can claim to represent authentically the newer campfires of industrial militancy, whether in the traditional sectors of labor action (e.g., auto) or those most novel (e.g., postal service).

Thus the predictions of Marxist and anti-Marxist observers a half century ago as to the future course of labor have been proved inadequate. Specifically, the relationship which Leftists hoped would be established between intellectuals and workers has been least prophetic. Within the United States (as compared to Europe), such a relationship has not even a past. The influence of intellectuals has, indeed, at all points been so slight as to be virtually irrelevant to the main course of labor, and insignificant to radicals save in what they choose to believe about their movements' future in guiding the working class. In part, the socialists and communists have denied this reality, or chosen to explain it as a result of the (always "temporary") power of conservative "misleaders" over the ranks of labor. In part, labor's anti-intellectualism has been internalized by the Left and constitutes a major peculiarity of the American radical movement. More than in any European counterpart, American radicals deeply mistrust the expense of time and energies for the reproduction of mere ideas. Similarly, those few exceptional Leftists who as individuals influenced the labor movement from within were more commonly than in other nations openly indifferent to ideological fineries. Even in the short-lived overtly revolutionary wing of American labor, the IWW, politicians and ideologues were suspect where not actually objects of derision.

There have been interrelationships between Left "intellectuals" and labor, and these are worth some detailed consideration. One cannot successfully find clues to the real nature of the implications for both forces, however, in framing the question as instrumentally as Perlman or even Sturmthal. Rather, it is necessary to assess the ways in which the transformation of the labor movement, particularly in the early period of American radicalism, shaped the role of the intellectuals and established the limitations of the formal Marxist movements.

As is well known, the American labor movement emerged in the late nineteenth century as a preeminently "practical" (i.e., nonsocialist) stratum of the working class, removed by skills and to some extent ethnicity from the bulk of workers. External "intellectuals" from the Socialist Labor Party exerted a certain influence upon the collapse of the Knights of Labor and the rise of the American Federation of Labor, but were in no sense decisive to the course of either organization. The case of Daniel De Leon in regard to both has been central to the historical discussion of the intellectuals' role, and has been sufficiently studied that we may draw general conclusions as to the meaning of his efforts.

From his entry into the socialist movement in 1890 until well after the turn of the century, De Leon saw the union as an essentially defensive institution which could *at best* provide socialist indoctrination for workers stripped of their livelihood by the collapse of the capitalist system. With the support of the more politically oriented socialists, De Leon set out to free the workers from the "Labor Fakirs." De Leon's influence manifested itself first nationally with the *coup de grâce* to the faltering Knights at the 1895 convention, where the leadership denied De Leon a seat and the SLP concessions previously promised. Utilizing the socialist forces withdrawn from the hapless labor organization, De Leon sought in 1895 to create an alternative organization to the American Federation of Labor, where socialist influence had also been turned back. De Leon's efforts proved however to be in vain, and by the late 1890s even the leaders of the SLP's pet Socialist Trade and Labor Alliance were denounced by De Leon as crooks and fakirs. De Leon gained real influence within the labor movement only by reversing his tactical position, in assuming and then brilliantly elucidating a quasi-syndicalist position toward unions, in which political organization was to serve only as an educational arm of the revolutionary struggle. Despite the temporary influence he achieved within the IWW, De Leon was doomed again by the indifference of the labor movement toward political chimeras.[3] At the end of his life, De Leon found himself the leader of a mere propaganda sect, frustrated at every point from gaining real influence upon the working class.

The principles De Leon espoused for the IWW were later to be partially vindicated, with the formation of industrial unions. But in a different way than Perlman, De Leon saw only half the truth, for the SLP's revered "socialist industrial unionism" was never to be and the direct influence of De Leon's ideas assumed practical form only where forms of leadership were immediately lacking (as in the first days of the Paterson, New Jersey, strikes of 1912) or where De Leonists functioned essentially like other radical trade unionists (as with some Pennsylvania furniture workers in the late 1930s).[4]

De Leon was indeed prophetic in his understanding that the ascendance of "state socialism" (the ideology of the stratum from the middle class or the skilled working class who saw in the growth of the state a solution to all social problems) within the radical movement would not draw the mass of workers into political struggles. His final alternative, the reshaping of radical forces from below (at the industrial level), was at least a plausible solution for the inability of socialists to organize within the new work force of foreign-speaking immigrants during the Progressive period. Yet at the point of his clearest expression of revolutionary strategy, De Leon pointed toward a theory in which all "outside" forces *including his own SLP* were growingly obsolescent if not already unnecessary.[5] Here the great contradiction of socialist intellectuals was forcefully exposed: the more one sought in objective class forces the actual liberation of workers, the more the intellectual's role seemed relegated to observer or at best respected adviser on the great events of the time.

Mainstream socialists who determined to play a reformist role in the day-to-day life of the working class scarcely escaped this dilemma. Two counterparts to De Leon will serve as an illustration of the opposite side of the contradiction: Max Hayes, editor of the Cleveland *Citizen;* and Victor Berger, "architect of victory" for Milwaukee municipal socialism, power in the local Federated Trades Council, and key ideologist for the Milwaukee *Leader.* Neither of these men qualifies as an "intellectual" in the sense of European theoreticians or even in the sense of De Leon. Hayes and Berger neither wrote nor translated books, nor even used the newspapers they influenced to further Marxist theory. On the contrary, they were commonly regarded among local workers and political activists as they saw themselves, eminently practical men operating within the historical framework of "material determinism" (in Hayes's phrase) toward the achievement of socialist society.

Hayes influenced the labor movement and thereby American socialism in a number of diverse ways. As editor of the *Citizen,* socialist-oriented organ of the Cleveland Central Labor Council, Hayes offered shrewd pronouncements on the political events around the nation and world through the editorial columns. His role during the 1890s was especially important, for he diligently sought to separate the potential working-class socialist movement from the stream of patrician reform organizations and causes that appeared on the scene. Unlike De Leon, Hayes saw no distinction between the immediate needs of the city's skilled workers and the long-run interests of the socialist movement. Hayes remained therefore an "AFL socialist," bitterly denouncing the IWW as "De Leon-dominated" splitters of labor unity. Yet Hayes was not in any simple sense the opportunist De Leon believed him to be: within the AFL, Hayes bitterly decried Gompers' pure-and-simple leadership of the organization and ran for president against the old leader. In later years Hayes left the Socialist Party because of his support of World War I, but returned to radical ranks in principled fashion as candidate for vice-president on the Farmer-Labor ticket in 1920.[6]

Hayes like Berger was prone to see his efforts within the labor movement on two levels. As a good trade unionist, he provided leadership and advice in a day-to-day fashion; and as a socialist, he offered educational opportunities to the most politically advanced workers. Berger elevated this approach to the level of pedestrian theory, conceptualizing a "two-armed labor movement" (one arm organized labor, the other arm socialist-political), the limbs of which were for some reason not coordinated systematically but acted in a merely fraternal manner toward each other. Inevitably, therefore, Hayes like Berger provided himself with a role which was self-limiting: a socialist ideologue could advise or even plead, but he could not direct trade unionist energies toward the capture of the political state. Since Hayes and Berger believed in capitalism's imminent economic decline, they perceived no conflict between their interests. But given American economic prosperity and the relative well-being of the AFL unions, this policy was bound to produce a split between political-ideological ethics and the harsh realities of labor stability.

Berger was never directly dependent upon his position within labor organizations, although labor support was indispensable for the Milwaukee Social Democratic political machine and its daily paper, the *Leader.* Berger's avowed opposition to World War I and the extensive opposition conducted by the Socialist Party for an early peace had an oddly liberating effect upon Berger, even as it destroyed for the last time his hopes to effect a coalition to overturn Gompers' AFL leadership. By 1920 Berger looked to the creation of some force similar to the IWW which could gather the unorganized workers including blacks and recent immigrants.[7] Berger could not, however, provide a socialist political strategy to embrace such workers, and in any case, after having defended the industrial conservatism of the AFL for so long, his reconsideration was mere sentiment.

Hayes's and Berger's relationship to the AFL had all the while been dominated by a *merely* political opposition toward Gompers. Advanced in their own eyes, the AFL socialists were for the most part socially conservative, suspicious of new ideas and new directions for socialist agitation. The major effect of Berger's and Hayes's efforts within the socialist movement was to reinforce the archaism of the party's class perspectives when it had entered into a crucial period for growth or decay. While the industrial proletariat became an increasingly foreign-speaking group born in eastern and southern Europe, the two defended and praised the characteristics of the "real American worker" (of previous migrations), the old-style skilled craftsman who was losing his central role within industry. At best, these men had thrown their considerable energies into developing a solid basis of working-class support for socialism within their communities, and had made at least persistent efforts to spread socialist doctrines throughout the AFL. At worst, Hayes and Berger failed to confront the changing realities of American labor which would render their political strategy shortsighted and their anti-immigrationist, racist bias suicidal for the future of the Left. Unlike De Leon, who had foregone substantive relationships with workers for the sake of a dreamed future, Hayes and Berger gave up the potentialities of the future for the sake of a working-class stratum moving into the past.[8]

The transformation of labor after the Debsian period did nothing to alter intellectuals' most fundamental dilemmas. Individual left-wingers learned that in order to be effective, they had to work in conjunction with the AFL, but that the very operation of that organization drastically limited their potentialities as radical leaders —thus William Z. Foster in the steel strike of 1919, or such lesser figures as A. J. Muste and Louis Budenz of the Brookwood Labor College and the Committee for Progressive Labor Action, ultimately renounced direct linkage to organized workers in order to speak more openly of revolution to the working class. When the CIO arose in the mid-1930s, in response to widespread spontaneous strikes and the opportunities presented by the Wagner Act, Leftists of all sorts rose to union leadership positions. But their predominance was neither gained nor maintained by the strength of a revolutionary political position; rather, they found their efforts frequently (and by the 1940s, often intolerably) dichotomized between "practical" and "political" work. Few ever derived a public formula so simplistic as Berger's "two-armed labor movement," but in practice their efforts remained essentially segregated.[9]

The outcome of the "Red decade" was different than the early period of socialist strength, insofar as labor had surged ahead to industrial organization while Left politics was effectively controlled and directed through the vacillating "line" of the Communist Party. Communists found themselves by dint of hard work and organizational skills near top levels of major CIO unions. Yet when postwar prosperity emerged, radicals of every variety faced the same predicament as socialists a generation or so earlier: they had gambled that capitalism would finally grind to a halt, and that workers would inevitably turn to their friends and guides for the opening political struggle. As American capitalism survived, strengthened—indeed, with a world empire in its grasp—and workers continued to turn away from Left political faiths, radicals again found that their economic and political chores could not be reconciled. They could become able functionaries with little or no political strength; or they could fight rearguard actions against political isolation, and hope for the best. The choice was in any case Hobbesian, for *as radicals* they were bound to lose either way.

Moreover, it should be noted that socialist and communist functionaries of the 1930s were if anything less classical "outside" intellectuals than the Debsian writers and organizers. Rather than being alien to the working class by virtue of their Marxism, they were frequently so close to their origins that political leaders were distressed. Particularly interesting in this regard is the case of the Minneapolis Trotskyists, who by their very persuasion were not as susceptible to charges of personal "opportunism" as communists or socialists. Half a decade after their leadership of the famous Minneapolis general strike, the Trotskyist militants fell under the criticism of Trotsky for their unquestionably sincere adaptation to the "progressive" wing of the Teamster hierarchy.[10] Even the most revolutionary European political formulas could not prevent radicals from succumbing to American reality. Similarly in the case of the communists, the hundreds of young people who left college as "intellectuals" to enter the trade unions did not emerge as leading figures in the left-wing unions. Rather, communists gained leadership where they discovered amenable figures from the rank and file, who for shorter or longer periods cooperated with party strategies.[11] The control of these strategies from the party itself through the "mass leaders" (of unions or political organizations) was so tenuous that in the waves of post-war crisis, when the party demanded leaders gather their forces to support Henry Wallace in 1948, the party's powerlines snapped. Whatever widespread relationships the communists had maintained with millions of workers dissipated rapidly, the strongest possible sign of underlying weakness in the communist union position.

The militancy of American workers two decades later, when there is emphatically no significant Left union leadership, points to the conclusion that the combative trade union movement arose largely independently of the intellectuals' and parties' efforts. The Left—including all the intellectuals worth consideration here—neither provoked the spontaneous strikes of the early 1930s nor did it in any real sense control the aims of the rank and file as the unions were being built. Only for an interim, and largely insofar as they reflected the immediate desires of the organized workers, did organized Leftists exert substantial influences upon the labor movement for the benefit of American radicalism.[12]

In the broad sense we may conclude that American workers' movements at best partially coincided with the efforts of radical parties (whose membership has been, by any standards, disproportionately intellectuals). The American situation is unique in degree, but it may, as Perlman suggested, contain universal qualities which still speak to the future of Western labor movements.

NOTES

1. Guy Debord, *Society of the Spectacle* (translation by Black & Red, published in the United States in *Radical America,* vol. IV, #5), paragraph #98. Emphasis omitted.

In passing, it should be noted that some scholars of Lenin have doubted that his attitude in *What Is to Be Done?* prevailed throughout his life or was intended as an all-inclusive formula (although it became so under Stalin). See, for instance, C. L. R. James, *Lenin, Trotsky and the Vanguard Party* (Detroit, 1964); and Raya Dunayevskaya, "The Shock of Recognition and the Philosophic Ambivalence of Lenin," *TELOS,* #5 (Spring 1970), pp. 44–57.

2. In a recent article on the Italian working-class struggles, Bruce Brown notes that

> . . . the general strike in France [in 1968 (PB)] was only the culmination of a dynamic of confrontation and industrial ferment whose beginnings can be traced back at least as far as the insurrectionary general strike which shook Belgium in 1960–61, and whose subsequent development has left an almost endless trail of disruptive strikes extending from West Germany to Great Britain. The recurrent characteristics of these struggles have been the spontaneous nature of their development, outside of and sometimes even in opposition to the existing trade-union organizations; their explosive violence, often verging on insurrection; and their emphasis on questions such as working conditions and even workers' control rather than on simple wage issues. "Revolution in Western Europe?", *Liberation,* 15 (Winter 1971), pp. 28–33.

3. In some ways, the best single account of De Leon's activities remains Rudolph Katz's memorial essay, "With De Leon since '89," in *Daniel De Leon: The Man and His Work, a Symposium* (New York: New York Labor News, 1919). See esp. pp. 17–31, 75–78, 150–53.

4. Michael Ebner, "The Paterson Strike of 1912 and the Two I.W.W.s," *Labor History,* 11 (Fall 1970), pp. 452–66; Paul Buhle, "Introduction" to *Labor Power* reprint (Westport, Conn.: Greenwood Press, 1970).

5. See Daniel De Leon, *As to Politics* (New York: New York Labor News, 1956), esp. pp. 57, 61.

6. James Weinstein, *Decline of Socialism in America, 1912–1925* (New York: Monthly Review, 1967), pp. 36, 227, 273–74.

7. James Weinstein, "The IWW and American Socialism," *Socialist Revolution,* I (September–October 1970), p. 28, n. 20.

8. See Charles Leinenweber, "The American Socialist Party and 'New' Immigrants," *Science & Society,* 32 (Winter 1968), pp. 6–16, 22–25, on the content and significance of nativism within the Socialist

Party. John H. M. Laslett's *Labor and the Left* (New York: Basic Books, 1970) suggests but does not comprehensively analyze the peculiar radicalism of the pre-World War I "labor aristocracy" of skilled workers. See esp. pp. 296–97.

9. An extremely valuable recent autobiography, Len DeCaux, *Labor Radical* (Boston: Beacon Press, 1971), indicates the political relations within the CIO which frequently frustrated left-wingers. See, for instance, pp. 315–16, 379–80.

10. Tim Wolhforth, *The Struggle for Marxism in the United States* (New York: Bulletin Publications, 1969), p. 32.

11. See DeCaux, op. cit., for comments on Harry Bridges, Mike Quill, and Joe Curran, pp. 301, 425–29, 422–23.

12. See the suggestive essay by George Rawick, "Working Class Self-Activity," *Radical America,* III (March-April 1969), pp. 23–31; and Staughton Lynd, "Rank-and-File Organizing in the 'Thirties'," *Radical America,* V (May-June 1971).

REPLY

Adolph Sturmthal

What is a revolutionary transformation of society? Apart from a few references to Lenin, Mr. Buhle's Comment has been limited to the U.S. experience. This is not surprising. In few countries has the discussion about the relationship of intellectuals to the labor movement been as voluminous and intense as in this country. Even in Czarist Russia, the discussion lasted only a short period, to be buried shortly afterward by issues of more momentous significance.

If I read Buhle's Comment correctly–and I am not quite sure that I do–he starts from the assumption that the influence of the intelligentsia on American labor was never very great and, more importantly, that it was this lack of influence which was responsible for the failure of socialist (and other radical) ideas to take hold in the American labor movement. It is of course true that neither De Leon nor Hayes, Berger, et al. exerted any profound or long-lasting influence on American workers. The facts themselves are thus not in dispute. What may be questioned is whether it was this lack of intellectual impact that caused the failure of socialism to establish itself in the ranks of organized labor, or, vice versa, whether outside circumstances were such as to make American workers singularly unreceptive to socialist propaganda. Although it would be difficult to produce conclusive evidence for either sequence of events, it would seem to me that the weakening of socialist consciousness in most Western countries during the long and extraordinary wave of prosperity that followed World War II would make it appear plausible that prosperity was equally at work in limiting socialist influence in the United States. This would be particularly likely to have been the case during the rapid industrial expansion that followed the Civil War.

Somewhat connected with this argument is a further question raised in Buhle's Comment: is there a new wave of militancy among industrial workers and what is the role of the current generation of intellectuals in this phenomenon? It would be difficult, I believe, to produce objective and measurable evidence that there is widespread disaffection with left-wing parties. Election returns in Western countries would not tend to confirm this view. Labour was turned out of office in England, but by a narrow margin, and against this stand socialist successes in West Germany, Austria, and most of the Scandinavian countries. More important: to the extent to which the left-wing parties lost, the benefit did not go to the extreme Left, but rather to conservative groups. More persuasive is the evidence as regards the trade unions. Since the French events in 1968 a large-scale movement of rebellion against union leadership has manifested itself in such traditionally well-disciplined countries as West Germany and Sweden, while in Italy the trade unions themselves have transformed their character so profoundly that they are now expressions of political dissatisfaction of the workers with all the various left-wing parties dotting the political landscape.

The events of the last three years—for which some modest counterparts could, with some effort, be found in the United States—do indeed raise an issue: did this radicalism originate with the workers themselves or did the students and other intellectual groups play a key role in the movements? Has Lenin (first version) come into his own or is Plekhanoff still to be trusted? Has Perlman's interpretation anything to offer for our understanding of recent history? Obviously, in this narrow frame we can only provide hints for an answer.

There is no question that trade union leaders of all kinds of political persuasion are engaged in a self-examination which has few parallels in recent labor history. True, so far few fundamental changes have occurred in union structure or leadership except possibly in Italy but perhaps these are still to come. Large organizations with a substantial history and a long tradition do not change rapidly; but the mere fact of soul-searching cannot be denied. What is doubtful, however, is whether this process is likely to lead any one of the labor organizations into a search for a new relationship to the intelligentsia. In the first place, because—France excepted—there is no evidence that the rebellion of the workers against their leadership was in any way inspired or engineered by students or other groups of intellectuals. The series of West German wildcat strikes, the strike movement in northern Sweden, the endless strike wave in Italy had little or nothing to do with intellectual influences. Second, even in France, where undeniably the student rebellion gave the signal for the vast strike movement and the occupation of plants by the workers, the attempts of the students to establish contact and cooperation with the striking workers ended in total failure. The Communist Party, which for a moment had lost control of the labor movement in the Paris area—the formerly Christian CFTD (Confédération Française du Travail Démocratique) proved quicker in moving along with the workers—rapidly reestablished its influence. It used its power to resist all revolutionary slogans that Leftist student groups were propagandizing, and succeeded in turning the strikes into ordinary bread-and-butter movements. Their main accomplishments were the achievement of old-standing union demands which the employers and the government had so far rejected and in particular the possibility of establishing union sections in the plants themselves—something American unions regard at least since 1936 as a matter of course and distinctly compatible with the functioning of a modern capitalistic society.

It is of course possible to regard these movements as evidence of a new radicalism of labor. But if this is done, it is well to keep in mind that this is still bread-and-butter radicalism, a demand for more of the same, at the most for a larger share in the gross national product. There is no evidence, as far as I can see, that intellectual influence has played a significant part in determining the direction in which the movements have been propelled.

Indeed, a rather careful investigation of the attitudes of the "affluent worker" by a group of British sociologists would tend to indicate that the main change that seems to have occurred among the new, prosperous, geographically mobile workers is a different view of their union and class party; a weakening of the social solidarity element and an inclination to regard first of all the union and to a lesser extent the party as an instrument for the achievement of higher living standards.[1] The crucial factor in this change, according to the authors, is less the affluence of the workers but their more intense social contacts with white-collar workers and middle-class families. In this "instrumental" view of labor organizations, radicalism in the pursuit of bread-and-butter aims would be a fairly obvious implication. This, however, should not be mistaken for a radical desire to change the foundations of the society which has provided these workers with the highest standard of living in history.

If there is any other new element in the picture it is the progressive unionization of white-collar workers, following with some considerable distance upon the growth of the share of white-collar workers in the total labor force. This fact may give increased influence to white-collar workers in determining the direction in which the entire movement is progressing. With some considerable degree of imagination the vigor with which the demand for "participation" (whatever this vague term is intended to signify) has been raised may be related to this new power center within organized labor. It is doubtful whether intellectuals have had any real part in this trend.

That there is a new kind of radicalism in the Western world cannot be denied. It can be traced clearly to blacks and other minority groups in the United States and to student groups all over the Western world. The first need no elaborate explanation in our context. The new radicalism of the youth, however, requires some comment.

In the Marxian perspective the breakdown of the capitalistic system was the result of its increasing failure to "deliver the goods," a view which has entered the English language under the horrible title of the "law of the increasing immiseration of the masses." No elaborate demonstration is required to show that in the Western, i.e., capitalistic world, the evolution has not followed the Marxian prediction. Whatever the still intolerable forms of poverty that exist in advanced industrial nations, it can hardly be denied that per capita incomes have increased tremendously since the days of Marx. Even in the modified version of "relative immiseration" –from which it would anyhow be considerably more difficult to infer the inevitability of an anti-capitalistic revolution–the theory can hardly be defended with any degree of precision. Indeed, apart from the obscure writings of an East German economics professor no such attempt has been made in recent years.

The "new radicals" do not fall into the trap of asserting increasing immiseration in either the absolute or the relative meaning of the term. The facts are too obvious. Instead, they have made a complete turnabout, or to use Marxian terminology, they have turned Marx upside down. The main charge against the contemporary society is not that it produces too little for too many, but on the contrary that it shows an obsessive concern with economic growth and material advancement. It is being accused of neglecting the environment, of being insufficiently concerned with cultural values, with the proper use of leisure. A good deal can be said in favor of these accusations and it is the proper role of intellectuals to bring these issues to public attention. If the forms in which this is done—e.g., by "dropping out"—are often objectionable and self-defeating, this may be regarded by many as the lesser evil compared with the ability of other social groups to live in extreme luxury surrounded by oceans of garbage, both literally and figuratively in the quality of the cultural environment. This criticism, although it often has its origin with left-wing intellectuals, has no ancestry that leads to Marx. Indeed, if anything, it contradicts Marx and is more closely related to some of the utopian socialists for whom Marx had so much disdain.

In this rebellion labor organizations so far have played no significant part. Indeed, it is not unfair to say that they have shown a distinct lack of concern with the issues which the Leftist student groups have emphasized, and sometimes even outright hostility. Yet the need of organized labor for the services of experts in various fields has increased far beyond anything the old craft unions of pre-World War I days could have ever envisaged, and some of the students, a few years later, have become such experts. Now, it is easy to say that these are hired hands which do not determine policy but merely help to produce intellectually respectable arguments to support policies determined by the workers themselves. At first sight, this is indeed a persuasive point often advanced by intellectuals who were deeply involved in the actual operations of labor organizations, especially in this country. Yet I maintain some doubts about its validity.

The difficulty with this kind of reasoning is that it is less and less clear where the boundary between expert advice and policy-making lies. If labor leaders appear before congressional committees and have to argue fine points regarding the international monetary system, are they not completely dependent, even in their policy-making capacity, upon the advice of professionals in the field? Yugoslav observers, friendly toward the system of "workers' management" in that country, are aware of the scarcity of managerial talent among the workers and point toward the danger of technocracy. Obviously, the relationship between labor and the intelligentsia is too complicated to be fitted into the simple rules that were derived from the experience of half a century ago.

This brings me to the last two points I should like to make. Mr. Buhle's Comment refers, rightly I believe, to the "invigorated struggle over the very conditions of social relations at the point of production." He means, I suspect, that in a number of Western countries the actual leadership of working-class protest has passed from the distant union officials to the shop stewards and workers' councils at the plant. The British Donovan Commission has made this one of the central points of its findings and has gone so far as to speak of a dual system of industrial relations, one represented by the nation- or area-wide collective agreements, the other by the more or less formal understandings at the plant level. Other studies of industrial nations have come to similar conclusions, although they are not as sharply articulated as in the Donovan Report. Whether this is in fact a new form of revolutionary development or not remains to be seen. If it were, it would represent, not a new form of Marxist rebellion, but rather a return to the syndicalist ideas which Marx so bitterly opposed in his lifetime. In a peculiar fashion, however, these apparently syndicalist movements of the last few years have managed to combine reliance upon the state with syndicalist forms of movement. It is only a half-truth to assert that there has been "a flight of the working class from the political arena." True: in the great movements of the last few years it was the unions, rather than the political parties, that finally took hold of popular rebellion and negotiated the ultimate settlement. But the fact cannot be overlooked that it was the French government in the *constats de Grenelle* which arranged for the meeting of unions and employers and set the tone for the principles of agreement that were embodied in the document of Grenelle. Nor should one overlook in an analysis of these events the fact that in France and in Italy the political representation of working-class interests is weakened by special circumstances.

The French Communist Party, the dominant working-class party of the country, is outside the system and thus prevented from functioning in any other capacity than as an expression of protest. No serious alternative to conservative governments is possible as long as the Left is prevented, by the very existence of a powerful Communist Party, from throwing its full weight into the political arena.

While the Italian Communist Party, having shown some slight signs of independence from Moscow, is less of an outcast than its French counterpart, the incredible divisions of the non-Communist Left (plus a few splinters on the Communist side) make the political representation of the Italian working class almost as ineffective as is the case in France. The unions have thus been compelled to take on political assignments which elsewhere would have been handled by more effective working-class or popular parties. Whether this is indeed a new form of working-class radicalism of a permanent nature or not is an open question. Nor do the results obtained so far indicate that this development is likely to "become decisive in the transformation of society as a whole." In the main, the workers in both countries have obtained rights which American workers have long enjoyed. Perhaps the main difference is the insistence in Western Europe upon far longer paid vacations than in the United States. This is most probably a wholesome achievement, but whether it can be classified as a transformation of society any more than most other improvements of working-class conditions seems to me doubtful.

NOTE

1. John M. Goldthorpe et al.: *The Affluent Worker: Political Attitudes and Behaviour* (Cambridge University Press, 1968).

Chapter 14

PLURALISM AND POLITICAL PARTIES*

Norman Thomas

No third party [in America] has ever grown like an oak from an acorn. The Republican Party is no exception. It became a second party in its first national election, it was the Whig Party which died. Why has there been this general failure of "third" parties?

The reasons are largely political and are to be found in America's history, and its Constitution. I have sometimes told English friends that had we had a centralized parliamentary government rather than a federal presidential government, we should have had, under some name or another, a moderately strong socialist party.

President Kennedy, reflecting on what a Democratic Congress has done to his program, might, with some justice, challenge my calling ours a presidential government. It is near enough to it in that the choice of the President is the major all-absorbing political issue. He is the man for or against whom everybody votes, or thinks he votes. But in legal form, citizens vote not directly for the presidential candidate, but for a college of electors. Each state has as many electors as it has representatives, plus its two senators. The system is so arranged that voting strength of small states is disproportionately high. In voting for electors, the citizens do not vote under uniform qualifications or rules for getting candidates on the ballot, but under the various laws and procedures of fifty states, some of which make it virtually impossible for a minor party to get or stay on the ballot. To be elected, especially in our times, a candidate must be backed by a party strong enough to raise millions of dollars. A single, hour-long, syndicated television program, costs more than the Socialist Party had in funds during any of my six campaigns.

To win, the candidate must win a majority vote of the electoral

* Chapter 8 from Norman Thomas, *Socialism Re-examined* (New York: Norton, 1963), originally entitled "Socialism in the U.S.A."

college, or, failing that, the election goes to the House of Representatives, in which each state has one vote, thus enormously increasing the already disproportionate electoral weight of the less populous states. Three times the candidate with the popular plurality has lost. In 1948 a small shift in three close states, Ohio, Illinois and California, would have elected Dewey, without destroying Truman's substantial plurality. The average American voter wants to take no chance on this. He may prefer a minor party candidate, but will cast his vote for one of the two major party candidates. His decision is based on how much he likes, or learns to like, one of the candidates, or on how much he dislikes or hates one candidate more actively than the other. Almost up to election day, he may think he will vote for his real preference, a minor party candidate who managed to get on the ballot in his state, but then he will decide that he can't take a chance, "lest that so-and-so get in." (How often I have been told just that!) If the President of the United States could be elected by a popular preferential ballot in which the voters numbered their choices, the Socialist Party would be a force to be reckoned with at the polls.

This opinion is bolstered by many considerations, one of them the fact that Gene Debs got his highest vote—6 per cent of the total—in 1912. Why? Partly, at least, because that year, voters were pretty sure that the winner would be Woodrow Wilson or Theodore Roosevelt, not William H. Taft, and they didn't believe that the difference between these two fairly progressive men was important enough to prevent their voting for their real preference, the outspoken socialist and labor man, the beloved Gene Debs. In 1916, when the Party itself was stronger, they gave no such vote to Allan Benson, the socialist candidate. For one thing, he wasn't Debs, but that is not the whole story.

It is easier to make the sort of choice I have described because of the logical absurdities of our two-party system. Each of them is a federation of state parties, held together by historic and sociological considerations, rather than by ideological principle. The leaders of both parties, especially the Democratic, since 1932, have shown considerable willingness to adopt measures once considered socialist or almost socialist. Within each party, differences are greater than, on the average, between them, so that one asks of a candidate for Federal office not so much whether he is a Democrat or a Republican but what kind of a Democrat or Republican.

Labor, since 1932, is fairly content that it has kept and increased its gains by picking individuals (usually Democrats), who, by conviction or for the sake of labor votes, will come nearest to its demands. It runs its political campaigns on this principle with fair, but far from total success.

The differences between the parties are sociological rather than philosophical. Let an observer find out the sex, geographical location, occupation, national origin, church connection of an American citizen, and, nine times out of ten, he can determine the voter's party preference. However, it by no means follows that the citizen will always vote according to the label.

Insofar as the parties claim to have historic principles, they have swapped them. On the whole, except in the South, the Democratic Party tends to support very strong federal government, while the Republican Party—with exceptions—mourns the continuing decline of state's rights. Alexander Hamilton, Abraham Lincoln, Thomas Jefferson, John C. Calhoun, would all be surprised by today's political parties. So little are the voters accustomed to honest thinking in terms of political preference, that the average Democrat and Republican, if asked to give reasons for voting as he does, wouldn't know what you were talking about.

If this extraordinary irrationality of our parties and lack of sharp division between them made it possible, under strong leadership like Roosevelt's in time of crisis, to work out a pragmatic peaceful near-social revolution, it has also made possible the flouting, not only of the advanced Democratic platform of 1960, but of most of the Democratic President's program by a Democratic Congress in which the generally conservative Southern Democratic senators and representatives hold, by virtue of seniority, most of the important committee chairmanships.

In spite of a political set up in which the cards are stacked against a third party, had Roosevelt's New Deal not given us a welfare state, which was in no way indicated by his 1932 campaign platform, the Socialist Party, the Communist Party, and perhaps some new party compounded of enthusiasts for Huey Long and Father Coughlin, would have acquired political strength. Roosevelt's great public support was not won during his first campaign, but began with his inaugural address in 1933. He was elected the first time simply because he wasn't Mr. Hoover, but that was not the only reason for his popularity. The New Deal averted popular disturbances of a serious sort, without solving the problems it ameliorated or without giving us the improvements in the mechanics of democracy which we needed. . . .

For many years I hoped, sometimes against hope, that the Socialist Party and its campaigns could serve as a catalytic agency to stir up and guide the kind of mass awakening which would give us a new party, basically a consciously farmer-labor party, increasingly socialist, and in the process, bring about an opposing conservative party. As late as 1932, there was nothing in the Republican or Democratic national platforms to indicate that this was impossible.

In 1924, we socialists staked a great deal on our gamble that our coalition with some labor and farm organizations and the Wisconsin Progressives would bring about an American farmer-labor mass party strong enough soon to supplant one of the old parties or bring about their merger. We knew that such a party would not immediately be socialist, but we hoped that the logic of the situation, and our efforts, would soon make it so in fact, if not in name.

The odds were always against us, but they multiplied even before the end of a good campaign because some of the labor organizations originally interested, virtually defected. One of the forces that held down the La Follette vote was the cry: A vote for La Follette is a vote to send the election to the House of Representatives.

Now, while I do not affirm the impossibility of the rise of a new party which, substantially would be backed by labor organizations, I think a major party, controlled by labor to the degree that it is in Britain, would be neither attainable nor desirable for reasons I have repeatedly suggested in discussing labor and its relations to socialism in America. Today I do not think that a new mass party, if it is to emerge at all, will call itself a labor party, nor will it be controlled by the same men who control the unions. While a strong new mass party with a socialist philosophy and program may seem remote, such a party may yet come to birth. If so, it will be concerned largely with the road to peace.

After the establishment of the welfare state under Roosevelt, there emerged the possibility that one of the old parties, probably the Democratic, could be helped to evolve into a party at least as socialist as the British Labor Party or the German Social Democrats. This would require either an honorable democratic political solution of the race problems in the South or a clean-cut break in the Democratic Party. It would also require the development of a decided change in the present climate of political action in the United States. This would begin with an active minority which accepts the revolutionary belief that plenty, peace and freedom for all are attainable by us imperfectly rational men and that to work for them is to find life's deepest meaning. To that minority, a dedicated socialism should furnish driving power and guidance.

Older generations of American socialists would never have used such words to frame their role. In Debs' time they expected the party as such to grow to major strength. After World War I, under Morris Hillquit's intellectual leadership, we hoped socialism would become a prime force in creating a labor or farmer-labor party. Hence, in 1924, the coalition with the La Follette forces, which included the Conference for Progressive Labor Action. With most of us, the hope for such a party, although postponed, still lingered.

Meanwhile, to educate the public, or even to keep socialist ideas alive after the failure of our plans in 1924, we nominated candidates. The 1932 campaign brought us new hope and strength, but after 1933, Roosevelt and the New Deal, communist pressure, and later, fear of nazism abroad and of fascist tendencies at home, greatly changed the external situation and socialist and labor reaction to it. Before 1936, the Party, bedevilled by our internal factions, had lost numerous sympathizers and members of right and left to the Democrats, or rather, to Roosevelt. In 1936, a section of the Party split off, nominally on the question of the way to handle the communist issue. Thereupon, in New York (and only in New York) ardent anti-communists, communists, and others, joined in building the American Labor Party, which could strengthen support of Roosevelt. Some years later that party split over the communist issue, and today the secessionists carry on as the Liberal Party, supported by some unions. The American Labor Party died. The Liberal Party exists only in New York State and usually simply nominates Democratic candidates. For this service it gets occasional recognition in nominations and jobs.

The Socialist Party, which remembered how well its opposition to the first world war was justified by events, also opposed entry into the second world war (but not on isolationist grounds). After Pearl Harbor, it gave critical support to the war, and concerned itself with an approach to peace. It was opposed to Roosevelt's simple slogan of unconditional surrender, and to Anglo-American concessions to Stalin in Central Europe.

I am perhaps prouder of our 1944 campaign and its platform than of any of my six presidential campaigns. Unhappily, it did not build the Socialist Party. I ran again in 1948, against my original intention, because I thought that we socialists should not allow the strange conglomeration of the Wallace Progressives, with a minority of communists rather cleverly playing the dominant role, to represent socialism to the American voters.

All this, while state laws, or the way they were enforced, made it harder and harder to stay on the ballot. The popular vote in 1948 was smaller than the reception accorded to me and to my colleague, Tucker Smith, had led us to expect. Wherefore, around 1950, I began a campaign within the Party to utilize our limited resources of money and manpower in campaigning for socialist ideas rather than for a presidential ticket doomed to little notice and humiliating defeat. By 1960, this became the prevailing opinion of the Party. The majority put its hope on the political front by working for a meaningful political realignment. Socialists are now allowed by their Party not only to vote, but to work for those candidates of other parties who come nearest to the socialist position. The reasoning behind this is that the welfare state has incorporated a great many socialist "immediate demands." In doing so, it has precluded, we hope, the necessity of immediate, if peaceful, internal "revolution." The difference between more or less good or bad political measures might now be very important, perhaps decisive, in terms of war or peace. We dare not hope to have an indefinite number of years free from war during which we can work for our version of a socialist society which can be achieved only by complete victory at the polls.

Neither can we afford to allow ourselves or our fellow citizens to lose sight of the great socialist goal. Within our American political-economic complex, our efforts to build a significant numerical force at the polls have failed as have also our efforts to precipitate a coming of a new mass party, strongly supported by organized labor. Our devoted efforts in 1952 and 1956 were scarcely noticed except sometimes to be pitied. It was time to look for other means, to be more flexible in cooperation, to recognize that the political realignment we wanted could be brought about by more than one method. At present we can contribute more by persuasively presenting well-thought-out programs and by campaigning for candidates of a numerically significant party who might be going our way. We have no intention of following the communist tactics of "boring from within" and denying our true loyalty. The very lack of a principled theoretical basis for either great party makes it possible for an avowed socialist to support those candidates who most accurately represent our ideals, but we must always combine our support with an insistence on the need of better political alignment.

Just how to work out this campaign for realignment is still a subject of much debate within the Socialist Party. I greatly doubt the wisdom of our nominating a presidential candidate. I would like us, however, to be in a position, in congressional campaigns, where old party candidates are very unsatisfactory and we cannot successfully nominate our own, to favor those independent candidates who emphasize our stand on foreign relations. At present, the average Democratic congressman, even one originally well disposed, somehow fails to do this with any vigor because he falls under heavy Administration pressure. Events can change this judgment.

Meanwhile, it is only fair to sympathize with socialists who find it difficult to support any candidate of a "capitalist" or "bourgeois" party. On the practical side they point out the difficulty of maintaining a political party which does not nominate candidates or give voters a chance for a protest vote. They say that it violates our American traditions to call ourselves a party while failing to nominate a presidential candidate. I confess to frequent attacks of nostalgia for those not-so-good old days. It is necessary, however, to change the pattern; to show how a socialist party, under present conditions, can introduce principle and program into political discussion without depleting its limited strength, and without alienating sympathizers by running candidates who would, inevitably, merely draw away votes from the better of the two major party candidates.

COMMENT 1

Michael Harrington

In *Socialism Re-examined,* Norman Thomas unquestionably stated an important truth about why there is no mass socialist movement in America. Yet I believe he overstated his point, turning a problem of socialism in this country into *the* problem. But even though I thus disagree with his analysis—or at least with its emphasis—I am very much in agreement with him on the urgent necessity of a party realignment in this country.

First of all, let me define the area of agreement.

Thomas wrote, "I have sometimes told English friends that had we a centralized parliamentary government rather than a federal presidential government, we would have had, under some name or another, a moderately strong socialist party." And he was quite right to stress the impact of the political structure on American radicalism in this way.

The American government was, of course, designed by the Founding Fathers to frustrate the will of majorities. The intricate system of checks and balances, the tripartite division of power, and the other conservative devices of the Founding Fathers were supposed to minimize conflict, or at least to prevent any single faction, even one representing most of the people, from imposing its will upon the society. To borrow Richard Hofstadter's brilliant phrase (he applied it to Calhoun), some of the *Federalist Papers* seem to have been written by a Marx of the master class.

One consequence of this system was to make the life of the minority party exceedingly difficult. Under a parliamentary system, by voting for the candidate of your choice in a single constituency, even if he were a member of a dissident opposition group, you still had a chance to influence the choice of the Prime Minister. But under the American system there was a logic of either/or which tended to subvert the third party on both the presidential and other levels of politics.

In the case of the presidency, as Thomas knew so well from his six campaigns for that office, the existence of a national constituency puts a premium on broad, amorphous parties which are capable of building a variegated coalition in a vast country. So it was that Thomas' strength invariably declined as the election neared, even though he himself was an extremely attractive leader and effective political speaker. For by November it would have become clear to the voter that the basic choice was between the nominees of the Democratic and Republican parties. And many who actually preferred Thomas–and would have voted for him as a socialist parliamentarian–turned to one of the major party candidates.

On the congressional level the same logic held. There were, at one time or another, various socialist enclaves of considerable strength in the United States: the Lower East Side of New York and Milwaukee, Wisconsin, with socialist members of the House (and in Milwaukee, a socialist mayor), Reading, Pennsylvania, and Bridgeport, Connecticut, with municipal administrations. But those areas could not, in the absence of a parliamentary system, serve as steppingstones to national power. And sooner or later all of them were absorbed by the major parties.

This, I think, explains much about the contrasting fate of socialism in the United States and Canada. Just to the north of this country there are farmers and workers quite like their American neighbors who have given a certain measure of political power to the old Canadian Commonwealth Federation and to the present New Democratic Party. In the case of the NDP the comparison is particularly revealing since many of the AFL-CIO unions in Canada back that social democratic party (it is affiliated to the Socialist International) but stick with the Democrats in the United States. In the Canadian parliamentary system one does not "waste" a vote by casting it for the NDP opposition, because its legislative delegation also has the power to influence the decisions of the executive.

This point, however, should not be made to bear excessive weight. If there are unquestionably advantages to parliamentary rule, in that it favors parties with a certain consistency and program and allows a minority opposition to have its effect, there are also problems in that system. It can lead, as in the French Fourth Republic, to a diffusion of political power which makes stable government impossible. It can tend, as it has been doing for some years in England, toward a covert mechanism of presidential rule, as the Liberal Party in that country can attest. Therefore, in agreeing with part of Norman Thomas' thesis I am not suggesting that a parliament is the answer for all of America's ills. (It will, in any case, never be adopted.) I am simply observing that the lack of one was certainly a factor in the failure of the Socialist Party of the United States.

But, and now I am moving into the area of my disagreement with Thomas, the American political structure was not the crucial element in the socialist defeat.

There was, and is, a class struggle in the United States, and indeed it has been bloodier and more violent here than in Europe. And, beginning with the presidency of Woodrow Wilson, labor has been involved in mainstream politics on a class basis. The peculiarities of American political structure are one reason why this process did not culminate in a mass socialist movement. But there are many other factors. The Debsians had modeled themselves on the pre-World War I German social democracy, in which labor political organization preceded and dominated industrial organization. They therefore expected to become the central organizational expression of working-class political consciousness. But the American reality followed the English model. Unions which were officially pro-capitalist were gradually forced into a political struggle for reforms, often against their will. As a result, and it was fateful that too few socialists understood the fact, the Socialist Party was more often than not counterposed to the actual political organizations of the labor movement.

Some, like Hillquit, understood that it was therefore necessary to amend the Debsian perspective, and he helped bring about formal Socialist participation in the La Follette campaign of 1924. Thomas himself came to recognize this situation and in 1938 proposed that the Socialist Party abandon its electoral emphasis.[1] Had that been done, many of the trade unionists who felt that they were forced to choose between the party and union political action, and opted for the latter, might have been able to remain as active socialists. That would not have created a mass movement, but it would have provided the basis for a much more powerful socialist presence in American politics. Shortly after he came to this conclusion, the imminence of World War II turned Thomas back to the party's traditional stance of intransigent opposition to what were called—wrongly I think—Tweedledum and Tweedledee.

In the last period of his life, Thomas once more adopted the perspective he had briefly held in 1938. He was one of the leaders of the Socialist Party—as was this writer—who argued in 1960 that there was no sense in running a campaign every four years which only revealed the weakness of the movement and took a few votes away from liberal candidates to boot. And yet in my own relations with him, as comrade and friend, I always sensed a certain nostalgia for the old days. Thomas supported Johnson against Goldwater, backed Eugene McCarthy in 1968, and, with considerable reluctance, decided to vote for Hubert Humphrey in the general election of that year. But, as I know from conversations with him in 1967, he was exploring the possibility of an independent antiwar presidential campaign in 1968.

One of the reasons for his ambivalence is obvious from his essay. "Labor," he wrote, "since 1932 is fairly content it has kept and increased its gains by picking individuals (usually Democrats) who, by conviction or for the sake of labor votes, will come nearest to its demands." This is a fairly typical description of the unions as an interest group in the tradition of the Gompers maxim "Reward your friends, punish your enemies." Yet I do not think that it is accurate.

After that La Follette campaign in 1924, American labor veered back to the Gompers "voluntarism" it had abandoned right after World War I. It is quite sobering to remember that John L. Lewis, the architect of the CIO, voted for Herbert Hoover in 1932. But with the Roosevelt campaign of 1936, something unprecedented began to happen. The unions started to build an ongoing political apparatus. That process was marked by the creation of the CIO Political Action Committee and the AFL's League for Political Education in the forties. It was accelerated by the merger in the fifties and the appearance of the Committee on Political Education of the AFL-CIO. And in the campaigns of 1968 and 1970 it was obvious to most observers that union political organization was the single most important factor in the Democrats' effort.

The "English" pattern was unfolding and Thomas missed the fact. The labor commitment to politics was no longer individualistic and episodic, as he thought, but permanent and concerted.[2] And that made it possible to hope that, as in England, the pragmatic trade unionists would come to see the necessity of basic, structural change in the society. In fairness, though, I should add that there is another model which is not so encouraging from a socialist point of view: the Australian. In that country, the unions have been in politics for three quarters of a century, there is a long tradition of labor partyism—and yet the labor parties have never really become socialist.[3]

My criticism, then, is that Norman Thomas, by focusing too much on how the American political structure affected the Debsian perspective of a mass socialist party emerging in its own name, overlooked an alternative possibility: the politicalization of bread-and-butter unions as in the case of the British Labour Party. And yet I would not push that analogy too far, for I agree with Thomas that the Labour Party cannot be the model for American socialists. In what has gone before, my emphasis has been on the way in which a mass socialist movement developed in England—and could develop in America—not upon the actual structure which came into being.

And indeed in the 1960s, the Labour Party probably owed its electoral victories to the fact that it abandoned its narrow "laborite" identification. Harold Wilson projected the party as a modern institution appealing to the college-educated as well as to industrial workers. And that was the meaning of the German Social Democratic Party's change from a "party of the working class" to a "party of all laboring people" at the Bad Godesberg Congress in 1959. For in Europe, as in America, the class structure has evolved so that a party making an exclusively proletarian appeal is doomed to permanent minority status.

Moreover, there are specifically American reasons why the slogan of a "labor party" will not have great appeal. It is a profound tradition in this country to act upon the reality of class differences—the workers, as Seymour Martin Lipset pointed out in *Political Man,* vote more massively for the Democrats than their British counterparts for the Labour Party—but also to pretend that they do not exist. If American socialists want to advance their cause in terms of actual political power I believe that they will have to learn to tolerate a great deal of rhetorical imprecision. A party explicitly based on the working class in this country will not get very far; but a party implicitly based on the working class, but appealing to other groups as well, is the only vehicle for progressive political change.

That is why, finally, I agree with Thomas' political conclusion even though I disagree with elements in his analysis. Our present party counterposition, as I tried to show in *Toward a Democratic Left,* is based upon utopian pragmatism. It is assumed that providence has somehow designed social reality so that those fratricidal coalitions, the Republican and Democratic parties, will stumble down the middle of the road into the best of all possible futures. That is not the case. The invisible hand of Adam Smith will not guide a technology which is now producing more external diseconomies than economies. And a party system proud of its amorphousness will hardly be able to respond to complicated challenges at home and abroad. There must indeed be, as Thomas argues, a realignment.

The way to that realignment is through the liberal wing of the Democratic Party. It will not, in the near future at least, lead to the emergence of a mass socialist movement under its own, or any other, name. But it will finally allow Americans something like a relatively serious choice between conservatism and liberalism, the Right and Left limits of mass politics today. And it is only when such a confrontation has taken place that it will be possible to pose a socialist alternative in terms that tens of millions of Americans can understand.

Norman Thomas devoted a lifetime to the struggle for that alternative. He was not simply the "conscience" of his nation as so many of the obituaries insisted, for that suggests that he stood for principles good for Sunday sermons but not for the real political life of the society. On the contrary. He was profoundly, and practically, right about the necessity of restructuring the American political party system. He made his tactical errors in fighting for that ideal, but if this country ever does adopt the realignment he described in *Socialism Re-examined,* he will be seen as a precursor of a crucial American change, and one which will finally make it possible for this country to face up to its problems. Norman Thomas possessed a very practical conscience.

NOTES

1. Since Thomas rather quickly reverted back to the classic socialist position, many people are not aware of this interlude. It is documented in Bernard K. Johnpoll, *Pacifist's Progress: Norman Thomas and the Decline of American Socialism* (Chicago: Quadrangle Books, 1970), p. 203.

2. J. David Greenstone, *Labor in American Politics* (New York: Knopf, 1969) is a good description of this development.

3. This history is summarized in G. D. H. Cole's *History of Socialist Thought* (London: Macmillan's, 1956), vol. III, pt. 2, ch. XXIII; and vol. IV, pt. 2, ch. XXVIII.

COMMENT 2

Leon D. Epstein

To ask why there has been no large and durable American socialist party is a conventionally important question in comparative social and political analysis. It is unusual, however, to answer the question with Norman Thomas' emphasis on structural obstacles raised by constitutional and electoral arrangements. Social scientists generally, including historians, prefer broad sociological or economic causes rather than mechanistic political explanations. As must be apparent from the essays of this volume, the preference is not confined to Marxists or other economic determinists.

Understanding Thomas' emphasis is easier after a close look at the question as usually asked and then at Thomas' version of it. The "socialist party" absent in the United States is ordinarily conceived in British and Western European terms as an organization of numerous political activists capable of mobilizing mass electoral support for a program of economic redistribution antithetical, at least in the long run, to a prevailing capitalist system. In the traditional model, mass support as well as some of the leadership derives from industrial workers possessing a class consciousness sufficient for a political cause that is primarily their own. With industrialization, the working class develops not only the requisite consciousness of its interest and so of its political role, but also the numbers and strength of an electoral majority. Hence a socialist party is able to gain effective power in a nation whose policy makers are chosen by mass suffrage. And it is to exercise that power in the name of the majoritarian class that elected it, although, in democratic, non-Leninist socialism, with due regard for minority interests. The politics of socialism thus seem distinct from those of an American pluralism, in which interests are many rather than dichotomous, combined and compromised rather than sharpened as program commitments, and expressed electorally through loose and broad coalitions rather than through cohesive and disciplined forces.

A socialist party is not supposed to resemble the structure of the Republican or Democratic party. It is to have a large, organized, and ideologically recruited membership both for effective campaigning and for making the policy of the leaders whom it recruits and helps elect to public office. As such, a socialist party is the prototype "modern" party that Duverger, among other scholars, has found to exist in Britain and Western Europe but not in the United States.[1] It is also a prime example of the "responsible" party that non-socialist American political scientists like Schattschneider and Burns have advocated to replace the unprogrammatic, uncohesive brokerage structure characteristic of Republicans and Democrats.[2] Since, however, the responsible-party reformers would attempt to create a majoritarian party without reliance on class-conscious socialism, the difficulties of establishing a socialist party in the United States would only be relevant to their advocacy if those difficulties were of such a nature as to stand in the way of any strongly programmatic party seeking to win national power in the United States.

Usual explanations of American socialist party failure have been directed to the conditions uncongenial to socialism rather than to those uncongenial to "responsible" parties in general. Thomas himself, before discussing the structural obstacles, briefly notes the familiar factors (expanding frontiers, immigration, and social mobility) softening the impact of class in the United States. It is common to conclude that the weakness of American socialists, relative to European socialists, results from less class consciousness in the United States.[3] Not everyone would agree that there was less about which to be class-conscious, but the early, virtually pre-industrial "gift of the ballot" to white males seems to have reduced the potential.[4] And so did the nation's total wealth, making for fairly widespread affluence despite gross inequalities. Together these factors are thought to account both for late unionization of American labor and for its unresponsiveness to socialist party politics. And without formal or informal organizational ties to unionized labor, there is no basis for a socialist party on the British or European scale.[5]

Thomas, however, is not primarily concerned with an American socialist party conceived on that scale. Specifically, the British Labour Party, whose heavy trade union orientation has made it one of two major parties, is not his model. Thomas' aspirations seem to have been much more modest. He writes not of a failure to build a socialist party that would, like British Labour, have displaced one of the old parties in two-party competition and so have been able to achieve power as a majoritarian force. Rather he thinks in terms of "a moderately strong socialist party" that would at best be a substantial third or fourth party in a multi-party system, and at worst a consistently strong minor party in a weakened two-party system. It is true that Thomas wants a party whose socialist principles would make it even more cohesive and programmatic than the responsible-party school desires in a reconstituted Republican or Democratic party. Yet Thomas is significantly closer to a crucial assumption of American political practice: that the nation is too large and varied in its interests, regions, and ethnicity to provide a majority for a party committed to a doctrinal program that it will not compromise. Implicitly if not explicitly, Thomas accepts this assumption along with the usual socioeconomic explanation of why there has been no specifically socialist majoritarian party in the United States.

Consequently, in reality, he asks why there has been no substantial third or fourth party of American socialists, capable of regularly winning more votes than a "minor" party in essentially two-party competition. The European model, if there is one, seems to be not British but Continental, and to be limited to those multiparty situations in which socialists have remained well short of majority status. In this light, Thomas' question can be restated as an inquiry into the forces so preserving two-party competition as to discourage effectively the durable development of third parties. Here it is orthodox political science to stress structural features of the American Constitution and of election laws. In particular, Thomas is by no means the first or the last critic to focus attention on the presidential election system as a prime obstacle to those who would convert two-party competition to multi-party competition. Less common except among Anglophiles is Thomas' preference for "a centralized parliamentary government rather than a federalized presidential government." The difficulty here for anyone wanting several major parties rather than two is that there is nothing inherent in parliamentary government, as British experience demonstrates, that always produces multipartism. Combining proportional-representation elections with parliamentary government is a likelier means of facilitating multipartism, given the association of these institutions in Continental Europe, but the direction of the causation is by no means settled.

At any rate, parliamentary government, with or without proportional representation, receives only passing attention from Thomas. Whatever his preference on this score, he generally accepts the presidential form as a settled feature of American government and concentrates on proposing a change in the method by which Presidents are elected. He urges not only popular direct election, instead of the electoral college, but also a preferential ballot allowing voters to number their choices. The latter is naturally favored by the third-party advocate. Preferential voting, by allowing second choices to be added to first choices, does more than produce a winner without a runoff election. Simultaneously it encourages those who like a third- or fourth-party candidate to give him their first choice knowing that their vote is not thereby wasted just because he has no chance to win a majority of first choices. Even if he cannot pick up enough second choices for a majority, those who voted for him can still affect the outcome by their second choices–presumably cast for the lesser evil among the potential winners. Thus the preferential ballot sustains the third-party cause. Direct popular election of the President, as some of its present-day advocates understand, might itself work in the same direction. Even with a prospective runoff, additional party candidacies would be encouraged by the prospects of trading votes after the first inconclusive round. But the preferential ballot, Thomas recognizes, is the straightforward way to seek the multi-party end.

No technique exists for learning whether this tinkering with the election machinery would in fact produce an American multi-party voting pattern and along with it the strong socialist party that Thomas wants. It can be granted that the present election method, both in its coalition-imposing requirement of an electoral college majority and in its use of the standard simple-plurality principle of carrying a state, is well suited to the prevalent two-party competition. But that does not mean that two-party competition persists *only* because of the election method, or that it would fail to persist with a different election method. Nor is there any way to know that the established election method, however well suited to two-party competition, has really been crucial in frustrating socialist or other third-party hopes. Thomas himself ascribes his party's difficulties partly to financial shortages, and these would likely persist under any election method.

It can at least be argued that third-party efforts have been more successful, or less unsuccessful, in presidential elections than in other American contests. George Wallace's campaign is now added to those of Theodore Roosevelt and Robert La Follette as substantial twentieth-century efforts, besides that of Debs in 1912. None, it is true, secured many electoral votes, but their popular vote totals are impressive when compared to even the occasional victories of third-party candidates for Congress and for state offices. And, as George Wallace has been trying to teach us, even a small number of electoral votes might in a close election be transformed into effective bargaining power for the third-party candidate. To be more specific about Thomas' analysis, I cannot believe that difficulty in contesting presidential elections was a principal cause of Socialist Party failure. It cannot explain why the party's state and local electoral strength, peaking before World War I, should have declined instead of reviving in the 1920s and 1930s. Curiously the party faded almost completely at state, local, and congressional levels before Norman Thomas' presidential cause was abandoned.

Thomas is not unaware of the likely reasons, notably of Franklin Roosevelt's success in absorbing potential socialist strength under the banner of the New Deal and the welfare state. Since the absorption was within a coalition, namely a Democratic Party containing many decidedly non-socialist and non-New Dealish elements, Thomas can hardly regard the result as entirely satisfactory. Yet it may be inherently characteristic of American party politics. Each major party is not only ideologically broad but also structurally loose and open. New forces, once large and politically mobilizable, find it easier and more effective to enter an existing party than to start a new party. State and local organizations, when they cannot readily be taken over, are often bypassed. The direct primary is a nearly unique American device facilitating the process. State parties are reshaped and then used to influence national parties. Influence, of course, is not the same as control, and compromise is required as it is not in a new party reconciled to minority status.

To a considerable extent, this process seems to belong to any working two-party pattern and not just to American politics. Each of only two major parties must always be a fairly broad coalition capable of absorbing new interests and forces along with diverse older ones. Obviously it might become so broad as to be an ineffective political means to enact a positive program. That is the charge against American parties of the last few decades. Those who would reform them, within the two-party pattern, rest their hopes on emulating the apparently greater programmatic cohesion of British parties although it is achieved in a much less diverse society more readily permitting the maintenance of parliamentary party solidarity. Rejecting that kind of reform, while agreeing with the charge against American parties, leads, as it did for Norman Thomas, to the search for the means to build a third party. Neither as a political leader nor as a retrospective analyst did Norman Thomas discover the means. But it is likelier now than when he wrote that numerous successors will continue the search. American two-party politics is not presently enjoying its best days.

NOTES

1. Maurice Duverger, *Political Parties,* trans. Barbara and Robert North (New York: John Wiley, 1954).

2. E. E. Schattschneider, *Party Government* (New York: Rinehart, 1942); James MacGregor Burns, *The Deadlock of Democracy* (Englewood Cliffs, N.J.: Prentice-Hall, 1963).

3. David A. Shannon, *The Socialist Party of America* (New York: Macmillan, 1955), p. 263.

4. Selig Perlman, *A Theory of the Labor Movement* (New York: Augustus Kelley, 1949), pp. 167–68.

5. I have tried to explain the difference between American labor politics (in Canada and the United States) and European socialist parties in ch. VI of *Political Parties in Western Democracies* (New York: Praeger, 1967).

SELECTED BIBLIOGRAPHY

ARONOWITZ, STANLEY. *False Promises, The Shaping of American Working Class Consciousness*. New York: McGraw-Hill, 1973.

BEDFORD, HENRY. *Socialism and the Workers in Massachusetts, 1886–1912*. Amherst: University of Massachusetts Press, 1966.

BELL, DANIEL. *Marxian Socialism in the United States*. Princeton: Princeton University Press, 1967.

BUHLE, MARI JO. *Women and American Socialism, 1870–1920*. Urbana: University of Illinois Press, 1981.

BURBANK, GARIN. *When Farmers Voted Red, The Gospel of Socialism in the Oklahoma Countryside: 1910–1924*. Westport: Greenwood Press, 1976.

CANTOR, MILTON. *The Divided Left, American Radicalism: 1900–1975*. New York: Hill and Wang, 1978.

COCHRAN, BERT. *Labor and Communism, The Conflict That Shaped American Unions*. Princeton: Princeton University Press, 1977.

CONLIN, JOSEPH R. *Bread and Roses Too, Studies of the Wobblies*. Westport: Greenwood Press, 1969.

——— *Big Bill Haywood and the Radical Union Movement*. New York: Syracuse University Press, 1969.

DECAUX, LEN. *Labor Radical, From the Wobblies to the C.I.O.: A Personal History*. Boston: Beacon Press, 1970.

DICK, WILLIAM. *Labor and Socialism in America, The Gompers Era*. Port Washington: Kennikat Press, 1972.

DRAPER, THEODORE. *The Roots of American Communism*. New York: Viking Press, 1957.

——— *American Communism and Soviet Russia, The Formative Period*. New York: Viking Press, 1960.

DUBOFSKY, MELVIN. *We Shall Be All, A History of the I.W.W.* Chicago: Quadrangle Books, 1969.

EGBERT, D. D. AND S. PERSONS, eds. *Socialism and American Life*. 2 vols. Princeton: Princeton University Press, 1952.

FINE, NATHAN. *Labor and Farmer Parties in the United States, 1882–1928*. New York: Russell and Russell, 1961.

FONER, PHILIP S. *History of the Labor Movement in the United States*. 6 vols. New York: International Publishers, 1947–1982.

——— *American Socialism and Black Americans.* Westport: Greenwood Press, 1977.

——— ed. *The Bolshevik Revolution, Its Impact on American Radicals, Liberals and Labor.* New York: International Publishers, 1967.

GINGER, RAY. *The Bending Cross, A Biography of Eugene Victor Debs.* New Brunswick: Rutgers University Press, 1949.

GREEN, JAMES R. *Grass-Roots Socialism, Radical Movements in the Southwest: 1895–1943.* Baton Rouge: Louisiana State University Press, 1978.

HARTZ, LOUIS. *The Liberal Tradition in America, An Interpretation of American Political Thought Since the Revolution.* New York: Harcourt, Brace and World, 1955.

——— *The Founding of New Societies, Studies in the History of the United States, Latin America, South Africa, and Australia.* New York: Harcourt, Brace and World, 1964.

HERRESHOFF, DAVID. *American Disciples of Marx, From the Age of Jackson to the Progressive Era.* Detroit: Wayne State University Press, 1967.

HOWE, IRVING AND LEWIS COSER. *The American Communist Party, A Critical History.* New York: Frederick A. Praeger, 1962.

JOHNPOLL, BERNARD K. *Pacifist's Progress, Norman Thomas and the Decline of American Socialism.* Chicago: Quadrangle Books, 1970.

KARSON, MARC. *American Labor Unions and Politics, 1900–1918.* Carbondale: Southern Illinois University Press, 1958.

KEERAN, ROGER. *The Communist Party and the Auto Workers Unions.* Bloomington: Indiana University Press, 1980.

KIPNIS, IRA. *The American Socialist Movement, 1897–1912.* New York: Columbia University Press, 1952.

KRADITOR, AILEEN. *The Radical Persuasion, 1890–1917.* Baton Rouge: Louisiana State University Press, 1981.

LASLETT, J. H. M. *Labor and the Left, A Study of Socialist and Radical Influences in the American Labor Movement, 1881–1924.* New York: Basic Books, 1970.

LEVENSTEIN, HARVEY. *Communism, Anti-Communism, and the C.I.O.* Westport: Greenwood Press, 1981.

LIPSET, S. M. *Agrarian Socialism: The Cooperative Commonwealth Federation in Saskatchewan: A Study in Political Sociology.* Garden City: Anchor Books, 1968; reprinted Berkeley and Los Angeles: University of California Press, 1971.

———*The First New Nation: The United States in Historical and Comparative Perspective.* New York: Basic Books, 1963; reprinted in expanded form New York: W. W. Norton, 1979.

——— "Why No Socialism in the United States?" in S. Bialer and S. Sluzar, eds. *Sources of Contemporary Radicalism.* Boulder: Westview Press, 1977.

MOORE, R. LAURENCE. *European Socialists and the American Promised Land.* New York: Oxford University Press, 1970.

MYERS, CONSTANCE A. *The Prophet's Army, Trotsky in America: 1928–1941.* Westport: Greenwood Press, 1977.

PERLMAN, SELIG. *A Theory of the Labor Movement.* New York: Augustus M. Kelley, 1966.

POLLACK, NORMAN. *The Populist Response to Industrial America, Midwestern Populist Thought.* New York: W. W. Norton, 1966.

PREIS, ART. *Labor's Giant Step, Twenty Years of the C.I.O.* New York: Pioneer Publishers, 1964.

QUINT, HOWARD H. *The Forging of American Socialism, Origins of the Modern Movement.* Indianapolis: Bobbs-Merrill, 1964.

ROSENBLUM, GERALD. *Immigrant Workers, Their Impact on American Radicalism.* New York: Basic Books, 1973.

SHANNON, DAVID A. *The Socialist Party of America, A History.* New York: Macmillan, 1955.

——— *The Decline of American Communism.* New York: Viking Press, 1959.

SOMBART, W. *Why Is There No Socialism in the United States?* Edited by C. T. Husbands. White Plains: M. E. Sharpe, 1976.

STAVE, BRUCE M. *Socialism and the Cities.* Port Washington: Kennikat Press, 1975.

TRACHTENBERG, ALEXANDER, ed. *Letters To Americans, 1848–1895 by Karl Marx and Frederick Engels.* New York: International Publishers, 1953.

WARREN, FRANK A. *Alternative Vision, The Socialist Party in the 1930's.* Bloomington: Indiana University Press, 1974.

WEINSTEIN, JAMES. *The Decline of American Socialism, 1912–1924.* New York: Monthly Review Press, 1967.

——— *Ambiguous Legacy, The Left in American Politics.* New York: Franklin Watts, 1975.

YOUNG, ALFRED, ed. *Dissent, Explorations in the History of American Radicalism.* DeKalb: Northern Illinois University Press, 1969.

YOURBURG, BETTY. *Utopia and Reality, A Collective Portrait of American Socialists.* New York: Columbia University Press, 1969.

INDEX

Abbott, Wenonah Stevens, 321
Abell, Aaron, 87, 91
Adams, Henry, 341
Adams, John, 363; on abuse of power, 378
Adorka, R., 430–441
AFL. *See* American Federation of Labor
AFL-CIO, 524, 526. *See also* American Federation of Labor; Congress of Industrial Organizations; Trade unions
African Blood Brotherhood, 234
Agrarian tradition, 52–81
Agricultural Wheel, 77
Agricultural Workers' Organization, 197
Albi, study of glassblowers in (Scott), 416
Alger, Horatio, 349–350
Algerism, 334–335
Alienation, concept of, 364–365
Althusser, Louis, 402
Amalrik, Andrei, 429
American Chartism, 216
American Farm Bureau Federation, 70
American Federation of Catholic Services, 92
American Federation of Labor (AFL), 12; and Victor Berger, 503; "Bill of Grievances" presented by, 245; Catholic strength in, 83, 85–86, 87, 88–92, 93–95, 97–98, 103, 108–109; and Central Verein, 93–94; and Daniel De Leon, 120, 500; and Democratic Party, 135–136; and Father Dietz, 88–92; dissatisfaction with, 123; and Max Hayes, 502; on immigration, 245–248, 252, 255, 278, 286; and industrial unionism, 77; and Knights of Labor, 124; and lack of class consciousness, 472; National Civic Foundation and, 13; and Populist Party, 55–57; and socialism, 118–169. *See also* AFL-CIO; Congress of Industrial Organizations; Gompers, Samuel; Trade unions
American Freedom and Catholic Power (Blanshard), 113
American Labor Union, 120, 121
American Labor Unions and Politics (Karson), 113
American Socialist Party. *See* Socialist Party
American Syndicalism (Brooks), 195
Ameringer, Oscar, 242
Anabaptists, 9
Anatomy of Melancholy (Burton), 9
Anti-Boycott Association, 84
Appeal to Reason, 321
Asher, Robert, 278
Ashley, W., 335
Association of Catholic Trade Unionists, 105–106. *See also* Catholic Church
Atlanta Exposition, 221
Austria-Hungary, suffrage in, 488

Babeuf, Gracchus, 9
Bacon, Francis, 9
Bad Godesberg Congress, 47, 527
Baez, Joan, 204
Bakunin, Mikhail, 10; and Wobblies, 171
Barber, James, 441
Barnes, Mahlon, 258

Bayley, Bishop James Roosevelt, 107
Beard, Charles, 393, 394
Bebel, August, 291
Belgium, suffrage in, 488
Bell, Daniel, 3, 137; on foreign-language federations, 274
Bellamy, Edward, 13, 54, 195; on liberalism, 340
Bendix, Reinhard, 409–410, 440, 448
Benson, Allan, 137, 517
Bentley, Arthur F., 372
Berger, Meta, 297
Berger, Victor L., 19, 37, 220–221, 270; and Bernstein, 338, 341; on immigration, 249, 250–251, 253; on Milwaukee party, 256; and peaceful change, 341; and reform issue, 338; role of, in labor and socialist movements, 501–503, 504; on suffrage for Negroes, 223; and William E. Walling, 222; on women, 293
Berkeley, Governor, 489
Berlyn, Barney, 249
Bernstein, Eduard, 193, 338, 341, 485
Birth control, views of Socialist women about, 306
Bishops, of Catholic Church, 85–87, 107–108
Bismarck, Otto von, 469
Blacks: Congress on suffrage for, 223; constricted opportunities for, 410; and new radicalism, 511; political attitudes of, 165–166; Populism and, 78; social mobility of, 438; socialism and, 218–243; Socialist Party's approach to, 157, 164–165. *See also* National Association for the Advancement of Colored People; Race
Blanshard, Paul, 103, 113
Blau, Peter M., 428, 429, 433–434, 438
Blinov, N. M., 429
Bohn, William E., 171
Bolshevism, 21–26, 391; and trade unions, 121. *See also* Lenin, V. I.; Marxism
Boot and Shoe Workers Union, 119, 121, 138, 141, 143; contracts of, 134; and Knights of St. Crispin, 124; and socialism, 127–128; Union Stamp Contract of, 133, 134
Boston study (Thernstrom): on occupational mobility, 419–421; on property mobility, 421–424; on social mobility, 414–416
Boudin, Louis, 394
Bourgeois, Léon, 337
Bourne, Randolph, 394
Branstetter, Winnie E., 299
Branting, Jhalmar, 475
Brauer-Zeitung, 136
Brazier, Richard, 183
Brewery Workers Union, 119–120, 141, 143; and Democratic Party, 136; and ethnic assimilation, 132; joint affiliation of, 124; and jurisdictional conflicts, 123, 143; and socialism, 130–131, 132
Briand, Aristide, 341
Briggs, Asa, 215
Brissenden, Paul F., 205
Brody, David, 163–164
Brooks, John Graham, 195, 205
Brophy, John, 109
Browder, Earl, 25, 209
Bruehl, Father Charles, 86
Bryan, William Jennings, 36; and Populism, 72
Budenz, Louis, 504
Buhle, Paul, 279
Burke, Edmund, 379
Burns, James MacGregor, 531
Burton, Robert, 9

Calhoun, John C., 446, 518
Canadian Commonwealth Federation, 524
Capital (*Das Kapital*) (Marx), 11, 28, 46–47, 367
Capitalism, 6; economic rewards of, 452–483; equal treatment under, 460–463; flexibility of, 402
Cardinals, of Catholic Church, 83–84
Carey, James, 499
Carmaux, study of glassblowers in (Scott), 416
Carroll, Bishop John, 85–86
Cassidy, Frank, 253, 254, 270

Catholic Church: and AFL, 83, 85–86, 87, 88–92, 93–95, 97–98, 103, 108–109; anti-socialism of, 82–117, 156; bishops of, 85–87, 107–108; cardinals of, 83–84; Central Verein, 86–87, 92–95, 104; and immigrant radicalism, 277; influence of, in labor movement, 82, 83, 85–86, 88–92, 93–95, 97–98, 103–104, 107–108, 109, 156; Militia of Christ, 88–92, 100–101, 103–104, 115; press of, 95–97; priests of, 85–88. *See also* Association of Catholic Trade Unionists; Catholic Press Association; *Catholic Worker*; Papal encyclicals; *names of individual popes*
Catholic Press Association, 96–97
Catholic Trade Unionists, Association of, 105–106
Catholic Worker, 110
Central Blatt and Social Justice, 93
Central Verein, 86–87, 92–95, 104
Chartist movement, 489–490
Chatard, Francis S. M., 107
Checks and balances, 376
Chiliasm, 9–10
Chinese Exclusion Act, 250
Cigarmakers union, 12
CIO. *See* Congress of Industrial Organizations
Class consciousness, 27–28, 472–475
Clay, Henry, 446
Clayton Act, 135
Clergy. *See* Catholic Church
Cleveland Citizen, 501, 502
Coal mining industry: after Civil War, 129–130; and Slav miners, 166. *See also* United Mine Workers; Western Federation of Miners
Cobb, Ned, 236
Cochran, Thomas, 216
Coeur d'Alene, Idaho, strike in, 171
Cold War, 400
Collective bargaining, 134, 470–472. *See also* Trade unions
Collins, Peter W., 89, 94–95
Committee for a More Effective Congress, 32
Committee on Political Education, AFL-CIO, 526
Common Cause, The, 97
Commons-Wisconsin School, 155
Communism. *See* Bolshevism; Lenin, V. I.; Marx, Karl; Marxism
Communist countries, mobility in, 429–433
Communist Manifesto (Marx and Engels), 28, 370
Communist party, 21–26; in France, 213–214, 510, 513–514; in Italy, 514. *See also* Bolshevism; Marxism
Communist Party, U.S., 24–26, 34, 36; and immigrant radicals, 279; and race, 218, 235; and Sharecropper's Union, 235–236
Comte, Auguste, 336
Conditions of the Working Class in England, The (Engels), 4
Confédération Française du Travail Démocratique, 510
Conference for Progressive Political Action, 136
Conger-Kaneko, Josephine, 305, 321, 323; on separatist issue, 330
Congress, U.S., on Negro suffrage, 223
Congress of Industrial Organizations (CIO), 34, 49, 195, 279, 504, 526. *See also* AFL-CIO; American Federation of Labor; Trade unions
Conlin, Joseph Robert, 204
Conscience, ethic of, 8
Constitutionalism, 376
Coos Bay, Oregon, strike in, 208
Copenhagen, study of mobility in (Rishøj), 434, 448–449
Couch-Hazlett, Ida, 304; on separatist issue, 330
Coughlin, Father, 6, 518
Coxey movement, 61, 67
Craft unions. *See* American Federation of Labor; Trade unions
Cripple Creek, strike in, 171
Critique of Hegel's Philosophy of the State (Marx), 391
Critique of the Gotha Programme (Marx), 370
Croly, Herbert, 334, 336
"Culture of poverty," 172–173, 196, 210–211
Curti, Merle, 413, 416

Cutright, Philips, 428, 430
Czechoslovakia, social mobility in, 429

Darwin, Charles, 171
Dawson, Philip, 410–411
De Leon, Daniel, 36, 37, 113; and AFL, 120, 144, 500; and Americanism, 340; and dual unionist tactics, 118; ideology of, 500–501; and intellectuals, 500; on Thomas Jefferson, 343; and liberal goals, 350; on officeholders in unions, 152–153; and reform issue, 338. *See also* Socialist Labor Party; Socialist Trades and Labor Alliance
Debord, Guy, 498
Debs, Eugene V., 14–15; failure of, 447; highest vote for, 517; on immigration, 252–253, 263; influence of, 475; and IWW, 205; rhetoric of, 36–37; and trade unions, 33; on women, 294
Debs, Kate, 15
Decline of Socialism in America, The (Weinstein), 135
Deism, 4
Democratic Party: and AFL, 135–136; Blacks and, 237; farmers and, 53; Seymour Martin Lipset on, 527; Norman Thomas on, 517–518, 519–520
Depression. *See* Great Depression
Destley, Chester M., 125
Dewey, John, 517
Dietz, Father Peter E., 87–92, 103–104, 115
Disraeli, Benjamin, 349
Dobrynin, M., 432–433
Doherty, Robert, 414
Domingo, Wilfred A., 234, 238
Donald, David, 345
Donovan Commission (Britain), 513
Doree, E. F., 177
Dos Passos, John, 14
Douglas, Stephen, 446
Dreyfus affair, 341
Dual unionist policies, 118, 120, 153
Dubofsky, Melvyn, 166
DuBois, W. E. B., 221, 225
Duffy, Thomas, 89
Duncan, Otis Dudley, 428, 429, 433–434, 438
Dunham, Marion, 321
Duverger, Maurice, 531
Dwenger, Bishop John, 107

Easley, Ralph, 352
Eaton, Horace M., 128
Ebert, Justus, 174, 183
Economic and Philosophical Manuscripts (Marx), 390
Economic Interpretations of History, The (Seligman), 394
Economism, 485–486
Edgworth, W. J., 208
Education, 438–439; in Europe, 489–490
Effective freedom, 366
Eighteenth Brumaire, The (Marx), 11, 28
Ellison, Ralph, 219
Embree, A. S., 199
Engels, Friedrich, 4–5; on American working-class leaders, 163; on equality, 370–371; on liberty, 366; and SLP, 153; on system of Marxism, 381–382; on women, 291. *See also* Marxism
England. *See* Great Britain
Enlightened absolutism, 487, 488
Equality: American tradition of, 371–372; Marx on, 369–371
Ethics, 7–10
Ethnicity: and foreign-language federations, 259–262; socialism and, 244–290. *See also* Race
Ettor, Joe, 174, 179; on general strike, 190; on violence, 185
Eugene, Oregon, strike in, 207–208
European liberal reform, 335–338

Fabian Essays (Bellamy), 340
Fabians, 352
Farley, Cardinal John, 83, 84
Farmer-labor party, 61–62, 502, 519
Farmers, 52–81; census on number

of, 465; and Democratic Party, 53. *See also* Populism
Farmers' Alliance, 57–59, 77; merchants and, 79–80
Fascism, 17
Federal Farm Loan Act, 79
Federal Reserve Act, 79
Federal Warehouse Act, 79
Federalism, 376
Federazione Socialista Italiana, 275
Ferge, Sandor, 429
Feudal tradition, 346–347; legacy of, 487–488
Feuerbach, Ludwig, 390
Fieldman, Sol, 249
Finn Hall, 276
Flynn, Elizabeth Gurley, 110, 181, 187, 295
Foner, Philip, 113, 140; on IWW, 182; on racism, 232–233; study of Black socialist preachers by, 242
Foreign-language federations, 259–262; Daniel Bell on, 274; and Woman's National Committee, 301
Formal freedom, 366
Foster, William Z., 37, 504
Fourier, Charles, 3
Fox, Sister Mary Harrita, 115
France: Communist Party of, 213–214, 510, 513–514; and *constats de Grenelle*, 513; education in, 489; intellectuals in, 492–493; Paris Commune, 390–391; Popular Front in, 39; population studies of, 416; social mobility in, 410–411; and split in Marxism, 341; student rebellion in, 510; syndicalist movement in, 205–206
Free labor market, 367
Freedman, Estelle, 324–325, 326–327

Galleani, Luigi, 275
Garvey, Marcus, 237, 239
Gaylord, Winfield, 256
Genovese, Eugene D., 210
Geographical mobility, 412–416
George, Henry, 4, 54, 104
Germany: and Bad Godesberg declaration, 47, 527; collective bargaining in, 137; revisionist movement in, 485; Social Democratic Party of, 23, 38, 527; Socialist Party of, 39; standard of living in, 452–455, 457; strikes in, 509–510; suffrage in, 488
Gibbons, Cardinal James, 83–84
Ginger, Ray, 414
Giovannitti, Arturo, 186
Gleed, J. W., 61
Glennon, Archbishop John J., 89
Golden, John, 89
Goldman, Eric, 177
Goldwater, Barry, 526
Gompers, Samuel, 12–13; and Victor Berger, 503; as Catholic, 109; and Central Verein, 93–94; and farmers, 59; and Max Hayes, 502; hostility of, to socialism, 118, 119; on immigration, 245; and International Association of Machinists, 124; and Meyer London, 120; and Populism, 68–69; successes of, 447; Saul Yanovsky on, 155–156. *See also* American Federation of Labor
Gonner (Central Verein), 93
Gorz, André, 402, 403
Gramsci, Antonio, 38, 199, 402, 405
Grass-Roots Socialism: Radical Movements in the Southwest (Green), 242
Great Britain: collective bargaining in, 134; Donovan Commission of, 513; education in, 489; House of Lords of, 350–351, 358; lack of class solidarity in, 479; Liberal Party of, 525; property mobility in, 422; suffrage in, 474. *See also* Labor party
Great Depression, 6; occupational mobility and, 418; and Socialist Party, 48–49
Green, James R., 242
Green, T. H., 335
Greenback Labor Party, 56, 68
Greene, Victor, 166
Grenelle, constats de, 513
Grosse, Edward, 12
Grundy, Annie, 300

Guesde, Jules, 338, 341
Gulagin, Georgi, 432
Gutman, Herbert, 216; on homeownership, 421–422; on immigration, 272, 276

Haggerty, Father Thomas, 110
Hamilton, Alexander, 518
Handlin, Oscar, 166, 245, 246–247, 272
Hanna, Mark, 13, 156
Hansen, Marcus Lee, 13, 244, 279
Hardie, James Keir, 474
Harrington, Michael, 39–40, 105–106
Harrison, Frederic, 422
Harrison, Hubert H., 234, 238
Harrison, Royden, 418–419, 422
Hartz, Louis, 72, 209, 215
Hayes, Denis A., 89
Hayes, Max S., 154, 249, 501–504
Haywood, William M., 117, 155, 174; on direct action, 183; failures of, 447; on general strike, 190; on immigration, 255; and industrial unionism, 155, 192; on law, 184; and National Executive Committee, 193, 263; on passive resistance, 186; on revolution, 179, 180; on the state, 191; on strikes, 185; and women, 305
Hegel, G. W. F., 369
Henry Street Settlement House, 293
Herberg, Will, 193
Hicks, John, 72
Higgins, Monseignor George, 113
Hilferding, Rudolf, 31, 39
Hill, James, 108
Hill, Joe, 117, 170, 204
Hillquit, Morris, 19, 37, 139; on Asian immigration, 269–270; and Debsian perspective, 525; on foreign-language federations, 261–262; on immigration, 251–252, 269–270, 297; and La Follette campaign, 520, 525; leadership of, 520; *Messenger* supporting, 226; on organization of Socialist Party, 155; on separate representation of ethnic groups, 242; on socialist education, 157
History of the Labor Movement in the United States (Foner), 151
Hitler, Adolf, 17
Hoan, Dan, 19
Hobbes, Thomas, 378
Hobsbawm, E. J., 173, 178, 216; and labor aristocracy, 418–419; and "tramping artisans," 416
Hofstadter, Richard, 166, 523
Holm, N. F., 270–271
Holyoke, Massachusetts, study of textile workers in (Ginger), 414
Homeownership, 421–424
Homestead Laws, 465–466
Homestead Steel strike, 67
Hoover, Herbert, 526
Hourwich, Isaac, 245–246
Household budgets, 452–455, 457
Howells, W. D., 338
Hubbard, Elbert, 15, 334
Hueber, Anton, 475
Human Exploitation (Thomas), 18
Humphrey, Hubert, 526
Hungarian Socialist Society, 258
Hungary, social mobility in, 429–431
Hunter, Robert, 205, 262, 270
Husslein, Joseph, 96
Huthmacher, Joseph, 166
Hyndman, Henry, 340

ILGWU. *See* International Ladies' Garment Workers Union
Illinois Central and Harriman Lines strike, 152, 163
Illinois Federation of Labor, 155
Immigration, 5; AFL on, 245–248, 278; Asian, 250, 269–270, 271; and capitalism, 478–479; homestead laws and, 466; of labor leaders, 13; and social mobility, 437–438; Socialist Party and, 157–158, 244–290; Stuttgart resolution (1907) on, 248, 250, 252, 269–270; women and, 321. *See also* Ethnicity
Imperialist policies, 481
Independent, The, 153
Independent Labor Party (Britain), 340
Individualism, 383–384

Industrial Worker: on sabotage, 186–187; on syndicalism, 194; on violence, 185. *See also* Industrial Workers of the World
Industrial Workers of the World (IWW), 33, 170–216, 233, 304; AFL on, 155; and Victor Berger, 503; on contracts, 189–190; and Daniel De Leon, 501; death of, 204; and Max Hayes, 502; and hobo Wobbly legend, 170; ideology of, 176–177; immigrant radicals and, 279; and immigration, 255; "Internationale" of, 178; leadership of, 174; and non-benefit system, 174; and population turnovers, 424; and power doctrine, 181; and race, 233; on sabotage, 186–188; and Socialist Party, 192–195; *Solidarity*, published by, 171, 185, 186; on violence, 185–186; and Western Federation of Miners, 120–121; and women socialists, 304–305; and World War I, 207. See also *Industrial Worker*; Syndicalism
Intellectuals, 484–515; and syndicalism, 492
International Association of Machinists (IAM), 119, 121, 141, 142; and Democratic Party, 135–136; and Samuel Gompers, 124; leaders of, 152; and Populism, 67, 125–126; post-Civil War changes in, 128–129; and segregation, 142. See also *Machinists Monthly Journal*
International Ladies' Garment Workers Union (ILGWU), 121, 141; and ethnic assimilation, 132; *Justice*, published by, 155; and socialism, 130–131; and Socialist Party, 137, 138–139
International Machinists Union, 119, 142. *See also* International Association of Machinists
International Socialist Review, 113, 252, 294, 304
Ireland, Bishop John, 85, 108
Iron Heel, The (London), 181
Iskra, 486
"Isolated mass," in occupational environment (Kerr), 411–412
Italian Language Federation, 275
Italy: Communist Party of, 514; strike wave in, 510; suffrage in, 488
IWW. *See* Industrial Workers of the World

Jacksonian socialism, 333, 339
Jacobs, Paul, 134
James, Henry, 10
Jaurès, Jean, 338, 340, 341, 475
Jefferson, Thomas, 343, 518
Jewish community: and labor movement, 130–131; in New York, 132; and Socialist Party, 166
Jingoism, 481
John XXIII, pope, 114. See also *Mater et magistra*
Johnson, Lyndon, 526
Johnston, William H., 121, 152, 163
Justice (ILGWU), 155. *See also* International Ladies' Garment Workers Union

Karson, Marc, 156
Katz, Rudolph, 188
Kautsky, Karl, 3, 337
Kelley, Florence, 293
Kenkel, F. P., 93–94, 95
Kennedy, John F., 316
Kenrick, Archbishop Peter Richard, 108
Kerby, Father, 85
Kerr, Clark, 411–412, 416
Keyserling, Count Hermann, 5
Khrushchev, Nikita, 381
King, Martin Luther, Jr., 481
Kipnis, Ira, 137, 218–219, 262; on immigration, 269
Knights of Labor, 4, 56; and AFL, 124, 472; and Daniel De Leon, 500; effect of, 66; farmers and, 76; and Archbishop Kenrick, 108; membership growth of, 466–467
Knights of St. Crispin, 124

Kolko, Gabriel, 348, 349, 352
Ku Klux Klan, 227

La Follette, Robert M., 35, 519, 520; and Eugene Debs, 525; nomination of, 136; and third-party campaign, 534
La Follette Seamen's Act, 135
La Guardia, Fiorello, 278
Labor and the Left: A Study of Socialist and Radical Influences in the American Labor Movement (Laslett), 151
Labor Leader, The, 105
Labor party, 531–532; in Great Britain, 38, 341, 519, 527, 531–532; in U.S., 121, 519, 520. *See also* Farmer-labor party; Independent Labor Party
Labriola, Antonia, 3
Lafargue, Paul, 291
LaMonte, Robert Rives, 194
Larkin, "Big Jim," 179
Laski, Harold, 103
Laslett, John H. M., 72
Lawrence, Massachusetts, strike in, 196, 207
Leadville, strike in, 171
Lee, Algernon, 154
Leiserson, William, 247
Lenin, V. I., 22–24, 381, 391, 509; Guy Debord on, 498; on democracy, 379; on intellectuals and the labor movement, 485–487; and *Iskra*, 486; on Marxism, 382; and Plekhanoff, 487; and revolutionary putsch, 38; and trade union consciousness, 341; *What Is to Be Done?*, 22, 163, 486. *See also* Bolshevism; Marxism
Leo XIII, pope, 84, 88, 89, 92, 93, 96. See also *Rerum novarum*
Leonard, G. B., 353
Leonard, Sister Joan de Lourdes, 88
Levine, Louis, 205
Lewelling, L. D., 67
Lewis, John L., 475, 526
Lewis, Lena Morrow, 296, 299, 330; at Second International, 300; and women's groups, 326
Lewis, Oscar, 172–173, 175, 196, 210–211
Lewis, Tom, 270
Liberal Party, 520; in England, 525
Liberal tradition, 332–361
Liberal Tradition in America, The (Hartz), 345
Liberal-pluralism theory, 396
Liberty, 365–368, 369
Liebknecht, Wilhelm, 474–475
Lilienthal, Meta Stern, 300
Lillie, Bishop Thomas, 85
Lincoln, Abraham, 446, 518
Lipset, Seymour Martin, 215, 409–410; on Democrats, 527
Little (IWW official), 174
Live Issue, The, 97
Lloyd George, David, 38, 337, 469
Locke, John, 215, 346, 347; evolution of theory from, 400–401
London, Jack, 181
London, Meyer, 120; on suffrage for Blacks, 223–224; and women, 293
Long, Huey, 6, 518
Looking Backward (Bellamy), 195
Lorwin, Lewis, 154
Lowe, Caroline A., 300
Lukács, George, 402
Luther, Martin, 9, 31
Lynd, Helen, 215–216, 340
Lynd, Robert, 215–216
Lynd, Staughton, 210
Lyons, Eugene, 24

McAllister, W. W., 253–254
McArdle, Peter J., 89
McBride, John, 125
McCarthy, Eugene, 526
McClure, S. S., 352
McCraith (AFL anti-socialist), 109
McFaul, Bishop James, 85, 96
McGlynn, Edward, 104
McGrady, Father Thomas, 110
McGuire, Peter, 109, 110
Machiavelli, Niccolò, 378
Machinists Monthly Journal, 124–125; and Democratic Party, 136; on discontent, 129; and Populism, 126. *See also* International Association of Machinists
McKees Rock, strike in, 196

McKelvey, Blake, 413
McKinley, William, 37
MacPherson, C. B., 400
McQuade, Vincent, 83
Macy, Jessy, 61
Madison, James, 378
Madisonian social structure, 373
Maley, Anna A., 296
Malin, James C., 413
Malkiel, Theresa, 295
Mangan, John, 89
Mann, Tom, 216
Mannheim, Karl, 9, 10
Marseille, study on mobility in (Sewell), 418, 434
Martov, and *Iskra*, 486
Marx, Karl, 4, 11, 380–385; on American working-class leaders, 163; on Edmund Burke, 379; on class solidarity in England, 479; on consciousness of working class, 27–28, 441; on historic inevitabilism, 46–47; on imperialism, 481; on the state, 390–391; and syndicalism, 513. *See also* Marxism; *titles of individual works by Marx*
Marxism, 362–407; and equality, 369–371; and government, 376–380, 390–391; Populism and, 59–60; and social class, 372–375. *See also* Bolshevism; Marx, Karl
Marxism: The View from America (Rossiter), 398
Mater et magistra (Pope John), 108, 114
Material determinism, 502
Mattoon, Emma, 18
Matz, Bishop Nicholas, 108
Maurer, James, 135, 154
Mayer, Father Albert, 95
Maynard, Mila Tupper, 330
Meckel, Father, 95
Messenger, 225–226, 233–234, 238
Meyer, S., 479, 483
Michels, Robert, 163, 488, 490
Middletown (Lynd and Lynd), 215–216
Milič, Vojin, 431–432
Militia of Christ, 89–92, 100–101, 103–104; Sister Mary Harrita Fox on, 115. *See also* Catholic Church
Mill, John Stuart, 400–401
Miller, George Franzier, 234
Miller, Sally, 409–410
Mills, C. Wright, 372, 392
Milwaukee: German communities in, 132; Social Democratic Party of, 255–256
Milwaukee Leader, 503
Miner's Magazine, 113
Miners union. *See* United Mine Workers; Western Federation of Miners
Minneapolis, Trotskyists in, 505
Mitchell, John, 89, 103, 278
Mobility. *See* Social mobility
Modernization theory, 272
Moffat, John, 89
Molders Union, 157
Molly Maguires, 106, 107
Mooney, Tom, 110, 117
Moore, R. Laurence, 271
Morgan, James, 208
Morgan, Thomas J., 118–119
Mormon women, 304
Morris, William, 13
Morrison, John, 128
Moscow strike of 1895, 485
Mosely Commission, 462
Munzer, Thomas, 9
Muste, A. J., 504

National Association for the Advancement of Colored People (NAACP), 221, 222–223
National Civic Foundation, 13
National Economist, 57
National Executive Committee (Socialist Party): and William Haywood, 193, 263; and immigrant socialist groups, 257; women on, 293, 294, 296
National Farmers' Alliance. *See* Farmers' Alliance
National Labor Party, 121, 520
National Labor Union, 56
Nationalism, 581
Nativism, 245, 271, 286, 287
Nef, Walter, 197
Negroes. *See* Blacks
New Deal, 6; Norman Thomas on, 35, 518–519, 520

New Democratic Party (Canada), 524
New Left, 209–210
New radicalism, 511–512
New York: Jewish labor movement in, 130–131; Socialist Party in, 166
Newburyport study (Thernstrom), 413–414, 416–417; on property mobility, 421–424
Newspapers, Catholic, 95–97
Niagara Movement, 211
Niebuhr, Reinhold, 363
Nonpartisan League (North Dakota), 33
Northampton study (Doherty), 414

Occupational mobility, 416–421
O'Connell, Cardinal William, 83, 84
O'Connell, James, 89
O'Connor, T. V., 89
O'Hare, Kate Richards, 293, 295; on National Executive Committee, 296–297
Oklahoma Socialist Party, 235–242
O'Leary, Father Cornelius, 107
One Big Union concept (IWW), 196–197
Order and Progress (Harrison), 422
Ossowski, Stanislaus, 430, 431
Ovington, Mary White, 221–222, 232
Owen, Chandler, 225, 226, 233, 238

Pacem in Terris (Pope John), 114
Pacifism, 20
Pancner, John, 190–191
Papal encyclicals, 82–83, 85, 86–87, 88, 104, 105, 108, 114. See also *Rerum novarum*
Paris Commune, 390–391
Park, Robert Ezra, 275
Parker, Carleton, 172, 175
Paterson, New Jersey, strike in, 196
Payne, Laura B., 330
People, The (De Leon), 113
People's Council of America, 225–226
Perlman, Selig, 5–6, 30, 38, 474, 484; on AFL, 139; Paul Buhle on, 498–499, 501, 505; on Catholic Church, 83, 97–98; Adolph Sturmthal on, 484, 486, 487, 491–494, 509
Person, Carl E., 152
Phelps, J. G., 295
Philadelphia Longshoremen, 183
Pius X, pope, 86, 89
Pius XI, pope, 105
Place, Francis, 489–490
Plasticity, of human nature, 364
Plekhanoff, Georgi, 487, 509
Pluralism, 392–393; and political parties, 516–535
Poland, social mobility in, 429
Political Man (Lipset), 527
Political parties, 516–535
Political Parties (Michels), 163
Political Program of 1894 (Morgan), 118–119
Pollack, Norman, 55, 58
"Poor whites" psychology, 478
Popes. *See* Papal encyclicals; *names of individual popes*
Popper, Karl, 379
Popular Front, 25, 39
Populism, 33; and AFL, 55–57; and Blacks, 78; craft unions and, 68–69; failure of, 55; and formation of party, 54; and Samuel Gompers, 68–69; and IAM, 67, 125–126; and Marxism, 59–60; political alliance of, 62, 145–146; and Progressives, 79; radicalism of, 65–66; resistance to, 78; as single-issue party, 62; and Socialist Party, 72; and strikes of 1885–1895, 66–67; and trade unions, 67–70; of urban workers, 125–126; working class and, 69–70, 75–76. *See also* Farmer-labor party; Farmers; Farmers' Alliance
Populist Response to Industrial America, The (Pollack), 55
Pouget, Emile, 187
Poverty (Hunter), 262, 270
Powderly, Terence, 110

Presbyterian Department of Church and Labor, 156–157
Press, Catholic, 95–97
Prevey, Marguerite, 304–305
Priests, of Catholic Church, 85–88
Princess Casamassima (James), 10
Prison Notebooks (Gramsci), 38
Profit-sharing, 462–463
Progressives, 33, 333; and Catholic Church, 104; and Populism, 79; in Wisconsin, 519
Property mobility, 421–424
Prussia, suffrage in, 488
Pullman strike, 66–67, 68–69

Quality and Quantity (Rishøj), 448
Quigley, Bishop James, 85

Race: collective bargaining and, 471; new radicalism and, 511; and social mobility, 437–438; and socialism, 166–167, 218–243; women socialists and, 305. *See also* Blacks; Immigration
Randolph, A. Philip, 225, 226, 233, 238; on World War I, 239
Rauschenbusch, Walter, 19
"Red Decade," 24
Representative government, 376
Republican Party: and Blacks, 237; on immigration, 262–263
Rerum novarum (Pope Leo XIII), 83, 84, 88, 92, 93, 96, 108
Responsibility, ethic of, 8
Reuther, Walter, 475, 499
Revisionist movement, in Germany, 485
Revolutionary myth, concept of (Sorel), 10
Riesman, David, 372
Rishøj, Tom, 434, 448
Roberts, Peter, 456
Robinson, James Harvey, 394
Roddy, Edward G., 156
Rodgers, Daniel T., 272
Rogoff, Natalie, 433, 434
Roman Catholic Church. *See* Catholic Church
Roosevelt, Franklin D., 49, 518, 520, 534. *See also* New Deal
Roosevelt, Theodore, 334; and AFL "Bill of Grievances," 245; as conservative, 348; on socialist growth, 352; and third-party effort, 534
Rosenblum, Gerald, 272
Ross, E. A., 372
Rousseau, Jean Jacques, 369
Russell, Charles Edward, 222
Russia: abuse of power in, 379; education in, 490; Moscow strike of 1895 in, 485; social mobility in, 429, 432–433. *See also* Bolshevism; Lenin, V. I.
Ruthenberg, Charles, 260
Ryan, Father John A., 95

Sabotage, 186–188
Sabotage (Pouget), 187
Sadler, Kate, 304–305
Šaféř, Zdaněk, 429
St. John, Vincent, 174, 179, 184; on government, 191
St. Petersburg strike (1895), 485
Salpointe, Bishop John Baptist, 107
Sandgren, John, 174, 177; on syndicalism, 194
Saposs, David J., 82; on Militia of Christ, 90–91
Schattschneider, E. E., 531
Scheler, Max, 16
Schumpeter, Joseph, 428
Schuyler, George S., 234
Scott, Joan, 416
Second International, 300. *See also* Socialist Party
Seligman, E. R. A., 394
Separation of powers, 376
Settler movement, 480
Sewell, William H., Jr., 410, 417, 434
Sexual division of labor, 325. *See also* Women
Shannon, David, 137, 157; on foreign-language federations, 261
Shapiro, Gilbert, 411
Sharecropper's Union (Alabama), 235–236
Sherman, J. W., 127
Shoe industry, 126–127. *See also* Boot and Shoe Workers Union

Shoe Workers Journal, 138. *See also* Boot and Shoe Workers Union
Sieverman, Frank, 127
Simons, A. M., 256–257, 295
Simons, May Wood, 295, 308, 330; at Second International, 300
Singulari quadam caritate, 86–87. *See also* Pius X
Sklar, Martin, 348
Slav coal miners, 166
Smith, Adam, 401
Smith, Al, 278
Smith, Tucker, 521
Smith-Rosenberg, Carroll, 325
Social class, 372–375. *See also* Class consciousness; Social mobility
Social differentiation, 432
Social fascism, 23
Social mobility, 408–451; and class consciousness, 474; in communist countries, 429–433; and different systems, 436–439; and geographical mobility, 412–416; historical perspective on, 433–436; and occupational mobility, 416–421; and property mobility, 421–424
Social Mobility in Industrial Society (Lipset and Bendix), 448
Socialist Campaign Book (1912), 262, 270
Socialist Economics of Karl Marx and His Followers, The (Veblen), 394
Socialist Labor Party (SLP), 36; and dual unionism, 121; and Friedrich Engels, 153; intellectuals in, 500
Socialist Looks at the New Deal, A (Thomas), 35
Socialist Party: basis of, 16–20; and W. E. B. DuBois, 225; educational campaign by, 157, 164–165; and ethnicity, 244–290; future of, 521–522; and ILGWU, 137, 138–139; immigrants and, 157–158, 244–290; intellectuals in, 493; and IWW, 192–195; in Oklahoma, 235–242; Party Congress (1910), 248, 270; and parliamentary system, 525; peak of, 134–135; political demands by, 13–14; Populism and, 72; post-1919, 48–49; and preferential ballot, 533; and race, 157, 164–165, 166–167, 218–243; rightward drift of, 39–40; St. Louis Manifesto of, 34, 277; structure of, 530–531; and Western Federation of Miners, 123–124; and Woodrow Wilson, 134–135; and women, 291–330; World War I and, 32–33, 34, 277; World War II and, 520–521. *See also* Foreign-language federations; National Executive Committee; Woman's National Committee; *names of individual leaders*
Socialist Trades and Labor Alliance, 118, 120, 500. *See also* De Leon, Daniel
Socialist Woman, 307, 321
Solidarity (IWW), 171; on passive resistance, 186; on violence, 185. *See also* Industrial Workers of the World
Solidarity of class, 478, 479
Sombart, Werner, 5, 30, 38
Sorel, Georges, 10; and syndicalism, 194; transatlantic ties of, 206; and Wobblies, 171
Sorokin, P. A., 427, 428, 434
Southern Farmers' Alliance, 57–58
"Southern Filmerians," 350
Southern Tenant Farmers Union (Arkansas), 236
Soviet Union. *See* Russia
Spanish Civil War, 33, 34; and Loyalists, 16; Marxists and, 395
Spargo, John, 155, 342; on immigration, 248–249, 250, 286; on syndicalism, 194, 206; on women, 292–293, 322
Speed, George, 175, 181
Stalin, Josef, 370
Stalinism, 391
Standard of living: of American workers, 452–458, 468, 471, 477; economic growth and, 469–470; and world view, 457–458
Stelzle, Charles, 156
Stokes, Rose Pastor, 294–295
Strunsky, Anna, 222
Sturmthal, Adolph, 39
Stuttgart International Socialist

Congress (1907), resolution of, 248, 250, 252, 269–270
Suffrage: for Blacks, 223; class consciousness and, 473–474; in European countries, 487–488; for women, 301–302
Sumner, Graham, 372
Sweatshop conditions, 130–131
Sweden: social democratic regimes in, 39; strike movement in, 510
Syndicalism, 170–217, 513; and intellectuals, 492. *See also* Industrial Workers of the World
Syndicalism, Industrial Unionism and Socialism (Spargo), 155

Taft, Philip, 108, 115, 139
Taft, William Howard, 262–263
Talbot, Thomas W., 128
Theoretical System of Karl Marx, The (Boudin), 394
Theory of the Labor Movement (Perlman), 5, 139, 484; Paul Buhle on, 498–499
Theses on Feuerbach (Marx), 390
Third parties, 516–535
Thomas, Norman, 10, 16–20, 44; influence of, 475; as moral leader, 36–37; on New Deal, 35, 518–519, 520; Socialist Party and, 39–40; on third parties, 516–535
Thompson, Carl, 262
Thompson, E. P., 216, 288; on ethnicity, 273
Thompson, James P., 170; on economic power, 188; on revolution, 179–180; on sabotage, 187; on slavery, 184
Time contracts, 133–134
Tobin, John F., 127, 133, 134
Tocqueville, Alexis de, 439–440
Toryism, 335
Toward a Democratic Left (Harrington), 528
Trade unions, 118–169; and Catholic Church, 82–117; and political struggle, 525; and Populism, 67–70. *See also* AFL-CIO; American Federation of Labor; Collective bargaining; Congress of Industrial Organizations; *names of specific unions*
Trempeaulau County, study of occupational mobility in (Curti), 416
Tresca, Carlo, 275
Tridon, Andre, 205
Trotsky, Leon, 4, 505; and V. I. Lenin, 23
Tugwell, Rexford, 172, 175–176
"Turnover of the Farm Population in Kansas, The" (Malin), 413
Twining, Luella, 300

Ulam, Adam, 70, 340–341; on immigration, 272
Union Stamp Contract, 133, 134
Unions. *See* Trade unions
United Mine Workers (UMW), 121, 136, 141; contracts of, 133–134; dual affiliation of, 124; integration of, 224; and jurisdictional conflicts, 123; and Populism, 67–68, 125
United Mine Workers Journal, 136. *See also* United Mine Workers
Untermann, Ernest, 249, 250, 253–254; on AFL, 256
Utopian colonies, 4

Vanderveld, Émile, 475
Veblen, Thorstein, 343, 349, 372, 394
Verein. *See* Catholic Church; Central Verein
Villard, Oswald Garrison, 222
Vogt, A., 479, 483
Voluntarism, 526
Vyshinsky, Andrei, 370

Wagner, Robert F., 278
Wagner Act, 508
Walker, Jimmy, 18
Walker, John H., 135
Wallace, George, 534
Wallace, Henry, 25, 505
Walling, William English, 221–222, 232
War Labor Disputes Act, 493
Ward, Lester Frank, 336, 372
Ware, Norman J., 83
Warner, W. Lloyd, 372

Washington, Booker T., 221
Weaver, James B., 54
Weber, Max, 8, 31; on ethics and politics, 49–50; on World War I, 31–32
Weimar Republic, 31
Weinstein, James, 135, 137, 219, 348, 352
Weinstock, Harris, 184–185
Wells, H. G., 349
Western Federation of Miners, 120–121, 141, 143; and population turnovers, 424; and Populism, 125; and time contracts, 133; withdrawal of, from AFL, 123–124
Whalen, John S., 89
Wharton, Arthur O., 152
What Is to Be Done? (Lenin), 22, 163, 486
Whiggery, 350
White (Molders Union), 157
White, William Allen, 334
White Collar (Mills), 392
Why Is There No Socialism in the United States? (Sombart), 5
Why Negroes Should Be Socialists (Socialist Party), 227
Wilderspil, S. I., 429
Willard, Frances, 325–326
Williams, Ben, 171–172, 174, 177; on economic power, 188; on government, 191; on sabotage, 187
Williams, William A., 349
Wilson, Douglas, 126
Wilson, Woodrow, 36, 334, 352, 525; as conservative, 334, 348; and decline of Socialist Party, 134–136; and W. E. B. DuBois, 225; and Populism, 79; trade union support for, 135–136
Wilsonian Democrats, 33
Winthrop, John, 369
Wobblies. *See* Industrial Workers of the World
Woman's General Correspondent, 295–296
Woman's National Committee, 292; assessment of, 319–320; and foreign-language federations, 301; independent women's clubs and, 322–323; members of, 294; "Plan for Work" of, 297–298; projects of, 298–300; and suffrage movement, 301–302; undercutting of, 308
Women: and division of labor, 325; and socialism, 291–330; and suffrage movement, 301–302
Women and American Socialism (Buhle), 329
Women's Christian Temperance Union (WCTU), 325
Wood, Bishop James, 107
Woodbey, George Washington, 234
World War I: Black loyalty during, 239; and Catholic Church, 98; and IWW, 207; and A. Philip Randolph, 239; and Socialist Party, 32–33, 34; and Norman Thomas, 19; and Max Weber, 31–32
World War II, 17; and Socialist Party, 520–521; and Norman Thomas, 20
Wylie, Lawrence, 415

Yanovsky, Saul, 155–156, 163
Yugoslavia, social mobility in, 430, 431–432

Zetkin, Clara, 300, 306

DATE DUE

FE 26 '92			